THE GREEKS

HISTORY, CULTURE, AND SOCIETY

IAN MORRIS
STANFORD UNIVERSITY

BARRY B. POWELL
UNIVERSITY OF WISCONSIN-MADISON

PEARSON

Prentice Hall

Upper Saddle River, NJ 07458

Library of Congress Cataloging-in-Publication Data

Morris, Ian
   The Greeks : history, culture, and society / Ian Morris, Barry B. Powell.—1st ed.
      p. cm.
   Includes bibliographical references and index.
   ISBN 0-13-921156-X
      1. Greece—History—To 146 B.C. I. Powell, Barry B. II. Title.

   DF214.M69 2005
   938–dc22   2004058707

VP, Editorial Director: Charlyce Jones Owen
Executive Editor: Charles Cavaliere
Associate Editor: Emsal Hasan
Editorial Assistant: Shannon Corliss
Marketing Manager: Heather Shelstad
Marketing Assistant: Cherron Gardner
Managing Editor (Production): Joanne Riker
Production Editor: Jan H. Schwartz
Permissions Coordinator: Ron Fox
Permissions Researcher: Margaret Gorenstein
Manufacturing Buyer: Ben Smith
Cover Design: Bruce Kenselaar
Cover Illustration/Photo: Detail from one of the Riace Bronzes.
Photo Researcher: Linda Sykes
Image Permission Coordinator: Cynthia Vincenti
Composition: Interactive Composition Corporation
Printer/Binder: Courier/Stoughton
Cover photo/Frontis piece: Erich Lessing/Art Resource, NY.

Credits and acknowledgments borrowed from other sources and reproduced, with
permission, in this textbook appear on page C-1.

Pearson Education LTD.   Pearson Education Australia PTY, Limited
Pearson Education Singapore, Pte. Ltd   Pearson Education North Asia Ltd
Pearson Education, Canada, Ltd   Pearson Educación de Mexico, S.A. de C.V.
Pearson Education–Japan   Pearson Education Malaysia, Pte. Ltd

10 9 8 7 6 5 4 3 2 1
ISBN 0-13-921156-X

To our teachers Anthony Snodgrass and W. K. Pritchett

In 1972, a diver discovered two bronze statues off the south coast of Italy in shallow water, perhaps jettisoned during a storm. This is the face of one of them. Probably taken from Delphi to decorate a Roman's estate, they were made during the transition from the archaic to the early classic styles, c. 450 B.C., and are two of the finest sculptures to survive from the ancient world.

CONTENTS

MAPS

PREFACE

In this book we try to see ancient Greece as a whole: not just provide a narrative of events or an overview of culture, but history and culture taken together. From ancient Greece comes the modern conviction that through open discussion and the exercise of reason, a society of free citizens can solve the problems that challenge it. In one period of Greek history, a society just so governed produced timeless masterpieces of literature, art, and rational thought at the same time it waged terrible wars and countless other cruelties. If we understand the past, we can live better in the present. But the past is hard to understand.

We have organized the material chronologically in a continuous narrative, beginning at the end of the last Ice Age. We take the story through the palaces of Mycenaean Greece and the depressed centuries of the Dark Age to the birth of city-states in the Archaic Period. We describe the triumphs of the city-states in the Classical Period and their subjection to larger kingdoms in the Hellenistic Period, after Alexander the Great conquered the Persian Empire, and finally, their conquest by Rome. As we tell this story, we describe processes of social change and cultural achievements along with political events.

Two groups of imaginary readers look over our shoulders. For students we provide the names, dates, and details that you need to grasp Greek history, while avoiding technical jargon. Many of the names in this book will be unfamiliar. To assist with pronunciation, we provide an English pronunciation guide the first time each difficult name appears. (The pronunciation guides are repeated in the index.) We also use **bold** letters to highlight the most important names, places, and concepts. We repeat these names in a list of important terms at the end of each chapter, with page numbers of where the term first appears. We leave less important names in ordinary type, though we often give pronunciations for those as well. In the index we include capsule identifications for important names.

Our second group of imaginary readers is expert on ancient Greece. They can be tough critics. An expert's comment is, "Yes, but . . . ." There are countless places in a book like this where authorities would add that the evidence is ambiguous, the translation of key words debated, or there are exceptions to our generalizations. They are right to worry about complexities and scholarly debates, but in the end, we have told the story in our own way, as if this were the way it really happened. We hope that even they may find new ways of thinking about old problems—or, at least, will enjoy the read.

Our account differs in significant ways from the many excellent overviews of Greek history that already exist. First, we make special efforts to see the Greeks as part of a larger Mediterranean world. Older accounts tend to focus on the Aegean Sea, ignoring the Greeks of Sicily and southern Italy. We try instead to show how thoroughly linked developments were in eastern and western Greece. Most previous accounts also present non-Greek peoples like the Persians, Carthaginians, and natives of the west Mediterranean as cardboard characters, present only to defeat or be defeated. We try to make clear their motivations and their contributions to the larger story.

Second, we have rejected the prejudice that the only things worth knowing about Greece ended with the Peloponnesian War in 404 B.C., the death of Socrates in 399 B.C., or the battle of Chaeronea in 338 B.C. The final three centuries B.C. are vitally important in the story of the Greeks. The luxuries of Hellenistic Alexandria and the blood-soaked progress of Roman armies across the east Mediterranean are as much a part of the story as the insights of Pericles and the beauty of the Parthenon.

Third, because so much of antiquity is apprehended through the eye, we include abundant maps and photographs of landscapes, objects, and buildings. Archaeologists' discoveries have changed the ways we understand ancient Greece, and we emphasize material culture throughout.

As often as possible, we let the Greeks speak for themselves by including generous quotations from ancient authors. No supplements to this book are necessary to understand who the Greeks were and what they accomplished, but more extended readings from Homer, the historians, the tragedians, and the lyric poets would certainly complement the text. We make suggestions on further reading in modern scholarship as well as in the ancient sources at the end of each chapter.

Ian Morris
Willard Professor of Classics
Stanford University
imorris@stanford.edu

Barry B. Powell
Halls-Bascom Professor of Classics
University of Wisconsin-Madison
bbpowell@wisc.edu

ACKNOWLEDGMENTS

We are grateful to the many colleagues and students who have helped in writing this book, but particularly to Eric Cline (The George Washington University) and Carole Thomas (University of Washington), who read the entire manuscript and improved it with their advice. Also heartfelt thanks to Paul Cartledge (Cambridge University), Jenny S. Clay (University of Virginia), Stewart Flory (Gustavus Adolphus College), John Kroll (University of Texas at Austin), David Leitao (San Francisco State University), Kathryn A. Morgan (University of California at Los Angeles), D. Brendan Nagle (University of Southern California), Josiah Ober (Princeton University), and Christine Renaud (Carthage College). We also thank Charles Cavaliere, our editor at Prentice Hall, for his patience and guidance; and Jan Schwartz, who supervised the production of the manuscript.

We have made use of many fine translations of ancient texts, most of which we cite in full at the end of the first chapter in which the author is quoted. Occasionally we make small changes (usually restoring the original Greek) in order to make some point. Above all we have used translations published in the Penguin series: Aeschylus, Robert Fagles, S. Bernadete; Appian, J. Carter; Aristotle, P. J. Rhodes, T. A. Sinclair, J. A. K. Thomson, H. Lawson-Tancred; Arrian, Aubrey de Selincourt; Demosthenes, A. N. W. Saunders Euripides, Philip Vellacott; Herodotus, Aubrey de Selincourt; Hesiod, Dorothea Wender; Hippocrates, G. E. R. Lloyd; Hippocrates, J. Chadwick, W. N. Mann; Livy, Aubrey de Selincourt; Menander, Norma Miller; Pindar, C. M. Bowra; Plato, W. K. C. Guthrie, Hugh Tredennick, Harold Tarrant, D. Lee; Plutarch, Richard Talbert, Ian Scott-Kilvert, Rex Warner; Polybius, Ian Scott-Kilvert; Quintus Curtius, John Yardley; Solon, P. J. Rhodes; Sophocles, Paul Roche; Theocritus, Robert Wells; Theognis, Dorothea Wender; Thucydides, Rex Warner; Xenophon, Hugh Tredennick.

Where Penguins are unavailable, we have used translations from the Loeb Classical Library: Aristophanes, J. Henderson; Aristotle, W. H. Fyfe, G. C. Armstrong, H. Rackham, W. Ogle; Cicero, E. Shuckburgh; Demosthenes, J. H. Vince; Dio Cassius, Earnest Cary, Herbert B. Foster; Diodorus of Sicily, C. H. Oldfather, C. Bradford Welles, R. Geer; Hesiod, Hugh G. Evelyn-White; Homer, A. T. Murray; Homeric Hymns, Hugh G. Evelyn-White; Plato, P. Shorey; pseudo-Lucian, K. Kilburn. From texts published on the web by the Perseus Project (*http://www.perseus.tufts.edu/*) we are grateful to D. Svarlien for translation from Bacchylides and T. A. Buckley for translation from Euripides' *Bacchae*. We have made use of the following other translations: Aristophanes, D. Parker; Aristotle, H. W. Butler; Epictetus, W. Agard; Epicurus, H. M. Howe; Galen, M. T. May; Gilgamesh, S. Dalley; Hippocrates, H. M. Howe; Old Oligarch, C. W. Gray; Plato, H. M. Howe; Theocritus, B. Wells; Tyrtaeus, R. Lattimore; Vitruvius, H. M. Howe.

ABOUT THE AUTHORS

Ian Morris is the Jean and Rebecca Willard Professor of Classics, Professor of History, and Director of the Archaeology Center at Stanford University, where he teaches large lecture courses on ancient empires and Greek history. He is either the author or the editor of eight books on ancient history and archaeology, and directs a major archaeological excavation in Sicily. His latest book, *The Ancient Economy: Evidence and Models,* appears in 2005. He has lectured at universities all across America and Europe, and recently appeared on the History Channel's *Command Decisions: The Battle of Marathon* and the National Geographic special *Quest for the Phoenicians.*

Barry B. Powell is the Halls-Bascom Professor of Classics at the University of Wisconsin-Madison, where he is well known as a teacher of large lecture classes in ancient civilization and myth. He has lectured in many countries and is the author of the bestselling *Classical Myth* (4th edition), widely used in college courses. His popular introductory text *Homer* appeared in 2004. He is best known as the author of *Homer and the Origin of the Greek Alphabet,* which argues that the Greek alphabet was invented in order to record the poems of Homer. With Ian Morris he has published the internationally admired *A New Companion to Homer* (1997) as well as written numerous other books, articles, screenplays, and poetry. Recently, he appeared on the History Channel special *Troy: The True Story.*

CHAPTER 1

A SMALL, FAR-OFF LAND

Fair Greece! sad relic of departed worth!
Immortal, though no more! though fallen, great!

LORD BYRON,
Childe Harold's Pilgrimage (1812–18),
canto 2, stanza 73

Byron was just twenty-five when he wrote *Childe Harold's Pilgrimage*. He was handsome and dashing, a wealthy lord in the most powerful nation on earth, and already one of England's most famous poets. The world was at his feet. Yet within a decade, he turned his back on it all. He sailed to Greece to join its uprising against the mighty Turkish Empire (Map 1.1).

Lord Byron died in 1824, hundreds of miles from home and family, in a terrible siege in central Greece. Why did Byron feel so strongly that he gave his life for Greek freedom? Why did thousands of others flock to join him? Why, in our own time, do millions travel to see the ruins that dot Greece's landscape? And why do people spend so much time studying Greek history, culture, and society? In this book, we try to answer these questions.

HISTORICAL SKETCH

In the half-millennium 700 to 200 B.C.,[1] the Greeks engaged in a remarkable experiment. They built societies that were communities of equal citizens who systematically applied their reason to explaining the world. In the process, they created

1

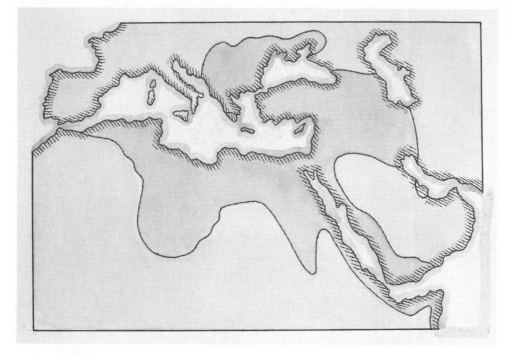

Map 1.1   The Ottoman Empire. Between A.D. 1300 and 1919, the Ottoman Turkish Empire controlled the eastern and southern territories of the old Roman Empire. Though hated by some, the Ottomans were gifted administrators under whose sway Islamic culture produced some of its finest achievements.

masterpieces of literature and art. Democracy, philosophy, history writing, and drama began in ancient Greece, and the Greeks developed science, mathematics, and representational art in previously unimagined directions.

Two hundred years ago, Byron died for an idea, a vision of the ancient Greek spirit. His vision was idealized; he and his contemporaries saw in Greek art and literature timeless truths that laid bare the meaning of life. In 1820, on the eve of the Greek uprising against the Turks, his fellow poet John Keats (1795–1821) thought he grasped the world's ultimate truths by simply gazing at painted Greek vases (Figure 1.1).

> O Attic° shape! Fair attitude! With brede
> Of marble men and maidens overwrought,
> With forest branches and the trodden weed;
> Thou, silent form, dost tease us out of thought
> As doth eternity: Cold Pastoral!
> When old age shall this generation waste,
> Thou shalt remain, in midst of other woe
> Than ours, a friend to man, to whom thou say'st,
> "Beauty is truth, truth beauty,—that is all
> Ye know on earth, and all ye need to know."

Keats, "Ode on a Grecian Urn"
(1820), stanza 5

°*Attic:* From Attica, the countryside around Athens.

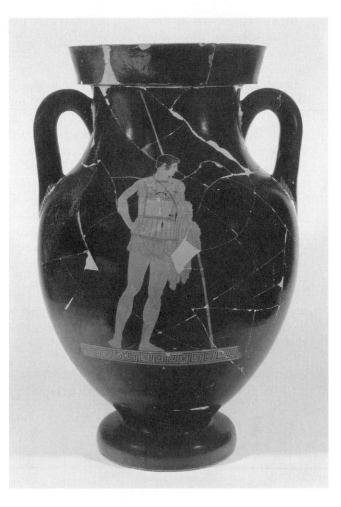

Figure 1.1 No single Greek vase lay behind Keats's poem; he drew inspiration from seeing hundreds of pots in English museums before his death in Rome at the age of just twenty-six. This pot is the kind he had in mind, an Athenian "red-figure" vase, circa 450 B.C.

The great poet saw deeply, but thanks to two hundred years of scholarship, we now see more. For Byron and Keats, ancient Greece was a simple and pure world of love and truth. But nowadays we understand the Greeks for what they really were. Theirs was an astonishing culture, but no utopia. The achievements of some Greeks rested on the backbreaking labor of others, often slaves from overseas. Their democracies excluded women. They fought endless wars and committed terrible acts of violence. Yet far from making us turn from the Greeks in revulsion, these discoveries make them more fascinating still. The Greeks lived in the real world, where they struggled with the same basic problems about freedom, equality, and justice that we face. Their difficulties show us that there are no simple answers.

Let us take the story back five thousand years, to a time when great **Bronze Age** civilizations (see Chronological Chart on page A-1 for this and other historical terms) had arisen in **Mesopotamia**[2] (what is now Iraq) and Egypt.

The Mesopotamian kings claimed that they had special relationships with the gods and that unless they interceded, the gods would not smile on humans. The kings of Egypt went further, claiming that they themselves *were* gods. By 2000 B.C., similar societies formed in Greece. Their palaces flourished until 1200 B.C., but then were burned along with cities all over the east Mediterranean. We still do not know why this destruction occurred, but its consequences were momentous. In Mesopotamia and Egypt, the old order of godlike kings revived, but in Greece that way of doing things was over. From about 1200 until 800 B.C., writing disappeared from Greece; the country's population shrank and was isolated from the wider world. The present book focuses on the Greek societies that emerged from this **Dark Age** in the eighth century B.C., creating a new Greek world that had little in common with the Bronze Age.

This world had several radical features. First, most Greeks now organized themselves in small city-states called *poleis* (this is the plural form; the singular is *polis*), not in large kingdoms. Second, as population grew in the eighth century, some Greeks responded by sailing off and creating new *poleis* around the shores of the Mediterranean (see Map 1.2). Third, Greeks saw their city-states as communities of equal, free males. Fourth, they refused to believe that the gods gave any individual or narrow elite a divine right to rule.

These developments presented the Greeks with problems and opportunities absent in other ancient societies. If the gods had not put sacred kings on earth to tell mortals what to do, just what *was* the relationship between mortals and the divine? Most Greeks thought that the gods were powerful and wise, that the world

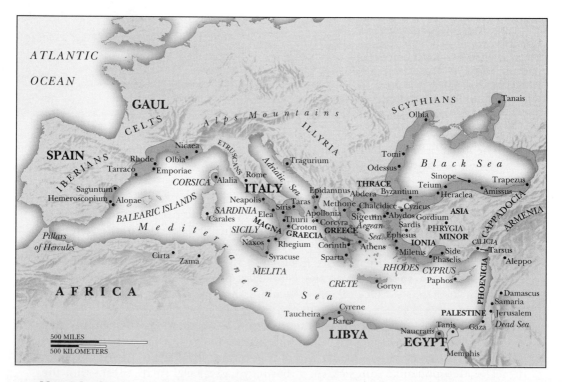

Map 1.2   Greek colonies.

was full of spirits and ghosts, and that a few oracles and priests could give access to the supernatural. This access was distorted and open to challenge, and oracles and priests could not use it to dominate others. How, then, could mortals really know what was true?

These conditions created a fundamental conflict that we call **the Greek problem.** Without God or gods to rule and to reveal, many Greeks concluded that human reason was the only guide to truth. If no king had special access to truth, then all males[3] must be roughly equally well qualified to discuss it, and the only source of good decisions must be the whole male community. By 500 B.C., this theory led to the world's first democracies (democracy comes from the Greek word *dēmokratia* [dē-mo-kra-**tē**-a], meaning "power of the people"), in which all male citizens debated and voted on the major issues.

Other Greeks drew different conclusions from the Greek problem. Some thought that elites should rule; the richest men, with the most respected family connections, could be trained in the skillful exercise of reason on behalf of the whole community. The conflict between mass and elite—democracy and experts—was a driving force in Greek history and one that remains familiar today. What is the place of intellectuals in a democracy? How should wealth be distributed? What do equality and freedom mean?

But while these philosophical debates raged, the Greeks still had to live in the real world. Like us, they had a growing population and conflicting demands on their resources. Leading men in every *polis* competed for power and wealth, and the rich as a group were often at loggerheads with the poor. Neighboring *poleis* fought for land and other resources, sometimes polarizing into great power blocs. The Greeks as a whole fought with powers like Persia, a great empire in western Asia, and with Carthage, a great trading city in what is now Tunisia. Different *poleis* found different solutions to the problem of working out a civil society independent of rule by gods and their agents, but always did so against the material realities of the southern Balkan Peninsula. Sparta developed a militaristic society, suppressing debate in the interests of security. Athens turned toward democracy and pluralism, glorying in open expression. Syracuse in Sicily alternated between Athenian-style creativity and rule by brutal tyrants.

These diverse responses to the Greek problem produced two results. First, there was constant intercity warfare, as different *poleis* promoted their own interests and their own visions of the good society. In the fifth century B.C., it looked as if Athens might defeat all comers, unite Greece, and become its capital city. But after Sparta overcame Athens in 404 B.C., the wars only intensified, becoming increasingly expensive and destructive.

The second consequence of living with the Greek problem was more positive. Thinkers needed to explain not only how the universe worked independent of divine whim, but also why there was such variety in it. As early as the sixth century B.C., Greek intellectuals in Ionia on the west coast of Asia Minor (modern Turkey; see map on the inside of the back cover) developed rational models of the mechanics of the cosmos, accepting that the gods created the universe but assuming that the physical world continued to work because natural forces acted on each other. Their questions initiated Greek science and philosophy. In the fourth century B.C., they led to the epoch-making work of Plato and Aristotle, and in the third century B.C., to the mathematical discoveries of the engineer Archimedes (ar-ki-**mēd**-ēz). Other thinkers extended logical, rational analysis, asking why Greek *poleis* were so different from each other and why Greece as a whole was so different from the Persian Empire and from other foreign peoples. This questioning gave us the writings of Herodotus and Thucydides, and the origins of history, anthropology, and political science. At the same time, poets and artists struggled to define man's relationship to the gods. At the end of the Dark Age, during the eighth century B.C., Homer sang his *Iliad* and *Odyssey,* set in ancient days when men and gods walked together, and Hesiod (**hē**-sē-od) related the gods' own history. In the fifth century B.C., the great tragedians Aeschylus (**ē**-ski-lus), Sophocles (**sof**-o-klēz), and Euripides (ū-**rip**-i-dēz) retold Greek legends to explore profound moral problems, the sculptor Phidias (**fid**-ē-as) gave visual expression to new ideas of man's place in the cosmos, and Athens built the Parthenon, one of the world's aesthetic masterpieces.

The upheavals, triumphs, and tragedies of the Greeks in the **Archaic Period** (seventh and sixth centuries B.C.) and **Classical Period** (fifth and fourth centuries B.C.) were driven by the Greek problem—if we cannot rely on the gods to tell us what is true, how do we know what to do? But sudden and unexpected changes began to make the problem irrelevant in the late fourth century B.C. A new king named Philip modernized and centralized Macedonia, a large but loosely organized kingdom on the edge of the world of the *poleis,* and used its wealth and manpower to defeat the Greek cities. Conquering Greece was merely a sideshow to Philip, who planned to overthrow Persia itself. After his murder in 336 B.C., his dynamic son Alexander did just this.

Philip's and Alexander's conquests seemed superhuman. Both kings certainly saw their own triumphs as godlike, and in 324 B.C., Alexander ordered the *poleis* to worship him as a divinity. The great Greek experiment in founding society on reason was evolving into new forms. In many ways, the third century B.C. was the Greeks' golden age (a description often reserved for fifth-century Athens). The Greeks were more numerous and richer than ever. Their cities spread as far as Afghanistan. Their culture triumphed from the borders of India to the Atlantic, and their scientists and engineers made amazing breakthroughs. Such successes seemed to prove that the Greeks had answered old questions about where truth came from; but in the **Hellenistic Period** (from Alexander's death in 323 B.C. to Cleopatra's death in 30 B.C.), new problems arose. Above all, Greeks asked: How should we live together with the peoples we have conquered? And, as Roman armies cut a bloody path around the Mediterranean after 200 B.C., how should we live in a world with just one superpower?

WHY STUDY THE GREEKS?

These problems fascinate people today because we share many of them with the ancient Greeks. Around A.D. 1500, at the end of the European Middle Ages, kings in Europe claimed that they ruled through divine right (as had the kings of ancient Mesopotamia), supported by a Church that monopolized truth (as the temples guaranteed Mesopotamian kings' power). But during the eighteenth-century European Enlightenment, philosophers and scientists challenged such beliefs. Like archaic and classical Greeks, they again asked how humans could know the truth and govern themselves well if they could not rely on divinely justified kings and all-knowing priests to tell them what to do. They came to much the same conclusion as the Greeks: Only through the exercise of reason, unhindered by respect for custom and tradition, could they find the way forward.

The American and French revolutions elevated constitutions—written by mortal men—ahead of sacred books. They held, as so many Greeks had done before them, that a state was a community of equal (male) citizens, founded on reason, aiming at the pursuit of happiness. In the nineteenth century, the right of free, equal citizens to rule themselves—in short, democracy—became a burning social question, and, just as in ancient Greece, great debates sprang up that revolutionized philosophy, science, history writing, literature, and art. People asked once again how they could make sense of the world through reason and found that the Greeks had already asked these questions and had offered compelling answers. The spread of democracy in the twentieth century made the Greek experience of global interest; and in the twenty-first century, we find that our need to build a diverse society was also anticipated by the Hellenistic Greeks.

The Greeks do not provide a blueprint for how to live, and we often learn as much from their failures as from their successes. For example, they recognized that the freedom and equality of male citizens were logically incompatible with the subjection of slaves and women, but they did nothing about it. We have gone much further. Between A.D. 1860 and 1865, 675,000 Americans died fighting, largely to decide whether anyone had the right to hold slaves. The Greeks might have recognized America's problem, but its solution would have astonished them.

We might say, then, that the Greeks are *good to think with*. They conducted astonishing experiments in freedom, equality, and rationality, from which we can learn and upon which we can improve.

WHO WERE THE GREEKS?

Who exactly were these people, "the Greeks"? For about two hundred years—since Byron's time—the world has divided itself into nation-states. The theory behind nation-states is simple. Everyone belongs to an ethnic group defined by shared language and culture, and descent from common ancestors. Each group—Germans, Americans, Japanese, and so on—should govern its own destiny by forming a self-determining territorial state. The boundaries of the ethnic nation and the political state should coincide so that we find Germans in Germany, French in France, and Chinese in China.

In practice, things are not so simple. At the start of the third millennium A.D., the world is a complex ethnic patchwork. For example, while the largest concentration of Greek-speakers on the planet is in the city of Athens, the second largest is in Melbourne, Australia. You can get as authentic a Greek meal in Chicago as anywhere in the nation-state of Greece. Some Greek citizens feel strongly that the population of southern Albania is ethnically Greek and should be part of the Greek state (Map 1.3). Other Greeks feel that Greece's frontiers enclose too many ethnic Albanians, who should be made to go away, even if they hold Greek citizenship. Many Greeks wait nervously to see whether the former Yugoslav Republic of

Map 1.3 Modern Greece and the Balkans.

Macedonia will claim that the ancient region of Macedonia, within the boundaries of northern Greece, should be part of their new Republic. A war was fought partly over this issue in 1913.

Defining a "people," then, is never easy, but the one-people-one-state equation has dominated modern history. From it came the Holocaust and "ethnic cleansing." The Kurds' longing for a state to go with their ethnicity has destabilized the Middle East since the First World War. Ethnic pride has been a major force in turning Afghanistan into a slaughterhouse and the Balkans into a powder keg. Faith in the nation-state based on ethnic identity is one of the most powerful forces of our age.

If we ask what a people was in antiquity, we see that much has changed. The concept of the nation-state simply did not exist in ancient Greece. Greek-speakers who called themselves **Hellenes** (strangely, our word *Greek* comes from the name the Romans gave them) lived in cities scattered from Spain to the Ukraine (see Map 1.2). They agreed that their ancestral home, **Hellas,** lay around the Aegean Sea (roughly the area of the modern Greek nation-state plus the west coast of modern Turkey). Yet a Greek from Sicily felt just as Greek as one from Athens.

The notion that all ethnic Greeks should be politically unified had little appeal. The biggest *polis,* Athens, had a territory of just one thousand square miles, while the tiny island of Kea, covering barely one-tenth that area, was divided into three independent *poleis.* Greekness had nothing to do with belonging to a particular political unit. So what was Greekness? Most modern nations define ethnic identity in terms of common ancestors, language, and culture. Such beliefs are sometimes patently false nationalist myths, and within any nation people may choose among competing and contradictory stories to suit the needs of the moment. The Athenian Thucydides (thu-**sid**-i-dēz), one of the great thinkers of the ancient world, writing around 400 B.C., described similar behavior in Greece:

> My view is that . . . before the time of Hellên,° the son of Deucalion, the name Hellas did not exist at all, and different parts were known by the names of different tribes, with the name "Pelasgian" predominating. After Hellên and his sons had grown powerful in Phthiotis° and had been invited as allies into other states, these states separately and because of their connection with the family of Hellên began to be called "Hellenic." But it took a long time before the name ousted all the other names. The best evidence for this can be found in Homer, who, though he was born much later than the time of the Trojan War, nowhere uses the name "Hellenic" for the whole force. Instead he keeps this name for the followers of Achilles who came from Phthiotis and were in fact the original Hellenes. For the rest in his poems he uses the words "Danaäns," "Argives," and "Achaeans." He does not even use the term *barbaroi,*° and this, in my opinion, is because in his time the Hellenes were not yet known by one name, and so marked off as something separate from the outside world. By "Hellenic" I mean here both those who took on the name city by city, as the result of a common language, and those who were later all called by the common name.
>
> Thucydides 1.3 (R. Warner)
>
> °*Hellên* (**hel**-ēn): In myth, the ancestor of all the Hellenes (that is, the Greeks), who gave his name to Hellas (Greece).   °*Phthiotis* (thī-**ō**-tis): An area in central Greece.   °*Barbaroi:* Greeks conventionally called all foreigners *barbaroi,* the root of our word barbarians, because they thought foreign languages sounded like people saying "bar-bar-bar."

Thucydides applied his reason to the text of Homer to draw conclusions about the past: In Homer's day, the Greeks were not a single people. Just a few lines before introducing this model, he had explained that the Athenians claimed a different ancestry from other Greeks. They alone, they said, were *autochthonous* ("born from the soil"): they had always lived in Athens. Yet we know that other Athenians believed that their ancestors had at some time invaded their territory from outside, cohabiting with and then expelling people called the **Pelasgians** ("peoples of the sea"). There were competing stories and only a limited sense of Greekness. Most of the time, ancient Greeks identified primarily with the *polis* that they lived in. If you could have stopped them as they went about their business and asked who they were, they would normally have said Syracusan, Athenian, Spartan, and so on, not Hellenic.

Sometimes, usually during serious wars, groups of *poleis* would recognize a larger identity. When Athens and Sparta began the terrible Peloponnesian War in 431 B.C., those who considered themselves **Ionians** (descendants of Ion, a legendary ancestor) generally sided with Athens, while those who called themselves **Dorians** (descendants of the sons of the hero Heracles[4] (**her**-a-klēz), who, according to myth, had conquered much of Greece in the distant past) supported Sparta (Map 1.4).

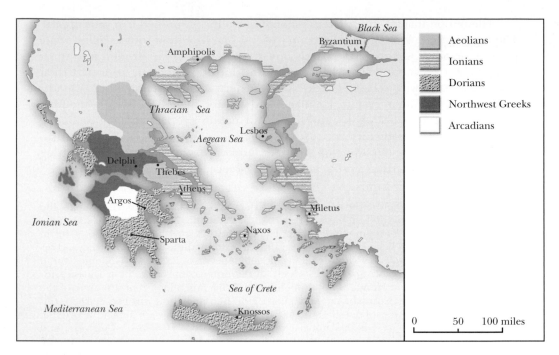

Map 1.4 Distribution of Greek ethnic groups during the Classical Period. The groups were the Aeolians, Ionians, Dorians, Northwest Greeks, and Arcadians, and each group shared a dialect.

Occasionally, people could put aside regional and kinship identities to unite as Hellenes. Whether or not Hellên really existed, he became a potent symbol at such moments. In a great crisis in 480 B.C., when Persia invaded Greece and Carthage invaded Sicily, many Greeks ignored their local myths and united around a presumed common heritage as the sons of Hellên. Herodotus (her-**o**-do-tus), writing at Athens around 420 B.C. and describing a critical moment in the war with Persia, spoke of

> our common Greekness: we are one in blood and one in language; those shrines of the gods belong to us all in common, as do the sacrifices in common, and there are our customs, bred of a common upbringing.
>
> Herodotus 8.144 (A. De Selincourt)

Blood, language, religion, and customs are the foundations of modern nation-states. Greeks often felt distinct from peoples around them who did not speak their language or live like them, and wars with Persia and Carthage highlighted these distinctions. But they never translated this sense of Greekness into political unity, and in Hellenistic times, the distinction between Greek and foreigner partly broke down. Thousands emigrated from Greece to the Near East[5] and Egypt, though few learned the languages of the peoples they settled among. By contrast, native-born Egyptians, Syrians, and others learned Greek, took Greek names, spoke and wrote in Greek, wore Greek clothes, and acted in Greek ways. Who was to say, or know, after a few generations had passed, that one family was more "Greek" than another?

By the time Rome conquered the East Mediterranean in the second and first centuries B.C., Greekness was widely diffused and was taking on new meanings.

THE STRUCTURE OF THIS BOOK: HISTORY, CULTURE, AND SOCIETY

In the next twenty-two chapters, we tell the Greeks' story. The subtitle of our book—*History, Culture, and Society*—sums up our method. First, our format is narrative history, focusing on the half-millennium 700 to 200 B.C. Only by seeing individuals, events, and intellectual discovery in context can we understand them. Second, in the course of our narrative history, we emphasize Greek culture: This is what makes this small, far-off land so important. We describe literature, art, philosophy, and beliefs in their historical context. Third, as our narrative unfolds, we explain Greek culture by looking at the larger Greek society. This means exploring the institutions and economics of each period, along with the Greeks' endless wars and their clashes with other powers. Out of these many conflicts—between rich and poor; free and slave; male and female; Athens and Sparta; and Greeks, Persians, Carthaginians, Macedonians, and Romans—a remarkable culture grew, triumphed, and disintegrated.

KEY TERMS

Attic, 2
Bronze Age, 3
Mesopotamia, 3
Dark Age, 4
polis, 4
the Greek problem, 5
dêmokratia, 5
Archaic Period, 6

Classical Period, 6
Hellenistic Period, 6
Hellenes, 8
Hellas, 8
autochthonous, 9
Pelasgians, 9
Ionians, 9
Dorians, 9

FURTHER READING

Byron and the Greeks

St. Clair, Roger, *That Greece Might Still Be Free* (London 1972). Vivid account of the Greek War of Independence and the romantics who joined it. A great read.

General Reviews of Greek History

Bury, J. B., and Russell Meiggs, *A History of Greece* (3rd ed., London 1975). Bury first published this classic in 1901. It remains the standard resource for the facts of politics and war, though it says little about social, economic, or cultural history, and is dense reading.
Camp, John, and Elizabeth Fisher, *The World of the Ancient Greeks* (London 2002). Brief text by two archaeologists, with beautiful illustrations.
Cartledge, Paul, ed., *The Cambridge Illustrated History of Greek Civilization* (Cambridge, UK, 1998). Essays on various aspects of Greek culture by nine leading specialists, with excellent illustrations. It does not give a continuous narrative of Greek history, but, like Sparkes' book (see below), makes a useful supplement to the other works in this list.
Freeman, Charles, *The Greek Achievement* (London 1999). Readable survey by a journalist-turned-historian.

Pomeroy, Sarah, Stanley Burstein, Walter Donlan, and Jennifer Roberts, *Ancient Greece: A Political, Social, and Cultural History* (New York 1998). Much more readable survey than Bury and Meiggs. Also concentrates on political history, but takes a serious look at social trends.

Sparkes, Brian, ed., *Greek Civilization* (Oxford 1998). A collection of nineteen essays on the Greeks, including a useful section of four essays taking the story from the end of the Roman Empire through the twentieth century A.D.

Ethnicity

Hall, Jonathan, *Hellenicity: Between Ethnicity and Culture* (Chicago 2002). Sophisticated discussion of the evolution of Greek ethnicity.

Malkin, Irad, ed., *Ancient Perceptions of Greek Ethnicity* (Cambridge, MA, 2001). Wide-ranging essays on how the Greeks perceived themselves in antiquity.

CHAPTER 2

COUNTRY AND PEOPLE

What was it like to live in ancient Greece? In this chapter, we look at the basic rhythms of Greek life: geography, diet, health, and standards of living. In the next chapter, we describe the family, the basic building block of Greek society in ancient Greece. These two chapters provide the foundations for making sense of Greek history and culture.

In ancient times, economic changes generally happened too slowly for people to perceive them. Yet by the end of the period covered in this book, most Greeks lived longer, ate better, were sick less often, inhabited finer houses, and had more opportunities than their ancestors five hundred years earlier. Life in Hellenistic times was still nasty, poor, brutish, and short by modern standards, but Greeks of this era were better off than those of the Dark Age.

GREEK GEOGRAPHY, CLIMATE, AND AGRICULTURE

Plato, the Athenian philosopher of the fourth century B.C., described the Greeks as "frogs around a pond." Ninety percent of Greeks lived within a day's walk of the Mediterranean. That was where the best farmland was, and people living inland were effectively cut off from the greater world. According to a Roman inscription set up in A.D. 301, it cost less to move a load of grain by ship the thousand miles from one end of the Mediterranean to the other than it did to pile it on wagons and drag it seventy-five miles inland. "The land divides, the sea unites," according to an old saying. The sea was the lifeblood of Greek civilization.

Nearly all Greeks, whether they lived in Athens, Sicily, or Spain (see maps at front and back of book), knew much the same climate and geography, what we now

Figure 2.1 Snow-capped summer peaks in the rugged Pindus range, which runs like a backbone down the center of Greece, dividing the land into small plains usually open to the sea. In the center is a small church.

call a "Mediterranean" environment. The Greek homeland around the Aegean Sea was a world of small coastal plains, cut up by hills and often backed by forbidding mountains (Figure 2.1). The plains were heavily cultivated, while scrub and brush covered the hills (Figure 2.2). Some mountains were homes to pine forests; others were bare and hostile. In the 320s B.C., after Alexander's conquests, Greeks settled in Egypt and Mesopotamia, where they encountered the great Nile, Tigris, and Euphrates rivers. Here farming depended on harnessing rivers through irrigation, but in the north Mediterranean, farmers relied on rainfall to water their crops.

Consequently, to most Greeks, nothing mattered more than rain. Greek writers' comments about the weather, combined with evidence like tree rings from fragments of ancient wood, suggest that the Mediterranean climate of twenty-five hundred years ago was quite like that of today. The hot, dry summers that draw modern tourists to Greek beaches were lazy days for ancient farmers. In July and August, it hardly ever rains, and temperatures reach ninety degrees Fahrenheit. **Hesiod,** an oral poet who may have sung around 700 B.C., tells us in his strange poem of agricultural and moral advice called the ***Works and Days*** that

> When the thistle blooms and on the tree
> The loud cicada sits and pours his song
> shrill and continuous, beneath his wings,
> exhausting summertime has come. The goats
> are very fat, the wine is very good.
> Women are full of lust, but men are weak,

Figure 2.2 The rich Thessalian plain spreads before Mount Olympus, the highest mountain in Greece. Beyond Olympus lies Macedonia.

> their heads and limbs drained dry by Sirius,
> their skin parched from the heat. But at this time,
> I love a shady rock, and Byblos wine,°
> a cake of cheese, and goat's milk, and some meat
> of heifers pastured in the woods, uncalved,
> or first-born kids. Then may I sit in the shade
> And drink the shining wine, and eat my fill.

Hesiod, *Works and Days*, 582–93
(D. Wender)

°*Byblos wine:* Byblos was a trading city in Phoenicia (modern Lebanon); this is special, imported wine.

The cool, wet winters were the busy season. It can snow in December and January in the Greek plains (but rarely does), and the mountains can get blizzards. Hesiod describes Lenaion, the Greek month covering late January and early February:

> The horned and hornless creatures of the wood
> in pain, with chattering teeth, flee through the brush,
> one care in all their minds, to find a cave
> or thickly covered shelter. Like the man,
> three-legged with his staff, with shattered spine,
> whose head looks to the ground, like him they go
> wandering, looking for shelter from the snow.
>   Then put your body in a shelter too;
> a fleecy coat and tunic to the ground,
> woven with thicker woof than warp; do this
> so that your body's hair lies still and does
> not shudder and stand up all over. Next,
> bind on your feet the fitted oxhide boots,
> lined with thick felt. And when the chilly time
> approaches, stitch the hides of newborn kids
> with sinews from an ox into a cape

to keep the rain from falling on your back.
A fitted cap of felt upon your head
keeps your ears dry; when Boreas° attacks
the dawn is cold. . . . Finish your work;
get home ahead of him, so you will not
be swallowed up in that black cloud from heaven
and come home dripping, your clothing soaked.
be on your guard: this is the hardest month.

Hesiod, *Works and Days,* 529–57
(D. Wender)

°*Boreas:* The North Wind.

On average, Athens gets just eight to twenty-four inches of rain each year, while the mountains of Arcadia, less than one hundred miles to the southwest but towering to three thousand feet, get five times as much. But the rain in the plains is not just low: it is also unpredictable. Farmers who sowed their fields with wheat would see their crop fail on average one year in four: That is, when they harvested their grain, they recovered less than they had used as seed. Barley is hardier and failed only one year in twenty, so although Athenians preferred wheat bread to hard barley, most of them made do with gnawing on barley loaves.

The small plains were the prime grain-growing areas, but the thinner soil on the hills supported olives and vines. One of the pleasures of traveling in Greece today is stumbling across hidden upland valleys where farming flourishes. But on the whole, the mountains supported few crops and were used most by herdsmen leading flocks of sheep and goats between high summer pastures and lowland winter grazing. Goats provided milk, cheese, meat, and cloth from their hair; sheep provided meat and wool. The few cattle, so expensive to feed, were used to pull plows and, occasionally, for meat.

The Mediterranean environment made Greek civilization possible but also set limits on what could be done. Greeks liked to talk about how poor they were. At the end of the fourth century B.C., the Athenian comic poet Menander described one character by saying

Poor man, what a life he leads. That's your genuine Attic farmer. He struggles with stony soil that grows thyme and sage, getting a good deal of pain and no profit.

Menander, *The Grumpy Old Man,* 604–606
(N. Miller)

Hesiod, who lived four hundred years before Menander, also warns that only constant struggle and backbreaking labor could yield a living:

The gods desire to keep the means of life
hidden from us. If they did not, you could
work for a day and earn a year's supplies;
you'd pack away your rudder, and retire
the oxen and the laboring mules . . .
    O noble Perses,° keep my words in mind,
and work till Hunger is your enemy
and till Demeter,° awesome, garlanded,
becomes your friend and fills your granary.
For Hunger always loves a lazy man;

°*Perses:* Hesiod's brother, to whom he addresses the poem.   °*Demeter:* The goddess of grain.

both gods and men despise him, for he is
much like the stingless drone, who does not work
but eats, and wastes the efforts of the bees.[6]
But you must learn to organize your work
so you may have full barns at harvest time.
From working, men grow rich in flocks and gold
and dearer to the deathless gods. In work
there is no shame; shame is in idleness.

Hesiod, *Works and Days,* 42–46, 298–311
(D. Wender)

DEMOGRAPHY

When we want to know the facts of life in modern societies—life expectancy, health, population—we consult the government census. Such documents did not exist in ancient times. The educated Greeks who produced the surviving literary texts were not much concerned with such matters. They wrote tragedies, philosophy, and legal speeches, not statistical reports. Nonetheless, by combining the brief literary references to daily life that do survive with archaeology and comparisons with other premodern societies, we can sketch a credible picture of ancient Greek **demography.**

Demography is the study of the biological aspects of human societies: their size, distribution, growth, rates of birth and death, marriage, and disease. Demographers have shown how a tremendous change began in all these aspects of life in western Europe in the eighteenth century A.D. and spread from there to most of the world. Before then, mortality and fertility rates were high, and life expectancy at birth low, typically in the early twenties. Then, in the eighteenth-century "demographic transition," mortality sharply declined. For a while, this made population grow rapidly; then people restricted their fertility through later marriage and contraception, creating the quasi-equilibrium that we are familiar with today, with low fertility rates, low mortality, and high life expectancy at birth (over eighty in the United States). In premodern societies, about one-third of all babies born alive died before their first birthday. Barely half survived to five years. Those who made it through early childhood had a reasonable chance of living into their thirties, but fewer than one in six of the people born reached sixty, and just one in twenty made it to seventy.

These statistics broadly apply to ancient Greece, judging from the evidence of ancient skeletons. The fourth-century-B.C. philosopher Aristotle observed that "most [deaths] occur before the child is a week old." Cemeteries include depressing numbers of infants and young children, often buried inside broken clay wine jars that served as makeshift coffins. In some periods, the very young were buried so casually that we recover few traces at all. Perhaps people dealt with death on this scale by trivializing it to reduce the emotional costs of seeing their young children die. Plutarch (**plū**-tark), a Greek writing in the Roman Empire around A.D. 100, suggests as much:

We neither bring drink nor offerings of drink to those who die in infancy nor do we do for them the things which it is customary to do for the dead; for they had no part in this world or in the things of this world; nor are we devoted to their graves and monuments, nor to the laying out of their bodies, nor do we sit by their bodies; for the laws do not allow us to mourn those of such an age.

Plutarch, *Moralia* 612A
(W.C. Helmbold)

In our own times, the death of a newborn baby can be a catastrophe, causing terrible psychological scars. In ancient Greece, it was just part of life. Every family experienced it, over and over again. High mortality demanded high fertility. To keep population stable in a society with high infant mortality, women had to average four or five live births. Given that some women did not marry, and that in some marriages one or both partners were infertile, many women must have had seven or more live births. But most ancient Greek women died in their mid-to-late thirties, after a childbearing life of just eighteen to twenty years: Bearing and rearing children utterly dominated their lives.

While child mortality was common in ancient Greece, the death of adolescents and young adults from natural causes was not. The Greeks called those who died in these years *aôroi,* "the untimely ones," and bitterly mourned their loss. Their ghosts were powerful, and curse tablets were sometimes buried with them. A young man's death in battle was celebrated as glorious and honorable; but for disease or accident to carry off a young man or woman was simply unfair.

Ancient Greek skeletons suggest that most adults died in their thirties or early forties. Only a few reached their sixties, but we might hesitate to think of these as fortunate. Severe arthritis tormented many. Some Greek poets said they wanted to live into old age, but stressed that they wanted *healthy* old age. Some despaired and prayed to die before they got old. Yet the most famous ancient Greeks generally reached the age of seventy—the philosophers Socrates and Plato, the dramatists Sophocles and Euripides, and perhaps Aeschylus and Aristophanes (ar-is-**tof**-a-nēz). The historians Herodotus and Thucydides, the philosopher Aristotle, the statesman Pericles, and the sculptor Phidias all lived past sixty. Perhaps only those lucky enough to live a long time in good health could establish reputations and rise to the top ranks of achievement.

But demography is not static. There was an upward trend in adult life expectancy across the Stone and Bronze Ages, a decline during the Dark Age, then a peak in Classical and Hellenistic times. By 300 B.C., adults typically lived four or five years longer than those five hundred years earlier lived. If adult women live through more of their fertile years, there is potential for population growth, and this is just what happened. Combining written evidence, excavations, and the study of surface artifacts, we can estimate that population increased about tenfold between 900 and 300 B.C. Around 900 B.C., there were probably no more than 350,000 Greeks, concentrated mainly around the western shores of the Aegean. By 300, 3 million to 3.5 million people called themselves Greeks, lining the coasts of the Mediterranean from Spain to Syria, with some living far up the Nile and in the mountains of Afghanistan.

What caused these long-term changes? We review three main factors: migration, disease, and nutrition.

MIGRATION

Maybe population grew so much because people moved into the Greek homelands from outside, but that does not seem to be the case. The main form of migration into Greece was forced migration: Beginning in the sixth century B.C., some *poleis* imported non-Greek slaves into Greece. Most of the slaves came from the northern

Balkans and from Asia Minor (modern Turkey). Athens was the largest purchaser of imported slaves, and at the height of this practice, in the fourth century B.C., probably had some fifty to eighty thousand slaves. Some were born in Greece in captivity, but most were newly imported in each generation. If we add in all the other Greek states importing slaves, our best guess (it can be no more than that) is that twenty-five hundred to three thousand slaves were imported into Greece per year in the fourth century. This represents 1 to 2.5 percent of the total population of Greece: a lot of people, but nowhere near enough to account for the overall population growth. In fact, the main patterns of migration involved Greeks moving *out* from their old homelands. Between about 750 and 650 B.C., Greek colonization in the west Mediterranean probably involved some thirty thousand adult males (assuming that single men went, finding brides among the natives), or about 2 to 3 percent of the adult males in the Aegean; and between about 330 and 250 B.C., another one hundred to two hundred thousand males emigrated to newly conquered Egypt and the Near East, mostly as soldiers of fortune.

These were important movements of people, both inward and outward, but they account for only a small part of the changes in populations during this period. To know why population grew, we must examine other factors.

HEALTH AND DISEASE

The ancient texts tell us that terrible epidemics could rage through Greece. The historian of the Peloponnesian War, the Athenian **Thucydides** (c. 460–400 B.C.), described a plague that broke out in Athens in 430 B.C., while Spartan armies besieged the city. It killed Pericles, Athens' great leader. Thucydides himself caught it, but survived. His description shows his exceptional powers of observation, which he shared with Greek medical writers:

> Previously attacks of the plague had been reported from many other places in the neighborhood of Lemnos° and elsewhere, but there was no record of the disease having been so virulent anywhere else or causing so many deaths as it did in Athens. At the beginning the doctors were quite incapable of treating the disease because of their ignorance of the right methods. In fact mortality among the doctors was highest of all, because they came more frequently into contact with the sick. Nor was any other human art or science any help at all. Equally useless were prayers made in the temples, consultation of oracles, and so forth; indeed, in the end people were so overcome by their sufferings that they paid no further attention to such things.
>
> The plague originated, so they say, in Ethiopia in upper Egypt,° and spread from there into Egypt itself and Libya and much of the territory of the King of Persia. In the city of Athens it appeared suddenly, and the first cases were among the population of Piraeus,° where there were no wells at that time, so that it was supposed by them that the Spartans had poisoned the reservoirs. Later, however, it appeared also in the upper city,° and by this time the deaths were greatly increasing in number. As to the question of how it could first have come about or what causes can be found adequate to explain its powerful effect on nature, I must leave that to be considered by other writers, with or without medical experience. I myself shall merely describe what it was like, and set down the symptoms, knowledge of which will enable it to be recognized, if it should ever break out again. I had the disease myself and saw others suffering from it.

°*Lemnos:* An island in the Aegean.   °*upper Egypt:* Up the Nile, that is, in southern Egypt. °*Piraeus:* The harbor of Athens, about seven miles from the city.   °*upper city:* That is, Athens.

That year, as is generally admitted, was particularly free from all other kinds of illnesses, though those who did have any illness previously all caught the plague in the end. In other cases, however, there seemed to be no reason for the attacks. People in perfect health suddenly began to have burning feelings in the head; their eyes became red and inflamed; inside their mouths there was bleeding from the throat and tongue, and the breath became unnatural and unpleasant. The next symptoms were sneezing and hoarseness of voice, and before long the pain settled on the chest and was accompanied by coughing. Next the stomach was affected with aches and with vomitings of every kind of bile that has been given a name by the medical profession, all this being accompanied by great pain and difficulty. In most cases there were attacks of ineffectual retching, producing violent spasms; this sometimes ended with this stage of the disease, but sometimes continued long afterwards. Externally the body was not very hot to the touch, nor was there any pallor. The skin was rather reddish and livid, breaking out into small pustules and ulcers. But inside there was a feeling of burning, so that people could not bear the touch even of the lightest linen clothing, but wanted to be completely naked, and most of all would have liked to plunge into cold water. Many of the sick who were uncared for actually did so, plunging into the water-tanks in an effort to relieve a thirst which was unquenchable; for it was just the same with them whether they drank much or little. Then all the time they were afflicted with insomnia and the desperate feeling of not being able to keep still.

In the period when the disease was at its height, the body, so far from wasting away, showed surprising powers of resistance to all the agony, so that there was still some strength left on the seventh or eighth day, which was the time when, in most cases, death came from the internal fever. But if people survived this critical period, then the disease descended to the bowels, producing violent ulceration and uncontrollable diarrhea, so that most of them died later as a result of the weakness caused by this. For the disease, first settling in the head, went on to affect every part of the body in turn, and even when people escaped its worst effects, it still left its traces on them by fastening upon the extremities of the body. It affected the genitals, the fingers, and the toes, and many of those who recovered lost the use of these members; some, too, went blind. There were some also who, when they first began to get better, suffered from a total loss of memory, not knowing who they were themselves and being unable to recognize their friends.

Words indeed fail one when one tries to give a general picture of the disease; and as for the sufferings of individuals, they seemed almost beyond the capacity of human nature to endure. . . .

These, then, were the general features of the disease, though I have omitted all kinds of peculiarities that occurred in various individual cases. Meanwhile, during all this time there was no serious outbreak of any of the usual kinds of illness; if any such cases did occur, they ended in the plague. Some died in neglect, some in spite of every possible care being taken of them. As for a recognized method of treatment, it would be true to say that no such thing existed. What did good in some cases did harm in others. Those with naturally strong constitutions were no better able than the weak to resist the disease, which carried away all alike, even those who were treated and dieted with the greatest care. The most terrible thing of all was the despair into which people fell when they realized that they had caught the plague; for they would immediately adopt an attitude of utter hopelessness, and, by giving in in this way, would lose their powers of resistance. Terrible, too, was the sight of people dying like sheep through having caught the disease as a result of nursing others. This indeed caused more deaths than anything else. For when people were afraid to visit the sick, then they died with no one to look after them. There were many houses in which all the inhabitants perished through lack of any attention. When, on the other hand, they did visit the sick, they lost their own lives, and this was particularly true of those who made it a point of honor to act properly. Such people felt ashamed to think of their own safety and went into their friends' houses at times when even the members of the households were so overwhelmed by the weight of their calamities that they had actually given up the usual practice of making laments for the dead. Yet still the ones who felt most pity for the sick and dying were those who had had the plague themselves and had recovered from it. They knew what it was like and at the same time felt themselves to be safe, for no one caught the disease twice, or, if he did, the second attack was never fatal. Such people were congratulated on all sides, and they themselves were so elated at the time of their recovery that they foolishly imagined that they could never die of any other disease in the future.

Thucydides 2.47–51 (R. Warner)

Thucydides adds a telling note:

A factor that made things much worse than they were already was the removal of people from the country into the city,° and this particularly affected the newcomers. There were no houses for them, and, living as they did during the hot season in badly ventilated huts, they died like flies. The bodies of the dying were heaped one on top of the other, and half-dead creatures could be seen staggering about in the streets or flocking around the fountains in their desire for water.

Thucydides 2.52 (R. Warner)

°*into the city:* Because of the Spartan invasion.

This plague was so severe because Athens was under siege. People were crammed into unsanitary conditions, and the plague—which we cannot identify, in spite of Thucydides' precise description—spread like wildfire.

Such disasters happened only when people were unusually crowded. Most of the time, the main factors limiting life spans were not spectacular epidemics but everyday sicknesses that are no longer major threats in the developed world. By our standards, Greek waste disposal was primitive, and there was little control over drinking water. Thucydides describes how plague victims threw themselves into public water tanks. This was exceptional behavior, but every day people with running sores, diarrhea, and other infectious complaints polluted each other's drinking water. Public health was almost nonexistent. And as if this were not enough, tuberculosis and malaria, whose ancient forms resembled modern ones, were common and deadly, and even minor injuries could turn septic and prove fatal. Young children were particularly at risk, which explains the high infant mortality. Women often died in childbirth from infection and complications. Skeletons suggest that ancient Greeks spent much of their time feeling unwell, infested with internal parasites, their joints painful from heavy labor, and their teeth worn down from eating coarse foods (although with no sugar in their diet, they had few cavities).

This explains why Greeks died so much younger than modern people, but not why their numbers grew so quickly after 800 B.C. The reason is that although their health seems terrible to us, by ancient standards it was quite good. One factor may have been that Greek medical skills were relatively advanced. The most famous Greek doctor was **Hippocrates,** who lived in the late fifth century B.C. He is a shadowy figure, but probably came from the island of Cos, where there was a kind of hospital in Classical and Hellenistic times, and a great temple to the healing god Asclepius. Hippocrates is said to have written the famous Hippocratic Oath that physicians take to this day:

I swear by Apollo the healer, by Asclepius,° by Health and all the powers of healing, and call to witness all the gods and goddesses that I may keep this oath and this promise to the best of my ability. . . .

°*Asclepius:* The god of medicine.

I will use my power to help the sick to the best of my ability and judgment; I will abstain from harming or wronging any man by it.

I will not give a fatal draft to anyone if I am asked, nor will I suggest any such thing. Neither will I give a woman the means to procure an abortion.

I will be chaste and religious in my life and in my practice.

I will not use surgery, even on [those suffering from] stones, but I will leave such procedures to the practitioners of that craft.

Whenever I go into a house, I will go to help the sick and never with the intention of doing harm or injury. I will not abuse my position to indulge in sexual contacts with the bodies of women or of men, whether they be free or slaves.

Whatever I see or hear, professionally or privately, which ought not to be divulged, I will keep secret and tell no one.

If, therefore, I observe this oath and do not violate it, may I prosper both in my life and in my profession, earning good repute among all men for all time. If I transgress and forswear this oath, may my lot be otherwise.

Hippocrates, *The Oath* (G. E. R. Lloyd)

Hippocrates was the greatest Greek physician, but he had many competitors.[7] The kings of Persia would use only Greek doctors and gave them huge gifts. The top doctors were among the richest men in Greece. Around 530 B.C., the ruler of a Greek island paid a doctor one hundred *minai* for his services—what a skilled laborer would earn in forty years!

Greek doctors excelled at diagnosis and prognosis, categorizing illnesses into complex typologies and predicting their course and outcome. But they were less skilled on the causes of diseases, and worse still at actually treating them. They lacked microscopes, which transformed the treatment of disease in modern times. Their knowledge of the body was crude, and they had little interest in dissection. Hippocrates summed it up by saying, "Life is short. Art is long. Opportunity is brief. Experiment is dangerous. Judgment is difficult." Aristotle—living a hundred years later—conceded that "The internal parts of the body, especially those belonging to humans, are unknown."

If you survived childhood in ancient Greece, you would probably make it through your twenties and thirties unless you suffered an injury or a particularly virulent infection came your way. After forty, your chances steadily declined. If you were rich, a doctor might stave off some threats, and upper-class Greeks had better health care than others. If you were poor, you were on your own.

NUTRITION

Resistance to disease depends on health, and health depends on diet. Most ancient Greeks ate simply. Barley bread was the basic food. Poets called humans "bread-eating mortals"; meat was a luxury, and Greeks rarely ate it. There is roughly a ten-to-one conversion ratio between grains and animals, meaning that every calorie you get from eating beef has cost ten calories in grains to produce (there is a further ten-to-one conversion ratio between herbivores like cows and carnivores like lions, which is one reason why people do not rear lions for meat!). In Greece, animals were raised more for muscle-power than for meat, except at religious sacrifices, which required the slaughter of animals (Figure 2.3). Sheep and goats were the principal sacrificial victims, as they were the most common domestic animals, along

Figure 2.3 At the sacrificial altar. A line of five women and one man, perhaps dancing, approaches an altar on which a fire burns. The priest is about to cook the meat of the sacrificial victim in the fire, from an Athenian wine cup, circa 540 B.C.

with pigs, although there were regional specialties. In Boeotia (bē-ō-sha) in central Greece, giant eels were popular for sacrifices.

Homeric heroes scorned fish as a food, and in one episode in the *Odyssey*, a hero preferred death to eating fish. But in classical times, fish were considered a delicacy. In comedy, the standard way to portray someone as decadent was to have him eat lots of fish. Small fry like sardines and sprats were cheap, and no doubt people living on the coast ate plenty of them. The best that people living inland could hope for was salted fish, while bigger fish like tuna, mackerel, and sturgeon were rare and expensive for everyone.

The most important supplements to cereals were olives and wine (Figure 2.4). Bread, olives, and wine made up the **Mediterranean triad,** the core of the Greek diets from the third millennium B.C. until the twentieth century A.D. So far, archaeologists have found little evidence of significant changes in the types of grains, olives, and vines grown throughout the first millennium B.C.

The typical diet was monotonous and protein-poor, but healthy and tasty. Garlic, onions, grapes, goat cheese, and some kinds of sausage were common. Rich Greeks spiced up their bread with sauces and dips and, by the late fifth century B.C., developed a varied cuisine. In the fourth century B.C., a Sicilian chef not only won an international reputation but wrote a mock epic poem about a culinary tour of the Mediterranean.

Historians of modern economies have found a strong correlation between the quality of children's nutrition and their height as adults. Modern historians

Figure 2.4 Olive harvest; on a black-figure *amphora* ("jar with two handles") by the Antimenes painter, circa 520 B.C. Three men knock olives from trees, while a fourth puts olives into a basket. *Courtesy of the Trustees of the British Museum.*

generally study abundant records of army recruitment or factory hiring giving individuals' heights. No such documents exist from ancient Greece, of course, but we can calculate heights from excavated skeletons. Ancient Greeks were short: In the Classical Period, men typically stood about five feet, six inches, and women five feet, two inches. Back in the Dark Age, Greeks had been shorter still—the average man by an inch and a half, and the average woman by two inches. Nutrition clearly improved between about 900 and 300 B.C., and sources of food became more reliable, so children went hungry less often. Compared to modern Mediterranean populations, classical Greeks were quite well nourished. As recently as 1949, recruits into the Cypriot army were shorter than Greek men of the fifth and fourth centuries B.C.

Part of the explanation for Greek population growth lies, therefore, in nutrition. As they moved from the Dark Age to classical times, Greeks ate better, lived longer, and multiplied. Life in the fourth century B.C. was hard, but it was better than life in the ninth century B.C.

Standards of Living

A major element in the material quality of life—perhaps the most important, after food itself—is shelter. In the Dark Age, houses were simple. Most were one-room structures, with the back end often curved in a shape called *apsidal,* saving the builders from having to construct corners. All activities—cooking, eating, sleeping—went on either in the one main room or in the open air. The walls were too thin to support a second floor. Six hundred years later, the basic materials— mud brick walls on stone foundations—were the same, but now houses had tile roofs and internal courtyards, shady in summer and sheltered from the rain in winter (Figure 2.5). They had functionally distinct rooms: cooking went on in one, eating in another, drinking in another still. Many had paved floors, simple latrines and drains, and staircases to the second floor. The roofed part of the ground level covered some twenty-four hundred square feet in typical houses, about the norm for contemporary American housing and five times the area of the typical Dark Age house. Depending on how much of the upstairs part was roofed, it may have been twice this size, a commodious and pleasant house by any standards.

As well as living longer and eating better, then, classical Greeks had richer and more varied domestic goods than Dark Age Greeks. Greece had increased significantly in wealth: A fourth-century house must have cost five to ten times as much as one built in the tenth century.

The public amenities of Greek cities also improved drastically. By the sixth century B.C., major centers like Athens and Syracuse had underground pipes bringing drinking water to the downtown areas, and even quite small cities had fountain houses. Magnificent temples, beautiful statues, and strong fortifications were found all over Greece. In the tenth century B.C., Athens probably had an urban population under two thousand; in the fifth century, she reached forty thousand; and in the

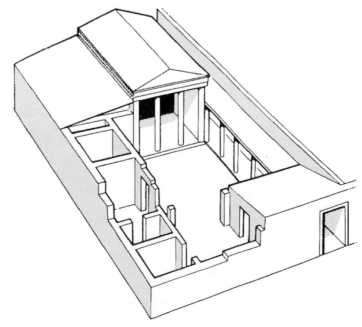

Figure 2.5 Reconstruction of a house of circa 850 B.C., from Nichoria in southwest Greece. This simple hut had a rough stone foundation, mudbrick walls, and a thatched roof.

fourth century B.C., Syracuse was twice that size. What caused these improvements in the material bases of life in Greece?

ECONOMIC GROWTH IN ANCIENT GREECE

The last 250 years have witnessed a revolution in human life. Eighteenth-century Europeans learned to harness the power of fossil fuels, beginning with steam produced by burning coal. As this technology spread, inventors made increasingly radical breakthroughs. We nowadays take it for granted that technology drives economic growth, but this was not so in ancient Greece. In the Classical and Hellenistic Periods, the basic technologies—plows and manure in agriculture, ships and carts in transport, bronze armor and iron weapons in war—had been around for centuries. There were steady, small improvements, but not until the third century B.C. did scientists in the Greek city of Alexandria in Egypt make inventions that could really improve production (see Chapter 21, "Hellenistic Culture, 323–30 B.C."). The economic growth that took place between the Dark Age and the Classical Period depended on changes in the way society was organized, not on new technology.

Such changes were not the result of conscious economic planning. Even the great Aristotle had only the vaguest understanding of economics. Rather, while pursuing other goals, Greeks accidentally set free forces of growth that most other ancient societies had kept in check. One of the most important was the increasing personal freedom of the Greek citizen. In the Classical Period, ordinary citizens had better legal protection than citizens of most ancient civilizations. It was difficult (though not impossible) for wealthy neighbors or agents of the state to defraud them, seize their property, or sell them into slavery. Shielded to some extent from arbitrary plunder, they had more incentive to invest effort and resources into farming or to add to their income through trading and craft.

Ancient Greeks fought for the freedom of the citizen because they thought it was morally right, not because they thought it would stimulate economic growth. Such unintended consequences are important themes in historical study. As we shall see, alphabetic writing was probably adapted from the Phoenician system and developed to record poetry in the eighth century, but it also simplified traders' record-keeping. Coinage, apparently introduced around 600 B.C. as a form of political propaganda, also facilitated exchange. Athens passed a law around 425 B.C. requiring all subjects in her empire to use Athenian weights, measures, and coins, no doubt to make collecting imperial tribute easier; but the law also promoted trade between cities. Little by little, the Greek world became more economically integrated. Wheat and barley moved from Sicily and the Ukraine to feed urban Athens; finished goods like decorated pots and olive oil flowed in the reverse direction. Piraeus, Athens' harbor town, became the greatest market in the Aegean. According to one Athenian around 440 B.C., "Whatever is sweet in Sicily or in Italy, in Cyprus, Egypt, or Lydia, in Pontus or the Peloponnesus or anywhere else—all these are gathered here in one place."

As wealth increased, people improved their diets and housing. Health improved and mortality declined; and as these processes unfolded, population increased.

Growing numbers meant a more sophisticated division of labor. Individuals, towns, and whole regions specialized, exploiting the unequal distribution of personal skills and natural endowments. The division of labor improved efficiency and created more wealth, allowing people to eat and live better still, leading to further reductions in mortality, which stimulated more population growth . . . and so on, in a self-reinforcing cycle. By our best guess, classical Greeks on average consumed 50 percent more wealth than their Dark Age predecessors.

Without this economic growth, the cultural achievements that fill this book could not have happened. But let us close this chapter by stressing two facts. First, although conditions were better for the typical Greek in the fourth century B.C. than they were in the tenth century B.C., life was still hard by our own standards. Even in the best of times, Greeks were stunted and malnourished compared to people in modern developed countries. Economic growth reached a ceiling, slowed, and finally stopped. You can go only so far by reorganizing institutions. Without technological advances, there are limits to growth. The Greeks reached these limits and never went further.

Second, Greek economic growth was linked to slavery. Only a minority of the population of Greece were slaves, but they played an essential role. People who could afford slaves could add labor to enterprises when they needed it and then dispose of unprofitable workers. Some wealthy people bought gangs of slaves and rented them to entrepreneurs for difficult and dangerous work like mining. Classical Greek civilization could not have existed without slavery, which gave an elite group the freedom to fashion a remarkable civilization. We ourselves use labor-saving machines to create comparable leisure, leaving us free to abominate slavery. How, then, should we evaluate the Greek achievement, given the different material circumstances in which they lived?

KEY TERMS

Hesiod, 14	Thucydides, 19
Works and Days, 14	Hippocrates, 21
demography, 17	Mediterranean triad, 23

FURTHER READING

Physical World

Osborne, Robin, *Classical Landscape with Figures* (London 1987). Good introduction to the natural environment of ancient Greece.

Daily Life

Garland, Robert, *Daily Life of the Ancient Greeks* (Westport, CT, 1998). Excellent survey of all aspects of everyday life. The best introduction to many of the topics in this chapter.

Demography

Scheidel, Walter, "The Demographic Background of the Greek Expansion." In *Journal of Hellenic Studies* 103 (2003) 40–60. Excellent overview of demographic trends in Greece.

Health and Disease

Grmek, Mirko, *Diseases in the Ancient Greek World* (Baltimore 1989). A detailed introduction.

Nutrition

Dalby, Andrew, *Siren Feasts: A History of Food and Gastronomy in Greece* (London 1996). Overview of Greek dietary habits and the growth of a sophisticated cuisine.

Davidson, James, *Courtesans and Fishcakes: The Consuming Passions of Classical Athens* (New York 1997). Amusing look at Athenian food, sexuality, and elite culture.

Garnsey, Peter, *Food and Society in Classical Antiquity* (Cambridge, UK, 1999). Excellent summary of food, nutrition, and health.

Standards of Living and Economic Growth

Morris, Ian, "Archaeology, Standards of Living, and Greek Economic History," In Joe Manning and Ian Morris, eds., *The Ancient Economy: Evidence and Models* (Stanford 2005). A first attempt to estimate changes in the standard of living in Greece.

Ancient Texts

Hesiod, *Works and Days*. In *Hesiod and Theognis* (Harmondsworth, UK, 1973; tr. Dorothea Wender). Agricultural poem.

Hippocrates, *Airs, Waters, Places*. In *Hippocratic Writings* (New York 1978; ed. G. E. R. Lloyd). Account of climate and disease, probably written around 400 B.C.

Thucydides, *The Peloponnesian War* (Harmondsworth, UK, 1954; tr. Rex Warner).

CHAPTER 3

THE GREEKS AT HOME

If land was the economic foundation of ancient Greece, the *oikos,* "house/family" (root of our word *eco*nomic) was its social foundation. The *oikos* was broader than our concept of family, because it included slaves, close relations, and the house and its contents. Nonetheless, the basis of the *oikos* was a monogamous union of man and woman to produce and rear legitimate children. We therefore begin with Greek relationships between the sexes.

GENDER RELATIONSHIPS: IDEALS AND REALITIES

Throughout Greek history, virtually all the men who wrote our texts agreed on a few points about marriage. Men should wed around the age of thirty; women, as teenagers. Brides should be virgins (no man would marry a woman who was not). A marriage (Figure 3.1) was contracted between a groom and the parents of his bride-to-be, who gave their daughter a dowry to help set up the new household. A wife should obey her husband and not act independently, except within the *oikos,* where she was responsible for preparing food, rearing children, and producing cloth. Laws varied from *polis* to *polis,* but usually women owned little or no real estate, the basic economic resource. In most cities, laws limited women to trivial financial transactions and denied them access to the legal system, an all-male preserve. Some ancient authors took it for granted that husbands would beat disobedient wives (although no source actually describes a beating).

Of course, all our sources are texts produced by men for men. Scrappy evidence suggests that some females found ways around the laws on property and used males to get access to the courts. Scholars have assiduously examined the few dozen lines that survive of the extraordinary, almost unique, female poet **Sappho,** who lived

Figure 3.1 A woman, named as Thalea, prepares for her wedding on a red-figure *pyxis*, a box for keeping trinkets, circa 440 B.C. A servant (off photo to the right) offers the bride a chest, perhaps containing toiletries, while another approaches from behind to tie her hair with a ribbon. A third servant stands on the far left. Notice the bronze mirror on the wall, indicating an interior setting.

around 600 B.C., hoping to detect evidence for a female viewpoint on gender, but little can be said except that the tone of her poetry is similar to that of her male contemporaries. Sappho celebrates love and marriage as woman's primary concerns (Figure 3.2). She addressed some poems to other women, suggesting to readers since Roman times (but never to Greeks) that she celebrated homoerotic love: hence our term *lesbian* (because Sappho lived on the island of Lesbos). However, her voice is never personal: She wrote poems to be memorized and performed by others at weddings, the only time in a respectable woman's life when her sexuality could be publicly celebrated without shame. The men may have made the rules, but the respectable women—mothers, grandmothers, aunts—enforced them.

Our male sources often represent women as an evil influence, virtually a separate species. Such **misogyny** ("hatred for women") is an important theme in Greek culture. Hesiod justified it with a story of how Zeus, ruler of the gods, created the dreaded race of females to punish men for having accepted the theft of fire from heaven (Figure 3.3). Zeus says

> "I'll give another gift
> To men, an evil thing for their delight,
> and all will love this ruin in their hearts."
> So spoke the father of men and gods, and laughed.
> He told Hephaestus° quickly to mix earth
> and water, and to put in it a voice
> and human power to move, to make a face
> like an immortal goddess, and to shape
> the lovely figure of a virgin girl.

°*Hephaestus:* The lame, ugly god of craftsmen (better known today by his Roman name Vulcan).

Figure 3.2 Sappho, as imagined by a red-figure painter around 460 B.C., perhaps 150 years after she flourished. The figure is labeled "Sappho." She sits on a folding chair and studies a papyrus with a poetic text (we cannot read it). A woman standing before her offers the lyre that accompanied many forms of Greek poetry. *Sappho. Detail of a Greek vase painting, c. 440 B.C. The Granger Collection, New York.*

Athena° was to teach the girl to weave,
and golden Aphrodite° to pour charm
upon her head, and painful, strong desire,
and body-shattering cares. Zeus ordered, then,
the killer of Argos, Hermes,° to put in
sly manners and the morals of a bitch.
The son of Cronus° spoke, and was obeyed.
The lame god° molded earth as Zeus decreed
into the image of a modest girl,
gray-eyed Athena made her robes and belt,
divine Seduction and the Graces gave
her golden necklaces, and for her head
the Seasons wove spring flowers into a crown.
Hermes the messenger put in her breast
lies and persuasive words and cunning ways;
the herald of the gods then named the girl
Pandora,° for the gifts which all the gods

°*Athena:* The virgin goddess of war and handicrafts, who sprang fully formed from Zeus's head.   °*Aphrodite:* The beautiful goddess of sexual attraction (Roman Venus).   °*Hermes:* Messenger of the gods, and god of trickery, trade, and travel (Roman Mercury); Argos was a monster with a hundred eyes that Hermes killed.   °*Cronus:* The son of Cronus was Zeus. °*lame god:* Hephaestus.   °*Pandora:* "all-gifted."

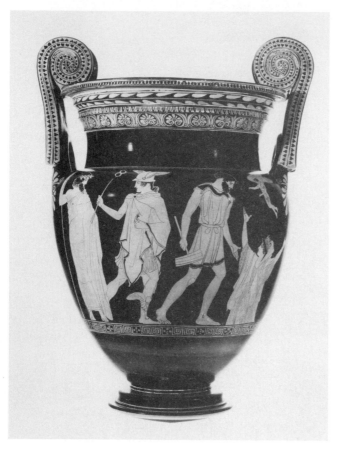

Figure 3.3 Epimetheus, brother of Prometheus, takes Pandora's hand as she rises from the earth; on a red-figure Athenian *krater* (wine-mixing vase), circa 450 B.C. On the far left, Zeus oversees his plan to punish man by inventing woman. The messenger god Hermes carries his wand and wears a magic cap and shoes. *Ashmolean Museum, Oxford, England, U.K.*

had given her, this ruin of mankind.
The deep and total trap was now complete:
the father sent the gods' fast messenger
to bring the gift to Epimetheus.°
And Epimetheus forgot the words
his brother said to take no gift from Zeus,
but send it back, so that it would not injure men.
He took the gift and understood, too late.
Before this time men lived upon the earth
apart from sorrow and from painful work,
free from disease, which brings the death-gods in.
But now the woman opened up the jar°
and scattered pains and evils among men.
Inside the jar's hard walls remained one thing,
Hope, only, which did not fly through the opening.
The lid stopped her, but all the others flew,
thousands of troubles, wandering the earth.
The earth is full of evils, and the sea.

°*Epimetheus:* Epimetheus (epē-mē-thūs), a mortal whose name means "afterthought," was the brother of Prometheus (pro-mē-thūs, "forethought") and was constantly being tricked. Epimetheus ended up marrying Pandora, and all humans descend from their union.   °*jar:* Apparently a gift from Zeus. A medieval mistranslation led to the phrase "Pandora's box."

Diseases come to visit men by day
and, uninvited, come again at night
bringing their pains in silence, for they were
deprived of speech by Zeus the wise. And so
there is no way to flee the mind of Zeus.

Hesiod, *Works and Days* 57–105
(D. Wender)

Hesiod makes women's inferiority and dangerous intentions part of Zeus' cosmic plan to punish wicked mortals, embodied in the lovely but untrustworthy female Pandora ("all-gifted"), so called because many gods endowed her with gifts. Later Greek writers offered more nuanced interpretations. The most interesting was written soon after 400 B.C. by **Xenophon** (**zen**-o-fon), an Athenian aristocrat and professional soldier, as part of a larger treatise describing a fictional conversation between Socrates and a man named Ischomachus (is-**kom**-a-kus). Figure 3.4 supports Xenophon's observations.

"I've got a question on this too, Ischomachus," I [Socrates] said. "I'd be very glad if you could tell me whether you personally taught your wife how to be a model wife, or

Figure 3.4 Women drawing water from a well house; on an Attic black-figure vase, circa 530 B.C. One woman fills her amphora while two others, jugs balanced on their heads, gossip. A third woman faces the other way. Drawing water was a regular chore.

whether when her parents gave her to you she already knew how to manage her sphere of responsibility."

"How on earth could she know that when I received her, Socrates?" he asked. "She wasn't yet fifteen years old when she came to me, and in her life up till then considerable care had been taken that she should see and hear as little as possible. Don't you think one should be content if all she knew was how to turn wool into a cloak, and all she'd seen was how wool-spinning is assigned to the female servants? I was content, Socrates," he added, "because when she came, she'd been excellently coached as far as her appetite was concerned, and that seems to me the most important training, for the husband as well as the wife."

"What about all the other things she needed to know, Ischomachus? . . . Please tell me where you started, Ischomachus," I said. "What did you teach her first? I'd rather hear you describe this than the most spectacular athletic competition or horse-race!"

"All right, Socrates," said Ischomachus in reply. "I waited until she'd been broken in and was tame enough for a conversation, and then I asked her something along the following lines. 'Tell me, my dear, have you realized yet why I married you and why your parents gave you to me? I mean, I know, and it's clear to you too, that it wouldn't have been difficult for each of us to have found someone else to share our beds. But for my part, I was considering whom it was in my interest to get as the best person to share my home with and my children, and your parents had your interest at heart. So I chose you, and your parents apparently preferred me to all other eligible candidates. Now, as far as children are concerned, we will wait to see if the god grants us any before thinking about how best to bring them up. One of the advantages we will share with each other is having them to support us and look after us as well as they can when we grow old. But what we share now is this home of ours, and we share it because I make all my income available for both of us, and you have deposited all that you brought with you in the same common pool.° There's no need to add up which of us has made the greater contribution quantitatively, but we much appreciate that whichever of us is the better partner contributes more qualitatively.'

"To this, Socrates, my wife replied, 'What assistance can I be to you? What can I do? It's all up to you. My mother told me that my job was to be responsible.'

"'Yes, my dear, of course,' I said. 'My father gave me the same advice. But you should know that responsible people of either sex should act in such a way as to ensure that their property is in the best possible condition and is increased as much as fair and honest dealings permit.'

"'And what can I do to increase our estate?' asked my wife. 'Can you see anything I can do?'

"'Yes, I surely can,' I replied. 'You can try to utilize to the best of your ability the talents which the gods have implanted in you and society approves.'

"'What talents do you mean?' she asked.

"'Ones which, in my opinion,' I said, 'are far from worthless—unless the jobs over which the queen bee of a hive presides are worthless! I'll tell you what I'm getting at, my dear. I think that the gods exercised especially acute discernment in establishing the particular pairing which is called "male" and "female," to ensure that, when the partners co-operate, such a pair may be of the utmost mutual benefit. In the first place, this pairing with each other is established as a procreative unit so that animal species might not die out. In the second place, human beings, at any rate, are supplied with the means to have supporters in their old age as a result of this pairing. In the third place, human life, unlike that of other animals, which live in the open, obviously requires shelter. But if people are to have something to store in this shelter, then they need someone to work out in the open: plowing, sowing, planting, and pasturing are all open-air jobs, and they are the sources of the necessities of life.

"Now, when these necessities have been brought under cover, then in turn there is a need for someone to keep them safe and to do the jobs for which shelter is required. Looking after newborn children requires shelter, as does making bread from grain and clothes from wool.

°In the form of a dowry, conventional in Greek marriage.

"'Because both of these domains—indoor and outdoor—require work and attention, then the god, as I see it, directly made woman's nature suitable for the indoor jobs and tasks, and man's nature suitable for the outdoor ones. For he made the masculine body and mind more capable of enduring cold and heat and travel and military expeditions, which implies that he ordained the outdoor work for man; and the god seems to me to have assigned the indoor work to woman, since he made the female body less capable in these respects.

"And knowing that he had made it the woman's natural job to feed newborn children, he apportioned to her a greater facility for loving newborn infants than he did to man. And because he had assigned to the woman the work of looking after the stores, the god, recognizing that timidity is no disadvantage in such work, gave a larger share of fearfulness to woman than he did to man.'"

Xenophon, *The Estate Manager* 7.4–20
(H. Treddenick, R. Waterfield)

Unlike Hesiod, Xenophon does not represent woman as man's punishment, but does believe that the gods made men superior to women: tougher, more disciplined, and more suited to an outdoor life. Yet marriage is a partnership. The husband is in control, yes, but he and his wife must work together. A virtuous husband can educate his wife so that her contribution to the household becomes equal to his own. Socrates is so impressed by the description that he interjects, "Good heavens, Ischomachus! On your evidence, your wife has a mind as good as a man's!"

Another Athenian writer, Andocides (an-**dos**-i-dēz) (fourth century B.C.), gives a different account of Ischomachus' wife and tells us her name, Chrysilla. In Xenophon's version, she happily stays home, trying to live up to Ischomachus' standards. In Andocides' version, she begins an affair with a man named Callias, who marries Ischomachus' daughter while sleeping with Chrysilla—his own mother-in-law—at the same time! Chrysilla then moves in with Callias and his wife (her daughter). The distraught daughter attempts suicide before leaving Callias, who throws out Chrysilla, now pregnant with his child. Later, Callias takes Chrysilla back and adopts their son, and they all live together (though perhaps not happily). Perhaps Xenophon idealized Chrysilla to exemplify what he (and many Athenian men) thought marriage *ought* to be like.

SEXUALITY

Ischomachus says that he chose his wife because she was "the best person to share my home and my children." A wife's success was judged largely by her ability to produce sons. After all, a stable population required the average woman to have four or five live births, as we have seen; during periods of population growth, as in the fifth century, the average was seven to eight. Marriage followed swiftly on menarche, pregnancy swiftly on that. Most women remained pregnant or nursing for their whole married lives.

Male writers often refer to sexual activity in marriage as "work," the work of producing heirs. Impregnation they saw as a farmer plowing seed in a field. Sex outside marriage was available to men in various forms, but was a catastrophe for women. Many men owned slaves, and sexual relations between master and slaves (female and male) were commonplace. But adultery with a free woman was dangerous. The woman's guardian—her father, husband, brother, or son—could, and sometimes did, kill the adulterer (though he usually spared the adulteress). Most *poleis* took steps to prevent retaliation from turning into blood-feuds by imposing heavy fines on the adulterer. In Athens, for example, the fine for adultery was twice that for rape, apparently because a rapist committed a one-time assault, while a seducer turned a woman's mind against her *oikos,* inflicting a permanent scar on another man's property and reputation. Worse still, a seduced wife might pass off the adulterer's son as a legitimate heir, thereby stealing the entire household.

Prostitutes were a more attractive source of sexual pleasure for the male, and there were many of them in major *poleis* like Athens and Corinth. Greeks divided prostitutes into two categories: *hetairai,* or "courtesans," and *pornai,* or "whores" (root of *porn*ography, "whore-writing"). A courtesan named **Aspasia** (as-**pas**-ē-a), Pericles' mistress, conversed with the day's leading intellectuals, and Plato joked that she wrote some of Pericles' speeches. A few courtesans made fortunes from their trade. But most sex-workers were *pornai* (singular form, *pornê*), whose lives were not glamorous (Figure 3.5).

Comic writers in fifth-century Athens make prostitution sound fun-filled, but we occasionally glimpse another side. The fourth-century Athenian speechwriter Andocides tells of a slave girl who slept with her master. He got tired of her and decided to sell her to a brothel (most *pornai* were slaves). The slave was so terrified that she poisoned him and, accidentally, a visiting friend too. When her plot was discovered, she was tortured and executed.

We know little about Greek brothels. A possible brothel of around 400 B.C. has been found in Athens, but its identification remains controversial (it is not obvious

Figure 3.5 An aging *pornê* masturbates a client; from a red-figure Athenian *kylix,* circa 510 B.C. *Phintias (Painter), "Attic Red-Figure Kylix," The J. Paul Getty Museum, Villa Collection, Malibu, California. Malibu 80. AE31 © The J. Paul Getty Museum.*

what archaeologists could dig up to prove that an ancient building was used for commercial sex). The Athenian building had a maze of small rooms, and finds include many images of Aphrodite, the sex-goddess, and ornaments from Asia Minor and the northern Balkans, the source of many slaves in Greece. Other finds suggest that the building was an inn and a center for weaving—other sides of brothel life, according to literary sources.

Greek men also had sexual relations with boys and, occasionally, with men of their own age. In modern times, male homosexuality is sometimes coyly called "Greek love," but Greek same-sex relationships were different from modern homosexual behavior. In its usual (and usually respectable) form, a mature male was the sexually active partner (the *erastês,* or "lover"), while a prepubescent passive partner (the *eromenos,* or "beloved") received the erect penis of the *erastês* between his thighs (so-called intercrural intercourse). Such **pederasty** ("boy-love") grew out of the social environment of the Greek **symposium,** or "drinking party," where prepubescent males served wine and prepared to become men. It was, however, shameful to remain an *eromenos* after sexual maturity. The fifth-century B.C. comic poet Aristophanes savagely ridiculed men who put themselves in the position of a woman, that is, were the recipients in anal intercourse with other males.

In Greek pederasty, the adult *erastês* introduced his younger *eromenos* to the ways of polite society, establishing social contacts for help later in life (Figure 3.6). If the *eromenos* was wealthy, talented, from a famous family, or particularly handsome, he would reflect back honor onto his *erastês.* Some Greek writers, notably Plato, thought that the relationship should remain chaste (hence the expression "Platonic love"), focusing on intellectual development; others thought that the relationship should be explicitly sexual but come to an end when the *eromenos* reached puberty and the first traces of a beard appeared.

Figure 3.6 Pederastic scene; from an Attic black-figure *kylix,* circa 530 B.C. An older *erastês* touches a younger *eromenos.*

We know a fair amount, then, about male sexual life, but our sources, written by men, say little about female sexual life. Athenian law required that women convicted of adultery be divorced, whether their husbands wanted it or not. The adulteress was disgraced and sent back to her parents, if they still lived. She was also forbidden to attend public religious festivals, the equivalent of males being banned from political life. With little chance of finding a new husband, women caught in adultery faced ruin and poverty.

Occasionally, comic writers joked about free women having sex with male slaves, and comedies and vase painting made great play out of women finding pleasure in dildoes. Many erotic illustrations survive—only Japanese art showed a parallel concern with sexual and pornographic art. Of course, such vessels were painted for male amusement. The illustrations suggest that the Greeks were not prudish about sex, but they were meant for men's eyes alone in the sometimes licentious environment of the symposium. True, in art men are usually shown naked, unlike in any earlier society, but such conventions do not appeal to a prurient interest. Respectable women in art, by contrast, are clothed until the fourth century B.C., for it was shameful to see a woman's body. Some men felt that respectable women should be veiled in public. Parents were anxious for the safety of their children's bodies, and strict rules prohibited seduction within the gymnasium, where men and boys were naked and females forbidden. Greek erotic art probably represents general Greek attitudes toward sexuality no better than contemporary pornography represents modern attitudes.

ADULTS AND CHILDREN

According to Euripides, one of the great tragedians of fifth-century B.C. Athens, children were the center of life. "Both the best of mortals and those who are nobodies love children. They differ in material things. Some have property and some do not; but the whole race is child-loving." Typically, married couples were surrounded by small children for most of their lives together.

Different *poleis* imposed different educations and customs on their citizens. Sparta, especially, was distinct. We will discuss Spartan customs in detail in Chapter 10, "A Tale of Two Archaic Cities: Sparta and Athens, 700–480 B.C." We know far more about Athens than other *poleis,* but can perhaps generalize about "Greek customs" from our study of Athenian customs.

The burden of child-rearing fell on the mother. Xenophon explains:

> The husband both supports his partner in childbearing and provides for the children that are to be born everything that he thinks will be an asset to them in life, and he provides it as fully as he can. The wife conceives and carries this burden, bearing the weight of it, risking her life and giving up a share of her own nourishment. And after all her trouble in carrying the child for the full time and bringing it to birth, she feeds and cares for it, although the child has never done her any good and does not know who his benefactor is. He cannot even communicate what he wants; his mother's attempts to supply what will be good for the child and give pleasure depend on her power of guessing. And she goes on rearing him for a long time, putting up with drudgery day and night, without knowing whether she will receive any gratitude.

Xenophon, *Memoirs of Socrates* 2.2.5
(H. Treddenick, R. Waterfield)

Birth and the first few days of life were hazardous for children and dangerous to the mother. There were no hospitals, let alone epidurals or caesarian sections, but midwives no doubt had plenty of experience and the folk wisdom that comes from experience. All the same, Euripides, in his tragedy the *Medea,* has the heroine proclaim that she would rather stand three times behind a shield in battle than give birth once.

Fathers had the right to decide whether to keep newborn babies or to expose them to die. Our information is poor, but apparently girls were exposed more than boys. Unwanted babies were left in a well-known spot that slave-traders would check and would either die of exposure or be sold into a lifetime of servitude. Many prostitutes began life in this way. The famous myth of Oedipus begins with his being exposed to die as an accursed child.

Wanted babies who survived their first few days underwent rituals that brought them into the community in a formal way. The most important was the ***amphidromia,*** or "running around." Holding the baby in his arms, the father walked around the hearth, presenting the baby to **Hestia** (**hes**-ti-a), goddess of the hearth (her name means "hearth"). The *amphidromia* established the child's legitimacy and its future status as a citizen. Friends and neighbors brought gifts of octopus and cuttlefish. The parents hung an olive branch outside the front door if the child was a boy, and a tuft of wool for a girl. Whatever the sex, they smeared the walls with black tar to turn away hostile spirits released by the bloody fluids that attend childbirth.

Many parents named the child at this fifth-day festival, but those who could afford to hold a second party delayed naming until the *dekatê,* the "tenth day," when women danced and honey cakes were passed around. Unlike in most modern societies, Greeks gave children only one name, used in conjunction with the father's name—for example, "Pericles, son of Xanthippos." Firstborn sons often took their father's father's name; other sons commonly took variants on their father's name. As in our own world, names went in and out of fashion.

Greek medicine was superior to others in the ancient world, but riddled nonetheless with superstition. For example, Galen, a famous second-century-A.D. doctor (see Chapter 21, "Hellenistic Culture, 323–30 B.C."), advised against giving babies protein-rich colostrum, the premilk fluid which comes from a mother's breast before the milk itself and prevents infection. Families that could afford it gave their children to wet nurses, although mothers' milk is best. Swaddling was common, although it can deform bones if babies have a poor diet. Doctors recommended weaning at dangerously early or dangerously late ages, hardly ever at appropriate ones. Microscopic analysis of teeth shows that most Greek children experienced periods of malnutrition.

Whatever the medical disadvantages, intense bonds might develop between a child and its wet nurse. A wet nurse in a play by Aeschylus says:

My own Orestes, he wore me out.
I raised him, taking him from his mother.
Oh, the many and troublesome tasks
when he cried out to me in the night
waking me up, fruitless though I endured them . . .
For you must nurse the senseless thing

> like a dumb beast the best you can,
> What else can you do? While still in diapers,
> a babe has no speech at all, whether it is hungry,
> or thirsty, or wants to make water.
> The young insides of children go on their own way.
> Often I could tell, but just as often I was deceived
> and had to wash the child's linen, as much laundry-maid as nurse.
> Performing these twin duties, I raised up Orestes
> for his father. And now to learn, cursed that I am . . .
> that he is dead!
>
> Aeschylus, *Libation Bearers* 749–63 (B. B. Powell)

Boys and girls were reared together until somewhere between five and seven, spending most of their time with their mothers. At this age, they might learn their letters (though even in Athens, where literacy was most widespread, probably only one man in ten, and far fewer women, could read), but probably spent most of the time helping around the house and playing. Ball games were popular, although the best balls available were inflated pigs' bladders. They were not very round but could be improved by heating in the embers of a fire. There were board games too, and games with dice and the squarish shaped knuckle-bones of pigs (*astragaloi*), which adults used for gambling.

Death or divorce often ended marriages while children were still young. Men typically died ten to fifteen years after they married, in their forties. Their widows either moved back in with their birth family or remarried, leading to all kinds of legal complications. Far more children were orphans than in our world. Wealthy orphans had guardians to look after their estates, which could lead to acrimony and, when the child matured, years of lawsuits. Poor orphans relied on relatives, although if the father had been killed in war, they might get community support. For most orphans, life was very hard. In the cities, they easily fell into the underworld of prostitutes and thieves.

Around the age of seven, boys and girls with parents to support them began to be segregated. Most boys now spent more time in the fields (with their fathers if they were lucky), and girls learned the weaving and housekeeping skills they would need as wives. In wealthy families, boys (and a few girls) got formal schooling, concentrating on poetry (especially Homer), rhetoric, and music. An educated man was expected to have some skill in these areas, but not too much. Most professionals in primary education were slaves, and no one wanted to be skilled enough to be mistaken for a slave.

Educated slave chaperones accompanied schoolchildren at all times and helped the children with their studies. These slaves and the schoolmasters spent a lot of time just keeping their pupils under control. Physical punishment was common, although aristocratic boys were not always happy being slapped around by slaves. There are stories of pupils attacking their teachers: In myth, Heracles killed his music teacher by using his lyre as a club, then was acquitted on grounds of self-defense!

With the onset of puberty around fourteen, this kind of schooling ended. There was nothing like what we think of as higher education. By the late fifth century, wealthy young men could attach themselves to intellectuals, sometimes following them around and listening to them talk, at other times hiring them for a fee, but few did this.

In many city-states, boys spent at least a couple of years between their fourteenth and eighteenth birthdays in formal military training under the supervision of mature men. This training involved garrison duty and experience sleeping in the rough, as if on campaign. Such behavior was most refined in Sparta (see Chapter 10).

Greek literature is full of stories of conflict between fathers and rebellious teenage sons, and an Athenian legal speech by Demosthenes describes juvenile delinquents calling themselves "the hard-ons" going around at night attacking older citizens. Like most premodern societies, *poleis* had no police, but depended on fathers and other older kin to control wild male teenagers. Girls, by contrast, were already married at this age and under the control of a husband (and the husband's mother).

Technically, boys became adults and were admitted to the ranks of the citizen warriors at age eighteen. Fewer than half would have a living father by then and may have already been masters of their own affairs for some time.

KEY TERMS

oikos, 29

Sappho, 29

misogyny, 30

Xenophon, 33

Aspasia, 36

pederasty, 37

symposium, 37

amphidromia, 39

Hestia, 39

FURTHER READING

Dover, Kenneth, *Greek Homosexuality* (Cambridge, MA, 1978). The book that made scholarly study of this field respectable. A classic.

Garland, Robert, *Daily Life of the Ancient Greeks* (Westport, CT, 1998). Excellent survey of all aspects of everyday life. The best introduction to many of the topics in this chapter.

Golden, Mark, *Children and Childhood in Classical Athens* (Baltimore 1990). Much the best survey of the evidence.

Halperin, David, Jack Winkler, and Froma Zeitlin, eds., *Before Sexuality* (Princeton 1990). Important collection of essays on different aspects of sexuality in Greece.

Hubbard, Thomas, *Homosexuality in Greece and Rome: A Sourcebook of Basic Documents* (Berkeley 2003). Collects Greek and Latin texts that inform us about same-sex activities.

———, *Greek Love Reconsidered* (New York 2000). Four scholars reconstruct Greeks' attitudes toward pederasty and their evolution.

Patterson, Cynthia, *The Family in Greek History* (Cambridge, MA, 1998). Good survey.

Ancient Texts

Aeschylus, *The Oresteia* (New York 1984; tr. Robert Fagles). Aeschylus' trilogy on the House of Atreus.

Hesiod, *Works and Days* and *Theogony*. In *Hesiod and Theognis* (Harmondsworth, UK, 1973; tr. Dorothea Wender). The basic poetic accounts of the origins of mortals and immortals.

Plato, *The Symposium* (Harmondsworth, UK, 1951; tr. W. Hamilton). Entertaining account of a drinking party and sexual mores in early fourth-century B.C. Athens.

Xenophon, *Conversations of Socrates* (New York 1990; eds. Hugh Treddenick and Robin Waterfield). Some of the best sources for daily life and values in Athens, early fourth century B.C.

CHAPTER 4

THE GREEKS BEFORE HISTORY, 12,000–1200 B.C.

In Chapter 2, "Country and People," and Chapter 3, "The Greeks at Home," we described some of the foundations of classical Greek life: the environment, demography, standards of living, and the family. But conditions of life in Greece were always changing. Let us trace such changes, beginning with the long centuries that scholars call "prehistoric": times for which we have little or no written information, for which archaeology is our major source of evidence. Let us travel back some fourteen thousand years.

THE END OF THE LAST ICE AGE, 12,000–11,000 B.C.

Climate has a history. In the last 150 years, human activity has raised the average temperature on earth. But natural climatic changes are well attested in the geological record. There have been several Ice Ages in the last two million years, for unclear reasons; shifts in the earth's axis may have created these periods of intense cold. A drop in average temperature of just eight degrees Fahrenheit would leave one-third of the world covered year round by ice. The most recent Ice Age began about thirty-five thousand years ago, ending just thirteen thousand years ago (Map 4.1).

Greece stayed warmer than the rest of Europe, but at the coldest point, around 18,000 B.C., its winters were longer and colder than anything classical Greeks had to complain about. The average winter temperature in Athens around 15,000 B.C. was roughly thirty degrees Fahrenheit; today, it is closer to fifty degrees Fahrenheit.

The earliest evidence of humans in Greece dates back two hundred thousand years; fully modern humans (*homo sapiens sapiens*) probably entered thirty-five thousand years ago. The population was tiny. Finds from caves suggest that people lived in bands of fifteen to twenty-five members. The few edible wild plants were available only in summer, so the tiny population was constantly moving, following

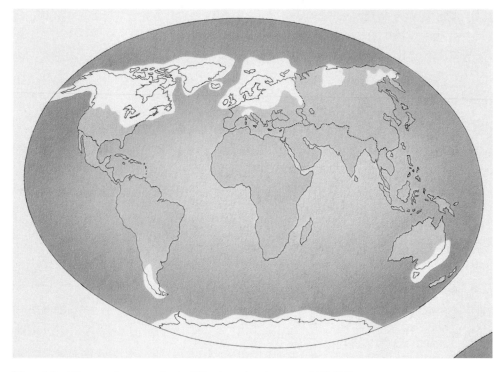

Map 4.1   The maximum extent of the ice sheet, around 18,000 B.C.

herds of animals that migrated into the mountains in summer and came down onto the plains in winter. Each band needed a huge territory to feed itself, and the whole of Greece probably supported only a few thousand people.

THE ORIGINS OF AGRICULTURE, 11,000–5000 B.C.

By 10,000 B.C., temperatures reached levels close to modern ones. The wet mixed woodlands of Ice Age Greece gave way to the sparse and dry vegetation that we described in Chapter 2, and in the **Fertile Crescent** in the Near East, changes were underway that were to transform Greek life (Map 4.2).

As temperatures rose in the hill country that is now northern Iraq and eastern Turkey, an area that gets low but reliable rainfall (ten to twelve inches each year), wild grains were evolving. Some had large seeds that could be crushed into porridge and bread. People gathering these grains could support larger populations per square mile than was possible in the Ice Age. Bands got larger and split into more bands until once again they pressed against the limits their territories could support. Around 9000 B.C., dwellers in the northern foothills of the mountains that bound the Fertile Crescent began selectively breeding wild grasses to produce better strains, creating the first genetically modified crops. In this revolutionary period, they also experimented with animal husbandry, taming cattle, sheep, pigs, and goats.

Such profound changes in food supply required equally profound changes in ways of life. Instead of constantly wandering in search of food, possessors of these new resources settled in permanent villages. Instead of moving around to collect

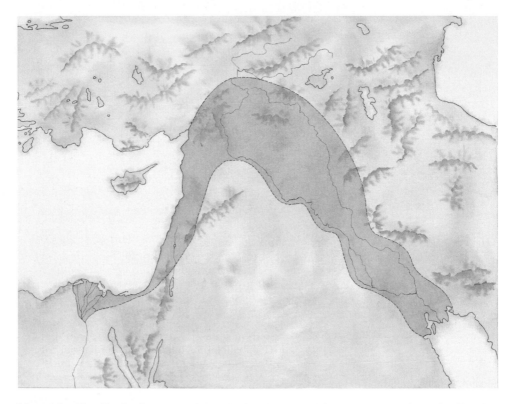

Map 4.2 The Fertile Crescent: A band of well-watered land stretching from the Persian Gulf in the east (modern Kuwait and southern Iraq), northwest along the Tigris-Euphrates rivers (modern Iraq, Syria, and southeastern Turkey), then down the Mediterranean coast (modern Lebanon and Israel) to Egypt.

whatever seeds and berries were available seasonally, dwellers in the Fertile Crescent now planted crops, weeded them, and harvested them. Agriculture was more work than gathering and hunting, but by offering higher and more dependable returns, it created an inexorable pressure to modernize: With hungry children to feed, who could resist settled agriculture? Population grew steadily in the settled communities until farmers vastly outnumbered the small bands that followed the old ways. When farmers wanted the thinly populated territory of food-gatherers—land that was empty most of the year as its occupants moved around collecting different re-sources—there was little that the gatherers could do.

As settled populations grew and lived cheek-by-jowl with new strains of domesti-cated animals, amid evil conditions of sanitation, new viruses appeared that were devastating when introduced into the smaller bands. The choices were clear. One could continue to live as a hunter-gatherer and perish of disease or starvation; settle down and join the farmers; or move away from them. Native Americans faced simi-lar choices when faced by European colonists, inheritors of an economic revolution by then twelve thousand years old.

By 7000 B.C., villages in Syria had hundreds of inhabitants, and by 6000 B.C., a settlement in Turkey called Çatalhöyük (cha-tal**hu**-yūk) had perhaps five thousand residents. The entire population of Ice Age Greece might have fitted into this one town. We call this complex of changes—the domestication of crops and animals and the shift toward sedentary village life—the **Neolithic Revolution** (see Chronological Chart, A-1). The Neolithic economy reached northern Greece around 7000 B.C., as the inhabitants harvested crude forms of barley and wheat and kept semidomesticated sheep and goats.

GREEKS AND INDO-EUROPEANS

Some archaeologists believe that this Neolithic expansion may answer a big question raised in Chapter 1, "A Small, Far-Off Land": *Who Were the Greeks?* To explain their arguments, we need to make a short digression.

In 1783, Sir William Jones arrived in India from England to take up a High Court post in the colonial regime. Jones decided to learn Sanskrit, the language of the oldest Indian texts. He already knew Greek, Latin, and of course English. When he started studying Sanskrit, he was surprised at how easy it was—the grammar was similar to the languages he knew already. He soon found that Irish, Gothic, and Old Persian worked in similar ways. In a lecture in 1786, he announced that all these tongues formed a single family of languages, which we now call **Indo-European.**

The major languages of modern Europe, and important languages in the Near East and even in China, are Indo-European, but there are also pockets of unrelated speech (Map 4.3), and every country, including Greece, has non-Indo-European

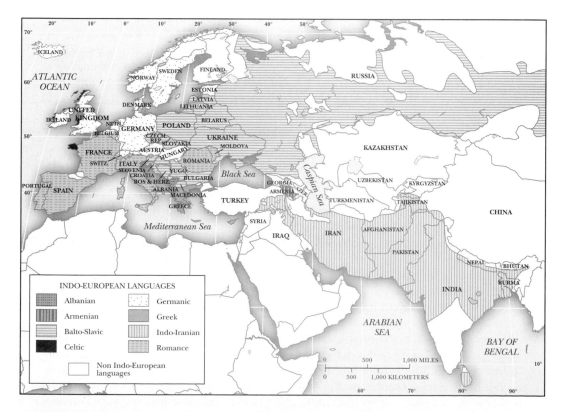

Map 4.3   Branches of the Indo-European family.

place-names. The simplest explanation is that at some time in prehistory, a single group spoke a **proto-Indo-European** language. It migrated across Europe and south Asia, displacing or replacing earlier inhabitants and their languages.

For 150 years, archaeologists have tried to discover when this language dispersal began and where the proto-Indo-Europeans came from. But while the pottery, stone tools, houses, and burials that archaeologists dig up *may* be related to ethnicity and language, they do not *have* to be. The spread of a new pot shape *might* indicate a migration, but there are other explanations.

Some archaeologists argue that the first farmers, living in what is now eastern Turkey, spoke proto-Indo-European and spread Indo-European languages across the Old World as they took over new land. There is some archaeological evidence for movements of new peoples, beneficiaries of the Neolithic revolution, who moved into Greece in the seventh millennium B.C. But other archaeologists think that proto-Indo-Europeans dispersed much later, around 2000 B.C. Geneticists can now extract ancient DNA from skeletons, which may one day resolve the question. Whichever theory is right, origins are a small part of the Greeks' story. The languages of the first farmers in Greece bore little resemblance to the language of Sophocles and Plato spoken six thousand years later. The important question is: How did society develop across this period?

NEOLITHIC SOCIETY AND ECONOMY, 5000–3000 B.C.

If people could get by gathering wild foods, they would, working harder (breeding crops, herding animals) only when necessary. A major innovation was the invention of the plow, which allowed farmers to turn the soil of larger areas than they could with handheld hoes or digging sticks. The drawback of plows was that farmers needed oxen to pull them; and the oxen needed their own food, which meant plowing even more land and working harder still. But as population grew, the new technology spread. There are signs that plows were in use in the Danube valley around 4500 B.C., in Poland and in England by 3500 B.C., and in Spain before 3000 B.C. The data from Greece are ambiguous, but plows were probably common by 3000 B.C.

The ox that drew the plow was no longer raised just for meat. Farmers who raise cattle for meat kill them young; but animal bones from excavations show that after 3500 B.C., Greek farmers started keeping their animals longer. Archaeologists call this change the **secondary products revolution,** a shift toward raising animals as much for traction, milk, and wool as for meat.

The plow allowed large-scale grain cultivation. In Greece, the Mediterranean triad of grain, olives, and grapes that we described in Chapter 2 was in place by 3000 B.C. It increased caloric output, improved health, and supported population growth. It also made agriculture more labor-intensive. People were working *much* harder by 2500 B.C. than hunter-gatherers had done around 6500 B.C. Progress had costs as well as benefits.

Archaeologists interpret mute artifacts by drawing analogies with living societies at the same technological level. In modern times, hunter-gatherer societies are communal: there is little private property (because there is not much to own) and little hierarchy. Farming societies, on the other hand, recognize private property; the family is a core institution; and gender, age, and class distinctions become pronounced.

Plow technology marks a critical threshold because a good piece of land suddenly becomes valuable. People want to keep particular fields and pass them on to their children. Defining legitimate heirs becomes important. Unlike in simpler economic systems, men start worrying about female premarital virginity, because they want to be sure that children come from the husband and should rightfully inherit his property.

As a family with good land marries its children to those of an equally advantaged family, the best land is concentrated in the hands of a few, creating permanent inequalities of wealth. When some end up with no land at all, the only way for them to live is by working rich families' fields. Not only do some eat better than others, but some must toil all their lives, while others live in leisure. Hunter-gatherers wander an empty landscape. If band members argue, some can leave and gather berries elsewhere. A world based on farming cannot work like this. Farmers need seed, labor, animals, and a place to store food to see them through until the next harvest. They need organization. A village provides this, but the villagers must find ways to live together.

Anthropologists find that hunter-gatherer bands of a dozen or so people deal with most problems through face-to-face discussion. But once populations reach a couple of hundred, some individuals start to wield more influence than others. In villages of one thousand people, permanent chiefs appear. This seems to have happened at some sites in Greece by 4500 B.C., when chiefs' houses, bigger than anyone else's, appear.

By 3000 B.C., someone—probably one of these chiefs—was mobilizing food surpluses to support craftsmen. We find pots as early as 6000 B.C., but around 3000 B.C. come rapid artistic advances, clearly represented in the abundant finds from Sesklo (Map 4.4).

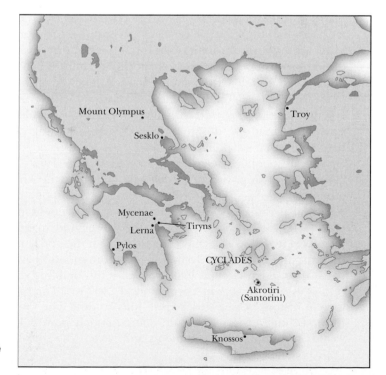

Map 4.4 Sites in Greece mentioned in this chapter.

THE EARLY BRONZE AGE, 3000–2300 B.C.

The **Early Bronze Age** saw further changes. Craftsmen learned to mix copper with tin or arsenic to produce bronze, far harder than copper; from this metal the period takes its name (see Chronological Chart on page A-1). Yet most bronze and gold relics from this early period come from just a few graves. In the early third millennium B.C., an elite separated itself from the masses and obtained power and wealth.

The Early Bronze Age also saw advances in architecture. From bigger-than-usual Neolithic houses, we move to monumental buildings. At **Lerna,** the **House of Tiles,** built around 2800 B.C., measured eighty by forty feet. Named for the clay roof tiles that covered it, the house contained storerooms and had a second floor. A number of clay sealings were found within the building, small clay lumps made by impressing a hardstone seal into clay, usually to seal documents or stores of food; perhaps the House of Tiles was an administrative center. It had plastered walls decorated with rectangular panels. There were wooden doors and stairs, and accurately laidout corners. We have found the ruins of similar buildings from this period at Troy in Asia Minor and on the island of **Crete;** and at Tiryns, near Lerna, there is a strange round building ninety feet across with mudbrick walls five feet thick.

When inequalities in wealth appear within communities, inequalities between communities always follow. Military tensions are reflected in a high wall studded with towers that protected the House of Tiles, and coastal sites were regularly fortified. There was wealth to be taken, and there were those ready to use violence to take it.

Culture in the Early Bronze Age

Harder work, inequality, war—if these were the fruits of civilization, why bother? Perhaps ambitious and clever men forced others to work for them and held communities together through violence. But naked force never works for long. It is too difficult to compel everyone to obey. Rulers must persuade the ruled that they are better off despite the inequalities. Greece was close to the old, splendid civilizations of the Near East. Perhaps contact with eastern Mediterranean rulers helped Aegean rulers secure their power. As with the adoption of farming, carrying on with simple ways of life might be unsafe if you lived within striking range of societies with fortifications, metal weapons, and armies.

In Mesopotamia, early rulers owed much of their power to the claim of a close relationship with divine beings. In Egypt, the kings *were* gods. Mighty religious structures—*ziggurats* (Mesopotamian tall-stepped mountains with temples on top) and pyramids (tombs for the pharaoh)—benefited everyone by pleasing the gods, but also provided proof of the power and magnificent wealth of society's leaders. The rulers' special relationship with the gods justified building great monuments; and their ability to build great monuments proved this special relationship to be true. Such circular logic underlies the building of the immense Great Pyramid of Khufu (**ku**-fu) in Egypt around 2400 B.C. The only bigger manmade structure in history is New York's Fresh Kills landfill! The message is clear: No ordinary human, but only a god, could manifest such power. The Greeks never had the wealth to build such monuments and lacked the social structure that lay behind their construction.

Figure 4.1 Cycladic marble female figurine, circa 3000–2500 B.C. Note the incised pubic area and the stylized presentation of the female form.

By 2500 B.C., life in Lerna was faster paced, more sophisticated, and more exciting than in a small village. There would have been music, pomp, and pageant, and architecture to entrance the eye. We have some direct testimony to Early Bronze Age culture in the beautiful and enigmatic marble figurines found in the Cycladic islands, hence called **Cycladic figurines.** Most are female (Figure 4.1), but one (Figure 4.2) shows a man playing a lyre, a stringed instrument later used to accompany sung poetry (like Homer's). We know very little about the Early Bronze Age Cyclades, but evidently poetry was already important. The figurines' clean lines and abstract symmetry are striking, and inspired the modernist British sculptor Henry Moore (1898–1986), but the originals had eyes, mouths, genitals, and other details painted on. The Cycladic peoples, whoever they were, must have been expert seamen, going to and fro among the Cyclades, Crete, the mainland, and the East (see map on inside cover). Some artifacts preserve pictures of their long boats.

Most of these figurines come from just a few graves. Culture helped separate an elite, who had access to beautiful things, from the masses. Although Greek culture might have seemed primitive to visiting Egyptians, civilization was changing the Greeks' way of life.

Figure 4.2 Cycladic marble figurine of a man playing a lyre, circa 3200–2200 B.C., from Keros, Greece.

THE MIDDLE BRONZE AGE, 2300–1800 B.C.

Around 2300 B.C., the House of Tiles burned to the ground, along with most major sites in mainland Greece. By 2200 B.C., figurines had disappeared from graves in the Cyclades, and by 2000 B.C., settlement had contracted to just a few sites. None had monumental buildings, and long-distance trade virtually stopped.

Something important happened around 2300 B.C., derailing social complexity on the mainland and in the Cycladic islands, but not, as we shall see, on Crete. The sophisticated mainland and island elites of the Early Bronze Age disappeared. For the next five hundred years, around 2300 to 1800 B.C., people lived simpler, village-level lives. We do not know much about this period, which we call the **Middle Bronze Age,** a dark age obscure to modern scholars and characterized by social regression.

One explanation is that newcomers invaded Greece around 2300 B.C., with perhaps a second wave entering around 2000 B.C. The pottery, bronzes, houses, and graves we find after 2300 B.C. are different from those before, and violent conquest would explain the fiery end of Lerna and other sites. There were also upheavals in Anatolia and possibly big population movements. Some archaeologists believe that it was at this time, and not around 6000 B.C., that Indo-European speakers entered Greece. Instead of a gradual wave of advance by farmers, made up of countless shifts of just a few miles spread over centuries, they envisage a single great invasion from a homeland in the Ukraine. One version of this theory sees the invading Indo-Europeans as "patriarchal" and warlike destroyers of a gentle "Old European" civilization focused on mother-goddesses, perhaps represented by the Cycladic female figurines. However, such interpretations go beyond the evidence. What really happened is shrouded in mystery and will probably remain so.

THE AGE OF MINOAN PALACES, 2000–1600 B.C.

The Middle Bronze Age recession on the mainland meant little to Cretans. If it had affected them too, the development of Greek culture would have been very different. But on Crete, separated from the mainland by seventy-five miles of water, the centralization of power and development of art and ceremony that began in Neolithic times continued without interruption. Around 2000 B.C., people at **Knossus** and a few other sites built structures so large, and with so many similarities to buildings in the Near East, that we call them palaces (Figure 4.3 and Map 4.5).

These sites remained in use for centuries, and the foundations and basements of later phases severely damaged the remains of the earliest phases. Knossus probably had third-millennium B.C. structures just as grand as those at Lerna and Tiryns, but they are lost. The first palaces had massive storage capacities, spacious courtyards, and elaborate façades. Europe's first experiments with writing took place here. The oldest writing, around 2000 B.C., is a pictographic script of about 135 symbols representing recognizable objects, mostly found on hard stone seals to be impressed on clay. We cannot read the script or even say what language it encoded (though we doubt that it is Greek).

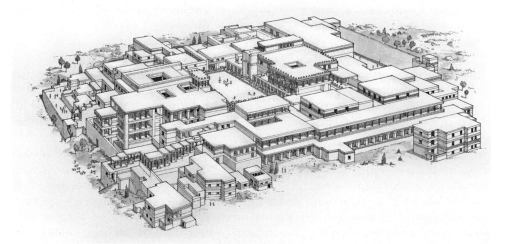

Figure 4.3 Reconstruction of the palace at Knossus as it may have appeared around 1500 B.C., comprising hundreds of rooms and covering several acres.

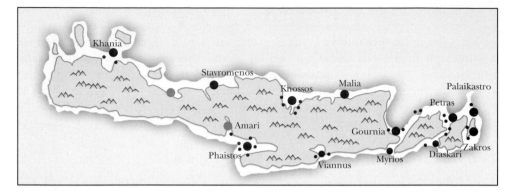

Map 4.5   Map of Crete showing where ruins of Minoan palaces have been found.

Another development coincides with the first palaces. Some Cretans started climbing mountains and building altars, where they offered pottery and figurines to the gods. Some figurines they threw into chasms, perhaps to send them to the underworld; others they hung in shrines, particularly models of human limbs, perhaps in gratitude for healing (still seen today in rural Greek churches). Some peak sanctuaries had elaborate and expensive architecture. Again, religion and ceremony aided the concentration of power.

A great problem in studying the Bronze Age is how to interpret stories that Greeks wrote about it a thousand years later, during the Classical Period. Most Greeks thought that Crete was once ruled by a great king named **Minos,** after whom we sometimes call the Bronze Age civilization on Crete **Minoan.** These stories provide details that archaeology never could. According to the most famous story, Minos once failed to sacrifice a special bull to the god Poseidon. The god caused Minos' wife (herself the daughter of the Sun) to fall in love with the very bull. She hid inside a wooden cow, which the bull then mounted, and from their strange union came the half-man, half-bull, man-eating **Minotaur** ("bull of Minos"). Minos then built a maze called the Labyrinth and kept the Minotaur in it.

Archaeologists sometimes suggest that stories about the Labyrinth were attempts to make sense of the mazelike ruins of the palace at Cnossus, and that the Minotaur began in distorted memories of a bull-leaping game played in the palaces (Figure 4.4). Some also think the story of the Cretan queen's intercourse with a bull represents a religious ritual in which a queen pretended to (or really did) have intercourse with a bull.

Comparing legends and archaeological finds reveals the difficulty of understanding the past. Sometimes we have sources of information produced by people actually present during the period described. These we call **primary sources.** Every reliable historical account must rest on primary sources. At other times, we have only documents produced by people who were not present—either because they lived somewhere else or just happened not to be there that day, or because, like ourselves, they lived much later. Thucydides, the famous Athenian historian active around 400 B.C., wrote about King Minos but had no access to Minoan primary sources. Lacking such sources, he had to concede that "I have found it impossible,

Figure 4.4 Bull-jumping fresco from Cnossus, circa 1500 B.C., height including border about 25 inches. A red-painted figure balances on the back of a galloping bull, evidently somersaulting into the arms of a white-painted figure, while another white-painted figure, preparing to somersault, grips the bull's horns. The white figures seem to be female, while the red figure is male, following an artistic convention borrowed from Egypt.

because of the remoteness in time, to acquire a really precise knowledge of the distant past or even of the history preceding our own period."

We call texts that are not primary sources **secondary sources.** Whenever we look at a secondary source, we must ask how the author knew anything about the subject. Did the author have access to primary sources? If not, then to a secondary source that itself drew on primary sources? Unless we can answer one of these questions in the affirmative, there is no reason to believe anything a secondary source says.

The myths about Minos are entertaining, but they are secondary sources. Archaeological discovery must remain the major source of information about Bronze Age Crete. After a century of research, beginning with the pioneer archaeologist Arthur Evans, who started digging at Cnossus in 1899, we have real information about the Cretan economy and way of life. The world of Cnossus' rulers was sophisticated and glamorous. Their craftsmen made elegantly painted eggshell-thin vases (Figure 4.5) and painted geometric designs and marine motifs on the palace walls. The elite wore delicate gold jewelry, and tombs show that even common folk had bronze ornaments. After 1800 B.C., typical Minoan houses became much larger and were well built. Standards of living were (by ancient standards) rising.

By 1800 B.C., the palaces were in direct communication with the Near East, mainly through the great trading city of Ugarit in north Syria. Minoan palaces look quite like Near Eastern ones, and an eighteenth-century B.C. clay tablet from the great Bronze Age city of Mari on the Euphrates River in Syria may be the first written reference to the Aegean. The tablet notes that the king of Ugarit had sent weapons, cloth, sandals, and pots from "Kaptara" as a gift to the king of Mari. Kaptara was probably Crete. Another tablet from Mari records that some of the gifts

Figure 4.5 "Octopus vase" from Palaikastro, Crete, circa 1500 B.C., height 11 inches. Marine motifs were common in Minoan art.

sent to Mari by the Cretans, including a pair of sandals, were sent on to the famous King Hammurabi of Babylon, who created a law code in the eighteenth century B.C.

The Cretans were minor players in Near Eastern diplomacy, but for the Minoan elite, these contacts were crucial. Their agents brought home tin, without which there would be no bronze, and exotic objects from distant, rich kingdoms. Cretan leaders basked in luxury in their palaces and communed with gods on mountaintops, but dramatic events around 1750 B.C., in the Middle Bronze Age, undid some of this work. Some archaeologists think that devastating earthquakes struck (several fault lines run through Crete); others, that an internecine war destroyed the palace at Cnossus, after which the reorganized Cnossians defeated everyone else and fashioned a single Minoan state. We do not know, but the palaces were quickly rebuilt on an even grander scale than before.

This **Second Palace Period** is the best-known phase of Minoan history. The palace at Cnossus covered an area the size of two football fields. To enter, visitors crossed a wide courtyard to reach an elaborate two-story façade (Figure 4.6). We may be sure that the palace made a strong impression on Cretan peasants and on traders from the rude villages of mainland Greece; surely the beings who lived in such houses were closer to the gods than were mere mortals.

The grand entrance to the palace led to a twisting, winding corridor which abruptly let out into a huge paved courtyard, 150 feet long and 75 feet wide,

Figure 4.6 Arthur Evans' reconstructions of portions of the walls of the Cnossus palace, circa 1400 B.C., as shown here triggered criticism, but give a sense of what this splendid palace may have looked like.

surrounded by towering blank walls. This too seems designed to astonish visitors. Tucked away in one corner was the throne room itself, where a high stone chair was flanked by wall paintings of griffins, a Near Eastern motif (Figure 4.7).

The most remarkable parts of the palace would have been closed to visitors. There were bathrooms with a drainage system for disposing of human waste, the oldest attested example in the world. There were anterooms and storerooms, waiting rooms and dressing rooms, airy light wells and dark crypts, towering staircases and subterranean vaults (Figure 4.8). Walls, floors, and even ceilings were painted in dazzling colors, often with beautiful naturalistic scenes of dolphins, birds, monkeys, fish, octopuses, and rulers in elaborate costumes (Figure 4.9).

Beneath all this gaiety lay the palace's economic realities. Everywhere were narrow chambers packed with pots and stone bins for storage. Each palace held vast quantities of grain, oil, and wine as well as metals, wood, and materials of war. The rulers kept track of it with a new writing system that we call **Linear A** (Figure 4.10)—"linear" because the signs are made up of lines, and "A" to distinguish it from a later linear system. We do not have enough samples yet to decipher the script, but like its pictographic predecessor, most tablets are economic accounts.

The Minoan palaces, like those of the Near East, were **redistributive centers,** and Linear A allowed the rulers to run a centralized **command economy.** In theory,

Figure 4.7   An alabaster throne with scalloped backrest and incised patterns sits on a dais between benches lining the walls of the Throne Room at Cnossus in Crete, circa 1400 B.C. On either side of the throne are reconstructed frescoes of griffins in fields of lotuses, symbols of royal power. *Hellenic Republic Ministry of Culture, Archaeological Receipts Funds.*

it worked like this: If one valley was well suited for wheat, that was all it grew; if a hillside was placed just right for olives, it was given over to them. (In practice, command economies do not work so neatly: It is difficult to tell people what to grow.) The harvested crops were brought to the palace, where they were recorded. Bureaucrats kept accounts in Linear A, skimmed off what the rulers needed, and sent back to each village a selection of goods that the rulers deemed necessary for the local people. The palaces did not control the entire economy, of course, and there would have been local systems of barter and rural markets. But from 2000 through 1400 B.C. or later—hundreds of years—the Cretans ran a wealthy and complex command economy, without the use of coinage, which was not invented until 600 B.C.

Remarkably, no fortifications have been found at Cretan sites, unlike the well-protected dwellings of the Greek Mycenaeans on the mainland. Evidently, the Minoans faced no credible threats; the historian Thucydides in the fifth century B.C. described their power as a **thalassocracy,** "kingdom of the sea," and his explanation remains plausible. Nor did they fear internal attack, suggesting that the various Minoan palaces scattered around Crete belonged to a single state, run from Knossus.

The eighteenth and seventeenth centuries B.C. were the high point of Minoan civilization. Typical houses were well made, covering two thousand to three thousand square feet. Mainland Greek houses did not equal these dimensions until the fourth century B.C. The aristocracy lived even better: The hilltops of Crete were dotted with

Figure 4.8 Reconstruction of a light well in the central palace, supported by columns thicker at the top than at the bottom. Notice in the corridor paintings of "figure-eight" shields made of oxhide, also found in mainland art, and the rosettes surrounding the door, a typical Minoan motif.

Figure 4.9   Arthur Evans' reconstruction of the dolphin fresco over the "queen's apartments" in a lower floor of the palace (some archaeologists think the fresco could have fallen from the floor above). Dolphins swim amidst tuna in a scene rich in nature, fantasy, and movement. A typical frieze of rosettes bounds the bottom of the picture.

Figure 4.10 Linear A signs on a potsherd from Palaikastro, circa 1500 B.C. These signs probably designate a commodity of some kind, but Linear A remains undeciphered.

villas, often decorated with wall paintings like those in the palaces, and filled with precious objects. Minoans had more contacts than ever with the East. Egyptian paintings show men called Keftiu—almost certainly Cretans—bearing gifts, and Minoan-style wall paintings, one even showing bull-leaping, are known from Egypt, Syria, and Israel.

The Cretan Middle Bronze Age was truly an international age. The Minoans thrust their culture into the Aegean. **Akrotiri** on the Cycladic island of Santorini, miraculously preserved when buried in volcanic ash in 1628 B.C., is a Minoan Pompeii, giving us unique insights into daily life. Its people had time to flee with their valuables, but their ruined houses stand two floors high (Figures 4.11 and 4.12). Archaeologists have found so much Minoan pottery at Akrotiri and some other Cycladic sites that we must conclude that these sites were Cretan trading posts or colonies.

Was this a Minoan empire, then? Later Greek writers thought so, especially Thucydides:

> Minos, according to tradition, was the first person to organize a navy. He controlled the greater part of what is called the Hellenic Sea;° he ruled over the Cyclades, in most of which he founded the first colonies, putting his sons in as governors after having driven out the Carians.° And it is reasonable to suppose that he did his best to put down piracy in order to secure his own revenues.

Thucydides 1.4 (R. Warner)

°*Hellenic Sea:* The Aegean Sea.   °*Carians:* Caria was an area in southwest Anatolia (modern Turkey). Thucydides believed that the Carians were the original settlers of the Cyclades.

But without primary sources, Thucydides could not be certain of the distant past. Archaeology helps less when we move from economic and cultural facts to political ones. Linear A tablets have turned up at Akrotiri and other Cycladic sites. They may be evidence for colonial administration, but perhaps independent bureaucracies copied Minoan methods.

Figure 4.11 Partially excavated house at Akrotiri on the island of Santorini (ancient Thera). The walls are mudbrick, set between beams resistant to earthquake. Storage jars still stand where they stood when the island volcano blew up in 1628 B.C., burying the town in ash (some have thought this catastrophe stands behind the legend of Atlantis).

Figure 4.12 Fresco in a house at Akrotiri shows boats rowing into a harbor backed by multistory houses. From the windows and rooftops, the inhabitants watch the fleet's return.

THE RISE OF MYCENAEAN GREECE, 1750–1500 B.C.

Between 1750 and 1700 B.C., as Minoan power reached its height, something strange was happening in the mainland town of **Mycenae.** People dug a great round pit into the rock, seventy-five feet across, and lined it with stones. Over the next century and a half, they buried thirty-five people in this pit—what we now call Grave Circle B. The richest burial was marked by two gravestones, one of them carved. This burial held four adults, one of them a man six feet tall—a giant in 1700 B.C. Chemical analysis of his bones suggests that he ate a lot of meat and some fish. The fill of the shaft contained some forty pots. Accompanying the dead were fourteen bronze weapons, a bronze vase, two gold cups, gold attachments sown onto the clothes of the dead, a silver-coated wooden box, an extraordinary death mask made of electrum (a natural mix of gold and silver), and many lesser treasures. Greece had never before witnessed such wealth and artistry, even in the heyday of the House of Tiles.

A wealthy and warlike elite had taken control of Mycenae. They may have grown rich trading with Minoan Crete or won their power leading resistance to Crete. Whatever the source of their wealth, around 1650 B.C., while Grave Circle B was still in use, the Mycenaeans built a second monument, **Grave Circle A,** 150 yards uphill (Figure 4.13). Heinrich Schliemann, Troy's original excavator, sank his first trench directly into these graves in 1874. It remains one of the most amazing archaeological discoveries ever made.

The six shaft graves in Grave Circle A were stuffed with gold, jewels, silver, bronze, and pottery. The five gold death masks found here (Figure 4.14) still freeze

Figure 4.13 Grave Circle A. In the deep shafts, Schliemann found one of the greatest archaeological treasures ever.

Figure 4.14 Mycenaean gold death mask. When Heinrich Schliemann saw this mask, with its noble features, beard, and mustache, he reportedly wired that he had "gazed upon the face of Agamemnon" (in fact, the graves are four centuries too early to have held Agamemnon's body).

Figure 4.15 Dagger from Mycenae Grave Circle A, seventeenth century B.C. Bronze inlaid with gold, iron, and electrum, length about 9 inches. Warriors carrying shields attack lions.

visitors to the spot in front of their case in the National Museum in Athens. There are so many other precious objects that the museum cannot display them all. The workmanship is astounding, from inlaid dagger-blades (Figure 4.15) to carved gems so tiny the naked eye can scarcely make them out. Many of these objects are Minoan, or inspired by Minoan art. At the very height of the power of the Cretan palaces, a rival dynasty, representing itself in death as violent and aggressive, had appeared on the mainland.

We call the civilization of the **Late Bronze Age** on the mainland **Mycenaean** (mī-sen-ē-an) after this site, but similar developments were underway elsewhere. In Messenia, seventy-five miles to the southwest, a large town grew up at **Pylos** by 1600 B.C., and for several generations its wealthy nobility buried their dead in vaulted stone chambers called **tholos tombs,** which resemble underground stone beehives. In the sixteenth century B.C., the rich lords of Mycenae built similar tombs, though much larger. All were looted long ago, but their original wealth must have been very great.

There were palaces on the Greek mainland by 1500 B.C., which used a writing system called **Linear B,** derived from Minoan Linear A. Large caches of clay tablets inscribed in Linear B (Figure 4.16) have been found. In 1952, a British architect named Michael Ventris deciphered Linear B and showed, to everyone's surprise, that it encoded an early form of Greek. Ventris was not a professional classicist, but his hobby was code-breaking. Linear B was not an alphabet like our own, where each sign stands for a single sound, but a **syllabary** of eighty or so signs, where each sign stands for a syllable (e.g., *ba, be, bi, bo, bu*). The tablets are economic records, and no literature of any kind survives. The Mycenaeans adapted Minoan Linear A, which recorded an unknown language, and created Linear B, which recorded an early form of Greek, to aid them in running and recording their own redistributive economy.

Figure 4.16 Linear B tablets from Cnossus. Linear B reads from left to right, scratched along horizontal lines. The tablets record economic accounts, mostly lists of commodities from a single year, and survived because they were fired when the palace of Cnossus burned, probably around 1400 B.C.

All over Greece, new men had seized power, brutal warlords no doubt, but connoisseurs of the best Minoan art, who understood the value of bureaucracy. Linear B tablets call the kings *wanakes* (singular, *wanax*). The tablets tell us little about these kings, because their intended audience—other scribes—already knew who the *wanakes* were. But the architecture of Minoan and Mycenaean palaces and the art on their walls suggests that, as in the Near East, the *wanakes* had persuaded their subjects that they were closer to the gods than others. The *wanakes* divided Greece into several kingdoms; from the Pylos tablets we know that the one based there covered eight hundred square miles. Around 1600 B.C., Mycenaean civilization was still in the shadow of the Minoans, but by 1400 B.C., Linear B was in use at Cnossus. Mycenaean Greeks now sat in the throne room of the greatest Cretan palace.

THE END OF MINOAN CIVILIZATION, 1600–1400 B.C.

The volcanic eruption that destroyed Akrotiri may have played a part in the decline of Minoan civilization, but we cannot be sure of details. The delightful ring-shaped island of Santorini, southernmost of the Cyclades and today a favorite for tourists, was once a solid circle of land with a small volcanic mountain at its center. But in 1628 B.C. (judging from tree rings in California bristlecone pines, which correlate with high acidity in ice cores from Greenland), the volcano blew up the middle of the island—the greatest eruption attested to in the geological record.

The prevailing winds would have carried the worst of the ash cloud east, dumping it into the sea, but some of the red-hot dust blew south. The Cretans must have lived through days of darkness when death fell from the skies, fires raged out of control, and tidal waves thrust inland. A layer of ash twenty feet thick buried Akrotiri. The Minoan palaces survived this disaster, but it must have weakened them. Some have connected this geological event with Plato's legend of Atlantis, but the connection cannot be proven.

Then, around 1450 B.C., the Minoan palaces did burn, perhaps by enemy action. Only Knossus, and perhaps Chania in the west, survived. Minoan material culture disappeared from the Cyclades, now replaced by Mycenaean finds. Perhaps the eruption of 1628 B.C. shook Minoan strength, then internal wars or uprisings, or further natural disasters, gave the mainland Mycenaean Greeks an opening. They occupied Knossus, leaving the other palaces in ruins. Then Knossus itself was burned around 1400 B.C., preserving our earliest large horde of Linear B tablets and proving that Greek-speakers had by then occupied the island. Gradually, the fine townhouses of the eighteenth and seventeenth centuries decayed, and standards of living declined. The ancient Minoan social order was gone forever.

MYCENAEAN GREECE: ARCHAEOLOGY, LINEAR B, AND HOMER

By the mid-second millennium B.C., then, Mycenaean Greeks dominated the Aegean. Their palaces looked different from the non-Greek Minoan ones: they were on hilltops and heavily fortified. Crete produced nothing like the famous Lion Gate at Mycenae (Figure 4.17).

Minoan palaces were designed around a central courtyard, but Mycenaean palaces focused on a **megaron**, a rectangular building with a porch on the front and

Figure 4.17 Victorian visitors at the Lion Gate at Mycenae, constructed around 1250 B.C. The sculpture—the oldest architectural sculpture in Greece—may be an emblem of royal power. It shows lionesses (probably) flanking a pillar. The king as "lion" is an old Near Eastern motif, as is the arrangement of two animals on either side of a central image. *German Archaeological Institute, Athens, Greece.*

a round hearth in the middle (Figure 4.18). Mycenaeans painted their palace walls, as did Minoans, but enjoyed warlike as well as pastoral scenes. The main similarities between Minoan and Mycenaean palaces were the prominence of storerooms and written records.

In addition to their physical ruins, we have two potential sources of information about the Mycenaean palaces. The first is the Linear B tablets. They were temporary records scratched onto damp clay, meant to be transferred later to another medium—probably papyrus from Egypt—which has not survived. Once the data had been transferred, the tablets would be moistened, scraped clean, and used again. But when the palaces were destroyed around 1200 B.C., the fires that raged through them accidentally preserved the tablets that happened to be in use, baking them hard like pottery. The tablets probably tell us only about transactions that took place just before the palaces were destroyed.

Most tablets are dull economic records. A typical example reads "21 spinning-women, 25 girls, 4 boys; 1 *ta*."[8] What is the record for? Another records "20 woolen cloaks that are to be well boiled," as if every minutia of palace property and personnel needed to be tracked. But we can learn a lot from these texts. For example, Table 4.1 shows the number of animals recorded on Linear B tablets from Knossus.

Even from our random sample of records, we witness the impressive scale of the palace's economy, a complex organization run by dozens of officials whose names and titles fill the tablets. Beneath the *wanax* at the top was a finely graded hierarchy in which everyone had a place. A tablet from Pylos lists "16 fire-kindlers, 10 *meridum-ate*, 3 *mikate*, 4 riggers, 5 armorers; Xanthos. 23 fire-kindlers, 6 *meridamate*, 5 riggers,

Figure 4.18 Reconstruction of the throne room at Pylos. In the center is a great circular hearth beneath an opening in the roof supported by four pillars. Frescoes decorate the walls (after a painting by Piet de Jong).

Table 4.1 Totals of sheep, goats, pigs, oxen, and stags recorded in the Linear B tablets excavated at Knossus. The tablets do not explain what the palace administration was doing with the animals.

	Male	Female	Unclear sex	Total
Sheep	8,217	1,554	386	10,157
Goats	1,004	771	50	1,825
Pigs	57	234	249	540
Oxen	0	0	8	8
Stags	0	0	16	16

6 *mikata*, 3 armorers, 3 bakers. 4 *porudamate*. For Pallas, Purkolos, Axotas, Priameias, Eniausios, Ptejori, Qotawo, Anthas, Theopompos." Although we do not understand the meaning of many of these words, we can see that professions were carefully distinguished and the names of every professional recorded. The tablets suggest that in Mycenaean society everyone owed obligations to superiors, while claiming

certain goods or services from those below them. The bureaucracies at the center tried to keep everything under control, for their own advantage and the betterment of the community.

A second potential source of information about the Mycenaeans is Homer, the great epic poet. The twenty-eight thousand verses of his *Iliad* and *Odyssey* tell of a Greek war against the city of Troy. The leading Greek cities in Homer's account were major centers in the Bronze Age, and Agamemnon, the Greek commander, came from Mycenae. Although there is no consciousness of historical time in the epics, they seem to be set in what we call the Mycenaean Period. But Homer lived in the eighth century B.C., four hundred years after the end of the Mycenaean palaces. He is very much a secondary source. Writing disappeared from Greece between 1200 and about 800 B.C., so we know that Homer had no primary accounts from the Bronze Age. How could he know anything about the Bronze Age?

Homer tells us exactly what his sources were in the following passage, when he prepares to list the Achaeans (the Greeks) who fought at Troy:

> Sing to me now, you Muses who hold the halls of Olympus!
> You are goddesses, you are everywhere, you know all things—
> who were the captains of Achaea? Who were the kings?
> The mass of troops I could never tally, never name,
> not even if I had ten tongues and ten mouths,
> a tireless voice and the heart inside me of bronze,
> never unless you Muses of Olympus, daughters of Zeus
> who shield his rolling thunder, sing, sing in memory
> all who gathered under Troy.
>
> Homer, *Iliad* 2.484–92 (R. Fagles)

Homer knows about the past because goddesses, the Muses (see Chapter 6, "Homer"), tell him about it! In Chapter 6, we have more to say about how Homer composed his epics; for the moment, we simply note that most historians think Homer knew little about the Bronze Age, in spite of his claim to divine guidance. Bits and pieces of information (like the names of famous settlements) were passed down by word of mouth, true, but Homer tells us more about what eighth-century poets thought about the world than about actual Mycenaean life. Homer spoke to an eighth-century audience and drew on experiences from his own times, embellished by exaggeration (heroes are stronger, braver, and better-looking than men today) and by fantasy (talking rivers and horses, personal appearances by gods).

When we compare the poems with archaeological evidence, we quickly see how different Homer's world is from that of the Mycenaeans. For example, at one point Telemachus (tel-**em**-a-kus), son of the great hero Odysseus, wants to sail off to find news of his father, missing for twenty years. Homer describes his preparations:

> Telemachus went down to his father's high-roofed
> storeroom, broad, where lay gold and bronze
> and cloth in chests and scented oil.
> There were jars of old sweet wine
> having a divine unmixed substance within
> lined up all in a row along the wall, in case Odysseus

should return home, after his agony.
The two doors, tightly fitted, were shut,
and a woman housekeeper both night and day
watched over it, who guarded all in wisdom of mind,
Eurycleia, the daughter of Ops, the son of Pisenor . . .
Straightaway she drew off wine into jars,
and poured in barley from well-stitched bags.
Telemachus went back to the hall and mixed with the suitors.
Bright-eyed Pallas,° the goddess, thought of one more thing.
In the likeness of Telemachus, she went throughout
the city, and standing beside each man she spoke,
and urged them at night to gather at the swift ship.
She asked Noemon the illustrious son of Noemon
to lend her a ship. He gladly agreed.

Homer, Odyssey 2.337–47, 379–87 (B. Powell)

°*Pallas:* Another name for the goddess Athena, who helps Telemachus prepare the trip.

But Bronze Age palaces were not like this. They were massive redistributive centers with dozens of storerooms, not a single room. The economic nerve center in Homer's vision of Odysseus' palace is a big room with double doors, guarded by an old lady. There is no bustling bureaucracy, no rows of underground storage bins. And when Telemachus gets his supplies, it sounds as if the king's palace does not even own a ship, but must borrow one from a neighbor! The *Iliad* and *Odyssey* were myths that eighth-century Greeks told themselves to explain, at least in part, the physical ruins surviving from the past, visible in many places. The Homeric poems are important sources for understanding eighth-century Greek culture, but not for making sense of the Mycenaean world.

The archaeological record and the Linear B tablets tell us that Mycenaean society was more warlike than Minoan, and wealth less widely diffused. The Mycenaean *wanakes* were great rulers, whose civilization spread north to the slopes of Mt. Olympus. Mycenaean pottery has been found in Sicily and Sardinia. Shipwrecks found off southern Turkey show that Mycenaean Greece was involved in far-flung commercial networks. Ships moved all kinds of goods, from food, to bronze ingots, to writing tablets. For the kings, soldiers, and traders (but not for the ordinary village-dwellers) this was a big, cosmopolitan, international world. State archives of the Hittite Empire in central Anatolia complain about a western kingdom called **Ahhiyawa,** probably a twisting of **Achaea** (a-kē-a), later the name of a region of Greece, which Homer remembered as one of three names for the Greeks. In the thirteenth century B.C., Hittite kings wrote to the rulers of Ahhiyawa as equals. The Mycenaeans were important players on an international stage.

THE END OF THE BRONZE AGE, CIRCA 1200 B.C.

A visitor from another planet around 1300 B.C. might have predicted that palatial civilization would continue expanding north and west. The Mycenaeans and Hittites were stronger than ever, and trade routes pulsed with life. But in the thirteenth century, Mycenaean metalworkers used raw materials more sparingly, and Linear B tablets suggest shortfalls in tax collection around 1200 B.C. Fortifications at major sites expanded, and people drifted from vulnerable villages to the security of defended settlements. Then, between 1225 and 1175 B.C., fires gutted the palaces. Over the next few centuries, dust blew over the ruins, which were slowly buried, then forgotten until the 1870s, when archaeologists exposed their secrets.

What happened? Thucydides says that

> after the Trojan War, Hellas was in a state of ferment; there were constant resettlements, and so no opportunity for peaceful development. It was long before the army returned from Troy, and this fact in itself led to many changes. There was party strife in nearly all the cities, and those who were driven into exile founded new cities.
>
> Thucydides 1.12

Thucydides believed that the ten-year siege of Troy destabilized Greece, adding that "many years passed by and many difficulties were encountered before Hellas could enjoy any peace or stability, and before the period of shifting populations ended." Homer and Thucydides both treat the Trojan War as important, but when we scrutinize Thucydides' account (a secondary source, who wrote around 400 B.C.), we find that his main source of information was Homer (another secondary source!). Homer believed that the Muses inspired him, and Thucydides copied Homer.

The Linear B tablets are our only primary sources, written in the dying moments of the palaces. One text from Pylos describes a religious ceremony. The scribe began on one side, scratched through what he had written, then turned the tablet over, dashed off a few lines, then went back to the original (erased) side, adding more, before the text trails off unfinished:

> PYLOS: perform an action at the shrine of Poseidon and . . . the town, and bring the gifts and bring those to carry them. One gold cup, two women . . .
>
> PYLOS: perform an action at the shrines of the Dove-Goddess and of Iphimedeia and of Diwja, and bring the gifts and bring those to carry them. To the Dove-Goddess: one gold bowl, one woman. To Iphimedeia: one gold bowl. To Diwja: one gold bowl, one woman. To Hermes: one gold cup, one man.
>
> PYLOS: perform an action at the shrine of Zeus, and bring the gifts and bring those to carry them. To Zeus: one gold bowl, one man. To Drimios the priest of Zeus: one gold bowl, one man (?).
>
> In the month of Plowistos: PYLOS: perform an action at the place Pakijane, and bring the gifts and bring those to carry them. To the Mistress: one gold cup, one woman. To Mnasa: one gold bowl, one woman. To Posidaeia: one gold cup, one woman. To the three-times-hero: one gold cup. To the Lord of the House: one gold cup.
>
> Pylos tablet Tn 316

In later Greek mythology, Poseidon was the god of the sea, and this tablet shows that he, Hermes, Zeus, and Hera were already worshiped in the Bronze Age (though we do not know how beliefs about these gods might have changed). The other divinities mentioned in this tablet were not worshiped in later periods. The offerings of people to gods may describe human sacrifice in response to a crisis. Another tablet from Pylos may also refer to an impending disaster that called for extreme measures:

> As follows, the watchers are guarding the coastal area.
> Command of Maleus at Owitono:
> Ampelitawon, Orestas, Etewas, Kokkion.
> 50 *suweowijo* men of Owitono at Oichalia.

Command of Nedwatas: Echmedes,
Amphieta, and the *marateu,* Taniko.
20 Kyparissian *kekide* men at Aruwote,
10 Kyparissian *kekide* men at Aithalewes,
and with them the follower Kerkios.
Aeriqhoitas, Elaphos, Rimene.
30 men from Oichalia to Owitono,
and 20 *kekide* men from Apuka,
and with them the follower Aikota.

                                                    Pylos tablet An 657

Some specialists see this tablet as describing a last-ditch defense of the coast against invaders; others suggest that these 130 men were just a routine force.

The ruins of the palaces give more hints. Sometimes huge walls collapsed or were bent at strange angles, houses had fallen off foundations, and bodies were found under rubble, perhaps the consequence of earthquakes. The destructions of the Greek palaces seem to have been spread between 1225 and 1175 B.C., so there cannot have been a single giant earthquake; but there could have been what geophysicists call an "earthquake storm," spread over many years. Battered by repeated collapses, each causing fires, the Mycenaean ruling class may have lost control.

But the Greek disasters were not just local. Ugarit, the greatest emporium on the Mediterranean, was destroyed around 1200 B.C., and the Hittite Empire collapsed at the same time. Of the great ancient civilizations, only Egypt survived. An inscription at Karnak, the Egyptian capital four hundred miles south of modern Cairo, says that in 1209 B.C. the pharaoh Merneptah defeated an invasion of Libyans and their allies. In his slightly later funerary temple, pharaoh Ramses III put up similar inscriptions, saying that in 1176 B.C., he fought a coalition of invaders that had wiped out precisely those Asian sites that archaeology reveals were destroyed at this time:

Year 8 under the majesty of Ramses III . . . The foreign countries made a conspiracy in their islands. All at once the lands were removed and scattered in the fray. No land could stand before their arms, from Hatti [kingdom of the Hittites in central Anatolia], Kodê [Cilicia in southern Anatolia], Carchemish [on the Euphrates River], Arzawa [probably in southern Anatolia], and Alashiya [Cyprus] on, being cut off at one time. A camp was set up in one place in Amor [probably in Syria]. They desolated its people, and its land was like that which has never come into being. They were coming forward toward Egypt, while the flame was prepared before them. Their confederation was the Peleset [probably the Philistines], Tjeker [?], Shekelesh [perhaps Sicilians], Denyen [probably the same as Danaans, a word Homer used to mean Greeks], and Weshmesh [?] lands united. They laid their hands upon the lands as far as the circuit of the earth, their hearts confident and trusting: "Our plans will succeed!"

Now the heart of this god [Ramses III], the Lord of the Gods, was prepared and ready to ensnare them like birds. . . . I organized my frontier at Djahi [in the Nile delta] prepared before them: princes, commanders of garrisons, and *maryanu* [important military leaders]. I had the river-mouths prepared like a strong wall, with warships, galleys, and coasters, fully equipped, for they were manned completely from bow to stern with valiant warriors carrying their weapons. The troops consisted of every picked man of Egypt. They were like the lions roaring upon the mountain tops. The chariotry consisted of runners, of picked men, of every good and capable chariot-warrior. The horses were quivering in every part of their bodies, prepared to crush the foreign countries under their hoofs. . . .

Those who reached my frontier, their seed is not, their heart and their soul are finished forever and ever. Those who came forward together on the sea, the full flame was in front of them at the river-mouths, while a stockade of lances surrounded them on the shore. They were dragged in, enclosed, and prostrated on the beach, killed, and made into heaps from tail to head. Their ships and their goods were as if fallen into the water.

I have made the lands turn back from even mentioning Egypt; for when they pronounce my name in their land, then they are burned up.... I have taken away their land, their frontiers being added to mine. Their princes and their tribes people are mine with praise, for I am on the ways of the plans of the All-Lord, my august, divine father, the Lord of the Gods [that is, Amon, god of the state at this time].

Funerary text of Ramses III, Medinet Habu
(J. A. Wilson, ANET)

We call these invaders the **Sea Peoples.** They were probably involved in the destructions in Greece too; the Pylos tablet describing naval defenses may allude to them. The Sea Peoples included the Peleset, probably the **Philistines** well known from the Hebrew Bible. Philistines settled five towns in what is now the Gaza Strip and southern Israel after Ramses III defeated them. Some of their towns have been excavated: The finds are almost identical to those from Greece in the twelfth century B.C. The Philistines were probably Mycenaean Greek refugees. Merneptah's inscription of 1209 B.C. names a group which could have been pronounced Akaiwasha (Egyptian writing does not express vowel sounds), very like the Ahhiyawa in the Hittite texts. Egyptian texts also mention the Danuna, perhaps the same as Homer's Danaans (for the Greeks), and the Shardana, perhaps men from Sardinia. Shekelesh sounds like the Greek *Sikeloi,* or Sicilians.

Later authors say that the Dorians—to whom all Dorian Greeks (see Chapter 1) traced their ancestry—entered Greece after the Trojan War, though archaeological research has not documented this. Still, such a movement may have been linked to the depredations of the Sea Peoples. Migrations may have coincided with ferocious earthquakes and possibly other natural disasters. Faced with economic collapse and starvation, bands of Mycenaean Greeks may have joined a broader tide of displaced peoples, as irresistible as any modern refugee movement. As one kingdom after another crumbled before them, the tide became a flood that engulfed Near Eastern civilization, until Ramses III stopped it in 1176 B.C.

We would like to know what impelled the Sea Peoples to move and why their attacks had such devastating effects against well-fortified positions. A wave of violence swept across the Aegean and passed into the Near East circa 1200 B.C. Without the palaces, the *wanakes* had no function. Without the *wanakes* and their bureaucrats, Linear B writing disappeared. The artistic works favored by the kings ceased to exist. Population plummeted. By 1000 B.C., most traces of Mycenaean civilization had disappeared from the old centers of power. An age of darkness had descended on Greece.

KEY TERMS

Fertile Crescent, 43
Neolithic Revolution, 45
Indo-European, 45
proto-Indo-European, 46
secondary products
    revolution, 46
Early Bronze Age, 48

Lerna, 48
House of Tiles, 48
Crete, 48
Cycladic figurines, 49
Middle Bronze Age, 50
Knossus, 51
Minos, 52

FURTHER READING

Neolithic and Early Bronze Age Greece

Broodbank, Cyprian, *An Island Archaeology of the Early Cyclades* (Cambridge, UK, 2000). Reviews social developments in the islands in the fourth and third millennia.

Diamond, Jared, *Guns, Germs, and Steel: The Fates of Human Societies* (New York 1997). Pulitzer Prize-winning essay on the evolution of society and how the Neolithic revolution in the Near East set the framework for subsequent human history.

Mithen, Steve, *After the Ice: A Global Human History, 20,000–5000 B.C.* (Cambridge, Mass., 2004). Fascinating review of humanity's responses to the end of the Ice Age.

Renfrew, Colin, *Archaeology and Language: The Puzzle of Indo-European Origins* (London 1987). Archaeological arguments that Indo-European languages were spread by Neolithic farmers before 6000 B.C.

Minoan Crete

Doumas, Christos, *The Wall Paintings of Thera* (Athens 1992). Well-illustrated study of the wall paintings from Akrotiri on Santorini.

Hägg, Robin, and Nanno Marinatos, eds., *The Function of the Minoan Palaces* (Stockholm 1987). Papers on the archaeology and art history of the Minoan palaces.

Mycenaean Greece

Cullen, Tracey, ed., *Aegean Prehistory: A Review* (Boston 2001). Up-to-date review of discoveries in the Neolithic and Bronze Age Aegean.

Dickinson, Oliver, *The Aegean Bronze Age* (Cambridge, UK, 1994). Accurate survey of the evidence, although the organization sometimes makes it difficult to use.

Rutter, Jeremy, *Greek Prehistory (http://devlab.dartmouth.edu/history/bronze_age)*. Online textbook, completely up-to-date as of January 10, 2004.

van de Microop, Marc, *A History of the Ancient Near East* (Oxford, 2004). Excellent brief summary of Near Eastern history.

The Aegean and the Near East

Chadwick, J., *The Decipherment of Linear B*, 2nd ed. (Cambridge, UK, 1970). Exciting tale of the decipherment by one of the principals.

Cline, Eric, and Diane Harris-Cline, eds., *The Aegean and the Orient in the Second Millennium* (Liège 1998). Proceedings on a conference on Bronze Age Greek connections with the Near East.

Kuhrt, Amélie, *The Ancient Near East, c. 3000–330 B.C.* (2 vols., New York 1995). Volume 1 has an excellent survey of the period down to 1200 B.C. The standard work.

Pritchard, J. B., ed., *Ancient Near Eastern Texts Relating to the Old Testament*, 3rd ed. (Princeton 1969-*ANET*). Standard collection of texts.

CHAPTER 5

THE DARK AGE, 1200–700 B.C.

To Greeks of the Classical Period, the Bronze Age was another world, its ruins dotting the landscape, and stories about the heroes who lived in them surviving only on the lips of singers. Only modern research has made possible any real understanding about what happened after the great disasters, and even now the five centuries that follow 1200 B.C. offer more mysteries than certainties.

THE COLLAPSE OF THE OLD STATES

At the end of the Bronze Age, the whole east Mediterranean was in crisis. In central Anatolia, the collapse of the Hittites opened the floodgates to invaders who overran the countryside. But urban civilization survived, and by 1100 B.C. powerful new kingdoms—Phrygia (**fri**-ja) in the west and Urartu (ur-**ar**-tu) in the east—emerged (Map 5.1). Both had wealthy and literate courts, although few texts survive. Along the southeastern fringe of the old Hittite empire, in northern Syria, tiny "neo-Hittite" kingdoms formed (the Hittites mentioned in the Bible). In **Assyria,** a major Bronze Age state on the upper Tigris River in what is now northern Iraq, the royal family dissolved into murderous, feuding factions in the twelfth century B.C. A strong-man finally killed all his rivals and reunited the country, but when he died in 1076 B.C., the kingdom fell into anarchy. Its king lists break off, and we hear no more about Assyria until almost 900 B.C.

Population movements convulsed the Near East through the twelfth and eleventh centuries. The Sea Peoples were part of a larger pattern. Semitic-speaking pastoralists (sheep herders, goat herders) called Aramaeans (ar-a-**mē**-anz), also known from the Bible, had for centuries gone back and forth between the Syrian desert and the settled plains. They exploited Assyria's decline to settle in Damascus (once called Aram), which became one of antiquity's greatest cities.

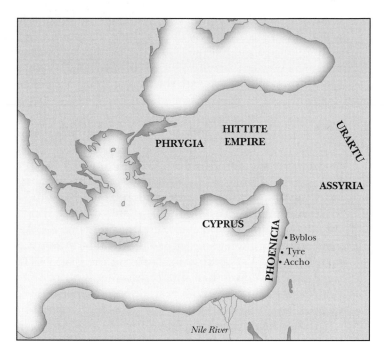

Map 5.1 East Mediterranean areas mentioned in this chapter.

Despite Ramses III's victory over the Sea Peoples, Egypt lost its empire in the Levant in the eleventh century B.C. We can get a sense of the changes by comparing two texts. One, written by a petty prince on the coast of Palestine to the pharaoh around 1350 B.C., begins: "To the king, my lord, the sun god from heaven: Thus Zatatna, prince of Accho [modern Akko], your servant, the servant of the king, and the dirt under his two feet, the ground which he treads . . . seven times, seven times I fall, both prone and supine!" In the second text, written soon after 1100 B.C., the pharaoh sent an agent on a diplomatic mission to Byblos (**bib**-los) in Phoenicia (modern Lebanon). The prince of Byblos told him bluntly. "As for me—me also—I am not your servant! I am not the servant of him who sent you either!" As its empire slipped away, Egypt broke up into two kingdoms, sometimes ruled by invaders from the western deserts or the Sudan.

Everywhere in the twelfth and eleventh centuries B.C. were movements of population, the fall of states, and economic chaos. The old established states of Egypt and the Near East fared better than Anatolia, but the Greek states fell hardest and took longest to recover. By 1000 B.C., the population of Greece was one-third what it was in 1300 B.C. After 1100 B.C., if there was a food shortage in one area, there was no one to relieve it by bringing in food from another area. Agriculture declined and monumental stone architecture disappeared, as did writing. There were migrations into and out of Greece. Long-distance trade faded away, a thing of the past.

LIFE AMONG THE RUINS

Bronze-makers needed tin from eastern Anatolia, but after 1100 B.C. the supply dried up. The inhabitants of Cyprus had known for centuries how to work iron, but rarely did so when bronze was abundant. Iron ores are widely distributed in the East

Mediterranean but require very hot temperatures to refine, unlike the copper from which bronze is made. As the tin trade declined, Cypriote smiths improved their techniques around 1050 B.C., building very hot fires using pitch-soaked pine, and iron became a serviceable alternative to bronze. Only gradually did steel develop, which requires mixing carbon with the iron ore. Greek steel never achieved the standards found in the Far East or in medieval Europe. The Dark Age was also the Iron Age, simultaneously a period of advance and retrogression.

The darkest stretch of the Greek Dark Age is the hundred years from roughly 1025 through 925 B.C. Ironworking was established, but the Greek peninsula was cut off from the outside world. Even within Greece, communications were limited, and regions developed local patterns of behavior. On Crete, Minoan-Mycenaean styles of houses, burials, art, and religion continued on a small scale, as did Mycenaean-style burials in the depopulated backwoods of western Greece. But in the old centers of power around the shores of the Aegean, the Mycenaean heritage was forgotten. The biggest towns, like Athens, **Argos,** and Thebes on the mainland and **Lefkandi** (lef-kan-**dē**) on the island of **Euboea** (ū-bē-a) (Map 5.2), numbered no more than one or two thousand people, and most Greeks lived in villages of a few dozen, rarely staying in one location for more than a generation or two.

In this shrunken world, cut off from the Mediterranean and daily reminded of how far it had fallen by a landscape full of Mycenaean ruins, a new society took shape at the end of the eleventh century B.C. We know it only from archaeology, and there is little of that—just a few graves and the foundations of flimsy houses. Some social distinctions, at least, survived. Most villages had one or two well-off families who

Map 5.2 Greek sites mentioned in this chapter.

claimed the best land and flocks, while their neighbors scraped by as dependents. In bigger towns like Athens, there may have been something like an aristocracy.

The Linear B tablets mentioned a local official called a *qasireu* (kas-**ir**-e-u), and in Homer's eighth-century-B.C. poetry, the leading man in each community is called a **basileus** (ba-**sil**-us), derived from the Mycenaean *qasireu*, often translated "king." Perhaps after the collapse of the upper social levels of Mycenaean society, the *qasireu* was the most elevated rank that still meant something, and these village headmen evolved into a minor nobility, the *basileis* (plural).

DARK AGE HEROES

The leaders of Dark Age communities represented themselves in their funerals as a homogeneous group. There is little variation in their simple graves or their plain, one-room houses. Religious behavior has left few traces. People continued visiting Bronze Age sacred places, but set up no temples or altars and left few offerings.

But some stood out. In 1981, archaeologists made a remarkable discovery at Lefkandi, a large building dating around 1000 to 950 B.C., unlike any other found anywhere in Greece at this time. Its plan is typical of Dark Age houses, but at 150 feet long, it is five times as big as a normal house (although it would have fit easily into the central courtyard of the Minoan palace at Cnossus). Under its floor were two burials: the cremation of a man in a decorated bronze urn—a two hundred-year-old heirloom from Cyprus—along with his iron weapons; and the inhumation (that is, burial without burning) of a woman adorned with gold jewelry (Figure 5.1).

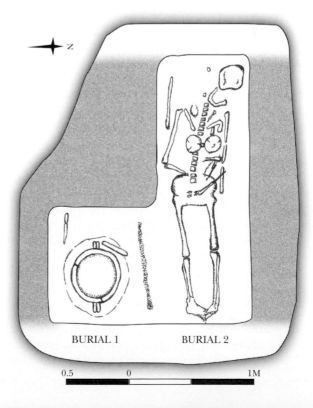

Figure 5.1 The burials under the Lefkandi hero shrine. Burial 1 is the male cremation in a bronze urn; burial 2 is the female inhumation.

BURIAL 1   BURIAL 2

0.5   0   1M

In an age when gold grave goods are almost unheard of, hers were remarkable. She wore a Babylonian gold chest piece that was already a thousand years old, an heirloom. Next to her was an iron knife with an ivory handle. Inhumation is rare at Lefkandi, and she may have been a human sacrifice at the man's funeral. In a second shaft were four horses. A huge pot stood over the graves, and soon after the funeral, the large house was deliberately filled with earth and converted into a giant mound.

This extraordinary site stands out from all other Dark Age finds. Later Greek literature perhaps explains it. The texts are full of stories about the *heroes,* men born from the sexual union of gods and mortals. Greece once was peopled by a race of heroes. According to **Hesiod,** perhaps living around 700 B.C., the gods created five successive races on earth: of gold, silver, bronze, heroes, and iron. He tells us that after the gods destroyed the bronze race,

> Zeus the son of Cronus made another, fourth,
> upon the fruitful land, more just and good,
> a godlike race of heroes, who are called
> the demi-gods—the race before our own.
> Foul wars and dreadful battles ruined some;
> some sought the flocks of Oedipus, and died
> in Cadmus' land, at seven-gated Thebes;
> and some, who crossed the open sea in ships,
> for fair-haired Helen's sake, were killed at Troy.
> These men were covered up in death, but Zeus
> the son of Cronus gave the others life
> and homes apart from mortals, at earth's edge.
> And there they live a carefree life, beside
> the whirling Ocean, on the Blessed Isles.
>
> Hesiod, *Works and Days,* 157–71 (D. Wender)

The war of the Greek heroes against Troy was central in Greek myth and provides the setting for Homer's *Iliad* and *Odyssey* (see Chapter 6, "Homer"). Greeks seem to have placed the heroes and the Trojan War in the days of the Mycenaean palaces, but they also thought that heroes could be born in their own age and recognized in various ways: by glorious death in battle, by successfully founding a colony, by a great athletic victory, or sometimes for no reason except that an oracle said that some man deserved heroic honors.

The Greek countryside was dotted with heroes' tombs and shrines. A man would be cremated and his ashes placed in a bronze urn, accompanied by his weapons and perhaps his horses. His grave was marked by a mound and sometimes a huge gravestone and offerings left at it. But the burial at Lefkandi is the earliest known example of someone accorded heroic honors at death and the most splendid throughout the entire Dark Age. Who was this man, and is any memory of him preserved in Greek myth? We would like to know.

ART AND TRADE IN THE DARK AGE

New artistic styles emerged. Around 1025 B.C., potters, whose work we know best because of fired clay's durability, developed a highly abstract style called **Protogeometric,** "first Geometric," because it preceded the more linear Geometric style that appeared

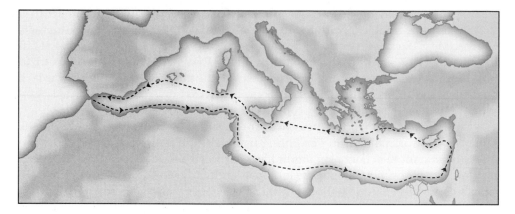

Map 5.3 Phoenician trade routes in the Mediterranean.

around 900 B.C. Protogeometric pottery is characterized by concentric circles and semicircles. It was simple, plain, and austere, but the results could be pleasing. Weavers probably used similar designs, but only scraps survive. Bronze workers made delicate pins to fasten clothes, of which we have some examples, but few other forms of art have come down to us.

Developments in the east Mediterranean were about to change conditions in Greece. Phoenicia had been a major trading center before 1200 B.C. and was reviving. The Bible notes that kings Solomon of Israel (c. 950 B.C.) and Hiram of Tyre, a major Phoenician port city, combined to trade with the land of Ophir (perhaps in the Red Sea) and Tarshish, probably in southern Spain. Before 900 B.C., Near Eastern objects reappear in Greece (particularly in graves at Lefkandi, Athens, and Cnossus), probably brought by Phoenicians, and Greek pottery is found at Tyre, up the coast in Syria, and even inland around the Sea of Galilee. The Greeks were drawn into an expanding economic system with a center in Phoenicia (Map 5.3). Probably few ninth-century Greeks traveled far, but this handful of adventurers had a disproportionate influence. Exotic objects not seen in Greece for centuries were again available. In a few places, Greeks began—for the first time since the Late Bronze Age—to make valuable gifts to the gods, particularly at **Olympia** in the wooded, virtually uninhabited backcountry of the western Peloponnesus, later site of the Olympic Games. Many of the earliest bronzes at Olympia were made in Argos, across the rugged mountains of Arcadia. By making pilgrimages to distant Olympia, across such tough terrain, wealthy Argives displayed their piety and affluence.

The pace of life quickened in the ninth century B.C. as towns grew, new forms of riches appeared, and foreign faces, speech, and customs again became familiar in some centers. There were experiments in art, housing, burial, and the worship of gods, but nothing to prepare for the explosion of innovation that would come in the eighth century, sometimes called the Greek Renaissance.

THE EIGHTH-CENTURY RENAISSANCE: ECONOMY

From Iran to Spain, population grew rapidly in the eighth century. Evidence from polar ice cores, sediments on the beds of lakes and bogs, and pollen surviving from ancient plants shows that after 800 B.C. average temperatures fell a few degrees, and winter rains increased. Crop yields probably rose, and mortality declined. In a slightly more favorable environment, population doubled in eighth-century-B.C. Greece. Most Dark Age Greeks had a few dozen neighbors in their tiny villages, but by 700 B.C. villages of a hundred were common. Towns like Athens and Argos had five thousand residents. Having twice as many mouths to feed from the same area of land means disaster for many unless property is redistributed or output increases. When those who have adequate property resist change, conflict is inevitable.

Land hunger led to more intensive use of resources—getting more food from the same land by working harder—manuring the fields, and plowing and weeding more often. Hesiod took such labors for granted. "Pile work on work, and still more work," he said. When possible, people brought new land into cultivation by using land previously considered marginal. But only hard work could make rocky soil yield a living. Better to find good land in a new place. Greeks were trading with Italy and Sicily by 800 B.C. and saw good harbors and fields there. In the 740s B.C., the Phoenicians founded trading posts in Sicily, Tunisia, and Spain, and seafaring Greeks competed and associated with them in the far west. Around 775 to 750 B.C., Greeks from Euboea settled at **Pithekoussai** ("monkey-island"), a little island in the Bay of Naples (modern Ischia) (see Map 5.2), the first western Greek settlement. The settlement was probably a home to traders. Judging from the short inscriptions in Phoenician scripts on pottery from this site, Phoenicians lived intimately with Greeks.

In 734 B.C., Greeks emigrated to the east coast of Sicily, seizing unoccupied land, driving off the local population, or enslaving them. Probably thirty thousand Greek men headed west between 750 and 650 B.C., taking native wives when they arrived (see Map 5.4). Many communities received information about where to

Map 5.4 The Greek colonies. Shown in the darker shade, the colonies spread from southern France and Spain to Sicily, southern Italy, northern Africa, and the coasts of the Black Sea.

colonize from Apollo's shrine at Delphi, a clearinghouse for stories about foreign lands. Founders of colonies often went to Delphi before setting out, to receive the god's approval and sponsorship. By 700 B.C., colonists had created a new Greek world in Sicily and southern Italy. In the *Odyssey*, a poem about seafaring to the distant and dangerous west, Homer describes how land-hungry Greeks might have felt that resources were being wasted by those who did not know how to exploit them properly:

> Now there is a level island that stretches across the harbor,
> not close to the shore of the Cylops'° island,
> nor far out, wooded. Wild goats without number
> roam there, for the footfall of men does not drive them away
> nor do hunters go there as they stalk the peaks of mountains,
> panting mightily. The island is not held by flocks,
> nor is the land plowed, but unsown, unharvested,
> it knows not the hand of man, but nourishes only
> the bleating goats. Nor do the Cyclops have ships
> with red-painted prows, nor do shipwrights live among them,
> who might make for them well-benched ships,
> which might accomplish for them every thing,
> carrying them in ships to the cities of men, as men
> travel often across the sea to visit others.
> Such artisans, too, would have made this
> a nice place to live. It is not bad in any way,
> and would bear every kind of crop in season.
> The sea-meadows run, well-irrigated, gentle,
> along the shores of the sea. Your vines would
> never give out. There is level plow land,
> where you would forever reap deep crops in season,
> so rich is the soil beneath.
>   There is a harbor good for mooring,
> no need of a cable, nor for anchors, nor to tie up the prow.
> There you can bring your ship ashore and wait
> until your seamen again feel the urge to travel
> and the winds blow fair. At the head of the harbor flows
> a noble spring, gushing from a cave. Around it poplars grow.
>
> Homer, *Odyssey* 9.116–41 (B. Powell)

°*Cyclops:* One-eyed giants.

We call the overseas Greek settlements "colonies," but they were independent *poleis,* not satellites of their mother-cities. Some grew larger and richer than the Aegean *poleis.* The territory they seized doubled the amount of good land under Greek control, and they chose sites with fine harbors, like the island Homer described. At first, the position of the Greek colonies was precarious. Some sites failed and had to relocate; some disappeared altogether (like Jamestown in sixteenth-century America). Those that survived flourished in the second generation. The houses are bigger, and temples appear. More settlers kept coming, and some colonies, like Syracuse in Sicily, sent out subcolonies of their own. The new settlements spread Greeks all round the Mediterranean and Black Sea.

One could also extend production in a time of burgeoning population by stealing neighbors' land. There were several wars for land around 700 B.C. The most famous was Sparta's invasion of **Messenia** in the late eighth century. Messenia is a territory that lies west of Sparta across a high mountain range (see Figs. 10.1 and 10.2). After a long struggle, the Spartans annexed Messenia, enslaved its population, and divided its land among themselves. The Messenians now worked the land for Spartans, handing over most of the produce. The reduction of Messenia to servitude was an extreme response to population growth and made Sparta peculiar among the Greek city-states (see Chapter 10, "A Tale of Two Archaic Cities: Sparta and Athens, 700–480 B.C."), but many Greek states used force on a smaller scale to take control of disputed border zones.

Another response to growing population was *more efficient organization.* The Minoans and Mycenaeans had refined their organization by inventing a form of writing and imitating the bureaucratic structure of literate Near Eastern economies. Making use of written records, they told some people what to grow to get the most out of their land, and they set up others in workshops. The palaces moved goods between the occupational groups, raising efficiency through the division of labor. What the palaces accomplished through centralization, eighth-century Greeks did through markets. In this way, archaic-classical Greece differed profoundly from Bronze Age Greece. In the eighth century, no one was telling anyone what to grow, make, or trade, except in enslaved communities like Messenia. Free Greeks acted on their own authority and were governed, as we would say, by the forces of the marketplace, and served (in ways still unclear) by the revolutionary Greek alphabet. The results were better than in the Bronze Age. The population grew and lived better. But all these responses to growing population had social costs, some of them high.

EIGHTH-CENTURY RENAISSANCE: SOCIETY

To exploit their land more intensively, Greeks needed to increase the amounts of labor and capital (in the form of animals, manure, and better plows) that they put into each field. Rich people with a lot of land wanted poorer people to work it, while the poor wished to have enough land to employ their own labor effectively. If the rich could concentrate all land in their own hands, the poor would have to work for them; if the poor could distribute land equally, they could support themselves.

Some of the colonies in Sicily may have conducted a kind of social experiment, giving each man equal land and equal rights. Patterns of burials suggest that egalitarian ideals were in any event gaining ground everywhere in the eighth century. During the Dark Age, the elite received more formal burials than the poor, but after 750 B.C., most people began receiving equal treatment at death. As social power shifted from rich to poor, the divisions that would plague archaic Greece took shape as did struggles between those who thought that a small aristocracy should control land, labor, and the conduct of war and those who thought that all the men in a *polis* had an equal voice in such matters.

Extending the land under cultivation brought in more food but called for still more labor, while occupying someone else's land required force and the qualities that make force effective. Political boundaries—the divisions between territories—became more important and better defined. Competition for land made Greeks more aware of belonging to particular groups, such as the Athenians or the Corinthians, and in the new forms of organized violence, ever more was at stake.

Figure 5.2 Breastplate (*cuirass*), circa 650 B.C., from a burial. The bronze is modeled to the man's pectoral and abdominal muscles.

There were important advances in arms and armor. After 700 B.C., we begin to find fine bronze armor, the first seen since Mycenaean times (Figure 5.2), and fortifications proliferated and became stronger.

Warfare favors centralized power: someone has to muster fighters, design strategy, and see that orders are obeyed. In this new atmosphere, state institutions appeared, directing communal policies and monopolizing the use of violence. In some cases, the growing importance of war allowed Dark Age chiefs to become kings who made key decisions. Was Greece returning to Bronze Age monarchy?

We learn a good deal about these chiefs from Homer and Hesiod, who call them *basileis*. The poets thought that the *basileis'* authority came in part from closeness to the gods. To Homer, Odysseus was "godlike," and many heroes who fought at Troy were born from the union of gods with humans. Some of the most powerful men in the eighth century B.C. may have claimed to be sacred rulers, and Hesiod says that *basileis* in his own day (around 700 B.C.) enjoyed the divine favor of the Muses:

> When the daughters of great Zeus [the Muses] would bring
> honor upon a heaven-favored *basileus*
> and when they watch him being born, they pour
> sweet dew upon his tongue, and from his lips
> flow honeyed words. All people look to him
> when he is giving judgment uprightly,
> and speaking with assurance, he can stop
> great quarrels sensibly. Wise *basileis* are wise
> in this: when public harm is being done

> to the people, they can set things straight with ease,
> advising with soft words. And when a *basileus*
> comes into the assembly, he is wooed
> with honeyed reverence, just like a god,
> and is conspicuous above the crowd.
> Such is the Muses' holy gift to men.
>
> Hesiod, *Theogony* 80–93 (D. Wender)

Hesiod, no doubt, understood how to flatter his audience (these very *basileis*), but most *poleis* did away with kingship altogether in the seventh century B.C.

In an agricultural society, growth that can support a larger population depends on rulers strong enough to protect property rights, so people feel comfortable investing time and resources, but not so strong that they can simply help themselves to anyone's profit. The *basileis'* inability to provide conditions of security is clear in a story that Hesiod tells, and such failures undermined the *basileis*. Hesiod says that when his father died, he and his brother Perses divided their inheritance in two. But Perses bribed the *basileis* to award him a larger share:

> We split our property in half, but you
> grabbed at the larger part and praised to heaven
> the *basileis* who love to try a case like that,
> eaters of bribes. The fools! They do not know
> that half may be worth more by far than whole,
> nor how much profit lies in poor man's bread.
>
> Hesiod, *Works and Days* 37–41 (D. Wender)

The weakness of the *basileis* meant that Greek state-formation followed an unusual path. Institutions became stronger and more efficient, but the ordinary men in the community resisted the ambitions of would-be kings and haughty aristocrats. A good illustration comes from the peculiar situation at the start of Homer's *Odyssey*. The great hero Odysseus had been a good *basileus* on Ithaca, the tale runs, but the gods caused him to disappear for ten years on his way home after spending the previous ten years at Troy. For twenty years, Ithaca lived without a *basileus*. Most Ithacans presumed Odysseus dead, and got on with their lives. But a crowd of aristocratic suitors descended on Odysseus' house, vying for the hand of the beautiful Penelope, his supposed widow. They devoured his stored wealth and slept with his maidservants until, in the twentieth year of Odysseus' absence, his grown son Telemachus (tel-**em**-a-kus) decided to get rid of them:

> At once he ordered the clear-voiced heralds to summon
> to the assembly the Achaeans with their long hair.
> The heralds shouted out, and the Achaeans quickly gathered.
> And when they were gathered together and crowded
> the meeting ground, Telemachus entered the place of assembly,
> and in his hand he held a bronze spear. He was not alone;
> two swift hounds accompanied him. Athena cast a wondrous charm
> about him. Everyone looked at him as he entered.
> He sat down in his father's seat, and the elders made way.
> Then to them the hero Aegyptius began to speak,
> who was bent with age and knew many things . . .
>   "Hear me, men of Ithaca, what I have to say.
> Never have we held an assembly or met in session

since godlike Odysseus sailed in his hollow ships.
Who now has summoned us in this way? one of the youngsters?
or one of the old-timers? or has someone announced
some army that is coming, someone who can describe it clearly
because he first learned of it himself? or will he speak
of some other matter of public concern and address us?

Homer, Odyssey 2.6–16, 25–32 (B. Powell)

Homer took it for granted that men from important families, like Telemachus, were the center of attention in politics. Odysseus even had his own seat in the assembly. Aegyptius said there had been no assembly since Odysseus left for Troy twenty years before, so we might assume that Odysseus had dominated Ithacan politics; on the other hand, Aegyptius had no idea which Ithacan called this meeting, so not only a basileus could call assemblies. Aegyptius thinks of "the Ithacans" as a corporation responsible for communal well-being.

Telemachus stands up and explains that it was he who summoned the assembly. He describes the suitors' outrages:

". . . Thronging our house day after day
they party on and on. They drink the shining wine
as if there was no tomorrow. Everything wasted.
No longer is there a man such as Odysseus was,
who might expel this curse from my household.
Surely I could not accomplish it. I would only appear
ridiculous and knowing nothing of power.
If I did have the power, I would do something about this.
Their deeds are intolerable! It's no pretty sight,
what they've done to my house! You should
take shame, all of you, and be mortified in the eyes
of all those who live around us. Fear the anger of the gods,
or seeing these evils they will whirl against you!
I beg you in the name of Zeus on Olympus,
and Themis too, who dissolves and gathers assemblies:
Stop! my friends, and leave me alone
to be worn away in sorrow—if ever my father,
the excellent Odysseus, ever did harm with evil intent
to the well-greaved Achaeans—now,
I suppose, you repay it by the harm
you do to me, with evil intent,
encouraging these men. It would be better for me
if *you* consumed my wealth and my cattle. At least
if *you* ate them, one day there would be recompense.

Homer, Odyssey 2.55–76 (B. Powell)

In Ithaca, state institutions are weak. There is no police. Since there is no third party to enforce justice, and Telemachus lacks the strength to fight the suitors himself, he appeals to the community's moral sense. They should be embarrassed to allow such goings-on in Ithaca and concerned that the gods will punish them. Telemachus marvels that the Ithacans tolerate such behavior, and he pretends to wonder whether Odysseus had done them some wrong. Telemachus presents himself as the champion of justice and advocates the community's right to judge even the mightiest among them, including the young, rich, arrogant suitors.

One of the suitors replies that it is not their fault. Telemachus should send his mother back to her father, and the suitors would then approach him about a re-marriage. Telemachus denounces the scheme, and Zeus sends an omen: Two eagles fight in the sky above. An old man says this means that Odysseus will return and punish the suitors. Unlike in Assyria or in Egypt, there are no professional omen-interpreters in this society. Eurymachus, a suitor, speaks up:

> "Hey old man, why don't you go home
> and prophesy to your kids? In case they might
> suffer something or other in times to come.
> I'm a better prophet than you are. There are birds
> aplenty soaring through the rays of the sun,
> but they are not all signs from another world.
> Odysseus, come on, died in some far place,
> and you should have died with him.
> You wouldn't rant your prophecies then,
> nor would you be stirring up this angry young man,
> thinking you might get some gift from him.
> Now I prophesy to you, and what I say shall come to pass.
> If you, so filled with wisdom, so knowing of life,
> with your fancy words stir up this young man to run riot,
> *he* will be the first to pay. Nor will he be able to do
> a thing about it. As for you, we'll slap on a fine that
> won't be fun to pay. You'll wish you'd never been born."
>
> Homer, *Odyssey* 2.178–93 (B. Powell)

Unlike Telemachus, Eurymachus is full of threats and shows contempt for the gods in saying that the sign means nothing. Another Ithacan, Mentor, sadly observes:

> "Hear me, men of Ithaca, what I have to say.
> Let no scepter-bearing *basileus* willingly
> be kind and gentle, knowing how one should act,
> but let him be always hard and the doer of evil things!
> As it is, no one remembers godlike Odysseus
> from all the people he ruled, how gentle,
> how like a father he was.
>   I don't begrudge the well-born suitors
> if they want to commit acts of violence in the perversity
> of their minds: they lay their heads on the line
> when with violence they consume
> the house of Odysseus, whom they think
> will never return. But I hold it against *you*
> as you sit there, every man in silence,
> and you refuse to speak and to
> put an end to the suitors' outrage, who are few
> in number, while there are many of you."
>   Leocritus, son of Euenor, answered.
> "Mentor! You fool! Crazed, mad! What do you mean,
> urging us to lay off? It's a rough game to fight
> against more men than yourself, over a meal!
> Even if Odysseus the Ithacan himself should come
> home and rage in his heart to expel the suitors
> who dine in his house, I don't think his wife
> would take much pleasure in him, No,
> however much she wanted to. No, here,

on the spot, he'd meet an ugly death,
if he fought against our multitude.
What you say is gibberish . . .
Enough of that! Now go to your homes
—each one of you!"
   . . . So he broke up the assembly in a jiffy,
and everyone went home to his house.
But the suitors returned to the house of godlike Odysseus.

Homer, Odyssey 2.229–59 (B. Powell)

Mentor thinks the community should stop the rich and impious suitors, but the Ithacans do nothing, and Leocritus abruptly dismisses them. Homer took it for granted that Ithaca should have a *basileus,* but also assumed that the *basileus* must act justly and that Ithaca's men would decide what counted as just behavior. The assembly could in theory denounce the elite, but they hold back. Institutions are weak and the suitors are ready to resist anyone who attacks them. Although the suitors retain control, battle lines are drawn between the mass of Ithacans, including virtuous leaders who stand for decency and self-interested aristocrats out for selfish gain. In his description of events on Ithaca, Homer appears to reflect similar divisions in his own society of the eighth century B.C.

The same social divisions appear in Hesiod's poem, *Works and Days,* although Hesiod offers a very different perspective. He presents himself as a hardworking farmer dispensing advice on how to live a good life. We earlier quoted his criticism of the *basileis* for taking bribes, after which he continues:

O Perses, follow right; control your pride.
For pride is evil in a common man.
Even a *basileus* finds it hard to bear;
it weights him down and leads him to disgrace.
The road to justice is the better way,
for justice in the end will win the race
and pride will lose: the simpleton must learn
this fact through suffering. The god of oaths
runs faster than a crooked verdict; when
justice is dragged out of the way by men
who judge dishonestly and swallow bribes,
a struggling sound is heard; then she returns
back to the city and the homes of men,
wrapped in a mist and weeping, and she brings
harm to the crooked men who drove her out.

Hesiod, Works and Days 37–41, 213–24 (D. Wender)

Hesiod denounces the *basileis* of his small village of Ascra (not far from Thebes) for their injustice. They ignored *dikê* (**dē**-kā), "justice," and their impiety caused the gods to abandon mankind. Hesiod champions the moderate, middling farmer, like himself, who has a clear sense of right and wrong, and pursues wealth fairly:

                    . . . If a man gets wealth
By force of hands or through his lying tongue,
as often happens, when greed clouds his mind
and shame is pushed aside by shamelessness,
then the gods blot him out and blast his house
and soon his wealth deserts him.

Hesiod, Works and Days 320–25 (D. Wender)

Around this same time the prophets of the Hebrew Bible denounced the kings of Israel and Judah for similar injustices, predicting that God would bring punishment. Comparable sentiments turn up much earlier in Egyptian and Mesopotamian literature. But Homer and Hesiod differ from the Near Eastern authors. Whereas the Hebrew prophets Amos and Isaiah believed that they should point out the rulers' faults, and Egyptian texts expected the pharaoh to correct injustice, Greek authors believed that ordinary men themselves had the right to correct injustice. It was up to the community of farmers to determine what was good and proper, and to resist the wicked *basileis*. From such extraordinary attitudes was to grow the male-citizen democracy of fifth-century B.C. Athens.

THE EIGHTH-CENTURY RENAISSANCE: CULTURE

Eighth-century social conflicts were intimately tied to cultural developments. Since 3000 B.C., Near Eastern kings alone mediated between this world and the gods. Kingship came from heaven. The Greeks separated religion from social power.

When Dark Age Greeks prayed to the gods, they met at a special place, killed an animal in the god's honor, poured drink offerings (libations), roasted the animal on a fire, and ate. Around 750 B.C., they began to build stone altars for the fire and to offer gifts at shrines. The Olympic Games were founded near this time, traditionally in 776 B.C., though we cannot verify the date. At the games, when warfare was suspended, Greek athletes from different towns competed. The earliest athletes came from near Olympia, but by the sixth century B.C. competitors came from all over the Greek world. Their gifts to the shrine of Zeus were rich, and by 700 B.C. included objects of bronze, silver, and gold.

During those same years, Greeks started building temples—houses for the gods' images. Temples were at first modest, though bigger and better built than the houses around them. Larger towns, like Eretria (e-**re**-trē-a) on the island of Euboea, built "hundred-foot" temples called **hekatompeda** in Greek, and soon after 700 B.C. Corinth and Argos built *hekatompeda* completely from stone. Seventh-century temples dwarfed all contemporary buildings. They were the biggest expenditures in capital, labor, and ambition since the Mycenaean palaces.

Dark Age ritual meals evolved into elaborate sacrifices and feasts with impressive dedications to the gods. After battles, winners might offer one-tenth of their plunder to a god, and great sanctuaries like Olympia, Delphi, and Delos filled up with such offerings. Periodically, the priests cleaned up the sanctuaries, digging big pits and burying the old but hallowed offerings. At many sanctuaries, archaeologists cannot put a trowel into the earth without turning up eighth- and seventh-century offerings. The increasingly self-conscious *poleis* marked out areas for the gods, communal sanctuaries that embodied local identity and pride. Most *poleis* set up two major sanctuaries, one in the heart of the main town and one on a frontier that helped define the community against its neighbors, solidifying its claim to the land.

At the same time that spending on religious architecture increased, rich grave goods declined. After 700 B.C., anyone who wanted to show off his wealth did so not by a huge grave mound or buried suits of armor, which would glorify the family alone, but by making gifts to the gods, which benefited the whole community. Private displays of wealth also declined. Shortly before 700 B.C., a few people built houses as big as twenty-five hundred square feet, with second floors, the size of a

Figure 5.3 The earliest figured art since Mycenaean times shows funerals and battles. On the top panel on this large Late Geometric vase from Athens, called a *krater* ("mixing bowl," for wine), circa 750 B.C., a body is laid out on a bier. On either side of the bier, mourners tear their hair. In a panel below, warriors ride in chariots.

modern American house. After 700 B.C., such mansions were rare until the fourth century B.C.

In a few places, people started leaving offerings in Bronze Age tombs, perhaps to honor the long-dead race of heroes. As well as redefining their relationships with the gods, eighth-century Greeks were rethinking their relationships with their ancestors. Another change, the revival of representative art in the **Late Geometric style** of vase painting (roughly 750–700 B.C.), may be connected with this development. Late Geometric paintings show humans in battles and at funerals (Figure 5.3), but the scenes may evoke the long-lost race of heroes as much as contemporary practices. Many of the well-known Greek myths were probably invented in this period, perhaps stimulated by the influx of images from Near Eastern art on objects made of cloth (now all lost) and on metal objects like armor and bowls.

But the greatest cultural innovation by far, which forever changed communication, was the invention of the **Greek alphabet.** As we have seen, Linear B syllabic writing, which recorded Greek, disappeared completely after 1200 B.C. Around 800 B.C., an unknown Greek or Near Easterner invented a new script based on an earlier Semitic script used in the Levant from around 1000 B.C. Sometimes called the Phoenician alphabet, the script on which the Greek alphabet was based was really an odd syllabary in which each sign stands for a consonant plus an implied vowel, to be provided by the native speaker. (To distinguish the Phoenician writing from the

Greek alphabetic writing, some scholars call Phoenician writing a *consonantal script.*) The Phoenician syllabary did not, however, belong to the Phoenicians alone, but was one of a family of closely related writings called **West Semitic writing** used all over the Levant, including Syria, Phoenicia, and Palestine. Possible forerunners to this family of writings, which includes Hebrew writing, have recently been found in southern Egypt, dating as early as 1800 B.C.

It takes a lot of skill to read something written in West Semitic script. West Semitic writing was revolutionary because it needed just twenty-two signs and because of a unique method of learning by memorizing a fixed sequence of names and signs. The consonantal value of a sign (but no vocalic values) was encoded in the name of the sign as the first sound of the name. We still say, in a somewhat similar fashion, "A is for apple, B is for brave, C is for cat. . . ." Because no vocalic values are encoded, you cannot pronounce West Semitic (including Hebrew) unless you speak the language. By stark contrast, anyone can pronounce a document in the Greek alphabet, even if he or she has no idea what is being said. The Greek alphabet was the first technology that preserved the approximate sound of speech.

Many scholars assume that Phoenicians developed their script for traders' record-keeping, but there is no direct evidence, not even a system of numbering, until much later when the Western Semites borrowed numbers from the Greeks. Rather, the writing seems to have been used to record political activity, family histories, prayers to the gods, and rules of behavior. Surviving West Semitic texts (including early forms of the Bible) were probably dictated rather than composed silently in the modern manner; for this reason, West Semitic writing paid exclusive attention to sound, ignoring the many nonphonetic aids to communication that earlier Mesopotamian cuneiform and Egyptian hieroglyphic writings employed. Small portions of the Hebrew Bible may go back as far as 1000 B.C. and, although most of the Bible is much later, the documents it contains probably reflect the range of records and literature kept in this widespread family of writings during the Dark Age, from which only the Hebrew scriptures have survived.

Archaeologists on Crete have found objects with Phoenician inscriptions from as early as 900 B.C., but not until after 800 B.C., in the midst of all the upheavals described previously, did someone adapt these symbols to suit the sounds of Greek poetry (Table 5.1). The adapter of the Phoenician script, the inventor of the Greek alphabet, no doubt lived in a bilingual community (perhaps the cosmopolitan island of Euboea). The adapter divided the Phoenician syllabic signs into two categories, one now to represent vowels (in Greek, literally "things sounded") and the second to represent the sounds that go with vowels, or consonants ("things that sound along with something else"), and added a few new signs to the end of the series. The adapter's radical invention was not so much the introduction of vowel signs, which

---

Table 5.1   The Phoenician and Greek writing systems. The Greek alphabet used the *waw* sign in two places: for the *digamma,* which had the sound of English *w,* and for one of the five new signs, the vowel *u.* Later, the Greeks dropped the *digamma,* but it has come down to us through the Latin alphabet (the Western form of the Greek alphabet) as the letter *F. San* was an alternate sign for the *s* sound and was soon dropped, as was *qoppa,* similar to *k,* but it survives as our letter *q.*

Phoenician Symbol (ca. 700 BCE)	Semitic Name	Approximate Semitic Sound	Greek Symbol (ca. 700 BCE)	Modern Greek Symbol	Greek Name
	'aleph	glottal stop (catch in voice)		A	alpha
	beth	b		B	beta
	gimel	g in glory		Γ	gamma
	daleth	d		Δ	delta
	he	h		E	epsilon
	waw	w		---	(digamma)
	zayin	z		Z	zeta
	heth			H	eta
	teth			Θ	theta
	yod	y in yellow		I	iota
	kaph	k		K	kappa
	lamed	l		Λ	lambda
	mem	m		M	mu
	nun	n		N	nu
	samekh	s		Ξ	xi
	'ayin	pharyngeal consonant (gagging sound)		O	omicron
	pe	p		Π	pi
	tsadhe	ts		---	(san)
	qoph	rough k		---	(qoppa)
	resh	r		P	rho
	shin	sh		Σ	sigma
	taw	t		T	tau
	waw	w		Υ	upsilon
				Φ	phi
				X	chi
				Ψ	psi
				Ω	omega

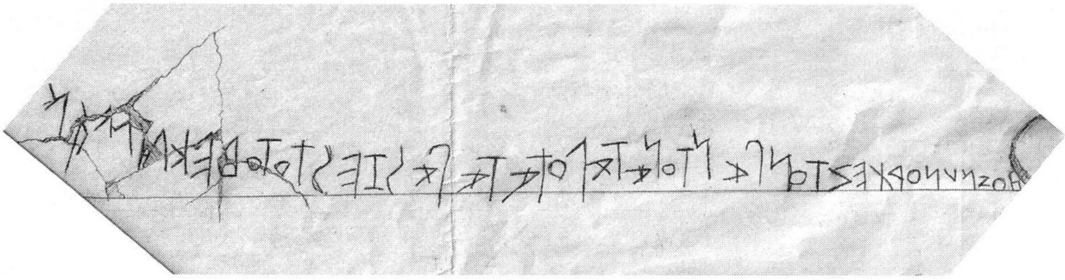

HOSNUNORXESTONPANTONATALOTATAPAIZEITOTODEK{M}M{N?}N
Whoever of all the dancers now dances most gracefully . . .

Figure 5.4 Transcription of one of the oldest Greek alphabetic inscriptions; on a jug found in Athens, circa 740 B.C. The inscription, reading from right to left, is a perfect hexameter, Homer's meter, plus a few puzzling signs at the end. The alphabet was used to record Greek verse from the beginning.

had existed in earlier writings including Linear B, as the spelling rule whereby a sign from one group, the vowels, must always accompany signs from the second group, the consonants. Where a Phoenician would write, "Tll m, Ms, f th mn f mn ws, wh ws drvn / fr jrns, ftr h hd sckd Trs scrd ctdl," the Greek alphabet could now write "Tell me, Muse, of the man of many ways, who was driven / Far journeys, after he had sacked Troy's sacred citadel"—the first two lines of Homer's *Odyssey*. In practical terms, the Greek alphabet was the first system of writing that you could pronounce, once you had learned the rules, whether or not you knew the underlying language. It could be used to record any language at all, and since its invention has become, in its Roman variation, the most widely used script in the world by far, recording hundreds of languages from Turkish to Chinese (in the so-called Pinyin script).

Why did the adapter go to the trouble of inventing a script with two kinds of signs and the rule that they must always work together? We can be confident that it was not to record lists of "woolen cloaks to be well boiled," like the Mycenaean record-keepers, nor to create a writing system capable of recording every human language. His motive appears to have been to write down Greek poetry, even the poetry of Homer, who seems to have lived at this time (Figure 5.4).

You can record poetry in consonantal, syllabic, or even hieroglyphic scripts, and Near Easterners and Egyptians had done so for two thousand years, but the Greek language, especially Greek poetry, uses complex clusters of vowels that cannot be represented by such systems. Linear B never records poetry, as far as we know. The alphabet gave Greeks the means to record the words of the greatest poets, and from this time on, literary evidence (almost all in the form of poetry until about 450 B.C.) survives in increasing quantities. The invention of the Greek alphabet and the recording of the Homeric poems separate Greek prehistory from Greek history.

CONCLUSION

Down to 1200 B.C., Greek society was not so different from the rest of the East Mediterranean. The Neolithic revolution had spread from the Near East to Greece by 6000 B.C.; the secondary products revolution arrived by 3000 B.C., and complex societies emerged soon after. The mainland societies collapsed around 2300 B.C., but by 2000 B.C., large palaces appeared on Crete, using Linear A writing to run complex bureaucracies. In the eighteenth and seventeenth centuries, Minoan society was rich and sophisticated, with ordinary people enjoying high living standards, and Minoan-type institutions spread through the Cyclades. By 1700 B.C., warlike societies gained great wealth on the mainland and at some point took over Crete. They too fell victim to unexplained disasters around 1200 B.C., and all the Mycenaean centers on the mainland burned.

Great kings and palaces revived in western Asia in the tenth century, but not in Greece. Although there are hints of recovery in the ninth century, the Greek Dark Age continued until the eighth century, and the city-states that then emerged were very different from Near Eastern societies. The *poleis* had a sense of community—so strong that would-be rulers could not claim that the gods had singled them out. In this inventive period appeared new forms of religious, artistic, and poetic expression. New *poleis* around the Mediterranean and Black Sea revolutionized the Greek economy and provided scope for social experiments. In place of the centralized, redistributive economies of the Bronze Age, eighth-century Greeks relied on individuals to exchange goods as they thought best.

Around 700 B.C., the *poleis* were small, poor, and weak by Near Eastern standards. They were internally divided by feuds within the aristocracy and by feuds between the aristocrats and the masses. They were also divided among themselves, as city-states competed for resources. In the next two chapters, we examine two of the cultural pillars that supported the new framework: the Homeric epics and Greek religion.

KEY TERMS

Assyria, 72

Argos, 74

Lefkandi, 74

Euboea, 74

basileus, 75

Hesiod, 76

Protogeometric, 76

Olympia, 77

Pithekoussai, 78

Messenia, 80

dikê, 85

hekatompeda, 86

Late Geometric style, 87

Greek alphabet, 87

West Semitic writing, 88

FURTHER READING

The Dark Age

Gitin, Seymour, Amihai Mazar, and Ephraim Stern, eds., *Mediterranean Peoples in Transition, Thirteenth to Early Tenth Centuries BCE.* (Jerusalem 1998). Papers from a conference on the Sea Peoples.

Sandars, Nancy, *The Sea Peoples* (2nd ed., London 1985). Standard account of the Sea Peoples and the upheavals around 1200 B.C.

Snodgrass, Anthony, *The Dark Age of Greece* (Edinburgh, UK, 1971; reissued 2001). Now out of date on recent finds, but still the best archaeological survey of the Dark Age.

Popham, Mervyn, Evi Touloupa, and L. Hugh Sackett, "The Hero of Lefkandi," *Antiquity* 56 (1982), 169–74. Brief excavation report on the tenth-century finds at Lefkandi.

Whitley, James, *The Archaeology of Ancient Greece* (Cambridge, UK, 2001). Chapters 5 to 10 are the best recent overview of Dark Age and Archaic archaeology.

The Eighth Century

Boardman, John, *The Greeks Overseas* (rev. ed., London 1999). The best introduction to the archaeological evidence for Greek colonies.

Burkert, Walter, *The Orientalizing Revolution* (Cambridge, MA, 1992; German original 1984). Stimulating study of literary and archaeological evidence for Greek contacts with the Near East in the eighth and seventh centuries.

de Polignac, François, *Cults, Territory, and the Origins of the Greek City-State* (Chicago 1995). Original analysis of the significance of religious changes in the eighth century.

Hurwit, Jeffery, *The Art and Culture of Early Greece* (Ithaca, NY, 1985). Excellent analysis of vase painting and poetry.

Langdon, Susan, ed., *New Light on a Dark Age* (Columbia, MO, 1997). Proceedings of a conference on art and culture in the age of Homer.

Morris, Ian, and Barry B. Powell, eds., *A New Companion to Homer* (Leiden 1997). The essays in Part IV discuss Homeric history and archaeology.

Powell, Barry B., *Homer and the Origin of the Greek Alphabet* (Cambridge, UK, 1991). Argues that alphabetic writing was invented specifically to record Homer's poetry.

———, *Writing and the Origins of Greek Literature* (Cambridge, UK, 2003). Describes the new possibilities that the alphabet offered and the relationship between art and song.

Snodgrass, Anthony, *Archaic Greece* (Berkeley 1981). Outstanding combination of archaeological and textual evidence.

———, *Homer and the Artists* (Cambridge, UK, 1998). Important and readable study of the interactions of poets and painters.

CHAPTER 6

HOMER

We quoted Homer several times in Chapter 4, "The Greeks before History, 12,000–1200 B.C.," and Chapter 5, "The Dark Age, 1200–700 B.C." Homer is the first known European poet and of such importance to the Greeks that we need to pause our historical narrative to look more closely at him and the controversies that have surrounded him.

Homer became the basis for Greek education (Figure 6.1), and has remained so to this day. He is also our best source for knowing what the Greeks were thinking in the eighth century B.C. as they fought each other and sailed across dangerous seas to found new *poleis* in alien lands. Who was Homer? When did he live? How were his works written down? What are his poems about? He seems to come from the void, a flare suddenly lighting up the Dark Age, illuminating a new world. Such problems constitute the **Homeric Question,** a central issue in humanistic study for the past two hundred years.

THE HOMERIC QUESTION

The oldest surviving texts of the *Iliad* and the *Odyssey* go back to around A.D. 1100, separated from the poet by nearly two thousand years. Scholars produced them in the late Roman capital of Byzantium, today Istanbul. Pieces, but only pieces, of *ancient* texts of Homer survive from the dry sands of Egypt, where Homer was read and loved by Greek-speakers who settled the Nile Valley after Alexander the Great's conquest in 333 B.C. Some fragments date back to the third century B.C.; more papyrus fragments of Homer survive than of any other poet, and twice as many fragments of the *Iliad* as of the *Odyssey*. The papyrus fragments sometimes have extra lines not found in our texts, but on the whole they are remarkably similar.

Figure 6.1 A boy recites a memorized epic poem to his schoolmaster, who checks his work against a text; on an Athenian red-figure drinking cup, 480s B.C. Behind the schoolmaster, a second pupil practices the lyre, which accompanied songs.

We know almost nothing about Homeric texts earlier than these papyri. We have no primary sources for Homer's life, for where he lived, or when, although traditions reaching back to the fifth century B.C. said he was born on the coast of Asia Minor or on the island of Chios, just off it. Scholarly books still today often describe Homer as an Ionian, someone from Asia Minor, but in fact we have no direct knowledge.

Friedrich August Wolf

Even in the ancient world, intellectuals noticed that nothing certain was known about Homer. He was an enigma, a mystery. But the modern form of the Homeric Question was cast in A.D. 1795 with the publication of a famous book, *Prolegomena ad Homerum* ("Introduction to Homer"), written in Latin by a German scholar, **Friedrich August Wolf.** Wolf was deeply influenced by revolutionary criticism then being applied to the Bible. Scholars asked, Where did the Bible come from? How old is it, and who wrote it? The name of God is given in different forms in the first five books of the Hebrew Bible (called the *Pentateuch*, "five rolls"), and scholars showed that Genesis, for example, consists of four strands, recognizable and to some extent separable from one another. Thus we can explain such inconsistencies as that woman was created twice, on the seventh day as man's peer and again from the rib of Adam. Hebrew scholars, working in exile in Babylon in the sixth century B.C., had evidently combined once independent written accounts to fashion something like the Bible that has come down to us.

Homer, too, contains strange inconsistencies. For example, in Book 9 of the *Iliad*, the Achaean commanders send a contingent to the angry Achilles to beg him to return to the war, which they are losing. As representatives, they select Odysseus, famous for his persuasive speech; Ajax, one of the greatest warriors; and Phoenix, Achilles' tutor. Two heralds will go along. Then, a few lines later, Homer informs us that "the two of them walked along the loud-resounding sea . . . ," although there were five (or three). In another passage, a warrior is killed, then later found fighting on the windy plain.

Such difficulties looked rather like those in the Bible. Wolf emphasized that writing was unknown to the Homeric warriors. Only once does Homer mention writing, and then in a confused fashion, as if he did not understand what it was. If Homer lived in a world without writing, Wolf asked, how could he have *written* his poems?

The "Pisistratean Recension"

Various authors, beginning with Plato (or someone imitating him) in the fourth century B.C., connected the Athenian tyrant **Pisistratus** (pī-**sis**-tra-tus, c. 590?–527 B.C.; see Chapter 10, "A Tale of Two Archaic Cities: Sparta and Athens, 700–480 B.C.") to the performance and perhaps the shape of the Homeric poems. Plato speaks of a kind of performer called a **rhapsode** whom Pisistratus required to "take up where the other left off." Rhapsode probably means "staff-singer," because he held a staff as he declaimed (Figure 6.2). Rhapsodes were sometimes professional reciters who

Figure 6.2 Rhapsode delivering an epic poem; on an Athenian red-figure vase, circa 470 B.C. A partial line of poetry comes from his mouth, "That once in Tiryns. . . ." © *Copyright The Trustees of The British Museum.*

memorized the Homeric texts and presented them at the Athenian festival of the Great Panathenaea ("all-Athenian") held every four years. Pisistratus used this festival to further his cultural program and enhance his political stature.

The illiteracy of Homer's world, combined with traditions that something happened to the *Iliad* and the *Odyssey* in sixth-century-B.C. Athens, led Wolf to conclude that the Homeric poems were the product of editorial activity in Pisistratus' time, similar to that which had produced the early books of the Bible (the theory of the so-called **Pisistratean Recension**). The Roman orator Cicero, in the first century B.C.—seven hundred years after Homer—says explicitly that Pisistratus assembled the books of Homer, previously scattered, to fashion the text we now have.

Once, Wolf thought, there must have been separate songs that someone combined to make up our poems. There was no Homer, any more than Moses "wrote" the first five books of the Bible. "Homer," a name that could conceivably mean "he who fits things together," is just a name applied to texts "fit together" by unknown editors, according to this manner of thinking. Wolf had evidence on his side, together with a modern method of inquiry that bore rich fruit in biblical studies. Serious scholars accepted his conclusions and devoted sustained effort throughout the nineteenth and early twentieth centuries to identifying where one song ended and the next began. Such scholars were called **Analysts** (from the Greek word for "dissolvers"). They divided the poem into "early" portions and "late" portions. Objections by the great German writer Wolfgang von Goethe (1749–1832) and others that a single poet stood behind the texts were dismissed; to oppose Homeric Analysis was to be a romantic amateur. But despite their scientific methods, Analysts could not agree on how to divide the poems into their constituent parts. In their long and heated disagreements, they failed to solve the mystery of the Homeric poems.

MILMAN PARRY AND ORAL POETRY

The terms of the Homeric Question changed through the work of the Californian **Milman Parry** (1902–1935), a scholar of Greek who died at the age of thirty-four of self-inflicted gunshots wounds (perhaps a suicide). He was the most influential classical scholar of the twentieth century. As an undergraduate, Parry noticed an inexplicable fact about the style of Homeric verse, each line of which contains six beats per line that scan long-short-short (or long-long), a meter called **dactylic hexameter.**[9] Within this highly stylized rhythmical pattern appear numerous fixed phrases attached to names—for example, "swift-footed Achilles" or "Hector of the shining helm." These fixed phrases are a distinctive feature of Homer's style, even in many English translations. Parry discovered that the different descriptive epithets (e.g., "swift-footed") are not used to clarify the dramatic situation—what is happening in the story—but vary simply according to *where* in the poetic line the phrase appears.

For example, Odysseus is called "godlike" when the poet needs to fill out the last five beats of the line, "much-knowing" to fill out the last seven beats, "much-suffering godlike" to fill out the last nine beats, and "descended-from-the-gods" to fill the first seven beats of the line. Similar epithet systems exist for other heroes and the gods. Rarely are there alternative epithets, but only a single one for each position in the line. Such a system of linguistic **formulas** was not explicable according to the familiar rules of poetic composition, nor to Homer's imitators in later Greek and Latin literature. The formula became the defining feature of oral poetry and a major discovery in the history of literary criticism.

Parry speculated that nonliterate poets used formulas to compose without writing. With a graduate student named **Albert Lord,** he traveled to Serbia, northwest of Greece, where oral singers still flourished. They were called *guslari* because they accompanied their songs by bowing a one-stringed instrument called a *gusle* (Figure 6.3). Parry and Lord befriended several *guslari*, questioned them about their lives, and took down their lyrics in writing and by means of a device for recording songs on wire, powered by the battery of their Model T Ford. The *guslari* were illiterate and learned to compose metrical song by prolonged exposure to older singers. We might compare the metrical speech of the *guslari* to a special kind of language in which a recurring rhythm is a part of the "grammar," that is, a structural component essential to communication but invisible without literate analysis.

Because they could not read and write, *guslari* did not think in terms of separate words when they sang. They insisted that they could reproduce exactly a song sung by another *guslar*, even after one hearing. This claim really meant that they could follow the same sequence of events, or themes, not the same words, as we think of them. The *guslari*, like Homer, composed metrically, although even the concept of "line," which also depends on writing, was unknown to them. Like Homer, they

Figure 6.3 Avdo Mejedovich, Milman Parry's best singer, bowing his one-string *gusle* in 1935.

often made their lines of fixed phrases and repeated whole lines (one in eight lines in Homer is repeated somewhere).

Parry argued from analysis of Homeric style that Homer's poetry was not the product of poetic composition as we know it, then provided an ethnographic analogy based on original fieldwork. Homer, Parry suggested, must have been like the Yugoslav *guslari*.

Parry's early death and World War II delayed the spread of his theories, but in the 1950s and 1960s, Lord's publications made them the standard interpretation of Homeric poetry. Parry and Lord discovered that in oral poetry there is considerable forgiveness for inconsistency, the sort of details that troubled the Analysts, because a live audience does not notice or care about them and there is no text against which to check the poem. Various type-scenes reappear in oral poetry (e.g., arming scenes, when warriors prepare to fight; assembly scenes, when men gather to discuss issues and make decisions; feasting scenes). These **type-scenes** enable poets to compose quickly at the level of the story, as the formulas enable them to compose at the level of the line, essential to entertain restless audiences.

Above all, Parry discovered, there is no such thing as a *fixed text*. Every time a poet sings "the same song," it is different, because nothing has been memorized. Composing oral poetry has more in common with playing in a rock band than with composing poetry in writing. The oral poet hears someone else's song and remembers its basic plot and themes (which are often highly stylized), just as a guitarist in a band picks up chord sequences for the verses and choruses of a song (which are also often highly stylized) by hearing them a couple of times. The oral poet would know certain useful formulas by heart and use them at convenient points in the line, just as the guitarist knows standard licks and inserts them as fillers to keep a solo going or to liven up the song. Above all, the oral poet and the improvising musician both know how to put well-known phrases together in new ways and to create new phrases. Some poets and some musicians are hacks, recycling what everyone else does; a few are creative geniuses, inventing powerful new expressions and giving new meanings to classic ones.

The poet composes as he goes, in a special language. Each time he sings a tale, he normally observes the same sequence of themes, but the words are different. In performance, the oral poet must constantly respond to the demands of the audience, who can be attentive or not, amused or bored. The average length of an oral poem is about seven hundred lines, equivalent to a couple of hours of performance.

Only writing can preserve the words of an oral poem, but it does not preserve emphasis, intonation, musical accompaniment, gesture, or the many other subtle communicative features of an oral poet's performance. Again, we might compare oral poetry with rock music; we think of a track recorded on a CD in a studio as somehow canonical, but seeing a good band perform live is an entirely different, and richer, experience. Writing creates from oral song something new and something different, a *text*, a material object marked with signs that can be made to deliver up an approximation of human speech, only one aspect of oral song. You can never speak of an oral poem as being passed down from one singer to another verbatim, word for word, because oral poems are composed afresh every time they are sung. Verbatim repetition of a poem depends on a text and cannot exist without it.

THE ORAL POET IN HOMER

The Greeks called oral poets **aoidoi,** "singers" (*aoidos* is the singular form). Homer himself, in the curiously self-conscious *Odyssey*, describes two *aoidoi*. One, named Phemius (fē-mē-us, meaning "famous"), is forced to entertain the suitors besieging Odysseus' palace. In the following passage, Athena, disguised as a seafaring merchant, has come to Odysseus' palace on Ithaca, to advise Telemachus, Odysseus' son, who is eager to show the stranger hospitality:

> Then in came the proud suitors, and sat down in rows on chairs
> and high seats. Heralds poured water over their hands,
> and maid-servants heaped by them bread in baskets,
> and youths filled the bowls brim full of drink; and they put forth
> their hands to the good cheer lying ready before them.
> Now after the suitors had satisfied their desire for food and drink,
> their hearts turned to other things, to song and to dance;
> for these things are the crown of a feast. And a herald
> put the beautiful lyre in the hands of Phemius, who sang against his will
> among the suitors, and he struck the chords in prelude to his sweet song.
>
> Homer, Odyssey 1.144–155
(A.T. Murray)

The suitors' affection for good food, good cheer, and good song probably reflects real tastes of Homer's eighth-century-B.C. contemporaries, although of course these men are morally corrupt and will pay a terrible price for their crimes. The portrait of the singer in their midst must reflect real custom too.

HEINRICH SCHLIEMANN AND THE TROJAN WAR

We noted earlier that most historians think that Homer tells us more about society in his own day than about Mycenaean times, when the Trojan War is supposed to have taken place. Oral poets of the eighth century B.C. had no access to primary sources from hundreds of years earlier. The only way Homer could have known about Bronze Age society is if oral poets had preserved details of institutions and culture intact for centuries, but that is unlikely.

Did the Trojan War really take place? Even if Homer knew little about Mycenaean society, could the story of the war itself be based on a real conflict? The comparative evidence is ambiguous. Twentieth-century-A.D. Serbian *guslari* often sang about the battle of Kosovo, a real battle between Christians and Turks in A.D. 1389—but they got the details wrong; and the *Song of Roland*, a famous French epic composed around A.D. 1100, focused on the real battle of Roncesvalles, fought in A.D. 776—although it got the details (and even the armies involved) even more badly wrong.

By the 1860s, Analyst scholars had convinced academics that "Homer" was an amalgam of different poets and that the Trojan War was a fiction. **Heinrich Schliemann** was not so sure. Schliemann had read Homer as a boy, made a fortune in business, retired early, and set out to prove the professors wrong. An American scholar had already dug some pits on a hill called Hissarlik in northwest Turkey, very near the Dardanelles (named after Dardanus, an early king of Troy), but found mostly Roman remains. From reading Homer, Schliemann convinced himself that Hissarlik was Troy, and in 1870 descended on the site with an army of workers. He

Figure 6.4 Heinrich Schliemann with Sophia Schliemann, who wears the "gold of Troy," an elaborate gold diadem and necklace. Taken from Berlin by Russian troops in 1945, the gold was thought lost until rediscovered recently in a museum in St. Petersburg. The jewelry dates to the Early Bronze Age, circa 2500 B.C., much too early for Helen of Troy!

was a reckless archaeologist by modern standards, and sometimes dishonest; but he took from the ground phenomenal Bronze Age treasures. At Troy, he found great walls surrounding a citadel on a promontory overlooking the Scamander plain and the Hellespont, just as Homer had described.

A consummate showman, Schliemann sent home photographs of his young Greek wife decked out in what he claimed was the very jewelry of Helen of Troy (Figure 6.4). Archaeology was such a new science that no one really knew what Schliemann was finding, and few specialists believed this could be Troy. We now know that a city at Hissarlik was in fact violently destroyed (whether by war or earthquake, we cannot say) around 1200 B.C., just when ancient scholars believed that Troy fell (although without records, they were only guessing). Hittite tablets refer to a place called Wilusa, which might be the equivalent of Ilion, the Greek name for Troy. Another Hittite text refers to someone whose name might be Alexander, another name for Paris, who in the Greek stories ran away with Helen and so began the war. Earlier, we referred to Hittite complaints about the Ahhiyawa, perhaps the land of the "Achaeans," and other parallels have been drawn between names found in Hittite accounts and names in the Greek tradition. A single piece of writing has now been found at Troy, a bronze seal with a name inscribed in a form of Hittite writing. Possibly there was a great siege at Troy; there had to be some reason why stories clustered around this particular city. But Homer's account may have little—if anything—to do with any actual war. His poems succeeded because they entertained and inspired.

THE TRAGIC *ILIAD*

What kind of stories are these poems, which have exacted so profound an influence? The *Iliad* takes place over a period of fifty-three days in the tenth year of the Trojan War, but only five days pass between Books 2 and 22 (out of 24 books). Although the epic is sprawling, its focus, even in time, is tight. The first word in the poem is *rage*, announcing a story about the consuming, self-destructive effects of this terrible human emotion:

> *Rage*—Goddess, sing the rage of Peleus' son Achilles,
> murderous, doomed, that cost the Achaeans countless losses,
> hurling down to the House of Death so many sturdy souls,
> great fighters' souls, but made their bodies carrion,
> feasts for the dogs and birds,
> and the will of Zeus was moving toward its end.
> Begin, Muse, when the two first broke and clashed,
> Agamemnon lord of men and brilliant Achilles.
>
> Homer, *Iliad* 1.1–6 (R. Fagles)

Everyone feels anger, but it is an emotion especially familiar to men who live by the sword. Anger can be a life-preserving force on the field of battle, enhancing courage in combat, but within a group, and to the individual, anger brings destruction. Such is the topic of Homer's poem. An offended Achilles knew he was right, and so did his companions. The outcome of his justified sense of grievance was the death of his best friend, Patroclus, and the certitude of Achilles' own imminent death. Homer's study in anger must have fascinated his audiences, who were warriors too.

Timê and Geras

To become angry about what is wrong, you need strong convictions about what is right. Moral systems can be ranged along a spectrum from **shame cultures** to **guilt cultures.** Heroic societies, such as Homer describes, are generally shame cultures. Shame comes from falling short of an ideal pattern of social conduct. If your companions think ill of you, you have "lost face." If the loss is serious enough, you may feel that your life has lost meaning. Guilt, on the other hand, is the consequence of transgression against internalized norms, often understood as the laws of God. Such is a modern point of view. The sanctions of shame are external, something physical, tangible, material, like medals or trophies. The sanctions of guilt, by contrast, are internal—feelings of remorse when wrong has been done.

In Homer's *Iliad*, a man's standing before others was called *timê* (**tē**-mā), translated as "honor, respect" or "value, price." Every warrior strove for *timê*. The external, tangible sign of *timê* was *geras* (**ger**-as) or "prize," ordinarily a material object, something tangible. A man could not have *timê* without *geras:* one implied the other.

The poem opens abruptly when a prophet of Apollo named **Chryses** (**krī**-sēz) comes to the Greek camp and begs for the return of his daughter Chryseïs (kri-**sē**-is), whom the Greeks captured in a raid. As we noted earlier, Homer does not call the besiegers of Troy Greeks, but Achaeans (perhaps the Mycenaeans called themselves this), Danaäns (descendants of Danaüs, a tribal name), or Argives (men from Argos, the plain on which stood the Bronze Age city of Mycenae). The assembled Greeks urge that the girl be returned to avoid conflict with the dangerous prophet. But Agamemnon, the principal *basileus* in an assembly of *basileis*, won the girl as his concubine in a division of the spoils. She is his *geras*, and to lose her would be to lose *timê*:

> Then all the rest of the Achaeans shouted assent,
> to show respect to the priest and accept the glorious ransom,
> yet that plan did not please the heart of Agamemnon, son of Atreus,
> but he sent him away harshly, and laid upon him a stern command:
> "Let me not find you, old man, by the hollow ships, either tarrying now
> or coming back later, for your prophet's staff and the wreath of the god
> will not protect you. I will not set her free. Sooner will old age
> come upon her in our house, in Argos, far from her native land,
> as she walks back and forth before the loom and serves my bed.
> But go, do not anger me, if you wish to get out of here with your life."
>
> Homer, *Iliad* 1.21–32
> (A.T. Murray)

Homer refers to people by such epithets as "shining," "swift-footed," or "of thick arms," but never describes their characters. Rather, he shows them in action, revealing who they are by how they speak and what they do. Agamemnon's refusal to accept ransom from the priest protected his *timê* but endangered the entire expedition, because the priest was in a position to harm them. Chryses prays to Apollo, who, as the god of plague, kills the Achaeans in large numbers. A much-alarmed Achilles, one of many *basileis* who with his followers make up the Greek army, speaks before a second assembly and urges that they consult a prophet about what to do. Agamemnon is unhappy with this plan, but allows Calchas (**kal**-kas), the army's prophet, to speak. As Agamemnon feared, Calchas explains that the plague has come from Agamemnon's refusal to surrender his *geras*, the daughter of Chryses.

The stage is set for Achilles' anger, because Agamemnon is caught in a double bind of his own making. If he gives up the girl, he loses *timê*. If he refuses, he loses *timê* anyway, for not caring about the expedition's well being. Blustering, desperate really, he announces that he will take someone else's *geras* to replace the one he's losing, for it would be unseemly for him to be without *timê*:

> With rage his black heart was wholly filled, and his eyes
> were like blazing fire. To Calchas first of all he spoke, and his look threatened evil:
> "Prophet of evil, never yet have you spoken to me
> a pleasant thing; ever is evil dear to your heart to prophesy, but a word of good
> you have never spoken, nor brought to pass. And now among the Danaäns
> you claim in prophecy that for this reason Apollo who strikes from afar
> brings woes upon them, because I would not accept the glorious ransom
> for the girl, the daughter of Chryses, since I much prefer to keep her in my home.
> For certainly I prefer her to Clytemnestra, my wedded wife, since she is not
> inferior to her, either in form or in stature, or in mind, or in any handiwork.
> Yet even so will I give her back, if that is better; I would rather
> the people be safe than perish. But provide me with a *geras* of *timê* right away,
> so that I alone of the Argives not be without one, for that would not be proper.
> You all see this, that my *geras* goes elsewhere."
> In answer to him spoke swift-footed brilliant Achilles:
> "Most glorious son of Atreus, most covetous of all, how will

the great-hearted Achaeans give you a *geras?* We know nothing of a hoard
of wealth in common store, but whatever we took by pillage from the cities
has been apportioned, and it is not right to gather these things
back from the army. But give back the girl to the god, and we Achaeans
will recompense you three and fourfold, if ever Zeus grants us to sack
the well-walled city of Troy."

Homer, *Iliad* 1.104–126
(A.T. Murray)

Achilles' political power is less than Agamemnon's, because he rules fewer people, yet he should have more (or at least as much) *timê* because of his greatness in
battle. We saw that Homeric Ithaca was a stateless society, where people had to rely
on their own strength to get things done. Similarly, the Achaean army has little of
what we would call military discipline. Achilles does not shrink from telling his supposed superior how he should approach the most important issue in a warrior's life,
the achievement of *timê.*

Achilles' Rage

Enraged, Agamemnon threatens to take Achilles' own *geras,* or that of another warrior. Through his intolerable behavior he offends Achilles, and the hotheaded
fighter draws his sword, thinking to cut down his commander in public view. The
whole expedition would then collapse in failure. Here is a great crisis, described in
lightning pace in the first few hundred lines of Homer's *Iliad.*

Only a god's intervention can prevent the inevitable, and Athena duly comes
from heaven and seizes Achilles by the hair, holding him back (but only Achilles can
see her). She promises that, if he restrains himself, he will receive in the future three
times the *timê* he already has. Flushed with anger, Achilles says what many have
thought when in a struggle with an unjust superior, words that will bring death to
many men:

"Yes, clothed in shame, thinking of profit, how will any man of the Achaeans
obey your words with a ready heart either to go on a journey or to fight
against men with force? It was not on account of the Trojan spearmen that I came
here to fight, since they have done no wrong to me. Never have they driven off
my cattle or my horses, nor ever in deep-soiled Phthia,° nurse of men,
did they lay waste the harvest, for many things lie between us
—shadowy mountains and sounding sea. But you, man of shame, we followed,
so that you might rejoice, seeking to win recompense for Menelaüs and for yourself,
from the Trojans, you dog-face. This you disregard, and take no heed of.
And now you threaten that you will yourself take my *geras* away from me,
for which I toiled so much, which the sons of the Achaeans gave to me.
Never have I *geras* like yours, whenever the Achaeans sack a well-inhabited citadel
of the Trojans. The brunt of furious battle my own hands undertake,
but if ever an apportionment comes, your *geras* is far greater, while small
if precious is the reward I take to my ships, when I have worn myself out
in the fighting. Now I will go back to Phthia, since it is far better
to return home with my beaked ships, nor do I intend while I am here
dishonored to pile up riches and wealth for you."

Homer, *Iliad* 1.148–170
(A.T. Murray)

°*Phthia* (**thī**-a): Achilles' homeland in southern Thessaly (central Greece)

Achilles does not go home. Instead, he prays to his divine mother, Thetis, and asks that she intercede with Zeus to turn the battle against the Greeks. They will be sorry that they allowed Agamemnon to treat him disgracefully! Achilles allows Agamemnon's men to take his *geras*, the girl named Briseïs, then sulks, waiting for the destruction to begin.

The Embassy and Achilles' Crisis

Homer takes the opportunity of Achilles' absence from the action to give considerable background about the war, including a list of all the ships that went there, with their commanders' names and how many men each had. After much fighting, the battle goes against the Greeks, thanks to Zeus, responding to the request of Thetis, Achilles' mother. Desperate, Agamemnon calls an assembly. He and the other war-leaders resolve that they must persuade Achilles to return to the fight, or they will all die. Fast-talking Odysseus, Ajax (a great fighter), and Phoenix (Achilles' former tutor) form an embassy to beg Achilles to return. Agamemnon offers Achilles *geras* aplenty, including the hand of his own daughter in marriage once they return to Greece, if Achilles will give over his anger. Here is the moment promised by Athena when she restrained Achilles from violence against Agamemnon—three times the *timê* that he had before. To everyone's astonishment, Achilles turns down the offer with contempt:

> He wouldn't dare to face me himself, though he has the look of a dog.
> I'll make no plans with him nor undertake anything, for he has deceived me
> and offended me. Never again will he trick me with words.
> He has done enough. Let him go to hell in his pleasure,
> seeing that Zeus the counselor has taken away his mind.
> I *hate* his gifts, I count them not worth a hair.
> Not even if he gave me ten times, or twenty times all that now he has
> and if yet others should be added to that from somewhere, not though it was all
> the wealth belonging to Orchomenus,° or to Thebes of Egypt,° where treasures
> in greatest store are laid up in men's houses—Thebes the city of a hundred gates
> and two hundred warriors with horses and cars pound through each
> —no, not though he gave gifts as great in number as sand and dust.
> Not even then would Agamemnon persuade my soul, until he has paid
> the full price of the disrespect that stings my heart!
>
> Homer, *Iliad* 9.309–326
> (A.T. Murray)

°*Orchomenus:* A city in Boeotia near Thebes, where important Bronze Age ruins have been found.   °*Thebes:* Not the Greek *polis* of that name, but a city in Egypt, capital of that country during the New Kingdom (circa 1650–1150 B.C.). Egyptian Thebes is four hundred miles south of Cairo.

Phoenix, Achilles' childhood tutor, offers other arguments for returning, concerned that through stubbornness Achilles will lose his *timê*. But Achilles will have none of it:

> Phoenix, old sire, like my father, nurtured of Zeus, in no way
> do I have need of this *timê*. I get my *timê* from Zeus!
> It will be mine amid the beaked ships as long as breath
> abides in my breast and my knees.
>
> Homer, *Iliad* 9.610–612 (A.T. Murray)

Achilles' companions are astonished at his refusal. Agamemnon had offered him great wealth and the honor that goes with it. But in the crisis of values that is a central concern of the poem (and must have reverberated with Homer's contemporaries), Achilles appears to reject the system on which the heroic shame culture was built. He has internalized his sense of value: it doesn't matter what men think, because he receives his *timê* from Zeus. Achilles has made his own small guilt culture in the midst of a sea of shame culture. As a crisis of values, his position is curiously modern. After his refusal to accept Agamemnon's offer, Achilles lives in his own world, ill attached to his companions. In his isolation, he is the type of tragic hero, progressively isolated until utterly alone in an impending death.

The Deaths of Patroclus and Hector

As the Trojans attack ever more boldly, Achilles' companion, Patroclus, upbraids his friend for his indifference to the suffering of their companions and begs Achilles to let him sally forth and break the Trojan attack. Achilles reluctantly agrees and lends Patroclus his armor. At first, Patroclus kills many, then comes up under the walls of Troy. Hector, the greatest of the Trojan princes, kills him and strips his armor.

When Achilles learns of Patroclus' death, which he himself has caused by refusing Agamemnon's offer, he falls into a paroxysm of grief, then rage against Patroclus' killer, Hector. He attacks the Trojan forces single-handedly and, in a surreal passage, even fights the River Scamander, whose waters he chokes with corpses. At last, he corners Hector under the walls and kills him. Hector's mother and father, Hecuba and Priam, look on from the walls above. Achilles binds Hector's corpse to his chariot and drags it to his camp.

The Ransom of Hector and the End of Achilles' Rage

Achilles accepts Agamemnon's gifts after the death of Patroclus, but with little interest. He has transferred his anger from Agamemnon to Hector, but even after Hector's death, Achilles burns with hate. Every day, he drags the body behind his chariot, punishing the flesh of the man who killed his friend. If only he himself had returned to the fight, Patroclus would still be alive.

In a scene charged with overtones of a descent into the land of the dead, old King Priam loads a cart with ransom and, protected by Hermes (guide of the souls to the other world), travels at night across the plain into Achilles' camp. To the astonishment of the great Achilles, the king appears suddenly at his tent. Achilles ought to kill him, as the father of the man who killed his friend, but he sees in the pathetic king, who has lost his sons, the image of his own father, who will soon lose his own son:

> Unseen of these great Priam entered in and coming close to Achilles
> clasped in his hands his knees and kissed his hands, the terrible man-killing hands
> that had killed his many sons. And as when blindness of heart comes upon a man,
> that in his own country he kills another and escapes to a land of strangers,
> to the house of some man of substance, and they wonder who look upon him,
> even so did Achilles wonder at the sight of godlike Priam, and seized with wonder
> were the others too, and they glanced at one another. But Priam made a plea,
> and spoke to him, saying,

> "Remember your father, O Achilles like to the gods,
> whose years are like mine, on the painful threshold of old age.
> No doubt those who live near are treating him badly,
> nor is there any to ward off ruin and evil. Still, so long as he hears that you are still alive
> he has joy at heart, and he hopes day by day that he will see his dear son
> returning from Troy-land. But I—I am utterly unblest, seeing I fathered
> the best sons in the broad land of Troy, yet I swear that not one of them is left.
> Fifty I had, when the sons of the Achaeans came. Nineteen were born
> of the self-same womb, and the others from women of the palace.
> Furious Ares has loosed the knees of these, as many as they were,
> and he that alone was left me, that by himself guarded the city and the men,
> him you killed just now as he fought for his country, Hector. For his sake
> have I now come to the ships of the Achaeans to win him back from you,
> and I bear with me ransom past counting. Have respect for the gods, Achilles,
> and take pity on me, remembering your own father. Truly, I am more piteous than he,
> and have endured what no other mortal on the face of earth has endured,
> to reach forth my hand to the face of him that has killed my sons."
> Thus he spoke and in Achilles roused desire to weep for his father.
> He took the old man by the hand and gently put him from him. So the two
> thought of their dead, and wept, the one for man-killing Hector, while he groveled
> at Achilles' feet, but Achilles wept for his own father, and now again for Patroclus,
> and the sound of their moaning went up through the house.
>
> Homer, *Iliad* 24.479–642 (A.T. Murray)

Achilles persuades Priam to eat with him, and each man admires the other. Achilles accepts the ransom and puts Hector on the wagon to be carried back to Troy. The poem ends with the burial of horse-taming Hector.

Thus Achilles abandons rage against his companions and against his bitterest enemy. In the eighth century B.C., Homer's Achilles rejected a system of values based on *geras* and *timê*, by which others lived. Even in classical times, three hundred years later, Greeks judged a man by his ability "to help friends and harm enemies." In a precocious moral vision, Homer shows us Achilles finding a common humanity in both King Priam and his own father, united by suffering.

HOMER AND THE INVENTION OF PLOT

Although Homer's poems are the oldest surviving examples of western literature, there is little in Homer that cannot be anticipated in earlier literatures in the Near East, except the transcendence of plot. In Near Eastern literature, events are strung one after the other as beads on a string. Homer is the first poet who worked with a recognizably modern plot. Aristotle, writing in the fourth century B.C., was first to notice that plot has three parts: beginning, middle, and end. In an essay on poetry called the *Poetics,* he says,

> A whole is what has a beginning and middle and end. A beginning is that
> which is not a necessary consequent of anything else but after which
> something else exists or happens as a natural result. An end, on the contrary,
> is that which is inevitably or, as a rule, the natural result of something else but
> from which nothing else follows. A middle follows something else and
> something follows from it. Well-constructed plots must not therefore begin and
> end at random, but must embody the formulas we have stated.
>
> Aristotle, *Poetics* 1450b (H.W. Butler)

Literature gives the impression of being like life, but it is not life: It has its own rules. A plot begins with the *setup*. We learn who the main character is and what is his or her "dramatic need," what he or she wants to possess, have, achieve, or accomplish. Characters are defined by their dramatic need. In the *Iliad*, Achilles is the main character, and his dramatic need is to satisfy his rage, first against Agamemnon, then against Hector. The beginning of a plot establishes the dramatic context, the backdrop against which the main character functions: in this case, the troubled camp of the Achaeans in the tenth year of a siege of Troy.

Then something happens to change the direction of the story, to begin the middle of the plot (its largest segment). In the parlance of the modern feature film, this event is a **plot-point.** In a feature film, normally 120 minutes long, the first plot-point occurs around the thirtieth minute. In the *Iliad*, the first plot-point comes early, when Achilles withdraws from the fighting and prays to his mother for revenge against the Achaeans. The plot is set, and now the real story begins, the working-out of Achilles' anger.

Conflict dominates the middle of a plot, presenting the main character in contention with forces opposing the fulfillment of his or her dramatic need. In the modern feature film, the middle is twice as long as the beginning and has its own plot-point, or midpoint, which binds together the two halves of the middle (it comes around the sixtieth minute). In the *Iliad*, the midpoint is when the Achaeans, devastated by Hector, send an embassy to Achilles to beg him to return to the fighting. He refuses, allowing a further working-out of his prayers for revenge: more fighting, more death, and more suffering by his former friends.

The middle portion of a plot, like the beginning, ends with a plot-point, an event that again turns the story in a different direction, toward the resolution of conflict. In the *Iliad*, Patroclus' death does this. Achilles kills Hector, hoping to satisfy his rage, which in the final scene he abandons: Along with Hector's body, he gives up the anger that caused him and those around him "ten thousand woes." The first word in the poem is *rage*, and the last scene shows how, through an intuition of the unity of all human experience, Achilles gave up his anger.

The *Odyssey* too has a tripartite plot, but moves more in spirals than in a straight line.

THE COMIC *ODYSSEY*

Whereas the *Iliad* describes a man at odds with his society, a man apart, the *Odyssey*, whose first word in Greek is *man*, describes a man who journeys far, suffers much, then returns to his proper place in society. The *Odyssey*'s pattern of renewal and reintegration into society is explicitly opposite to the *Iliad*'s pattern of progressive alienation. Whereas the *Iliad* is tragic, the *Odyssey* is comic, according to an old tradition of understanding these poems. In everyday speech, we use *comic* to mean humorous, but when literary critics say comic, they mean a story that ends in harmony and acceptance. Humor, of which there is a good deal in the *Iliad*, is not comedy, and there is little humor in the *Odyssey*. Because nothing expresses social integration better than a wedding, comedies—for example, those of Shakespeare—often end in weddings. So does the *Odyssey*, in a mock re-wedding between Odysseus and Penelope.

Whereas Achilles' concern in the *Iliad* is to win *timê* at all costs, in the *Odyssey* the hero strives to return home and to his former position there, at all costs. Whereas Achilles meets obstacles with violence, threatening to kill his own commander, then cutting down the greatest Trojan, Odysseus also overcomes obstacles through intelligence, trickery, and disguise. In the first line of the poem, he is "the man of twists and turns," who can approach a problem from different angles. Elsewhere, Homer uses an epithet for Odysseus that means "wily," "clever," or "devious." Achilles abhors such qualities and says so in the speech he gives to the embassy. In these respects, the *Iliad* and the *Odyssey* are utterly different, yet they complement one another in striking fashion: No episode described in the *Iliad* is repeated in the *Odyssey*, which provides considerable information about the Trojan War omitted in the *Iliad*—for example, the story of the Trojan Horse, the funeral of Achilles, and the return of Menelaüs and Helen to Sparta.

The Quest for Truth

The story of the man who wandered is not original to the Greeks. In the Mesopotamian ***Epic of Gilgamesh,*** already two thousand years old when Homer was born, the hero Gilgamesh wandered far from his home through the Mountains of Mashu to the place of the sun, then across demonic waters, seeking a way to escape mortality. Even the opening words of the Gilgamesh epic are similar to those of the *Odyssey:*

> Of him who found out all things, I will tell the land,
> of him who experienced everything, I will teach the whole.
> He searched lands everywhere.
> He who experienced the whole gained complete wisdom.
> He found out what was secret and uncovered what was hidden.
> He brought back a tale of times before the Flood.
> He had journeyed far and wide, weary and at last resigned.
>
> *Gilgamesh,* SBv 1 (S. Dalley)

Gilgamesh was a seeker of truth about the meaning of mortality. In the *Odyssey*, less explicitly, the hero is a seeker too:

> Tell me, O Muse, of the man of many devices, who wandered
> full many ways after he had sacked the sacred citadel of Troy.
> Many were the men whose cities he saw and whose mind he learned,
> Yes, and many the woes he suffered in his heart upon the sea,
> seeking to win his own life and the return of his comrades.
> Yet even so he saved not his comrades, though he desired it very much,
> for through their own blind folly they perished—the fools,
> who devoured the cattle of Helios Hyperion,° and he took from them
> the day of their returning. Of these things, goddess, daughter of Zeus,
> beginning where you wish, tell to us.
>
> Homer, *Odyssey* 1.1–5 (A.T. Murray)

°*Helios Hyperion:* The sun.

In fact, Odysseus seemingly learns nothing in his journeys. Yet the poem is a paradigm for truth-seeking, of wandering in search of knowledge, even though the hero knows no more when he ends than when he began.

The *Odyssey* and History

Homer may have inherited the story of the wanderer from the Near East, but his tale is massively colored by events of the eighth century B.C. The colonial movement that we described in Chapter 5 was particularly important. Between 775 and 750 B.C., Greeks founded Pithekoussai in the Bay of Naples, a settlement of perhaps five thousand occupants—a large number in so remote a place; and between the 730s and 650 B.C., probably another thirty thousand Greek males settled in Sicily and Italy. Taking an open boat from Greece to Italy was a stupendous adventure, and it is not surprising that monsters and magical creatures were lurking beyond the waves that fill the *Odyssey* (Figure 6.5).

The Greeks who settled the west went there for profit, a motive reflected in the first book of the *Odyssey*, when Athena comes to the palace in Ithaca disguised as a sailor named Mentês (**men**-tēz):

> I declare that I am Mentês, the son of wise Anchialus, and I am lord
> over the oar-loving Taphians. And now have I put in here, as you see,
> with ship and crew, while sailing over the wine-dark sea to men of strange speech,
> on my way to Temêsê for copper; and I bear with me shining iron.
> My ship lies yonder beside the fields away from the city, in the harbor of Rheithron,
> under woody Neion.°
>
> Homer, Odyssey, 1.180–85 (A.T. Murray)

°*Rheitron* and *Neion:* Perhaps Rheitron is one of the modern harbors on Ithaca; a mountain there is still called Neion (maybe because of the *Odyssey*).

The tiny island of Ithaca, where Odysseus' palace was sited, lay directly on the coasting route from Greece to Italy. Early Greek explorers headed down the narrow channel between Ithaca and Cephallenia, stopped in the Ithacan harbor on the southern side of the island, then veered north to the island of Corcyra (kor-**sī**-ra—called Corfu in English). The Corinthians founded a colony on Corcyra in 733 B.C.,

Figure 6.5 Warship on an Athenian vase, circa 520–515 B.C. While more advanced than eighth-century B.C. ships, it is still an open boat with rowers on either side, a single mast and sail, and a short deck for the helmsman, who steers with an oar. *Antimenes Painter, Greek, Attic, ca. 520–515 B.C. Black-figure terracotta, D. 50.8 cm © The Cleveland Museum of Art, 2002. John L. Severance Fund, 1971.46.*

Map 6.1 The Strait of Messina. Between the northeast corner of Sicily and the Greek city of Rhegion on the toe of the boot of Italy lies the Strait of Messina. To sail to the west coast of Italy, you must pass through these dangerous waters.

a sort of halfway house between the familiar world of Greece and "barbarian" lands beyond. Already, in the fifth century B.C., Thucydides thought Corcyra was the island Phaeacia, where Odysseus stops before reaching home and where he tells famous stories of his adventures.

Outward-bound sailors from Corcyra crossed open water to the heel of Italy (as early as 800 B.C., they were trading with the natives of this region), then headed south along the coast before passing through the dangerous **Strait of Messina,** from an early time thought to be Homer's Scylla and Charybdis (Map 6.1). Thence north they sailed along the Italian coast to the Bay of Naples, where the Greeks mixed with Phoenician seafarers and came into early contact with the Etruscans, who lived north of Rome. It would be no surprise if Homer himself had made this journey. He shows familiarity with the island of Ithaca (with some perplexities), which he surely knew.

The *Odyssey* and Folktale

As a trickster, Odysseus has many parallels in folklore throughout the world. We can view the poem as a kind of folktale. Following a common pattern, the hero, reduced to the lowest social class—a beggar in his own household—overcomes enormous odds (over one hundred suitors oppose him) to become king and marry the queen. The *Odyssey*'s inner meaning, though, is a story about a man who went to the other world and returned, reborn—also a folktale motif. There are strong folktale components too in Odysseus' famous adventures, the best-known part of the poem, in which the trickster hero's greatest enemy is Death, whom he seems to meet repeatedly, in many guises. Females, too, constantly threaten him or aid him. The poem is practically a study in female types, positive and negative. Yet the general setting is the same heroic world as in the *Iliad*, and many of the same heroes appear; or Homer directs his focus on the everyday world of Ithaca, populated by beggars, slaves, serving girls, and arrogant aristocrats.

Folktales contain folksy morals about how one should act, and they appeal to the universal instinct that the wicked should be destroyed. Early in the poem, Homer announces this theme in declaring that "the recklessness of their own ways destroyed" Odysseus' companions. Often in folktales, a violated prohibition leads to someone's destruction. Hence the companions perished because "they devoured the cattle of the Sun," which they were told not to do.

The poem's preoccupation with right, wrong, and punishment is clear in the announcement that Zeus makes near the beginning of the poem. Poseidon has gone to banquet with the blameless Ethiopians, while Zeus sits with the other gods in the halls of Olympus and reflects on the fate of Aegisthus (ē-**jis**-thus), a cousin of Agamemnon who committed adultery with Agamemnon's wife, Clytemnestra, and helped her to murder Agamemnon. Later, Orestes, the son of Agamemnon and Clytemnestra, grown to manhood, killed Aegisthus and his own mother to avenge his father's death:

> Among them the father of gods and men was first to speak, for in his heart
> he thought of noble Aegisthus, whom far-famed Orestes, Agamemnon's son,
> had killed. Thinking on him he spoke among the immortals, and said,
>   "Look you now, how ready mortals are to blame the gods.
> It is from us, they say, that evils come,
> but they even of themselves, through their own blind folly, have sorrows
> beyond that which is fated. Even as now Aegisthus, beyond that which was fated,
> took to himself the wedded wife of the son of Atreus,° and killed him on his return,
> though he well knew of sheer destruction, seeing that we spoke to him before,
> sending Hermes, the keen-sighted Argeïphontes,° that he should neither kill the man
> nor pursue his wife, for from Orestes will come vengeance for the son of Atreus
> when once he has come to manhood and longs for his own land."
> So Hermes spoke, but for all his good intent he did not prevail on the heart of Aegisthus,
> and now he has paid the price for it.
>
> Homer, *Odyssey* 1.28–42 (A.T. Murray)

°*wife of the son of Atreus:* The wife is Clytemnestra, the son of Atreus is Agamemnon.
°*Argeïphontes* (ar-jē-i-**fon**-tēz): "Argus-killer," an epithet of Hermes.

Zeus' observation is common in later Greek literature: Mortals are responsible for their own actions and should not blame the gods when things go wrong. We find no such speculations in the *Iliad*, where men die every day simply because Fate has so decreed, or because they are warriors, but not because of some evil they have done. What evil did Hector commit? This strong moral stance, a feature of folktale, underlies the *Odyssey*'s grand narrative of the destruction of the suitors. Some have wondered at the bloodthirsty slaughter that Odysseus, his son, and two slaves wreak on the men who have been flirting with Penelope, killing all but two (the *aoidos* and a herald are spared), but the suitors should not have behaved as they did and cannot expect better. The suitors were fools who violated Odysseus' property rights (as Odysseus' men did when they ate the cattle of the sun). They got what they deserved.

Telemachus, Son of Odysseus

After Zeus pronounces his view that men make their own fates, Athena rises in the divine assembly and objects that Odysseus, a righteous man, has been imprisoned for seven years on the island of the beautiful **Calypso** ("concealer") in the navel of the sea. Zeus agrees to send Hermes to set him free.

Then Homer switches the narrative to Ithaca. The next four books, sometimes called the *Telemacheia*, are devoted to the plight and education of Odysseus' only child, Telemachus. Telemachus is under siege by the rowdy suitors, who want to marry his mother and become the new king. The disguised Athena urges Telemachus to leave his father's house and go into the world to learn about his father's fate. He should take a boat to Pylos on the mainland coast, where King Nestor rules, who fought with Odysseus at Troy and perhaps now, ten years after the war, might know something. In his travels, Telemachus will become a man, fit to stand at his father's side, fit to inherit his father's house and power.

The Adventures of Odysseus

The *Telemacheia* provides the setup for the poem, describing the situation on Ithaca and the personalities involved, including the absent Odysseus about whom everyone speaks. Then, at plot-point one, Homer switches his story to Odysseus, who prepares to escape from Calypso. He builds a raft and sails away, but his enemy Poseidon—the sea-god—spots him and stirs a great storm. The raft breaks up, and for three days Odysseus swims in the rugged seas, then comes ashore on **Phaeacia,** where King Alcinoüs rules. The princess Nausicaä meets him on the shore and takes him to the palace.

For many days, no one asks the mysterious stranger who he is. At a banquet, the man of mystery asks the *aoidos* to sing the song of the Trojan Horse, a trick that Odysseus himself designed. Overcome with emotion when hearing the song, Odysseus weeps. "Why are you weeping?" the king asks. "Because *I*," he replies, "am Odysseus."

Here is set the basic pattern for the whole poem, a pattern repeated more than twenty times:

- Odysseus arrives somewhere in disguise or unrecognized

- He faces opposition, sometimes deadly

- He is recognized, in this case by his tears, but also by the story he tells and at other times by a "token" such as a scar on his leg

To the Phaeacians, who sit spellbound at the banquet, Odysseus recounts his wanderings, some of the most famous stories in the world. Nevertheless, they take up only one-sixth of the whole poem. Odysseus' journeys are presented in patterns of three: first two short tales, then a long one.

Figure 6.6 Odysseus, in white, leads his men in plunging a stake into Polyphemus' eye; on a large amphora from Eleusis, circa 670 B.C. (see also Chapter 9, "The Archaic Cultural Revolution, 700–480 B.C.," Figure 9.10). The cup that Polyphemus holds refers to the detail in the story that Odysseus first made him drunk.

After leaving Troy, he and his men, with twenty boats, come to the land of the Thracians northwest of Troy, but in a raid lose many men. They depart, but a storm drives them to the land of the **Lotus Eaters:** If you eat the lotus, you forget your purpose—in Odysseus' case, to go home again. He comes next to the land of the giant, one-eyed **Cyclops,** the most famous adventure, where he is imprisoned in a dark cave and nearly eaten alive. By a trick, he gets the giant drunk, puts out his eye with a stake, and escapes from the cave (Figure 6.6).

After a nearly successful journey home, courtesy of the Wind King, and a brief but deadly adventure with more cannibal-giants, Odysseus comes to the mysterious land of **Circê,** "hawk." Only his boat still survives. The witch Circê changes his men to pigs. When Odysseus defeats her with help from the god Hermes, Circê releases his companions from the spell. Odysseus and his men remain on the island for a year, when at last his followers remind him of his purpose, to reach home. Odysseus prepares to sail, and Circê tells him that first he must cross the river Ocean, which surrounds the world, and consult the spirit of the dead prophet **Tiresias** (tī-rē-sē-as) to learn what awaits him. Odysseus puts ashore in a misty land, fills a pit with lamb's blood, and speaks with the ghosts who gather around it, including Tiresias and Agamemnon. At first, Agamemnon praises Penelope, in contrast to his own murderous wife, then warns Odysseus that he, too, should be careful about returning home!

Figure 6.7 Odysseus and the Sirens on an Athenian red-figure jug, circa 450 B.C. Odysseus, bound to the mast, hears the Sirens' song while his men, their ears plugged with wax, row past the island. Note the apotropaic eye on the prow of the ship.

Traveling on, they pass the island of the **Sirens,** whose song, promising knowledge, no man can resist; Odysseus stuffs the ears of his men with wax but lashed to the mast, he alone hears the song and survives (Figure 6.7).

Now he must pass between the monster Scylla and the whirlpool Charybdis. The monster eats five men, but the rest escape and they come to the island of Helios, the Sun. Circê warned him not to eat the sun's cattle that graze there, but Odysseus' hungry men disobey. Even in the prologue, this incident is given as the archetype for the behavior of men doomed to a bad end, the motif of the violated prohibition.

Odysseus alone escapes, clinging to the ship's rudder. He is swept into Charybdis and nearly destroyed. At last he comes to the island of Calypso, where the poem began. Unlike the *Iliad*, which advances in a straight line, the *Odyssey* moves in spirals, repeatedly turning back on itself as characters recall things that happened before.

Important Themes in the Adventures of Odysseus

The adventures are folktales of independent origin that Homer adapted for his epic poem. Odysseus' first enemy is the sea and its god Poseidon. The vast sea, the water from which life emerges, is the negation of life; being lost on it is like death. When Odysseus comes ashore in Phaeacia after Zeus blasts his ship, he is naked like a baby; he takes refuge in a dark cave of bushes. A young girl, Nausicaä, with marriage on her mind, rouses him from sleep; he appears naked to her. Later, he says that she gave him life. The symbolism of rebirth, as elsewhere in the *Odyssey*, is strong. The *Iliad,* by contrast, never tells its story through action that has symbolic meaning.

As the sea obliterates all things, so does sleep (brother of death), or narcosis (the lotus), which stands between Odysseus and his return. He falls asleep just offshore from Ithaca after leaving the Wind King. He is asleep on the island of Helios while his men devour the sacred cattle. He is put ashore on Ithaca, wrapped in a deep sleep.

The adventures, like much folktale, preserve the child's vision of a world eating itself, in which eating and being eaten are the central experiences of life. The Cyclops eats Odysseus' men, the Laestrygonians do too and, although Homer does not say so, Circê's pigs, once men, are as edible as any swine. Scylla eats five of his men. In proper Greek society of Homer's day, one was bound to receive a wandering stranger with courtesy and food, a custom called **xenia,** "treatment of a stranger." The Cyclops inverts this custom; instead of offering his guest a meal, he makes a meal of them! Just so did the suitors violate *xenia.* Folktales are filled with monsters, and we find our share here, but also the seductive wiles of death-dealing females hold back the male from his goal. In the everyday world, Clytemnestra, who kills her husband Agamemnon in a bathtub, stands for the treacherous deadly woman. In the strange world of Odysseus' wandering, Circê, with her beauty, wishes to lure Odysseus into bed and castrate him. The Sirens are irresistible with the beauty of their song (like the beauty of Homer's own song), and only a trick allows him to escape. The monstrous Scylla is female.

On the other side are the "good females": Nausicaä, the princess who finds him, and the queen of the Phaeacians, who is eager to help. In the divine world, Athena favors Odysseus. In the everyday world, Penelope embodies the beneficent female. Like Clytemnestra, men want to sleep with her; she too has a teenage son. But she cleverly eludes those who cannot distinguish their own advantage from deadly folly.

ODYSSEUS AND HOMER

Homer builds his second plot-point around Odysseus's return to Ithaca. Henceforth we observe the working-out of Odysseus' revenge, the resolution of the conflict brewing since the beginning of the poem. Fully half of the *Odyssey* is devoted to the third part of Aristotle's tripartite plot structure—no modern audience, schooled in cinema, could tolerate so leisurely an ending, though Homer enlivens his story by repeated disguise, secret penetration, and mass murder.

Throughout, scenes of recognition permeate the *Odyssey,* and they continue on to Ithaca in rapid succession as Odysseus progressively strips off his lying exterior to reveal himself as Odysseus, the son of Laertes, the true king and true husband of the queen. First, he reveals himself to a faithful swineherd in a remote part of the island (Odysseus becomes master of his property); then to his son Telemachus, who has returned from abroad (Odysseus is now father to his son). He comes to the palace, where the dog Argus recognizes him (Odysseus, the noble sportsman). In the palace, the nurse recognizes him from a scar on his leg as she bathes his feet (Odysseus is master of the house). The suitors recognize him when he strings a powerful bow, his own, by which act Penelope declared she would judge who would be her next husband. With this very bow he begins the slaughter (Odysseus as king). Finally, Penelope recognizes Odysseus by a trick and a token. Witnessing the corpses of the suitors, she gratefully asks the nurse to bring out the master's bed for Odysseus to sleep in. "That's impossible," he protests, "I myself built it around an olive tree growing in the ground." By this token the husband again takes his wife (Odysseus as husband).

The poem ends with an artistically unsatisfying account of Odysseus' hasty, even mechanical, recognition with his father and a contrived brief skirmish with the family of the dead suitors, interrupted by a thunderbolt from Zeus. Order is restored to the family, to the household, and to the world, a comic vision of optimism and affirmation. The dark uncertainty of the *Iliad* is relieved in the resounding triumph of right over wrong. The *Odyssey*, not the *Iliad*, is the model for the ubiquitous plots of modern cinema, which needs an "up" ending to be successful.

KEY TERMS

Homeric Question, 93	guilt cultures, 101
Friedrich August Wolf, 94	*timê*, 101
Pisistratus, 95	*geras*, 101
rhapsode, 95	Chryses, 101
Pisistratean Recension, 96	plot-point, 107
Analysts, 96	*Epic of Gilgamesh*, 108
Milman Parry, 96	Calypso, 112
dactylic hexameter, 96	Phaeacia, 112
formulas, 96	Lotus Eaters, 113
Albert Lord, 97	Cyclops, 113
guslari, 97	Circê, 113
aoidoi, 99	Tiresias, 113
Heinrich Schliemann, 99	Sirens, 114
shame cultures, 101	*xenia*, 115

FURTHER READING

Cairns, D., ed., *Oxford Readings in Homer's Iliad* (Oxford 2001). Collection of influential essays on various aspects of the *Iliad*.

Dougherty, C., *The Raft of Odysseus* (New York 2000). Close reading of the *Odyssey* and the adventures in the west.

Edwards, M., *Homer: Poet of the Iliad* (Baltimore 1988). The clearest single book on the *Iliad*. Most helpful in its book-by-book commentary and its extensive bibliography.

Latacz, Joachim, *Troy and Homer* (Oxford 2004). Exciting up-to-date review of new finds at Troy and their relationship to Homer.

Malkin, I., *The Returns of Odysseus* (Berkeley 1998). Superior study of the *Odyssey*, colonization, and the place of Ithaca.

Morris, I., and Powell, B., eds., *A New Companion to Homer* (Leiden 1997). Scholarly essays on every aspect of modern Homeric scholarship.

Murnaghan, S., *Disguise and Recognition in the Odyssey* (Princeton 1987). Good treatment of this topic.

Powell, B. B., *Homer* (Oxford 2003). Concise, up-to-date synthesis of scholarship, with account of origins and analysis of both poems.

Tracy, S. V., *The Story of the Odyssey* (Princeton 1990). Synopsis of the complex story.

Ancient Texts

Homer, *The Iliad* (New York 1990; tr. Robert Fagles). Good verse translation.

Homer, *The Odyssey* (New York 1996; tr. Robert Fagles). Good verse translation.

The Epic of Gilgamesh (Harmondsworth, UK, 1960; tr. Nancy Sandars). The classic Near Eastern epic, dating back to the third millennium B.C.

CHAPTER 7

RELIGION AND MYTH

In Chapter 1, "A Small, Far-Off Land," we suggested that understanding religion is fundamental to making sense of the Greeks. Unlike most other ancient societies, Greeks generally refused to believe that anyone could have privileged access to the supernatural that would give them the right to rule human society. The "Greek problem" that this created, of how people could know what to do without divine direction, played a large part in shaping the story in this book.

Classical Greek religion seems to have taken shape largely in the eighth century B.C. It was not codified in a single book, as in the Bible or Koran; rather, the Greeks told countless stories which we call *myths* that had no sacred status. Myth comes from the Greek word *mythos*, but to the Greeks the word meant *saying* or *plot*. Nor did the Greeks have a word with quite the same meaning as our word *religion*. They normally did not think of religion as a category separable from daily life itself. Discussing Greek religion and myths, then, means seeking realities that the Greeks themselves might not have recognized. We must therefore be clear about what we take these words to mean.

DEFINITIONS OF RELIGION AND MYTH

Religion and myth are both forms of symbolic thought, chiefly expressed through speech, but also through visual art, music, and dance. The Romans explained their word *religio*, root of our word *religion*, in three different ways: first, as coming from *re-ligo*, "to bind someone back so they cannot do something," to establish a taboo;[10] second, as coming from *re-lego*, "repeat" a magical formula over and over so it is effective; or third, as coming from *re-linquo*, "to leave alone," to treat in a special way. We are no more sure than they were about the word's derivation, but in actual usage, Latin *religio* variously designates an external force, an internal emotion, a cult practice, or a taboo. It never refers to the combination of belief, ritual, and canons of moral behavior that religion implies for us.

The Christian and Moslem notions of religion grew out of these respective faiths' efforts to define themselves against each other and against Judaism. Every religion is different, but we might think of each as *a set of practices based on belief in supernatural beings.* Unlike political conviction, which also motivates action, religious belief implies acceptance of the reality of nonhuman, usually invisible beings. Normally, these beings know what we do, judge us, and are powerful.

People in most cultures hold notions like these, but the modern view that specific beliefs—accepting something unprovable as a basis for action—are the *core* of religion grew from the early Christian church's need to decide which of the many divergent interpretations of the life, teachings, and mission of Jesus were true. Some argued, for example, that Jesus was divine and therefore did not die on the cross, and a long, bitter, and divisive conflict raged over whether Jesus had a single divine nature (called Monophysitism) or a dual nature, both human and divine. The Nicene Creed of the fourth century A.D., still repeated in Christian churches, was written in Greek but called a creed from its Latin translation, which begins *credo,* "I believe." The creed was a definitive statement of what was true, or orthodox (from a Greek word meaning "right-seeming"), about Jesus' nature, rejecting other interpretations as heterodox ("wrong-seeming") or heretical ("choice" of the wrong interpretation). The Nicene Creed announced that God the Son was coeternal with God the Father, opposing influential theories that the son was inferior to the father.[11]

Just as our thoughts about religion would have puzzled ancient Greeks, so would our isolation of myth as a topic for discussion. The Greek *mythos,* meaning "saying" or "story," appears commonly in works of the poets, starting with Homer, but never with the modern meaning of "a fanciful tale to explain, justify, or amuse, involving gods or other supernatural beings." This meaning of myth goes back to the eighteenth-century European Enlightenment and to an influential collection of stories.[12] Still, in the fifth century B.C., intellectuals began distinguishing what we would call *history,* the rational search for truth about the past, from *myth,* a story without rational claims to the truth. The Athenian Thucydides, writing around 400 B.C., was the first author we know of to describe false stories as "mythical" (*mythôdes,* "like a *mythos*"):

> And with regard to my factual recording of the events of the war I have made it a principle not to write down the first thing I came upon, and not even to be guided by my own general impressions; either I was present myself at the events which I have described or else I heard of them from eye-witnesses whose reports I have checked with as much thoroughness as possible. Not that even so the truth was easy to discover: different eye-witnesses give different accounts of the same events, speaking out of partiality for one side or the other or else from imperfect memories. And it may well be that my history will seem less easy to read because of the absence in it of the *mythôdes.* It will be enough for me, however, if these words of mine are judged useful by those who want to understand clearly the events which happened in the past. . . .
>
> Thucydides 1.22
> (R. Warner, modified)

In dismissing the *mythôdes,* the "mythlike," Thucydides seems to criticize Herodotus' *History,* which appeared just a few years earlier and contained many fanciful tales. Early Christian theologians, thinking about the meaning of Jesus' life and death, were Thucydides' intellectual heirs: they too sought to know truth by understanding the past. So do we still, when scholars agonize over what is true and not true in, say, the story of the Trojan War. Myths may contain historical elements, but are not concerned with the truth about the past as such.

Whereas religion is a set of practices based on belief in invisible nonhumans, *myth is a story*, sometimes about such beings, but sometimes not. A long search for the essence of myth has proved fruitless. For our purposes, we may think of myth as a story that matters within a community, which is told and retold for that reason. The story of Oedipus, who killed his father and married his mother, is a good example. Homer mentions these details as if they were everyday knowledge.

One common approach divides myths into three categories. First are **divine myths,** stories in which gods are important, creating the universe and establishing its rules. Such stories explain where the world came from. Second are **legends** (or sagas), stories about heroes and the human past, analogous to our history. Third is **folktale,** similar to our novels and feature films; such stories are recognized as fictional, though they may contain moral advice. These distinctions are useful, although myths have a way of slipping in and out of the categories to which we assign them.

Because both myth and religion can be concerned with the external forces that surround and influence us, they are easily confused. Gods and goddesses are prominent in myths, endowed with personality and will. The confusion is worsened because myth and religion may focus on similar problems: how to understand through intellect, and express through language, otherwise incomprehensible phenomena.

Myths too can be central to religious practice. The Egyptians told a myth about how Osiris died but came back to life through the magic of Isis. By referring to this story in hieroglyphic writing and placing the writing next to the mummy, the Egyptian priest helped the individual to share a similar destiny. The Greeks told a story about the madness that befell Pentheus, king of Thebes, when he denied the power of Dionysus, the god of wine and revelry: such is the experience of all who refuse the god's revivifying power, the story seems to say. Although religion is not itself myth, but practice, the two can intertwine inextricably.

HESIOD'S MYTH OF THE ORIGIN OF THE GODS

Religion tries to establish good relations with invisible powers and provide insurance against misfortune, but before philosophy, only myths explained why religion was necessary at all, why things are the way they are. Such is the overall purpose in Hesiod's poem, the *Theogony,* created probably sometime around 700 B.C. Its opening lines raise the question of truth and falsity in myth. The Muses gave Hesiod the gift of song, but not everything the Muses sing is true, Hesiod says. Near the very beginning of Greek literature, then, appears the notion that poetry can be "just a myth":

> It was they [the Muses] who taught Hesiod beautiful song
> as he tended his sheep at the foothills of god-haunted Helicon.
> Here are the words the daughters of aegis-bearing Zeus,
> the Muses of Olympus, first spoke to me.
> "Listen, you country bumpkins, you swag-bellied yahoos,
> we know how to tell many lies that pass for truth,

and we know, when we wish, to tell the truth itself."
So spoke Zeus's daughters, masters of word-craft,
and from a laurel in full bloom they plucked a branch,
and gave it to me as a staff, and then breathed into me
divine song, that I might spread the fame of past and future,
and commanded me to hymn the race of the deathless gods,
but always begin and end my song with them.

Hesiod, *Theogony* 22–34 (H. G. Evelyn-White)

Hesiod distinguishes between true and false stories because he wishes to emphasize how his own story is true—inspired by the gods. In his story, his *mythos,* Hesiod will declare the greatness of Zeus by describing how Zeus came to power and established the customs that make up the world:

With their divine voices
the Muses first sing the glory of the sublime race of the gods
from the beginning, the children born to Gaea.
Tell me, O Muses who dwell on Olympus, and observe proper order
of each thing as it first came into being.

Hesiod, *Theogony* 108–115 (H. G. Evelyn-White)

At the beginning, according to Hesiod's influential account, appeared three beings. First there was **Chaos,** which means "gap," as if something had yawned, as if one thing had become two. Out came **Gaea** (jē-a), Earth, something to stand on. Tartarus, the darkness that is always down in the earth, also sprang from Chaos. **Eros,** the force of sexual desire, that restless, irresistible energy that drives all living things and creates new living things, came from Chaos as well.

Gaea begot her own consort **Uranus** (**u**-ra-nus), Sky, to form the first clear duality: Up and Down, Above and Below. Gaea/Earth made the mountains, the glades of nymphs, and then gave rise to Pontus/Sea. Male Sky is above, and female Earth is below. Pontus/Sea is wet, and male too, like semen, and lies hard against the Earth, embracing her. Hesiod's metaphors are explicitly sexual because the world is like we are. Only through sexual union, and the generations from it, can the world grow and change. The race of the gods is like the race of human rulers who are begotten, who beget others, who struggle, triumph, and fade away. The gods are within the world; they do not stand outside it.

The first duality, Gaea/Earth and Uranus/Sky, united in primal sexual embrace. From their union came a host of creatures of obscure nature and meaning, the race of **Titans.** Most Titans had no cult in Greek religion; they were entirely mythical beings. Two of them, **Cronus** and **Rhea** (rē-a), are critical to Hesiod's story. Uranus/Sky was a bad father:

All these awesome children born of Uranus and Gaea
hated their own father from the day they were born,
for as soon as each one came from the womb,
Uranus, with joy in his wicked work, hid it
in Gaea's womb and did not let it return to the light.
Huge Gaea groaned within herself
and in her distress she devised a crafty and evil scheme.
With great haste she produced gray iron

and made a huge sickle and showed it to her children;
then, her heart filled with grief, she rallied them with these words:
"Yours is a reckless father; obey me, if you will,
that we may all punish your father's outrageous deed,
for he was first to plot shameful actions."
So she spoke, and fear gripped them all; not one of them
uttered a sound. Then great, sinuous-minded Cronus
without delay spoke to his prudent mother:
"Mother, this deed I promise you will be done,
since I loathe my dread-named father.
It was he who first plotted shameful actions."
So he spoke, and the heart of giant Earth was cheered.
She made him sit in ambush and placed in his hands
a sharp-toothed sickle and confided in him her entire scheme.
Uranus came dragging with him the night, longing for Gaea's love,
and he embraced her and lay stretched out upon her.
Then his son reached out from his hiding place and seized him
with his left hand, while with his right he grasped
the huge, long, and sharp-toothed sickle and swiftly hacked off
his father's genitals and tossed them behind him—
and they were not flung from his hand in vain.

Hesiod, *Theogony* 154–182 (H. G. Evelyn-White)

On the surface, Hesiod's cosmic tale is about family dissension, so often the essence of Greek myth, but the tale of domestic abuse cloaks a description of creation as separation embodied in the name *Chaos,* "gaping" or "chasm." Hesiod's myth attempts, we might say, to explain by means of ordinary categories of thought what is otherwise inexplicable.

Uranus/Sky and Gaea/Earth begot children, but the children could not come forth because Uranus would not let them emerge from Gaea's womb, as if Sky and Earth were locked in constant sexual embrace. Uranus' fault was sexual in nature, which both Gaea and Cronus called "shameful things." One of the original three beings was Eros, sexual attraction; unless this cosmic attraction could be broken, female and male would forever be bound in sexual union, and there could be no world. When Cronus severed his father's penis, which joined Uranus/Sky to Gaea/Earth, Uranus rose upward, where he has been ever since. First there was one thing: Uranus and Gaea, masculine and feminine, locked in eternal embrace. Now there were two separate beings and a proper space between them wherein change could take place. But the beginning of the world in bloody castration of father by son would bring a legacy of danger, terror, and hate.

The ground was watered with Cronus' blood, and from it grew the **Furies** (or *Erinyes*), the angry persecuting spirits, especially of murdered members of one's own family; the Giants ("earth-born ones"), a blood-thirsty race who would one day oppose Zeus and his relatives; and the spirits of the trees which cover the earth, because only blood in the ground, as from sacrifice, could bring life to the mighty trees.

Most terrible of all was Aphrodite, "born from the foam" (Greek *aphros* "foam") that gathered around the severed penis of Uranus when it fell into the sea. It was a ghastly image. The foam that gathered around the severed penis was like foam that gathers around the penis of a man in human intercourse, but this penis has been sliced away. Such was Aphrodite: ferocious sexual attraction that arises from gore and brings bloody disaster in its wake. The danger of sexual attraction and of woman, who uses attractiveness as a weapon against the male, is a central theme in Greek myth.

The awful crime of Cronus, working with his mother against his father, bred more crimes, as Hesiod goes on to tell. Cronus proved to be just as wicked a father as Uranus before him. Uranus pushed his children back into Gaea (as if stuffing up the womb with his penis), but Cronus was a cannibal, swallowing his children whole. Gaea conspired with her son Cronus to overthrow her husband Uranus; then Rhea, Cronus' sister/wife, destroyed the power of her husband. She saved her last child, Zeus, from being eaten by Cronus by wrapping a rock in swaddling clothes and giving it to Cronus to swallow. Stupid Cronus fell for the trick while Zeus, his life spared, was raised on the island of Crete, hidden in a cave.

When Zeus grew up, he deposed Cronus and became king himself. Although threatened repeatedly, Zeus defeated his enemies and, unlike his father and grandfather, established a permanent disposition over the world we live in now. All praise to great Zeus, father of gods and men! Hesiod ends his poem.

Myth is a story that explains not only how things came to be, but why things are the way they are. Hesiod's complex story, of which we have examined a portion, explains the origin and role of the great forces that make up the world.

GREEK RELIGION IN HISTORY

Hesiod describes how Zeus came to power by overthrowing his father, who had previously overthrown his father. It is a story and does not require action. Greek religion was very different from myth and mostly independent of it, although stories were sometimes told in explanation of religious practice. Greek religion was **polytheistic,** "having many gods," and **anthropomorphic,** "imagining its gods in the form of humans." The powers that surround us have their own wills and psychology, mysterious and unpredictable but similar to our own. Greek religion was a typical form of religion, found in other ancient cultures, that originates from primitive fear, but you have to know something about the history of religion to understand how it worked.

Animals and humans alike have fear, but only humans have illusions. Combining fear with imagination, humans create religion. All humans have religion, even those who deny it. Through their illusions, humans have attached their religious fear to every conceivable kind of person, place, or thing, hoping by the stone of amazing color, the brilliant orb in the sky, the eerie spirit from beyond, or the amazing man, to be saved from the forces that relentlessly punish them.

Religion may begin in fear wedded to illusion, but there are two broad categories: **evolutionary religion** and **revealed religion.** An evolutionary religion embraces the totality of things feared by a social group at any one time and has no specific origin. Evolutionary religions are always polytheistic, like Greek religion, though not necessarily anthropomorphic. Evolutionary religions evolve from humans' constant changing response to the hostile world around them. Although such religions impose moral behavior, they have no teaching as such. Except for Judaism and Christianity, all ancient religions, including Greek, were evolutionary religions. Egyptian religion, for example, was a bewildering chaos of fetishes (objects with power), magic, symbols, gods, and powers, all of which coexisted without complaint.

There were books of spells and rituals, but no sacred book, and few myths. Greek religion was different from Egyptian, but shared these same general qualities.

Revealed religions, by contrast, have founders, men with special relations to the divine. The oldest revealed religion was that of the strange Egyptian pharaoh Akhenaten ("servant of the Aten," c. 1360 B.C.), who claimed a special relationship with Aten, the one God, and outlawed the evolutionary and polytheistic religion that had long guided Egypt and guaranteed personal happiness after death. Similarly, God was revealed to Moses, who founded the religion of Israel (although the race descends from Abraham). Saint Paul and the Apostles founded Christianity on the basis of the life of Jesus. Zoroaster founded a religion in Iran, and Sakyamuni founded Buddhism (if it is a religion, not a philosophy). Revealed religions are monotheistic, or close to it (Christianity is monotheistic, but admits three divine persons in one); no prophet ever came from the mountain to announce, "There are many gods!" Revealed religions are all tied to written documents—the "books of Moses," the Koran, the New Testament. Revealed religions can appear independently of writing (for example, the religion of the Paiute prophet Wovoka from Nevada in the late nineteenth century A.D.), but they do not last. The closest the Greeks came to revealed religion was the movement called Orphism, which had books, teachings, and an alleged founder (see the Section "Ecstatic and Mystical Religion," later in this chapter), but Orphism was restricted to a philosophic elite and was more what we would consider a cult.

Greek evolutionary religion embraced powers and fears of all kinds. As we have seen, its gods were within the world, which they did not create. These powers—gods, nymphs, and other spirits—did not die (ordinarily), but they were born. The Greek gods had favorite humans and intervened in human affairs, but did not live within the human heart. They were powerful, but their power had limits. All gods, including Zeus, were subject to **Fate** (Latin *fatum,* "that which has been spoken"), the way things must be.

FORMS OF GREEK RELIGIOUS PRACTICE

All religions, evolutionary and revealed, share common practices, although different religions emphasize different practices. Let us examine the most important religious practices to form a context for understanding Greek religion.

Magic

Our relation to the stupendous powers that govern every facet of life demands more than feeling and speculation. **Magic** forces such powers to do what we wish. Some scholars distinguish magic from religion, but the two are hard to disentangle. We might think of magical effects as dependent on magicians, who force gods to their will, whereas in religion, the gods act of their own will. Magic appears in Greek literature and in Greek society, but was less important in Greece than in other evolutionary religions. The educated elites who wrote Greek literature generally felt that magic was beneath them, but some Greeks did practice magic, and they left behind evidence of their spells and incantations.

Magic can work by imitation of the desired effect. If I wish to harm you, I make a wax doll and stick pins into it. Some Greeks did just this, then buried the dolls with criminals' corpses to increase the doll's power to do harm. Archaeologists have found such dolls in graves. In another form of magic, the magician may do on a small scale what is meant to happen on a large; sprinkling from a bucket of water will bring rain, and at one Attic festival, water was sprinkled during a prayer for rain. A third form of magic works by symbolism, assuming that the name of a thing and the thing itself are the same—thus the police shout, "Stop in the name of the law!" as they chase criminals down dark alleys. Cursing or blessing by name is a further example. By invoking the gods' names, we can compel them to obey our will; a body of Greek hymns survives whose purpose was to attract the gods' attention by naming them and telling stories about them. The biblical commandment against taking God's name in vain works similarly, and in Judaism, the written name of God is never pronounced because of its power. Magic is perhaps closer to primitive science with invalid axioms than to what we think of as religion, but it leaves its traces in all cults and many myths.

Persuasion

Magic might force invisible powers to obey one's will, but in dealing with very great powers, persuasion and propitiation by sacrifice can be preferable. Because the powers are like ourselves, we can persuade them to follow this or that course. We too are liable to flattery, bribery, and shame. The story of Chrysês in the first book of Homer's *Iliad* (see Chapter 6, "Homer") is a good example. This priest persuaded Apollo to punish the Achaeans when Agamemnon refused to release Chrysês' daughter and sent him away:

> The old man was terrified. He obeyed the order,
> turning, trailing away in silence down the shore
> where the roaring battle lines of breakers crash and drag.
> And moving off to a safe distance, over and over
> the old priest prayed to the son of sleek-haired Leto,
> Apollo, "Hear me Apollo! God of the silver bow
> who strides the walls of Chrysê and Cilla sacrosanct—
> lord in power of Tenedos—Smintheus, god of the plague!
> If I ever roofed a shrine to please your heart,
> ever burned the long rich bones of bulls and goats
> on your holy altar, now, now bring my prayer to pass.
> Pay the Danaäns back—your arrows for my tears!"
> His prayer went up and Phoebus Apollo heard him.
> Down he strode from Olympus' peaks, storming at heart
> with his bow and hooded quiver slung cross his shoulders.
> The arrows clanged at his back as the god quaked with rage,
> the god himself on the march and down he came like night.
> Over against the ships he dropped to a knee, let fly a shaft
> and a terrifying clash rang out from the great silver bow.
> First he went for the mules and circling dogs but then,
> launching a piercing shaft at the men themselves,
> he cut them down in droves—
> and the corpse-fires burned on, night and day, no end in sight.
>
> Homer, *Iliad* 1.33–50 (A.T. Murray)

Chrysês uses the magic of names to insure the god's attention: not any Apollo, but the well-known one who rules over the villages Chrysê (**krī**-sē) and Cilla (**sil**-la), locations unknown to us. This Apollo rules Tenedos (**ten**-e-dos) too, an island near the Trojan plain. He is Smintheus, meaning "of the mice," apparently because

Figure 7.1 The archer god Apollo and his sister Artemis kill the children of Niobê, who bragged of having more children than Leto, Apollo and Artemis' mother. The children—three boys and a girl—fall, pierced by arrows. Athenian red-figure pot, circa 450 B.C. *Musée du Louvre/Reunion des Musees Nationaux, Paris, France/Art Resource, NY.*

Apollo can bring plague or drive it away. Such local names pin down Apollo in the welter of the world, much as we dial a phone number; they get the god's attention and alert him to the need to destroy the Achaeans, who have offended his priest.

Chrysês then explains why he deserves this favor. He has, one, built a roof over Apollo's special place, and two, burned animal parts on Apollo's altar. Apollo owes Chrysês for his services, and Chrysês is calling in his marker. Apollo is persuaded and does as Chrysês asks.

Homer's description shows how closely related and easily confused are myth, religion, and magic. These lines are the earliest information we receive about Apollo, one of the most celebrated ancient gods. What do we learn about Apollo? He is a bowman and carries a quiver on his shoulder. He comes like the night, swift and dark, a killer. First, animals die, then humans—such is his power. That is what Chrysês wanted, what he prayed for, why he sacrificed at Apollo's shrine and roofed it, a religious act. Yet Chrysês is like a magician who creates his own effects through Apollo's agency; priests are dangerous and should not be meddled with. These special details are, however, part of a myth, the story of the Trojan War. From this passage derive subsequent representations of Apollo, often shown with a bow and arrows (Figure 7.1).

Homer gives a mythical description of what his audience would understand as plague, when animals and humans die mysteriously, as often happens on military campaigns. The cause was a magician allied with a god, who had shrines throughout Greece (Figure 7.2).

Sacrifice

Later in the *Iliad*, when the suffering Achaeans agree to return Chrysês' daughter so he will release them from disease, they restore relations with Apollo through **sacrifice**—the killing of an animal or offering of fruits and plants, the most visible

Figure 7.2   The shrine of Apollo at Delphi, one of the major Greek sacred sites. The oracle of Apollo at Delphi is important in many Greek myths (for example, Oedipus the king, who killed his father and married his mother). Visible in the center-left are columns from the god's temple; above, center-right, is the open-air theater from which a path led up the hill to an athletic stadium. Beyond the mountain in the background lies the Gulf of Corinth.

expression of religion in the ancient world. Sacrifice was what you did (Figure 7.3). The psychology of sacrifice is summed up in the Latin saying, *do ut des,* "I give that you might give." The Achaeans gave to Apollo so Apollo might allow them to live:

> Out went the bow-stones—cables fast astern—
> and the crew themselves climbed out in the breaking surf,
> leading out the sacrifice for the archer god Apollo,
> and out of the deep-sea ship Chryseïs ["daughter of Chrysê"] stepped too.
>   Then tactful Odysseus led her up to the altar,
> placing her in her loving father's arms, and said,
> "Chrysês, the lord of men Agamemnon sent me here
> to bring your daughter back and perform a sacrifice,
> a grand sacrifice to Apollo—for all Achaea's sake—
> so we can appease the god
> who's loosed such grief and torment on the Argives."
>   With those words he left her in Chrysês' arms
> and the priest embraced the child he loved, exultant.
> At once the men arranged the sacrifice for Apollo,

Figure 7.3 The sacrifice of Polyxena, a daughter of King Priam of Troy, over the grave of Achilles. A figure labeled Neoptolemus (Achilles' son) cuts the virgin princess' throat as if she were an animal, spilling the blood into the flame. Human sacrifice was extremely rare in classical Greece. © *The British Museum.*

making the cattle ring his well-built altar,
then they rinsed their hands and took up barley.
Rising among them Chrysês stretched his arms to the sky
and prayed in a high resounding voice, "Hear me, Apollo!
God of the silver bow who strides the walls of Chrysê
and Cilla sacrosanct—lord in power of Tenedos!
If you honored me last time and heard my prayer
and rained destruction down on all Achaea's ranks,
now bring my prayer to pass once more. Now, at last,
drive this killing plague from the armies of Achaea!"
   His prayer went up and Phoebus Apollo heard him.
And soon as the men had prayed and flung the barley,
first they lifted back the heads of the victims,
slit their throats, skinned them, and carved away
the meat from the thighbones and wrapped them in fat,
a double fold sliced clean and topped with strips of flesh.
And the old man burned these on a dried cleft stick
and over the quarters poured out glistening wine
while young men at his side held five-pronged forks.
Once they had charred the thighs and tasted the organs
they cut the rest into pieces, pierced them with spits,
roasted them to a turn and pulled them off the fire.
The work done, the feast laid out, they ate well,
and no man's hunger lacked a share of the banquet.
When they had put aside desire for food and drink,
the young men brimmed the mixing bowls with wine
and tipping first drops for the god in every cup
they poured full rounds for all. And all day long
they appeased the god with song, raising a ringing hymn
to the distant archer god who drives away the plague,
those young Achaean warriors singing out his power,
and Apollo listened, his great heart warm with joy.

Homer, *Iliad* 1.437–68 (A.T. Murray)

We can supplement Homer's description with other reports. First, the cattle that made up the sacrifice were grouped around the altar in a circle, a formation of magical power. Cattle were valuable, and their bequest to the god made a powerful impression. The officiants then purified themselves. Somebody brought a bowl of water ("they washed their hands"). Purification was religiously important because humans were constantly threatened by defilement from their own waste and from the fluids of intercourse and childbirth. Women were especially liable to impurity and dangerous to religious practice. Defecation, urination, intercourse, childbirth, menstruation, and death (which produces its own repulsive fluids) were strictly forbidden in religious precincts, in ancient Greece and elsewhere. The barley grains sprinkled on the animals provided the same magical purificatory function as the water, being a rain of the fruitful, life-bearing seed. The grain purified the animal and separated it from the everyday world. The Latin word *sacer* means "separated from everyday human usage," made over to a divinity, from which comes our words *sacred, consecrate, sacrifice, sacrament, sanctify,* and *saint.*

The animal's death would bring life to the men: *do ut des,* "I give that you might give." The sacrificial knife, we learn from other descriptions, lurked in the seed-filled basket from which the grain is scattered, awaiting the priest's hand. As the men sprinkled the grain, they told the god what they wished in return. The men drew back the head so the animal looked up, assenting to the shedding of its blood and stretching its throat taut (Figure 7.4). Priests in Greek religion (and most other ancient religions) were butchers, skilled in killing, skinning, and dismembering animals.

Figure 7.4   A bull led to sacrifice in the Athenian Panathenaic procession, illustrated on the Parthenon, 440s to 430s B.C. The bull rears its head, presenting its throat, a good omen. Marble, carved under the supervision of Phidias.

The animal was skinned and the thigh bones cut out and wrapped in juicy fat in a sort of sandwich. Pieces of meat from all parts of the animal were sprinkled over the fat (as Homer describes). The meat-sprinkled fat-sandwich represented the entire animal, whose good parts the hungry men ate, while the god received the undesirable fat and inedible bones. Chrysês burned this fat-sandwich on a spit and doused it with wine.

Meanwhile, someone roasted the entrails. The rest of the animal was sliced and roasted on forks. Most Greeks ate meat only at sacrifices. The excitement of killing a large animal; the prayers; the splash and stink of blood as it gushed out of the animal's throat into the flames of the altar (or was first caught in a bowl); the thick and redolent smoke from the burning blood, bones, and fat; and the scent of roasting meat—such was the essence of Greek religion from the Bronze Age until Saint Paul promulgated the voluntary self-sacrifice of Jesus, which obviated need for further sacrifices. The Greek calendar was largely a cycle of festivals to this or that divinity, when the people would taste sacrificed meat. Public sacrifices brought the community together, affirmed values, and added protein to the diet. The average Greek experienced religion in this and in no other way.

HESIOD'S MYTH OF SACRIFICE

Hesiod tells a myth explaining why, in Greek sacrifice, humans received the good parts and gods got the worst:

> When the gods and mortal men were settling their accounts
> at Meconê,° Prometheus cheerfully took a great ox,
> carved it up, and set it before Zeus to trick his mind.
> He placed meat, entrails, and fat within a hide
> and covered them with the ox's stomach,
> but with guile he arranged the white bones of the ox,
> covered them with glistening fat, and laid them down as an offering.
> Then indeed the father of gods and men said to him:
> "Son of Iapetus,° you outshine all other kings,
> but friend, you have divided with self-serving zeal."
>   These were the sarcastic words of Zeus, whose counsels never perish,
> but Prometheus was a skillful crook and he smiled faintly,
> all the while mindful of his cunning scheme,
> and said: "Sublime Zeus, highest among the everlasting gods,
> choose of the two portions whichever your heart desires."
> He spoke with guileful intent, and Zeus, whose counsels never perish,
> knew the guile and took note of it; so he pondered evils in his mind
> for mortal men, evils he meant to bring on them.
> With both hands he took up the white fat,
> and spiteful anger rushed through his mind and heart
> when he saw the white bones of the ox laid out in deceit.
> From that time on the tribes of mortal men on earth
> have burned the white bones for the gods on smoky altars.
>
> Hesiod, *Theogony* 543–558 (H. G. Evelyn-White)

°*Meconê* [me-**kō**-nē]: Sicyon, in the north Peloponnesus.   °*Iapetus:* A Titan, father of Prometheus.

Hesiod's myth is a good example of a story that explains the cause (Greek *aition*) of something—in this case, the division of the animal in sacrifice—called an **etiological myth.** Hesiod's *Theogony* ("begetting of the gods") is itself an etiological tale explaining how Zeus came to rule the world. Myth often explains, telling us why things are as they are; religion, the killing and eating of animals, is practice, a mode of action.

The conditions for sacrifice, which brings all good things to men, are now established. The basic facts of human life are tied to sacrifice: it brings us to the world of the gods and guarantees us its benefits.

GODS AND OTHER MYSTERIOUS BEINGS

Many scholars distinguish two broad categories of Greek religious practice. The first was directed toward the **Olympians,** gods who in poetic fancy lived on lofty Mount Olympus between Macedonia and Thessaly, Greece's highest mountain (9,573 feet; Figure 2.2). The second was **chthonic cult** ("of the earth," where the dead are buried), directed toward ghosts, underworld spirits, and various halfway supernatural beings like the heroes. Both forms of religion served similar ends, however, and in practice they overlapped, but for the sake of discussion we treat them separately here.

Greek Polytheism

The Greek word for god is *theos* (root of *theo*logy, "study of god"), possibly from the same root, meaning "bright," that gives us the name *Zeus* and the Latin *Ju*-piter and *deus* (root of *deity*). *Theoi* (the plural of *theos*) are the "shining ones," perhaps because they occasionally appear to humans as luminous beings. Whereas ghosts are the departed breath of the living, gods have very diverse origins and natures.

We get some inkling of how complex is the category "gods" by looking again at Hesiod's *Theogony,* our most important early source of information about Greek religion. In the following passage, we **italicize** each god (or group of gods) that Hesiod mentions:

> I begin my song with the Heliconian *Muses:*
> they have made Helicon, the great god-haunted mountain, their domain;
> their soft feet move in the dance that rings
> the violet-dark spring and the altar of mighty Zeus.
> They bathe their lithe bodies in the water of Permessus
> or of Hippocrene or of god-haunted Olmius.
> On Helicon's peak they join hands in lovely dances
> and their pounding feet awaken desire.
> From there they set out and, veiled in mist,
> glide through the night and raise enchanting voices
> to exalt aegis-bearing *Zeus* and queenly *Hera,*
> the Lady of Argus who walks in golden sandals;
> gray-eyed *Athena,* daughter of aegis-bearing Zeus,
> and Phoebus *Apollo* and arrow-shooting *Artemis.*
> They exalt *Poseidon,* holder and shaker of the earth,
> stately *Thetis* and *Aphrodite* of the fluttering eyelids,
> and gold-wreathed *Hebê* and fair *Dionê.*
> And then they turn their song to *Êos, Helius,* and bright *Selenê,*
> to *Leto, Iapetus,* and sinuous-minded *Cronus,*
> to *Gaea,* great *Oceanus,* and black *Night,*
> and to the holy race of the other deathless gods.
> It was they who taught Hesiod beautiful song
> as he tended his sheep at the foothills of god-haunted Helicon.
>
> Hesiod, *Theogony* 1–23 (H. G. Evelyn-White)

Figure 7.5 The poet Musaeus (mu-**sē**-us) on the left and a Muse on an Attic red-figure amphora. Musaeus, a legendary poet ("man of the Muse") wears a laurel wreath and a cloak. His name is inscribed above him. His right hand rests on a tortoiseshell lyre to accompany songs. Hesiod tells us the names of nine Muses; the one shown here is labeled Terpsichorê (terp-**sik**-o-rē, "delighter in dance"), usually thought of as the inspirer of lyric poetry and dance circa 450–420 B.C.

The Greeks called the **Muses** gods, *theoi*, or referred to a single god, the Muse (Figure 7.5). The Muse(s) personified the mysterious force that enabled *aoidoi* ("singers") to strum a lyre and tell an entrancing story in metrical song. We attribute similar abilities to inspiration, the "taking in of a spirit." The Muses favored some people and did not favor others, but the actual power to sing was never personal.

The Muses perhaps were gods who worked from without to create effects in people's lives, but they originated as much in a manner of speaking about artistic power as in the primitive fear at the heart of an evolutionary religion. They are a good example of the power of poetry to mold religious expression in early Greece. Highly local, they did not live in the sky or far away, but on Mount Helicon above the village of Ascra in southern Boeotia, where Hesiod lived some time in the eighth century B.C. Like young girls from Hesiod's village, the Muses bathed in an obscure stream called Permessus. No one outside a radius of a few miles could have heard of these places, or of Hippocrene (**hip**-ō-krēn, "spring of the horse"), probably a cold-water spring on Mount Helicon. The altar of Zeus around which they dance has never been identified.

Hesiod, therefore, begins his hymn to the universal Zeus with a hymn to the very local Muses, who themselves sing a hymn to Zeus and a long list of other gods, our earliest such list in Greek culture (except for some names on Linear B tablets). We examine these gods briefly and individually; some recur countless times in the culture of the ancient Greeks, while others may be unfamiliar.

The Olympians

"Gray-eyed Athena, daughter of aegis-bearing Zeus," "Phoebus Apollo," and "arrow-shooting Artemis" in Hesiod's list belong, with Hera and Zeus, to what became a canon of the twelve greatest gods, formalized by the early fifth century B.C. The canon may derive from an altar "To the Twelve Gods" set up in Athens. The twelve Olympian gods, sculpted on the Parthenon frieze, (part of which is shown in Figure 7.6) are listed here:

Figure 7.6 Gods on the Parthenon frieze. At center, the beardless youthful Dionysus (or Apollo) turns to speak to Poseidon (at left), while Demeter (at right) watches the procession. Marble, 440s to 430s B.C.

Zeus	Artemis
Poseidon	Apollo
Demeter	Athena
Hera	Hermes
Ares	Dionysus
Aphrodite	Hephaestus

Of these twelve gods, Hesiod's list does not include Demeter, Ares, Hermes, Dionysus, or Hephaestus—the gods of grain, war, travel, wine, and metalworking. Hesiod talks about these gods in other contexts, but does not seem to know about a canonical list.

Zeus and Hera

Head of the Olympians is *aegis*-bearing **Zeus.** *Aegis* means "goatskin" and refers to a magical implement, perhaps a shield, which Zeus carried, perhaps symbolic of the thundercloud (but in art, Athena is more likely to carry it). The undiscovered altar around which the Muses dance in Zeus' honor, according to Hesiod's account, was no doubt on the peak of Helicon, for such altars "on high places," as described in the Hebrew Bible, were the abode of weather gods all over the Mediterranean, hated by the Hebrew prophets because of their power and influence. Their shrines were often on mountaintops because storms gather there. The storm god had many names: Hadad in Syria, Marduk in Babylon, Teshub among the Hittites; but always, like Zeus, he was the great power of the sky felt in awesome storms that consume the earth with rain and blast trees and rocks to smithereens (Figure 7.7a, Figure 7.7b).

To Zeus, Hesiod joins "queenly **Hera,** the Lady of Argos who walks in golden sandals," a great goddess in her own right and already mentioned in Linear B tablets. She had an important sanctuary near Argos, to which Hesiod refers. She, like the Muses, had a local origin, but her power spread far and wide. As the bull symbolized Zeus, Hera was the cow, the female principle of fruitfulness. In Greek religion, she protected marriage.

Ancient goddesses were always defined by their relationship to fertility and reproduction (as were women in society), unlike gods, whose duties were not unified by a common thread (nor were those of men in society). In religion, Hera was an important goddess who received magnificent temples and rich sacrifices, but in Homeric myth, she is a nagging, snooping wife, always opposing the designs of her portentous and philandering husband Zeus. In the following passage, Hera complains to Zeus for scheming with another goddess behind her back to help the Trojans, whom Hera loathes:

"So, who of the gods this time, my treacherous one,
was hatching plans with you?
Always your pleasure, whenever my back is turned,
to settle things in your grand clandestine way.
You never deign, do you, freely and frankly,
to share your plots with me—never, not a word!"
    The father of men and gods replied sharply,
"Hera—stop hoping to fathom all my thoughts.
You will find them a trial, though you are my wife.
Whatever is right for you to hear, no one, trust me,
will know of it before you, neither god nor man.
Whatever I choose to plan apart from all the gods—
no more of your everlasting questions, probe and pry no more."
    And Hera the Queen, her dark eyes wide, exclaimed,
"Dread majesty, son of Cronus, what are you saying?
Now surely I've never probed or pried in the past.
Why, you can scheme to your heart's content
without a qualm in the world for me . . . "
    And Zeus who marshals the thunderheads returned,
"Maddening one . . . you and your eternal suspicions—
I can never escape you. Ah but tell me, Hera,
just what can you *do* about all this? Nothing.
Only estrange yourself from me a little more—
and all the worse for you . . .
Now go sit down. Be quiet now. Obey my orders,
for fear the gods, however many Olympus holds,
are powerless to protect you when I come
to throttle you with my irresistible hands."

Homer, *Iliad* 1.649–62 (A.T. Murray)

Athena, Apollo, and Artemis

Athena, Apollo, and Artemis are magnificent gods in Greek religion and myth. In religion, **Athena** protected Athens and several other cities. She encouraged arts,

(a)

(b)

Figure 7.7 (a) The Hittite storm-god Tarkhunzas carries an ax in one hand and a trident, emblem of the thunderbolt, in the other. Similar figures of storm-gods appear in the art of the Near East from the third millennium B.C. until late antiquity. (b) Zeus carries a similar forklike device, but pronged at either end: it is the thunderbolt, his special weapon. Tarkhunzas: basalt orthostat from Zinjirli, circa 900 B.C.; height 51 inches. Zeus: Nolan amphora by the Berlin painter, 460s B.C., height, 12 inches.

Figure 7.8   Athena stands between Odysseus, on the left, and princess Nausicaä and a friend, on the right. Her spear pointed downward, she looks toward her protégé. She wears the war helmet and the snaky-edged *aegis* around her neck. Odysseus has just emerged naked from the bushes and surprised the girls, washing clothes by the sea. *Staatliche Antikensammlungen und Glypthotek, Munich, Germany.*

especially women's weaving, even as Athens was preeminent in artistic production. In myth, Athena favored the Achaeans in the Trojan War and protected Odysseus on his journey home (Figure 7.8). On Greek pottery she often stands beside a hero, such as Perseus or Theseus.

Apollo was a complex god. Artists represented him as a beardless young aristocrat (Figure 7.6). He is the archer-god, but (unlike his sister Artemis) never hunts. He favored the Trojans and guided the arrow, fired by Paris, that killed Achilles. Apollo embodied aristocratic values and the power possessed by men of knowledge, like his priest Chrysês in the *Iliad*. His connections with the inner world made him the god of prophecy. As the divine aristocrat, Apollo brought success to those who sang and played lyres at elite drinking parties (artists often show him holding a lyre). The seventh-century-B.C. *Homeric Hymn to Apollo* celebrates his singing:

> I shall remember not to neglect Apollo who shoots afar.
>   The gods of the house of Zeus tremble at his coming,
> and indeed all spring up from their seats
> as he approaches, stringing his splendid bow.
> Leto alone remains by Zeus who delights in thunder
> and she is the one to unstring Apollo's bow and close the quiver;
> from his mighty shoulders with her hands she takes

the bow and hangs it up on a golden peg
on her father's pillar, and after that she leads him to a seat.
Then his father offers him nectar in a golden goblet
and drinks a toast to his dear son; and then
the other gods sit down as mighty Leto rejoices,
because she bore a valiant son who carries the bow. . . .
For everywhere, Phoebus, the field of singing is your domain,
both on the islands and the mainland which nurtures heifers.

Homeric Hymn to Apollo 1–20
(H. G. Evelyn-White)

Arrow-shooting **Artemis** received temples all over the Greek world, far more than Hera. She helped animals, particularly wild ones, to reproduce. Though a goddess of fertility, she is paradoxically virgin, because, more than others, virgins are poised to reproduce. In myth, the virgin Artemis was Apollo's twin sister, though no one has explained why. Hesiod also mentions their mother, Leto.

Artemis appears in many myths about hunting. Often, she is offended in some way and sends horrific retribution, like the Calydonian boar, which ravaged the countryside when a king forgot to sacrifice to her at his wedding. She enjoys human sacrifice: Agamemnon sacrificed his daughter Iphigenia to Artemis so that favorable winds would carry the fleet to Troy.

Other Gods

Hesiod's "Poseidon, holder and shaker of the earth," and "Aphrodite of the fluttering eyelids" belong to the later canonical list of twelve Olympian gods. **Poseidon** was the earthquake god and lord of the Aegean Sea. In religion he received the prayers of sailors and those who lived through the frequent and sometimes devastating earthquakes that plagued the eastern Mediterranean. In myth he persecuted Odysseus, whose enemy was indeed the sea, foreign lands, and death. Hesiod associates **Aphrodite's** name with *aphros,* "foam," but it also appears to be a corruption of Astartê, a Near Eastern goddess of sex and war. By 900 B.C., Astartê was established on Cyprus, brought there by Phoenicians. Hence, Cyprus was called Aphrodite's home, and she was often called the Cyprian.

Hesiod's "stately Thetis, gold-wreathed Hebê and fair Dionê" are scarcely known outside a few stories. Thetis is the mother of Achilles. Hebê is "Youth," a straightforward personification (Heracles married her on Olympus after he became immortal), and Dionê is a feminine form of Zeus, perhaps his original consort before being displaced by Hera. The Muses close their list with three personifications of nature, Dawn (Eos), Sun (Helius), and Moon (Selenê); with three gods who have little role in cult, Leto (mother of Apollo and Artemis), the almost unknown Iapetus (probably the same as Japheth in the Bible, a son of Noah), and sinuous-minded Cronus (father of Zeus); then three primordial beings, Earth (Gaea), the encircling waters (great Oceanus), and black Night.

In organizing our earliest testament to Greek polytheism, Hesiod worked backwards from the present world order, where Zeus and Hera reign together with their brothers, sisters, and children, to an earlier era, when gods less personalized and unfamiliar to contemporary Greek religion were in power. In the Muses' hymn, Hesiod carries us back to the beginnings of things in earth, water, and darkness.

CHTHONIC RELIGION

Cultism is what people do in religious contexts. However, a religious cult is not always directed toward anthropomorphic gods with a psychology more or less like ours yet with far greater power. There are also personal, hidden, envious, and dangerous ghosts and spirits. Most ancient peoples (and many modern) believed in ghosts and spirits, and much of what we think of as religion belongs to ancient ghost-cult, perhaps the earliest form of religious behavior.

The Breath-Soul

Greek **psychê** (sī-kē, pl. *psychai*), poorly translated as "soul," literally means "breath."[13] Spirit- and ghost-cult derives from the belief that when people die, they are not gone, but transformed. The obvious fact about a dead body is that it no longer breathes. The *psychê* has escaped. Death is the departure of the insubstantial breath-soul from the body.

The breath-soul, denied the pleasures of life and mindful of hurts received, is invisible and very dangerous. To avoid the ghost's displeasure, it is important to demonstrate anguish at its departure by wearing dark, unattractive clothing that hides our sexual natures (a source of pleasure). The living should either deny themselves food (which brings pleasure) or invite the ghost to a special feast in its honor. It is good to abuse your body in other ways, by biting off a finger (Orestes did this after killing his mother) or cutting your hair, and it is always good to destroy some property of the deceased; you cannot be shown to benefit from the person's death. Among their many functions, grave-offerings might prevent the ghost's displeasure over someone having taken its property.

Odysseus and the *Psychai*

Homer's *Odyssey* is informative about Greek conceptions of ghosts and the mechanics of appealing to them. When Odysseus and his men wanted to leave the beautiful witch Circê's island after a year, she told them how to cross the river Ocean (one of the gods Hesiod mentions) to consult the *psychê* of the famous prophet Tiresias:

> There, gaining that point, we beached our raft
> and herding out the sheep, we picked our way
> by the Ocean's banks until we gained the place
> that Circê made our goal.
>   Here at the spot
> Perimedes and Eurylochus° held the victims fast,
> and I, drawing my sharp sword from beside my hip,
> dug a trench of about a forearm's depth and length
> and around it poured offerings out to all the dead,
> first with milk and honey, and then with mellow wine,
> then water third and last, and sprinkled glistening barley
> over it all, and time and again I vowed to all the dead,
> to the drifting, listless spirits of their *psychai,*
> that once I returned to Ithaca I would slaughter
> a barren heifer in my halls, the best I had,
> and load a pyre with treasures—and to Tiresias,

°*Perimedes* and *Eurylochus:* Companions to Odysseus.

alone, apart, I would offer a sleek black ram,
the pride of all my herds. And once my vows
and prayers had invoked the nations of the dead,
I took the victims, over the trench I cut their throats
and the dark blood flowed in—and up out of Erebus° they came,
flocking toward me now, the ghosts of the dead and gone . . .
brides and unwed youths and old men who had suffered much
and girls with their tender hearts freshly scarred by sorrow
and great armies of battle dead, stabbed by bronze spears,
men of war still wrapped in bloody armor—thousands
swarming around the trench from every side—
unearthly cries—blanching terror gripped me!
I ordered the men at once to flay the sheep
that lay before us, killed by my ruthless blade,
and burn them both, and then say prayers to the gods,
to the almighty god of death and dread Persephonê.
But, the sharp sword drawn from beside my hip,
sat down on alert there and never let the ghost
of the shambling, shiftless dead come near that blood
till I had questioned Tiresias myself.

Homer, *Odyssey* 11.131–45 (A.T. Murray)

°*Erebus:* "Darkness," the underworld.

Figure 7.9 Odysseus and the ghost of Elpenor, who fell from a roof and broke his neck as the expedition departed. The figures are labeled. The unburied Elpenor's *psychê* emerges, its legs hidden from the knees down, raising his left arm against a crag. Odysseus sits beside the fleece of a sacrificed sheep, his sword ready to deflect the ghosts as he gazes sorrowfully into Elpenor's eyes. Attic red-figure jar, circa 440 B.C. *The Lyakon Painter, "Pelike (storage jar)," Greek, classical period, c. 440 B.C.; ceramic, red figure; height: 47.4 cm (18-11/16 in); diameter: 34.3 cm (13-1/2 in.)/Museum of Fine Arts, Boston, William Amory Gardner Fund, 34.79. Photograph © 2004 Muse.*

The *psychai* are thin, faint versions of their human selves; they have lost the vitality that blood, coursing through veins, gives to the living. Hence it is important, in sacrifice at tombs, to pour the blood of animals onto the grave, as Odysseus pours blood into a pit at the edge of the River Ocean (Figure 7.9). Wine, milk, honey, and water, the fluids of life, are excellent too. Beginning in the eighth century B.C., Greeks made offerings at ancient tombs, or to unknown heroes, or sometimes just "to the hero." Chthonic cults existed side by side with cults of the Olympian gods, and Greeks did not distinguish them strongly.

THE UNGRATEFUL DEAD AND THE LAYING OF THE GHOST

Although evanescent, ghosts are not innocuous and may persecute the living who have wronged them. A good example of ghost-persecution appears in the *Oresteia,* a group of three plays by Aeschylus, performed in Athens in 458 B.C. In the first play, *Agamemnon,* Clytemnestra, the queen of Argos, murders her husband, Agamemnon, when he returns victorious from Troy. The second play, the *Libation Bearers,* is set many years later. Clytemnestra has had a terrible dream: To appease Agamemnon's ghost, she sends a group of slaves to pour libations (drink offerings, a form of sacrifice) over his grave. But only the murder of Clytemnestra herself, blood for blood, will satisfy this ghost.

Ghosts, especially ghosts of the murdered, send bad dreams, but they may also appear to friends in dreams. In the *Iliad,* Achilles has avenged the death of his friend Patroclus by killing Hector, and that night Patroclus' *psychê* appears to him:

> Achilles lay down now, groaning deep from the heart,
> near his Myrmidon° force but alone on open ground
> where over and over rollers washed along the shore.
> No sooner had sleep caught him, dissolving all his grief
> as mists of refreshing slumber poured around him there—
> his powerful frame was bone-weary from chasing Hector
> straight and hard to the walls of windswept Troy—
> than the *psychê* of stricken Patroclus drifted up . . .
> He was like the man to the life, every feature,
> the same tall build and the fine eyes and voice
> and the very robes that used to clothe his body.
> Hovering at his head the phantom rose and spoke:
> "Sleeping, Achilles? You've forgotten me, my friend.
> You never neglected me in life, only now in death.
> Bury me, quickly—let me pass the gates of Hades.
> They hold me off at a distance, all the souls,
> the shades of the burnt-out, breathless dead,
> never to let me cross the river, mingle with them . . .[14]
> They leave me to wander up and down, abandoned, lost
> at the House of Death with the all-embracing gates.
> Oh give me your hand—I beg you with my tears!
> Never, never again shall I return from Hades
> once you have given me the soothing rites of fire."

Homer, *Iliad* 23.59–76
(A.T. Murray)

°*Myrmidon:* A follower of Achilles.

The ghost of Patroclus begs to be released from this world, where it still wanders: only proper burial can "lay the ghost." Then Patroclus will be gone. The obligation to lay the ghost ordinarily falls on the family, but Achilles serves this role for Patroclus while they are in a foreign land. After all, the family is first to receive an unhappy ghost's complaint, like Clytemnestra. The family's need to lay the ghost is the basis for Sophocles' celebrated tragedy *Antigonê* (441 B.C.), in which the king forbids the burial of a treacherous prince, bringing catastrophe down on everyone. The purposes of Greek religion were collective, not for the well-being of individuals; the penalty for leaving the ghost to wander would be visited on the whole family, or even the entire state.

Miasma

We saw earlier how Chrysês, through magic, invoked Apollo and brought disease to the Achaeans. The wandering or vengeful ghost, too, may stand behind every sort of misfortune. The ghost brings **miasma** (mī-**az**-ma) "stench," often translated as "blood-pollution," and anyone coming in contact with a murderer is liable to persecution as well. Such is the basis of the most famous story from antiquity, told in Sophocles' tragedy *Oedipus the King* (429 B.C.).

A priest appears before Oedipus the king to announce that plague has broken out:

> O ruler of my country, Oedipus,
> you see our company around the altar;
> you see our ages; some of us, like these,
> who cannot yet fly far, and some of us
> heavy with age; these children are the chosen
> among the young, and I the priest of Zeus.
> Within the market place sit others crowned
> with suppliant garlands, at the double shrine
> of Pallas and the temple where Ismenus°
> gives oracle by fire. King, you yourself
> have seen our city reeling like a wreck
> already; it can scarcely lift its prow
> out of the depths, out of the bloody surf.
> A blight is on the fruitful plants of the earth,
> a blight is on the cattle in the fields,
> a blight is on our women that no children
> are born to them; a god that carries fire,
> a deadly pestilence, is on our town,
> strikes us and spares not, and the house of Cadmus°
> is emptied of its people while black Death
> grows rich in groaning and in lamentation.
>
> Sophocles, *Oedipus the King* 14–30 (R. Fagles)

°*Ismenus:* That is, Apollo, who had an oracular shrine near the spring Ismenus.
°*House of Cadmus:* The royal house, descended from the legendary Cadmus.

The cause of the plague, we soon learn from an oracle, is the unavenged murder of King Laius, killed mysteriously at a crossroads: The ghost is abroad and wants blood. As Sophocles' story unfolds, we learn that Oedipus himself killed Laius and that Laius was Oedipus' own father, although he did not know it; worse, Oedipus married the widowed queen, his own mother, who hangs herself in horror. Appalled at his deeds, Oedipus blinds himself with pins taken from his dead wife/mother's gown. Murder would be simple were it not for the ghost's malevolence.

ECSTATIC AND MYSTICAL RELIGION

In Olympian and chthonic religion, the worshiper makes sacrifice, sings hymns, and says prayers to obtain what is desired. The ordinary devotee watches, content to follow the commands relayed. His or her share in worship is the proper performance of ritual. But in another kind of Greek cult, worshipers sought direct communion with deities, or even complete loss of self in the divine.

The Eleusinian Mysteries

Many people who know nothing about Greek religion have heard of the **Eleusinian mysteries.** Our very word "mystery" comes directly from descriptions of what happened at a temple to **Demeter** and **Persephonê** in the small town of Eleusis, five miles west of Athens. A *mystês* was a "person with closed eyes," required of those initiated into the rites of the temple. The mysteries functioned for over one thousand years, but no one ever described what happened in them. To do so was punishable by death.

We do know that every year a great procession went from Athens through the countryside to the temple. Ordinarily, a Greek temple was the god's house, containing its image. Sacrifice took place outside the temple, on an altar facing east. At Eleusis, by contrast, celebrants went into a unique rectangular building supported by a forest of columns (Figure 7.10). According to a late commentator, during the ceremony a flash of light, perhaps from a fire, came from a stone hut in the building's center. All Greeks—men, women, and slaves—were eligible for initiation into the mysteries, which promised a happier life in the afterworld.

The *Hymn to Demeter* (attributed to Homer, though actually written two centuries after his time) tells the myth of the founding of the cult at Eleusis. Hades, god of death, requested permission from his brother Zeus to marry his niece **Persephonê**, daughter of Demeter. Zeus agreed. While Persephonê played by the seashore with her friends, Hades appeared from the earth in his chariot, seized the girl, and carried her to the underworld.

Demeter, goddess of wheat-growing, searched everywhere for her daughter. She came to Eleusis disguised as an old woman and became nurse to the king and queen's child. At night, she placed the child on the flame of the hearth to burn away its mortal parts. One night, the queen saw them and cried out. Demeter revealed herself to the terrified queen and demanded that a temple be built on that spot.

Meanwhile, fertility had disappeared from the earth. Alarmed, Zeus arranged that Persephonê could return to the upper world, but only on condition that she had eaten nothing in the House of Hades. In fact, she had eaten one pomegranate seed, which Hades gave her. Therefore, she could spend only two-thirds of the year

Figure 7.10   Ruins of the temple at Eleusis. Behind the figure are seats for initiates and in front of the figure are the foundations of the small building from which emanated a flash of light. The large hall was nearly square, with seven rows of columns supporting the roof. Fifth century B.C.

above ground with her mother, the other third below it with her lawful husband Hades, king of the dead.

The myth, similar to very ancient Near Eastern stories about fertility, explains how the cult at Eleusis was founded, but tells us little about the rituals there. The myth promises new life in Persephonê's return to the upper world, but cautions that death is necessary. Demeter and Persephonê were called the Two Ladies, or just The Goddesses. They were two aspects of a single force, one making for life, the other for death.

The Orphics

As the cult at Eleusis claimed Demeter as its founder, the **Orphics,** the "followers of **Orpheus,**" claimed the legendary Orpheus. According to myth, Orpheus was the greatest of singers, whose song even entranced nature. His bride, Eurydice, died on his wedding day, bitten by a serpent. Orpheus descended to the underworld, charming the ghosts and the spirits and winning back Eurydice, on condition that he did not look back at her until they reached the upper world. He failed and so lost his beloved forever (Figure 7.11).

Whereas the Eleusinian mysteries were open to all, including slaves, the Orphics were a small, self-contained group, probably all male. Because Orpheus had gone to the underworld and returned, his followers claimed special knowledge about human destiny, about our relation to the divine, and about life after death. More philosophy than religion, Orphism taught that a spark of God dwells in every

Figure 7.11 Orpheus plays among the Thracians, who listen entranced. After losing his wife a second time, he wandered in Thrace associating only with men and, according to some accounts, invented homosexuality. In anger at his behavior, Dionysus' followers tore him to bits. Attic red-figure vase, circa 440 B.C. *Orpheus Painter (5th B.C.E.), "Orpheus among the Thracians," Red-figure crater from Gela, ca. 450 B.C.E.; H: 50.5 cm, view 1/2 INV. V.I. 3172. Photo: Johannes Laurentius. Antikensammlung, Staatliche Museen zu Berlin, Germany. Bildarchiv Preussischer Kultu.*

human. Only through a pure life—abstaining from sex, certain foods, and especially the bloody sacrifice that stained the altars of heroes and gods—could initiates achieve knowledge of the divine self locked in the tomb of flesh.

The Orphics were a countercultural movement, interpreting reality differently from most contemporaries. They never were many, but they deeply influenced Plato, who in turn influenced the early Christian church fathers. Plato wrote as follows about the body and soul:

> This too [the derivation of the word *sôma,* "body"] can be explained in several ways, it seems to me, if one changes the spelling a little. Some say that it is the tomb [*sêma*] of the soul, in which the soul is buried for the time being. . . . But it seems to me that the followers of Orpheus have been especially responsible for calling the body *sôma,* because it is the place where the soul pays the penalty for its misdeeds: the body is the enclosure in which the soul is kept [*sôzetai*] as in a prison. For that is just what the body is, as its name shows, an enclosure for the soul until it has paid the penalties it owes.
>
> Plato, *Cratylus* 400b (P. Shorey)

Hence the Orphic expression **sôma sêma,** "the body is a tomb." Such thoughts were widely discussed in the fifth century B.C. and lie behind modern notions of the soul trapped "in this mortal coil." Before Plato's refinement of Orphic and Pythagorean thought, the soul was the miserable and insubstantial *psychê;* after Plato, some philosophers saw the soul as a transcendent, eternal spark, more real than our bodies or this world. But these were always minority views.

The Cult of Dionysus

The Olympians lived far away in the sky or on a mountain, while ghosts lived beneath the ground, near their human bones. **Dionysus,** by contrast, lived within the yellow sap of the vine, the spirits of red wine, fructifying white semen, and nourishing white milk. You know Dionysus when he comes, when you are a sprig sprouting from the tree of life.

In the cult of Dionysus, also called **Bacchus,** followers tore apart wild animals alive and ate them raw: they behaved like animals, which they had become (Figure 7.12). Intoxicated, they left the human, moral realm. Dionysus, as the life-force, was not human and had no interest in human affairs. Women were believed to be especially susceptible to his power. Abandoning responsibilities to husband and family, **Bacchae** ("the female followers of Bacchus") followed the god, wandering in bands through wild places. The Greeks called their secret ceremonies *orgia,* origin of our word orgy. Drunkenness and sexual license awakened the god's power within.

Myths said Dionysus was snatched from the ashes of his mother Semelê's (**sem**-e-lē) womb, destroyed when Zeus appeared to her in his full glory. Jealous Hera had tricked Semelê into asking Zeus for this favor. Raised by nymphs, the

Figure 7.12 Dionysus in ecstasy. The god wears ivy in his hair and a leopard skin around his shoulders as he tears a deer in half. Followers of the god ate animals raw, and sometimes still alive, to imbibe the life-force; in myth they ate human infants. Attic red-figure vase, circa 450 B.C. © *The British Museum.*

young Dionysus wandered afar, then returned to Greece. Many rejected him and his cult of ecstatic identification with transhuman forces. They might as well have denied the tides of the sea or the hurricane, and those who denied him paid for their false understanding.

The most famous myth of resistance to Dionysus is in Euripides' tragedy, the *Bacchae* (403 B.C.), in which the foolish Pentheus, king of Thebes, rejects the god, goes mad, and is torn to pieces by *Bacchae* as he tries to watch their rituals. In the play, the chorus celebrates the god's power:

> You on the streets, You on the roads! Make way!
> Let every mouth be hushed. Let no ill-omened words
> profane your tongues. Make way! Fall back! Hush!
> For now I raise the old, old hymn to Dionysus.
> Blessed, blessed are those who know the mysteries of god.
> Blessed is he who hallows his life in the worship of god,
> he whom the spirit of god possesses, who is one
> with those who belong to the holy body of god.
> Blessed are they who keep the rite of Cybelê° the Mother.
> Blessed are the thyrsus-bearers, those who wield in their hands
> the holy wand of god.°
> Blessed are those who wear the crown of the ivy of god.
> Blessed, blessed are they: Dionysus is their god!

Euripides, *Bacchae* 69–82
(T. A. Buckley)

°*Cybelê:* A mother goddess in Phrygia, with whom Dionysus was associated.   °*wand of god:* The thyrsus, a phallic staff entwined with ivy.

Unlike the Olympians, Dionysus and the celebrant became one. Scant wonder that early Christians adopted Dionysiac imagery on tombs to celebrate the promise of renewed life offered by their own religion.

CONCLUSION

Greek religion had much in common with other ancient polytheistic religions, like those of the Egyptians and the Mesopotamians, but differed from Jewish revealed religion, which depended on written documents held to reflect God's will directly. The Greeks wanted to persuade the Olympian gods and to satisfy with sacrifice the host of other spirits and ghosts that filled the world. We get one version of Greek religion when we read Homer or examine the Parthenon, where gods and goddesses behave as personalities, and quite another from documents like the following calendar of sacrifices, where the gods are bare names in a list, set alongside obscure spirits and powers of the local landscape:

> In Boedromion [September/October] festival of the Proerosia: for Zeus Polieus ["Zeus of the City"] a choice sheep; women acclaiming the god, a piglet bought for holocaust sacrifice;° for the worshipper the priest will provide dinner; for Cephalus [an Athenian hero] a choice sheep; for Procris [an Athenian heroine], an offering-tray; for Thorikos [personification of a county], a choice sheep; for the Heroines of Thorikos, an offering-tray; at Sounion [near Athens] for Poseidon, a choice lamb; for Apollo, a choice goat; for Kourotrophos ["Nourisher of the Young"] a choice female piglet; for Demeter, a

°*holocaust sacrifice:* When the entire victim was burned.

full-grown victim; for Zeus Herkeios ["Protector of the fence" around the house], a full-grown victim; for Kourotrophos, a piglet; at the salt-marsh for Poseidon, a full-grown victim; for Apollo, a piglet.

G. Daux, *"Le Calendrier de Thorikos au Musée J.-P. Getty,"*
Antiquité classique 52 (1983) 122; quoted in Zaidman/Pantel, 82

The calendar stipulates sacrifices for but a single deme (roughly a village; there were 140 in Attica) for a single month. It says nothing about where the sacrifices will take place or who will pay for them, because everyone knew. Such was the everyday reality of Greek religion.

But the Greeks introduced two unusual elements to their rather conventional polytheism. The first was exuberant storytelling, outstanding for its inventiveness and continuing appeal. These myths deeply influenced the Greeks, who loved them, learned them by heart, and imitated them in art. Religion is something one does as well as believes; the Greeks prayed, then killed animals and ate them. Myths are stories; first one thing happened, then another. Because the actors in Greek stories were sometimes the recipients of religious sacrifice, Greek myth and religion intermingle in a bewitching (and exasperating) way.

The Greeks' second innovation, which we emphasize often in this book, was to separate religious from social power. The gods, heroes, spirits, and ghosts were important and (so the Greeks believed) intervened regularly in human affairs. However, no one could use special access to the supernatural to justify power in this world, as did the kings of the ancient Near East. As we shall see in the next chapter, this strange separation and radical innovation had massive consequences for Greek society.

KEY TERMS

mythos, 118
divine myths, 119
legends, 119
folktale, 119
Chaos, 120
Gaea, 120
Eros, 120
Uranus, 120
Titans, 120
Cronus, 120
Rhea, 120
Furies, 121
polytheistic, 122
anthropomorphic, 122
evolutionary religion, 122
revealed religion, 122
magic, 123
sacrifice, 125
etiological myth, 129
Olympians, 130

chthonic cult, 130
Muses, 131
Zeus, 132
Hera, 133
Athena, 133
Apollo, 135
Artemis, 136
Poseidon, 136
Aphrodite, 136
psychê, 137
miasma, 140
Eleusinian mysteries, 141
Demeter, 141
Persephonê, 141
Orphics, 142
Orpheus, 142
sôma sêma, 143
Dionysus, 144
Bacchus, 144
Bacchae, 144

FURTHER READING

Religion

Burkert, W., *Structure and History in Greek Mythology and Ritual* (Berkeley 1979). Astute analysis of problems in the study of myth, with dissection of structuralist theories.

———, *Greek Religion* (German original, 1977; Oxford 1985). The standard one-volume history, useful for reference.

Buxton, R., *Oxford Readings on Greek Religion* (Oxford 2001). Collection of important papers on Greek religion, mostly from the 1980s and 1990s.

Dodds, E. R., *The Greeks and the Irrational* (Berkeley 1959). How the Greeks interpreted the irrational in their own experience. A pioneering work.

Easterling, P. E., and J. V. Muir, eds., *Greek Religion and Society* (Cambridge, UK, 1985). Chapters by leading British scholars on aspects of Greek religion.

Garland, R., *The Greek Way of Death* (Ithaca, NY, 1985). Greek attitudes and practices concerning death and the dead.

Guthrie, W. K. C., *The Greeks and Their Gods* (London 1950). Dated but useful survey of the Olympians.

Johnston, Sarah Iles, *Restless Dead: Encounters between the Living and the Dead in Ancient Greece* (Berkeley 1999). Superior study of ghost-cult.

Mikalson, J., *Athenian Popular Religion* (Chapel Hill, NC, 1983). How the person-in-the-street understood religion.

Parker, R., *Athenian Religion: A History* (Oxford 1996). Scholarly treatment of religion in our best-known city-state.

Rice, D. G., and J. E. Stambaugh, *Sources for the Study of Greek Religion,* Sources for Biblical Study 14, The Society of Biblical Literature (1977). Useful collection of ancient texts.

Zaidman, L. B., and P. S. Pantel, *Religion in the Ancient Greek City* (Cambridge, UK, 1992; tr. P. Cartledge). Accessible summary of the major issues.

Myth

Edmunds, L., ed., *Approaches to Greek Myth* (Baltimore 1990). Useful essays on the interpretation of myth, with most schools of thought represented.

Kirk, G. S., *Myth: Its Meaning and Function in Ancient and Other Cultures* (Berkeley 1970). Good on schools of interpretation.

Powell, B. B., *Classical Myth* (4th ed., New York 2004). Review of all the Greek and Roman myths, with interpretation and historical background and many illustrations.

Veyne, P., *Did the Greeks Believe in Their Myths?* (French original, 1983; Chicago 1988). Complex essay on the nature of belief.

West, M. L., *Hesiod: Theogony* (Oxford 1966). Standard edition of the Greek text, with invaluable notes and introduction.

Ecstatic and Mystery Religion

Burkert, Walter, *Ancient Mystery Cults* (Cambridge, MA, 1987). With sections on the Orphics and the Eleusinian mysteries.

Mylonas, G. E., *Eleusis and the Eleusinian Mysteries* (Princeton 1961). Best book on the topic by the excavator of the site.

Ancient Texts

Aeschylus, *The Oresteia* (Harmondsworth, UK, 1966; tr. Robert Fagles). Three tragedies performed at Athens in 458 B.C., including *The Libation Bearers.*

Hesiod, *Theogony.* In *Hesiod and Theognis* (Harmondsworth, UK, 1973; tr. Dorothea Wender). The basic poetic account of the origins of the gods, composed c. 700 B.C.

Sophocles, *The Theban Plays* (Harmondsworth, UK, 1947; tr. E. F. Watling). Three tragedies about the legendary royal family of Thebes, including *Oedipus the King.*

CHAPTER 8

ARCHAIC GREECE, 700–480 B.C.: ECONOMY, SOCIETY, POLITICS

In Chapter 6, "Homer," and Chapter 7, "Religion and Myth," we discussed the twin props of early Greek culture, Homer and religion. In this chapter, we examine the development of the *poleis* between the upheavals of the eighth century B.C. and the great wars of 480 B.C., a period historians call archaic Greece. The patterns of life that we described earlier crystallized in this era: Living standards rose, equal citizenship became the core social principle, beliefs were systematized, and an intellectual revolution began. These were years of intense and sometimes violent conflict, both between *poleis* for control of larger regions, and within *poleis* where individuals and factions among the rich struggled for power while the poor struggled against them. This chapter and the next provide a broad sketch of historical and intellectual developments in this age, although there were many local differences.

GOVERNMENT BY OLIGARCHY

The Bronze Age Greeks had great kings, the *wanakes*. Weaker kings, *basileis*, replaced *wanakes* in the Dark Age. By the eighth century B.C., Homer and Hesiod took *basileis* for granted and even called them "dear to the gods"; but they also thought that *basileis* had to conform to community values. On Ithaca, Odysseus and Telemachus had to show that they were stronger than the other noblemen, who might also claim the title *basileus*. The *basileus* often seems to be merely the leading man among a group of feuding chiefs. In the *polis* of the seventh century B.C., the *basileis* lost their power to **oligarchies,** meaning "rule of the few."

An oligarchy could be a handful of men or a council of hundreds. Rule by oligarchy sets Archaic *poleis* apart from Greece's neighbors in western Asia, where typical states were monarchies ("rule by one man"). Rich men in Greek *poleis* liked to call themselves ***agathoi,*** meaning "the good people," and to call the poor ***kakoi,*** "the bad people"; but despite this divisive language, Greek oligarchs were in fact not greatly elevated above ordinary citizens. The balance of power between *agathoi* and *kakoi* varied through time and between one *polis* and another, but in general, poor, lowborn Greeks were more assertive than poor, lowborn Egyptians or Syrians. Across the seventh and sixth centuries B.C., more and more power came into the poorer citizens' hands. Even at the beginning of the Archaic Period, the rich could face stern criticism. In Chapter 5, "The Dark Age, 1200–700 B.C.," we saw how Hesiod abused his local *basileis* when they defrauded him, calling them "eaters of bribes" and "fools." He assumed there should be hierarchy, but he also claimed the right to judge the *basileis'* performance on the basis of traditional morality. When they violated such laws, only ruin could follow:

> . . . when Justice is dragged out of the way by men
> who judge dishonestly and swallow bribes,
> a struggling sound is heard; then she returns
> back to the city and the homes of men,
> wrapped in a mist and weeping, and she brings
> harm to the crooked men who drove her out.
>   . . . Often, all the city suffers for
> their wicked schemes, and on these men, from heaven
> the son of kronus sends great punishments,
> both plague and famine, and the people die.
> Their wives are barren, and their villages
> dwindle, according to the plan of Zeus.
> At other times the son of Cronus will
> destroy their army, or will snatch away
> their city wall, or all their ships at sea.
> You *basileis,* take notice of this punishment.
> The deathless gods are never far away;
> they mark the crooked judges who grind down
> their fellow-men and do not fear the gods.

Hesiod, *Works and Days* 220–24, 240–51
(D. Wender)

As the Archaic Period wore on, ordinary citizens increasingly challenged the right of any man, no matter how rich or talented, to make decisions for the entire community. For example, a poorly preserved inscription dating around 550 B.C. from the island of Chios (see Map 8.1) mentions a *basileus,* who clearly has significant functions, but then refers to a People's Council, which has major powers of hearing appeals and inflicting fines. The inscription says little else about this council or its tasks. But by about 525 B.C., we hear about the **dêmos,** "the people," as a whole making important decisions in several *poleis.*

The three main reasons why the archaic Greek *agathoi* had relatively little power in the face of the *kakoi* were economic, military, and ideological. Let us review each in turn.

Wealth

Land and labor were the bases of wealth within Greece. If a man had plenty of land and enough workers, he could produce more agricultural goods than his family needed, then exchange the excess for goods that they desired but could not or

Map 8.1   Sites mentioned in this chapter.

would not produce themselves. Such exchanges might be over short distances, giving food to blacksmiths or carpenters in return for specialized products, or might involve shipping produce across the Mediterranean in search of profitable outlets. Herodotus tells the story of a merchant blown off course by severe winds around 600 B.C. Arriving on the Atlantic coast of Spain, he found eager buyers at windfall profits for the exotic Greek goods he carried.

Of course, opportunities for amassing wealth varied according to local conditions. For example, the island of Thasos was suited to growing wine grapes. Families that planted more vines than they needed for domestic consumption could ship their surplus to places less favored for viticulture or could sell their grapes to specialist traders. By 600 B.C., large pots called amphoras used to ship wine and olive oil turn up far from their centers of manufacture. Most *poleis* had iron ore in their territory, but many lacked good timber or building stone. Only a lucky few, like Athens and Thasos, had silver. The need to move goods and materials offered opportunities to those who could sail ships and stomach the risks that came with trade across the high seas.

We can get a rough idea of how rich archaic aristocrats were. At the end of the Archaic Period, in 480 B.C., an Athenian named Kleinias equipped a warship at his own expense. This meant paying to build the ship, fit out the rigging, and support 180 to 200 men for a campaign of three to six months. In Athenian money, this cost between five and eight silver **talents,** a very large sum (enough to feed a village of a hundred people for a year). Herodotus, who told the story, regarded the outlay as spectacular, but he also knew that Kleinias was not the richest man in archaic Greece. Probably dozens of Greeks in Sicily could have outspent him. Sicily had better rainfall than Athens, and more arable land. The ruling class of Akragas in Sicily

Figure 8.1 Temple ruins at Akragas in Sicily, sixth century B.C. The Akragantines built seven enormous temples along a ridge. Today, many Greek temples in Sicily are better preserved than those in the Aegean.

grew rich from selling olive oil and wine to Carthage, the great Phoenician trading colony on the north coast of Africa in what is now Tunisia. Between 550 and 450 B.C., they built the most spectacular series of temples ever raised by Greeks (Figure 8.1).

Yet the richest Sicilian Greeks remained poor by comparison, for example, with even the minor nobility of the Persian Empire. Herodotus says that in the same year that Kleinias so impressed the Athenians by paying for a warship from his own pocket, the richest private individual in the Persian Empire offered to give the Persian king eighteen thousand silver talents—well over a million pounds of silver! The Persian king rewarded his favorites by giving them vast estates and the revenues of entire cities, dwarfing what was possible in Greece.

Greek communities were poorer than those in the Near East. There were no great mansions or imposing tombs. By 600 B.C., most new houses had three or four rooms around a small courtyard. Most tombs were individual burials without elaborate markers and with just a few pots as grave goods. The only real wealth found in archaeological investigations comes from sanctuaries. Some Greek temples were awe-inspiring (see Chapter 9, "The Archaic Cultural Revolution, 700–480 B.C."), and offerings to the gods included small amounts of gold and silver jewelry, and larger amounts of bronze armor, vessels, and ornaments. Most *poleis* had one or two grand sanctuaries with stone temples that received the finest offerings, and dozens of smaller shrines where local people dedicated pottery. The relatively narrow gap between rich and poor in archaic Greece is one reason why Greek aristocrats were weaker than those in many other ancient societies.

War

The second reason why archaic Greek aristocrats were relatively weak was military. The Greeks developed a peculiar way to fight, devastatingly effective in the right conditions but leaving little scope for aristocrats as heroic leaders. Tyrtaeus (tir-**tē**-us), a seventh-century B.C. poet from Sparta, described Greek tactics:

> Let a man take up a wide stance and stand up strongly against the foe,
> digging both heels in the ground, biting his lip with his teeth,
> covering thighs and legs beneath, his chest and his shoulders
> under the hollowed-out protection of his broad shield,
> while in his right hand he brandishes the powerful war-spear,
> and shakes terribly the crest above his helm.
> Our man should be disciplined in the work of the heavy fighter,
> and not stand out from the missiles when he carries a shield,
> but go right up and fight at close quarters and, with his long spear
> or short sword, thrust home and strike his enemy down.
> Let him fight toe to toe and shield against shield hard driven,
> crest against crest and helmet on helmet, chest against chest;
> let him close hard and fight it out with his opposite foeman,
> holding tight to the hilt of his sword, or to his long spear.

Tyrtaeus fragment 11, lines 21–30
(R. Lattimore)

The mainstay of archaic Greek armies was the heavy infantryman, or **hoplite** (**hop**-līt, from *hoplon,* "shield"). He normally wore fifty to seventy pounds of bronze armor—greaves on his shins, a solid breastplate, an enclosed helmet with horsehair crest, and a wooden shield faced with metal—and carried a spear six to eight feet long (Figure 8.2). Infantrymen in most countries surrounding Greece carried small shields of wicker or leather. Holding a single handle in the middle of the shield, soldiers could manipulate it to parry blows, but could not stop strong spear thrusts.

By contrast, the hoplite's round shield, about three feet across, was made of hardwood covered in bronze and could block all but the fiercest blows. It weighed about sixteen pounds, and short, poorly nourished ancient Greeks could not have held it up by a single, central handle for long. It therefore had two handles: one on the rim, gripped by the hand, and the second a broad strap in the center through which the forearm passed (Figure 8.3).

The ingenious invention created a new problem: Held this way, a shield covered only the left side of the fighter's body. Hence, hoplites massed shoulder-to-shoulder in a **phalanx,** a dense formation six or eight ranks deep, so that each hoplite shielded the right (unprotected) side of the man standing to his left. Only the man on the far right of each line remained exposed: a position of great honor. So long as it maintained formation, the hoplite phalanx presented the enemy with an unbroken wall of bronze shields many ranks deep and a forest of deadly spear tips, an overwhelming and catastrophic force, as the Persians were to learn.

To maintain formation, a phalanx had to move slowly and deliberately, and tended to creep crablike to the right as each man sought to stay well protected by the shield of his neighbor. Unlike Egyptian or Persian infantry, fighters trained together regularly, but even so, the phalanx could lose order on broken ground, leaving the hoplites vulnerable to lightly armed but more maneuverable troops

Figure 8.2 Bronze statuette of a hoplite; from Corinth, circa 500 B.C., height 8 inches.

Figure 8.3 Hoplite phalanxes clash to the music of a flute player on a Protocorinthian wine jug, the "Chigi Vase," around 650 B.C. Height 4 inches. Notice the round shield with central strap and rim strap on the central figures.

who would skirt their flanks. Herodotus has a Persian general make fun of hoplite warfare, saying:

> From what I hear, the Greeks are pugnacious enough, and start fights on the spur of the moment without sense or judgment to justify them. When they declare war on each other, they go off together to the smoothest and most level bit of ground they can find, and have their battle on it—with the result that even the victors never get off without heavy losses, and as for the losers—well, they're wiped out.
>
> Herodotus 7.9 (A. de Selincourt)

Hoplites almost never stormed fortifications or fought in hills, but met on flat ground, as if war were a sporting event. The two phalanxes advanced deliberately to within two hundred yards of each other, raised a chant, then waited to see if the enemy lost his nerve. Homer describes men waiting to launch an ambush from hiding, but his words probably apply just as well to the tense moments before a hoplite battle:

> The skin of the coward changes color all the time,
> he can't get a grip on himself, he can't sit still,
> he squats and rocks, shifting his weight from foot to foot,
> his heart racing, pounding inside the fellow's ribs,
> his teeth chattering—he dreads some grisly death.
>
> Homer, *Iliad* 13.279–83 (R. Fagles)

If neither phalanx lost its nerve, they advanced again, now running, trying to keep order. They charged the last few yards, smashing head-on, the front ranks shoved forward by the mass of men behind, lunging with their spears just before the bloody collision. Most spear points would skid off the protective bronze, but some bit home over or under the wall of shields, finding exposed throats and groins. Bronze clashed on bronze; spears shattered into splinters, or their points were driven into the enemy's heavy armor. A hoplite battle was a gigantic, deadly scrimmage. According to one Athenian, in the main phase of battle, "throwing up their shields, they tuck their left shoulders inside them, and deliberately pushing, they fight, they kill, they die." When their spears fell useless in the crush of bodies, the men at the front drew short swords and daggers and hacked away, kicking, choking, and punching. The fighters could not see or hear much inside their closed helmets. Their bodies ran with sweat as they fought for their lives, their blood rising in an orgy of killing.

There was no way to direct this kind of fighting. Only discipline, strength, and courage counted. The initial spear-thrust before the actual collision opened gaps in both front lines into which the leading hoplites pushed. If they kept their heads and their order, they could widen these breaches, pushing over the fallen bodies, deeper into the opposing mass. After a few moments or many minutes, one side would start to give way. The men in the front ranks, packed together, could not run away; decisive panics began in the rear as men in the fifth or sixth rank suddenly confronted a murderous, raging enemy. In an instant, the phalanx could dissolve into a hysterical mob as men broke from the back and fled. Any who stood their ground were bowled over by the weight of the surging and now victorious enemy. The battle was over and the slaughter began, as the Spartan poet Tyrtaeus explains:

> Those who, standing their ground and closing their ranks together,
> endure the onset at close quarters and fight in the front,
> they lose fewer men. They also protect the army behind them.

Once they flinch, the spirit of the whole army falls apart.
And no man could count over and tell all the number of evils,
all that can come to a man, once he gives way to disgrace.
For once a man reverses and runs in the terror of battle,
he offers his back, a tempting mark to spear from behind,
and it is a shameful sight when a dead man lies in the dust there,
driven through from behind by the stroke of an enemy spear.

Tyrtaeus, fragment 11.11–20 (R. Lattimore)

In this final phase, the rear ranks of the victorious phalanx leaped past their exhausted colleagues, stabbing at exposed backs as their shattered foes threw away their heavy shields and ran for their lives. According to an old saying, a Spartan mother handed her son his shield before campaign, telling him to come back "with this, or upon it"—victorious or a corpse.

Some think this style of warfare evolved gradually across the ninth, eighth, and seventh centuries B.C., whereas others suggest that hoplite armor was invented around 650 B.C. when an older, aristocratic style of war abruptly became obsolete. In any event, the new tactics depended on rising standards of living, because each hoplite bought his own expensive armor. By about 600 B.C., probably a quarter or a third of the citizens of a typical *polis* could afford their own armor. In the eighth century B.C., the few wealthy men with bronze armor had significant advantages over poorer fighters, but in the seventh and sixth centuries, they lost these advantages. In the phalanx, aristocrats and better-off small holders fought and died side by side. Archaic Greek aristocrats could not define themselves against the mass of citizens in either economic or military terms. If Greek aristocrats had had enough wealth to equip an effective cavalry, they might have become an elite of military virtuosos, like Japanese samurai or medieval European knights. Or, if they had armed bands of hoplites at their own expense, they might have dominated archaic warfare, but they could not afford it. They could not claim that the community depended on them for survival.

Ideology

The most important reason for the relative weakness of archaic Greek aristocrats, however, was ideological. No ruling class—no matter how rich or how necessary in war—can maintain power by coercion alone. Even totalitarian regimes prefer propaganda to compulsion because the costs of forcing everyone to do what he or she is told, all the time, are just too high. As we saw in Chapter 4, "The Greeks before History, 12,000–1200," in the Bronze Age, Near Eastern rulers justified their power by claiming special ties to the gods, but in archaic Greece, such claims were not persuasive. The poet Sappho, writing around 600 B.C., imagined herself and her friends communing with the gods, sharing golden cups brimming with wine, and dining at the same glittering tables. She and other poets claimed to be equals of the great kings of the East. But for every Greek poet who asserted special connections to the gods, another rejected such pretensions. Eastern luxury and divine honors were both unattainable and undesirable. In the Near East and Egypt, normally only a few religious specialists, drawn from powerful families, could perform sacrifices. In Greece, by contrast, anyone could do so. When Herodotus visited Persia, he was amazed to discover that no sacrifices could take place unless a religious professional called a Magus presided.

Economics, war, and ideology reinforced each other. Had Greek aristocrats been as rich as the rulers of Babylon, they might have convinced ordinary citizens of their close relationship with divinity, through displays of pomp and glory. Or had a warrior elite been able to slice through enemy phalanxes, they might have seemed godlike. Conversely, if an elite had controlled access to the gods, they might have been able to establish claims to more resources; and perhaps few would have dared stand against them in battle.

Although the richest men did run politics during the Archaic Period, their grip was weak. Some claimed the right to rule because they were godlike, but most *agathoi* merely claimed to have superior moral qualities, moderation, and wisdom. They deserved privilege, including control of politics, because their talents exemplified a middle way in life. By 500 B.C., ordinary citizens in several *poleis* had rolled back even this limited elite domination of politics and moved toward male democracy, but aristocrats nonetheless tried to maintain cultural forms that set them apart from the masses. In the next section, we examine the most important of these.

ELITE CULTURE

Drinking

The upper-class authors of the surviving literature rarely refer to public bars, but curse tablets make it sound as if there was one on every corner. For example,

> I bind Callias the barman and his wife Thraitta, and the bar of the bald man, and Anthemion's bar near [. . .][15] and Philo the barman. Of all these I bind their soul, their trade, their hands and feet, their bars . . . and also the barman Agathon, servant of Sosimenes . . . I bind Mania the barmaid at the spring, and the bar of Aristander of Eleusis.
>
> Cited in Davidson, *Courtesans and Fishcakes*, p. 55

All kinds of people (free and slave, male and female, rich and poor, young and old) frequented bars, though we know little about them. Patrons could buy wine in bulk to take home or in smaller measures to drink on the premises. Some bars were probably very pleasant: The one excavated building likely to have been a bar, from fourth-century-B.C. Athens, was spacious and contained fragments of wine amphoras from all over Greece. Even the highbrow philosopher Plato mentions one fourth-century barman's reputation for skill with wines.

But *agathoi* preferred private parties called symposia (sim-**pōz**-i-a, "drinking together"; singular form, **symposium**). A normal party included nine men. The host sent out invitations on wax tablets. The conventional starting time was after sunset, and the party could continue till dawn. They gathered in a room called an ***andrôn*** ("men's room") in a house or sometimes rented a room (often from a sanctuary). The symposiasts lay on couches placed against the walls around a central altar (a seating custom copied from the Near East) and ate dinner from tables set up by each couch. Then the drinking began.

The symposium had elaborate rules. The party chose a toastmaster by rolling dice. He made two key decisions: what ratio of wine to water to use and how many cups each guest should drink. Greeks thought that drinking neat (unmixed) wine drove men mad, and given the length of a symposium and the variable quality of wines, mixing one or two parts of water to each part of wine was no doubt a good plan. The rule about how many cups to drink was meant to keep all the guests roughly equally sober. The toastmaster then announced a libation, an offering to the gods, by pouring a small amount of wine onto the ground. Every act of drinking—even solitary drinking under a shady tree in the heat of summer, according to Hesiod—began with a libation.

There could be entertainers, including musicians, dancers, acrobats, and clowns. Cities even passed laws about what entertainers should be paid and how long their shifts should be. Earlier we saw examples of sexual behavior in the Greek symposium, and written sources confirm that sexual activity—whether between guests and prostitutes or between male drinkers and younger boys who served wine—was common (Figure 8.4).

If the symposium lasted all night, the participants could become very drunk. According to one Athenian comic poet,

> The first cup is to health, the second to love and pleasure, the third to sleep, the fourth to violence, the fifth to uproar, the sixth to drunken revel, the seventh to black eyes, the eighth to the lawyer, the ninth to bile, and the tenth to madness and throwing chairs around.
>
> Euboulos (cited in Garland, *Daily Life,* p. 101)

Parties could end with the revelers wandering the streets, starting fights, and generally raising hell. Yet symposium culture was part of aristocratic identity, and

Figure 8.4 The symposium ("drinking party"). On an early-fifth-century B.C. Athenian vase, a naked *hetaira* entertains the male diners on a double flute. On the far right, a diner plays a game called *kottabos;* the drinker twirls a large, shallow drinking cup called a *kylix* on his forefinger, then flings the dregs of the wine across the room to knock down a small statuette, usually of a satyr. The diner to his left reaches for the *hetaira,* while on the far left, two elderly men are deep in their cups; one holds two *kylikes.*

severe stigma attached to those who did not know how to act at symposia—and to
those who did not drink in symposia at all. A poet named **Theognis** (thē-**og**-nis), who
probably lived in Megara (between Athens and Corinth) in the sixth century B.C.,
describes how to be a good toastmaster:

> Don't hold the unwilling guest, Simonides,
> but don't expel the friend who wants to stay.
> Don't rouse your drunken comrade whom sweet sleep
> has caught, but let the wakeful stay awake.
> All force is disagreeable. Stand by
> ready to pour for those who want to drink—
> we cannot have a party every night.
> Still, because I am moderate in my use
> of honeyed wine, I reach my house before
> I think of soothing sleep, and I make clear
> how fine a beverage for man is wine.
> I'm no teetotaler, but not a lush.
> The man who drinks too much cannot control
> his tongue or mind. He rambles foolishly
> embarrassing his sober friends. He's not
> ashamed of his behavior when he's drunk.
> Even though he was sensible before,
> now he's an ass. But you, who know all this,
> don't overdo your drinking. Quietly
> get up and go before you're drunk, or if
> you'd stay, then have no more to drink—don't let
> your belly master you as if you were
> a common laborer. That stupid word
> "Pour!" that you're always babbling has made
> you drunk. First, you drink to a friend,
> then, for a bet. Another's for the gods;
> the next, because—it's in your hand, you can't
> say no. The winner of a drinking bout
> really is one who drinks and still does not
> talk stupidly. All who stay beside
> the mixing-bowl, try to converse as well
> as possible. Let no hostility
> intrude; let your remarks be general,
> and you will have a fine symposium.
>
> Theognis 467–96 (D. Wender)

The man who could not hold his liquor in a symposium was no better than a
laborer, the antithesis of the aristocrat. Theognis was terrified that lower class behavior was infecting the ranks of those who set themselves apart by their cultivated
moderation. As Theognis saw it, the world was going wrong because everything was
now for sale. Men who lacked good birth, manners, and taste were gaining control:

> These things I tell you, Kyrnos, for your good.
> I learned them, as a boy, from gentlemen.
> Rule one: no honor, prize, or cash reward
> can justify a base or crooked act.
> The second rule: avoid "low" company,
> mix only with the better sort of men.
> Drink with these men, and eat, and sit with them,

and court them, for their power is great. From them
you will learn goodness. Men of little worth
will spoil the natural quality of your birth.
Do this and you'll acknowledge, in the end,
Theognis gave good counsel to his friend.

Theognis 27–38 (D. Wender)

A proper aristocrat conversed intelligently about politics, love, the gods, and other elevated topics, and did not act like a buffoon. Theognis was eager to suggest that his rivals lacked character and dignity.

Of course, anyone could claim that when he drank at home with friends, they were having a "symposium"; perhaps this is why rules proliferated, so that men like Theognis could set themselves above not only poor laborers but also hard drinkers who lacked moderation. In the fifth and fourth centuries B.C., Athenians often suspected that symposia were hotbeds of aristocratic plotting against democracy—and with good reason.

Athletics

Another major way some archaic Greeks tried to set themselves above others was through athletics. Many societies have some kind of sports, but archaic Greeks developed them in unusual ways. Watching athletics was entertaining, and taking part was exhilarating, but archaic Greek athletics also had important social functions. They defined who the Greeks were. Only Greeks could enter the greatest athletic competition, the games held at **Olympia** every fourth year. The judges were forced to make decisions about what it meant to be Greek. Athletics also defined a class of special Greek men: Only those with wealth and leisure could spend enough time training to stand a chance in the top games. Finally, athletics created a hierarchy within this class of gifted athletes: Only a few could win.

Athletics were important in Homer's vision of the heroic age, but they were informal. The funeral of the hero Patroclus in the *Iliad* involved boxing, wrestling, archery, javelin-throwing, and foot, horse, and chariot races so contentious that the competitors almost came to blows. On his long journey home from Troy, Odysseus was entertained after dinner on the island of Phaeacia with similar games, and when he declined to take part, one of the locals insulted him, saying he was not of the proper class. When Odysseus finally got home, he was pressed into an impromptu boxing match while disguised as a beggar.

Archaic aristocrats formalized the rules of athletics. A fourth-century B.C. scholar calculated that proper competitions began at Olympia in 776 B.C. At first, competitors came from near Olympia, but by the seventh century B.C., there were entrants from all over Greece. During the games, a sacred truce suspended all warfare. The Greeks took this so seriously that in 480 B.C., as a Persian army pushed its way into central Greece, several *poleis* refused to fight until the Olympic truce was over. In the sixth century B.C., other **Panhellenic games** ("all-Greek" games) sprang up at Delphi (where Apollo had his shrine), Isthmia (near Corinth), and Nemea (near the ruins of Bronze Age Mycenae), making a circuit, with at least one major festival every summer. Most cities had their own official games, and there were huge numbers of informal competitions.

Figure 8.5 Two naked athletes fight the *pankration* from a red-figure Athenian pot, circa 450 B.C.

Any Greek man could enter an athletic contest, and there were even a few events for unmarried girls (though women were not allowed near the Olympic games). We do not know what proportion of Archaic Greeks trained for athletics, but **gymnasia** ("naked places," so called because Greek men exercised naked) were common, and standards were very high. The story of Arrachion, who won the *pankration* ("all-in wrestling") at Olympia in 564 B.C., illustrates how far competitors would go (Figure 8.5).[16] The only rules in the *pankration* were no biting and no gouging out eyes (Spartans thought these rules too restrictive, and allowed everything except strangulation). The story runs that Arrachion's opponent caught him in a brutal hold, wrapping his legs around Arrachion's waist and crushing him while choking him with his hands. Arrachion started losing consciousness but managed to grab one of his opponent's toes. He wrenched the toe out of its socket and twisted it around. Arrachion was suffocating, but the agony of a dislocated toe proved too much for the opponent, who raised his hand in submission. The judges rushed over to award Arrachion the victory, only to find that he had died in his moment of triumph. The spectators were astonished at his bravery and determination; he became a folk hero, honored by paintings and statues still on display a thousand years later.

Another sixth-century athlete, Milo from Croton in Italy, won the olive crown for wrestling six times at Olympia, six times at Delphi, ten times at Isthmia, and nine times at Nemea. Milo was famous for eating vast quantities of meat. According to Pausanias, a Roman tourist of the second century A.D. who saw Milo's statue at Olympia seven hundred years after his death, Milo could snap a cord tied round his head simply by holding his breath to make the veins on his head bulge; and no man was strong enough to bend back even Milo's little finger.

Arrachion and Milo were exceptional, but they had many rivals. Serious athletes spent hours each day at the gymnasium with professional coaches, and even ordinary men dropped in regularly. The fascination with athletics turned gymnasia into social centers where older men talked in the shade and philosophers wrangled. But at the heart of them was competition between young men and a growing cult of the male body. Not surprisingly, pederasty was closely linked to athletic training:

> Happy the lover who exercises, then
> goes home to sleep all day with a handsome boy.
>
> Theognis lines 1335–36 (D. Wender)

According to legend, athletes competed naked (an alarming prospect for wrestlers and *pankratists*) because a man once lost an Olympic footrace when his loincloth fell off and he tripped. Whatever the truth, nakedness allowed men to assess each other's bodies, and many Greeks—though short and unhealthy by our standards—were in peak physical condition. Some people's admiration went to extraordinary lengths. After training, athletes rubbed themselves down with olive oil, then scraped off the mixture of oil, sweat, and dirt. Some believed that this residue contained the athlete's inner strength; some even ate it, to share this almost godlike power. Women adored athletic victors, as the early-fifth-century-B.C. poet **Pindar** (c. 522–c. 438 B.C.) reports about Telesicrates, winner of the race in armor at Delphi in 474 B.C.:

> Often, too, you have won
> at the returning mysteries of Pallas:°
> while maidens watched, and in silence each one wished
> you, Telesicrates,
> were her dearest husband, or her son;
> and at Olympia, and at the games
> of deep-bosomed Earth,°
> yes all the games of your country.
>
> Pindar, *Pythian Ode* 9.97–103 (C.M. Bowra)

°*Pallas:* At Athens, at the Panathenaic games. °*deep-bosomed Earth:* At Delphi, where Earth was said to have been worshiped before Apollo came.

Poleis voted public honors for athletic champions, including free meals, pensions, and statues. The oracle at Delphi ordered that some athletes should receive cult honors as *heroes* after their deaths. By 500 B.C., professional poets, including Pindar, specialized in victory hymns, charging enormous sums to immortalize athletes' fame. These victory odes tell us a lot about the values aristocrats linked to athletic prowess. The odes were publicly performed to music, with large choruses dancing intricate steps, and enjoyed by popular audiences. In one ode, Pindar contrasts the winner of the wrestling contest at Delphi to his defeated rivals:

> And now four times you came down with bodies beneath you,
> (You meant them harm),
> To whom the Pythian feast° has given
> No glad home-coming like yours.
> They, when they meet their mothers,
>
> °*Pythian feast:* The games at Delphi.

Have no sweet laughter around them moving delight.
In back streets out of their enemies' way,
They cower; disaster has bitten them.

Pindar, Pythian Ode 8.82–87 (C.M. Bowra)

Pindar and other professional ode-writers offered a service to those who could afford it. Great athletes' easy claim to godlike qualities aroused hostility and suspicion, so the poets explained that success was genetic and belonged to the victor's whole clan, going back to the heroic age. Pindar insisted that the entire city could take pride in its aristocrats' athletic triumphs. Victors were among the most famous men of their age. Their glory often earned them a special voice in the city, although they could face criticism for arrogance.

Intermarriage

The archaic elite also tried to mark itself off through selective breeding. Theognis was horrified that the elite of culture and taste (he and his friends) was being degraded by boorish behavior and that money mattered more even than a good bloodline:

You want to buy an ass? A horse?
You'll pick a thoroughbred, of course,
for quality is in the blood.
But when a *man* goes out to stud—
he won't refuse a commoner
if lots of money goes with her.
And vulgar oafs with brutish ways
can marry nobler girls, these days.
Good faith means nothing now, it's clear,
hard cash is all that's honored here,
while genteel blood unites with base—
the drachma's ruining our race.
You wonder, boy, that I disparage
the present state of civil marriage?

Theognis 183–92 (D. Wender)

Aristocrats of all ages have tried to restrict marriage to those they think meet their own standards of breeding. In the following example, set in the 560s B.C., expectations about refinement, athletic prowess, bloodlines, and marriage flow together:

Cleisthenes [**klī**-sthen-ēz],° the son of Aristonymos, grandson of Myron and great-grandson of Andreas, had a daughter, Agaristê [ag-a-**ris**-tē], whom he wished to marry to the best man in all Greece. So during the Olympic games, in which he had himself won the chariot race, he had a public announcement made to the effect that any Greek who thought himself good enough to become Cleisthenes' son-in-law should present himself at Sicyon within sixty days—or sooner if he wished—because he intended, within the year following the sixtieth day, to betroth his daughter to her future husband [see Map 8.2]. Cleisthenes had had a race-track and wrestling-ring specially made for this purpose, and presently the suitors began to arrive—every man of Greek nationality who had something to be proud of either in his country or in himself. From Sybaris in Italy, then at the height of its prosperity, came Smindyrides the son of Hippocrates, a man noted above all others for delicate and luxurious living, and from Siris, also in Italy, came Damasos the son of Amyris who was nicknamed

° *Cleisthenes:* Sole ruler, or tyrant, of the small *polis* of Sicyon near Corinth.

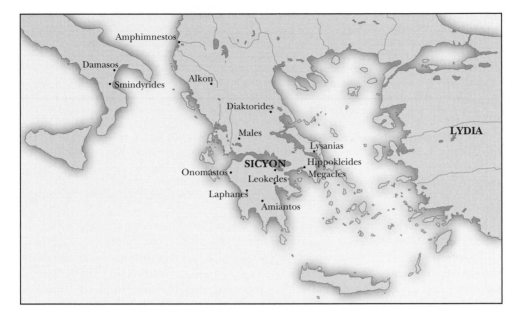

Map 8.2   The intercity aristocracy: origins of the suitors for Agaristê's hand.

the Wise. Then there was Amphimnestos, the son of Epistrophos, from Epidamnus on the Ionian Gulf, and Malês from Aetolia—Malês, the brother of Titormos who was the strongest man in Greece and went to live in the remotest part of Aetolia to avoid living with other human beings. From the Peloponnese came Leokedes the son of Pheidon. . . . Next there was Amiantos, the son of Lycurgus, from Trapezos in Arcadia, and Laphanes, an Azanian from Paios, whose father Euphorion, the story goes, received Castor and Pollux under his own roof and afterward kept open house for all comers; and then Onomastos of Elis, the son of Agaios. From Athens there were two: Megacles, whose father Alcmaeon visited the court of Croesus, and Tisander's son Hippocleides, the wealthiest and best-looking man in Athens. Euboea provided but a single suitor, Lysanias from Eretria, which at that time was at the height of its prosperity; then there was a Thessalian, Diaktorides, one of the Skopadai, from Krannon, and, lastly, Alkon from Molossia. This was the list of suitors.

Cleisthenes began by asking each in turn to name his country and his parentage; then he kept them in his house for a year, to get to know them well, entering into conversation with them sometimes singly, sometimes all together, and testing each of them for his manly qualities and temper, education, and manners. Those who were young he would take to the gymnasia—but the most important test of all was their behavior at the dinner-table. All this went on throughout their stay in Sicyon, and all the time he entertained them handsomely.

For one reason or another it was the two Athenians who impressed Cleisthenes most favorably, and of the two Tisander's son Hippocleides came to be preferred, not only for his manly virtues but also because he was related some generations back to the family of Cypselus of Corinth.°

At last the day came that had been fixed for the betrothal, and Cleisthenes had to declare his choice. He marked the day by the sacrifice of a hundred oxen, and then gave a great banquet, to which not only the suitors but everyone of note in Sicyon was invited. When dinner was over, the suitors began to compete with each other in music and in talking in company. In both these accomplishments it was Hippocleides who easily

°*Cypelus of Corinth:* Member of another family of tyrants, whom we discuss in the next section.

proved his superiority to the rest, until at last, as more and more wine was drunk, he asked the flute-player to play him a tune and began to dance to it. Now it may well be that he danced to his own satisfaction. Cleisthenes, however, who was watching the performance, began to have serious doubts about the whole business. Presently, after a brief pause, Hippocleides sent for a table.

The table was brought and Hippocleides, climbing on it, danced first some Spartan dances, next some Athenian ones, and ended by standing on his head and beating time with his legs in the air. The Spartan and Athenian dances were bad enough, but Cleisthenes, though he already loathed the thought of having a son-in-law like that, nevertheless restrained himself and managed to avoid an outburst. But when he saw Hippocleides beating time with his legs, he could bear it no longer. "Son of Tisander," he cried, "you have danced away your marriage." "Hippocleides doesn't care," came the reply. Hence the common saying, "Hippocleides doesn't care."

Herodotus 6.126–30 (A. de Selincourt)

Cleisthenes wanted to create an aristocracy of wealth, culture, sophistication, beauty, education, and athletic prowess that cross-cut the boundaries of individual city-states and stood above the mass of ordinary citizens. But the citizens understood the threat. By the fifth century B.C., several *poleis* passed laws denying citizenship to boys who had only one locally born citizen parent, thus blocking inter-*polis* dynastic loyalties. Wealthy Athenian families still could marry into other wealthy Athenian families, but if they made marriage ties with men like Cleisthenes of Sicyon, they would pay a price. Symposia, athletics, and intermarriage did open gaps between aristocrats and the nonaristocrats, but these gaps were narrow, weaker than the chasm between rulers and ruled in the Near East.

THE TYRANTS

Aristocrats channeled much of their rivalry into athletics, but such activities were sideshows to the real struggle: for political power. We described in Chapter 5 how increasing competition between communities in the eighth century B.C. encouraged ever-better organization and the creation of centralized institutions. As the classical state came into being, the more there was to gain from controlling public offices.

The story of Agamemnon and Achilles in the *Iliad* suggests that from early on Greeks were aware how damaging feuds between aristocrats could be. Some of the oldest surviving public inscriptions deal with preventing the pursuit of power from descending into violent conflict. A difficult inscription from Dreros on Crete, our very earliest Greek legal document, dating between 650 and 600 B.C., says,

> May the gods be kind. This has been decided by the *polis:* when a man has been *kosmos,* for ten years that same man shall not be *kosmos.* If he should become *kosmos,* whatever judgments he gives, he himself shall owe double, and he shall be useless as long as he lives, and what he does as *kosmos* shall be nothing. The swearers to this shall be the *kosmos,* the *dêmioi,* and the Twenty of the City.
>
> R. Meiggs and D. Lewis, *Greek Historica Inscription* (Oxford 1969), no. 2.

The *kosmos* seems to be the top official in seventh-century-B.C. Dreros, and other officials—the *dêmioi,* "men of the people," and the Twenty of the City—agree to restrict everyone to a single term as *kosmos* each decade. The agreement is the kind of law we ourselves are familiar with: It commits people to agreed limits. If one prominent man tries to hold on to power, the others agree not to cooperate. So long as everyone plays by the rules, no one can seize power. Most early Greek laws take this form, being more about procedure than substance.

Most aristocrats did play by the rules, but a few were ruthless enough and strong enough to ignore what others in the city thought. This became a core political problem in seventh- and sixth-century Greece. Setting themselves up as sole rulers, scorning agreements, these strong men were called *tyrannoi* (singular, *tyrannos*), from which our word **tyrant** derives.

One way to become a tyrant, in a world largely lacking standing armies or police, was to gather an armed force and bully other aristocrats into cooperating. It helped to have popular support, so aspiring tyrants often claimed to be defending the interests of ordinary citizens against other aristocrats. Theognis describes such a situation, seeing it (as always) through the eyes of the old aristocracy:

> Gentlemen never yet destroyed a town,
> but when the scum resort to violence,
> seduce the masses and corrupt the courts
> to line their pockets and increase their power,
> then, Kyrnos, you may know this tranquil town
> cannot remain unshaken very long.
> When wicked men rejoice in private graft
> the public evils follow. Factions rise,
> then a bloody civil war, until the state
> welcomes a tyrant. God save us from that fate!
>
> Theognis 43–52 (D. Wender)

Ruthless men found ingenious ways to raise armed forces. Several faked attacks on themselves and so persuaded their colleagues to authorize bodyguards, who then staged a coup. Others hired mercenaries. In one story, the aristocratic council running Akragas wanted to build a new temple. Following standard procedure, it raised funds, then offered them to whoever would build the temple to its specifications for the lowest cost. The winner of the auction took Akragas' money, used it to hire mercenaries, and seized the city. Yet another method was to marry into an established tyrant's family, then get him to back a coup.

Thucydides tells of a failed coup in Athens in 632 B.C.:

> In former times there was an Athenian called Cylon [sī-lon], a victor in the Olympic Games, belonging to a noble family, and a powerful man himself. He had married the daughter of Theagenes, a Megarian, who at that time was tyrant of Megara. Cylon went to Delphi to consult the god, and the reply he received was that he was to seize the Acropolis of Athens during the Great Festival of Zeus. Theagenes gave him some troops and, summoning his own friends to join him, when the time came for the Olympic festival in the Peloponnese, he seized the Acropolis with the intention of making himself tyrant. . . . However, when the Athenians discovered what had happened they all came in from the countryside in full force to resist Cylon's party and surrounded and blockaded them on the Acropolis . . . the besieged party of Cylon and his supporters were suffering badly from lack of food and water. Cylon and his brother managed to escape, but the rest, who were now in great straits, some of them actually dying from hunger, took their places as suppliants in front of the altar on the Acropolis. When they saw that they were dying in the temple, the Athenians who had been set there on guard persuaded them to leave their position on the understanding that they would not be harmed, took them out, and put them to death. They also killed some of them who, on the way past, took refuge at the altars of the Dread Goddesses [the Furies].
>
> Thucydides 1.126 (R. Warner)

But even if Cylon had succeeded, his problems would be only beginning. It was one thing to gather an armed gang and proclaim yourself sole ruler (no one ever called himself "tyrant," a term of abuse); it was another to maintain this position. Herodotus tells how Periander, tyrant of Corinth, sent an ambassador to Thrasyboulos, tyrant of Miletus, asking him how to maintain power:

> Thrasyboulos invited the ambassador to walk with him from the city to a field where wheat was growing. As he passed through this wheat field, continually asking questions about why the messenger had come from Corinth, he kept cutting off all the tallest ears of wheat that he could see, and throwing them away, until the finest and best-grown part of the crop was ruined. In this way he went right through the field, and then sent the messenger away without a word. On his return to Corinth, Periander was eager to hear what advice Thrasyboulos had given, and the man replied that he had not given any at all, adding that he was surprised at being sent to visit such a person, who was evidently mad and a wanton destroyer of his own property—and then he described what he had seen Thrasyboulos do. Periander understood at once. It was perfectly plain that Thrasyboulos recommended the murder of all the people in the city who were outstanding in ability or influence.
>
> Herodotus 5.92 (A. de Selincourt)

A different strategy was to cut deals with the top men, giving them government offices and sharing with them control of the state. Holding onto power required a delicate mixture of diplomacy and brutality, and most tyrannies fell after one or two generations. The men who founded them were ruthless, bold, and talented, but few of their sons and grandsons were so skillful. Power went to their heads. Our sources emphasize sexual scandals: tyrants forced themselves on the wives, daughters, and sons of prominent men, who formed alliances against them and sooner or later expelled or destroyed them.

Thucydides summed up the impact of tyranny on Greece:

> In the Hellenic states that were governed by tyrants, the tyrant's first thought was always for himself, for his own personal safety, and for the greatness of his own family. Consequently security was the chief political principle in these governments, and no great action ever came out of them—nothing, in fact, that went beyond their own immediate local interests, except for the tyrants in Sicily, who rose to great power.
>
> Thucydides 1.17 (R. Warner)

After 500 B.C., tyranny largely disappeared from Aegean Greece. Sparta opposed tyrants on principle, sometimes sending armies to help dissidents overthrow them. Feuding aristocrats learned to handle disputes without creating opportunities for someone to seize power. Athens even created an institution called **ostracism,** a kind of annual unpopularity contest in which the citizens exiled for ten years any man who looked like he might make himself tyrant (see Chapter 10, "A Tale of Two Archaic Cities: Sparta and Athens, 700–480 B.C.").

Thucydides singles out Sicily as the exception to his rule that tyrants performed no great deeds. Tyrants appeared in Sicily around 580 B.C. and were most common between about 490 and 465 B.C., just as they were disappearing in the Aegean. They returned in force around 400 B.C. We have noted several times in this chapter that the Sicilian *poleis* had many economic and sociological differences from the Aegean world, and we have more to say about Sicilian tyrants in later chapters.

THE STRUCTURE OF ARCHAIC STATES

If Archaic Greek aristocrats were relatively weak as a social class, so too were the institutions of the states they controlled. We are used to states with huge bureaucracies that control unimaginable finances. Modern governments have agencies to oversee employment, welfare, education, the arts, transportation, and are usually one of the biggest employers in a country. Before the twentieth century A.D., however, states had far fewer offices and concentrated on a handful of tasks. Oligarchs and tyrants took responsibility only for war and religion and for finding the money to pay for them.

Defending the State

If an enemy threatened the *polis,* officials called up the army. This meant sending out word that the hoplites should assemble on a certain day. In the fifth century B.C., the state might pay for food and hired men to carry the soldiers' armor, but probably did not do so in archaic times. Normally, a war was settled by a single battle. Campaigns were usually fought in the summer, the agricultural off-season, and were over in a week or two. Both sides needed to settle the matter and get home before the autumn planting. The costs were minimal. Armies lived off the land, and the side that won often made a profit. At the very least, the winners could sell bronze armor taken from the enemy dead; if they captured any towns, there would be loot.

Because all soldiers were amateurs, there were no peacetime standing armies and no need for states to borrow money or drain their treasuries to pay for long campaigns. Navies were tiny before the 480s B.C. The biggest state expense was fortifications, but even these were simple, and many cities had none. War was cheap for the state. Hoplites had to give up their time to train to keep order in the madness of battle, but the individual citizens bore the cost.

Religion

Religion could be more expensive than war. Before about 750 B.C., Greeks did not build temples or give the gods elaborate gifts. In the eighth and seventh centuries B.C., by contrast, hundreds of temples were built and millions of objects dedicated, but private individuals again bore most costs. State officials were involved mainly in building very large temples and putting on communal festivals. By 700 B.C., some communities had one or more of the temples called *hekatompeda,* "hundred-footers," as focuses for worshiping a patron divinity. In the seventh century B.C., rich states started building these from stone, with tiled roofs, and in the sixth century, lavish sculpture became common. Tyrants particularly liked advertising their power by building temples, and some Sicilian cities built great avenues of temples.

A big stone temple cost far more than a hoplite war, but the expense could be spread out over long periods. The enormous temple of Olympian Zeus at Athens (Figure 22.13 in Chapter 22, "The Coming of Rome, 220–30 B.C.") was begun around 530 B.C., but only finished 650 years later, by a Roman emperor! Temple-building correlated with successful wars, with plunder covering many of the costs.

Festivals could also be expensive. We know little about everyday Archaic religion, but in Classical times groups of local worthies administered village festivals, raising money for sacrificed animals, chiefly goats and sheep. Most citizens ate beef only when the state put funds into a larger festival. The state recouped some costs by selling the animals' hides to leather tanners, but a good calendar of state festivals would cost more each year than warfare.

Welfare and Infrastructure

Two obvious categories of modern state spending that were largely missing in archaic Greece are welfare and spending for such infrastructures as roads and bridges—things that make society function smoothly. Families took care of their own sick and elderly and educated their young. If you had no family, you had no chance in life, but would die young or become a wandering beggar. The closest thing to state intervention in employment was the redistribution of land and the loans that some tyrants made to farmers, driven by fear that landless men were potential revolutionaries. Poor citizens constantly demanded redistribution of land and sometimes states obliged. Some of the tyrants' public building projects made work for unemployed men who had drifted into the cities from bankrupt farms, and getting rid of such potential troublemakers was one purpose of overseas colonies.

Although the state generally took little interest in infrastructure, around 600 B.C. Corinth's tyrant built a stone road across the four miles of the Isthmus of Corinth so that ships could avoid sailing hundreds of miles around the Peloponnese (and so that Corinth could tax traders using the road). Around 530 B.C., an engineer named Eupalinos dug a mile-long tunnel, eight feet wide and eight feet high, through a mountain to bring fresh water into the town of Samos, and by 500 B.C. simple clay pipes did the same thing for several cities. But such projects were exceptions. Greece had only bad roads, and few cities (Corinth and Samos among them) invested in good harbors.

The one way in which Greek states did intervene energetically in economic behavior was by minting coins (Figure 8.6). Just before 600 B.C., the kingdom of Lydia in Asia Minor began issuing uniform pieces of electrum (a naturally occurring mixture of gold and silver) stamped with a symbol to guarantee their weight, and between 600 and 570 B.C. various Greek *poleis* followed suit. The earliest Greek coins were for such large denominations that they could hardly have had much financial use, and some historians suggest that they were made to advertise state authority or perhaps to simplify state pay to mercenary soldiers for long periods of service. Such motivations seem as much political as economic; but well before 500 B.C., the economic advantages of having tokens with guaranteed metal content had become obvious, and Greek cities were issuing small copper and bronze coins for everyday use.

Finance

In 2003, federal government outlays in the United States were almost one-third of the gross domestic product. In Britain, the figure was 40 percent; in Sweden, 59 percent. We have no figures from archaic Greece, but government spending probably never exceeded one or two percent of the gross domestic product. The state got nearly all its money from publicly owned property, indirect taxes (that is, harbor dues, customs and excise, market fees, as distinct from direct taxes on land or income), and "gifts." Condemned criminals often forfeited their property to the community, and such revenues met many military and religious expenses. Minerals

Figure 8.6 Two sides of a coin from Aegina, circa 560 B.C. These coins were known as "turtles" from the design shown on the left. On the right is a deep punch mark, perhaps to show that the coin was made of the same metal all the way through. © *The British Museum.*

normally belonged to the community, and some of the profits of mining went to the public treasury. Further, a tithe (10 percent) of plunder from wars was given to the gods and could be used to defray religious costs.

Much revenue came from imports and exports, with traders paying fees to use harbors and markets. In maritime cities like Corinth, such taxes probably brought in the bulk of state income. Inland communities did less well, but people always needed to exchange things and could be made to pay for the protection states gave to commerce. When there was a crisis, the richer citizens might be asked to contribute a percentage of their wealth to the community to pay for war or to finish a temple. Some burdens, like paying for parts of festivals, might be farmed out to rich citizens, who could win public respect by funding them. The rich needed a stable state and the gods' goodwill, so they were often willing to pay.

In the last fifty years, modern Western states have typically collected 33 to 50 percent of their tax revenue from income taxes. Archaic *poleis*, by contrast, brought in nothing from this source—or from inheritance taxes, land taxes, or poll taxes. A few tyrants imposed such direct taxes, but they were bitterly resisted as invasions of the citizens' freedom, tantamount to slavery. Indirect taxes encourage smuggling, but they met the *poleis'* modest financial needs better than direct taxes because they only required a small bureaucracy. Direct taxes were difficult to assess and collect. In following this path, *poleis* were like many pretwentieth-century states.

CONCLUSION

In some ways, archaic Greece was much like other ancient societies. Its economic base was agricultural, it was hierarchical, gender distinctions were strong, and it was polytheistic. But in other important ways it was unusual, or unique. The structures of hierarchy were weak. There were few kings or powerful priesthoods. The ruling aristocrats held power because they controlled political institutions, not because of great wealth, military supremacy, or kinship with the gods. A distinctive civilization was emerging.

KEY TERMS

oligarchy, 148	Theognis, 158
agathoi, 148	Olympia, 159
kakoi, 148	Panhellenic games, 159
dêmos, 149	gymnasia, 160
talents, 150	*pankration*, 160
hoplite, 152	Pindar, 161
phalanx, 152	tyrant, 165
symposium, 156	ostracism, 166
andrôn, 156	

FURTHER READING

De Angelis, Franco, *Megara Hyblaia and Selinous* (Oxford 2003). Survey of archaeological and textual evidence for two important Sicilian cities and their interactions with non-Greeks.

Davidson, James, *Courtesans and Fishcakes: The Consuming Passions of Classical Athens* (New York 1997). Lively study of popular culture.

Fisher, Nick, and Hans van Wees, eds., *Archaic Greece* (London 1998). Collection of essays on every aspect of Archaic Greece.

Forrest, W. G., *The Emergence of Greek Democracy* (London 1966). Now somewhat dated, but still one of the most readable accounts of archaic Greece.

Garland, Robert, *Daily Life of the Ancient Greeks* (New York 1998). The best review of the topic.

Hanson, Victor, *The Western Way of War* (New York 1989). Superb treatment of hoplite warfare from the soldier's point of view. A classic.

McGlew, James, *Tyranny and Political Culture in Ancient Greece* (Ithaca, NY, 1993). A study of how Archaic tyrants presented themselves.

Miller, Stephen, *Arete: Greek Sports from Ancient Sources* (Berkeley 1991). Useful collection of ancient texts about athletics.

Murray, Oswyn, *Early Greece* (2nd ed., Stanford 1993). Excellent overview of Archaic Greek civilization.

———, ed., *Sympotica* (Oxford 1990). Collection of essays about every aspect of the symposium.

Osborne, Robin, *Greece in the Making* (London 1996). A recent general survey of archaic Greece. Strong on archaeological evidence.

Pleket, Harry, and Moses Finley, *The Olympic Games: The First Thousand Years* (London 1976). Well-illustrated introduction to ancient Greek athletics from the perspective of the greatest festival.

Snodgrass, Anthony, *Archaic Greece* (London 1980). Outstanding essay on the development of Greek society, focusing on archaeological evidence.

Ancient Texts

The poems of Theognis. In *Hesiod and Theognis* (Harmondsworth, UK, 1973; tr. Dorothea Wender). Critical view of sixth-century-B.C. society, full of information on the symposium.

Pindar, *The Odes* (Harmondsworth, UK, 1969; tr. Maurice Bowra). Fine translations of these famously difficult poems, written c. 500–460 B.C., praising athletic victors.

Herodotus, *The Histories* (Harmondsworth, UK, revised edition 1996; tr. Aubrey de Selincourt). Written around 420 B.C., but full of stories about archaic Greece.

CHAPTER 9

THE ARCHAIC CULTURAL REVOLUTION, 700–480 B.C.

The Archaic *poleis* were small, open societies. Their weak oligarchs never established good claims to religious authority; ordinary people could, and did, criticize them without committing sacriledge. Debate was tolerated. In most *poleis*, aristocrats made political decisions through discussion in councils, and during the sixth century B.C. these councils expanded to include more citizens.

The Archaic *poleis* were open in another sense: Some of their members traveled far and wide, bringing home new ideas from overseas. In the sixth century B.C., something remarkable came from the combination of these forms of openness. For centuries learned men in Egypt and Babylon (Map 9.1) had thought about the world, compiled data, and developed analytical techniques. Sometime before 3000 B.C., someone in Egypt—needing to predict the annual floods of the Nile—established a 365-day calendar, today only slightly improved. In the second millennium B.C., Babylonian thinkers created a base-60 numerical system that we use still in the minutes of an hour and the degrees of a compass. Superior decimal systems emerged in first-millennium-B.C. Mesopotamia, although two thousand years passed before Arabs imported from India the crucial concept of zero (first discovered in Sumer) and standardized the simple symbols 1, 2, and 3 that the whole world now uses. Using their base-60 system, the Mesopotamians developed algebra, solved quadratic equations, and drew up logarithmic tables. By 1600 B.C., they recorded observations on the movements of the planet Venus in mathematical language; before 500 B.C., they systematically applied mathematical theory to observing the stars. Both Egyptians and Babylonians developed geometry to high levels, calculating the areas and volumes of different shapes and surveying field boundaries accurately. The rulers of the Assyrian Empire were patrons of learning and compiled collections of Babylonian scholarship, but when their empire collapsed in 612 B.C., their

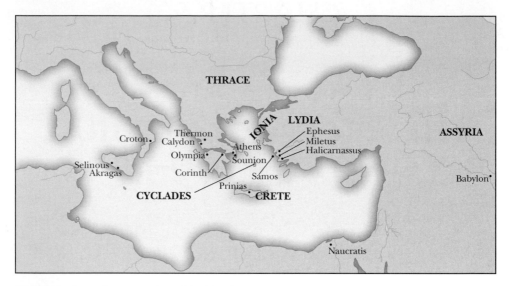

Map 9.1   Locations mentioned in this chapter.

scholars scattered far and wide. Some of them, apparently, came to the eastern shores of the Aegean Sea.

NATURAL PHILOSOPHY IN MILETUS

Early in the first millennium B.C., Greeks had settled in what is now western Turkey, emigrating through Athens to escape the problems of Dark Age mainland Greece. These Greeks claimed to be descendants of a man named Ion and therefore called the area they settled **Ionia.** Along this coast, and above all in **Miletus** (mī-lē-tus), ancient Mesopotamian learning and new Greek institutions fused in the sixth century B.C. in what we now call the **Ionian Enlightenment.** Scholars use the word "enlightenment" deliberately to evoke comparison with the European Enlightenment of the eighteenth century A.D., which saw enormous advances in scientific thought, the substitution of naturalistic explanations for religious ones, and the application of rational, scientific criticism to all spheres of life (including the creation of the American republic). In Miletus, such principles were articulated for the first time.

Milesian thinkers responded to Mesopotamian learning in three important ways. First, they asked different questions: not so much *how* things worked, but *why.* It was exciting to know how planets moved around the skies, but *why* did they do so? Second, rather than adding to Babylonian wisdom, they removed something: the gods. It was not good enough to say, "They move like this because the gods want them to." The Milesians first articulated the theory that "natural causes," independent of the will of this or that god, governed events in nature. Third, they systematized knowledge. Traditional thought had compartmentalized the world. The royal scholars of Assyria, in vast palatial bureaucracies, could hold incompatible theories, but in a little city like Miletus, where the town's old men gathered to talk every day in the main square (*agora*), theories that explained one part of the natural world needed to be consistent with those that explained another.

Little survives of the writings of the Milesian thinkers, and mostly we rely on what later Greek scholars, particularly Aristotle (384–322 B.C.), said about them. Aristotle tells us that there were three major thinkers: Thales (**thā**-lēz), Anaximander (an-ax-i-**man**-der), and Anaximenes (an-ax-**i**-men-ēz). Thales probably wrote nothing, while Anaximander may have produced the earliest prose treatise in Greek. According to Aristotle, all three men, and numerous followers, wanted to explain the material cause of things—where the world came from. They were the first natural philosophers.

Perhaps oversimplifying for clarity, Aristotle says that each man focused on one element as the source of everything. **Thales** (who flourished in the 580s B.C.) thought this primary element was water. Mesopotamian myth held that the primordial gods Tiamat and Apsu, from whom the world emerged, were water. Thales probably knew these stories. He suggested that all matter was water in one of three different states: solid, liquid, or gas. Unfortunately, we know little more about Thales except that (presumably by drawing on Mesopotamian records) he supposedly predicted a solar eclipse in 585 B.C. and that he calculated the height of the Egyptian pyramids from the length of their shadows.

Anaximander (550s B.C.) may have developed his theories as criticisms of Thales. Thales suggested that the earth floated on water; if so, what held up the water? Anaximander suggested that the earth hung freely in nothingness, kept in place by being equidistant from everything else in the cosmos. The primary element must, he thought, be the Infinite (Greek *apeiron*). According to one later source, Anaximander theorized how matter was created from the Infinite:

> He [Anaximander] says that which is productive from the eternal of hot and cold was separated off at the coming-to-be of this world, and that a kind of sphere of flame from this was formed around the air surrounding the earth, like bark round a tree. When this was broken off and shut off in certain circles, the sun and the moon and the stars were formed.
>
> Pseudo-Plutarch, *Stromata 2*
> (trs. Kirk, Raven, and Schofield)

Thales had suggested that everything came from water; Anaximander asked how water could turn into other things, such as its opposite, fire. Various sources suggest Anaximander, thought the Infinite had no qualities except boundlessness, but within the Infinite, four qualities were in competition: hot, cold, wet, and dry. Change comes from this competition as first one quality, then another, becomes ascendant. Water puts out fire, then the fiery sun dries up water. All change is cyclical, reflecting changes in the ascendancy of one quality over another—thus we move through spring, summer, autumn, and winter. The Infinite is in constant motion, a sort of wiggling, and because of this wiggling motion, opposite qualities congeal, producing sun and stars, which are hot and dry, and earth, which is wet and cold. The cosmos came into being through the Infinite's inbuilt tendency to wiggle. Life emerged from the warm slime, because the hot and wet make life. The earliest creatures, Anaximander claimed, were fish, and humans evolved from them.

Some of Anaximander's explanations have startling parallels to modern theory. Relying on reason, logical inference, and some evidence, Anaximander rejected earlier stories of how the gods made the universe, instead focusing on how the one original substance (the Infinite) became many and how the many things changed into other things. No agent is responsible for the movement of the Infinite, because motion is somehow a quality inherent in it. Not only was matter formed out of the Infinite, but the Infinite has generated worlds beyond number. Anaximander might have welcomed modern notions about the universe.

Using astronomical observations, Anaximander offered the first mechanical theory of the cosmos. The earth, he said, is shaped like a column drum, three times as wide as it is deep, suspended at the center of the Infinite. Around it are three rotating rings of fire shrouded by mists, but the mists have small gaps though which we glimpse the fire. The smallest ring is nine times the diameter of the earth, and we call the flecks of fire that we see through its numerous gaps stars. The second ring, eighteen times the earth's diameter, has one gap, which we call the moon. The third, twenty-seven times the earth's diameter, also has one gap, which humans call the sun. Spatial relationships were crucial to Anaximander, who produced the first known map of the world.

His fellow Milesian **Anaximenes** (520s B.C.) took over much of Anaximander's thought but found other explanations for how substances turned into new substances. He defined the Infinite more precisely, as air. Through eternally ongoing processes of rarefaction and condensation, he theorized, air condenses into liquid water, and liquid water condenses into solid ice. Heat reverses these processes, turning ice to water to air; so too all matter will return to air. The very soul of a man is a rarefied form of air, taken from the essence of the universe. The Greek word for soul, *psychê*, means "breath" as we have seen.

To Aristotle, living some two hundred years after Anaximenes, these theories seemed childish. Selecting water or air as the primary substance was arbitrary, and no Milesian integrated theory with observation very well, let alone developed experimental methods. We might call their attempts to explain change in nature by means of natural forces semiscientific, in a way that Babylonian or Egyptian analyses had not been. Anaximenes' processes of rarefaction and condensation required no divine intervention. Milesian models, too, were generalized, seeking to explain all of nature, not just bits of it. All theories were necessarily interrelated and were open to rational criticism.

The Ionian Enlightenment did not mean that suddenly every Greek sat down to argue over the Infinite. Few can have understood such obscure arguments, any more than most of us today grasp theoretical astrophysics. Anaximenes' principles of condensation and rarefaction seem almost common sense when compared to Heisenberg's uncertainty principle: that we cannot know a particle's position and velocity at the same time. But by 500 B.C., such speculations created a model for rational inquiry into the causes and nature of change that spread to other fields of inquiry.

PYTHAGORAS: PHILOSOPHY AND SOCIAL SCIENCE IN THE WEST

The Ionian Enlightenment began in Miletus, but other thinkers in Ionia shared in it. One was **Pythagoras** from the island of Samos, near Miletus. Many legends grew up around him, so it is hard to say what he really taught, but he seems to have pushed Milesian thought in three directions—toward mathematics, mysticism, and politics.

Pythagoras fled his native Samos in 531 B.C. to escape from its tyrant. He settled in Croton, a Greek city in southern Italy. Pythagoras emphasized both the differences and the connection between gods and mortals. The human soul, he said, was a spark of divinity. Through transmigration (reincarnation), the same spark dwelled within a sequence of fleshly containers, animal as well as human. Pythagoreans therefore never ate meat for fear of consuming a spark of the divine. Every human's job, Pythagoras said, was to turn away from the material dross enclosing the divine spark within us and, through moral purity and ascetic practice, to free the spark to rejoin its source in the divine infinite.

Pythagoras was the first to call the universe the *kosmos,* meaning "ordered whole." He saw the individual as a *kosmos* in miniature. The individual's goal was to attain in miniature the same order that governed the universe, and mathematics was the way to comprehend that order. The Greeks used letters to express numbers, which made arithmetic difficult, but Pythagoras made remarkable advances in geometrical thought about space and proportion. He discovered how to express the intervals of musical harmony as relations between the numbers one, two, three, and four. The octave, for instance, is a two-to-one ratio: If you pluck an open string on a guitar, then stop it at the halfway point (twelve frets up), the two notes are harmonious in the relation of the octave. If you stop the string so that the lengths of its two parts stand in a ratio of three to two, the note you get is a fifth, also harmonious with the base note or unstopped string. These relationships are the building blocks of musical harmony. They are not subjective, but inherent in the *kosmos* itself. Musicians do not need to know the mathematical basis of what sounds good, but the basis nonetheless exists, independent of human judgment. Pythagoras had exposed the structure of reality. Mathematics proves that the world is an ordered *kosmos.* Pythagoras and his followers made further discoveries, including the famous Pythagorean theorem that everyone learns in school: In a right-angled triangle, the square of the longest side is equal to the sum of the squares of the other two sides. Mathematics uncovered how reality worked, and Pythagoreans believed they were unlocking the universe's secrets.

Pythagoras saw two principles at work in the *kosmos:* the Unlimited, which was shapeless and bad, and the Limiting, as when a string limited by exact intervals produced ordered harmonies, which are good. A follower could attain perfection by replacing disharmony (unlimited intervals) in one's own life with harmony, achieving union with the *kosmos* and allowing the divine spark to rejoin the infinite. One (unity, the point), two (duality, the line), three (trinity = unity + duality, the plane), and four (quadrinity, the solid) add up to ten, the number of perfection in the *kosmos,* the universe, and in the microcosm, the individual. Ten is the number of perfect harmony.

Such mystical theories sound less concrete than the Milesians' speculations about matter, but where the Milesians cared about substance and how it changed—what the universe was made of and how one thing became another—Pythagoras cared about structure, the ordering of things. Number was the key to structure at every level, from the *kosmos* to the individual, including the level of politics. The openness of Greek society, served by alphabetic writing, compared to the royal courts of the Near East, served by complex and only partially phonetic systems of writing, allowed thinkers to develop systematic methods of analysis. Pythagoras (or his followers) seized Croton in Italy and several other cities, reorganizing society in a utopian effort to make it conform to their mathematical theories. We are poorly informed about details, but for a while Pythagorean aristocrats were the most powerful men in western Greece. Eventually, Pythagoras' utopias failed, generating bitter civil wars. But the application of scientific abstractions to society as well as to nature had come to stay, with enormous consequences.

HECATAEUS, HERODOTUS, AND *HISTORIÊ*

By 500 B.C., other schools of thought were developing in the Greek cities under Persian rule in Ionia and in the independent cities of southern Italy and Sicily. Some of them fused Milesian semiscience with Pythagoras' application of reason to human society. **Hecataeus** (hek-a-tē-us), also from Miletus, was an important innovator. He flourished around 500 B.C.; only fragments of his writings survive. He was steeped in Enlightenment speculation and improved on Anaximander's map of the world. He wrote two important prose works. One was a systematic account of the peoples around the Mediterranean basin, combining geography, ethnography, and politics. The second analyzed genealogies. Even in Greece, a few aristocrats claimed to have gods as ancestors and told stories to prove it. Hecataeus provided rational explanations for these stories. While not denying the gods' existence, Hecataeus underlined their separation from humankind, increasing the need for rational accounts of human behavior. A later writer preserves the memorable opening of his study of genealogies: "Hecataeus of Miletus speaks thus. I write these things as they seem to me to be true. For the tales of the Greeks are many, and, it seems to me, laughable."

Hecataeus seems to have pioneered a new genre of inquiry into the causes of human events, but his successor **Herodotus**' account of the Persian invasions of Greece at the end of the Archaic Period was the first systematic attempt to explain human events in human terms. Herodotus was born around 484 B.C., as archaic times ended, and hailed from Halicarnassus, thirty miles south of Miletus. Just as Anaximander wrote in response to Thales, and Anaximenes to Anaximander, Herodotus replied to Hecataeus, whom he mentions eighteen times, usually to correct him. Herodotus opened his great *Histories* by explaining that

> Herodotus of Halicarnassus here displays his *historiê* so that human achievements may not be forgotten in time, and great and marvelous deeds—some displayed by Greeks, some by barbarians°—may not be without their glory; and especially to show why the two peoples fought with each other.
>
> Herodotus 1.1 (A. de Selincourt)

°*barbarians:* As noted earlier, Greeks called all non-Greeks barbarians.

In Greek, *historiê* meant "inquiry," but has become our word *history,* a rational, orderly investigation into human events. We use it to describe the study of the past, but for Herodotus *historiê* included the present too.

Herodotus' book is not history as most of us think of it. He wished to preserve the memory of men's great deeds, much like Homer in the *Iliad*. Like Homer, Herodotus made up speeches at vital moments in the story, although he could not always have known what was said, or even whether a speech was given—as when he imagines a conversation between the Persian king and queen in their bed! In its purpose, length, ambition, and all-embracing curiosity about the world and the things in it, Herodotus' *historiê* resembles Homer's epic. If putting a fictional speech in a character's mouth was the way to get a point across, so be it.

The presence of the gods further distinguishes Herodotus' text from modern historical writing, as when Herodotus cheerfully tells us that the gods toppled mountains onto the Persians. Like other Ionian Enlightenment thinkers, he accepted the reality of the gods. Thales had famously remarked that the world was full of gods. But like Thales and his successors, Herodotus assumed that causes and effects nonetheless normally lay in the human realm, amenable to systematic analysis. After opening his book with the sentence quoted above, he relates various semimythical explanations for the origin of the conflict between East and West put forward by "learned men," ending with the Trojan War. He then adds a remarkable paragraph:

> So much for what the Persians and Phoenicians say, and I have no intention of passing judgment on its truth or falsity. I prefer to rely on my own knowledge and to point out who in actual fact first injured the Greeks. Then I will proceed with my *historiê*.
>
> Herodotus 1.5 (A. de Selincourt)

Herodotus leaps forward from the mythical Trojan War to the sixth century B.C., where he can rely on his own knowledge to make statements of fact. He believes in the gods and gives them their due when reasonable, but no Muses tell him what happened, as they had informed Homer. He traveled extensively and, like an investigative reporter, asked his own questions, weighed what he saw and heard, and explained events as he understood them. Truly, Herodotus was the father of history in the sense that he was the first to investigate systematically the human causes of human events.

MATERIAL CULTURE

The same furious energy that drove speculation about physical and social realities also powered a revolution in Greek material culture. Immigrant craftsmen were as important for introducing new art styles as eastern intellectuals were for introducing new forms of thought, but in art as in philosophy, transplanting Near Eastern traditions into the unusual sociology of the *poleis* encouraged developments in unprecedented directions.

Sculpture

Near Eastern and Egyptian kings had used stone sculpture to glorify themselves since the Bronze Age. Ninth-century-B.C. Greek travelers must have seen examples, but Greek *basileis* had neither the wealth nor the power to make such symbolism useful. The most lavish Greek sculptures from the impoverished Dark Age are little bronze figures of humans and animals, a few inches tall, dedicated at certain sanctuaries (particularly Olympia). The first experiments with stone carving took place on the island of Crete, where Near Eastern influence had always been strong. Early examples are rough heads and scenes in low relief on limestone blocks on Cretan tombs from around 700 B.C., strongly recalling Assyrian art. As states spent more money on public sanctuaries, they borrowed Near Eastern techniques (and perhaps hired Near Eastern craftsmen) to represent divinities in more elaborate ways. In early shrines, a simple plank of wood or block of stone may have represented the deity, and when carvers started making freestanding limestone statues of gods around 650 B.C., they retained a slab-like appearance. The Auxerre goddess (once kept in a museum in Auxerre, France; Figure 9.1), is a good example. Virtually two-dimensional, the figure stands in a frontal pose with feet together, left hand at the side, right hand held to the chest. She wears a short cape over a straight-sided, belted tunic from which her bare feet emerge. Her hair is arranged in thick ridges, terminating in corkscrew curls over her brow. The skirt is lightly incised (and

Figure 9.1 The Auxerre *korê* ("maiden"), a daedalic statue, circa 640–630 B.C. It is named after the French town Auxerre, where it used to be displayed, but was almost certainly made in Crete. Height 26 inches.

originally painted) with rectangular designs. The Near Eastern features, stiff posture, and Egyptian-like wig for hair characterize the **daedalic (dē-da-lik) style,** named after the legendary craftsman Daedalus, who built a labyrinth maze for King Minos, only to have Minos imprison him and his son Icarus in it. It is an odd term, because if Daedalus existed, he would have lived during the Bronze Age, a thousand years before the statues we call daedalic. Art historians use daedalic to mean early Greek art, with primitive features.

The daedalic style evolved rapidly as Cretan temples grew more elaborate in the late seventh century B.C. Near Eastern visitors to Crete around 620 or 610 B.C. would have found familiar-looking sculptures used in strange ways, on temples and occasionally in cemeteries, but never on palaces, as in the Near East. But Egyptian styles soon influenced Greek sculpture as innovation shifted from Crete to the Cycladic islands and the mainland. Around 670 B.C., the ruler of Egypt had ordered all Greek merchants in his country to operate out of a single port, at **Naucratis** in the Nile Delta. Various mainland, island, and Ionian *poleis* set up trading posts there. By 600 B.C., Naucratis was a major conduit for the transfer of styles and technique from Egypt to Greece.

For two thousand years, Egyptian craftsmen had carved statues to a standard format. They took a block of stone, often limestone, marked it out in squares on the flat faces of the stone according to a pattern book, then worked inward, as in a statue of Prince Ranefer ("Ra is beautiful"), from about 2300 B.C. (Figure 9.2). Ranefer's hands are clenched at his sides, holding an unknown object, and his left foot is slightly advanced. He wears a kilt and stares fixedly into space. In the sixth century B.C., nearly two thousand years later, Egyptian statues still looked similar, and in fact changed little until the Romans conquered Egypt, still five hundred years later. Such artistic conservatism depended on the statues' magical purpose as

Figure 9.2 Statue of Ranefer, an Egyptian official of the fifth dynasty, limestone, circa 2300 B.C. Limestone, height 5 feet.

Figure 9.3 *Kouros* from Anavyssos in Attica, circa 540 B.C. On the base is carved: "stand and grieve at the tomb Kroisos the dead,/in the front line killed by wild Ares." Height 6 feet. *Standing youth (kouros). Said to be from the neighborhood of Anavyssos. Marble. H: 76" (193 cm). ca. 580 B.C.E. The Metropolitan Museum of Art, Fletcher Fund, 1932. (32.11.1). Photograph © 1997 The Metropolitan Museum of Art.*

substitute bodies for the *ka,* or "vital essence," of the deceased in case the mummy was destroyed.

Greek carvers borrowed Egyptian techniques to produce new types of statue, which archaeologists call *kouroi* ("young men"; singular, ***kouros***) and *korai* ("young women"; singular, ***korê***). The similarities between Figures 9.2 and 9.3 are striking. Both have straight arms with clenched fists and an unnatural pose, with the left leg slightly advanced, both feet flat on the ground, and the body directly over the upright right leg (the pose is possible only for people whose left legs are longer than their right). Unlike the Egyptian statue, however, supported by a flat upright slab at the back, the Greek statue is freestanding. It is also naked, as Egyptian statues never were. Early Greek female statues, by contrast, were always clothed.

Egyptian sculpture changed little in three thousand years, but in Greece styles changed by the decade. Because they did not serve religious hierarchies like their Egyptian counterparts, Greek sculptors were free to experiment, softening the unnatural musculature of the *kouroi,* loosening their poses, raising their right heels from the ground, and introducing contemporary hairstyles, as in a fine example of about 480 B.C. (Figure 9.4). The sculptor has moved very far from his Egyptian prototypes. He observed the human body rather than working from sketchbooks.

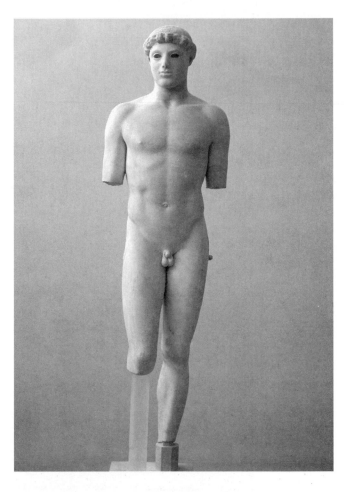

Figure 9.4 The Kritios boy, found on the Acropolis in Athens, circa 480 B.C., apparently the creation of a sculptor named Krito. Marble. Height 3 feet, 10 inches.

The anatomy has been modulated and made more naturalistic, as has the face. The muscles of the abdomen approximate real musculature. The statue seems alive, swelling with a vitality rare in Egyptian statues. Traces of paint remain on the hair, and pubic hair would also have been painted on. The sculptor reached out to create in stone an idealized naked Greek youth.

The female *korê*, "young girl," corresponded to the male *kouros*. The *korê* was always fully clothed. An extraordinary series of these charming statues was found on the Athenian Acropolis in pits where the Athenians swept debris after Persians sacked the city in 480 B.C. Figure 9.5, carved about 530 B.C., is called the Peplos *Korê* from the woolen dress (*peplos*) she wears. Like the *kouroi*, she has an "archaic smile," a fixed grin found on most sixth-century statuary. Long braided locks, painted red, fall on either side of her full breasts, outlined by the *peplos*, which ends just above her belted waist. Her drapery is complex and naturalistic, and her face is thoughtful. Unlike the *kouroi*, the *korai* stand with feet side by side. In this statue, the sculptor has boldly freed the figure from the block of stone by attaching an extended left arm (now missing).

Figure 9.5 The Peplos *Korê;* from Athens, circa 530 B.C. Marble, height 48 inches.

As with natural philosophy, transplanting Near Eastern and Egyptian practices to a very different social setting gave Greeks the freedom to innovate. Sculpture was expensive; only the rich could hire skilled carvers and pay to move large blocks of stone. In Assyria, such spending was the preserve of kings and nobles. But in Greece, there were few kings and no grand palaces. A few nobles put *kouroi* and *korai* over their graves (like Figure 9.3), but most were placed in sanctuaries (e.g., Figures 9.4, 9.5). Greek sculptors took their basic techniques from Egypt and Syria but, because they made up new rules for the use of statues, they did not feel bound by conventions. Cycladic and Athenian masons innovated by using hard marble, abundant in both areas, rather than soft limestone, as was common in Egypt. The driving question in archaic Greek culture—what is humanity if we are separated from the gods?—may have encouraged sculptors to think about what made the human body what it is. They faced similar issues as the philosophers, but gave answers in stone, not words.

Architecture

Sociological changes drove architectural innovations too. The most important was the separation of religious and secular space around 700 B.C. As we noted in Chapter 5, "The Dark Age, 1200–700 B.C.," the gods may have been worshiped in chiefs' houses in the Dark Age. Presumably, the chiefs' special ties to gods are reflected in Hesiod's sense that Zeus gave special favor to good *basileis*. After 700 B.C., *basileis* disappeared, and as egalitarian ideals developed, the worship of the gods was largely separated from the homes of mortals.

Some of the earliest sanctuaries consisted of a simple altar under the open sky, where an animal could be killed and cooked. By 750 B.C., communities began adding buildings for the god's image near the altar. The earliest temples, like Dark Age houses, had one curved end. Already by 700 B.C., some were a hundred feet long. Early in the seventh century, craftsmen learned how to make clay roof tiles, and temple-builders replaced thatch with this superior material. The heavy tiles required strong walls, now often built entirely from carefully cut stone blocks with columns helping to carry the weight. The building was divided into a long main room (*cella*), where the cult statue stood, and a short back porch (*opisthodomos,* "back-house"), unconnected to the cella, where treasure was stored, with a row of columns down the middle. Still more columns (a *colonnade*) surrounded the building, the whole built on a platform (*stylobate*).

Such temples required much wood and stone and were enormously expensive by Greek standards. But the communities that sponsored the buildings took civic pride in their construction. Seventh-century temples often used huge blocks of stone, much bigger than in later times, despite having only simple cranes. It seems as if the *poleis* rejoiced in the difficulty of the task they set themselves to honor the gods and to celebrate the local community. The new building styles gave new opportunities for elaboration in decorating the upper part of the temple with painted plaques and molded faces.

By 600 B.C., distinct canons of temple building had evolved, familiar to us today, called the **Doric** and **Ionic orders** after the two principal Greek ethnic divisions (Figure 9.6). A third order, the Corinthian, with elaborate capitals of acanthus leaves, first appears in the fifth century B.C. (Chapter 18, "Greek Culture in the Fourth Century B.C.").

Regardless of order, temples had three parts. At the top was the **entablature** ("superimposed board") made up of a pitched, tiled roof, a decorated frieze beneath it, and a plain support of stone blocks called the **architrave** (**ar**-ki-trāv, "chief beam"). At the front and back ends of the temple, the triangular areas under the roof (the end gables), called **pediments,** often had sculpture.

The second architectural element was the columns, where the main difference between the orders lay. All types of columns tapered toward the top, but Doric columns had no bases, were less fluted than Ionic, and had a very plain top (what architects call the capital). A Doric capital was called an *echinus,* which meant sea urchin, because its cushion shape reminded Greeks of that creature, so common on their beaches. Ionic columns had fancier capitals, with curved volutes ("rolls") and Corinthian columns had the fanciest capitals of all. The third element was the temple's base. The columns stood on a *stylobate* (**stī**-lō-bāt, "column-walk"), which stood on a series of progressively larger slabs forming steps, and finally on a leveling course.

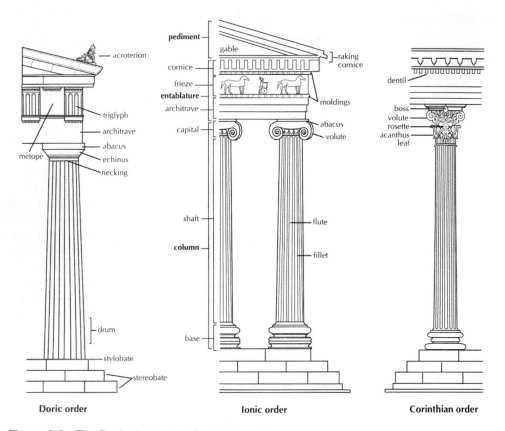

Figure 9.6 The Doric, Ionic, and Corinthian orders.

The Doric and Ionic orders had only a loose connection to Dorians and Ionians as ethnic groups. Greeks thought the Doric order was more masculine, and it was generally preferred on the mainland and on Sicily in both Ionian and Dorian cities. The more elegant or feminine Ionic order was preferred in Greek cities on the coast of Asia Minor. Corinthian columns were uncommon until the Roman period.

Temple design grew out of Dark Age house design, but no one could confuse sixth-century temples with private houses, which had followed their own line of development. By about 550 B.C., nearly all new houses had half a dozen rooms grouped around a shady courtyard, entered through a small door from the street into the courtyard. Houses therefore presented only blank walls to the outside world. Temples inverted this arrangement by having their shady colonnades on the outside, where anyone could walk. The decoration of houses grew progressively simpler in the sixth and early fifth centuries B.C., while that of temples got more lavish. Offering statues to the gods and making donations to the *polis'* funds for building new temples were praiseworthy ways for sixth-century aristocrats to show off their wealth; the donor not only honored his own name by making a gift, but won the god's favor for the whole city (like the Olympic victors discussed in Chapter 8, "Archaic Greece, 700–480 B.C.: Economy, Society, Politics"). As a result, temple architecture developed rapidly.

The best temples had pedimental sculptures by famous artists, marble façades, and clever use of curvature to charm the eye. Cities built ever-larger structures to show their wealth and power. The old hundred-footers were dwarfed by temples over one hundred yards long. The rich cities of Ionia and Sicily particularly favored gigantic constructions. We can trace competition between *poleis* on Sicily, where Selinous and Akragas built avenues of rich temples. Each time Akragas put up a super-temple, Selinous would start a new one a few feet longer—only for Akragas to add another, longer still. Figure 9.7 suggests what the famous temple of Artemis of Ephesus, one of the largest Greek temples and one of the Seven Wonders of the ancient world, looked like. For the first time, Greek architecture competed with Near Eastern and Egyptian in scale and expense; and it outdid them in sophistication and beauty.

Painting

There are no archaic parallels to the beautiful Bronze Age wall paintings whose fragments we examined in Chapter 4, "The Greeks before History, 12,000–1200 B.C." The fact that we lack archaeological contexts like the Santorini eruption partly explains this, but it also seems that wall painting was less important in archaic

Figure 9.7 Hypothetical reconstruction of the Ionic temple of Artemis at Ephesus, begun around 560 B.C., with the roof cut away to reveal the *cella* and the cult statue within. Note the tiny size of the human figures, crowding like ants before the magnificent portal.

Greece than in the Bronze Age, in accordance with the unostentatious lifestyle of Greek aristocrats.

Remains of painted pottery, however, are superabundant. Several million examples survive, mostly decorated with simple bands or solid blocks of black paint. Starting around 750 B.C., a tiny minority had figured scenes. Near Eastern influence then became so strong that we speak of an **orientalizing phase** in Greek art, lasting through the seventh century B.C. Corinth was one of the main trading cities in archaic Greece and, not surprisingly, was also the main center for orientalizing vase painting. A style called Protocorinthian painting flourished between about 725 and 625 B.C. The finest examples are miniatures (Figure 9.8). Unlike the Late Geometric figures in Chapter 5, Figure 5.3, the warriors here are flowing and energetic, in multicolored paint. The craftsmanship is extraordinary, the figures less than an inch tall. Corinthian workshops produced millions of such vessels to hold the scented oils that athletes used in the gymnasium. Greeks associated perfume with the luxurious east, which made orientalizing decoration appropriate for its containers.

By 625 B.C., Corinthian painting settled down into the Ripe **Corinthian** style, favoring a dense texture of detail of Eastern inspiration (c. 625–550 B.C.; Figure 9.9). The effect is rich, like tapestry: band after band of repetitive animals, and every square inch of background stuffed with floral filling ornaments. The designs are not applied with paint, but with a thin "slip," a watery clay that, when fired, became part of the pot. Through allowing oxygen into the kiln, then blocking the vents, then

Figure 9.8 A Protocorinthian aryballos (a-rib-**al**-os), or perfume flask, circa 650 B.C. This vase is known as the Macmillan aryballos, after a British art collector. It is less than 3 inches tall. © *The British Museum.*

Figure 9.9 Corinthian *olpê* (wine jug), circa 600 B.C. Height 18 inches.

again permitting oxidation, the thin slip and the body of the pot take on different colors. After firing, the potter used a sharp tool to scratch detail within the black figures and ornaments, often adding red or white highlights in actual paint.

Athens, by contrast, developed a wild seventh-century style known as **Protoattic** (Figure 9.10). Protoattic painters put their best work on large vessels. Figure 9.10 shows one of the most extraordinary. On the neck (also shown in Figure 6.6 in Chapter 6, "Homer"), Odysseus blinds the Cyclops. On the shoulder, a lion attacks a boar, and on the belly are Gorgons, mythical female creatures whose gaze turns a viewer to stone. Unlike the disciplined Protocorinthian vases, this scene has random filling ornaments floating in the background. The drawing is loose and sketchy. The rigid Athenian Late Geometric style had dissolved into a kind of chaos. In its day, Corinthian work was much more successful, being sold all over the Mediterranean, but the future lay with Athens.

In the early sixth century B.C., Athenian painters wedded the inventiveness of Protoattic with the order and precision of Corinthian in an extraordinary new **black-figure** style. Athenian potters continued to portray mythical characters, but

Figure 9.10 The Eleusis Vase, a famous Protoattic amphora, circa 675 B.C., found at Eleusis near Athens, where it had been used as a baby coffin. (Figure 6.6 shows a detail from the neck.) Height 4 feet, 9 inches.

learned from and then surpassed the Corinthians' neatness and tight composition. One of the most famous ancient pots, the François Vase (Figure 9.11), shows in the main scene, on the shoulder, the marriage of Achilles' parents; on the neck are the funeral games of Achilles' friend Patroclus; and on the lip, the killing of a giant boar that, according to legend, terrorized the town of Calydon in the generation before the Trojan War. Beneath the main scene is a procession of Dionysus, the god of wine, and below that a frieze of winged monsters called griffins. Even the foot has a figured scene, of a mythical battle between pygmies and cranes. The pot has two hundred figures, dozens of them with names painted in. Among the names we can read are *KLEITIAS EGRAPSE*, "Kleitias painted it," and *ERGOTIMOS EPOIESE*, "Ergotimos made it" (although we do not know whether "made it" means that Ergotimos physically threw the pot or owned the workshop). Animal scenes were now relegated to providing subsidiary ornament, as the human form became the vase painter's main subject.

   Pottery was cheap compared to sculpture, but by 550 B.C. a few Athenian painters raised the medium to the status of a serious art (Figure 9.12). Exekias was perhaps the greatest of these artists. Figure 9.12 shows a powerful moment from the Trojan War story. After Achilles was killed, all the Greek heroes wanted his armor. The great hero Ajax lost his mind with rage when the other Greeks refused to award it to him. Blind

Figure 9.11 The François Vase, a black-figure Athenian krater of about 570 B.C., named after the man who discovered it in the nineteenth century. Kleitias and Ergotimos signed the vase and covered it with mythological details. Kleitias painted in the names of dozens of characters. Height 2 feet, 2 inches.

Figure 9.12 The suicide of Ajax on an Athenian black-figure amphora by Exekias, circa 540 B.C. Height 10 inches. *Chatteau Museum, Boulogne-sur-Mer, France.*

with fury, he attacked them; but when his wits returned, he found that he had actually slaughtered a flock of sheep, not the other Greeks, who stood laughing at him. Dishonored, he planted his sword in the ground and threw himself on it, a popular subject for black-figure painters. Most showed Ajax impaled on his sword, kicking and squirting blood, but Exekias fills the scene with impending tragedy. The great but flawed hero smooths the earth around his deadly sword, his brow furrowed in concentration. A solitary palm to the left, indicating the outdoor setting, and the carefully stacked arms to the right evoking the armor that drove Ajax to this end frame the majestic central figure. Ajax's own eyeless helmet appears to watch with chilling disinterest. Only a great artist could achieve such a harrowing effect in a simple medium.

Top Athenian craftsmen competed to sell their wares and innovated constantly. Black figure worked by painting the figures in slip, then firing the pot so that the background preserved the color of the reddish clay while the painted slip oxidized black. In a new **red-figure** style, painters simply reversed the procedure, painting the background with slip and leaving the figures in the color of the pot. By using slips of different density, they could add subtler details than incision allowed. At first, red figure was perhaps a novelty style; some of the earliest examples show the same scene in black figure on one side and in red figure on the other. But within a few years, the best painters switched to red figure. In Figure 9.13, the painter

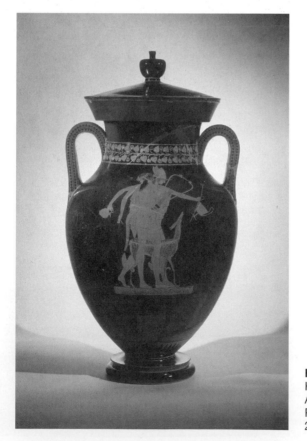

Figure 9.13 Red-figure scene of Hermes, a satyr, and a fawn; on an Athenian amphora, by the Berlin Painter,[17] circa 480 B.C. Height 20 inches.

realizes the full potential of the technique, using different lines, shading, drapery, and nudity to superimpose a satyr, a fawn, and the messenger god Hermes—a complex design impossible in black figure. It lacks the profundity of Exekias' best work but is a delightful, virtuoso scene.

ART AND THOUGHT IN SIXTH-CENTURY GREECE

From Ionia to Sicily, Greeks of the sixth century B.C. began remarkable explorations of the human condition. The Milesian natural scientists worked in such a rarefied intellectual environment that only a few Greeks understood them, while sculptors created art that thousands saw and appreciated. Philosophers were highly educated, while vase painters were artisans, worrying about getting the best clay and keeping kilns firing at the right temperature. These painters came from all over Greece, and even beyond. A leading painter at Athens in the 550s B.C. signed his work Lydos, "the Lydian," while a workshop owner in the 480s signed his vases as Brygos, "the Brygian." Lydia was a kingdom in western Asia Minor, and the Brygians were a Thracian people, living in modern Bulgaria. Both regions supplied many slaves to Greece (see Map 10.2 in Chapter 10, "A Tale of Two Archaic Cities: Sparta and Athens, 700–480 B.C."), and it is likely that Brygos and Lydos came to Athens as slaves.

In eastern kingdoms, representational art circulated in royal and other elite contexts, adorning palaces or temples to which few were admitted. Archaic *poleis,* by contrast, were cities of images open to all: Thought-provoking sculpture, architecture, and paintings were everywhere. Pythagoras put his theories into action in politics, and Herodotus perhaps gave public readings. The weak hierarchy of the Archaic *poleis* created an unusual open society. The ancient learning and art of Mesopotamia and Egypt were transformed. In Ionia, new knowledge created the first natural philosophy and semiscientific analyses of society. By 500 B.C., Greek society looked different from its neighbors, and Greek culture was winning admirers from Persia to the Straits of Gibraltar.

KEY TERMS

Ionia, 172
Miletus, 172
Ionian Enlightenment, 172
Thales, 173
Anaximander, 173
Anaximenes, 174
Pythagoras, 174
Hecataeus, 176
Herodotus, 176
historiē, 176
daedalic style, 178
Naucratis, 178
kouros, 180

korē, 180
cella, 183
Doric order, 183
Ionic order, 183
entablature, 183
architrave, 183
pediments, 183
orientalizing phase, 186
Corinthian, 186
Protoattic, 187
black-figure, 187
red-figure, 190

FURTHER READING

Philosophy

Barnes, Jonathan, *The Presocratic Philosophers* (2 vols., London 1979). Barnes relies on modern analytic philosophy to discuss ancient philosophers.

Furley, David, *The Greek Cosmologists: The Formation of the Atomic Theory and Its Earliest Critics* (vol. 1, Cambridge, UK, 1989). Sophisticated analysis of Milesian philosophy.

Guthrie, W. K. C., *The Greek Philosophers: From Thales to Aristotle* (London 1950). Superb short review by a leading scholar.

Lloyd, G. E. R., *Demystifying Mentalities* (Cambridge, UK, 1990). One of the best studies of the relationships between philosophy and other forms of thought in Archaic Greece.

Lloyd, G. E. R., *Early Greek Science: Thales to Aristotle* (London 1970). Very clear brief survey.

Historiography

Harrison, Thomas, *Divinity and History: The Religion of Herodotus* (Oxford 2000). Outstanding reassessment of the place of religion in Herodotus' history-writing.

Luraghi, Nino, ed., *The Historian's Craft in the Age of Herodotus* (Oxford 2001). Wide-ranging essays on how Herodotus composed his *History*.

Thomas, Rosalind, *Herodotus in Context* (Cambridge, UK, 2000). Analysis of Herodotus' achievements against their contemporary intellectual background.

Art

Hurwit, Jeffrey M., *The Art and Culture of Early Greece, 1100–480 B.C.* (Ithaca, NY, 1985). Excellent interpretive study of painting, poetry, sculpture, and architecture in Dark Age and Archaic Greece.

Moon, Warren G., ed., *Ancient Greek Art and Iconography* (Madison, WI, 1983). Essays on Greek painting.

Osborne, Robin, *Archaic and Classical Greek Art* (Cambridge, UK, 1998). Imaginative interpretation of Greek art.

Pedley, John Griffiths, *Greek Art and Archaeology* (2nd ed., New York 1998). Standard introductory textbook, well illustrated.

Rasmussen, Tom, and Nigel Spivey, eds., *Looking at Greek Vases* (Cambridge, UK, 1991). Essays by experts, covering different ways of approaching painted pottery.

Stewart, Andrew F., *Greek Sculpture: An Exploration* (2 vols., New Haven, CT, 1990). Comprehensive analysis of Greek sculpture, with very thorough illustrations.

Ancient Texts

Kirk, G. S., J. E. Raven, and M. Schofield, eds., *The Presocratic Philosophers* (2nd ed., Cambridge 1983). The Greek text and good translations and explanations for all the sixth-century B.C. philosophers.

Miller, Andrew, *Greek Lyric* (Indianapolis 1996). Good translations of a selection of archaic poetry.

CHAPTER 10

A TALE OF TWO ARCHAIC CITIES: SPARTA AND ATHENS, 700–480 B.C.

In Chapter 8, "Archaic Greece, 700–480 B.C.: Economy, Society, Politics," and Chapter 9, "The Archaic Cultural Revolution: 700–480 B.C.," we reviewed developments across Archaic Greece as a whole; but in fact, no two *poleis* followed exactly the same path. In this chapter we look in detail at the two best-documented *poleis*, Sparta and Athens. These cities dominated the classical Aegean, but they were among the most unusual archaic *poleis*.

Like all *poleis*, Sparta and Athens faced conflicts within their ruling elites, between these elites and the masses, and between the community as a whole and neighboring states. Both responded by creating internally egalitarian male citizen communities, but in very different ways. In Sparta, state-owned serfs called **helots** worked the land while citizens followed a life-long program of military training in centralized institutions. Athens, on the other hand, encouraged markets and democratic practice; monogamous families were the core institution of Athenian society. While Spartan men were occupied within military institutions, Spartan women developed parallel all-female groups. Athenians, by contrast, drew boundaries within the household, headed by the senior male. Spartans and Athenians both defined citizenship in ethnic terms, but whereas Spartans saw themselves as a conquering race ruling over indigenous helots, most Athenians believed they had always lived in their own land. Whereas Spartans used helots as dependent labor, Athenians turned to non-Greek chattel slaves imported from overseas and privately owned. Sparta and Athens were equally "Greek," but their different ways of being Greek, each with its own institutions, were to tear the Aegean world apart in the fifth century B.C.

SPARTA

The Spartan Mirage

Ancient historians usually complain about not having enough evidence, but with Sparta we almost have too much evidence. Greeks and Romans loved writing about Sparta and created an idealized version of it that we call the **Spartan mirage.** The mirage was a vision of stability, hierarchy, and order in which all knew their place. Greeks regularly contrasted Sparta with Athens, the archetype of undiscipline, freedom, and disorder. Some Greeks (like some moderns) hated the image of Spartan authoritarianism; others loved it. But the stereotype of Sparta was not its reality, which the Spartans themselves deliberately concealed.

The Spartan mirage begins with the story of **Lycurgus** (lī-**kur**-gus), said to have created perfect laws for Sparta. He made all Spartan men equal, regulated their lives, and forged the ultimate fighting machine, according to the story. Around A.D. 100, the learned Greek Plutarch wrote an admiring biography of Lycurgus, but even he conceded that

> Generally speaking it is impossible to make any undisputed statement about Lycurgus the lawgiver, because conflicting accounts have been given of his ancestry, his travels, his death, and above all his activity with respect to his laws and government; but there is least agreement about the period in which the man lived.
>
> Plutarch, *Life of Lycurgus* 1 (R. Talbert)

We do not know how much in the stories that Plutarch and others tell is true and how much is romantic fiction.

SPARTIATES, *PERIOIKOI,* AND HELOTS

Archaeology reveals that Sparta was a major Bronze Age center. In later legends, Helen, who ran off with Paris and thus began the Trojan War, came from Sparta (see Chapter 6, "Homer"). Whatever the truth behind such legends, Sparta was in fact destroyed by fire around 1200 B.C., and **Laconia**—the region around Sparta (see Map 10.1)—declined. There are few Dark Age sites, and only around 900 B.C. do new settlements appear.

The Spartans spoke the dialect of Greek called **Dorian.** According to legend, the Dorians were a distinct people who invaded southern Greece in the twelfth century B.C., soon after the fall of Troy (see Map 1.4 in Chapter 1, "A Small, Far-Off Land"). Archaeologists have argued for a century over whether this Dorian invasion is visible in the material record, but have reached no agreement. So far as archaic and classical history is concerned, though, the Spartans *believed* that they descended from conquering Dorians and that this descent gave them the right to dominate the defeated indigenous peoples.

Probably in the ninth century B.C., Sparta conquered Laconia, reducing its population to dependence (Figure 10.1). The luckier Laconians were called *perioikoi* (peri-**oi**-koi), meaning "dwellers-around." They lived in dozens of independent villages, paid tribute to Sparta, and served in the Spartan army, but did

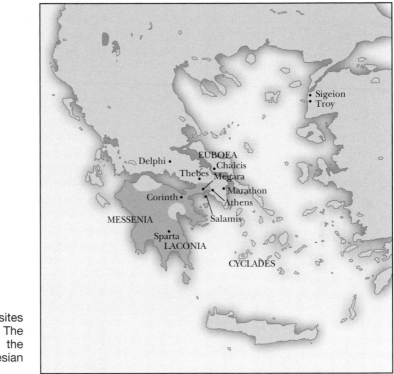

Map 10.1 Regions and sites mentioned in this chapter. The darker area represents the sixth-century Peloponnesian League.

not contribute to decisions about when and where Sparta went to war. The less fortunate Laconians became helots, state-owned slaves. The full Spartan citizens (called **Spartiates**) divided up the land, and the helots worked it for them. The seventh-century Spartiate warrior-poet Tyrtaeus said helots were "like donkeys exhausted under great loads: under painful necessity to bring their masters fully half of the fruit their plowed land produced."

Like the *perioikoi*, helots had their own villages and could marry, but were subject to many disabilities. Plutarch called helotage "the cruelest and most lawless system," and other ancient writers agreed. Helots were sometimes made to wear ridiculous outfits, paraded drunk in public, and whipped. Every year, Spartan officials declared ritual war against them, removing religious pollution for killing a helot, in effect making murder legal. To make the relationship brutally clear, Plutarch explains:

> Periodically the overseers of the young Spartiate men would dispatch into the countryside in different directions the ones who appeared to be particularly intelligent; they were equipped with daggers and basic rations, but nothing else. By day they would disperse to obscure spots in order to hide and rest. At night they made their way to roads and murdered any helot whom they caught. Frequently, too, they made their way through the fields, killing the helots who stood out for their physique and strength.

Plutarch, *Life of Lycurgus* 28 (R. Talbert)

Figure 10.1 The mountain road from Sparta southeast to Kalamata, a typical landscape in southern Greece.

This extreme system, aimed at terrorizing the helots into obedience (they probably outnumbered Spartiates five to one), only partly succeeded. The helots and *perioikoi* hated the Spartiates. Xenophon said that they "showed clearly enough, if there was ever any mention of the Spartiates, they would be glad to eat them, even raw." The helots rebelled whenever they got a chance. The Spartiates' fear of uprisings shaped every aspect of their society.

In the eighth century B.C., population growth increased pressure on resources. Feuds within the elite, struggles between rich and poor, and wars between communities escalated. Some Greeks sent out colonies, but the Spartans' earlier success in conquering Laconia perhaps convinced them that war was the answer to their own problems. Between 740 and 720 B.C., Sparta overran the large, fertile territory of **Messenia,** to the west of the Spartan valley of Lacedaemon, across high mountains (Figure 10.2). They reduced its population to *perioikoi* and helots, probably doubling the land and labor under Spartan control.

Occupied Messenian land and labor made the Spartiates relatively rich. The great challenge was how to distribute the spoils of war. Some Spartans were shut out from the profits: A group called the *Partheniai*, which means "born of virgins," planned a coup in 706. Their name may mean that they were not considered full

Figure 10.2 The wooded slopes of Mount Taygetos, elevation 6,000 feet. The valley of Lacedaemon lies at the bottom of the slope and the plains of Messenia, which the Spartans conquered in the eighth century B.C., on the other side of the mountains.

citizens and were therefore denied a share of the plunder. Whatever the details, when the plot was discovered, the entire group was exiled. Shifting from conquest to colonization, the *Partheniai* sailed to southern Italy and founded a colony there. New wars of expansion after 700 B.C. met with limited success and demands grew for a redistribution of land. A Spartan king was assassinated. Around 650 B.C., the Messenians rose up, to be crushed with unrelenting savagery. Tyrtaeus' military poems (quoted earlier) were composed against the background of that war.

PLUTARCH'S SPARTA

The Spartiates responded to the complex problem of maintaining peace among their own citizens while suppressing the helots by becoming full-time warriors. They believed that Lycurgus designed this system, but modern historians suspect that it took shape gradually, perhaps beginning in the ninth century, when Sparta conquered Laconia, or in the late eighth, during the first Messenian War. Spartan society was certainly militarized by the late seventh century B.C., after a second Messenian War. The Spartan war machine and the society built to support it reached its highest form in the sixth and fifth centuries B.C., then declined in the fourth, as we shall see.

For the details of Spartan society, the most influential account is found in Plutarch's *Life of Lycurgus*:

Lycurgus' . . . most revolutionary reform was his redistribution of the land. For there was dreadful inequality. Many destitute people without means were congregating in the city, while wealth had poured completely into just a few hands. In order to expel arrogance, envy, crime, luxury, and those older and yet more serious political afflictions, wealth and poverty, Lycurgus persuaded the citizens to pool all the land and then redistribute it afresh. Then they would all live on equal terms with one another, with the same amount of property to support each, and they would seek to be the first only in merit. There would be no distinction of inequality between individuals except for what censure of bad conduct and praise of good would determine.

Acting on his word, Lycurgus distributed the rest of Laconia to the *perioikoi* in 30,000 lots, and divided the part subject to the city of Sparta into 9,000. This was the number of lots for Spartiates. . . . There is a story that at some later date when [Lycurgus] was passing through the country just after the reaping and saw the heaps of grain side-by-side and all equal in size, he smiled and remarked to the bystanders that the whole of Laconia had the look of a property which many brothers had recently divided among themselves.

He attempted to divide up their movable property too, in order to remove inequalities and contrasts altogether. But when he saw their adverse reaction to outright expropriation, he went about this in a different way and devised constitutional measures against their greed. First he declared that all gold and silver coinage was now invalid and decreed that only iron should be used as currency; and then he assigned a low value to even a great weight and mass of this, so that a sum of ten *minas*° demanded substantial storage space in a house and a wagon to shift it. Once this was made the legal tender, many types of crime disappeared from Sparta. For who would set out to steal, or accept as a bribe, or rob, or plunder something which could not be hidden, excited no envy when possessed, and could not even profitably be chopped up? For the story is that Lycurgus doused the surface of the red-hot iron with vinegar, thus removing whatever other use and strength it might have, and making it fragile and intractable. . . .

With the aim of stepping up the attack on luxury and removing the passion for wealth, he introduced his third and finest reform, the establishment of common dining messes. The intention was that the Spartiates should assemble together and eat the same specified meat-sauces and cereals. This prevented them from spending their time at home, lying at table on expensive couches, being waited upon by confectioners and chefs, fattened up in the dark like gluttonous animals, and ruining themselves physically as well as morally, and by giving free rein to every craving and excess which demanded lengthy slumbers, warm baths, plenty of rest, and, in a sense, daily nursing. . . .

The boys, too, used to frequent the messes. For them it was like being brought to a school for self-discipline, where they both heard political discussion and witnessed the kind of entertainments appropriate for free men. For their own part they would grow used to making fun and joking without becoming indecent, as well as not taking offense when they were the butt of the joke. In fact this ability to take a joke would seem to be very Spartan. If a joke was too much for someone to take, he could plead with the person making it, and the latter left off. . . .

The food they think most highly of is black broth. Thus the older men do not even ask for a helping of meat but leave it to the young ones, while they have broth poured out for themselves and make a meal of it. There is a story that one of the kings of Pontus° even bought a Laconian cook for the sake of the broth, but after tasting it was not pleased. At this the cook declared, "This is broth to be savored, O king, by those who have bathed in the Eurotas."°

After moderate drinking they depart without a torch. Neither for this journey nor for any other are they allowed to walk with a light, so that they should grow used to the darkness and to traveling cheerfully and fearlessly by night. This, then, is how the messes are organized. . . .

°*ten minas:* Enough money to feed a family of four at a basic level for three years. Plutarch's point is that while you could put ten *minas* in coins in your pocket, in Sparta this much money would be unmanageable.   °*Pontus:* A kingdom on the north coast of modern Turkey.   °*Eurotas:* A river running through Sparta.

Since Lycurgus regarded the upbringing of children as the greatest and noblest responsibility of the legislator, at an early stage he took his start from that by showing much concern for matters relating to marriages and births. Aristotle claims wrongly that he tried to discipline the women but gave up when he could not control the considerable degree of license and power attained by women because of their husbands' frequent campaigning. At these times the men were forced to leave them in full charge, and consequently they used to dance attendance on them to an improper extent and call them their Ladyships.

Lycurgus, rather, showed all possible concern for them too. First he toughened the girls physically by making them run and wrestle and throw the discus and javelin. Thereby their children in embryo would make a strong start in strong bodies and would develop better, while the women themselves would also bear their pregnancies with vigor and would meet the challenge of childbirth in a successful, relaxed way.

He did away with prudery, sheltered upbringing, and effeminacy of any kind. He made young girls no less than young men get used to walking nude in processions, as well as to dancing and singing at certain festivals with the young men present and looking on. On some occasions the girls would make fun of each of the young men, helpfully criticizing their mistakes. On other occasions they would rehearse in song the praises that they had composed about those meriting them, so that they filled the youngsters with a great sense of ambition and rivalry. For the one who was praised for his manliness and became a celebrated figure to the girls went off priding himself on their compliments; whereas the jibes of their playful humor were no less cutting than warnings of a serious type, especially as the kings and elders attended the spectacle along with the rest of the citizens.

There was nothing disreputable about the girls' nudity. It was altogether modest, and there was no hint of immorality. Instead it encouraged simple habits and an enthusiasm for physical fitness, as well as giving the female sex a taste of masculine gallantry, because it too was granted equal participation in both excellence and ambition. As a result the women came to talk as well as to think in the way that Leonidas' wife Gorgo is said to have done. For when some woman, evidently a foreigner, said to her, "You Laconian women are the only ones who can rule men," she replied, "That is because we are the only ones who give birth to men."

There were then these inducements to marry. I mean the processions of girls, and the nudity, and the competitions that the young men watched [Figure 10.3], attracted by a compulsion not of the intellectual type, but (as Plato says) a sexual one.

In addition Lycurgus placed a certain civil disability on those who did not marry, for they were excluded from the Festival of the Naked Boys. In winter the magistrates would order the unmarried men to parade naked in a circle round the town square, and as they paraded they sang a special song composed about themselves, which said that their punishment was fair because they were flouting the laws. In addition they were deprived of the respect and deference which young men habitually showed their elders. Thus nobody objected to what was said to Dercyllidas, even though he was a respected general. When he approached, one of the young men did not give up his seat to him, but said, "You have produced no son who will give his seat to me."

The custom was to capture women for marriage—not when they were slight or immature, but when they were in their prime and ripe for it. The so-called "bridesmaid" took charge of the captured girl. She first shaved her head to the scalp, then dressed her in a man's cloak and sandals, and laid her down alone on a mattress in the dark. The bridegroom—who was not drunk and thus not impotent, but was sober as always—first had dinner in the mess, then would slip in, undo her belt, lift her and carry her to the bed. After spending only a short time with her, he would depart discreetly so as to sleep wherever he usually did along with the other young men. And this continued to be his practice thereafter: while spending the days with his contemporaries, and going to sleep with them, he would warily visit his bride in secret, ashamed and apprehensive in case someone in the house should recognize him.

Figure 10.3 Running girl, bronze, circa 520–500 B.C., found in Serbia but probably made in Sparta. She is not naked like the girls in Plutarch's account, but bares one breast, and both knees are exposed. Height about 4 inches. © *The British Museum.*

His bride at the same time devised schemes and helped to plan how they might meet each other unobserved at suitable moments. It was not just for a short period that young men would do this, but for long enough that some might even have children before they saw their own wives in daylight. Such intercourse was not only an exercise in self-control and moderation, but also meant that partners were fertile physically, always fresh for love, and ready for intercourse rather than being sated and pale from unrestricted sexual activity. Moreover some lingering glow of desire and affection was always left in both.

After making marriage as modest and orderly as this, Lycurgus showed equal concern for removing absurd, unmanly jealousy. While excluding from marriage any kind of outrageous and disorderly behavior, he made it honorable for worthy men to share children and their production, and derided people who hold that there can be no sharing of such things, and who avenge any by assassinations and wars. Thus if an older man with a young wife should take a liking to one of the well bred young men and approve of him, he might well introduce him to her so as to fill her with noble sperm and then adopt the child as his own. Conversely a respectable man who admired someone else's wife noted for her lovely children and her good sense, might gain the husband's permission to sleep with her—thereby planting in fruitful soil, so to speak, and producing fine children who would be linked to fine ancestors by blood and family. . . .

The father of a newborn child was not permitted to make his own decision about whether to rear it, but brought it in his arms to a particular spot called a *leschê* where the eldest men of his tribe° sat. If after examination the baby proved well built and sturdy they instructed the father to bring it up and assigned it one of the 9,000 lots of land. But if it was puny and deformed, they dispatched it to what was called "the place of rejection," a steep spot by Mount Taygetos,° thinking it better both for itself and for the child that the child should die if right from its birth it was poorly endowed for health or strength. And that is why women would test their babies' constitutions by washing them in wine instead of water. The effect of the unmixed wine on ailing and epileptic children is said to be that they lose their senses and their limbs go stiff, whereas healthy ones are toughened by it and acquire a hardier constitution.

The children's nurses exercised special care and skill. To allow free development of limbs and physique, they dispensed with swaddling clothes. They trained children to eat up their food and not be fussy about it, not to be frightened of the dark or of being left alone, and not to be prone to fits of ill-bred temper or crying. . . .

Lycurgus did not put Spartiate children in the care of any tutors who had been bought or hired. Neither was it permissible for each father to bring up and educate his son in the way he chose. Instead, as soon as boys reached the age of seven, Lycurgus took charge of them all himself and distributed them into troops: here he accustomed them to live together and be brought up together, playing and learning as a group. The captaincy of the troop was conferred upon the boy who displayed the soundest judgment and the best fighting spirit. The others kept their eyes on him, responded to his instructions, and endured their punishments from him, so that altogether this training served as a practice in learning ready obedience. Moreover, as they exercised boys were constantly watched by their elders, who were always spurring them on to fight and contend with one another: in this their chief object was to get to know each boy's character, in particular how bold he was, and how far he was likely to stand his ground in combat.

The boys learned to read and write no more than was necessary. Otherwise their whole education was aimed at developing smart obedience, perseverance under stress, and victory in battle. So as they grew older they intensified their physical training and got into the habit of cropping their hair, going barefoot, and exercising naked. From the age of twelve they never wore a tunic and were given only one cloak a year. Their bodies were rough, and knew nothing of baths or oiling; only on a few days in the year did they experience such delights. They slept together by squadron and troop on mattresses that they made themselves from the tips of reeds growing along the river Eurotas, broken off by hand without the help of any iron blade. During winter they added thistledown and mixed it into the mattress, since it was a substance thought to give out warmth.

By this age the boys came to be courted by lovers from among the respectable young men. The older men, too, showed even more interest, visiting the gymnasia frequently and being present when the boys fought and joked with one another. This was not just an idle interest. Instead, there was a sense in which everyone regarded himself as the father, tutor, and commander of each boy. As a result everywhere, on all occasions, there would be somebody to reprimand and punish the boy who slipped up. In addition a Trainer-in-Chief was appointed from among the men with outstanding qualities. They in turn chose as leader for each troop the one out of the so-called Eirens who had the most discretion and fighting spirit. Those who have proceeded two years beyond the boys' class are called "Eirens."

Such an Eiren, twenty years of age, commands those under him in his troop's fights, while in his quarters he has them serve him meals like servants. The burlier boys he instructs to bring wood, the slighter ones to collect vegetables. They steal what they fetch, some of them entering gardens, others slipping into the men's messes with a fine mixture of cunning and caution. If a boy is caught, he receives many lashes of the whip for proving to be such a clumsy, unskilled thief.

°*Eldest men of his tribe: Poleis* divided their citizens into kinship groups called *phylai*, which historians translate as "tribes." Dorian cities had three tribes, and Ionian cities four.
°*steep spot by Mount Taygetus:* Excavations in the 1970s located this gorge, and bones were found there.

The boys also steal whatever provisions they can, thereby learning how to pounce skillfully upon those who are asleep or keeping guard carelessly. A boy is beaten and goes hungry if he is caught. The aim of providing them with only sparse fare is that they should be driven to make up its deficiencies by resort to daring and villainy. While this is the main purpose of their scanty diet, a subsidiary one is claimed to be the development of their physique, helping them in particular to grow tall. . . .

The care which the boys take over their stealing is illustrated by the story of the one who had stolen a fox cub and had it concealed inside his cloak. In order to escape detection he was prepared to have his insides clawed out by the animal, and even to die. This tale is certainly not incredible, judging from the Spartan young men today. I have witnessed many of them dying under the lashes they received at the altar of Artemis Orthia°. . . .

Whether a boy's standing was good or bad, his lover shared it. There is a story that once when a boy had let slip a despicable cry in the course of a fight, it was his lover whom the magistrates fined. Sexual relationships of this type were so highly valued that respectable women would in fact have love affairs with unmarried girls. Yet there was no rivalry. Instead, if individual males found that they desired the same person, they made this the foundation for mutual friendship and eagerly pursued joint efforts to perfect their loved one's character.

Boys were further taught to express themselves in a speaking style that was sharp, yet at the same time attractive and suited to concise exposition of a variety of points. While in the case of his iron money, as I have explained, Lycurgus arranged for heavy weight to be matched by low value, he did the opposite for the currency of speech. Here he developed the technique of expressing a wide range of ideas in just a few, spare words. In his scheme boys, staying silent most of the time, were led to give pithy, well trained answers. By contrast the talk of the person who babbles constantly turns out vapid and mindless, just as excessive sexual activity for the most part leads to barrenness and sterility. Indeed when some Athenian made a joke about how short Laconian swords were, and spoke of the ease with which theatrical conjurors swallow them, King Agis retorted, "All the same, we certainly reach the enemy with these daggers." While the Laconian style of speech may seem brief, in my view it certainly does penetrate to the heart of a matter and makes a forcible impression upon its hearers' minds.

Plutarch, *Life of Lycurgus* 8–19 (R. Talbert)

°*Artemis Orthia:* A local cult, where initiation rites were performed.

Plutarch deeply admired Sparta, yet his account can horrify modern readers. Sparta sounds like a place where brutalized, half-starved, illiterate child molesters bullied the weak, stole, and repressed all common decency. Did husbands really allow other men to sleep with their wives to breed better warriors? Or for the first year or two of marriage, pretend they were not married? Possibly Spartan customs recognized several different kinds of unions, and Plutarch—writing centuries later—misunderstood and combined them into one peculiar kind of marriage. Of course Plutarch placed these curious customs in the distant past. The claim was always that Lycurgus wanted the Spartans to do this or that, but modern times had corrupted his sacred institutions. Xenophon, writing about Sparta five hundred years before Plutarch, thought that the Spartans' ancestral ways were disappearing. Already in the fifth century, some Spartans were rich enough to win Olympic chariot races, the pinnacle of glory for the wealthy. The story that Lycurgus suppressed wealth and inequality cannot be literally true, but it defined the Spartans to themselves. Dedication to "the good old days" reminded the Spartiates of what being a Spartan meant and explained away inequalities as recent aberrations.

We should not believe every word in Plutarch, but archaic Sparta was different from most *poleis*. We can draw some general conclusions from Plutarch's account.

The Spartan claim that luxury, wealth, and debt were recent departures from an older equality encouraged martial valor in a state that was a band of brothers. Boys grew up in single-sex paramilitary institutions; girls grew up at home, with few men around. Pederasty flourished and perhaps women had more license than elsewhere, in the conviction that such behavior would produce stronger sons. To make sure their sons grew up brave, tough, and disciplined, Spartans undermined the nuclear family, the basis of society elsewhere in Greece. Every *polis* wanted effective warriors, but no other was willing to pay so high a price. As Xenophon observed, "The most extraordinary thing of all is that despite the universal praise for this code of behavior, not a single city is willing to copy it."

SPARTAN GOVERNMENT

Sparta had an unusual political system, with four main political institutions: the kings, the Council of Elders, the Council of Ephors, and the Assembly. By 700 B.C., most *poleis* discarded kings, but Sparta, always different, had a **double monarchy.** Two families, the Agiads and the Eurypontids, each provided a king, possibly a relic of some compromise in Sparta's early history. The kings had authority in war and were the highest religious officers. The two rulers had equal standing and in archaic times led the army jointly, until one king left the other king in the lurch in a war against Athens in 506 B.C. A new law decreed that only one king could be with the army at a time.

The two kings also served with twenty-eight other members on the **Council of Elders.** The Council settled all serious lawsuits and determined what questions to put before the Assembly, which consisted of the male Spartiate citizens. Because Sparta had no written laws, the power of the Elders went beyond that of modern judges and juries combined. The Assembly elected the Elders. When there was a vacancy, all men over sixty (when they ceased to be eligible for military service) paraded before the Spartiates, and whoever got the loudest shout was chosen.

Being made an Elder was the greatest honor in Sparta. Only about five percent of the population lived until their sixtieth birthday, so we estimate that roughly one in ten men still alive in their sixties would attain this rank. Very few Elders lived to serve on the Council for more than ten years, whereas a king who came to the throne as a youth could serve for forty years or more. The kings' influence on the Council waxed and waned.

Each year the Assembly also elected by acclamation five **Ephors,** or Overseers. Ephors served for one year and could not be re-elected. They supervised the kings and Elders, with authority to impeach or depose them if they broke the (unwritten) laws. Two Ephors always accompanied the kings on campaign, and Ephors also supervised Assembly meetings. They held formidable powers, but at the end of his year in office, each Ephor had to go through a judicial review by the new Ephors. This meant that Ephors had to be very careful about whom they offended while in office.

The **Assembly** included all Spartiate men aged over thirty and met outdoors at each full moon. The Elders made proposals and the citizens shouted approval or disapproval, without discussion.

The Spartans prided themselves on their balanced constitution, in which different institutions exercised checks and balances on each other. The kings controlled war and religion, the Elders controlled law, and the Ephors ensured fair play. In theory, the citizens made the final decisions, although as early as the seventh century, a law was added that allowed the kings and Elders simply to adjourn the Assembly and proceed without its approval if they felt that the citizens were making "a crooked choice."

Political power was in the hands of a tiny elite. The Spartiates made up less than five percent of the population of Laconia, and the effective decision-makers were barely one percent of the Spartiates. Because each institution within this political elite depended on the others, drastic change was difficult, and the Spartan consti-tution was stable from the seventh or sixth until the third century B.C. The absence of a hierarchy of offices, however, combined with Spartan deference to authority, meant that charismatic individuals could gain great power. Kings who did well in war and diplomacy extended their influence into civil society; when the kings were weak, enterprising Ephors or Elders did the reverse. Backroom deals, favoritism, and betrayal were common. When Sparta had strong leaders, the system worked well, but when leadership was weak, it worked poorly. Because of the habit of defer-ring to authority, indecision was easier than action. Sparta relied on oracles when its leaders could not decide, and other *poleis* bribed oracles to mislead Spartans.

Yet Sparta never had a tyrant, avoided serious civil unrest for half a millennium, and for generations no one defeated its hoplites in the field. For much of this period, Sparta was the greatest military power in Greece. Its leaders continued the policy of annexation that had worked in Messenia, but after setbacks around 560 B.C., they abandoned it. Thereafter, they worked with oligarchies in other cities, offering them military support against popular uprisings, would-be tyrants within their own ranks, and rivals in other *poleis*. In return, the cities joined a Spartan alliance that modern historians call the **Peloponnesian League** (see Map 10.1). The allies swore "to have the same friends and enemies, and to follow the Spartans wherever they lead." They did not pay tribute and could not be forced to go to war. The League was bicameral, with the Spartan Assembly voting first, then the allies as a group having the right of veto. Even if the allied assembly agreed on war, individual allies could still reject Spartan plans. The League was basically defensive and rarely acted north of the Isthmus of Corinth. By 500 B.C., the combination of the Spartiates' ferocity and the numbers of allied hoplites meant that no Greek state dared challenge Sparta directly. As we shall see in Chapter 11, "Persia and the Greeks, 550–490 B.C.," and Chapter 12, "The Great War, 480–479 B.C.," even the greatest foreign powers did so at their own risk.

ATHENS

Archaic Athens faced many of the same problems as Sparta, but responded differ-ently. The result—a *polis* based on equal male citizenship—was similar in both cases. But Athenians and Spartans each defined *citizens* and *equal* in their own way. The two cities were as different as was possible within ancient Greece.

THE SEVENTH-CENTURY CRISIS

As population grew in the eighth century B.C., both Athens and Sparta had more mouths to feed. Whereas Sparta had a tradition of military expansion, Athens did not. Its neighbors were more populous, richer, and better organized than Messenia. Nor did Athens follow the example of its neighbors and send colonies to Sicily, al-though we are not sure why. Rising population put greater pressures on farmers. In the precarious ancient economy, drought, a run of bad harvests, poor planning, or simple bad luck could force a farmer to seek help. As Hesiod explains, the first step was to ask relatives, friends, and neighbors:

> . . . Measure carefully
> when you must borrow from your neighbor, then
> pay back the same, or more if possible,
> and you will have a friend again in time of need.
>
> Hesiod, *Works and Days* 349–51 (D. Wender)

But what if you could not pay back what you had borrowed?

> Give to him who gives, but not, if he does not.
> We give to generous men, but no one gives
> to stingy ones. Give is a lovely girl,
> but Grab is bad, and she takes only death.
> . . . don't let it be
> that you should take your children and your wife
> and beg with downcast spirit for your food
> from neighbors who refuse to care. You may
> succeed two times or three. But after that,
> you'll bother them in vain, and all your words
> will come to nothing, and your argument will fail.
>
> Hesiod, *Works and Days* 354–56, 399–403 (D. Wender)

Hesiod assumes that borrowers and lenders alike were farmers living close to the margin. But rather than going to an equally poor neighbor, a failing farmer might approach someone richer, who could demand the borrower's land—or even his person—as security. If he failed his obligations, the borrower could take his land or make him a debt-slave. This is what happened in seventh-century Attica, according to an important document ascribed to Aristotle (fourth century B.C.):

> The Athenians' society was oligarchic in all other respects, and in particular the poor were enslaved to the rich—themselves and their children and their wives. The poor were called "dependents" and "sixth-parters," because it was for the rent [or tribute] of a sixth that they worked the fields of the rich. All the land was in the hands of a few, and if the poor failed to pay their rents both they and their children were liable to seizure. All loans were made on the security of the person until the time of Solon: he was the first champion of the people. The harshest and bitterest aspect of the society for the masses was the fact of their enslavement, though they were discontented on other grounds too. It could be said that there was nothing in which they had a share.
>
> Aristotle, *Constitution of Athens* 2 (P.J. Rhodes)

The concentration of wealth in the hands of the rich generated resistance. In Sparta, as we saw, there was a failed coup in 706 B.C., but the Spartiates maintained cohesion and reorganized society around their triumphant hoplite army. In Athens, by contrast, the ruling elite, called the *Eupatridai* (yu-pa-**trē**-dī, "well born ones"), basically fell apart. In 632 B.C., a young Olympic victor named Cylon (**sī**-lon) launched a coup, helped by his father-in-law, the tyrant of Athens' enemy Megara down the coast (we quoted Thucydides' account of this incident in Chapter 8). When Cylon failed, the Athenians massacred his followers, although they had promised them safe passage. The recriminations that followed deepened divisions within the aristocracy, and the Athenian Assembly laid down a curse on the important **Alcmaeonid** (alk-**mē**-o-nid) family for its part—with unexpected repercussions to follow a century later.

In 621 B.C., **Dracon** (**drā**-kōn) was empowered to set up a new law code (famous for prescribing death for virtually every crime—hence our word *draconian*), but the code did not reduce tensions. This divided society was poorly suited to providing patriotic soldiers, and Athens lost wars with several neighbors over the next twenty years. Megara seized the large island of Salamis off Athens' harbor, worsening Athens' land shortage and exacerbating conflicts at home. The *Eupatridai* were in such disarray that rather than planning reconquest of the island, they passed a law condemning to death anyone who mentioned the loss. As Johnny-come-latelies to Greek colonization, the Athenians sent a colony to the north Aegean, but in 607 B.C., it was defeated and ignominiously thrown out.

SOLON

Athens had lost territory, its aristocracy was racked by feuds, and class warfare was breaking out when in 594 B.C. the *Eupatridai* chose **Solon** (**sō**-lon), one of their number, to work out a compromise with the rebellious poor. Solon produced a new law code, as comprehensive as that which the Spartans attributed to Lycurgus. Solon, however, certainly existed; some three hundred lines of his poetry survive, and the wooden boards recording his laws could still be seen in the fifth century. In the fourth century B.C., lawyers liked to claim that any laws favoring their clients had been passed by Solon, to make them sound more weighty, but the main outlines of his reforms are clear enough.

Solon, like the Spartans, saw the ideal society as a band of brothers. The Spartans made their system work by stealing their neighbors' land, turning the former owners into serfs, and breaking down family structures to support the warrior brotherhood. No such options were available to Solon, who reorganized the existing economy and society by redefining property rights.

He began with Athenians' ownership of their own bodies. From now on, no one could own another freeborn Athenian. All current debt-bondsmen were freed; those sold into slavery abroad were brought home; no loan could ever again be secured on someone's person; and all outstanding debts were canceled. He then redistributed land, although we are not sure how. In one poem, he appeals to "the mighty mother of the Olympian gods, dark Earth, whose boundary stones fixed in many places I once removed; enslaved before, she is now free," but in another, he says, "It gives me no pleasure to act with the violence of tyranny or to share the country's rich land equally between *kakoi* and *esthloi*."[18] Probably he did not redistribute the land into equal-sized plots, as Lycurgus was thought to have done at Sparta, but returned to its original owners land that had been used as security on loans and then lost. We know that there were still big landowners in the later sixth century, but also a broad class of peasant freeholders. Solon also defended the right of landowners without children to sell, give, or will their land to whomever they wished, regardless of what their relatives thought. Plutarch, who wrote a *Life of Solon* as well as of Lycurgus, recognized that "the effect of this law was to make every man's possessions truly his own."

Athenians called Solon's reforms the ***seisachtheia*** (sās-ak-**thē**-a), or "shaking-off-of-burdens." But there were still too many people and not enough land, and just ending debt-bondage could easily have made things worse: If the poor could not borrow on the security of their persons, the rich had less reason to lend in bad years. But Solon promoted a sounder economic base. He banned the export of grain from Attica. Bad harvests can turn into famines if rich landowners get a better price for their wheat abroad, so Solon required them to sell all grain at home. Much Athenian soil was not good for growing cereals, but was excellent for olives and vines: Solon encouraged these crops. He clarified weights and measures to simplify exchange, required fathers to teach their sons a trade, and established incentives for craftsmen to come to Athens.

Archaeological finds reflect an increased prosperity after Solon. Sculpture and pot painting reached new heights of excellence in early sixth-century Athens. Athenian clay vessels for olive oil, called "SOS amphoras" after the design on their necks, are widespread around the Mediterranean, and after 550 B.C. Athenian fine pottery turns up everywhere from Spain to Syria. Athens expanded her silver mining, exporting silver coin and importing more and more food (Figure 10.4). Athens not only survived her crisis, but flourished.

Solon overhauled the political system by dividing all citizens into four census classes based on wealth:

1. The *pentakosiomedimnoi,* "five-hundred-measures men," whose land yielded over 500 *medimnoi* of produce each year. They could hold all political offices in the state.

2. The *hippeis,* "horsemen," who produced 300 to 499 *medimnoi.* They could hold all offices except treasurer.

Figure 10.4 Two sides of an Athenian silver coin, circa 525–500 B.C. On the left is the goddess Athena in her trademark helmet; on the right are other symbols of Athens—an olive branch, an owl, and three Greek letters spelling "Athe," in abbreviation for Athens. These coins, known as *owls,* are found all over the Mediterranean and attest to Athens' export of silver to pay for imports (particularly food and slaves).

3. The *zeugitai*, "yokemen" (probably meaning they had enough land to need a full team of oxen), producing 200 to 299 *medimnoi*. A *zeugitês* could hold lower political offices but could not serve as treasurer or as archon (**ar**-kon), "leader."

4. The *thêtes*, or "poor," producing less than 200 *medimnoi*. They could not hold political offices but attended the Assembly and served as jurors.

Nearly all Athenians were *thêtes*. A *medimnos* was a measure of volume equivalent to about seventy-five pounds of barley or ninety pounds of wheat, so the requirements for belonging to the upper classes were high. A typical peasant farm in classical Attica was about five hectares (one hectare is about two and a half acres), but to qualify as a *zeugitês,* a man would need ten to twenty hectares, and as a *pentakos-iomedimnos* at least twenty-five to fifty hectares. Although the top property class was poor by Near Eastern standards, probably only one in ten Athenians qualified.

Nine **archons** were elected each year from the top two classes. One served as chief archon, with extensive powers. A man could be archon only once, but after his year in office he became a life-member of the council known as the **Areopagus** (a-rē-**op**-a-gus, "stake of Ares"), named after the hill beneath the west end of the Athenian Acropolis where the council met (the Acropolis was the fortified hill that dominated Athens, where stood the major temple of Athena). This upper-class body tried major lawsuits, especially murder, and had general judicial oversight.

As a balance against its power, Solon created juries manned by citizens of all classes to hear appeals against the Areopagus. He allowed any Athenian, regardless of census class, to bring suit against anyone else before these juries. According to Aristotle, he deliberately worded the laws vaguely so the juries had maximum control over legal interpretation (his most democratic reform, Aristotle thought).

The Assembly, apparently open to all citizens who wanted to attend the meetings, probably decided war and peace and elected the archons, and perhaps dealt with other major decisions. In Sparta the citizen assembly simply shouted yes or no to proposals made by the Elders, and if the Elders did not like the assembly's response, they could overrule it. But Solon designed a **Council of 400** men chosen from all four property classes to prepare agendas for the Assembly. Whoever controlled the agenda controlled the meeting, so this act gave even the poorest citizen a voice in politics.

Solon wanted to strike a balance between rich and poor and to restrain elite feuding. He advised the rich:

> Quiet the strong spirit in your hearts,
> you who have glutted yourselves with many good things,
> and in moderation set aside your ambition.
> We shall not allow you to proceed like this.
> To the masses I gave as much privilege as is sufficient,
> neither taking away from their honor nor adding more to it.
> And as for those who had power, and were envied for wealth,
> I took care that they too should receive no indignity.
> I stood holding a strong shield about both the parties,
> and did not allow either to win an unjust victory.
>
> Solon fragments 4c, 5 (P.J. Rhodes, modified)

Solon departed most strongly from the Spartans in seeing the ideal community as an agglomeration of independent households, with the male heads of these households coming together in ritual, war, and politics to constitute a brotherhood. Solon had no interest in Spartan-type public dining messes, but worked to strengthen the nuclear family and the authority of its male head. Plutarch says that Solon limited dowries to reduce fortune-hunting men marrying for money and insisted on the sexual basis of honest marriage, decreeing that "an heiress' husband should have intercourse with her at least three times a month. Even if they have no children, this is a mark of honor and affection that a man owes to a chaste wife; it removes many of the frustrations that arise in such cases and prevents their differences from bringing about a complete estrangement." He also regulated women's behavior and travel, restricting them to the domestic sphere under a man's control. Unlike the Spartiates, Athenian men combined the roles of husband, father, farmer, warrior, trader, and citizen. They would support themselves through their own enterprise, not through the labors of state-owned helots.

PISISTRATUS AND THE CONSEQUENCES OF SOLON'S REFORMS

At first Solon's reforms appeared as ineffectual as Dracon's thirty years earlier. In 590 B.C. and again in 586, elite conflicts were so severe that no archon could be appointed. A certain Damasias, elected archon in 582, refused to step down in 581, probably seeking a tyranny, but was forced out. In the 570s, three factions formed, known as the parties of the Plain, Shore, and Hill, combining regional and class solidarities to support individual aristocrats. Aristotle says, "In general the Athenians remained in an unhealthy state in their relations with one another. Some had the cancellation of debts as the origin and explanation of their discontent, because they had been impoverished by it; others were discontented with the constitution because of the great change that had been made; others were motivated by personal rivalry."

Solon's cancellation of debts must have thrown the upper class into chaos, giving windfall profits to some and ruining others. Many lost land they thought their own, and most lost their ability to coerce labor. There was little reason to have a large estate if there was no one to farm it. A normal family can effectively work only a few acres—nowhere near enough to qualify as *zeugitai*, let alone as *pentakosiomedimnoi*. Solon's poetry gives the impression that few *Eupatridai* cared to spend all day in the hot sun behind a heavy plow. They might hire workers, but they would need to make enough profit from selling produce to pay competitive wages. With a large, landless population the cost of labor is low, but by returning land to the poor Solon effectively increased the price of labor. People preferred working their own land to being wage earners. To compound the problem, the times when large landowners needed labor most—the seasons of sowing and harvesting—were the same times that small farmers also needed labor.

The Athenian aristocracy solved their problem in the early sixth century B.C. by importing foreign slaves. In the seventh century, it was cheaper to reduce the local poor to serfdom than to import and maintain slaves, but in sixth-century Athens slavery became structurally necessary to society. Cheap slaves were available

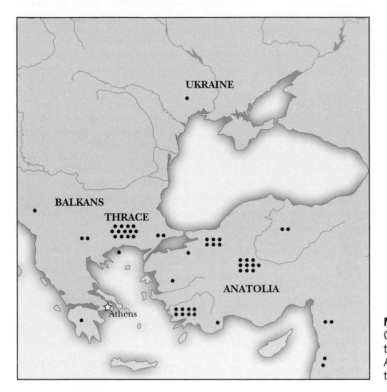

Map 10.2 Two groups of Classical Athenian inscriptions tell us the origins of fifty-four Athenian slaves. Each dot on the map represents one slave.

from the Balkans, the Ukraine, and Anatolia (Map 10.2). When Herodotus listed the customs of the Thracians (living in modern Bulgaria), he matter-of-factly said, "They carry on an export trade in their own children."

Slaves allowed rich Athenians to stay rich without driving the poor back into serfdom. Ironically, freedom and slavery depended on each other in ancient Greece—the free Spartiates depended on enslaved helots, the free Athenians, on imported slaves. By the fourth century B.C., probably one in four residents of Attica were slaves, who could be found in nearly every walk of life, particularly crafts, mining, and agriculture. Even modestly wealthy households would own a slave.

In 561 B.C. a powerful aristocrat named **Pisistratus** (pī-**sis**-tra-tus) launched a bloodless coup and established a tyranny. Pisistratus had won popularity by recapturing the island of Salamis from Athens' rival Megara. Following a strategy for seizing power described in Chapter 8, he pretended to have been attacked by rivals so that the Assembly allowed him a small bodyguard armed with clubs. Like most *poleis*, Athens had no standing army or police. Pisistratus then simply announced that he was now in charge. Nonetheless, Aristotle says, "He administered affairs more like a citizen than a tyrant," governing through political alliances more than the implied threat of his club-bearers.

Sometimes the difference between being a tyrant and being the most influential oligarch was subtle, and when in 556 B.C. two rivals—Megacles and Lycurgus (not the same as the legendary Spartan of the same name)—pushed Pisistratus aside, he remained in Athens and continued to play a role in politics. Soon after, Lycurgus pushed Megacles aside too, so in 551 B.C. Megacles made Pisistratus an offer: If Pisistratus married Megacles' daughter, Megacles would help him regain the tyranny. Herodotus tells the strange story:

> Pisistratus agreed to the terms that Megacles proposed, and then, to bring about his return to power, they devised between them what seems to me the silliest trick that history has to record. The Greeks have never been simpletons; for centuries past they have been distinguished from other nations by their superior wits, and of all Greeks the Athenians are considered to be the most intelligent: yet it was at the Athenians' expense that this ridiculous trick was played. In the village of Paeania there was a beautiful woman named Phyê [**fu**-ē], nearly six feet tall, whom they fitted out in a suit of armor and mounted in a chariot. Then, after getting her to pose in the most striking attitude, they drove into Athens where messengers who had preceded them were already, according to their instructions, talking to the people and urging them to welcome Pisistratus back because the goddess Athena herself had shown him extraordinary honor and was bringing him home to her own acropolis [Figure 10.5]. They spread this nonsense all over the town, and it was not long before rumor reached the outlying villages that Athena was bringing Pisistratus back, and both villagers and townsfolk, convinced that the woman Phyê was indeed the goddess, offered her their prayers and received Pisistratus with open arms.

> Herodotus 1.60 (A. de Selincourt)

Figure 10.5 Chariot driven by Athena with Artemis as passenger. Artemis wears a decorated gown and holds a bow. Athena wears a cloak, but no helmet or other attribute. Both figures are named. Archaic Athenian black-figure vase, 3 feet high, signed by Sophilos, circa 580 B.C. © *The Trustees of The British Museum.*

Pisistratus again relied on alliances to keep power, but soon lost Megacles' support. Pisistratus worried that any children he had by Megacles' daughter might stand in the way of his sons, already grown. So,

> To prevent his new wife from having any children he refused normal intercourse and lay with her in an unnatural way. For a time his wife said nothing about this insult, but later—perhaps in answer to a question—she told her mother, and her mother told Megacles, who was so angry at the slight upon himself and his daughter, that he made up his quarrel with his political enemies. This new threat persuaded Pisistratus to get out of the country altogether.
>
> Herodotus 1.61 (A. de Selincourt)

In exile, Pisistratus went over the situation with his sons. He borrowed money and soldiers from rich men and tyrants in other cities and hired mercenaries. In 546 B.C. he and his men landed in Attica on the beach at Marathon (site of the later famous battle against the Persians in 490 B.C.). Various malcontents joined him. For a while, the Athenians ignored him, then finally sent out an army but had little heart for a fight. Pisistratus surprised them while they ate lunch or napped. He persuaded the remnants to go home, then confiscated all weapons in private hands.

Pisistratus had again triumphed, but this time his grip was tighter, and he brought many benefits to the city. Later, Athenians remembered his reign as a golden age of peace and security. By the time Pisistratus died in 527 B.C., Athens was richer than in Solon's time, houses better built, public facilities improved, petty industry and mining flourishing, and Athenian goods widely exported. By the 520s, Athenian "black glaze" drinking vessels were the most common traded wares in the whole Mediterranean Sea. The city's growth to perhaps twenty-five thousand people, many of them artisans, meant that Athenian farmers always found buyers for their produce, while the high value of Athenian manufactured goods meant that farmers from other *poleis*, or even outside Greece, could get so good a price for their grain that it was worth shipping to Athens. Athenian farmers exchanged high-value olive oil for imported food, and the painful conflicts of the seventh century slipped away.

Pisistratus feared aristocratic plots. Rather than following Thrasyboulos' advice to kill the outstanding men in the city (Chapter 8), he wisely made them part of the successful enterprise, allowing potential rivals to hold office and to profit from the regime. He also elevated poorer citizens, listened to the Assembly, and followed the laws. He instituted new taxes, something everyone hated about tyrants, but from the revenue he provided loans for farmers to develop their land and he constructed ambitious public buildings. Some, like fountain houses and drains, benefited everyone. He overhauled the legal system, creating local justices who reported directly to him. In reducing aristocratic power he strengthened institutions of the centralized state.

When Pisistratus died in 527 B.C., his sons ruled as a junta, but the oldest of them, **Hippias,** wielded the real power. He and his brother **Hipparchus** continued to promote Athens as a cultural center, inviting great poets to their court. Pisistratus had himself instituted festivals, including the Panathenaea, and perhaps he introduced public recitations of Homer based on complete texts (see Chapter 6). Athens was the leading center for innovation in sculpture and painting. However, in 514 B.C., Thettalos, the youngest of Pisistratus' sons, fell in love with a boy named **Harmodius,** who was in turn the beloved of the mature **Aristogeiton** (a-ris-tō-jī-ton). Harmodius rebuffed Thettalos, who then used his influence to exclude Harmodius' sister from the great Panathenaic festival, a massive insult to Harmodius' family. He and Aristogeiton decided to murder the tyrants. The plot misfired, and they killed only Hipparchus. Guards cut down Harmodius on the spot. Aristogeiton was captured and tortured to death.

In the fifth century B.C., many thought Harmodius and Aristogeiton had overthrown the tyrants (which they did not), and they were honored as champions of freedom—even though their real motives were sex, anger, and revenge (Figure 10.6). Their descendants were exempted from taxes and had the right to dine at public expense. Popular songs celebrated them as Athens' saviors. In fact, their attack earned only a crackdown. Hippias executed or exiled many noblemen

Figure 10.6 Harmodius and Aristogeiton. When Hippias fell in 510 B.C., the Athenians set up statues of Harmodius and Aristogeiton in the Agora. The Persians took the original group in 480 B.C. (Alexander the Great later returned it), so the Athenians set up new statues. These too are now lost, but this photograph shows a Roman copy, today in Naples. The clean-shaven Harmodius holds a sword in his upraised left hand while his bearded lover Aristogeiton extends a rock in his left hand, a protective cape draped over his arm.

and soon lost the support of leading families. He appealed to the curse laid on the Alcmaeonid family in 632 B.C. to exile this powerful clan. Exploiting Sparta's opposition to tyrants and faith in oracles, the Alcmaeonids bribed the Delphic priests to give the same response to every Spartan who sought advice: "First free Athens." The Alcmaeonids rebuilt the temple of Apollo, recently damaged by fire, and paid for a top-grade marble façade out of their own pockets. Sparta and the Pisistratids had good relations, but Sparta's attitude, Herodotus says, was "no matter—the commands of the god are more important than human ties."

An initial Spartan raid on Athens in 511 B.C. failed when Hippias' friends in Thessaly sent a thousand cavalry, who routed the Spartans. But the next year, Sparta's king Cleomenes returned with a larger army and defeated the Thessalians. Many Athenians now joined the Spartans, and Hippias withdrew to the acropolis. The Spartans captured Hippias' sons and exchanged them for Hippias' pledge to go into exile. The tyrants had fallen.

DÊMOKRATIA

The Spartan king Cleomenes promptly went home (510 B.C.), and Athens returned to the kind of aristocratic politicking that Pisistratus had suspended in 546. Soon **Cleisthenes** (klī-sthen-ēz, one of the Alcmaeonids) emerged as the strongest man in the state. Throughout Archaic times, aristocrats had mobilized ordinary citizens to overthrow their rivals, putting new oligarchs or a tyrant in their place, but after about 525 citizens insisted on taking parts of government for themselves. Cleisthenes ceded power to ordinary Athenians in return for their help. Cleisthenes' first step was to break up the four old "tribes" (*phylai*), kinship groups that had been sources of aristocratic power. Cleisthenes divided Attica into thirty units called *trittyes* ("thirtieths"). Modifying the regional groupings so important in politics since the 570s, he clustered the *trittyes* into three groups of ten, one group each from the coastal, inland, and urban areas (Map 10.3). Each *trittys* contained several villages or city neighborhoods, designated by the word *dêmos* ("people," but when used to describe one of Cleisthenes' units, we translate it **"deme"**). Formerly, Athenian men were known by their personal name (they had only one) and their father's name (for example, Hippias son of Pisistratus). From now on, they were known by their name and deme (for example, Pericles of Cholargus).

Solon's Council of 400, which drew up the agenda for the Assembly, had one hundred men from each of the old four tribes. Cleisthenes replaced it with a **Council of 500,** composed of fifty men selected by lot from each of ten new tribes. Councillors had to be over thirty, served for a year, and could serve only twice in their lifetimes. This meant that almost every Athenian citizen would have to serve. Men were chosen by lot to serve as president of the Council for twenty-four hours. Roughly three out of every four citizens would fill this position at some point in their lives; and about one citizen in twelve would hold the position on a day when there was a meeting of the full Assembly, in which case he would preside over six thousand or more of his fellow citizens as they made life-and-death decisions about war and peace or the food supply.

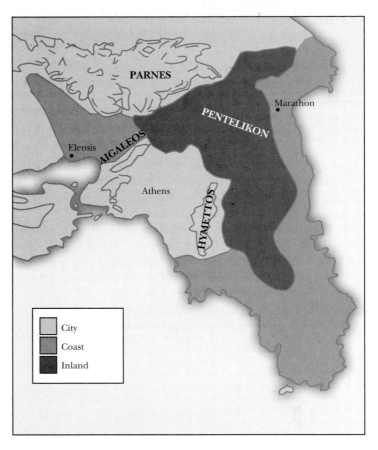

Map 10.3 The complicated political landscape created by Cleisthenes' reforms. The map shows the city, coast, and inland areas. The circles represent demes; the links between them show *trittyes.*

Athenians eventually termed their new political system *dêmokratia,* "power of the people." Our word democracy of course comes from this word. *Dêmokratia* looks undemocratic today: The *dêmos,* "people," excluded women, children, and slaves. But from an ancient Greek perspective, it was a radical system. The men on the Council came from every walk of Athenian life, from peasants to politicians. Cleisthenes himself might sit in the Council next to a farmer who had never been more than a day's walk from his home, and both were expected to have something to say. The constitution *required* that all citizens be involved. Fewer than one citizen in ten could read. But Athenians wanted ordinary citizens to set the agenda.

All citizens were free to come to the Assembly, discuss the issues, vote, and put decisions into action. Political power did not depend on winning elections every four years, but on coming to the Assembly, speaking, and persuading people on the day of the vote. Politicians had to keep turning up at meetings of the Assembly; a single vote could wipe out years of work. Political leaders could attempt bribery and make secret deals, but after the citizens took over Athens' government in 508, real power came from speaking well in the Assembly. If a man lost the people's support, they might fine, exile, or even execute him.

Athenians recognized the importance of individual leaders. In Chapter 8, we mentioned the remarkable annual unpopularity contest called **ostracism,** designed to prevent anyone being *too* popular and (like Pisistratus) using the Assembly as a stepping-stone to tyranny. Each year, the Athenians could vote to send one man away for ten years, a punishment in anticipation of a crime (but the ostracized man's property remained intact until he returned). First the Assembly voted on whether there should be an ostracism that year. If six thousand citizens voted and the majority said yes, then each citizen took a fragment of broken pottery (an *ostrakon* in Greek, hence ostracism) and wrote a name on it. Those who could not write could buy prewritten potsherds (Figure 10.7). Whoever got the most votes had to leave town for ten years.

Athenians went to extraordinary lengths to minimize the political advantages that education, experience, or contacts gave some men. They wanted all men to be involved in making decisions that affected the group, and even used complicated lottery machines to randomize participation. The Athenians would not have thought our political systems democratic. If rich people with years of experience in professional government, law, or business make the major decisions, these systems are oligarchies, not democracies, even if we vote every four years on which wealthy professionals govern us.

Figure 10.7 An *ostrakon* with the names of the famous Themistocles, who led the Athenians to victory against Persia in 480 B.C., and the unknown Odeadeios. Over two hundred *ostraka* inscribed "Themistocles" were found in a single deposit, evidently to be passed out to those who could not write.

Dêmokratia developed archaic traditions, but also broke with them. The sense of community was strong in early Greece, where the *aristoi* never really distanced themselves from the *kakoi* and were always answerable to them. The Greeks rejected divine kingship and increasingly turned to public discussion to solve problems. Cleisthenes and democratic reformers in other *poleis* extended such principles. Formerly, aristocrats were answerable to the people, but claimed to act as guardians. In the late sixth century, the citizens began to doubt that aristocrats had no advantage in wisdom. Sometimes a rich man would have the best idea; sometimes a poor man. Because all citizens shared wisdom, the sensible way to run a state was to make its institutions as open as possible.

Few Greek texts spell out this new vision explicitly, because most literate people were ambiguous about or even hostile toward democracy. The clearest statement comes in one of Plato's philosophical dialogues, probably written in the 390s B.C. In it the thinker Protagoras explains the logic of democracy to Socrates (who later challenges it). Protagoras casts his explanation as a myth, not an abstract argument. When the gods created the world, he said, they told Epimetheus ("afterthought") to hand out attributes to the animals. To some he gave claws and teeth; to others, protective shells; to others still, speed. By the time he came to humans, he had given away all the available powers. But his brother Prometheus ("foresight") stole fire and arts such as speech and house-building from the other gods and gave them to humans as their special gift.

> Thus provided for, the humans lived at first in scattered groups; there were no cities. Consequently they were devoured by wild beasts, because they were in every respect the weaker, and their technical skill, though a sufficient aid to their nature, did not extend to making war on the beasts, for they had not the art of politics, of which the art of war is a part. They sought therefore to save themselves by coming together and founding fortified cities, but when they gathered in communities they injured one another for want of political skill, and so scattered again and continued to be devoured. Zeus therefore, fearing the total destruction of our race, sent Hermes to impart to men the qualities of respect for others and a sense of justice so as to bring order into our cities and create a bond of friendship and union. Hermes asked Zeus in what manner he was to bestow these gifts on men. "Shall I distribute them as the arts were distributed—that is, on the principle that one trained doctor suffices for many laymen, and so with the other experts? Shall I distribute justice and respect for their fellows in this way, or to all alike?" "To all," said Zeus. "Let all have their share. There could never be cities if only a few shared in these virtues, as in the arts. Moreover, you must lay it down as my law that if anyone is incapable of acquiring his share of these two virtues he shall be put to death as a plague to the city."
>
> Thus it is, Socrates, and from this cause, that in a debate involving skill in building, or in any other craft, the Athenians, like other men, believe that few are capable of giving advice, and if someone outside those few volunteers to advise them, they do not tolerate it—rightly so, in my submission. But when the subject of their counsel involves political wisdom, which must always follow the path of justice and moderation, they listen to every man's opinion, for they think that everyone must share in this kind of virtue; otherwise the state could not exist. That, Socrates, is the reason for this."
>
> Plato, *Protagoras* 322B–323A (W.K.C. Guthrie)

If Protagoras' logic holds, then democracy is the only rational way to run a community. But to critics, democracy maximized the input of ignorant people. What right did Cleisthenes have to bring the rabble onto the political stage, to gain his own advantage? One Isagoras—Cleisthenes' major rival in Athenian political circles—asked Sparta's king Cleomenes to return to Athens and set things straight. Cleisthenes fled as in 508 B.C. as Cleomenes marched in with a small force and banished seven hundred families. Isagoras wanted to set up a ruling Council of 300 men to run Athens with himself at its head. He asked Cleomenes to disband the current Council responsible for setting the Assembly's agenda. But the city rose up in a mob. Cleomenes and Isagoras fled to the Acropolis and for two days crowds raged outside its gates. On the third day, Cleomenes and Isagoras quietly surrendered, selling out their friends in return for safe passage to Sparta.

ATHENS SUBMITS TO PERSIA

The new democracy was saved, but there was no guarantee of its future. Sparta's enraged King Cleomenes roused the Peloponnesian League to attack Athens and—contrary to Sparta's traditions of opposing tyranny—planned to install Isagoras as tyrant. He arranged a triple attack in 506 B.C., with armies from Thebes and Chalcis invading at the same time as Sparta. Athens seemed doomed, until Sparta's Corinthian allies discovered the plan to make Isagoras tyrant and refused to fight. When Demaratus, co-king with Cleomenes, discovered why the Corinthians had withdrawn, he marched back to Sparta. Never again would the Spartans send two kings into the field at once. In the chaos, the other allies withdrew. The Athenians wheeled their army around, caught first the Thebans, then the Chalcidians, and destroyed them utterly.

Cleomenes dropped Isagoras and invited Hippias—the last of the Pisistratid tyrants, whom he had himself deposed in 510 B.C.—to Sparta, promising to restore him to power. In 505 B.C. he mustered a second Peloponnesian army, but the Corinthians again refused to join. This army too dissolved. The Thebans sought revenge for the previous year's defeat without Spartan help, only to be routed a second time. Athens' victory astonished Greece:

> Thus the Athenians went from strength to strength, and proved, if proof were needed, how noble a thing equality before the law is, not in one respect only, but in all. For while they were oppressed by tyrants they had no better success in war than any of their neighbors, yet, once the yoke was flung off, they proved the finest fighters in the world. This clearly shows that, so long as they were held down by authority, they deliberately shirked their duty in the field, as slaves shirk working for their masters; but when freedom was won, then every man amongst them was interested in his own cause.
>
> Herodotus 5.78 (A. de Selincourt)

Athens had come far since Solon's reforms a century earlier, but after expelling Cleomenes in 508, Herodotus tells us, the Athenians made a terrible blunder:

> They were well aware that they were now in a state of war with Cleomenes and Sparta, so to strengthen their position they sent representatives to Sardis,° in the hope of concluding an alliance with Persia. When they got there and delivered their message,

°*Sardis:* The capital of the kingdom of Lydia in western Turkey. Persia conquered Lydia in 546 B.C., and Sardis became the base of the governor of Persia's western province (see Chapter 11).

Artaphernes the son of Hystaspes, the governor, asked in reply who these Athenians were that sought an alliance with Persia, and in what part of the world they lived. Then, having been told, he put the Persian case in a nutshell by remarking that, if the Athenians would signify their submission by the usual gift of earth and water, then King Darius would make a pact with them; otherwise they had better go home. Eager that the pact should be concluded, the envoys acted on their own initiative and accepted Artaphernes' terms—for which they were severely censured on their return to Athens.

Herodotus 5.73 (A. de Selincourt)

From fear of Sparta, Athens had voluntarily submitted to Persia, the greatest empire the world had seen. Giving earth and water acknowledged that the Persian god, Ahuramazda, was supreme being in the heavens, and that their king, Darius, was his embodiment on earth with a right to rule over it. Submission was final and permanent. Backing out was rebellion against the divine order, and Darius was bound by the laws of heaven to punish rebels of any kind. The facts that Persia did not help Athens in 506 or 505, and that the Spartan threat failed to materialize, were beside the point. The Athenians had no idea what they had gotten into, but they were about to find out.

KEY TERMS

helots, 193
Spartan mirage, 194
Lycurgus, 194
Laconia, 194
Dorian, 194
perioikoi, 194
Spartiates, 195
Messenia, 196
double monarchy, 203
Council of Elders, 203
Ephors, 203
Assembly, 203
Peloponnesian League, 204
Alcmaeonid, 206
Dracon, 206
Solon, 206

seisachtheia, 206
archons, 208
Areopagus, 208
Council of 400, 208
Pisistratus, 210
Hippias, 212
Hipparchus, 212
Harmodius, 213
Aristogeiton, 213
Cleisthenes, 214
deme, 214
Council of 500, 214
dêmokratia, 215
dêmos, 215
ostracism, 216

FURTHER READING

Sparta

Cartledge, Paul, *The Spartans* (New York 2002). Highly readable overview of Spartan history by the world's foremost authority.

Finley, Moses, "Sparta and Spartan Society," in Moses Finley, *Economy and Society in Ancient Greece* (New York 1981). This essay, first published in 1968, is the inspiration for most modern work on Sparta. It turned attention away from fanciful reconstructions of Spartan prehistory and toward concrete analysis of how institutions functioned.

Hodkinson, Steve, *Property and Wealth in Classical Sparta* (London 2000). Scholarly study of Spartan economics and society, penetrating behind the Spartan mirage.

Manfredi, Valerio Massimo, *The Spartan* (New York 2001). A novel set in ancient Sparta. More accurate than most historical novels.

Pomeroy, Sarah, *Spartan Women* (Oxford 2002). Straightforward and sensible account of a complex subject.

Powell, Anton, ed., *Classical Sparta: Techniques Behind Her Success* (London 1989); Anton Powell and Steve Hodkinson, eds., *The Shadow of Sparta* (London 1994); and Steve Hodkinson and Anton Powell, eds., *Sparta: New Perspectives* (London 1999). Proceedings of three major conferences on different aspects of Spartan history.

Whitby, Michael, ed., *Sparta* (Edinburgh 2002). Collection of classic articles spanning thirty-five years.

Athens

Finley, Moses, *Ancient Slavery and Modern Ideology* (Chapter 2, London 1980). Sparkling account of the Solonian crisis.

Gallant, Tom, *Risk and Survival in Ancient Greece* (Stanford 1991). Models the life-cycle of Athenian farming families. Excellent use of modern comparative agricultural data.

Murray, Oswyn, *Early Greece* (2nd ed., Stanford, 1993). Excellent survey of the Archaic Period.

Shapiro, H. Alan, *Art and Cult under the Tyrants* (Mainz, Germany, 1989). Study of Pisistratus' use of religion, architecture, and propaganda.

Ancient Texts

Aristotle, *The Athenian Constitution* (New York 1984; tr. P. J. Rhodes). The main narrative for sixth-century-B.C. Athenian history. Written at Athens, 330s or 320s B.C.

Plato, *Protagoras and Meno* (Harmondsworth, UK, 1957; tr. W. K. C. Guthrie). Two influential dialogues, early fourth century B.C.

Plutarch, *Life of Lycurgus*, and Xenophon, *Spartan Society*. In *Plutarch on Sparta* (New York 1988; tr. Richard Talbert). The most important sources for Spartan society. Plutarch wrote around A.D. 100; Xenophon, in the early fourth century B.C.

CHAPTER 11

PERSIA AND THE GREEKS, 550–490 B.C.

Through conquest, colonization, trade, and internal reorganization, archaic Greece adjusted to population growth. The Greeks learned to manage elite feuds, conflicts between rich and poor, and wars between states. By 500 B.C., the Greeks were richer, more stable, and more creative than ever before. For centuries they had faced no external threats, but that was about to change.

Expanding population, trade, and wealth across the whole Mediterranean basin made the interstate environment more competitive. As tax revenues grew, rulers spent more on war, forcing their neighbors to do the same. Ruthless kings carved out empires in western Asia. In the 550s, Lydia forced the Ionian Greek cities to pay tribute; a decade later, Sparta was drawn into Near Eastern affairs when Persia reached the Aegean. In the 510s, Persia entered mainland Europe, and, as we have seen, received Athens' formal submission in 506. In 490, Persia attacked Athens. At the same time, the growing power of the Sicilian Greeks alarmed the Phoenician city of Carthage in North Africa, in modern Tunisia. In both east and west, tensions erupted in the fateful year of 480 B.C. Persia and Carthage both sent huge forces against the Greeks. The Greeks triumphed, but the effort of doing so changed their world forever.

EMPIRES OF THE ANCIENT NEAR EAST

Assyria

What did these foreign powers want, and why did they attack the Greeks? We must detour back into Near Eastern history. In the tenth century B.C., while Greece was

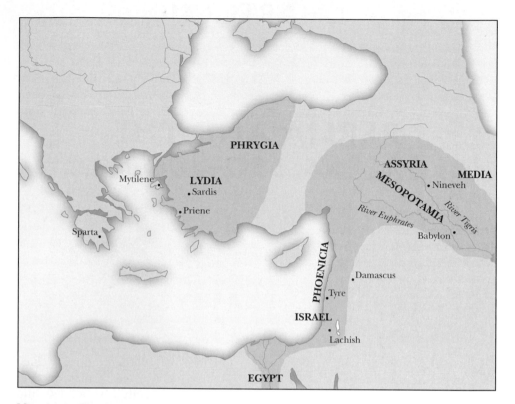

Map 11.1   The Assyrian and Lydian Empires.

still home to small, shifting populations isolated from the larger world, a new empire arose in the Near East. In the 930s B.C., the Assyrians, an agricultural people who lived along the upper banks of the Tigris River in what today is northern Iraq (Map 11.1), began raiding their neighbors for plunder. Within fifty years, these bandit-kings had reached the Mediterranean coast, an extraordinary achievement. These kings believed that their god **Ashur** ruled the heavens and wanted all humans to recognize this. The Assyrian aristocracy provided troops, and the kings rewarded them with plunder. The enriched nobles then provided more troops, who won more victories. Armed with formidable new siege engines (Figure 11.1) and supply trains feeding vast forces, the war machine rolled on. Over defeated peoples Assyria installed a friendly client-king or put in an Assyrian governor/tax-collector. Some rulers simply submitted to Assyria and paid tribute. They avoided devastation and might themselves join the Assyrian elite, receiving Assyrian support in local disputes (Figure 11.2).

But some peoples were more difficult to conquer. In 739 B.C., Assyria took Babylon, the greatest city in Mesopotamia, but it repeatedly rebelled. The little kingdoms of Israel and Judaea also resisted fiercely; they believed their god Yahweh was even more jealous than Ashur and had sent Assyria to punish them for disobedience to Moses' laws. In 722 B.C., Assyria wiped Israel (the northern Hebrew Kingdom) from the face of the earth[19] and burned Babylon in 689 B.C.

Figure 11.1 Assyrian siege warfare, depicted in Tiglath-Pileser III's palace at Nimrud, circa 730 B.C. A wheeled siege engine, protected by hides and armed with rams, advances up a slope to break the city's walls. The fate of the city's inhabitants—impalement on stakes—is foreshadowed at the upper left. To the right, Assyrian bowmen stand behind wicker frames. © *The British Museum.*

Figure 11.2 Jehu of Israel submitting to the Assyrians in 841 B.C., from the Black Obelisk of Shalmaneser III. In the only known depiction of an Israelite king, Jehu prostrates himself before Shalmaneser. Between Jehu and Shalmaneser, the god Ashur (depicted as a winged sun disk) and the goddess Ishtar (a star) hover. Jehu submitted in return for Assyrian protection against the king of Damascus. Black marble, height 5 feet. *Jehu, King of Israel, prostrating himself before King Shalmaneser III of Assur. Basalt bas-relief. Black stele of Shalmaneser III. British Museum, London, Great Britain. Erich Lessing/Art Resource, NY.*

The Assyrians reserved their greatest rage for vassals who submitted, then rebelled. Such people had broken their word to Ashur:

> I built a pillar over against his city gate and I flayed all the chiefs who had revolted, and I covered the pillar with their skin. Some I walled up within the pillar, some I impaled upon the pillar on stakes, and others I bound to stakes round about the pillar. And I cut the limbs off the officers, the royal officers who had rebelled.
>
> Many captives from among them I burned with fire, and many I took as living captives. From some I cut off their noses, their ears, and their fingers, of many I put out the eyes. I made one pillar of the living and another of heads, and I bound their heads to tree trunks round about the city. Their young men and maidens I burned in the fire. Twenty men I captured alive and I walled them up in the wall of his palace. The rest of their warriors I consumed with thirst in the desert.
>
> Ashurnasirpal II ("Ashur Is Guardian of the Sun") 883–859 B.C. (D.D. Luckenbill, *Ancient Records of Assyria and Babylon*, Ancient Records Series 1, in Geoffrey T. Bull, *The City and the Sign: An Interpretation of the Book of Jonah*, London, 1970, 109–110)

The kings decorated their palaces with such inscriptions, describing violence in honor of Ashur, and with relief carvings showing the fate of conquered peoples

Figure 11.3 Assyrian relief showing refugees from Lachish in Judea (701 B.C.), in the palace of Sennacherib at Nineveh, Mesopotamia (Iraq). At the top exiles flee, carrying provisions; at the bottom Assyrian soldiers skin alive a rebel whose arms are pinned to the ground. *Relief, Israel, 10th-6th Century: Judean exiles carrying provisions. Detail of the Assyrian conquest of the Jewish fortified town of Lachish (battle 701 B.C.). Part of a relief from the palace of Sennacherib at Niniveh, Mesopotamia (Iraq). The British Museum.*

(Figure 11.3). The Hebrew Bible records terror inspired by the mighty Assyrians, who became a byword for irresistible might. The same Byron whose verses on Greece opened this book famously imagined what the Israelites saw:

> The Assyrian came down like a wolf on the fold
>   And his cohorts were gleaming in purple and gold;
> And the sheen of their spears was like stars on the sea,
> When the blue wave rolls nightly on deep Galilee.
>
> Lord Byron, *The Destruction of Sennacherib* (1815), stanza 1

Assyria fed on war, and Assyrian demands transformed western Asia. To pay off the Assyrians, and to escape depredation, the Phoenicians who lived on the coast of modern Lebanon intensified trade and settlement in the west Mediterranean: in western Sicily, Sardinia, and—most importantly—at **Carthage** ("new city"), near modern Tunis. They brought metals, food, and slaves home from the west, exchanging them for such transportable manufactured objects as textiles, carved ivory, and perfumes. Phoenicia grew rich while buying protection from Assyria, and Carthage became the greatest city in the West.

Greece in the age of Homer was a poor, weak cluster of towns in the shadow of Near Eastern power and wealth. When Assyria attacked Egypt in the 660s B.C., Egypt's king hired formidable Greek hoplites as mercenaries, but the Greeks never had to defend themselves against Assyria, because in 612 B.C. Babylonian rebels and a warrior people from the mountains of western Iran called the **Medes** (mēdz) burned Assyria's capital at Nineveh (near modern Mosul in Iraq). One consequence of the turbulence was the flight of Mesopotamian thinkers to Ionia, which was about to be drawn into the world of the Near Eastern empires.

LYDIA

Few Greeks ever saw Nineveh, but **Phrygia** (Map 11.1) was close enough to inspire tales about **King Midas,** who—the stories ran—turned everything he touched into gold. Midas was a real man (Assyrians called him Mita) who reigned around 700 B.C. In the 1950s, American archaeologists excavated his tomb under a mound 150 feet high and forensic experts even reconstructed his face.

Lydia, whose capital was only seventy-five miles from the Aegean Sea, was nearer still. Lydia's wealth amazed the Greeks, who told legends about **Gyges** (gī-jēz), a usurper who seized Lydia's throne in the 680s. Herodotus thought that Gyges was originally the king's bodyguard, but the king, obsessed by his wife's beauty, ordered Gyges to hide in a closet to see her naked, so that someone else would know what a lucky man the king was. Unfortunately, the wife spotted Gyges and calmly told him that to avenge her honor, either he or her husband must die. Soon, Gyges was the new king, married to his predecessor's widow. (Plato heard a different story: that Gyges was a shepherd who found a magic ring on a superhuman corpse. The ring made its wearer invisible. Using it, Gyges seduced the queen and, with her help, killed the king and took the throne.)

Gyges and his successors forced the Ionian Greeks to pay him tribute. When one city refused around 590 B.C., Lydian engineers heaped a great mound against its walls (discovered by modern archaeologists). When the mound reached the top, troops poured into the city, massacring the Greeks.

Lydia drew Greece into an increasingly international world. One Greek courtesan made a fortune in Egypt; Greek mercenaries traveled up the Nile and scratched their names on the legs of already ancient statues (vandalism then, an important historical source now); and the poet Sappho's brother fought as a mercenary for Babylon. In 583 B.C., Babylon destroyed Tyre in Phoenicia, breaking Tyre's colony Carthage from dependence on its mother city. A hundred years later, a powerful and assertive Carthage will challenge the Greeks for control of Sicily.

In 560 B.C., a new king named **Croesus** (**krē**-sus) assumed Lydia's throne. Herodotus blamed him (not Gyges) for the subsequent clash of East and West. After reviewing myths explaining why Greece and Persia came to blows, Herodotus wrote:

> So much for what the Persians and Phoenicians say; I have no intention of passing judgment on its truth or falsity. I prefer to rely on my own knowledge and to point out who it was in actual fact that first injured the Greeks. Croesus of Lydia, son of Alyattes, was the first foreigner so far as we know to come into direct contact with the Greeks, both in the way of conquest and alliance, forcing tribute from the Ionians, Aeolians, and Asiatic Dorians, and forming a pact of friendship with the Spartans. Before Croesus' time all the Greeks had been free.
>
> Herodotus 1.5–6 (A. de Selincourt)

Croesus took the coastal Greeks into his empire, taxed them, and installed client-tyrants. Herodotus says he planned further conquests:

> Croesus forced all the Asiatic Greeks to pay him tribute, and then turned his attention to shipbuilding in order to attack the islanders. However, when everything was ready to begin building, something happened which persuaded him to desist. A certain Bias, of Priene°—or some say that it was Pittacus, of Mytilene°—came to Sardis,° and in answer to Croesus' request for news from Greece, told him that the islanders were raising a force of ten thousand horses to attack him in Sardis.
>
> Croesus took the remark literally and exclaimed, "What? The islanders mean to attack the Lydians with cavalry? I only wish they would!"
>
> "Sire," the man replied, "I think you are longing to catch the islanders on horseback on the continent. Indeed, you are perfectly justified. But they know your intention of building a fleet to attack them—and what do you think they want more than a chance of catching the Lydians at sea? It would give them their revenge for their brothers on the mainland, whom you have enslaved."
>
> This way of putting the matter tickled Croesus' fancy. Moreover, it seemed so much to the point that he abandoned the idea of building a fleet, and formed a treaty of friendship with the Ionian islanders.
>
> Herodotus 1.27 (A. de Selincourt)

°*Priene* (prī-**e**-nē): A Greek colony on the coast.   °*Mytilene* (mi-ti-**lē**-nē): The principal Greek city on the island of Lesbos, just off the Ionian coast. Later Greeks canonized a group of seven archaic wise men. Bias and Pittacus were two of them.   °*Sardis:* The capital of Lydia.

Croesus stopped his westward expansion; events further east were about to command his full attention.

CYRUS AND THE RISE OF PERSIA, 559–530 B.C.

When Croesus inherited Lydia's throne in 560 B.C., Persia in southwest Iran was a minor client-state of **Media.** Forty years later, Persia ruled the greatest empire the world had seen, stretching from Egypt to Afghanistan (Map 11.2). Interactions with Persia would dominate Aegean history for the next two centuries.

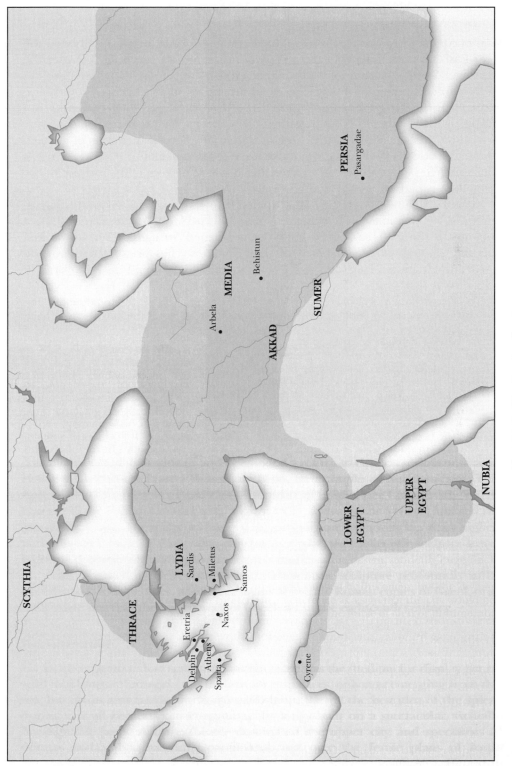

Map 11.2 The Persian Empire.

Herodotus' colorful account, our main source, says that **Astyages** (as-tī-a-jēz), king of Media, dreamed that his daughter urinated so much that she flooded the Near East, so Astyages married her off to an insignificant man in Persia. After the marriage, Astyages had another dream, that a vine grew from his daughter's genitals and engulfed his empire. Interpreters said the dream meant her son would seize Astyages' throne. Astyages commanded his relative **Harpagus** to kill the child. But Harpagus asked himself, What if Astyages dies and his daughter comes to power? What then? Instead of killing the child, he gave it to a herdsman, instructing *him* to expose the boy. The herdsman's wife had just delivered a stillborn baby. The herdsman switched babies, showed Harpagus the corpse of his own child as proof of the deed, then raised Astyages' son as his own.

The truth came out ten years later when the king's unrecognized grandson pretended to be king in a village game. He played his part too well, even punishing a nobleman's son for breaking the rules. News reached Astyages. When he worked out that Harpagus had not killed his grandson, Astyages pretended to forgive Harpagus. He invited Harpagus to dinner but asked him to send his son over first:

> As soon as Harpagus reached home, he sent his son—his only son, a boy about thirteen years old—to Astyages' palace, with instructions to do whatever the king wanted. Then in high glee he told his wife everything that had happened.
>
> When Harpagus' son arrived in the palace, Astyages had him butchered, cut up the joints and cooked them, roasting some, boiling the rest, and having the whole properly prepared for the table. Dinnertime came and the guests assembled, with Harpagus among them. Dishes of mutton were placed in front of Astyages and everyone else—except Harpagus. To Harpagus was served the flesh of his son: all of it, except the head, the hands, and the feet, which had been put separately on a platter covered by a lid.
>
> When Harpagus thought he had eaten as much as he wanted, Astyages asked him if he had enjoyed his dinner. He answered that he had enjoyed it very much indeed, whereupon those whose business it was to do so brought in the boy's head, hands, and feet in the covered dish, stood by Harpagus' chair, and told him to lift the lid and take what he fancied. Harpagus removed the cover and saw the fragments of his son's body. As he kept control of himself and did not lose his head at the dreadful sight, Astyages asked him if he knew what animal it was whose flesh he had eaten. "I know, my lord," was Harpagus' reply, "and for my part—may the king's will be done." He said no other word, but took up what remained of the flesh and went home, intending, I suppose, to bury all of it together. And that is how Harpagus was punished.
>
> Herodotus 1.119 (A. de Selincourt)

Astyages now sent his grandson (renamed **Cyrus**) to live with his birth mother (Astyages' daughter). Cyrus grew up and became chief of the Persians. Harpagus, who had stayed on as Astyages' top assistant, burned for revenge and secretly urged Cyrus to revolt. When he did, Astyages foolishly sent Harpagus against him at the head of his army. Harpagus promptly joined the rebels, and in 550 B.C. Cyrus overthrew Astyages and took the empire, just as Astyages' dreams had predicted.

Such bizarre tales are typical of Herodotus. To him, the story illustrated a fundamental difference between *poleis* and the eastern empires. In a *polis,* no man stood so far above the other citizens that he could treat them so brutally, while the eastern rulers—Assyrian, Median, Lydian, or Persian—took such difference in status for granted. Greek belief that no man could be truly free under Persian rule was to have profound consequences when Persia attacked the Greeks.

However Cyrus actually came to power, he quickly overran the Medians' large empire. In 546 B.C., as Pisistratus launched his third coup at Athens, Cyrus moved beyond Astyages' frontiers to threaten Croesus of Lydia. Seeing danger looming, Croesus asked two Greek oracles (one at Delphi) what to do, perhaps trusting them because they were not beholden to any political power:

> The Lydians who were to bring the presents to the temples were instructed by Croesus to ask the oracles if he should undertake a campaign against Persia, and if he should strengthen his army by some alliance. On their arrival, therefore, they offered the gifts with proper ceremony, and put their question in the following words: "Croesus, king of Lydia and other nations, in the belief that these are the only true oracles in the world, has given you gifts such as your power of divination deserves, and now asks you if he should march against Persia and if it would be wise to seek an alliance." To this question both oracles returned a similar answer; they foretold that if Croesus should attack the Persians, he would destroy a great empire, and they advised him to find out which of the Greek states was the most powerful, and to come to an understanding with it.
>
> Croesus was overjoyed when he learned the answer that the oracles had given and was fully confident of destroying the power of Cyrus.
>
> Herodotus 1.53–54 (A. de Selincourt)

Croesus contracted an alliance with Sparta, hired mercenaries, and marched against Cyrus. After an indecisive battle late in the year, Croesus returned to Sardis, intending to expand his alliance in the following spring. Assuming that Cyrus would go into winter camp, as was normal for ancient armies, and wanting to save money, Croesus disbanded his mercenaries. But Cyrus followed Croesus and suddenly appeared before Sardis. In a panic, Croesus wrote to Sparta, asking for immediate assistance. But by the time the Spartans set sail, Sardis had fallen.

Cyrus decided to burn Croesus alive. As Croesus sat on top of the pyre, waiting for the flames (Figure 11.4), he remembered a time when the wise Athenian lawgiver Solon had visited him. "Consider no man happy until he is dead," Solon had advised, indifferent to Croesus' power and prosperity. Croesus thought him a fool, but now he understood what Solon meant. "O Solon, Solon!" he cried. Cyrus, who was enjoying the execution, wanted to know what he meant and ordered the pyre put out. But the flames had taken hold. Croesus wept and called on Apollo—who had sent him the oracle about destroying a great empire—to save him. Rain fell from the clear sky, extinguishing the fire.

The fairytale theme of the reversal of fortune dominates Herodotus' stories about the eastern empires. Croesus, miraculously saved, now became Cyrus' closest adviser. Croesus sent an angry embassy to find out why (as he thought) the oracle had lied. Herodotus reports the Delphic priestess' reply:

> As to the oracle, Croesus had no right to find fault with it: the god had declared that if he attacked the Persians he would destroy a great empire. After an answer like that, the wise thing would have been to send again to inquire which empire was meant, Cyrus' or his own. But as he misinterpreted what was said and made no second inquiry, he must admit the fault to have been his own.
>
> When the Lydians returned to Sardis with the priestess' answer and reported it to Croesus, he admitted that the god was innocent and he had only himself to blame.
>
> Herodotus 1.91 (A. de Selincourt)

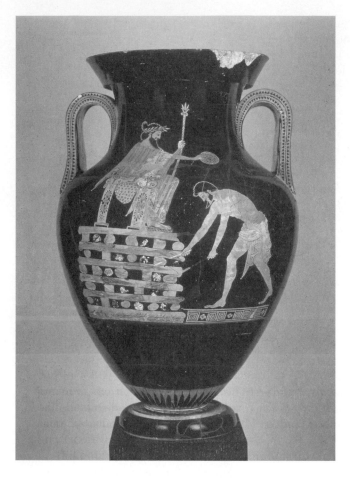

Figure 11.4 Croesus on the funeral pyre; from an Athenian red-figure vase, circa 490 B.C. Croesus, holding his kingly scepter, pours a libation while his servant lights the fire.

Some Ionian Greeks thought that Cyrus' destruction of Lydia might bring them freedom. They asked Sparta for help, but the Spartans sent only observers. Yet, even this caused trouble:

> The most distinguished of the men on board, a man called Lacrines, was sent to Sardis to forbid Cyrus, on behalf of the Spartans, to harm any Greek city, or they would take action. The story goes that when Cyrus heard what the herald said, he asked some Greeks who happened to be with him who the Spartans were, and what were their numbers that they dared to send him such a command. On being informed, he gave the following answer to the Spartan herald: "I have never yet been afraid of men who have a special meeting place in the middle of their city, where they swear this and that and cheat each other. Such people, if I have anything to do with it, will not have the troubles of Ionia to chatter about, but their own."

> Herodotus 1.153 (A. de Selincourt)

For now, Cyrus turned back to Mesopotamia and attacked Babylon, at this time the greatest city in the world. Two accounts of its fall in 539 B.C. survive. Herodotus says that Cyrus defeated a Babylonian army, then besieged the city. But the Babylonians had large stores of food. The innovative Cyrus dug a huge canal and drained the Euphrates into a nearby marsh. The Babylonians had not guarded the gates along

Figure 11.5 The Cyrus Cylinder, discovered in Iraq in 1879. Inscribed in Old Persian, the text tells of Cyrus' conquest of Babylon. Nine inches high, 538 B.C.

the river, and tunnels normally filled with water now became dry passages for Cyrus' troops under the city's walls. Herodotus adds that "The Babylonians themselves say that owing to the great size of the city the outskirts were captured without the people in the center knowing anything about it; there was a festival going on, and they continued to dance and enjoy themselves, until they learned the hard way." Cyrus had enough men to divert one of the world's great rivers, thereby capturing the world's biggest city. His resources dwarfed those of the Greeks.

The other account of Babylon's fall, the official Persian version that survives in an inscription on a clay cylinder (Figure 11.5), illustrates the very different role of religion in Persia from its place in Greece. In his account, Cyrus says that there was no battle. Rather, Babylon's chief god Marduk *wanted* Cyrus to conquer the city, to correct the Babylonians' improper conduct of their religion:

> Marduk, the great lord, a protector of his people, beheld with pleasure [Cyrus'] good deeds and his upright mind [and therefore] ordered him to march against his city Babylon. He made him set out on the road to Babylon going at his side like a real friend.

Without any battle, he made him enter Babylon, sparing Babylon any calamity. He delivered into [Cyrus'] hands Nabonidus, the king who did not worship [Marduk]. All the inhabitants of Babylon as well as of the entire country of Sumer and Akkad, princes and governors, bowed to [Cyrus] and kissed his feet, jubilant that he [had received] the kingship, and with shining faces.

> From the Cyrus Cylinder (*Ancient Near Eastern Texts Relating to the Old Testament*, 3rd ed., J. B. Pritchard, Princeton 1969, 315–16)

The Assyrians believed they had to subjugate others in order to make this world parallel Ashur's heavenly dominance. Cyrus followed a dualistic religion called **Zoroastrianism** (which still exists). Its prophet Zoroaster claimed that the universe was a battleground between **Ahuramazda,** the principle of light and goodness, and Ahiram ("The Lie"), the force of darkness. Ahuramazda had chosen Cyrus' family, the **Achaemenids** (a-kē-men-idz), to lead the struggle in this world. Like the Assyrians, Zoroastrians accepted that other gods existed and that good gods understood the supremacy of Ahuramazda. Thus, Marduk wanted Cyrus to take Babylon and restore proper religious observances there. The Persians fought not only for conquest and its benefits, but to hasten Ahuramazda's victory over The Lie. Vast military resources and religious persuasion fueled Cyrus' rapid conquests and made Near Eastern warfare completely different from the sportsman-like hoplite battles we described in Chapter 8, "Archaic Greece, 700–480 B.C.: Economy, Society, Politics."

CAMBYSES AND DARIUS, 530–521 B.C.

The world had never seen a conqueror like Cyrus. He carried Ahuramazda's name to the Aegean Sea and the borders of Egypt, then died in battle in Afghanistan in 530 B.C. fighting a nomadic warrior queen (Figure 11.6).

Cyrus' son **Cambyses** (kam-**bī**-sēz) continued the Achaemenid crusade, attacking Egypt in 525 B.C. The country fell quickly. Cambyses raced west to Cyrene, a Greek city in Libya, and south to Nubia in the Sudan. He planned to go further, to attack Carthage and the Ethiopians, whom he called "the tallest and best-looking people in the world."

As with Cyrus' attack on Babylon, we have two versions of Cambyses' adventures in Egypt, both informative about Persian imperialism. First, we consider a long inscription set up between 520 and 510 B.C. by Udjahorresne (u-ja-hor-**es**-nā), who had been an Egyptian general until 525 B.C.

> The Great Chief of all foreign lands, Cambyses, came to Egypt, and the foreign peoples of every foreign land were with him. When he had conquered this land in its entirety, they established themselves in it, and he was Great Ruler of Egypt and Great Chief of All Foreign Lands.
>
>   His majesty assigned to me the office of Chief Physician. He made me live at his side as Companion and Administrator of the Palace.
>
>   I made a petition to the majesty of the King of Upper and Lower Egypt,° Cambyses, about all the foreigners who dwelled in the temple of Neith,° in order to have them expelled from it, so as to let the temple of Neith be in all its splendor as it had been

°*King of Upper and Lower Egypt:* The traditional title of the pharaoh since the days of Narmer, the first pharaoh of all Egypt, around 3000 B.C.   °*Neith:* Early war goddess whose attribute was two crossed arrows.

Figure 11.6 The Tomb of Cyrus, in Pasargadae, southwest Iran. Cyrus' embalmed body lay in a gold sarcophagus on a gold couch beside which stood a treasure-laden golden table, but the tomb was looted long ago. After the seventh-century-A.D. Arab invasion, the empty mausoleum was known as the Tomb of the Mother of Solomon. Fifteen feet square, set on a stepped stone plinth.

before. His majesty commanded to expel all the foreigners [who] dwelled in the temple of Neith, to demolish all their houses and all their unclean things that were in this temple.

His majesty commanded to give divine offerings to Neith-the-Great, the mother of god, and to the great gods of Sais,° as it had been before. His majesty commanded [to perform] all their festivals and all their processions, as had been done before. His majesty did this because I had let his majesty know the greatness of Sais, that it is the city of all the gods, who dwell there on their seats forever.

The one honored by the gods of Sais, the chief physician, Udjahorresne, he says:

The King of Upper and Lower Egypt, Cambyses, came to Sais. His majesty went in person to the temple of Neith. He made a great prostration before her majesty, as every king has done. He made a great offering of every good thing to Neith-the-Great, the mother of god, and to the great gods who are in Sais, as every beneficent king has done. His majesty did this because I had let his majesty know the greatness of her majesty Neith, that she is the mother of Ra° himself.

Statue Inscription of Udjahorresne 11–27
(M. Lichtheim, *Ancient Egyptian Literature III,* Berkeley 1980, 37–41)

° *Sais:* A city in the central Egyptian delta where Neith had an ancient temple, and capital of Egypt after its liberation from Assyria in 664 B.C.   ° *Ra:* The sun god.

The inscription suggests that after conquering Egypt, Cambyses ruled as if nothing had changed, acting "as every king has done" and adopting traditional Egyptian royal titles like "King of Upper and Lower Egypt." As Cyrus had done at Babylon, Cambyses represented himself as defender of the gods. Udjahorresne accepted Cambyses' claim and changed sides: he could influence Cambyses to protect and enrich the temple of Neith, which Udjahorresne cared about deeply.

Persia needed men like Udjahorresne to run her empire. In return, local notables willing to change sides got Persian support against their own enemies, for example the foreigners living in Neith's temple. Some collaborated; others resisted, particularly in Egypt and Babylon. These wealthy regions had a strong sense of ethnic identity and hovered constantly on the brink of rebellion. To control the Greeks, Persia would need similar collaborators.

Our second account comes from Herodotus. He heard about priests who had resisted Cambyses, not about men like Udjahorresne. Herodotus says that Cambyses had always been strange, but in Egypt went completely mad. Instead of the piety that Udjahorresne praises, Herodotus says that Cambyses insulted Egypt's gods and even stabbed a sacred bull, whose death presaged Cambyses' own doom. Both accounts contain some truth: Cambyses rewarded Egyptians who worked with him and punished those who did not, and different people had different stories to tell. Herodotus says that Egypt's gods now pushed Cambyses into self-destruction. He married his own sister, then killed her by kicking her when she was pregnant. He buried noblemen alive upside down. He misinterpreted a dream and concluded that his brother Smerdis back in Persia was plotting against him. Cambyses had Smerdis murdered, and the Magi, Persia's ritual experts, hatched a plot. In 522 B.C., one of the Magi—by an implausible coincidence also named Smerdis—impersonated the dead Smerdis, whose killing had been covered up, and raised a revolt. Cambyses jumped on his horse to return to Persia, but accidentally stabbed himself in the thigh, just as he had stabbed the sacred bull in the thigh. As he traveled, the wound festered and he died.

Back in Persia, the false Smerdis reigned for seven months until a nobleman's daughter in the harem unmasked him. Royal ideology held that the Achaemenids were on earth to perfect the world for Ahuramazda, so a pretender undermined the whole cosmic order. Seven aristocrats overthrew the false Smerdis, then argued about who should replace him. They would let a divine omen settle the matter: "They proposed to mount their horses on the outskirts of the city, and he whose horse neighed first after the sun came up would have the throne." One of them, **Darius** (da-rī-us), hatched a plan with his groom Oebares (ē-bar-ēz):

> Oebares, accordingly, as soon as it was dark, took from the stables the mare that Darius' horse was particularly fond of and tied her up on the outskirts of the city. Then he brought along the stallion and led him round and round the mare, getting closer and closer in narrowing circles, and finally allowed him to mount her. Next morning just before dawn the six men, according to their agreement, came riding on their horses through the city suburb, and when they reached the spot where the mare had been tethered on the previous night, Darius' horse started forward and neighed. At the same instant, though the sky was clear, there was a flash of lightning and a crash of thunder, as if it were a sign from heaven; the election of Darius was assured, and the other five leapt from their saddles and bowed to the ground at his feet.

That is one account of how Oebares made the horse neigh. The Persians also have another, namely that he rubbed the mare's genitals and then kept his hand covered inside his breeches. When the sun was rising and the horses were about to be released, he drew his hand out and put it to the nostrils of Darius' horse, which at the smell of the mare at once snorted and neighed.

> Herodotus 3.85–87 (A. de Selincourt)

These stories sound like mere gossip, but Herodotus' account of what happened next is partly confirmed by a huge inscription that Darius put up in the mountains separating Mesopotamia from Persia (Figure 11.7a, b).

Set 340 feet above the ground, where only gods could see it, it was carved in three languages, perhaps for the gods of different peoples. In it Darius justified his seizure of power, emphasizing his legitimacy, piety, and justice. He insisted he was a genuine Achaemenid, fighting The Lie to make the world perfect.

> I am Darius the Great King, King of Kings, King in Persia, King of countries, son of Hystaspes, grandson of Arsames, an Achaemenid.
> Says Darius the King: My father was Hystaspes; Hystaspes' father was Arsames; Arsames' father was Ariaramnes; Ariaramnes' father was Teispes; Teispes' father was Achaemenes.

Figure 11.7a The great king Darius sits enthroned. Detail from the Behistun inscription (see Figure 11.7b).

Figure 11.7b   The Behistun inscription, circa 520 B.C. The huge billboard, seventy-five feet by fifty feet, records the struggles Darius faced in gaining the throne. Behistun lies 250 miles southwest of Tehran on the Silk Road from China to Babylon. The inscription is too high up the cliff to be read—except by Ahuramazda and other interested gods.

Says Darius the King: For this reason we are called Achaemenids. From long ago we have been noble. From long ago our family has been kings.

Says Darius the King: eight of our family were kings before. I am the ninth. Nine in succession we have been kings.

Says Darius the King: By the favor of Ahuramazda I am King; Ahuramazda bestowed the Kingdom on me.

A list follows of pretenders to the throne whom Darius punished, in variations on the following theme:

Says Darius the King: One man by name Tritantaechmes, a Sagartian—he became rebellious to me. Thus he said to the people, "I am king in Sagartia, of the family of Cyaxares."°

°*Cyaxares:* The father of Astyages of Media, who reigned 624–585 B.C.

Thereupon I sent off a Persian and Median army; a Mede by name Takhmaspada, my subject—him I made chief of them. Thus I said to them, "Go forth. The hostile army that shall not call itself mine, that do you strike!" Thereupon Takhmaspada went off with the army. He joined battle with Tritantaechmes. Ahuramazda helped me. By the favor of Ahuramazda my army struck that rebellious army and took Tritantaechmes prisoner and led him to me. Afterwards I cut off both his nose and his ears and put out one eye. He was kept bound at my palace entrance, and all the people saw him. Afterward I impaled him at Arbela.

Darius, Behistun inscription 1.1–12; 3.78–91
(R. Kent, *Old Persian Grammar Texts, Lexicon,*
New Haven 1953, DS of 22–58)

Cutting off noses, poking out eyes, impaling, crucifixion, and burying alive were standard tools of policy. Near Eastern kings were proud of their cruelty: It not only deterred other rebels but showed that the godlike Great King was free to act in any way he chose. In the citizen community of a Greek *polis*, such behavior was impossible. When everyone was equally human, violently dishonoring others—even slaves—was *hubris,* "violence," a punishable crime. Herodotus rightly saw that the *poleis* were very different from Persia.

PERSIA'S NORTHWEST FRONTIER AND THE IONIAN REVOLT, 521–494 B.C.

By 519 B.C., Darius had the empire under control. Cyrus and Cambyses were great conquerors, but now Darius saw the need for organization. The empire had thirty to thirty-five million inhabitants (ten to fifteen times as many as all the Greeks combined). Darius set up governors called **satraps** and made administration cheaper by shifting its costs onto them. Satraps were virtual kings within their provinces, so long as they kept the peace, kept taxes flowing to Darius, and provided troops when asked. The empire was so big that it took months or years for Darius to raise troops to respond to threats or rebellions, and it was the satraps' job to deal quickly and cheaply with local problems. In return, they could enrich themselves.

Persia's northwest frontier had been quiet since Cyrus met Sparta's envoy in 545 B.C., but Darius had ambitions in the west. He developed Persia's first fleet and cut a forerunner to the Suez Canal, linking the Mediterranean and Red seas. Herodotus says, "The greater part of Asia was discovered by Darius. He wanted to find out where the Indus River joins the sea—the Indus being the only river other than the Nile where crocodiles are found—and for this purpose sent off on an expedition down the river a number of men whose word he could trust. After this voyage was completed, Darius subdued the Indians and made regular use of the southern ocean."[20]

Around 521 B.C., even before he consolidated the throne, Darius seized the rich Greek island of Samos just off the coast of Asia Minor. Herodotus tells a famous story about how this happened. Polycrates, tyrant of Samos, was famous for his wealth and prosperity, but worried that his luck was bound to change. In the early 520s, before Cambyses' conquest of Egypt, he wrote about his fear to his friend the pharaoh, who advised him to destroy the thing he loved most: By doing himself intentional harm, he would forestall future harm. Polycrates chose a gold ring and threw it into the sea. A huge fish swallowed the ring. One of Polycrates' subjects caught the wonderful fish and presented it to the tyrant. When his servants cut up the fish for dinner, they found the ring, and Polycrates knew he was doomed. Sure enough, in 523 B.C., the Persian satrap tricked him, captured him, and crucified him on a rock in the hot sun. Darius killed this governor during his struggle for the throne, but also took over Samos.

Step by step, Darius moved north and west. The Scythian nomads of the Ukraine had long terrorized the Near East, and in 514 B.C. Darius launched a great punitive expedition. Darius pursued the Scythians for months without forcing them to give battle. As supplies grew scarce and he decided to withdraw, the Scythians went onto the offensive, cutting off his foraging parties. They rode up to Darius' only point of escape, a bridge over the River Danube, and tried to persuade the Greek subjects he left as guards to abandon it. If Darius and his army were destroyed, the Scythians urged, the Greeks could rebel.

The Greeks discussed this proposition, but **Histiaeus** (his-ti-ē-us), the pro-Persian tyrant of Miletus, opposed it.

> Histiaeus pointed out that each [Greek leader] owed his position as tyrant to Darius, and, in the event of Darius' fall, he himself would be unable to maintain his power at Miletus, nor would any of the rest of them. Each state would be sure to turn against tyranny and choose democracy. The meeting had begun by supporting [the Scythian proposal], but no sooner had Histiaeus put forward this view than everyone present changed his mind and it was unanimously adopted.
>
> Herodotus 4.137 (A. de Selincourt)

As Histiaeus saw things, he was in a similar position to Udjahorresne: It was better to be a tyrant under Persia than a private citizen in a free *polis*.

To fool the Scythians, the Greeks demolished part of the bridge, but left enough intact that they could easily repair it. Darius raced to reach the bridge before the Scythians cut him off.

> The Persians . . . had great difficulty in reaching the crossing. It was dark when they arrived, and the discovery that the bridge was broken caused a panic, for they at once supposed that the Ionians had left them in the lurch. Darius, however, told an Egyptian he happened to have with him, a man with a tremendous voice, to stand on the river bank and shout for Histiaeus, who heard him at the very first hail, set all the ships to the task of ferrying the army over, and made good the broken section of the bridge. In this way the Persians got safely out of the country. . . . The Scythians have a low opinion of the men of Ionia in consequence of all this: to consider them as a free people, they are, they say, the most despicable and craven in the world; and, considered as slaves, the most subservient to their masters and the least likely to run away.
>
> Herodotus 4.140–42 (A. de Selincourt)

Despite the close call, Darius' Scythian expedition did stop the Scythian raids. He was acutely aware of what he owed Histiaeus and asked him what he would like as a reward. Histiaeus requested—and received—a small territory in a timber-rich area of the north Aegean. Darius left an army in Europe to subdue the tribesmen in Thrace (roughly modern Bulgaria) and the Greek cities along the north shore of the Aegean, and as its general wound up his campaign in 512 B.C., he noticed Histiaeus' new territory. It struck him as a natural fortress, and he warned Darius that Histiaeus must be planning a revolt. Darius made Histiaeus an offer he could not refuse: to live with him at the imperial court as an honored advisor. "Forget about Miletus and this new settlement of yours," Darius said; "come with me to Susa [the Persian capital]. All I have there will be yours. You will eat at my table and be my counselor." Histiaeus was heartbroken about leaving Miletus, but knew refusal meant death. He gave Miletus to his nephew Aristagoras (a-ris-**tag**-or-as) and began the long journey east.

The Persian Empire was now firmly established in the Aegean, and Darius' satraps eagerly exploited opportunities to extend their power. Consequently, when Athenian envoys offered earth and water to Artaphernes (satrap in Sardis and also Darius' brother) in 506 B.C., hoping for Persian support against Sparta, he readily accepted. As the Persians saw it, the Athenians were now the Great King's slaves and recognized Ahuramazda's primacy. Persia was swallowing the Greeks.

In 499 B.C., the northwest frontier exploded. The troubles began in 500 B.C., when democrats seized the wealthy Greek island of Naxos in the central Aegean. They exiled the former oligarchs, who fled to Miletus and asked its new tyrant, Aristagoras, to restore them. Aristagoras asked the satrap for troops to capture Naxos for the empire, saying he could repay the expenses from plunder. Artaphernes agreed, but after four months the siege failed. Aristagoras was now terrified. He could not repay the money Artaphernes had advanced him, and he would probably be executed—painfully—for his blunders.

Histiaeus, Aristagoras' uncle and the former ruler of Miletus but now trapped in Darius' court, took a gamble.

> The various causes of alarm were already making Aristagoras contemplate rebellion [against Persia], when something else occurred to confirm his purpose: this was the arrival from Susa of a slave, sent by Histiaeus, the man° with the tattooed scalp, urging him to do precisely what he was thinking of, namely, to revolt. Histiaeus had been wanting to make Aristagoras take this step, but was in difficulty about how to get a message safely through to him, as the roads from Susa were watched; so he shaved the head of his most trustworthy slave, pricked the message on his scalp, and waited for hair to grow again. Then, as soon as it had grown, he sent the man to Miletus with instructions to do nothing when he arrived except to tell Aristagoras to shave his hair off and look at his head. The message found there was, as I have said, an order to revolt. What prompted Histiaeus to do this was his distress at being detained in Susa, and he hoped that, if a rebellion were started, he might be sent down to the coast to deal with it, whereas if nothing of the sort occurred he had little expectation of ever seeing Miletus again.
>
> Herodotus 5.35 (A. de Selincourt)

°*The man:* Herodotus' phrasing makes it sound like this was a well-known story.

Aristagoras started talking to other Ionian cities about revolt. Ionia had flourished under Persian rule, but many Ionians identified Persia with repressive, old-fashioned tyranny. Feeling the winds of change, Aristagoras surrendered his tyrannical powers to the ordinary citizens and helped other Ionian cities overthrow their tyrants. Then he sailed to mainland Greece, hoping for a general Greek struggle against Persia. Sparta, who had warned Cyrus in 545 B.C. not to hurt the Greek cities, declined to help, but Athens, a vassal state in Persian eyes, sent twenty ships. Nearby **Eretria,** on the island of Euboea, sent another five. As Herodotus observed, "These ships were the beginning of evils for Greeks and barbarians."

The Ionians burned Sardis, and the uprising spread to Cyprus. As usual in Persia, the local satraps tried to crush the revolt. Gradually the tide turned, and the Athenians, disillusioned at Ionian incompetence, returned home. Darius, impatient at the satraps' slow progress, began gathering a huge imperial army. This was Histiaeus' chance: He persuaded Darius to send him back to the Aegean to help suppress the uprising.

By this point, in 497 B.C., some Ionians regretted their decision to rebel. Aristagoras, always attuned to popular mood, fled Miletus to the property in the north Aegean that Histiaeus had received as his reward from Darius. Within a few months, he was killed by treachery. Histiaeus defected from Persia, but Miletus did not want another tyrant and drove him off. After more adventures, he became a sort of pirate king at Byzantium.

The Persians were closing in. In 494 B.C., Darius ordered his forces against Miletus, the rebellion's center. The Ionians staked everything on the war at sea and elected the experienced sailor **Dionysius** from Phocaea, the northernmost Ionian city in Asia Minor, to organize their resistance.

Naval warfare, ancient as much as modern, required efficient organization. The ships, called **triremes** (**trī**-rēmz; Figure 11.8), had three banks of oars down each side. They were long, thin, and—without a keel—unstable, but with trained crews could move quickly and were maneuverable. Each ship had archers and slingers, plus marines to board enemy vessels, but their main weapon was a ram—a wooden spike sheathed in bronze on the prow, just below the waterline. The basic tactic was to row full speed into an enemy ship, driving this ram through its hull. A curved beak above the ram prevented entanglement so the attacker could back away, while water flooded through the hole into the enemy ship. To maneuver deftly and break

Figure 11.8 A modern reconstruction of a trireme, with a student crew.

the enemy's line required stamina and discipline. Disorganized sailors—like the Ionians, drawn from several independent *poleis,* with no clear command structure— were helpless against organized forces. Herodotus explains what happened:

> The Ionians agreed to take orders from Dionysius, who at once got to work. Every day he had ships and crews out training, making the fleet sail in line ahead, keeping the troops on board under arms, practicing the oarsmen on the maneuver of breaking the line, and insisting that all ships, for the remainder of the day, should lie to their anchors instead of being hauled ashore. Thus the men got no rest from morning to night. For seven days they continued to obey orders; but after that, being unaccustomed to such hard work and worn out with toiling away under the hot sun, they began to grumble. "What god have we offended," they said, "to be punished like this? We must have taken leave of our senses, to have put ourselves in the hands of this swollen-headed Phocaean who provides no more than three ships for the fleet! Yet here he is, taking complete charge; the way he treats us is outrageous; we shall never recover from it—many of us are ill already, and many more expect to be. Anything would be preferable to the misery we now endure— if it's a choice between two sorts of slavery, then the one we are threatened with, however bad it turns out to be, could hardly be worse than what we are putting up with now. Now then—let us refuse to obey his orders."
>
> It was no sooner said than done. Every seaman in the fleet refused duty. They pitched tents, like soldiers, in the island, lounged about in the shade, and refused to go aboard the vessels or to continue their training in any way whatsoever.
>
> The commanders of the contingent from Samos, when they realized how the Ionians were behaving and were aware of the complete lack of discipline among them, were convinced that it would be impossible to get the better of the Persian fleet.
>
> Herodotus 6.12–13 (A. de Selincourt)

When the Persians attacked, the Samians deserted, and the Greek line broke up. Some crews fought heroically but were destroyed all the same. The Persians burned Miletus and its temples and deported the survivors two thousand miles away to the Persian Gulf.

In spring 493 B.C., the army devastated the other Ionian cities (except for island Samos, rewarded for her treachery with survival). The adult men were massacred, the best looking boys castrated to make eunuchs, the prettiest girls sent to the royal harem, and many others sold into slavery. Darius committed acts of savage terror but also listened to Ionian grievances from among the survivors. He replaced the hated tyrants with democracies, set up regional courts to suppress lawlessness, and commissioned a comprehensive land survey. Nonetheless, Ionia's cities, which had been among Greece's richest in the sixth century and had made original contributions to philosophy, never recovered from the devastation.

Histiaeus, whose machinations had inflicted so much suffering on Greeks and Persians alike, came to a bad end. When the Persians caught up with his pirates:

> The Greeks fled; and Histiaeus, who did not expect Darius to punish his fault with death, made a last bid to save himself. He was overtaken by a Persian as he ran, and, just as he was about to be speared, he cried out, in Persian, "I am Histiaeus, of Miletus." Now if after his capture he had been taken to Darius, he would not, in my opinion, have found himself in serious trouble, but Darius would have pardoned him; but as it was, for this very reason—to prevent him, that is, from rising once more to a position of influence in Darius' court—Artaphernes, the governor of Sardis, and Harpagus,° his actual

°*Harpagus:* A Persian general, not to be confused with the Harpagus who helped Cyrus to power in 559 B.C.

captor, resolved upon his death. As soon as he reached Sardis he was impaled; his head was cut off, pickled, and sent to Darius in Susa. Darius, when he learned what Artaphernes and Harpagus had done, was angry with them for not bringing Histiaeus to him alive. He gave orders for the head to be washed and tended, and buried with all the honor due to a man who had done good service to Persia and the king. So ends the story of Histiaeus.

Herodotus 6.29–30 (A. de Selincourt)

THE BATTLE OF MARATHON, 490 B.C.

The Ionian Revolt was a turning point for the Greeks. Athens had openly renounced her submission to Ahuramazda and Persia, and the Athenians knew that Darius would punish them as he had the Ionians. When Phrynichus, a leading playwright, produced a tragedy called *The Sack of Miletus,* Herodotus says that "the audience in the theater burst into tears. The author was fined a thousand drachmas[21] for reminding them of their own evils, and they forbade anybody ever to put the play on the stage again."

In 492 B.C., Darius sent his son-in-law Mardonius along the north coast of the Aegean with a fleet (Map 11.3), announcing his intention to punish Athens and Eretria for supporting the revolt. Herodotus says that "although these two places were the professed object of the expedition, in fact the Persians intended to subjugate as many Greek towns as they could." Everyone in Mardonius' path surrendered,

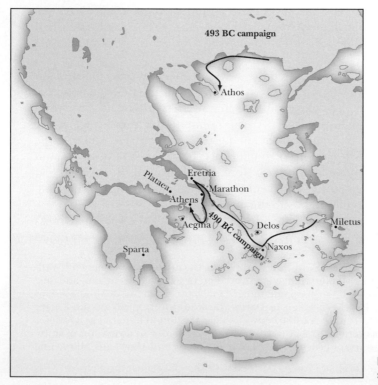

Map 11.3 The Persian invasions of 493, 490 B.C.

but he sailed into a terrific storm. According to Herodotus, "something like 300 ships were lost with over 20,000 men. The sea in the neighborhood of Athos is full of monsters, so that those of the ships' companies who were not dashed to pieces on the rocks were seized and devoured. Others, unable to swim, were drowned; others still died of cold."

Undeterred by the disaster,

> Darius now began to test the attitude of the Greeks, and to find out whether they were likely to resist or surrender. He sent heralds to the various Greek states to demand earth and water for the king, and at the same time he sent orders to the Asiatic coast towns, which were already tributary, for the provision of warships and transport vessels to carry cavalry. While these were being prepared, the heralds in Greece obtained what they had asked from many of the towns on the mainland and from all the islanders whom they visited with their request.
>
> Herodotus 6.48–49 (A. de Selincourt)

Many *poleis* submitted. Some aristocrats preferred being tyrants under Persia to living in free democracies, while the oligarchs of Aegina (ē-jī-na) hoped for revenge on neighboring Athens, their ancient enemy. The Athenians, by contrast, executed Darius' heralds (against sacred custom), and the Spartans told them that if they wanted earth and water, they should get it themselves, then pitched them head-first down a well. Aegina and Athens went to war with each other even as the Persians closed in on them. There seemed little hope that such disorganized people, who did not even have a professional army, could resist the greatest empire the world had ever seen.

In summer 490 B.C., Darius sent a small force by Persian standards—perhaps thirty thousand men—straight across the Aegean to avoid storms. Hippias, Athens' ex-tyrant, was with them; Darius planned to reinstate him. The Persian fleet stopped on Naxos, which had triggered the 499 revolt, and burned everything to the ground. They occupied the sacred island of Delos. After a few days, they reached Eretria, just miles from Athens. Athens sent four thousand men in Eretria's defense—nearly half her hoplites—but

> in spite of the appeals to Athens, things at Eretria were not in a healthy state; there was no firm resolve, and counsels were divided; one party proposed abandoning the town and taking refuge in the hills, another—having an eye to some gain from the Persians—was preparing to betray the city. When Aeschines the son of Nothon, one of the leading men of Eretria, came to know of what was afoot, he at once proceeded to act: he disclosed the whole situation to those of the Athenians who had already arrived and urged them to go home again before they were caught up in the catastrophe that was bound to come. They took Aeschines' advice and got safe away by crossing to Oropos.
>
> . . . The Eretrians had no intention of leaving their defenses to meet the coming attack in the open; their one concern (the proposal not to abandon the town having been carried) was to defend their walls—if they could.
>
> The assault soon came, and there was weight behind it. For six days fighting continued with many killed on both sides. Then, on the seventh, two well known Eretrians, Euphorbos the son of Alkimachos and Philagros the son of Kyneas, betrayed the town to the enemy. The Persians entered and stripped the temples bare and burned them in revenge for the burned temples at Sardis; and, in accordance with Darius' orders, carried off all the inhabitants as slaves.
>
> Herodotus 6.100–101 (A. de Selincourt)

Athens was next. The Persians sailed down the coast and soon after dawn on September 8, 490 B.C., landed on the beach of **Marathon.** There they organized their forces for an easy march to Athens. Fire signals flashed across the dry hills of Attica to warn the Athenians. The Assembly convened to discuss the crisis. The Athenians ran their army the way they ran their city, democratically. Each year they elected ten generals, who formed a committee that voted on tactics. They took turns chairing for a day each, a recipe for indecision, but at this critical moment one of the ten, **Miltiades** (mil-$\bar{\text{ti}}$-a-d$\bar{\text{e}}$z), took charge. At his urging, Athens' nine thousand hoplites took whatever food they had and headed straight for Marathon. The generals sent a runner named **Pheidippides** (f$\bar{\text{i}}$-**dip**-i-d$\bar{\text{e}}$z) to tell Sparta that the storm had broken.

> Pheidippides reached Sparta the day after he left Athens[22] and delivered his message to the Spartan government. "Men of Sparta," the message ran, "the Athenians ask you to help them, and not to stand by while the most ancient city of Greece is crushed and enslaved by a foreign invader; for even now Eretria has been enslaved, and Greece is the weaker by the loss of one fine city." The Spartans, though moved by the appeal, and willing to send help to Athens, were unable to send it promptly because they did not wish to break their law. It was the ninth day of the month, and they said they could not take the field till the moon was full. So they waited for the full moon, and meanwhile Hippias, son of Pisistratus, guided the Persians to Marathon.
>
> Herodotus 6.106–107 (A. de Selincourt)

Historians still debate whether it was really respect for religion or a secret desire to see Athens humbled that held Sparta back. The Athenian generals had better luck with another runner, who went to the little city of Plataea on the border between Athens and the powerful Boeotian city of Thebes. The messenger reminded the Plataeans how Athens had saved them from a Theban attack thirty years before. Plataea's full force of one thousand hoplites raced grimly to join the Athenians at Marathon.

The men of Athens marched all night, reaching Marathon around dawn on September 9, 490 B.C. To get from the beach to Athens, the Persians would have to pass through the low hills that the Athenians occupied. The Athenians quickly set up a strong position across the Persians' line of march, and that night or the next morning the Plataeans joined them. The two armies waited. The Persians hoped that traitors would betray Athens, saving them a troublesome uphill attack, while the Athenians hoped that the Spartans would come. On September 11, Pheidippides staggered back into Athens with the awful news: The Spartans would not come for another week.

The Athenian leadership split down the middle. Five of the ten generals, stunned by the size of the Persian force, urged a return to Athens to sit out a siege. Although the Persian infantry was lightly armed, and no match for hoplites, these generals feared that Persia's cavalry and archers would destroy the Greek phalanx before it ever came to hand-to-hand combat. The other five generals, led by the forceful Miltiades, feared that if they withdrew without fighting, the city would be betrayed to massacre, slavery, and death. An eleventh official, the archon known as the War-Archon, accompanied the army and had a tie-breaking vote. The War-Archon voted for war.

The face-off lasted a week. Even those generals who supported Miltiades hesitated to take responsibility for the actual battle, so the Athenians waited until it was Miltiades' turn to chair the generals' committee. Before dawn on September 17, Miltiades mustered the Athenians and Plataeans. To keep from being outflanked, he extended their line in the dark until it covered nearly a mile, the same length as the Persian front:

> One result of the disposition of Athenian troops before the battle was the weakening of their center by the effort to extend the line sufficiently to cover the whole Persian front; the two wings were strong, but the line in the center was only a few ranks deep. The dispositions made, and the preliminary sacrifice promising success, the word was given to move, and the Athenians advanced at a run toward the enemy, not less than a mile away. The Persians, seeing the attack developing at the double, prepared to meet it, thinking it suicidal madness for the Athenians to risk an assault with so small a force—rushing in with no support from either cavalry or archers. Well, that was what they imagined. But the Athenians came on, closed with the enemy, and fought in a way not to be forgotten. They were the first Greeks, so far as we know, to charge at a run, and the first who dared to look without flinching at Persian dress and the men who wore it; for until that day came, no Greek could even hear the word "Persian" without terror.
>
> The struggle at Marathon was long drawn out. In the center, held by the Persians themselves and the Sakai,° the advantage was with the foreigners, who were so far successful as to break the Greek line and pursue the fugitives inland from the sea, but the Athenians on one wing and the Plataeans on the other were both victorious. Having got the upper hand, they left the defeated enemy to make their escape, and then, drawing the two wings together into a single unit, they turned their attention to the Persians who had broken through in the center. Here again they were triumphant, chasing the routed enemy, and cutting them down till they came to the sea, and men were calling for fire, and taking hold of the ships. It was in this phase of the struggle that the War-Archon Callimachus was killed, fighting bravely, and also Stesilaos, the son of Thrasylaos, one of the generals. Kynegiros too, the son of Euphorion,° had his hand cut off with an ax as he was getting hold of a ship's stern, and so lost his life, together with many other well known Athenians. The Athenians secured in this way seven ships, but the rest got off, and the Persians aboard them.
>
> Herodotus 6.111–15 (A. de Selincourt)

°*Sakai:* Scythians.   °*son of Euphorion:* Another son of Euphorion also fought at Marathon that day: the tragedian Aeschylus. On his epitaph, Aeschylus was prouder of being in this battle than of all his dramatic triumphs.

Herodotus tells us, "In the battle of Marathon some 6,400 Persians were killed; the losses of the Athenians were 192."[23] But most of the Persian army was intact, and as the ships carried it safely off the beach, the Athenians saw a flash of light from the hills behind them: Someone was using a brightly polished shield as a mirror, catching the sun's rays to signal to the Persians. Traitors were ready to betray the city. The Persian fleet hoped to reach Athens while the hoplites were still at Marathon, catch it undefended, and win the war.

The Greek soldiers, bone-tired, immediately set off back to Athens, a grueling twenty-six-mile forced march through the mounting heat of the day. Ahead, they sent Pheidippides, the same man who had run 140 miles from Athens to Sparta and back again in three days. Now his mission was more desperate: to tell the men in the city to hold on. Their brothers-in-arms had won a triumph worthy of Homer, and they would not let the city fall.

Pheidippides' run inspired the modern marathon race when the Olympic Games were reinvented in 1896. It takes a modern professional runner over two hours to cover twenty-six miles. Pheidippides—underfed, drained from his previous run—ran to save his city from betrayal and destruction. He delivered the astounding news of victory, but after staggering into the *agora,* collapsed and died.

The Athenians in the city manned their defenses, put a watch on the gates, and waited. The Persians had to sail seventy miles, at top speed nine or ten hours; the Athenians had to cross twenty-six miles of hills "as fast as their legs would carry them," according to Herodotus, requiring about the same time.

The Athenian hoplites approached their city as evening fell. They saw no flames or pall of smoke, no Persian ships darkening the bay. They took up position outside the city and prepared to fight. The Persian fleet came into view. The Persians would now have to fight their way ashore through the very men who had slaughtered their friends just hours before. The sailors rested on their oars and the commanders debated. As darkness fell, they sailed back to Asia.

Outnumbered, abandoned by Sparta, surrounded by traitors, the Athenian amateurs had annihilated a professional Persian army. The Spartans were impressed:

> After the full moon, 2,000 Spartans set off for Athens. They were so anxious not to be late that they were in Attica on the third day° after leaving Sparta. They had, of course, missed the battle, but such was their passion to see the Persians that they went to Marathon to have a look at the bodies. That done, they praised the Athenians on their good work and returned home.
>
> Herodotus 6.120 (A. de Selincourt)

°*third day:* They covered fifty miles per day!

Marathon was *the* moment for Athens. Nearly seventy years later, when the comic poet Aristophanes wanted to express Athenians' pride in their city, his chorus (old men dressed as wasps to symbolize their ferocity) harked back to Marathon:

> For virulent virility, we remain unmatched. At pest removal,
> the city has not known our peer in sheer belligerence, as witness
> the coming of the Persians.
>   Their aim was simple—to drive us from our hives
> and to put the entire city to the torch to supply the smoke.
> Straightaway, forth we swarmed, our bravery bolstered with gall.
> We took our stand with shield and spear in single combat,
> and ground our jaws with rage as they blotted out the sun with arrows.
> But the owl of omen° flew over our ranks before the attack,
> and when evening blotted the sun in truth, the Persians bolted,°
> routed. We raced behind and riddled their Oriental rears,
> while their jaws and brows ballooned, harpooned by our Sting. Wherefore,
> since men are known by their attributes, throughout barbarian lands
> we are famed as the manliest race alive: the ATTIC WASP.
>
> Aristophanes, *Wasps* 1077–1090
(D. Parker, *Aristophanes: Three Comedies,* Ann Arbor 1969)

°*Owl of omen:* The owl was the symbol of Athena, the city's patron goddess. °*the Persians bolted:* Aristophanes apparently conflated the battle in the morning and the Persians' retreat from Athens in the evening.

Athens was saved—for now.

KEY TERMS

Ashur, 222

Carthage, 225

Medes, 225

Phrygia, 225

King Midas, 225

Lydia, 225

Gyges, 225

Croesus, 226

Media, 226

Astyages, 228

Harpagus, 228

Cyrus, 228

Zoroastrianism, 232

Ahuramazda, 232

Achaemenids, 232

Cambyses, 232

Darius, 234

hubris, 237

satraps, 237

Histiaeus, 238

Eretria, 239

triremes, 240

Marathon, 244

Miltiades, 244

Pheidippides, 244

FURTHER READING

Boardman, John, N. G. L. Hammond, David Lewis, and Martin Ostwald, eds., *The Cambridge Ancient History IV: Persia, Greece, and the Western Mediterranean c. 525 to 479 B.C.* (2nd ed., Cambridge 1988). Encyclopedic survey of the Greek world, Persia, Italy, and Carthage, with excellent chapters.

Briant, Pierre, *From Cyrus to Alexander: A History of the Persian Empire* (Winona Lake, IN, 2002). Superb detailed history of the Persian Empire.

Burn, A. R., *Persia and the Greeks* (2nd ed., London 1984). Very readable review of the Persian War, with an excellent appendix by David Lewis dealing with the evidence from the Persian side.

Kuhrt, Amélie, *The Ancient Near East* II (London 1995). A masterly survey of Assyrian and Persian history. The best introduction.

Sancisi-Weerdenburg, Heleen, Amélie Kuhrt, and others, eds., *Achaemenid History Workshops* (10 volumes, 1987–1994). Series of major conferences covering all aspects of Persian history. Indispensable for serious research.

Vidal, Gore, *Creation* (New York 1981). A novel set against the vast backdrop of the Persian Empire at the end of the sixth century B.C., ranging from Greece to China. Gripping and historically well informed.

Wiesehöfer, Josef, *Ancient Persia: From 550 B.C. to 650 A.D.* (New York 1996). The best brief survey of the three ancient Persian Empires, with focus on primary Persian sources. Fresh look at Persian history from its Near Eastern perspective.

Ancient Texts

Herodotus, *The Histories* (New York, rev. ed., 1996; tr. Aubrey de Selincourt). Books 1 through 6 narrate the rise of Persia to the battle of Marathon.

CHAPTER 12

THE GREAT WAR, 480–479 B.C.

When Darius surveyed his vast empire in 490 B.C., Marathon was a minor setback in the grand scheme. Persia's casualties were lower than in the storm of 492 B.C., and the expedition had punished the sinful Eretria, as intended. Nonetheless, the defeat was a setback, and Darius needed to act swiftly to reassert his authority.

Herodotus describes the situation in the Persian court:

> When news of the battle of Marathon reached Darius, son of Hystaspes and king of Persia, his anger against Athens, already great enough on account of the assault on Sardis, was even greater, and he was more than ever determined to make war on Greece. Without loss of time he dispatched couriers to the various states under his dominion with orders to raise an army much larger than before; and also warships, transports, horses, and grain. So the royal command went round; and all Asia was in an uproar for three years, with the best men being enrolled in the army for the invasion of Greece, and with the preparations.
>
> Herodotus 7.1 (A. de Selincourt)

But luck was with Athens. First, Egypt rebelled, and this was more important than Greece. Then Darius died in 486 B.C. Babylon rose up. Darius' son **Xerxes** (**zer**k-sēz) suppressed the revolts but was inclined to leave the western frontier alone. However, some advisors—particularly Mardonius, commander of the disastrous naval expedition in 492 B.C.—urged him to renew the attack. Xerxes agreed, then canceled his plans, then (because of a frightening dream, according to Herodotus) decided to invade after all. The Greeks had gained a vital breathing space.

STORM CLOUDS IN THE WEST

It was now 483 B.C. Diodorus of Sicily, a historian living in the first century B.C., tells the following story:

> Xerxes, being won over by Mardonius and desiring to drive all the Greeks from their homes, sent an embassy to the Carthaginians to urge them to join him in the undertaking and closed an agreement with them, to the effect that he would wage war upon the Greeks who lived in Greece, while the Carthaginians should at the same time gather great armaments and subdue those Greeks who lived in Sicily and Italy. In accordance, then, with their agreements, the Carthaginians, collecting a great amount of money, gathered mercenaries from both Italy and also from France and Spain, and in addition to these troops they enrolled their own citizens from Carthage itself and from the whole of Libya. In the end, after spending three years in constant preparation, they assembled more than 300,000 infantry and 200 warships.
>
> Diodorus of Sicily 11.1 (C. H. Oldfather)

Herodotus does not mention this alliance, and it may be that Greeks later simply assumed that simultaneous attacks from Persia and Carthage *must* have been coordinated. Certainly both great powers were concerned about the Greeks. As we saw in Chapter 11, "Persia and the Greeks, 550–490 B.C.," Sparta and Persia exchanged sharp words in 545 B.C., and in 499 Athens backed the Ionian rebellion. In the West, the Greek cities were not only powerful, but very rich. Compared to the Aegean, Sicily had rather few *poleis,* each with a large territory. The land was good and the rainfall reliable. Sicilian Greeks, like Sparta, could solve some social problems by conquering surrounding lands, and by 500 B.C. had taken over the best coastal plains (Map 12.1).

They pushed some indigenous peoples into the inland hills and reduced others to serfdom. Sicilian merchants grew rich selling grain to Aegean Greece and wine to Carthage, and taxes on trade through their harbors paid for breathtaking temples at Selinous, Akragas, and **Syracuse.** Perhaps because they were so rich, Sicilian aristocrats distanced themselves from the lower classes more than did Aegean nobles (though hardly anything like Egyptians or Persians). The forces that produced democracy in the Aegean were felt in Sicily, but the aristocrats' greater strength there led to violent civil wars, and around 500 B.C.—when tyranny disappeared in the Aegean—super-rich Sicilians exploited the constant unrest to install themselves as tyrants. Fifth-century Sicilian tyrants were stronger than their sixth-century Aegean predecessors because the states they ruled were more centralized and richer. With this wealth they hired mercenaries, reducing their need for support from citizen hoplites and enabling them to push still further inland at the natives' expense.

In western Sicily, relations between Greeks, natives, and Phoenicians were tense at the end of the sixth century (Table 12.1). The Phoenicians lived in three independent western Sicilian cities at **Motya,** Panormos, and Soloeis. These trading centers enjoyed good relations with the native Elymians, but not always with the Greeks. Around 510 B.C., a Spartan adventurer—King Cleomenes' half-brother—tried to set up a colony very near Motya. The Sicilian Phoenicians combined with the Elymians to destroy the colony and kill its leader. Meanwhile, Greek pirates were hurting

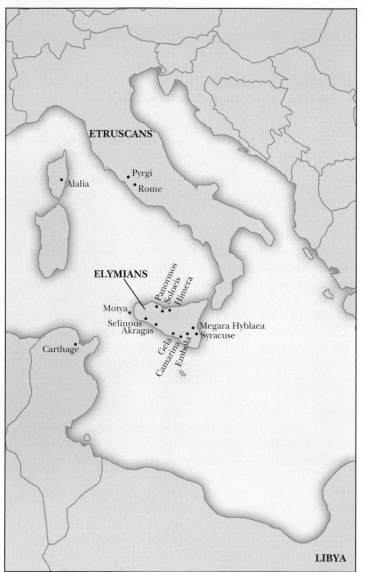

Map 12.1 West Mediterranean sites mentioned in this chapter.

Phoenician trade. Back in 535 B.C., Carthage had crushed the pirates in a sea battle near Corsica, but by 500 the raids were worse than ever. The same Dionysius who had tried to organize the Ionian fleet in 494 fled to Sicily after the disaster and became a pirate king, robbing only Phoenicians, never Greeks.

In the 490s, the tyrant of the small city of **Gela** (jē-la) on the south coast of Sicily, instead of attacking the natives, attacked other Greeks. He quickly built an empire covering most of eastern Sicily. When he died in 491, his former cavalry commander **Gelon** (jē-lon), took his place. In 485 the poorer citizens of the great city of Syracuse on the east coast of Sicily combined forces with native serfs to expel

Table 12.1 Events in the west, 535–480 B.C.

Date B.C.	Event
535	Battle of Alalia: Carthaginians defeat Greek pirates
510	Dorieus' expedition: Spartan adventurer tries to establish Greek colony near Motya
498	Hippocrates, tyrant of Gela, creates empire in eastern Sicily
494	Dionysius of Phocaea emigrates to Sicily and becomes pirate leader
491	Gelon succeeds Hippocrates as tyrant of Gela
485	Gelon becomes tyrant of Syracuse and gives Gela to his brother Hieron
c. 483	Gelon moves populations from Camarina, Gela, Megara Hyblaea [hi-**blē**-a], and Sicilian Euboea to Syracuse
483	Theron, tyrant of Akragas, overthrows Terillos, tyrant of Himera
481	Embassy from Aegean Greeks to Gelon
480	Hamilcar of Carthage invades Sicily; battle of Himera

the aristocracy. Gelon used his army to restore the nobles, then seized Syracuse for himself.

> The acquisition of Syracuse made Gelon much less interested than before in Gela. He handed it over to his brother Hieron and himself proceeded to strengthen Syracuse, which had now become the apple of his eye. At once Syracuse shot up and budded like a young tree; Gelon brought to it all the people of Camarina, which he had razed to the ground, and gave them citizen rights, and he did the same for more than half the population of Gela. Megara Hyblaea, too, had to make its contribution—the town had been at war with Gelon and had surrendered on terms. The men of substance, who had started the war, naturally expected death at Gelon's hands, but they were transferred instead to Syracuse and given citizen rights like the rest. The Megarian commoners, who imagined that they would be treated well because they had had no share of responsibility for the war, were also brought to Syracuse and then sold as slaves abroad. The Sicilian Euboea suffered similar treatment, the same distinction being made between men of property and the common people. In both cases Gelon's motive was his belief that the masses are very disagreeable to live with. In these ways Gelon rose to be tyrant and wielded very great influence.
>
> Herodotus 7.156 (A. de Selincourt)

Gelon acted more like an Assyrian or Persian king than a Greek leader, wiping out whole cities, moving populations around to build up his own city, and putting his brother in charge of Gela without reference to the citizens' wishes. Like an Achaemenid, he ran politics as a family business. He made marriage alliances with Theron, tyrant of Akragas, the second greatest city in Sicily. Between them, Gelon and Theron dominated eastern and central Sicily. Matters came to a head in 483 B.C. when Theron overthrew Terillus, the tyrant of **Himera** on the north coast of the island. Terillus had had good relations with Carthage, and by replacing him with a government less friendly to Carthage, Theron effectively closed down Phoenician traders' access to central Sicily.

The Carthaginians may have written their own histories, but when Rome destroyed this proud city in 146 B.C. (see Chapter 22, "The Coming of Rome, 220–30 B.C."), virtually all its literaure was lost. Our meager knowledge of Carthage comes from hostile comments by Greek and Roman authors and from archaeological excavations since the 1970s. Carthage was run by an oligarchy. Its great harbor provided an ideal center for traders shipping goods between the east and west Mediterranean, and the city flourished. As early as 508 B.C., Carthage made a treaty with Rome (then a minor power), regulating access to markets in central Italy, and negotiated similar deals with the more powerful cities of Etruria, north of Rome. Carthage was not going to allow adventurers, pirates, or ambitious Greek tyrants to disrupt her profitable trading system. The Carthaginian oligarchs may not have wanted to conquer Sicily, but they could not turn away when Theron of Akragas deposed Terillus of Himera and shut them from the island. Carthage needed to put the Greeks in their place.

STORM CLOUDS IN THE EAST

By 483 B.C., western and eastern Greeks knew that war was imminent. They should put aside their local squabbles. Cooperation was easier in Sicily than in the Aegean, because Sicily had fewer cities and the ruling families in Syracuse and Akragas, linked through marriage, dominated the island. In the Aegean, by contrast, both Athens and Sparta claimed leadership. Their inability to cooperate in 490 B.C. inspired little confidence, and many cities submitted to Darius without a murmur.

Sparta did nothing when Xerxes started gathering forces. An Athenian named **Themistocles** (the-**mis**-tō-klēz) saw the need to act. Chance intervened. There were rich veins of silver in Attica, which the state leased to private entrepreneurs, taking a cut of the profits. In 483 or 482 B.C., a silver strike brought the state a windfall of one hundred talents—a huge sum. Like a modern government with a budget surplus, Athens needed to spend the money:

> The Athenians proposed to share out amongst themselves the money at the rate of 10 drachmas a man. Themistocles, however, persuaded them to give up this idea and, instead of distributing the money, to spend it on the construction of 200 warships for use in the war with Aegina. The outbreak of this war at just that moment saved Greece by forcing Athens to become a maritime power. In point of fact the 200 ships were not employed for the purpose for which they were built, but were available for Greece in her hour of need.
>
> Herodotus 7.144 (A. de Selincourt)

While Themistocles worked behind the scenes to supervise construction of the fleet, and other Greeks dithered, Xerxes finished his preparations. Herodotus says that Xerxes raised 5,283,200 men, not counting eunuchs, cooks, and prostitutes! Five million troops would be 20 percent of the entire empire. By Herodotus' reckoning, they required four thousand tons of grain per day (four hundred thousand tons for a three-month campaign), drank rivers dry, and bankrupted cities with a single dinner. Modern historians guess that Xerxes' host was actually five hundred thousand or less, still the largest army the ancient world had ever seen. A force that size could not carry enough food and water to stay alive in Greece in summer, and Greece did not produce enough to support the Persian host. Ships would be decisive, because only a fleet coasting the shore could carry provisions for such a host. If the Greeks could disable Xerxes' fleet, his army would starve.

Xerxes hoped to avoid fighting by terrifying the Greeks into submission. He undertook massive engineering works, bridging the Hellespont and cutting a canal through the Athos peninsula where Mardonius was wrecked twelve years before. In October 481 B.C., Xerxes' envoys arrived in Greece. The Delphic oracle advised the Greeks to make terms, and several important *poleis* sent earth and water in submission. Only in November 481, when Xerxes reached Sardis, did Sparta at last summon the Greeks to resist. Only thirty-one *poleis* responded.

Despite mutual hostilities, Athens accepted Spartan leadership. The allies sent an embassy to Gelon in Syracuse for help. He offered 200 warships, 20,000 hoplites, 4,000 light infantry, 4,000 cavalry, and all the food the Greeks needed—but only if he, Gelon, would be commander-in-chief. The Aegean Greeks balked and Gelon withdrew.

> Gelon himself was afraid that Greece would be unable to survive the Persian invasion. At the same time, as tyrant of Sicily, he could not bring himself to go to the Peloponnesus and submit to taking orders from Spartans. Accordingly he chose a different course. As soon as news came that Xerxes was over the Hellespont, he sent three small ships under the command of Cadmus, the son of Skythes, a native of the island of Cos, with instructions to go to Delphi, where, equipped with a large sum of money and plenty of friendly words, he was to wait and see how the war would go. If the Persians won, he was to give the money to Xerxes together with earth and water of Gelon's dominions. If the Greeks won, he was to bring the money back again.
>
> Herodotus 7.163 (A. de Selincourt)

THE STORM BREAKS IN THE WEST: THE BATTLE OF HIMERA, 480 B.C.

Hamilcar (**ham**-il-kar), the Carthaginian general, had modest aims in 480 B.C. Rather than destroying the Sicilian Greeks, he wanted to reopen the island for trade. He raised huge sums of money and hired a host of mercenaries. Violent storms sank many of his transport ships, but his reduced force nevertheless easily defeated a Greek army outside Himera on the north coast of Sicily and besieged the city. Theron of Akragas, on the south coast of the island, wrote to Gelon in Syracuse, asking him to come at once. Gelon set off with 50,000 infantry and 5000 cavalry.

Hamilcar had problems feeding his large army, and when Gelon reached Himera, Hamilcar's men had scattered to find food. Gelon's cavalry captured thousands. The Greeks in Himera expected destruction at any moment, but Gelon's success revived their spirits. The Greeks gained the initiative, and Gelon sought a decisive battle. Diodorus of Sicily (first century B.C.) tells the story:

> Gelon's own ingenuity was greatly aided by an accident, because of the following circumstances. He had decided to set fire to the enemy's ships; and while Hamilcar was occupied in the naval camp preparing a magnificent sacrifice to Poseidon, cavalrymen came from the countryside bringing to Gelon a letter-carrier who was carrying dispatches from the people of Selinous,° which said that they would send the cavalry on the

° *Selinous:* A major Greek city in western Sicily, which generally pursued pro-Carthaginian policies.

day that Hamilcar had asked them to. That was the day on which Hamilcar planned to celebrate the sacrifice. And on that day, Gelon sent out cavalry of his own, who were under orders to skirt the immediate neighborhood and to ride up to the naval camp at daybreak, as if they were the allies from Selinous, and once they had got inside the wooden palisade, they were to kill Hamilcar and set fire to the ships. He also sent scouts to the hills that overlook the city, ordering them to raise the signal as soon as they saw that the horsemen were inside the wall. For his part, at dawn he drew up his army and waited for the sign that was to come from the scouts.

At sunrise the cavalry rode up to the Carthaginian naval camp, and when the guards admitted them, thinking them to be allies, they at once galloped to where Hamilcar was busy with the sacrifice, cut him down, and then set fire to the ships; and then the scouts raised the signal and Gelon advanced with his entire army in battle order against the Carthaginian camp. The commanders of the Phoenicians in the camp at first led their troops out to meet the Sicilians and as the lines closed they put up a vigorous fight; at the same time in both camps the trumpets sounded the signal for battle, and shouts rose from the two armies one after the other, each eagerly striving to outdo their enemies in the volume of their cheering. The slaughter was great, and the battle was swaying back and forth, when suddenly the flames from the ships began to rise up high and various people reported that the general had been killed. Then the Greeks were emboldened, and with spirits elated by the rumors and by the hope of victory, they pressed with greater boldness against the barbarians, while the Carthaginians, dismayed and despairing, turned in flight.

Since Gelon had given orders to take no prisoners, there followed a great massacre of the enemy in their flight, and in the end no fewer than 150,000 of them were killed.[24] All who escaped the battle and fled to a strong position at first beat off the attackers, but the position they had seized had no water, and thirst forced them to surrender.

After the battle at Himera twenty warships made their escape, being those which Hamilcar, to serve his routine requirements, had not hauled up onto the shore. Consequently, although practically all the rest of the combatants were killed or captured, these vessels managed to set sail before they were noticed. But they picked up many fugitives, and while heavily laden on that account, they encountered a storm and all were lost. Only a handful of survivors got safely to Carthage in a small boat to give their fellow citizens a brief statement: "All who crossed over to Sicily have perished."

Diodorus of Sicily 11.21–22, 24 (C. H. Oldfather)

Gelon's victory at Himera made him the most influential man in Sicily. Hailed as savior of the Greeks, his word was law. For Carthage, it was a disaster. Terrified that Gelon would invade North Africa, the Carthaginians offered a huge indemnity in return for which Gelon left Motya, Panormos, and Soloeis untroubled. Akragas also profited mightily by enslaving thousands of Carthaginian soldiers who fled across interior Sicily. Diodorus says that "there was such a multitude of captives that it looked as if the island had made the whole of Libya prisoner."

So ended Hamilcar's invasion. More than seventy years would pass before Carthage again challenged the Greeks.

THE STORM BREAKS IN THE EAST: THE BATTLE OF THERMOPYLAE, 480 B.C.

Xerxes was more ambitious than Hamilcar: He wanted to destroy Greece totally. His strategy was simple—march directly to Athens; burn it; do the same to Sparta. The goal was not just to destroy property, but to force the Greeks to fight (and lose) a decisive battle. Judging from past experience, the Greek alliance would break up before Xerxes actually had to fight.

The Greek strategy was equally simple: Stop this from happening. They could not hope to win an open battle, so they would defend one of the passes along the coast that Xerxes would have to cross if he stayed in contact with his fleet. Man for man, light-armed Persians were no match for Greek hoplites, but holding off Xerxes was not the same as defeating him. Persia had a huge fleet: If blocked at a pass, they could sail around it toward Athens and Sparta.

There were only three places where the Greeks might hold the Persians (Map 12.2). The first was the beautiful Vale of Tempe (**tem**-pē), between the towering mountains Olympus and Ossa at the northern border of Thessaly, whose cavalry the Greeks badly needed. Ten thousand hoplites and a hastily assembled fleet, including the two hundred new Athenian triremes, rushed north, only to learn that there was a second way into Thessaly, and that if they took a stand at Tempe, they would be outflanked. The Greeks therefore fell back, and Thessaly, undefended, surrendered to Darius.

The next natural defensive position was **Thermopylae** (ther-**mop**-i-lē, "the hot gates") between Thessaly and the district of Locris, where seemingly impassable mountains came within a few yards of the sea. Thermopylae was a logical place to make a stand because it was north of Athens and the Greek fleet could block the narrow straits of Artemision just off the coast, separating the northern tip of the island of Euboea from the mainland. On the other hand, Xerxes might get there

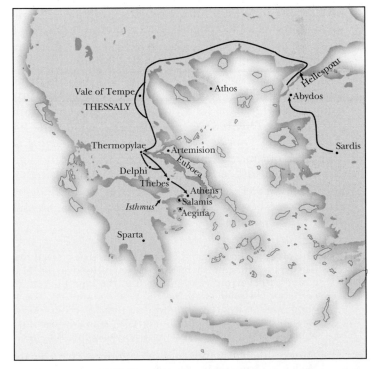

Map 12.2 The Aegean campaign of 480 B.C.

before the Greeks, or by sailing around the south end of the long island of Euboea, he could trap a Greek fleet at Artemision and destroy it. The third option was to abandon central Greece altogether and withdraw to the Isthmus of Corinth. That meant giving up Athens, perhaps destroying the alliance. In any event, Xerxes could easily outflank the Isthmus and land his army wherever he liked in the Peloponnese. Sparta nonetheless consistently favored this dangerous plan.

Furious arguments paralyzed the Greeks in the crucial spring of 480 B.C., as Xerxes' vast forces marched inexorably on. Unable to decide what to do, the Greeks sent troops to Thermopylae, but only a tiny force—just three hundred Spartans led by King **Leonidas,** and three thousand, nine hundred allies. Leonidas, convinced of the need to take a stand at Thermopylae, rushed to get there before the Persians. He repaired an old wall across the narrow pass while the entire Greek fleet took up a position off Cape Artemision. The Greek fleet and army faced terrifying odds, yet the Spartans, true to their reputation, showed almost reckless bravery as they awaited the onslaught. A story circulated that when the Persians shot their arrows, they blocked out the sun. "That's good," one Spartiate commented. "If the Persians hide the sun, we shall have our battle in the shade."

In this moment of crisis, the Greeks turned to their gods. An Athenian oracle recommended praying to Boreas, god of the north wind. As if in answer, a terrible storm hit the Persian fleet. Xerxes had so many ships that they had to ride at anchor eight rows deep, and when a fierce wind sprang up, it smashed four hundred ships against the rocks. Thousands died. Persia's fleet pressed on, only to discover the Greeks blocking the straits at Artemision. They expected the Greeks to flee, leaving Thermopylae exposed. **Eurybiades** (yu-ri-bī-a-dēz), the Spartan commander of the fleet, was tempted, but the Euboeans secretly gave Themistocles thirty talents to persuade Eurybiades to fight at Artemision, thus protecting Euboea. Themistocles gave five talents to Eurybiades, who then agreed, and pocketed the difference, making a fortune while achieving his own military aims.

Greek sailors were more skilled than Xerxes' Phoenicians, but after a week, half the Athenian ships were damaged. The Persians kept up the pressure at Artemision and sent a large naval force around the south end of Euboea to trap the Greeks in the channel. On land, Xerxes advanced against the handful of hoplites holding Thermopylae. Four days in a row, he awoke expecting to find that the Greeks had run away, but instead the naked Spartans lay in the sun, combing their long hair. Xerxes, Herodotus says, did not know what to make of this: "The truth, namely that the Spartans were preparing themselves to die and to meet death with all their strength, was beyond his comprehension." On the fifth morning, astonished at their behavior, Xerxes ordered a frontal assault:

> The Medes° charged, and in the struggle that ensued many fell; but others took their places, and in spite of terrible losses refused to be beaten off. They made it plain enough to everyone, and not least to the king himself, that he had in his army many men, but few soldiers. All day the battle continued. The Medes, after their rough handling, were at length withdrawn and their place was taken by Hydarnes and his picked Persian troops—the King's Immortals°, who advanced to the attack in full confidence of bringing the business to a quick and easy end. But, once engaged, they were no more

°*Medes:* Although the Medes were a distinct people from the Persians, Greek writers used Medes as a synonym for Persians. °*Immortals:* An elite force of ten thousand infantry.

successful than the Medes had been; all went as before, the two armies fighting in a confined space, the Persians using shorter spears than the Greeks and having no advantage from their numbers.

On the Spartan side it was a memorable fight. They were men who understood war pitted against an inexperienced enemy, and amongst the feints they employed was to turn their backs in a body and pretend to be retreating in confusion, whereupon the enemy would pursue them with a great clatter and roar, but just as the Persians were on them the Spartans would wheel and face them and in the new struggle inflict innumerable casualties. The Spartans had their losses too, but not many. At last the Persians, finding that their assaults upon the pass, whether by divisions or by any other way they could think of, were all useless, broke off the engagement and withdrew. Xerxes was watching the battle from where he sat; and it is said that in the course of the attacks three times, in terror for his army, he leapt to his feet.

Herodotus 7.210–12 (A. de Selincourt)

The next day, Xerxes hurled still more men against the phalanx, and the slaughter continued. Leonidas rotated contingents in and out of line so that they never tired, while mounds of the Persian dead grew around them. Xerxes' best men were falling, and the fleet he sent south around Euboea had not returned. Unknown to him, it had run into yet another storm, losing hundreds more ships.

A Greek traitor named Ephialtes turned the tide. He told Xerxes of a path over the mountains, coming out behind the Spartans. That night, Hydarnes led the Immortals over the path, brushing aside the few defenders. A runner informed Leonidas. Realizing that all was lost, he sent the allies away. But he and the three hundred Spartans had been ordered to fight, and whatever happened, they would honor their word. Seven hundred men from the small town of Thespiae near Thebes also refused to leave; they joined the Spartans for the last stand.

As the Persian army advanced to the assault, the Greeks under Leonidas, knowing that they were going to their deaths, went out into the wider part of the pass much further than they had done before; in the previous days' fighting they had been holding the wall and making sorties from behind it into the narrow neck, but now they fought outside the narrows. Many of the barbarians fell; behind them the company commanders plied their whips indiscriminately, driving the men on. Many fell into the sea and were drowned, and still more were trampled to death by one another. No one could count the number of the dead. The Greeks, who knew that the enemy were on their way round by the mountain track and that death was inevitable, put forth all their strength and fought with fury and desperation. By this time most of their spears were broken, and they were killing Persians with their swords.

In the course of that fight Leonidas fell, having fought most gallantly, and many distinguished Spartans with him—their names I have learned, as those of men who deserve to be remembered. In fact, I have learned the names of all the three hundred. Amongst the Persian dead, too, were many men of high distinction, including two brothers of Xerxes, Habrokomes and Hyperanthes, sons of Darius by Artanes' daughter Phratagune. Artanes, the son of Hystaspes and grandson of Arsames, was Darius' brother; as Phratagune was his only child, his giving her to Darius was equivalent to giving him his entire estate.

There was a bitter struggle over the body of Leonidas. Four times the Greeks drove the enemy off, and at last by their valor rescued it. So it went on, until the troops with Ephialtes were close at hand, and then, when the Greeks knew that they had come, the character of the fighting changed. They withdrew again into the narrow neck of the pass, behind the wall, and took up a position in a single compact body on the little hill at the entrance to the pass, where the stone lion in memory of Leonidas stands today. Here they resisted to the last, with their swords, if they had them, and, if not, with their hands and teeth, until the Persians, coming on from the front over the ruins of the wall and closing in from behind, finally overwhelmed them with missile weapons.

Herodotus 7.223–25 (A. de Selincourt)

Over their bodies, the Greeks later set up a famous inscription:

Go, tell the Spartans, passerby
That here, obedient to their wishes, we lie.

THE FALL OF ATHENS

The battered fleet escaped the trap set by the Persians and withdrew to the narrows around the island of **Salamis** near the harbor of Athens, while the Spartans held back the Greek army at the Isthmus. In 481 B.C., a Delphic oracle had advised Athens to "trust its wooden walls," which Themistocles took to refer to the fleet. Most Athenians fled to the ships at the Persian advance, but some Athenians imagined that "wooden walls" meant they should barricade the Acropolis with wooden planks. The Persians sent fire arrows into this wooden wall, then climbed the almost impregnable rock by a back path. Still the Athenians held out:

When the Athenians saw the Persians on the summit, some leapt from the wall to their death, others sought sanctuary in the inner shrine of the temple, but the Persians who had got up first made straight for the gates, flung them open, and slaughtered those in the sanctuary. Having left not one of them alive, they stripped the temple of its treasures and burned everything on the Acropolis.

Herodotus 8.53 (A. de Selincourt)

Athens was a smoldering ruin. The Spartan naval commander Eurybiades wanted to sail back to the Isthmus, join the land army, and there await the Persian attack, but Themistocles understood that the Greeks' only chance was to provoke Xerxes into a naval battle. If they could lure Xerxes into the narrows around the island of Salamis, his numbers would be neutralized, as they had been at Thermopylae. The stakes were very high. Athens was already destroyed. If the fleet fought and won, the city might be rebuilt; if not, it would remain in Persian hands forever.

Themistocles rounded on Eurybiades.

"As for you," he cried, "if you stay here and play the man—well and good. Go, and you'll be the ruin of Greece. In this war everything depends on the fleet. I beg you to take my advice. If you refuse, we will immediately put our families aboard and sail for Siris in Italy—it has been ours for a long time, and the oracles have foretold that Athenians must live there some day. Where will you be without the Athenian fleet? When you have lost it you will remember my words."

Herodotus 8.62 (A. de Selincourt)

Eurybiades relented, for the time being.

THE BATTLE OF SALAMIS

There was no good reason for Xerxes to fight at Salamis. Victory there would end the war quickly, but if he just sailed to the Isthmus, the Greeks would have to follow. He could meet them on his own terms. Herodotus says that **Artemisia,** the only woman commander in the war, gave Xerxes precisely this advice. While Xerxes deliberated, the Greek generals criticized Eurybiades for agreeing to stay at Salamis. They demanded a second meeting. Seeing they were going to give up Salamis, Themistocles sent a slave to Xerxes, with this message:

> "I am the bearer of a secret communication from the Athenian commander, who is a well wisher to your king and hopes for a Persian victory. He has told me to report to you that the Greeks are afraid and are planning to slip away. Only prevent them from slipping through your fingers, and you have at this moment an opportunity of unparalleled success. They are at daggers drawn with each other, and will offer no opposition—on the contrary, you will see the pro-Persians among them fighting the rest."
>
> Herodotus 8.75 (A. de Selincourt)

Xerxes took the bait and ordered his fleet forward, cutting off the Greeks' escape. There would be battle at Salamis. If the Greeks won, Themistocles would be the hero, but if Xerxes won, Themistocles could claim to be the author of his victory.

At dawn, the Persians rushed into the narrows. The 380 Greek ships were outnumbered two to one. Terrified, they backed water, but ran out of room. For a moment the line seemed about to break when one ship—Athenian or from Aegina—lunged forward and rammed a Persian. The navies fell upon each other. Aeschylus, one of the great Athenian dramatists, fought in the Greek fleet that day, and eight years later, in his play *The Persians,* a messenger describes events from the Persian side:

> Warships struck their brazen beaks
> together: a Grecian man-of-war began
> the charge, a Phoenician ornamented stern
> was smashed; another drove against another.
> First the floods of Persians held the line,
> but when the narrows choked them, and rescue hopeless,
> smitten by prows, their bronze jaws gaping,
> shattered entire was our fleet of oars.
> The Greek warships, calculating, dashed
> round and encircled us; ships showed their belly:
> no longer could we see the water, charged
> with ships' wrecks and men's blood.
> Corpses glutted beaches and the rocks.
> Every warship urged its own anarchic
> rout, and all who survived that expedition,
> like mackerel or some catch of fish,
> were stunned and slaughtered, boned with broken oars
> and splintered wrecks. Lamentations, cries
> possessed the open sea, until the black
> eye of evening, closing, hushed them. The sum
> of troubles, even if I should rehearse them
> for ten days, I could not exhaust. Rest
> content: never in a single day did
> so great a number die.
>
> Aeschylus, *The Persians,* 408–432 (P. Vellracott)

Herodotus gives an even-handed account:

> The greater part of the Persian fleet suffered severely in the battle, the Athenians and Aeginetans accounting for a great many of their ships. Since the Greek fleet worked together as a whole, while the Persians had lost formation and were no longer fighting on any plan, that was what was bound to happen. Nonetheless they fought well that day—far better than in the action off Euboea. Every man of them did his best for fear of Xerxes, feeling that the king's eye was on him.
>
> There were Greek casualties, but not many, for most of the Greeks could swim, and those who lost their ships, provided they were not killed in the actual fighting, swam over to Salamis. Most of the enemy, on the other hand, being unable to swim, were drowned. The greatest destruction took place when the ships that had been first engaged turned tail; for those stationed behind fell foul of them in their attempt to press forward and do some service before the eyes of the king.
>
> Herodotus 8.86, 89 (A. de Selincourt)

The Persian fleet scattered. The Greeks towed the disabled and captured ships to safety and waited for Xerxes to renew the battle. Even after losing hundreds of vessels, he outnumbered the Greeks. The second attack never came. Xerxes feared that the Greek fleet would break out from Salamis and cut the bridges to Asia. The Greeks might even capture him. His general **Mardonius,** sure to be blamed for persuading Xerxes to invade Greece, volunteered to stay behind with the best soldiers while Xerxes retreated. The next night, the Persian fleet slipped away to protect the Hellespont bridges. Jubilant, the Greeks raced after them. Themistocles urged attacking the Hellespont, but Eurybiades let them go. Why repeat Xerxes' mistake, risking everything on an unnecessary battle against a desperate foe? The ever-resourceful Themistocles sent a second message to Xerxes saying it was his idea to allow him to escape, in case Xerxes might some day return the favor!

Xerxes stayed a few days in Athens, then began the retreat. He left Mardonius in Thessaly with three hundred thousand men, according to Herodotus (most historians think the force was less than half that size). Without a supporting fleet carrying supplies, the Persian withdrawal became a rout:

> He reached the Hellespont crossing in 45 days, but with hardly a fraction of his army intact. During the march the troops lived off the country as best they could, eating grass where they found no grain, and stripping the bark and leaves off trees of all sorts, cultivated or wild, to stay their hunger. They left nothing anywhere, so hard were they put to it for supplies. Plague and dysentery attacked them; many died, and others who fell sick were left behind in the various towns along the route.
>
> The Persians, having passed through Thrace, reached the passage over the Hellespont. Food was more plentiful in Abydos° than what they had had on the march, with the result that the men over-ate themselves. This, combined with the change of water, caused many deaths in what remained of the army.
>
> Herodotus 8.115, 117 (A. de Selincourt)

°*Abydos:* A city in Thrace.

The campaign was a disaster. Xerxes had poured out the empire's blood and gold. Tens or hundreds of thousands had died, the fleet was broken, all for nothing.

THE END OF THE STORM: BATTLES OF PLATAEA AND MYCALE, 479 B.C.

Herodotus, writing fifty years later, saw that after Salamis, the war was as good as over:

> I find myself compelled to express an opinion that I know most people will object to; nevertheless, as I believe it to be true, I will not suppress it. If the Athenians, through fear of the approaching danger, had abandoned their country, or if they had stayed there and submitted to Xerxes, there would have been no attempt to resist the Persians by sea; and, in the absence of a Greek fleet, it is easy to see what would have been the course of events on land. However many lines of fortification the Spartans had built across the Isthmus, they would have been deserted by their confederates; not that their allies would have willingly deserted them, but they could not have helped doing so, because one by one they would have fallen victims to Persian naval power. Thus the Spartans would have been left alone—to perform great deeds and to die nobly. Or, on the other hand, it is possible that before things came to the ultimate test, the sight of the rest of Greece submitting to Persia might have driven them to make terms with Xerxes. In either case the Persian conquest of Greece would have been assured; for I cannot myself see what possible use there would have been in fortifying the Isthmus, if the Persians had command of the sea. In view of this, therefore, one is surely right in saying that Greece was saved by the Athenians. It was the Athenians who held the balance: Whichever side they joined was sure to prevail. It was the Athenians too, who, having chosen that Greece should live and preserve her freedom, roused to battle the other Greek states which had not yet submitted. It was the Athenians who—after the gods—drove back the Persian king.
>
> Herodotus 7.139 (A. de Selincourt)

But in autumn 480 B.C., this fact was far from clear. Mardonius still had a huge army in Thessaly, and for all the Greeks knew, Xerxes would return with a fleet the next year. Mardonius hoped to exploit such fears and offered Athens generous terms to change sides. The Athenians gave an impassioned reply:

> "There is not so much gold in the world nor land so fair that we would take it for pay to join the common enemy and bring Greece into subjection. There are many compelling reasons against our doing so, even if we wished: The first and greatest is the burning of the temples and images of our gods—now ashes and rubble. It is our bound duty to avenge this desecration with all our might—not to clasp the hand that did it. And then there is the Greek nation—the community of blood and language, temples and ritual, and our common customs; if Athens were to betray all this, it would not be well done. We would have you know, therefore, if you did not know it already, that so long as a single Athenian remains alive we will make no peace with Xerxes."
>
> Herodotus 8.144 (A. de Selincourt)

Stirring words, but when spring came, Mardonius burned Athens again (Map 12.3). The Spartans continued to fortify the Isthmus, but otherwise did nothing. Athenian messengers begged Sparta to march north, but each day the Ephors said they would answer tomorrow. After Salamis, the Isthmus was secure, so why should Spartans risk their lives for Athens? After two weeks, the Athenians reminded Sparta who had won security for the Isthmus and delivered an ultimatum—despite their hatred of Xerxes, they would defect. The Spartans feigned shock at the

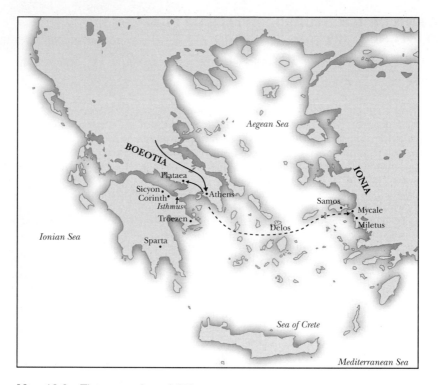

Map 12.3   The campaign of 479 B.C.

Athenians' lack of faith: just hours before, the Spartan army had at last set out under Pausanias (pow-**sā-nē**-as), regent for Leonidas' infant son, to seek out and destroy the Persian army.

When Mardonius heard that the Greek armies were marching north, he fell back to Boeotia, where the terrain was good for his cavalry. The Greeks took up position in the foothills near **Plataea,** hoping that the rough ground would neutralize Mardonius' cavalry (Map 12.4).

They had the largest army the *poleis* ever assembled, consisting of forty thousand hoplites and seventy thousand light troops, but (as always) few horsemen. Pausanias and Mardonius both wanted a decisive battle, but when they consulted the omens, each received the same answer: If you defend, you win; attack, and you lose.

Thus the armies faced each other for seven days. Every day the Persian cavalry rode out to lure the Greeks down from the hills, without success. But the Greeks had little food and less water in the barren foothills. On the eighth day, the Persians intercepted a huge Greek supply train of five hundred mules. Two days later, Mardonius committed his cavalry more heavily, making it hard for the Greeks to reach their only water supply.

The Greek position was desperate. Pausanias ordered an overnight withdrawal to a point between two branches of a river, with plentiful water and protection from the Persian horsemen. But no one was really in charge. Some Greeks panicked and fell

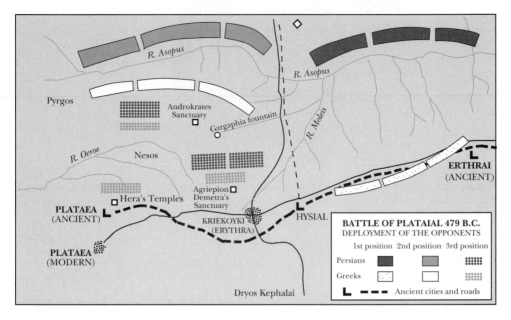

Map 12.4   The Battle of Plataea. At the right are the two armies' initial positions. After several days of skirmishing, the Greeks moved to a second position, at the top left of this map, where there was better water; the Persians moved to oppose them. After the Persians intercepted a Greek supply train, the Greeks fell back in disarray to the positions at the bottom left corner of the map. The final battle took place here.

back all the way to Plataea, whereas one Spartan commander refused to retreat at all. The Athenians waited to see what would happen. By dawn, Pausanias had persuaded everyone to move in the same direction, but a steep ridge now separated the main force of five thousand Spartiates, thirty-five thousand helots, and fifteen hundred Tegeans (Tegea was a town in the Peloponnesus) from the eight thousand Athenians, and the rest of the Greeks were nowhere to be seen. Mardonius took his chance and closed on the Spartans while on the other side of the ridge Greek mercenaries fighting for Persia attacked their fellow Greeks, the Athenians. The Persians facing Pausanias set up a barricade of shields and loosed a hail of arrows. Pausanias, still trying to obtain favorable omens, held his men back as he opened the entrails of sheep after sheep. The impatient Tegeans rushed forward. Just at that moment, Pausanias got his good omen and ordered the Spartan attack. (See Figure 12.1.)

> First there was a struggle at the barricade of shields; then, the barricade down, there was a bitter and protracted fight, close by the temple of Demeter, for the Persians would lay hold of the Spartan spears and break them. In courage and strength they were as good as their adversaries, but they were deficient in armor, untrained, and greatly inferior in skill.
>
> Sometimes singly, sometimes in groups of ten men—perhaps fewer, perhaps more—they fell upon the Spartan line and were cut down. They pressed hardest at the point where Mardonius fought in person, riding his white charger, and surrounded by his thousand Persian troops, the flower of the army. While Mardonius was alive, they continued to resist and defend themselves, and struck down many of the Spartans; but after

Figure 12.1   Greek warrior stabbing a Persian on a red-figure Athenian amphora, circa 475 B.C. The Greek wears bronze armor, while the Persian has a leather suit and cap with long flaps. *Greek. Vase, Red-figured. Attic. c. 480–470 B.C. Neck amphora, Nolan type. SIDE 1: "Greek warrior attacking a Persian." Said to be from Rhodes. Terracotta. H. 13-11/16 in. The Metropolitan Museum of Art, Rogers Fund, 1906. (06.1021.117) Photograph © 1986 The Metropolitan Museum of Art.*

his death, and the destruction of his personal guard—the finest of the Persian troops—the remainder yielded to the Spartans and took flight. The chief cause of their defeat was their lack of armor, fighting without it against hoplites.

The Persian force broke and fled to its fortified camp.

When the Spartans arrived, a struggle of some vigor began, but, as they have never mastered the art of attacking defensive works, the Persians kept them out and had much the better of it, until the Athenians reached the scene of the action. Then, with the arrival of the Athenians, the fight for the palisade was long and violent, until at last, by courage and perseverance, they forced their way up and made a breach, through which the rest of the army poured. Once the palisade was down, the Persians no longer kept together as an organized force; soldierly virtues were all forgotten; chaos prevailed and, huddled in thousands within that confined space, all of them were half dead with fright. To the Greeks they were such an easy prey that out of the 300,000 men (excluding the 40,000 who fled with Artabazus) not 3,000 survived.[25]

The Spartan losses in the battle amounted to 91 killed; the Tegeans lost 16, the Athenians 52.

Herodotus 9.62–63, 70 (A. de Selincourt)

On the very same day, another battle was fought on the Asian side of the Aegean, smaller than Plataea, but with consequences equally profound. Greeks from Samos had brought news to the Greek fleet (now at Delos, center of the Cyclades) that all Ionia was ready to throw off Persian rule (see Map 12.4). All the fleet needed to do was sail to Samos and defeat the few Persian ships there. They set sail, but the Persians, forewarned, retreated to a promontory on the coast near Samos called **Mycalê** (**mi**-ka-lē), beached their ships, and fortified an enclosure around them. The Greeks pursued, beached their ships, and disembarked. Shouting into the Persian camp, they invited the Persians' Ionian allies to defect. The Persians, suspecting the Ionians, sent most of them away and marched out alone to engage the Greeks.

The Greeks advanced in two columns. The Athenians arrived first:

> The Persians, so long as their line of shields remained intact, successfully repelled all attacks and had by no means the worst of things. Soon, however, the Athenians and their neighbors in line, wanting the credit for the day's work for themselves rather than for the Spartans, passed along the word and made a great effort—and from that moment it was a very different matter. They burst through the line of shields and fell upon the enemy in a mass assault. For a time, indeed, the assault was held, but in the end the Persians were forced to retreat within the protection of their fortification. The Athenians and men from Corinth, Sicyon, and Troezen forced their way inside on the heels of the enemy. That was the end; for once the barricade had fallen, the enemy made no further serious resistance. All the non-Greek Persian allies turned and fled, except only the Persians, who, in scattered groups, continued to fight against the Greeks who were still pouring in through the breach in the barricade.
>
> The Spartans arrived with the rest of their division while the Persian troops were still holding out, and took their share in what remained of the fighting. The Greek losses were also considerable, especially among the Sicyonians, whose commander Perilaos was killed. The Samians who were serving with the Persians and had been disarmed, seeing right from the start that the result of the battle was in doubt, did all they could to help the Greeks, and the other Ionians, following the Samian lead, deserted their Persian masters and attacked them. The men of Miletus had been ordered to watch the paths through the hills as a precaution to enable them to act as guides to the safety of the hills, in the event of a disaster for the Persians such as in fact occurred. They had also, it will be remembered, been assigned this task for another reason—namely to prevent them from causing trouble for the Persian army. In any case, what they actually did was the exact opposite of their orders; for when the Persians were trying to escape, they led them the wrong way by tracks that brought them back amongst the enemy, and finally joined in the slaughter and proved their bitterest enemies. Thus this day saw the second Ionian revolt from Persian domination.[26]
>
> Herodotus 9.102–104 (A. de Selincourt)

The hard-won victory at Mycalê eliminated the last viable Persian force in the Aegean Sea. The Ionians were free.

CONCLUSION

Herodotus says that he wrote "so that human achievements may not be forgotten in time, and great and marvelous deeds—some displayed by Greeks, some by barbarians—may not be without their glory." He succeeded better than he could have imagined. Twenty-five hundred years later, Marathon, Thermopylae, and Salamis are three of the most famous names in history. Leonidas' courage and Xerxes' hubris are not forgotten.

Herodotus, in his grand *inquiry* (Greek *historiê*), wanted to explain how and why the Greeks defeated the Persians. At one level, he told a highly moralistic story: *satiety* (Greek *koros*) from too much wealth and power excited the *envy* (Greek *phthonos*) of the gods, who sent *atê*, "madness," so that men forgot their inherent limitations, committed *violence* (Greek *hubris*), and suffered *retribution* (Greek *nemesis*). Thus did Croesus, Polycrates, Cambyses, Darius, and Xerxes come to grief. But at another level, Herodotus emphasized very material factors—the hoplites' superiority, the Spartans' discipline, the Athenians' determination, and

Themistocles' genius. Against all odds, they broke the grandest army the world had ever seen.

Was the sacrifice worth it? They had preserved their freedom. Xerxes intended to destroy Athens and Sparta utterly; the war saved them. Yet only thirty-one *poleis* risked fighting Persia, and some of the greatest cities—Selinous in the west, Thebes in the east—helped the invaders. Persia and Carthage cared little what their subjects did so long as they paid their taxes. Ionia flourished for half a century under Persian rule, until the brutal destructions of 494 B.C. In return for taxes, Persia provided peace and freedom from random violence. Anaximenes and Hecataeus worked in cities loyal to Persia, and the Persians let the Ionians set up democracies in 493 B.C. Would it have made much difference to Greek culture if Persia had won at Marathon or Salamis, or Carthage at Himera? In the west, a Carthaginian victory might have made little difference: Hamilcar aimed only at restoring the status quo. In the Aegean, so long as Persia continued its policy of leaving its subjects alone, a victorious Darius in 490 B.C. might have changed little in the broader development of Greek culture. However, a victorious Xerxes in 480 would surely have prevented the explosion of intellectual and artistic achievement in Athens that we examine in the next chapter.

In 479 B.C., Syracuse stood alone as the dominant power in Sicily, and Sparta and Athens stood together as triumphant but uneasy allies. Gelon needed only to extort concessions from Carthage; Sparta and Athens needed to defend Ionia against renewed Persian attacks. Whatever the long-term consequences of Carthaginian and Persian victories might have been, in the short run, the Greek victories created a whole new set of problems.

KEY TERMS

Xerxes, 248

Syracuse, 249

Motya, 249

Gela, 250

Gelon, 250

Himera, 251

Themistocles, 252

Hamilcar, 253

Selinous, 253

Thermopylae, 255

Leonidas, 256

Eurybiades, 256

Salamis, 258

Artemisia, 258

Mardonius, 260

Plataea, 262

Mycalê, 264

atê, 265

hubris, 265

FURTHER READING

In addition to the books listed in Chapter 11, the following are recommended:

Briant, Pierre, *From Cyrus to Alexander: A History of the Persian Empire* (London 2002). The standard work on Persian history.

Burn, A. R., *Persia and the Greeks* (2nd ed., London 1984). Very readable review of the Persian War, with an excellent appendix by David Lewis dealing with the evidence from the Persian side.

Harrison, Thomas, *The Emptiness of Asia* (London 2000). Excellent treatment of the evidence of Aeschylus' play, *The Persians*.

Lancel, Serge, *Carthage* (Oxford 1995). Review of the city's history by a prominent archaeologist.

Strauss, Barry, *The Battle of Salamis* (New York 2004). Lively account of the crucial battle, by a leading military historian.

Ancient Texts

Aeschylus, *The Persians*. In *Prometheus Bound and Other Plays* (Harmondsworth, UK, 1961; tr. Philip Vellacott). Aeschylus' tragedy, written in Athens in 472 B.C., describing the battle of Salamis from the Persian perspective.

Diodorus of Sicily, *The History*, book 11. In *The Library of History* IV (Loeb Classical Library; Cambridge, MA, 1946; tr. C. H. Oldfather). Parallel Greek and English texts. Writing in the first century B.C., Diodorus describes the war in Sicily in 480 B.C.

Herodotus, *The Histories* (New York, rev. ed., 1996; tr. Aubrey de Selincourt). Books 7 through 9 describe the war of 480–479 B.C. Written at Athens, c. 420 B.C.

CHAPTER 13

DEMOCRACY AND EMPIRE: ATHENS AND SYRACUSE, 479–431 B.C.

As the fierce summer cooled to autumn in 479 B.C., no one was sure what would happen. In the West, Gelon was becoming the greatest tyrant Greece had known, seemingly bent on creating a new kind of Greek state where many cities were ruled by a single king—somewhat like the Persian Empire. In the East, the war left Athens dominant at sea and Sparta on land. But Xerxes would seek revenge; could the alliance survive?

Aegean and western Greeks underwent similar experiences in the nearly fifty years from 479 through 431 B.C. (when the Peloponnesian War began). Syracuse and Athens both extended the power of their state institutions, finding new ways to raise money, fund warfare, and control the peoples around them. Both East and West saw (by ancient standards) strong economic growth; and Athens and Syracuse became great cultural centers. But in the details, the two regions were quite different. Syracuse totally dominated Sicily. Athens, by contrast, built her power by leading an anti-Persian alliance, slowly taking over more functions within the alliance until she became virtually the capital city of a multicity state. Athens did not dominate Old Greece: Sparta remained a formidable and increasingly hostile rival. Athens and Syracuse differed economically. Sicily prospered by exporting cereals; Athens, by importing them and selling silver and manufactured goods. The different bases of wealth were to have major repercussions. Although the Theban poet Pindar called Syracuse "the fairest Greek city," no one doubted that Athens was the wonder of the world—"the school of Greece," in the words of Thucydides. Although small by modern standards, with about forty thousand people covering just one square mile, Athens led an intellectual and aesthetic revolution without parallel.

Historians sometimes call this exhilarating time a golden age, but it had a dark side too. Economic and political expansion fueled Athens' cultural triumphs, but threatened Sparta. War drew in not just Athens and Sparta, but also Syracuse, Persia, and Carthage. Let us first review political and economic developments in western Greece, then turn to the Aegean. Our coverage is necessarily uneven, because so much more evidence survives from Athens than from Syracuse.

THE EXPANSION OF THE SYRACUSAN STATE, 479–461 B.C.

In Chapter 12, "The Great War, 480–479 B.C.," we left Gelon in his moment of triumph. Having defeated Carthage at Himera, he campaigned in the 470s to persuade Aegean Greeks that his victories were as great as theirs against Persia. He dedicated a golden tripod at Delphi to glorify his success. The stone base survives, inscribed "Gelon son of Deinomenes, the Syracusan, dedicated this to Apollo." It contrasted sharply with the Aegean Greeks' victory monument, another gold tripod whose bowl was supported by a bronze column in the form of a serpent. Part of the column survives today in Istanbul, where it was transported in the fourth century A.D. Its inscription reads: "By these the war was fought," followed by a list of thirty-one cities. While the Aegean cities fought as communities of citizens, Gelon *was* the state.

Gelon died at the height of his glory, in 478 B.C. His spectacular funeral drew mourners from all over the Mediterranean. His brother **Hiero** (**hī**-er-ō), whom Gelon had left in charge of Gela in 485, now moved to Syracuse, handing Gela to another brother, Polyzalos (po-lī-**zā**-los). Gelon and Hiero propelled Sicily toward a different political structure from the Aegean, with tyrant families ruling multicity states, using relatives to govern smaller cities, and treating everyone as subjects. Both tyrants depopulated entire cities when it suited them, moving their people to Syracuse or selling them into slavery. They used mercenaries to fight their wars, turned them against the citizens if their power was threatened, and settled exmercenaries on the lands of cities they emptied.

Hiero maintained peace with Carthage, making no moves against the Phoenicians in Sicily, or even against Selinous (Map 13.1), which had sided with Carthage in 480 B.C. However, he did win a great sea battle against the Etruscans in 474 near Cumae, in the Bay of Naples, and resumed Gelon's glorification of Sicilian achievements. When his team won the chariot race at Delphi in 470 B.C., Hiero hired Pindar to commemorate it in typically complex verse, claiming that the battles of Himera and Cumae were equivalent to Plataea and Salamis, and that Gelon and Hiero had therefore saved Greece from slavery:

> . . . Grant, I beg,
> O son of Cronus,° that the Phoenician
> and the Tyrrhenians'° war-cry
> keep quiet at home; they have seen what woe to their ships
> came of their pride before Cumae,
> and all that befell when the lord of Syracuse routed them,
> who out of their swift-sailing ships
> cast down their youth in the sea
> —delivering Hellas from grievous slavery.

°*son of Cronus:* Zeus.   °*Tyrrhenians:* Another name for the Etruscans.

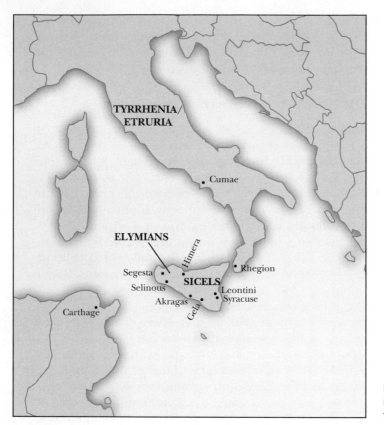

Map 13.1 Western Mediterranean sites mentioned in this chapter.

From Salamis I will win as my reward the gratitude of the Athenians,°
and in Sparta from the battles before Cithaeron,°
for there the Medes° gave way with their bended bows:
but by Himera's well watered banks
a song composed for Deinomenes'° sons,
which their valor earned
when the hosts of their enemies gave way.

Pindar, *First Pythian Ode* 71–80 (C.M. Bowra)

°*Athenians:* Pindar will win credit with the Athenians by celebrating in song the battle of Salamis.   °*Cithaeron:* This mountain stands behind Plataea.   °*Medes:* The Persians. °*Deinomenes' sons:* That is, Gelon and Hiero.

In the 470s, Etruria, Carthage, the Sicilian Phoenicians, and even their long-time native allies the Elymians in western Sicily declined before the growing power of Syracuse. The tyrants had defeated their non-Greek enemies, but two old problems—elite feuds and class conflict—came back to haunt them. Polyzalos chafed at being stuck in provincial Gela and persuaded Theron of Akragas, Syracuse's most important ally, to join him in challenging Hiero. When Theron died in 472, his son Thrasydaeus attacked Syracuse. Hiero crushed Thrasydaeus so thoroughly that the citizens of Akragas expelled him and set up a democracy. Thrasydaeus' former mercenaries, fearing they would not be paid, then tried to seize Akragas. They lost the war that ensued, but captured a smaller city and hung on for years. When Hiero died in 467 B.C., the Syracusans first expelled the tyrant's family, then fought a brutal civil war against their former mercenaries.

Tyrants fell all over Sicily, and Greeks forcibly transferred from one city to another returned home to wage civil war against those (often exmercenaries) who had taken their land. Bloody war raged from 466 until 461 between the "old" and "new" citizens. Finally, all the Sicilian cities signed a **Common Resolution** in 461 B.C.: Old citizens won the right of return, and exmercenaries won partial citizen rights. Syracuse's old network of alliances broke up, and, in theory, the Sicilian *poleis* were again free and equal.

THE WESTERN DEMOCRACIES, 461–433 B.C.

The Common Resolution created large and diverse *poleis*, mixing old and new citizens, former mercenaries, and naturalized natives. Many cities set up democracies as soon as they were freed from tyranny, but their citizen communities were less cohesive than those in the Aegean, and aristocrats preserved greater power. At Syracuse, a board of elected generals was particularly important and regularly opposed the **demagogues** ("leaders of the people"). Violence broke out in 454 when officials condemned a demagogue for organizing a bodyguard of poor citizens, and Syracuse introduced its own version of ostracism, here called *petalismos* because names were written on *petaloi* (olive leaves), not *ostraka* (potsherds).

For nearly three hundred years, the Sicilian Greeks had been taking over the best land, driving the natives off or reducing them to serfdom. Like all small peoples on the fringes of empires, the natives could either submit or resist, normally by copying the aggressors' own institutions. Indigenous Sicilians did both. In western Sicily, the Elymians abandoned their villages and concentrated in a single city at **Segesta,** which would play a major role in Mediterranean politics in the fifth century B.C. In eastern Sicily, a charismatic native leader named Ducetius used war and persuasion to forge a league of native Sicels. They created a Sicel army, issued coins, and in 453 B.C. founded a new city at a spectacular holy site where sulfur springs had formed two giant craters.

The Common Resolution had created a power vacuum, and Ducetius tried to exploit it. In 451, he attacked a fortress belonging to Akragas, which then joined with Syracuse to smash the emerging Sicel state. Ducetius fled into exile at Corinth, but returned in 446 B.C., apparently as a Syracusan client king. When he died in 440 B.C., Syracuse overran the Sicel League, selling thousands of Sicels into slavery. Even without her tyrants, Syracuse remained the largest and richest Sicilian *polis*, fueled by taxes on the Sicels and harbor dues from booming trade. In 439 B.C., she expanded her army and navy. She bullied and persuaded most Dorian-speaking Greeks in eastern Sicily to support her, and by the decade's end threatened non-Dorians too.

Such developments alarmed Athens. In 433 B.C., Athens allied with the cities of Leontini (in eastern Sicily) and Rhegion (on the tip of the boot of Italy). Leontini, surrounded by Syracuse's renewed alliance, was under intense pressure; Rhegion, facing the Strait of Messina, had long been Syracuse's enemy. By this move, Athens set eastern and western Greece on a collision course.

ECONOMIC GROWTH IN WESTERN GREECE, 479–433 B.C.

Despite political turmoil, the Greeks in Sicily and southern Italy flourished in the fifth century. Population boomed, probably doubling to reach 600,000. Syracuse, the largest city, had around 40,000 residents by 415 B.C. (as many as Athens), and Akragas and Selinous at least 20,000. Fifth-century houses were spacious, typically having four to eight rooms around a shady courtyard. Many had a second floor. Diodorus (first century B.C.) says that

> In Sicily, as soon as the tyranny of Syracuse had been overthrown and all the cities of the island had been liberated, the whole of Sicily was making great strides toward prosperity. For the Sicilian Greeks were at peace, and the land they cultivated was fertile, so that the abundance of their harvests enabled them soon to increase their estates and to fill the land with slaves and domestic animals and every other accompaniment of prosperity, taking in great revenues but spending nothing upon the wars to which they had been accustomed.
> Diodorus of Sicily 11.72 (C. H. Oldfather)

The wealth came largely from exporting produce grown on land taken from the natives. The Greeks worked it intensively, often with slave labor, and sold grain, olives, and wine to the land-poor Aegean and to Carthage. We know most about Akragas. Taxes on trade with Carthage paid for the most spectacular temple-building program in Greek history, and some landowners grew very rich. Diodorus says that when one of them won a victory in the games at Olympia in 412 B.C.,

> he was conducted into the city in a chariot and in the procession there were, not to speak of other things, 300 chariots each drawn by two white horses, all belonging to the citizens of Akragas. Speaking generally, they led from youth onward a manner of life that was luxurious, wearing as they did exceedingly delicate clothing and gold ornaments and, besides, using strigils° and oil flasks made of silver and even of gold.
>
> °*strigils:* Scrapers, usually made of iron or bronze. After exercising, athletes would oil themselves, then scrape off the oil, dirt, and sweat with a strigil.

One house was so grand that its wine cellar had "300 great casks hewn out of the rock itself, each of them with a capacity of about 900 gallons, and beside them was a wine vat, plastered and with a capacity of 9,000 gallons, from which the wine flowed into the casks." In amazement, Diodorus noted that

> when Akragas was under siege [in 406 B.C.], they passed a decree about the guards who spent the night at their posts, that none of them should have more than one mattress, one cover, one sheepskin, and two pillows. When this was their most rigorous kind of bedding, you can get an idea of the luxury that prevailed in their living generally.
> Diodorus of Sicily 13.81, 84 (C. H. Oldfather)

A complicated economic system was gaining strength. Sicily and south Italy sold food to Aegean Greece and Carthage, in return getting finished goods and silver. They developed their own urban centers, and standards of living and population rose everywhere. Even the indigenous peoples shared in the new wealth.

CIMON AND THE CREATION OF THE ATHENIAN EMPIRE, 478–461

As the rejoicing died down after the battles of Plataea and Mycalê, the Spartans apparently imagined that conditions would return to the way they were before the war. They tried to persuade Athens not to build new city walls, saying that Athens could rely on Sparta's protection. The wily Themistocles kept the Spartans negotiating while the Athenians secretly finished new walls. Thwarted, Sparta turned to Ionia. Only a fleet could protect the Ionians from Persia, but the fleet was dominated by Athenian ships. Sparta now proposed that the Ionians should relocate to mainland Greece. The result of defeating Persia would be to abandon their homes and their fertile land! No: The Ionians must stay, and a Greek fleet must protect them.

Sparta tried to keep control of the allied fleet. Pausanias, the hero of Plataea, took charge of it in 478 B.C., drove the Persians from Cyprus, then sailed north and captured Byzantium, guarding the entrance to the Black Sea (Map 13.2). But Pausanias' arrogance offended the other Greeks. Reportedly, he wrote to Xerxes, offering to betray Greece in return for Xerxes' daughter's hand and the position of satrap. The Ephors replaced Pausanias, but the Ionians refused to work with another Spartan. Consequently,

> the Spartans went back, and afterwards the Spartans sent out no other commanders. They feared that when their officers went overseas they would become corrupted, as they had seen happen in the case of Pausanias, and at the same time they no longer wanted to be burdened with the war against Persia. They regarded the Athenians as perfectly capable of exercising the command and as being also at that time friendly toward themselves.
>
> So Athens took over the leadership [of the fleet], and the allies, because of their dislike of the Persians, were glad to see her do so.
>
> Thucydides 1.95–96 (R. Warner)

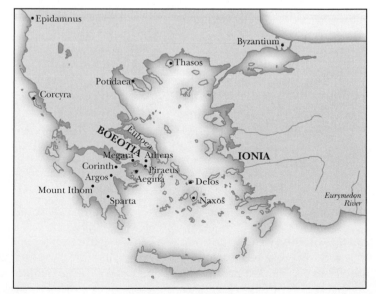

Map 13.2 Sites in Aegean Greece mentioned in this chapter.

It was a bloodless coup. Athens' leading politicians—Themistocles, his rival Aristides (a-ris-tī-dēz), and a young man named **Cimon** (kē-mōn or sē-mōn)—saw an opportunity to take control of an Aegean-wide alliance and use its navy to protect Athenian trade routes. By 500 B.C., Attica's population had passed the 120,000 to 150,000 that (in a good year) it could feed from its own resources. Athens now depended on grain imports, especially from the Ukraine and the Crimea north of the Black Sea. Athens' need to secure her grain route became *the* strategic issue in fifth-century Greece.

Athens and her allies met on the holy island of Delos, where Aristides presented a plan for waging war against Persia. A permanent fleet would cost far more than any *polis* could afford, he explained, so some cities (especially Athens) would provide ships and men, and the smaller ones could contribute money. His plan was fair: The small states bought cheap security and the big states received subsidies for their fleets. Dozens of cities accepted Athenian leadership (Map 13.3).

The obvious choice for commander was Themistocles, victor of Salamis, but his fellow-citizens feared he aimed at tyranny. In 477 B.C., they exiled him. Meanwhile, Sparta's ephors found Pausanias guilty of treason, and he starved to death in a temple where he took refuge. The ephors alleged that Themistocles was also plotting with Persia, so the Athenians agreed to find and kill him. Given Themistocles' behavior in 480 B.C., their mistrust was understandable, but hunted all across the Aegean, he could only hope to escape to Xerxes, who enriched and honored him.

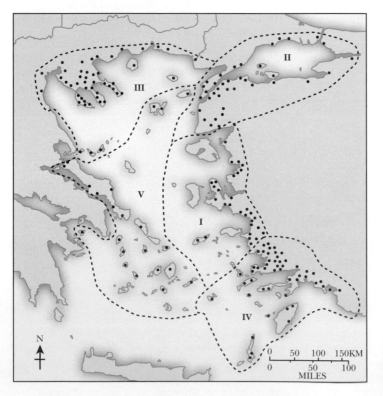

Map 13.3 Cities in the Athenian alliance, 449 B.C.

The dashing young Cimon now took command of the fleet and stormed the remaining Persian bases in the north Aegean. His strategy was to hound the Persians out of the Aegean while capturing as much plunder as possible; but no one enjoyed the fleet's protection without paying. Cimon attacked towns that refused to join the alliance, and when Naxos decided to withdraw in 476 B.C., Cimon compelled the island to keep paying.

> [Naxos] was the first case when the original constitution of the alliance was broken and an allied city lost its independence, and the process was continued in the cases of other allies as various circumstances arose. The chief reasons for revolts were failures to produce the right amount of tribute or the right numbers of ships, and sometimes a refusal to produce any ships at all. For the Athenians insisted on obligations being exactly met, and made themselves unpopular by bringing the severest pressure to bear on allies who were not used to making sacrifices and did not want to make them. In other ways, too, the Athenians as rulers were no longer as popular as they used to be: they bore more than their fair share of the actual fighting, but this made it all the easier for them to force back into the alliance any state that wanted to leave it. For this position it was the allies themselves who were to blame. Because of this reluctance of theirs to face military service, most of them, to avoid serving abroad, had assessments made by which, instead of producing ships, they were to pay a corresponding sum of money. The result was that the Athenian navy grew strong at their expense, and when they revolted they always found themselves inadequately armed and inexperienced in war.
>
> Thucydides 1.98–99 (R. Warner)

Athens was converting the alliance into an empire. Diodorus says that some Spartans thought they had been fools to surrender naval command in 478, and in 475 B.C. the Council of Elders discussed attacking Athens. In the meanwhile, Xerxes planned revenge and in 469 gathered 200 ships and an army at the Eurymedon River in southern Asia Minor. Cimon engaged both forces on the same day and won shattering victories.

The Eurymedon battles made many Greeks wonder whether they any longer needed the naval alliance—and Athens' growing power. In 465 B.C., in a dispute with the island of Thasos in the northern Aegean (one of her richest allies) over markets and mines, Athens sent in the fleet and started a siege. The Spartan Council secretly voted to invade Attica to force the Athenians to withdraw. But just after the vote, a major earthquake hit Sparta, killing many Spartiates. The helots and some *perioikoi* rose up in the fiercest revolt in Spartan history. Far from attacking Athens, Sparta now sought Athenian help against the helots.

Athens' mood had changed since 479 B.C. She was now the greatest naval power in the Mediterranean (or in the world). She had humbled Xerxes. New men, insisting that Athens did not need Sparta, won the Assembly's confidence. Cimon, Athens' greatest general, vigorously opposed this view.

> . . . when the Athenians' power had grown and they [the new politicians] saw that Cimon was wholeheartedly attached to the Spartans, they resented this, not least because of his tendency to sing the praises of Sparta to the Athenians whenever he had occasion to reproach them or spur them on. At these moments, so Stesimbrotos° tells us, he would say: "But that is not what the Spartans would do." This habit alone created a great deal of jealousy and dislike of him among the Athenians.

°*Stesimbrotos:* An author of the fifth century B.C.

When the Spartans asked for help in 464 after the earthquake,

> Ephialtes° opposed the request and exhorted the Athenians not to attempt to rescue or restore a city that was their rival but rather to let Sparta's pride be trampled underfoot. Cimon, on the other hand, put Sparta's interests before his own country's aggrandizement and persuaded the Athenians to send a large force of hoplites to her aid. Ion° actually records the phrase used by Cimon that did most to sway the people: he appealed to them "not to allow Greece to go lame, or their own city to be deprived of its yoke-fellow."
>
> °*Ephialtes:* A rising politician (see below).   °*Ion:* A historian from the island of Chios who lived at this time.

Cimon helped Sparta push the rebellious helots back to rugged Mount Ithomê, where the war became a siege. Athens' siege of Thasos and Sparta's of Ithomê dragged on in parallel. Thasos fell in 463 B.C., but in 462 Sparta had to ask for help again.

> The Athenians once more came to their support, but their boldness and enterprise frightened the Spartans, who singled them out from among all the allies as dangerous revolutionaries and sent them away. They returned home in a fury and proceeded to take public revenge on the friends of Sparta in general and Cimon in particular. They seized upon some trifling pretext to ostracize him and condemned him to exile for ten years.
>
> Plutarch, *Life of Cimon* 16–17 (I. Scott-Kilvert)

THE FIRST PELOPONNESIAN WAR, 460–446 B.C.

As we saw in Chapter 10, "A Tale of Two Archaic Cities: Sparta and Athens, 700–480 B.C.," leaders in the Athenian Assembly had to persuade the Assembly to support their plans day-in, day-out, in constant debates. Cimon had lost touch with the city's mood. His rivals, **Ephialtes** (ef-ē-**al**-tēz) and the young **Pericles** (**per**-i-klēz), had turned the Assembly against Cimon. In 461, Ephialtes convinced the Assembly to transfer crucial powers from the Council of the Areopagus, consisting of exarchons who served for life, to the Assembly, thus undermining conservative leaders' power and broadening the democracy. Ephialtes was soon murdered by Cimon's friends. Athens teetered on the brink of civil war.

Domestic and foreign policy were tightly linked, and the radicalized Assembly turned against Sparta. Apparently, some Athenians believed that the only way to protect democracy was to break up the Peloponnesian League so that Sparta could no longer help reactionaries within Athens. Athens' hoplites could never defeat Sparta in the field, but by allying with disaffected League members, Athens aimed to encircle Sparta's most important ally, Corinth. If Corinth came over to Athens' side, Sparta would be crippled. Athens' strategy led to the so-called First Peloponnesian War (460–446 B.C.), a kind of cold war fought almost entirely between Athens' allies and Sparta's allies. By 457, Argos, south of Corinth, and Megara, north of Corinth, had voluntarily joined Athens, and the island of Aegina and the cities of Boeotia northwest of Attica had been forced to submit. The noose was tight around Corinth.

Athens had not switched from anti-Persian to anti-Spartan policies; she pursued both at the same time. In 460 B.C., Egypt revolted from Persia. Egypt had vast wealth and supplies of grain. Athens sent two hundred ships—a huge force—to help the rebels. The struggle dragged on for six years, with Athens sending more and more ships. Despite her exertions in the cold war with Sparta and the hot war with Persia, Athens still found resources to build fortifications called the **Long Walls** linking Athens and its harbor of Piraeus, about five miles distant. Now no matter what the Spartans did on land, Athens could never be starved out.

In Chapter 10, we quoted Herodotus' comment that after Athens threw off tyranny in 508 B.C., freedom unleashed the citizens' strength and she became a great power. The reforms around 461 B.C. triggered a second extraordinary outpouring of Athenian energy. A casualty list from 459 B.C. shows that Athenians were fighting all over the east Mediterranean that year (Map 13.4). With Athens so fully committed, the Corinthians raided Attica, but the men too young or too old to be away with the army rushed out of Athens and inflicted a humiliating defeat. According to Thucydides, a Corinthian speaker later contrasted Athenian energy with Spartan caution:

> You Spartans have never yet tried to imagine what sort of people these Athenians are against whom you will have to fight—how much, indeed how completely, different from you. An Athenian is always an innovator, quick to form a resolution and quick at

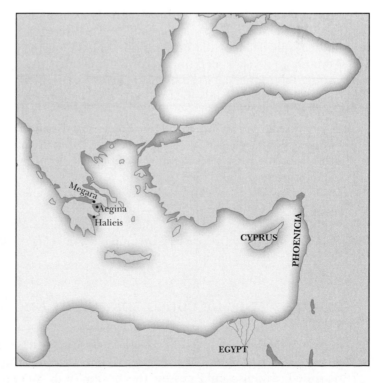

Map 13.4 Theaters of war where Athenians of the Erechtheid tribe died fighting in 459 B.C. Some fell close to home (Halieis, Megara, Aegina); others died far away (Cyprus, Phoenicia, Egypt). The Erechtheids were just one of ten Athenian tribes (*phylai*); Athenian soldiers may have fought in other theaters that we do not know about.

carrying it out. You, on the other hand, are good at keeping things as they are; you never originate an idea, and your action tends to stop short of its aim. Then again, Athenian daring will outrun its resources; they will take risks against their better judgment, and still, in the midst of danger, remain confident. But your nature is always to do less than you could have done, to mistrust your own judgment, however sound it may be, and to assume that dangers will last forever. Think of this too: while you are hanging back, they never hesitate; while you stay at home, they are always abroad; for they think that the farther they go the more they will get, while you think that any movement may endanger what you have already. If they win a victory, they follow it up at once, and if they suffer a defeat, they scarcely fall back at all. As for their bodies, they regard them as expendable for their city's sake, as though they were not their own; but each man cultivates his own intelligence, again with a view to doing something notable for his city. If they aim at something but do not get it, they think that they have been deprived of what belonged to them already; whereas, if their enterprise is successful, they regard that success as nothing compared to what they will do next. Suppose they fail in some undertaking; they make good the loss immediately by setting their hopes in some other direction. Of them alone it may be said that they possess a thing almost as soon as they have begun to desire it, so quickly with them does action follow upon decision. And so they go on working away in hardship and danger all the days of their lives, seldom enjoying their possessions because they are always adding to them. Their view of a holiday is to do what needs doing; they prefer hardship and activity to peace and quiet. In a word, they are incapable either of living a quiet life themselves or of allowing anyone else to do so.

Thucydides 1.98–99 (R. Warner)

The first setback came in 454 B.C., when Persia destroyed the Athenian expeditionary force in Egypt, leaving Athens' fleet so weak that the alliance's treasury was moved from Delos to the Acropolis in Athens, from fear that a Persian raid could carry off the silver. The situation stabilized in 451, when Cimon returned from exile and handily defeated the Persians on Cyprus. Fourth-century-B.C. authors say that Athens and Persia signed the Peace of Callias after this (probably in 449), formally ending their long war. Even if this treaty was a later fiction, as some think, Cimon's campaign in Cyprus did effectively end the Persian Wars. Fighting with Persia dwindled to nothing.

Why then pay tribute for defense against a threat that no longer existed? Some Boeotian cities rebelled in 447 and defeated an Athenian force sent against them. Athens looked weak. The island of Euboea, vital to Athens' communications and a major source of grain, rose up in 446. Megara turned on Athens, and Sparta prepared to invade. Pericles, now the leading figure in the Athenian Assembly, moved quickly. He reconquered Euboea before Sparta intervened, and late in 446 B.C. negotiated a treaty with Sparta, called the Thirty Years' Peace. Athens renounced all claims to mainland Greece, as if turning back the clock to the days when Sparta was the greatest Greek power.

PERICLES AND THE CONSOLIDATION OF ATHENIAN POWER, 446–433 B.C.

Pericles championed a subtle strategy: hold on to the allied cities, avoid entanglements, keep collecting tribute, and continue centralizing power. Eventually, he reasoned, Athens would possess the resources to overwhelm Sparta. Athens was becoming a capital city, reducing formerly independent *poleis* in the Aegean to provincial centers. The allies' tribute was effectively a tax paid for security. When there were revolts, Athens took over the cities' legal or financial administration, often sending out garrisons and officials or confiscating land for Athenians. Athens made decisions on foreign policy without consulting the cities involved and tried major lawsuits in Athens. Athens insisted that everyone use her weights, measures, and coinage, and claimed originally to have founded all the Ionian cities.

Pericles' successes made him the most powerful politician Athens had seen:

> Pericles had said that Athens would be victorious if she bided her time and took care of her navy, if she avoided trying to add to the empire during the course of war, and if she did nothing to risk the safety of the city itself. . . . Pericles, because of his position, his intelligence, and his known integrity, could respect the liberty of the people and at the same time hold them in check. It was he who led them, rather than they who led him, and, since he never sought power from any wrong motive, he was under no necessity of flattering them; in fact he was so highly respected that he was able to speak angrily to them and to contradict them. Certainly when he saw that they were going too far in a mood of over-confidence, he would bring back to them a sense of their dangers; and when they were discouraged for no good reason he would restore their confidence. So, in what was nominally a democracy, power was really in the hands of the first citizen.
>
> Thucydides 2.65 (R. Warner)

Athens consistently followed his policies. Athens' only major war between 446 and 431 B.C. was to crush a serious revolt on the island of Samos in 440 to 439.

The slow expansion of Athenian state power was the most important development in classical Greek history. Back in the eighth and seventh centuries B.C., Sparta made herself more than a normal city-state by conquering Messenia, but in the sixth century her expansion stalled, and Sparta stabilized as the head of a Peloponnesian alliance. In the 480s, the tyrants of Syracuse and Akragas created multicity states in Sicily, but they proved unstable and collapsed in the 460s. Now Athens was creating a new and uniquely powerful multicity state.

ECONOMIC GROWTH IN THE AEGEAN

Greek population probably doubled during the fifth century B.C., perhaps reaching 2.5 million in the 430s. Paradoxically, more people meant more wealth for everyone, as the growth of Athenian power fueled rising standards of living.

Trade

Most of the tribute that Athens took from other cities was spent on the fleet. Most ships were built in Piraeus, Athens' harbor, and most sailors were Athenians. Cash flowing into Athens ended up in the hands of oarsmen, riggers, and other state employees. Some of these men were part-time farmers, while others did no agriculture; all bought food. Because Athenians had money to spend, foreign importers brought food to Piraeus. Because grain came in from Sicily, Egypt, and the Ukraine, Athenian farmers could specialize in more profitable crops like olives, fruits, and legumes, selling them in urban markets and buying imported grain. Because Athens' markets flourished, artisans concentrated there, producing textiles, metalwork, pottery, and other goods that the grain traders could buy and carry back to sell in their home cities, making profits at both ends of their voyages.

Most Greeks were still farmers, consuming at home most of the food they grew. But the increasing integration of regions through seaborne trade meant that each region could concentrate on the activities for which it was best suited. Economic growth was driven by the big cities, whose citizens reaped the greatest benefits, but country people benefited too. Even small villages now had well-built houses.

As Athenian purchasing power increased, the population of Attica reached around 350,000, with 40,000 living in the city itself. The fleet suppressed piracy and guaranteed the trade routes. Around 440 B.C., an anonymous writer, known today as the **Old Oligarch** because of his hostility toward democracy, described the material benefits from naval power (see Map 13.5):

> Those who are most powerful by land have difficulty enduring the crop diseases that are sent by Zeus, but those powerful by sea endure them easily. For not every country is diseased at once, so that for sea-rulers food comes from a healthy place.
>   If I need to mention even minor matters, by virtue of domination of the sea the Athenians have in the first place discovered all sorts of good cheer through mingling with various foreigners. Whatever is sweet in Sicily or in Italy, in Cyprus, Egypt, or Lydia, in Pontus, or the Peloponnesus, or anywhere else—all these are gathered in one place through domination of the sea.
>   *The Old Oligarch* 2.7 (C. M. Gray, in Adkins/White, *The Greek Polis*)

The Old Oligarch describes a cosmopolitan Athens, but even small cities had regular visitors from overseas. Many Greeks involved in trade chose to settle in *poleis* other than their own before coming home as rich men. Such men were called **metics** (from the Greek verb *metoikein,* "to live with"). Metics had to pay residence taxes and usually could not own real estate in their adopted community. Many were menial workers, but a few were wealthy. Aristotle, for example, spent much of his life as a metic in Athens, and metics and slaves (some of them women) ran the major banks in Athens (though rich citizens usually owned the banks).

Slavery

We saw in Chapter 10 that Solon's ban on debt bondage made the use of foreign slaves a logical response, and in the fifth century B.C., the slave trade boomed. By the 430s, a quarter of the population of Attica—some seventy-five thousand people—may have been slaves, imported mainly from the Balkans and Asia Minor (see Map 10.2). Large landowners often found it easier to buy or rent slaves than to hire free labor. Hundreds of small workshops in Athens each employed a handful of slaves (Figure 13.1). Anyone who could afford it would have a slave or two as domestic servants (Figure 13.2), while up to twenty thousand men at a time served

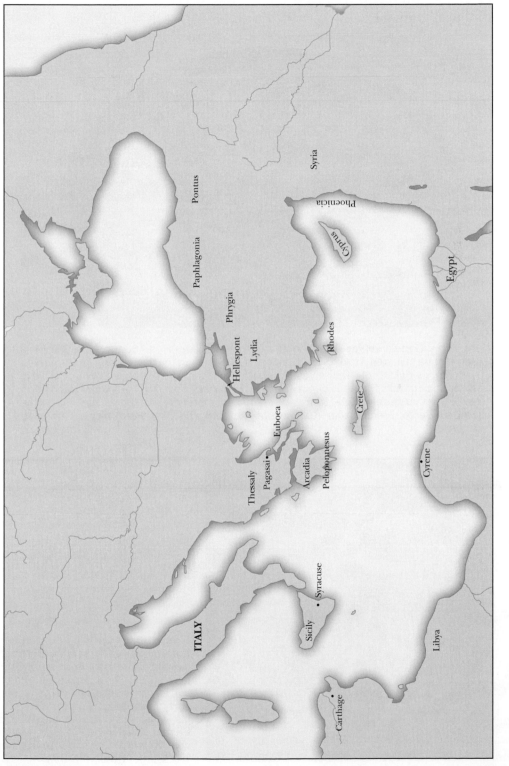

Map 13.5 Sources of Athenian imports mentioned by the Old Oligarch and Hermippus.

Figure 13.1   Red-figure vase painting of a bronze foundry, circa 480 B.C. Note the tools hanging above the men stoking the furnace, and the sculptor hammering out a statue. Many workers would have been slaves. Diameter 12 inches. The painter is known, from this vessel, as the Foundry Painter. *Foundry Painter. "A Bronze Foundry," red-figure decoration on a kylix from Vulci, Italy. 490–480 B.C.E. Ceramic, diameter of kylix 12" (31 cm). Staatliche Museen zu Berlin, Preussischer Kulturbesitz, Antikensammlung. Foto: Ingrid Geske/Art Resource, NY.*

Figure 13.2   On this Athenian cup from about 480 B.C., a Thracian slave girl (her origins are shown by her red hair, and her servile status by its shortness) holds a young partygoer's head while he vomits up his wine. Attributed to the Brygos Painter. Diameter 12 inches. *Martin von Wagner Museum der Universitat Wurzburg. Photo: K. Oehrlein.*

out their days in the narrow, airless shafts and inhuman conditions of the Athenian silver mines.

Greek slavery was very different from pre-1865 American slavery. Most obviously, American slave owners justified their institution by claiming that all African Americans were inferior to all European Americans. The Greeks had no such clear ideology. In the fourth century B.C., Aristotle did propose a theory of "natural slavery," holding that the gods had made non-Greeks inferior to Greeks, and that they therefore deserved to be enslaved, but the theory had many critics (see Chapter 18, "Greek Culture in the Fourth Century B.C."). Except in the mines, Greek slaves worked in small groups, often alongside their masters. Greece was unsuited to plantations with gangs of hundreds of laborers, such as on the American cotton and sugar plantations. Finally, whereas three-quarters of American slaves in 1850 were field hands, Greek slaves worked in virtually every occupation, and many were skilled workers. Thucydides says that in 413 B.C., twenty thousand skilled slaves—probably a quarter of the slave population—ran away from Athens.

The Rich

Some Athenians prospered from trade and lands taken from rebellious subject cities, but strong democratic ideals restrained people from showing off their wealth. Aegean houses were generally spacious and comfortable, but none stands out as lavish; burials were plain and uniform. Citizens erected few monuments to their own importance. The rich performed *litourgiai*, "public services," paying for festivals, sacrifices, or rigging warships. Rich politicians curried favor with the people by spending more than they had to on these **liturgies.** For example,

> Cimon was as rich as a tyrant: he performed the public liturgies lavishly; and he maintained many of his fellow-demesmen, for any man of Laciadae° who wished to could go to him each day and obtain his basic needs, and all his land was unfenced, so that anyone who wished could enjoy the fruit.
>
> Aristotle, *Constitution of Athens* 27 (P.J. Rhodes)

°*Laciadae:* Cimon's deme.

Not everyone applauded this system, including the Old Oligarch:

> As for equipping choruses and gymnasiums and warships, [the poor] know that the rich equip choruses, while the *dêmos* is part of them, and that the rich equip the gymnasiums and the warships, while the *dêmos* have gymnasiums and warships provided for them. Therefore the *dêmos* thinks it appropriate to receive money for singing and running and dancing and sailing in the ships, so that it gets the money and the rich get poorer.
>
> *The Old Oligarch* 1.13 (C. M. Gray)

Normally in ancient societies, those who had the wealth also controlled the political offices. In fifth-century Athens, the poor exercised enormous power. As the Old Oligarch saw it, the poor controlled Athens because they rowed in the fleet. Because Athens' safety depended on them, they could run the city through democratic institutions, and even exported democracy to the subject cities. In Athens, the struggle for power was between old aristocrats and the Athenian people (*dêmos*) as well as between Athens and her subjects. As the Old Oligarch explains,

> About the political system of the Athenians, that they actually chose such a system—I don't congratulate them for it. For in so choosing they have chosen that the *kakoi* do better than the *aristoi*.° I certainly don't congratulate them for that. But since it pleased them to do so, I will demonstrate how well they protect their system and successfully pursue the rest of their policies, though they're wrong policies in the eyes of other Greeks.
>
> First I'll say this—it's fair enough that the poor and the *dêmos* amount to more there than the well born and rich, for this reason: because the *dêmos* operates the ships and bestows power on the city. Steersmen and stroke-callers and unit captains and prow-men and shipwrights—these are the ones who bestow power on the city, much more than hoplites, *aristoi*, and people of substance. Since that's the way it is, it seems to be right for everybody to have a share in public office, both elective and by lot, and to let any citizen speak who wants to. . . .
>
> About the allies and the fact that when the *dêmos* sail out [to the allied cities] they bring malicious prosecutions and generally hate the *aristoi:* knowing that the ruler is necessarily hated by the ruled, and that, if the rich and powerful are strong in the cities, the rule of the Athenian *dêmos* will be short-lived, therefore they get the better sort sentenced to deprivation of their civic privileges, and they take away their money and drive them out and kill them, and they build up the *kakoi*. But the meritorious Athenians protect the meritorious people in the allied cities, knowing that it is always good for them to preserve the *aristoi* in the cities. . . .
>
> One thing they lack. For if the Athenians ruled the sea from an island base, they could do evil if they wanted to and suffer none, so long as they ruled the sea and could avoid having their own country ravaged and having to face enemies there. But as it is, the farmers and the rich Athenians are apt to fawn on the enemy, while the *dêmos,* since it knows that they won't burn or wreck anything of its own, lives without fear and does not fawn on them. . . .
>
> Since, then, they didn't have the luck to inhabit an island originally, here's what they do now: they put their property on the islands for safekeeping and trust to their dominance of the sea, and they disregard the Attic countryside's being cut to pieces, knowing that if they take pity on it they will be deprived of other, greater goods. . . .
>
> In this respect also the Athenians do not seem to me well advised. They side with the *kakoi* in cities torn by civil dissension. But they do this on considered opinion. For if they sided with the *aristoi* they would side with those who don't see things the way they do. In no city are the *aristoi* kindly disposed toward the *dêmos*, but the *kakoi* in every city are friendly toward it. For similar people have a friendly attitude toward similar people. Thus the Athenians opt for what fits them.
>
> The Old Oligarch 1.1–2, 14; 2.14, 16; 3.10 (C. M. Gray)

°*Kakoi* and *aristoi:* "bad people" and "best people." The Old Oligarch uses these words to express moral judgments, but also as synonyms for "poor" and "rich."

Athens transferred power and property downward from the old elites to the masses, and inward from the subject cities to Athens. The democratization of social power unleashed tremendous energy and wealth, but fueled old hostilities within the elite and between rich and poor. In the 420s, as we shall see, class hostilities combined with interstate conflict turned murderous.

THE EDGE OF THE ABYSS, 433–431 B.C.

Athens and Syracuse were exceptional places by the 430s B.C.—bustling, prosperous, and powerful democracies in which philosophical, literary, and artistic revolutions were almost commonplace. Artists and scholars moved back and forth between them. If any society merits the term golden age, it was surely that of Syracuse and above all Athens in the middle of the fifth century B.C. Crowds flocked to watch dramatic masterpieces. Day by day, great buildings rose higher in both cities. With Pericles at the helm, the Athenian ship of state seemed on course. The city's walls were strong, the fleet ruled the seas, and peace reigned. But "what made war inevitable was the growth of Athenian power and the fear that this caused in Sparta," as Thucydides put it, while Athens feared Syracuse, a rich, grain-exporting Dorian state with a navy.

In 433 B.C. (as we saw), Athens made treaties with Rhegion and Leontini (Map 13.1) to counterbalance Syracuse's revived power in eastern Sicily. In the same year, she entered a complicated dispute concerning **Corcyra** (modern Corfu), a large island off Greece's northwest coast (Map 13.2). Corcyra, like Syracuse, was a Corinthian colony, and in 435, Corcyra had sought Corinthian help against Corcyra's own colony Epidamnus, in what is now Albania. By 433, no help had come, so Corcyra approached Athens. The Athenians debated at length, then decided that because Corcyra had its own large fleet and was a convenient base for potential action against Syracuse, they would make the alliance. They broke Pericles' rule of avoiding new entanglements, but the risk seemed worthwhile.

The Corinthians, angry at being bypassed, sent ships to help Epidamnus. In 433 B.C., Athenian ships, supporting Corinth's colony on Corcyra, fought Corinthian ships, supporting Corcyra's rebellious colony **Epidamnus.** The battle was a draw, but the war had begun. In 432, a dispute broke out over yet another Corinthian colony, Potidaea in the north Aegean, now an Athenian subject city. Athens put the rebellious city under siege, trapping Corinthian visitors inside.

The Athenians calculated that Sparta would not break the Thirty Years' Peace (made fifteen years earlier) for Corinth's sake, but Athens' treatment of her little neighbor Megara tipped the balance. Following a minor disagreement over borders, Pericles persuaded the Assembly to ban Megarians from all harbors in cities that Athens controlled. Like many cities in the 430s, Megara had a small territory and a large population and relied on trade to bring in food. Athens' embargo brought hunger and desperation, but the Athenians merely laughed (see Chapter 14, "Art and Thought in the Fifth Century B.C.," for Aristophanes' jokes about Megarian hunger).

The Spartans could not allow Megara to fall under Athenian control. Sparta put pressure on Pericles by invoking the curse passed on the aristocratic Athenian Alcmaeonid family after Cylon's failed coup nearly two hundred years before (Chapter 10). Sparta demanded that the Alcmaeonids—including Pericles—should again be expelled. Athens must also raise the siege of Potidaea, Sparta demanded; "but," Thucydides tells us, "the chief point and the one that they made most clear was that war could be avoided if Athens would revoke the Megarian decree."

According to Plutarch,

> The real reasons which caused the decree [against Megara] to be passed are extremely hard to discover, but all writers agree in blaming Pericles for the fact that it was not revoked. Some of them, however, say that his firm stand on this point was based on the highest motives combined with a shrewd appreciation of where Athens' best interests lay, since he believed that the demand had been made to test his resistance, and that to have complied with it would have been regarded simply as an admission of weakness. But

there are others who consider that he defied the Spartans out of an aggressive arrogance and a desire to demonstrate his own strength.

Plutarch, *Life of Pericles* 31 (I. Scott-Kilvert)

Aristophanes included jokes in his plays that preserve contemporary rumors. He suggested that Pericles was protecting his foreign girlfriend Aspasia, two of whose call-girls had been abducted by Megarians; and that Pericles provoked war to divert attention from his efforts to protect his close friend, the great sculptor Phidias (see Chapter 14), under prosecution for embezzling. Although he had dominated Athenian politics for twenty years, Pericles' enemies had recently successfully prosecuted his friends (including Phidias, who died in prison). In any event, the Spartans had decided that unless they fought Athens now, the balance of power would tip further in Athens' favor. That is how Thucydides understood the breakout of war in 431 B.C.:

> The Spartans voted that the treaty had been broken and that war should be declared not so much because they were influenced by the speeches of their allies as because they were afraid of the further increase of Athenian power, seeing, as they did, that already the greater part of Greece was under the control of Athens.
>
> Thucydides 1.88 (R. Warner)

KEY TERMS

Hiero, 269

Common Resolution, 271

demagogues, 271

Segesta, 271

Cimon, 274

Ephialtes, 276

Pericles, 276

Long Walls, 277

Old Oligarch, 280

metics, 280

liturgies, 283

kakoi, 284

aristoi, 284

Corcyra, 285

Epidamnus, 285

FURTHER READING

Boedeker, Deborah, and Kurt Raaflaub (eds.), *Democracy, Empire and the Arts in Fifth-Century Athens* (Cambridge, MA, 1998). Collection of essays by leading scholars.

Davies, John, *Democracy and Classical Greece* (2nd ed., New York 1993). Good analysis of fifth-century geopolitics with a strong focus on the role of states other than Athens and Sparta.

Kagan, Donald, *The Outbreak of the Peloponnesian War* (New York 1969). First volume of a four-book series, covering the period 478 to 431, from a master of political and military history.

Meiggs, Russell, *The Athenian Empire* (Oxford 1972). Careful analysis based heavily on inscriptions. Very good on details, though the main thesis is now partly outdated because of the redating of many of the inscriptions.

Powell, Anton, *Athens and Sparta* (London 1989). Probably the best introductory survey of the period covered in this chapter.

Ste. Croix, Geoffrey de, *The Origins of the Peloponnesian War* (Ithaca, NY 1972). Excellent study of Athenian-Spartan power politics, with a particularly good analysis of Sparta.

Ancient Texts

Adkins, W. H., and Peter White, *The Greek Polis,* University of Chicago Readings in Western Civilization, vol. 1 (Chicago 2002).

Diodorus of Sicily, *The History,* books 11 and 12. In *The Library of History* IV (Loeb Classical Library; Cambridge, MA, 1946; tr. C. H. Oldfather). Parallel Greek and English texts describing Sicilian history, written in the first century B.C.

Fornara, C., *Translated Documents of Greece and Rome* I: *Archaic Times to the End of the Peloponnesian War* (2nd ed., Cambridge, UK, 1983). Documents 59 through 126 translate difficult but important inscriptions and obscure literary texts from the period 479 to 431 B.C.

Plutarch, *Lives* of Themistocles, Aristides, Cimon, and Pericles. In *The Rise and Fall of Athens* (Harmondsworth, UK, 1960; tr. Ian Scott-Kilvert). Much important information on fifth-century Athens in biographies written around A.D. 100.

Strassler, Robert (ed.), *The Landmark Thucydides* (New York 1996). The abundant maps and excellent endnotes make it easy to follow Thucydides' account.

Thucydides, *The Peloponnesian War* (Harmondsworth, UK, 1954; tr. Rex Warner). Book 1 describes the years down to 431 B.C. Written at Athens in the late-fifth century B.C.

CHAPTER 14

ART AND THOUGHT IN THE FIFTH CENTURY B.C.

As late as the Persian Wars, a traveler who wanted to meet the leading Greek intellectuals and artists needed to visit dozens of *poleis,* from Elea (el-ê-a) in southern Italy to Ephesus (**ef**-e-sus) in Ionia. By the 430s B.C., our traveler could catch most of them with just two stops, at Athens and Syracuse. Athens became what Thucydides called "the School of Hellas." Everyone who was anyone spent time there. In the 430s B.C., about one Greek in ten lived in Attica, yet more than half the cultural figures whose names have survived were Athenian; and more than half the non-Athenians spent substantial parts of their careers in Athens. Plato's philosophical dialogues give a sense of this extraordinary, cosmopolitan intellectual world, where Socrates could drop by a friend's house for dinner and run into leading artists and thinkers from all over Greece. One man wrote a comedy about how it felt to return to his hometown after making it big in Athens. Just as actors, artists, and musicians congregate in New York and Los Angeles in our own times, so in fifth-century Greece all roads led to Athens and Syracuse. Astounding achievements in philosophy, art, drama, and historical thought made Athens' creative geniuses—Aeschylus, Aristophanes, Phidias, Socrates, Sophocles, Thucydides, and many others—widely known twenty-five hundred years later. We devote two chapters to this remarkable cultural explosion, showing how Greeks, responding to particular problems, permanently changed human thought and art. In this chapter, we examine how Syracuse and above all Athens displaced older centers of philosophy and art; and in the next, we describe the invention of a whole new art form, drama.

PHILOSOPHY

Heraclitus and Anaxagoras, the Last Ionian Giants

The terrible Persian destructions in 494 B.C. ended Ionia's role as the center of Greek thought. **Heraclitus** (her-a-**klī**-tus) of Ephesus (Map 14.1), profound but inscrutable, was the last important thinker there. He grew up before his city's sack, but did most of his work between 494 and about 475 B.C. He took issue with previous theories about the cosmos. More of his writings survive than those of the earlier Ionian philosophers (he deposited a book of them in the temple of Artemis in Ephesus), but his brief and cryptic sayings ("The path up and down is one and the same") can strain comprehension.

Heraclitus criticized his predecessors for focusing on sensory perceptions, arguing that "Eyes and ears are bad witnesses if the soul is without understanding"— that is, we cannot learn the truth about the world through our senses. Truth, he argued, lies in the *logos*—"order," "word," or "reason," a philosophical term with a very long future before it: In the Christian gospel of John, *logos* is equated with God. The unseen *logos* arranges that all things exist through conflict, which for Heraclitus was good. The world is like a bow. Strung taut and leaning against a wall, it seems static, but really the bow is a tension of opposites striving against each other, as becomes clear if the string should snap. When things appear to be at rest, opposing and conflicting forces are in balance. "Everything flows," Heraclitus said in one of his most famous pronouncements. The world is change, so "you cannot step into the same river twice," because the water is constantly moving. So too, said Heraclitus, is all reality.

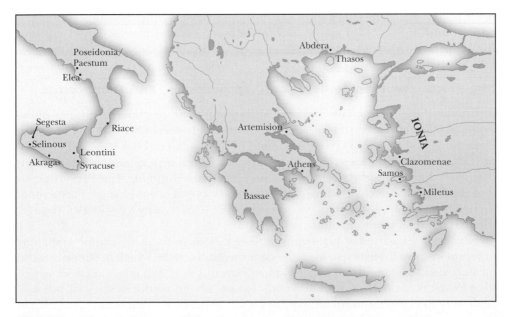

Map 14.1 Sites mentioned in this chapter.

Because all is change, all that lives does so at the expense of something else: "Fire lives the death of air, and air of fire; water lives the death of earth, and earth the death of water." Heraclitus' notion of fire, air, water, and earth as basic qualities looks back to Anaximander's four qualities, and like the Milesians before him, Heraclitus identified one element as the basis of everything. He called it *fire.* "The world is an ever-living fire, kindled in some measures and going out in equal measures." For Heraclitus, fire, which he seems to identify with the *logos,* symbolizes the strife and never-ending flux of the world. Fire lives through consuming, and although it may look the same, its substance is ever-changing. Fire is like the *logos,* the divine intelligence that motivates the world.

Ionia's ruin in 494 B.C. discouraged intellectual vigor, but by the time of the Persian Wars, debates begun in the sixth century had in any event reached a dead end. Heraclitus disagreed with Pythagoras over the nature of the universe, but had no way to resolve the disagreement. As intellectuals drifted toward Athens, they began to ask new and different questions. **Anaxagoras,** from Clazomenae in Ionia, was a crucial transitional figure. Born around 500 B.C., he moved to Athens probably in 456 and befriended Pericles. He must have formulated many of his theories in Ionia, but became famous only in Athens. Like some sixth-century Ionians, Anaxagoras asked, "Where do things come from?" He began his only book by saying, "All things were together": Initially there was a unity, but the action of pure mind (***nous***) separated matter into the variety we now see. The separation was not complete so that everything contains a little bit of everything else. "As things were in the beginning," he wrote, "so now are they all together." The only pure force is *nous,* "mind" itself.

Anaxagoras' important contribution to scientific thought was to distinguish between matter, that which is moved, and mind, that which moves. In his own day, he was more famous for challenging conventional beliefs about the gods. The sun was not a god, but a giant glowing rock. Even sophisticated Athenians were offended, and around 437 B.C. they exiled him for impiety. Pericles himself could not save Anaxagoras.

The Pluralists: Parmenides, Zeno, Empedocles, and Democritus

At the same time that Heraclitus and Anaxogoras were teaching, a distinct philosophical school grew up in southern Italy, where in the sixth century B.C. the great Pythagoras had emigrated from the island of Samos to establish a sacred community. **Parmenides** (par-**men**-i-dēz) of Elea (south of Naples) agreed with Heraclitus that our senses mislead us, but where Heraclitus thought that they trick us into thinking that reality is stable, whereas in fact its essence is change, Parmenides thought that our senses trick us into thinking that reality consists of change, whereas in fact it never changes.

Parmenides arrived at his surprising conclusions by focusing on the ambiguity inherent in speech. He began from the Greek word "is" (*esti*), which in Greek can also mean "exists." In English we might put his point this way: "What is" (in Greek *esti,* or what exists) is obviously not "what is not" (*ouk esti,* what does not exist), so if "what is" (*esti*) were to change into something else, it would become "what is not" (*ouk esti*); in which case "what exists" (*esti*) would become "what does not exist" (*ouk esti*)—which of course is nonsense. Things either "exist" (*esti*) or they do not (*ouk esti*), and there can be no in-between stages, which the concept of change requires. Therefore, motion cannot exist, since motion is a form of change. Space does not exist either, because space is that "which is not" and that which is not cannot be "that which is."

Parmenides exalted pure reason over dependence on the senses, laying the basis for future abstract thinking—thought that reaches conclusions independent of (and sometimes contrary to) external appearances. Parmenides' follower **Zeno** of Elea (c. 490–430 B.C.) went still further with famous puzzles, the **paradoxes of Zeno**, "proving" that motion, and hence change, is illusory. Imagine that Achilles, known for swiftness, wanted to overtake a tortoise, known for slowness. He could never do so, because first he would have to reach the point where the tortoise was when the race started, by which time the tortoise would have moved on a short way. When Achilles reached the tortoise's second position, it would have moved on again, and so on, *ad infinitum*. Similarly, you cannot get from here to there because first you must get halfway there, then cross half that distance, then half of that, and so on forever, never reaching your goal. Certainly arrows appear to soar through the sky, but at any one moment the arrow is someplace on its arc, hence has no opportunity to get anyplace else. The arrow appears to move, but cannot. The logical errors in Zeno's paradoxes are not obvious and were not clarified until the seventeenth century A.D.

Parmenides and his followers rejected Ionian theories tracing the variety of the world back to one substance, because such a description required that one thing change into another. Yet their conclusion, that things in the world do not exist, sticks in the throat; it just cannot be true. His immediate successors are called **pluralists** because they reasoned that if there is no one thing whence many derive, then the world must be made of many things in the first place. The important pluralists were Empedocles, Anaxagoras, and Democritus (de-**mok**-ri-tus).

The extraordinary **Empedocles** (em-**ped**-o-klēz; c. 492–432 B.C.) lived in Akragas in south-central Sicily. Active in politics and an Olympic athlete, he behaved like a shaman, claiming that his knowledge worked wonders, controlled the winds, and even raised the dead. He explained his theories in highly complex poetry, engaging in a kind of international dialogue with Pythagoras and Parmenides. He identified four original substances: earth, air, fire, and water, in this respect echoing Anaximander, but added that all things that are, are combinations of these four "roots." Bone, for example, is two parts earth, two parts water, and four parts fire. Motion is possible even without space, because things move like fishes through water, the water enclosing them and touching them at all times.

The Ionians thought that the single original substance moved by itself, as in the inherent wiggle of Anaximander's Infinite, but Empedocles (like Anaxagoras) saw the need for an external force to cause motion. This force was dual, Love and Strife, one joining the elements, the other breaking them apart. Yet these forces are inherent in the elements, not separate from them: Love is "equal in length and breadth to the world," he said.

Seeing no creative intelligence standing behind reality, Empedocles explained the complexity of the world's forms, and the suitability of such organisms as eyes and ears to their purpose, by saying that once, through chance encounter, there had been all sorts of unsuitable creatures and things (for example, humans with cows' heads), but that the fittest experiments survived, an anticipation of Charles Darwin's theory of evolution through natural selection (but unlike Darwin, Empedocles offered no evidence).

Such refined intellectual debates flourished in the far west, but Aegean thinkers followed them. **Democritus** of Abdera in Thrace (460–380) was a strange man who shunned fame (he visited Athens, but, he said, "no one knew me," so he went home again, and lived in a tiny room in his father's garden). He devised an **atomic theory**—of course without experimental evidence—in a form that changed little until the nineteenth century A.D. Instead of Empedocles' four changeless elements in constant recombination, he postulated a plethora of tiny "uncuttable" (*atomos*) things eternal in themselves, which recombined with other tiny things to form the phenomenal world. These tiny things were "atoms" because to isolate the very tiny things of which the world is made, one must keep slicing it until it cannot be sliced anymore. That last uncuttable thing is the *atom*.

The atoms are similar, but have different sizes and shapes. Democritus denied Parmenides' argument about the nonexistence of space, saying, "*What is not* does exist, no less than *what is*." The atoms, floating in space like motes in a sunbeam, drift into contact, stick together, and form the things of the world, though why the atoms move at all, Democritus does not say.

Different qualities derive from the density and shape of the atoms. In soft things, the atoms are far apart, with plenty of space; and in hard things, they are compacted together. Sharp atoms taste "bitter," whereas smooth atoms taste "sweet." Colors depend on the shape of the atoms and how they reflect light, which itself is a stream of atoms. The soul is made of atoms too, the finest of all. At death they break up, and the soul dissolves into its constituent atoms. There can therefore be no question of an afterlife or of reincarnation, as Pythagoreans believed.

Rhetoric, the Sophists, and Socrates

In this extraordinary intellectual environment, supported by the revolutionary technology of the Greek alphabet, thinkers who lived in Ionia argued with thinkers who lived in Sicily as if attached to an Internet. Both philosophical schools pushed sixth-century debates to new levels of sophistication, but by 450 philosophers in Athens and Syracuse asked different kinds of questions: How could they help men succeed in the democratic societies that rationalism helped create? Athenians called the intellectuals who flocked to their city **sophists** (*sophistai*), "wise men," really teachers whose instruction could improve a citizen's chance of gaining influence in the *polis*. The sophists did not constitute a philosophical school but shared a dedication to practical affairs. They claimed that they could teach *aretê* (**ar-e-tē**), "virtue" or "excellence." They were skeptical about traditional explanations and, noting that conflicting claims about the nature of reality were unresolvable, they questioned whether anyone could know anything for sure. We know through our senses, yet they are untrustworthy. The object of our knowledge is the world, yet its nature or even existence is open to debate. If "hot" and "cold" do not exist, but result only from the accidental mixture and meeting of invisible atoms, as Democritus maintained, then "good" and "evil" may also be relative, conventional categories. The sophists' **moral relativism** shook Greek intellectual life to its foundations. Socrates and Plato, often confused with the sophists by contemporary Greeks, dedicated their life work to dispelling this skepticism.

In Syracuse, where the return of exiles after the fall of the tyrants in the 460s B.C. generated thousands of lawsuits over property, philosophers began thinking about and teaching the art of rhetoric. Fortunes hung on the ability to speak well. Democracies assumed that the best way to make decisions was to gather a large number of citizens in assemblies or lawcourts; but if nothing about the external world could be known for sure, and right and wrong were merely conventions, then the art of persuasion, not facts, was the basis for power in the democratic assembly. Rhetoric therefore seemed the highest form of philosophy.

The first handbooks on persuasion, the art of making something seem true whether it was or not, appeared in Syracuse around 450 B.C. When the famous teacher of rhetoric **Gorgias** of Leontini (near Syracuse) first spoke at Athens in 427, he created a sensation and sparked a rash of imitators. When Aristophanes made fun of sophists in his play *The Clouds* (414 B.C.), he particularly mocked their claims to make false arguments stronger than true ones.

Hippias and Protagoras were the most famous sophists. Plato wrote dialogues now called by their names. **Hippias** is remembered for saying that (1) nothing exists; (2) if it did exist, you could not know it; and (3) if you knew it, you could never tell anyone about it. The versatile **Protagoras** coined the phrase "Man is the measure of all things," meaning that one man views the world in one way, another in another way, and that neither is right. Truth is relative and so are the moral categories of good and bad, although Protagoras insisted that some forms of behavior are more practical than others.

Protagoras pushed human-centered secularism to its limits. In Babylon, Egypt, and Israel, laws, rules for behavior, were justified as coming from the gods. By the late fifth century B.C., some Greeks concluded that all laws were in fact merely conventions made by men and could thus be changed by men, just as decisions were made and unmade in the democratic assembly. Protagoras defined the secular social contract by which we live today, the thesis that laws exist to serve social good; they do not reflect timeless values of right and wrong. If tradition, custom, and law are inconvenient, we can—indeed, should—sweep them aside.

Socrates (469–399 B.C.) vigorously opposed such moral relativism. He wrote nothing himself, but is the principal speaker in Plato's numerous dialogues. Scholars disagree about how far the opinions Plato ascribed to Socrates were really Socrates' and how far they were Plato's own, but most agree that Socrates maintained that "*aretê* is knowledge." The saying was directed against the sophists' assertions that they could teach *aretê*, which really means "efficiency at a particular task," while at the same time they held that nothing could be known. Socrates liked to speak in homely terms and would ask, "What is the *aretê* of a shoemaker?" Obviously, to make shoes. But in order to make shoes, you need to know the end in view, why you are making them—the facts that feet are soft, the ground is hard, and we are happier when well shod. Then you can proceed to the knowledge of how to make shoes. When the sophists claimed to teach *aretê* as a general concept, a quality that enriched a man's whole life, they implied that humans, too, must have an end, a purpose, an "efficiency for some task." But what is that task? What *is* the function of man?

Socrates never answered this question. The Socratic method meant convincing his interlocutors that when they thought they had an answer, they really did not. It is easy to see why Athenians disliked Socrates and confused him with the sophists. The sophists taught that nothing could be known; Socrates showed how no one knew anything, so long as their minds were cluttered with grand but ill-defined concepts like justice, love, and courage. When your mind is clear, then maybe you can acquire real knowledge. You simply must define your terms. If you know what justice is, you can act justly, but not before.

Hence, Socrates' second famous dictum, that vice is the result of ignorance, is really a backhanded way of repeating that *aretê*, virtue, is knowledge. Socrates encouraged the **inductive method** for discovering general definitions. From a large body of acts that people consider "just" you should be able to distill an essence, the thing all such acts have in common: "justice." Plato's most famous dialogue, *The Republic* (360 B.C.), is dedicated to discovering just such a definition.

Conclusion

Serious speculation about the physical world began in the sixth century B.C. among Greeks under Lydian and then Persian rule. By the late sixth century, rival schools of thought were flourishing in Sicily and southern Italy, with a scattering of major thinkers across other Greek cities. By the late fifth century, the centers of gravity had shifted to Athens and, to a lesser extent, Syracuse. As wealth flowed into these cities, some people spent it to attract leading thinkers; and when the thinkers arrived, they made themselves useful to Athenians and Syracusans. The philosophers' debates affected both cities, but Athenian and Syracusan society, politics, and culture also affected philosophy.

Intellectuals turned to issues that mattered in their host cities: how to pursue truth and wisdom in a democracy and how to use truth and rhetoric to gain power and wealth. The evolution of philosophy into a system for persuasive thought gave Greek politics an intellectual dimension absent in many civilizations. Where Assyrian or Egyptian kings could simply claim that they acted as the gods willed, Greek statesmen (even tyrants) were obligated to defend their positions on philosophical grounds.

MATERIAL CULTURE

A classic is something timeless, which transcends the particular conditions of its moment of creation and attains a wider relevance for humanity. In the midst of their wars, personal hatreds, and sometimes crass pursuit of wealth and power, a few hundred men in Athens and Syracuse broke through the normal constraints of humdrum experience to change the world. In classical art, as in philosophy, innovation was increasingly centralized in Athens and Syracuse, where the most important architects, sculptors, and painters gathered. Like philosophers, there they responded to the issues of the day, including the Athenians' and Syracusans' sense of themselves as saviors of Hellenism from barbarian threats, and the tensions between this self-image and the crude realities of the power they exercised over other Greek cities. As they dealt with historically specific problems, they forged masterpieces that speak across the gulf of centuries.

Sculpture

In the years after the great wars of 480 and 479 B.C., sculptors tried to bring out a new sense of idealized humankind. The Greeks had freed themselves from foreign threats, and artists struggled to express a sense of mastery over the world in the **severe style** whose serenely calm facial expressions on statues contrast with the earlier frozen smiles of the Archaic Period (contrast Figures 14.1 to 14.5 with Figures 9.5 to 9.8 in Chapter 9, "The Archaic Cultural Revolution, 700–480 B.C."). We know more about Greek sculpture from carved marble statues because the originally common bronze statues were long ago melted down for their metal. For bronze sculpture we have to rely on chance finds from shipwrecks, which saved the statues from being recycled (as on the cover of this book).

Sculptors cast these extraordinary bronze works by a very ancient method of casting called the lost-wax technique. First, the sculptor made a rough model of clay, then coated it with wax. He shaped the soft wax in detail, then coated it with a second layer of clay, leaving holes at the top and bottom of the second clay layer. He poured molten bronze in the top hole. The melted wax ran out through the bottom hole as the bronze filled the space the wax had occupied. The sculptor then shattered the outer layer of clay, revealing (when he got it right) a beautiful hollow statue of thin bronze. He could leave the clay core inside the bronze statue, or chip it away through small openings.

Casting large lost-wax bronze statues required exceptional skill and cost a great deal of money. Bronze workers cast elaborate figures in several pieces, then soldered them together. Bronze was lighter than stone and gave sculptors more freedom. The statue in Figure 14.1 could not have been carved from marble; the stone is not strong

Figure 14.1 Zeus (or Poseidon), found in the sea off Cape Artemisium, circa 460 B.C. Bronze, height 6 ft. 10 in. *The Striding god from Artemisium is a bronze statue dating from about 460 B.C.E. National Archeological Museum, Athens.*

enough to support the weight of outstretched arms. The sculptor would have to keep the arms down or add such unsightly supports as tree trunks to bear the load.

Larger than life-sized, Figure 14.1 perfectly embodies the qualities of grace, restraint, dignity, self-control, and perfected manhood that fifth-century Greeks saw as ideal, a superb example of the severe style. The heel of the right foot is raised, the left hand extends to take aim, the right hand is cocked to cast the thunderbolt (or trident). Fully bearded, the figure is naked, like the archaic *kouroi*, and its hair bound by a braid. The pubic hair is realistically portrayed. The archaic smile is gone, replaced by a magisterial calm. The muscles of its beautiful body resonate with an inner intensity.

One of the most extraordinary archaeological finds of the twentieth century was two bronze warriors in the severe style, probably thrown overboard as ballast to lighten a ship during a storm near the toe of Italy. Figure 14.2 (and the cover) shows one of them. These statues are not signed, but their date, style, and perfection

Figure 14.2a Bronze statue of a young man with helmet, perhaps by Phidias (c. 460 B.C.). Larger than life-sized, found in 1972 in the Bay of Riace, Calabria, Italy. The statue was probably taken from the sanctuary at Delphi.

lead many archaeologists to think that they were early works of **Phidias,** the most famous Athenian sculptor. As we will see in Chapter 22, "The Coming of Rome,
220–230 B.C.," in the second and first centuries B.C., the Romans looted Greece's art
treasures; these objects were probably among the plunder. Restored after eight
years of painstaking labor, the statues hint at the enormity of our loss of classical
sculpture. They once held shields attached to their left arms and held spears or
swords in their right. The figure shown here wore a metal helmet. The eyes are
made of ivory and glass paste, the lips and nipples of copper, and the teeth of one
statue of silver plate. The sculptor combined stylization of the hair and beard with
exceptional naturalism in the rendering of the veins in the groin, in the inner el-
bows, and in the calves and feet. In a casual, relaxed poise, the weight shifted to the
right foot, pelvis raised correspondingly on one side, their bodies in gentle S-curves,
they represent the pinnacle of concentrated masculine power and stand among
art's greatest achievements.

By the 450s B.C., increasingly more sculptors were congregating in Athens,
but by no means all. There was enough money in other *poleis* to support independent schools, some excellent. The museums of Syracuse are full of fragments

Figure 14.2b *Pheidias (c. 490–430
B.C.E.). Bronze statue of a young man
with helmet. More than life-size,
found in 1972 in the bay of Riace,
Calabria, Italy. Museo Archeologico
Nazionale, Reggio Calabria, Italy. ©
Erich Lessing/Art Resource, NY.*

Figure 14.3 The birth of Aphrodite from the Ludovisi Throne, circa 460 B.C., marble, width 56 in.

of fine fifth-century statues, but Figure 14.3 shows one panel of the so-called Ludovisi Throne, a better-preserved example from a Greek city in southern Italy. It may represent Aphrodite's birth from the sea, assisted by two female figures. The sheer garments that enclose her, sometimes called *wet drapery,* reveal her body beneath, a device found in fifth-century sculpture to show women's forms without representing them as naked. To an Athenian eye, this panel would have seemed provincial and erratic: It combined the latest style of drapery on the central figure with old-fashioned hairstyles and much stiffer drapery on the two attendants.

We can make stylistic comments like these because sculpture developed so rapidly in the fifth century B.C. By 450 B.C., artists in Athens were softening the severity of early fifth-century faces, loosening the poses, refining anatomy, and imbuing their statues with a greater unity and sense of purpose. Archaeologists call the style of the mid-fifth century **high classical,** to many tastes the zenith of ancient art. Beautiful and moving examples survive, but the best known come from buildings on the Athenian Acropolis.

After Xerxes destroyed the archaic temples atop the Acropolis in 480 and 479 B.C., the Athenians vowed not to replace them until they had exacted revenge; but after 449, perhaps because a peace treaty had now been signed with Persia, they rebuilt their holy places on a massive scale. Their patron goddess Athena received a spectacular new temple, the **Parthenon,** whose architecture we examine in the next

Figure 14.4 One possible reconstruction of Phidias' gold-and-ivory statue of Athena in the Parthenon, circa 439–432 B.C.

section. Inside was a statue of Athena Parthenos ("the virgin"), forty feet high (Figure 14.4). It had a wooden frame with ivory-coated flesh parts and gold-plated clothing. The statue survived for over a thousand years, although without its valuable coverings; eventually it was taken to Constantinople, where it was lost in the Middle Ages.

We know of this statue only from Roman copies. The Parthenon had a secondary sculptural program on a series of high-relief carved panels. They decorated the pediments (the triangular openings at front and back) and the top of the high cella walls, some forty feet above the ground, hard to see (Figure 14.5). Because the Parthenon remained in use from the fifth century B.C. to modern times (becoming a church to Mary Mother of God in the Byzantine Empire, then a mosque under the Turks from the fifteenth century A.D. through the nineteenth), these sculptures were never broken up for reuse. They were damaged during the Venetian siege of Athens in 1687, when a mortar shell blew up gunpowder the Turks had stored in the mosque, but they were still more or less intact in the late eighteenth century, when western Europeans first became interested in owning ancient Greek sculpture. In

Figure 14.5 Water-carriers on the inner frieze of the Parthenon. Probably, they were part of the Panathenaic festival that happened every fourth year, when Athena's statue was presented with a new robe. Aristocratic girls played special parts in the procession. Parthenon, north side, slab VI, height 43 in.

1799 Lord Elgin (**el**-ghīn), a British diplomat in Constantinople, received permission to dig on the Acropolis and remove finds. He tore down every piece of sculpture he could find and shipped it back to London, hoping to sell the statues and make his fortune. English aesthetes, more familiar with Roman copies than Greek originals, did not know what to make of the treasures. The British Museum curators argued for years over whether the nation wanted such things, and Elgin died bankrupt. Eventually, the British Museum bought the statues, and the **Elgin Marbles** became world-famous.[27]

The Elgin Marbles were carved around 435 B.C., reaching unsurpassed levels of technical skill and artistic power. Figure 14.6 shows a marvel of stone cutting, the surviving part of a figure of Iris, messenger of the gods, from the west pediment (see Figure 14.11). The sculptor used innovations to make Iris' form more naturalistic. Artificially high ridges on the folds of the drapery create an effect of transparency where it clings to the body. When real drapery folds over a limb, it does so in straight lines, but the Parthenon sculptor deliberately curved the lines of the folds, which paradoxically looks more real than straight lines would. The great Phidias oversaw

Figure 14.6 The body of Iris, from the Parthenon west pediment, Acropolis, Athens, circa 435 B.C.

the sculptural program but did not himself carve the statues. By chance, inscriptions survive that record payments for the carving; skilled slaves worked alongside free men at every stage.

Architecture

By 500 B.C., Greek architects rivaled the builders of Egypt and the Near East in sophisticated and beautiful constructions. Some sixth-century Greek temples are bigger than anything built in the fifth century, but the craftsmanship, beauty, and expense of fifth-century temples surpassed anything before. Through their buildings, architects expressed the ideal of the city-state as a community of citizens, equal in balance and harmony, honoring the gods while proudly displaying mastery over nature. Like fifth-century philosophy and sculpture, architecture reflected the new social force of democracy and the new wealth of empire. Syracuse was famous for its fifth-century temples, but like Syracusan sculpture, these are poorly preserved. The best known monuments are clustered on the Athenian Acropolis (Figure 14.7).

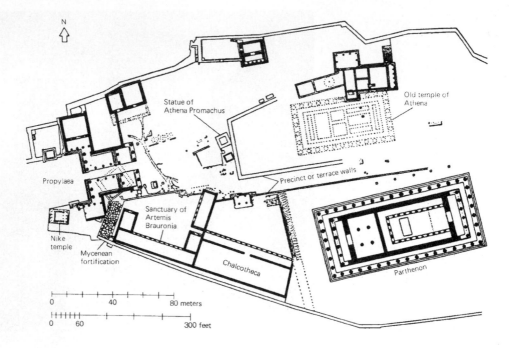

Figure 14.7a Plan of the Athenian Acropolis, circa 400 B.C., showing the Parthenon (lower right), Erechtheum (upper right), and Propylaea (left), and outlines of the old temple destroyed by the Persians (faded lines, center).

Plutarch explains that these buildings were very much part of Pericles' political program:

> Pericles ... was anxious that the unskilled masses, who had no military training, should not be debarred from benefiting from the national income, yet should not be paid for sitting about and doing nothing. So he boldly laid before the people proposals for immense public works and plans for buildings, which would require many different arts and industries and require long periods to complete, his object being that those who stayed at home, no less than those serving in the fleet or the army or on garrison duty, should be enabled to enjoy a share of the national wealth. The materials to be used were stone, bronze, ivory, gold, ebony, and cypress-wood, while the arts or trades which wrought or fashioned them were those of carpenter, modeler, copper-smith, stonemason, dyer, worker in gold and ivory, painter, embroiderer, and engraver, and besides these the carriers and suppliers of the materials, such as merchants, sailors, and pilots for the sea-borne traffic, and wagon-makers, trainers of draught animals, and drivers for everything that came by land. There were also rope-makers, weavers, leatherworkers, road builders, and miners. Each individual craft, like a general with an army under his separate command, had its own corps of unskilled laborers at its disposal, and these worked in a subordinate capacity, as an instrument obeys the hand, or the body the soul, and so through these various demands the city's prosperity was extended far and wide and shared among every age and condition in Athens.

Figure 14.7b　Aerial view of the Athenian Acropolis. In the left foreground are the ruins of the theater of Dionysus. Portions of the circuit walls date back to the Bronze Age. The Erectheum can be seen right of the Parthenon, and the Propylaea can be seen slightly on the left-hand promontory. The small theater visible in the left center (still used for modern performances) was built by Herodes Atticus in Roman times. The modern city spreads over the plain in all directions.

The new temples symbolized Athens' new power and were also shaped by it. No city had ever had the wealth or self confidence to pursue such a coherent and striking architectural vision:

> So the buildings arose, as imposing in their sheer size as they were inimitable in the grace of their outlines, since the artists strove to excel themselves in the beauty of their workmanship. And yet the most wonderful thing about them was the speed with which they were completed. Each of them, men supposed, would take many generations to build, but in fact the entire project was carried through in the high summer of one man's administration. . . . It is this, above all, which makes Pericles' works an object of wonder to us—the fact that they were created in so short a span, and yet for all time. Each one possessed a beauty which seemed venerable the moment it was born, and at the same time a youthful vigor which makes them appear to this day as if they were newly built. A bloom of eternal freshness hovers over these works of his and preserves them from the touch of time, as if some unfading spirit of youth, some ageless vitality had been breathed into them.
>
> Plutarch, *Life of Pericles* 12–13 (I. Scott-Kilvert)

The program began with the Parthenon in 447 B.C. (Figure 14.8). Pericles worked closely with the architects and with Phidias. The temple was dedicated in

Figure 14.8 The majestic ruins of the northwest corner of the Parthenon tower over loose blocks and broken columns strewn around its base. Acropolis, Athens.

438 and the sculpture finished in 432. Meanwhile, work had begun on the great gate called the **Propylaea** (pro-pi-lē-a, "fore-gates") in 437 (Figure 14.9); it too was finished in 432. The strange but wonderful temple called the **Erechtheum** (e-rek-thē-um) was also begun in the 430s, probably on the foundations of a Bronze Age palace. The financial stress of the Peloponnesian War, which broke out in 431 B.C., slowed construction; most of the work was done between 409 and 406 B.C. Finally, a beautiful little temple to **Athena Nikê** ("victory") was built in the 420s B.C., with a celebrated figure of Nikê (victory personified) adjusting her sandal added later (Figure 14.10b). This figure, with its transparent drapery and complex pose, shows high classical art at its best. Although it is the smallest building on the Acropolis, the temple of Athena Nikê is a compact masterpiece whose graceful Ionic columns perfectly balance the stern Doric of the Propylaea.

Following no overall design, Pericles' team reused the foundations of earlier buildings on the Acropolis, giving a chaotic appearance to the complex. Entering through the Propylaea (Figures 14.7a, 14.9), the visitor first encountered an enormous statue of Athena, which Phidias cast from the bronze of captured Persian armor (Figure 14.7a, just left of center). Behind this, to the visitor's left and at a

Figure 14.9 The west end of the Athenian Acropolis. The building in the upper left was an art gallery, part of the Propylaea, "gateway" to the Athenian Acropolis. Its Doric columns rise in the center. In the upper right is the small temple to Nikê, "victory."

Figure 14.10a The Ionic temple of Athena Nikê, circa 425 B.C. The blocks were later used as fill, and the temple was reconstructed in modern times. Notice the continuous frieze above the columns, characteristic of Ionic architecture (in Doric temples, the frieze is interrupted by blocks imitating beam-ends called *metopês*).

Figure 14.10b Nikê adjusting her sandal, circa 410–405 B.C., from the Nikê temple.

higher level, was the oddly shaped Erechtheum, "house of Erechtheus," an early king of Athens (Figure 14.12). Opposite the Erechtheum, on the south, was the Parthenon. The Athena Nikê temple stood south of the Propylaea, on an outcropping (Figure 14.9).

The Parthenon was made entirely of a beautiful translucent marble from nearby Mount Pentelicus. In general design, it was a Doric temple, with eight columns on the short sides and seventeen on the long (Figure 14.11). Designed with astonishing subtlety, the Parthenon has no straight lines. The stylobate ("column platform") swells in the middle, the columns lean inward, and the upper works lean slightly out. The columns at the ends are slightly closer together than in the middle. Such adjustments compensate for the optical illusion that makes truly straight lines appear to sag and give to the Parthenon a lightness and liveliness not found in any other Greek temple. It seems to grow organically from the rock.

The Parthenon raised architectural beauty to new heights, but the Erechtheum (Figure 14.12) was a very unusual structure, consisting of three rooms. Some scholars think this was to venerate three deities: Athena, Poseidon, and the hero Erechtheus. Others suggest its shape preserves the outlines of a Mycenaean palace that once stood on the Acropolis, which Athenians believed to have been Erechtheus' home.

The Erechtheum is in an elaborate Ionic style, with elegant carving around the doorways often imitated in later centuries by Romans. The building's most famous

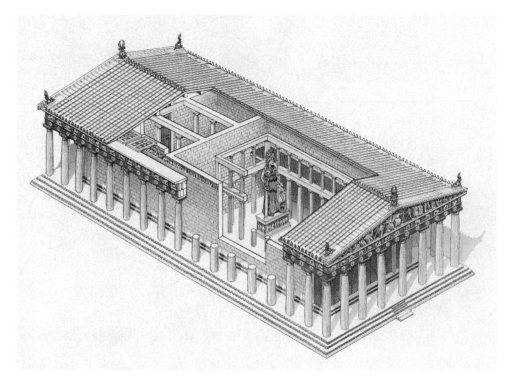

Figure 14.11 Sectioned plan of the Parthenon, with wall and roof cutaway to depict internal structure, the *cella* with the gold-and-ivory statue of Athena, and behind the *cella,* separated by a solid wall, the "treasury" or *opisthodomos* ("house behind").

feature is its south porch, where statues called **caryatids**[28] (kar-i-**a**-tidz) replace the normal fluted columns, women carrying the weight of the porch as if they were carrying baskets or water (Figure 14.12). Much copied by later architects, the women probably held offering cups in extended hands and may represent girls who served the cult of Athena.

Outside Athens, Greeks built hundreds of other remarkable temples in the fifth century B.C. Even remote hilltops were beautified in the gods' honor. Figure 14.13, for example, shows the temple of Apollo at Bassae in Arcadia, the wild central portion of the Peloponnesus, so far from centers of population that, although it survives almost intact, its very existence was forgotten except by local shepherds until a French adventurer stumbled on it in 1765. In the fifth century B.C., such new temples in perfect classical proportions arose in every part of the Greek world. Travelers in Sicily and southern Italy today can see many of them, in far better condition than most Aegean examples, in great avenues at Poseidonia (Paestum, in southern Italy), Selinous (western Sicily), and Akragas (south-central Sicily). At Segesta, the non-Greek Elymians of western Sicily built a perfect high classical temple in the 430s; many think that the Elymians hired the same architects who designed the Parthenon.

Figure 14.12   The Erectheum, with its famous caryatid porch. The modern olive tree on the left stands where the ancient olive grew, sacred to Athena, miraculously regenerated after the Persian sack.

Temples were not the only monumental buildings from the fifth century B.C. At the same time, the Greeks built theaters, administrative centers, and mile after mile of fortifications. They revolutionized the physical appearance of such cities as Athens and Syracuse, sweeping away the simpler monuments of archaic times and making them places fit for democratic citizens who felt they had no rivals on earth. The Greeks' reason, will, and bravery had transformed the world they lived in.

Painting

Ancient literary sources describe numerous fifth-century wall paintings, but almost no examples survive. According to Roman writers, the greatest fifth-century painter was **Polygnotus** (po-lig-**nō**-tus), born around 500 B.C. on the island of Thasos in the north Aegean. By 480, he had moved to Athens where he did his best work. Polygnotus is said to have represented individual character (what the Greeks called *êthos*) in his paintings, unlike the stiff representations in ancient Near Eastern and earlier Greek art. Polygnotus struggled to express depth and realism. The discovery of true perspective in painting did not come for another eighteen hundred years, but Polygnotus took the revolutionary steps of raising figures off the baseline and adding scenery.

Figure 14.13   The temple of Bassae in Arcadia, circa 420 B.C. Ictinus, architect of the Parthenon, designed it. Today an ugly canvas tent protects the temple. Its friezes, now in the British Museum, preserve important sculpture.

We get some sense of painting from this period from tombs at the Greek city of Poseidonia in Italy (modern Paestum). Here, Greeks buried some dead in large stone boxes that sometimes bore painted scenes on the interior walls and ceilings. Figure 14.14 shows an elegantly arched diver caught in midair, hinting at the vitality and energy of painting in this period. Stark trees stand on either side of the pool, the one on the right growing above the base line out of the picture's border, suggesting depth, as does the arching pool.

Contemporary vases are a far richer source for fifth-century painting. In Chapter 9, we noted the connections between vase painting and other arts and the concentration of the best vase painters in Athens. Vase painters rushed to exploit Polygnotus' innovations. In Figure 14.15, for example, Odysseus and his companions, scattered on different base lines, prepare the stake. At the right, a satyr fills a wine cup, alluding to Polyphemus' drunkenness. Vase painters also imitated sculptors, trying (often clumsily) to draw flimsy, semitransparent drapery as on the Parthenon sculpture.

Constantly innovating to stay ahead in a competitive market, Athenian vase painters developed a **white-ground style**, better suited than red figure for imitating the effects of wall painting. Artisans covered the surface of the vase with a chalky white pigment, then drew in the figures with fine black lines and filled them with thin washes of red, yellow, blue, and other colors. The best examples, produced expressly to accompany the dead, are very beautiful. In Figure 14.16, a servant presents a jewelry box to the dead woman, with whom the vase was buried.

Figure 14.14   The Tomb of the Diver, in Paestum (Italy). Ceiling block from a sarcophagus, circa 480 B.C. Height 40 inches.

Figure 14.15   South Italian scene of the blinding of Polyphemos, by the Cyclops Painter, circa 420–410 B.C. Height 18 inches. © *The British Museum.*

Figure 14.16 A white-ground oil flask (*lekythos*) by the Achilles Painter, circa 420 B.C., showing a servant bringing a box to the deceased.

Conclusion

The concentration of resources and talents in Syracuse and above all Athens in the fifth century fueled feverish cultural experiments. Both were democratic, imperial cities; both saw themselves as the saviors of Greece. In their different ways, dramatists, historians, philosophers, sculptors, painters, and architects tried to represent a new vision that put triumphant mankind at the center of the universe. They faced the problems of how Greeks should exercise power justly, how they could know right from wrong, and how great and talented men should fit into triumphant, egalitarian, male citizen communities. Although twenty-five hundred years have passed and the world has changed beyond recognition, achievements of the Greek Classical Period continue to speak directly to humanity's central concerns.

KEY TERMS

Heraclitus, 289

logos, 289

Anaxagoras, 290

nous, 290

Parmenides, 290

Zeno, 291

FURTHER READING

Philosophy: General

Buxton, R., ed., *From Myth to Reason? Studies in the Development of Greek Thought* (Oxford 1999). Engaging discussion of classical Greek thought.

Guthrie, W. K. C., *The Greek Philosophers: From Thales to Aristotle* (London 1950). Superb short review by a leading scholar.

Presocratics

Barnes, J., *The Presocratic Philosophers* (2nd vols., London 1979). Barnes relies on modern analytic philosophy to discuss ancient philosophers.

Kirk, G. S., J. E. Raven, and M. Schofield, eds., *The Presocratic Philosophers: A Critical History with a Selection of Texts* (2nd ed., Cambridge, UK, 1983). Contains the Greek text and good explanations.

Lloyd, G. E. R., *Early Greek Science: Thales to Aristotle* (London 1970). Excellent introduction to sixth- and fifth-century thought.

———, *Demystifying Mentalities* (Cambridge, UK, 1990). Thoughtful study by a leading historian of science.

Art

Boardman, John, *Greek Art* (rev. ed., New York 1985). Masterful overview by one of the world's leading ancient art historians.

———, *The Diffusion of Classical Art in Antiquity* (Princeton 1994). Shows how Greek styles of representation replaced earlier conventions, even influencing Buddhist art.

Hurwit, Jeffrey M., *The Athenian Acropolis: History, Mythology, and Archaeology from the Neolithic Era to the Present* (Cambridge, UK, 2000). The best book about the Athenian Acropolis.

Neils, Jenifer, ed., *Goddess and Polis: The Panathenaic Festival in Ancient Athens* (Princeton 1992). Beautifully illustrated study of this central festival.

Osborne, Robin, *Archaic and Classical Greek Art* (Cambridge, UK, 1998). Penetrating analysis with good photos.

Pedley, John Griffiths, *Greek Art and Archaeology* (2nd ed., New York 1998). The best textbook overview.

Pollitt, Jerome Jordan, *Art and Experience in Classical Greece* (Cambridge, UK, 1972). Discussion of ancient texts about art.

Rasmussen, Tom, and Nigel Spivey, eds., *Looking at Greek Vases* (Cambridge, UK, 1991). Walks the reader through the major issues in our study of illustrated pots.

Robertson, Martin, *A History of Greek Art* (2nd vols., Cambridge, UK, 1975). Comprehensive scholarly treatment.

———, *A Shorter History of Greek Art* (Cambridge, UK, 1981). Summary of Robertson's two-volume work.

Stewart, Andrew , *Greek Sculpture: An Exploration* (2nd vols., New Haven, CT, 1990). One of the best modern scholars of ancient Greek art.

———, *Art, Desire, and the Body in Ancient Greece* (Cambridge, UK, 1998). Addresses the social context of Greek art and its focus on the human body.

Ancient Texts

Kirk, G. S., J. E. Raven, and M. Schofield, eds., *The Presocratic Philosophers* (2nd ed., Cambridge, UK, 1983). The Greek text and good translations and explanations for the fifth-century B.C. philosophers.

CHAPTER 15

FIFTH-CENTURY DRAMA

In Chapter 14, "Art and Thought in the Fifth Century B.C.," we reviewed art and thought in fifth-century Greece. In this chapter, we focus on drama, the artistic form that many scholars think is fifth-century Greece's greatest achievement. Drama is so familiar to us that it is hard to imagine that it might not exist, yet all earlier societies lacked drama as we understand it—public presentations in which performers, pretending to be other people, speak in the first person, engage in conflict, and follow stories from beginning to end. The Greeks invented drama at the end of the sixth century B.C. It became one of antiquity's major art forms, but was at its peak in the fifth century B.C., when it provided a flexible and powerful artistic medium for reflecting on individuality, freedom, and responsibility.

The Greeks divided drama into two broad categories, tragedy and comedy. Athenian in origin, by 400 B.C. tragedy was becoming a Panhellenic art form, but the three great Athenian tragedians—Aeschylus, Sophocles, and Euripides—formed an unchallenged canon. Athens was also the main center for comedy, but had several challengers, above all in Sicily.

TRAGEDY

The genre's origins are obscure, but Athens and Syracuse were the major centers for production. All thirty-three surviving tragedies are Athenian—seven plays by **Aeschylus** (ē-ski-lus; 525–456 B.C.), seven more by Sophocles (sof-o-klēz; 496–406), and nineteen by Euripides (yu-**rip**-i-dēz; 485–406).[29] But most are lost. Each of these men wrote eighty or ninety plays, and all told, more than a thousand tragedies were performed between about 530 and 400 B.C.

General Features of Tragedy

In Greek, *tragoidia* seems to mean "goat song." Because goats were associated with Dionysus, at whose spring festivals in Athens tragedies were staged, the name may derive from songs performed while goats were sacrificed in the god's honor.

The script of a tragic play was in some ways like a modern screenplay. It was not meant to be read, but served as a prompt book for a live performance. After performance, copies of the scripts circulated. They were studied in schools and quoted to impress, but Greek literature was always meant to be heard, not read as you are reading this book.

Tragedy was popular entertainment, directed to the concerns of Athenian citizens, including their tastes for patriotic propaganda, horror, violence, and conflict between the sexes: themes that still draw audiences. Aeschylus is the earliest tragedian whose works survive. He loved long, elaborate descriptions, especially of foreign lands, and high-flown metaphors containing words of his own invention (the despair of modern students!). He used myth to explore grand moral issues like the conflict between individual will and divine destiny. His characters tend to be types, embodying some principle. Aeschylus lived through Athens' rise to greatness, and his epitaph (which he himself composed) says he fought at Marathon but does not mention his literary achievements. His play *The Persians* (472 B.C.) is the only surviving tragedy that does not have a mythical theme (though others did exist).[30] Setting tragedies in the heroic age allowed tragedians to experiment with stories that were already known to their audiences and to fill them with colorful kings, queens, and gods. By staging the core moral issues that faced democratic society against the backdrop of palaces or the Trojan War, poets could make their points much starker than if they told stories set in their own world.

Sophocles' career exactly coincides with the highpoint of Athens' political power. Born six years before Marathon, he died two years before Athens' defeat in the Peloponnesian War. His vivid characters are typically locked in bitter conflict. He liked to show the dignity of noble individuals caught in overwhelming crises with superior—often divine—forces. His heroes are lonely and unbending. They learn too late how to behave. He was deeply influenced by folklore: In all his plays, a prophecy or oracle predicts an unexpected outcome.

More of **Euripides**' work survives than of Aeschylus' and Sophocles' combined. He subjected traditional myths to rigorous scrutiny and sometimes severe criticism. His characters are often deflated heroes, mere mortals caught up in all-too-human squabbles. Aristotle remarked that Sophocles showed men as they ought to be, but Euripides showed them as they really are. Euripides reflected contemporary Athenian rhetoric more than did Sophocles or Aeschylus; most of his plays center on a long debate. He liked to celebrate emotion's power over reason.

In Aeschylus, inherited curses and divine will motivate action; in Sophocles, fate stands behind events; in Euripides, passionate, often erotic, and especially female emotion drives action. He is the most modern tragedian. His plays were often revived later in antiquity and are commonly performed today. His complex plots led directly to the conventions of so-called New Comedy, which we discuss in Chapter 21, "Hellenistic Culture, 323–330 B.C.," still important today in popular entertainment.

The Origins of Tragedy

According to the fourth-century philosopher Aristotle, whose *Poetics* is the earliest surviving work of literary criticism, tragedy developed in the late-sixth century B.C. out of **dithyrambs,** hymns to Dionysus danced and sung (presumably to accompany goat sacrifices) by choruses of fifteen or so members with a chorus-leader. Dithyrambs continued to be performed in the fifth century, and this example, from about 470 B.C., tells of the hero Theseus' arrival in Attica. The chorus sings and dances, and the chorus-leader, taking the part of Theseus' father Aegeus (ē-jūs), responds to them:

> **Chorus:** King of sacred Athens, lord of the
> luxurious-living Ionians,
> why has the bronze-belled trumpet
> just now sounded a war song?
> Does some enemy of our
> land beset our borders,
> leading an army?
> Or are evil-plotting robbers,
> against the will of the shepherds,
> rustling our flocks of sheep by force?
> What is it that tears your heart?
> Speak; for I think that you
> of all mortals have the aid
> of valiant young men at your disposal,
> son of Pandion and Creusa.
>
> **Aegeus:** Just now a herald arrived, having come
> by foot on the long road from the Isthmus.°
> He tells of the indescribable deeds
> of a mighty man. That man killed overweening
> Sinis,° who was the greatest of mortals in strength;
> he is the son of Lytaeus the Earthshaker,° son of Cronus. And he has
> slain the man-killing boar in the valleys of Cremmyon, and reckless
> Sciron. He has closed the
> wrestling school of Cercyon;
> Procoptes° has met a better man
> and dropped the powerful
> hammer of Polypemon.
> I fear how this will end.
>
> **Chorus:** Who is the man said to be,
> and from where? How is he equipped?
> Is he leading a great army
> with weapons of war?
> Or does he come alone

°*Isthmus:* The narrow neck of land joining mainland Greece to the Peloponnesus.
°*Sinis:* We now get a list of the deeds of Theseus, parallel to the Labors of Heracles.
°*the Earthshaker:* That is, Poseidon.   °*Procoptes:* Another name for Procrustes.

with only his attendants, like a traveler
wandering among foreign people,
this man who is so strong, valiant, and bold,
who has overcome the powerful strength
of such great men? Indeed a god impels him,
so that he can bring justice
down on the unjust; for it is not
easy to accomplish deed after deed
and not meet with evil.
In the long course of time all things come to an end.

Aegeus: The herald says that only two men
accompany him, and that he has a sword
slung over his bright shoulders . . . and two
polished javelins in his hands,
and a well-made Spartan hat
on his head with its fire-red hair.
A purple tunic covers
his chest, and a woolen
Thessalian cloak.
Bright red Lemnian fire flashes
from his eyes.° He is a boy in the
prime of youth, intent on the
playthings of Ares: war and
battles of clashing bronze.
He is on his way to splendor-loving Athens.

Bacchylides, *Dithyramb* 5 (D. Svarlien)

°*Fire flashes from his eyes.* The island of Lemnos was home to an ancient fire-cult.

The chorus is inquiring and speculative, whereas the voice of Aegeus is explanatory and authoritative. Actors and chorus had similar roles in tragedy. Something is happening: A stranger is coming to town, Aegeus' son, whom Aegeus has not seen from birth and does not yet recognize. In describing Theseus' glory, Aegeus unknowingly describes his own heir, so there is tension between what Aegeus knows and what the audience knows. This too is common in Greek tragedy. If this dithyramb resembles earlier dithyrambs, we can perhaps see how tragedy developed from it. Homer sang in the third person, saying that "Aegeus did such and such," but now a man pretends to be Aegeus and speaks as him. Some Greeks ascribed this radical innovation to Arion, a great sixth-century Corinthian singer. Arion visited Sicily and Italy (according to one story, unscrupulous sailors threw him overboard, but a dolphin, hearing his beautiful song, carried him safely home). But most Greeks attributed the crucial innovations to the Athenian **Thespis** (hence our word *thespian,* for actor), active in the 530s B.C. while Pisistratus was tyrant.

We might guess that Thespis (if it really was he) stepped forth from the chorus wearing a mask and pretended to be a mythical character. The use of masks in both tragedy and in the cult of Dionysus (Figure 15.1) may support Aristotle's statement that tragedy grew out of Dionysiac celebrations, but is more likely to have fulfilled a

Figure 15.1 Women followers dance and play flutes around an image of Dionysus consisting of a mask on a stake draped with robes; on a red-figure wine cup, circa 450 B.C. *Staatliche Museen zu Berlin/Bildarchiv Preussischer Kulturbesitz, Berlin, Germany/Photo by Ingrid Geske-Heiden/Art Resource, NY.*

wholly practical need. The actor selected a moment of choice in a hero's career. By changing his mask, he could be a second figure in the story, also speaking in the first person. The soul of *drama* ("things done") is conflict, and without choice, there is no conflict. The "hero in conflict" is the basic plot of Greek tragedies, and Thespis must have found some way of presenting it. In the dithyramb quoted above, there is no conflict and hence no drama.

For decades, tragedies remained highly stylized performances in which a single actor responded to the chorus' songs. Aristotle says that Aeschylus transformed the genre in the 470s B.C. by adding a second actor and reducing the chorus' role. The **protagonist** (literally, "first actor") could now come into direct conflict with another hero (the **antagonist**) and interact not just with the chorus. Aeschylus' surviving plays present dialogues between one actor and the chorus or the chorus-leader, while in his most famous works, a group of three plays (trilogy) called the *Oresteia* ("Story of Orestes," performed in 458 B.C.), he uses a third actor, an innovation that Aristotle attributes to Sophocles. Oddly, there never were more than three actors in a Greek tragedy.

Most tragedies were performed at the festival of the **City Dionysia,** which Pisistratus, who controlled Athens in the 530s B.C., reformed from an older festival. The City Dionysia, in honor of the god of wine, was a gigantic public symposium for the whole *dêmos* from which he drew political support. As poetry decorated the intimate aristocratic symposium, so did tragedy (and other poetry) decorate the symposium of the *dêmos*. As the aristocrats had formed and sealed political alliances in the intimacy of the "men's room," so now did the City Dionysia bring together the whole *dêmos* as a single political force under Pisistratus' leadership.

If Thespis did invent the new genre of tragedy, most likely Pisistratus exploited Thespis' invention for patriotic purposes. When the tyrants fell in 510 B.C., the popular tragic performances continued and spread, eventually, all across the Greek world. In Athens herself, tragedy became the quintessentially democratic art form, while in Syracuse the tyrants sponsored tragedies, just as Pisistratus had done. Hiero hired Aeschylus to write a play in 476 B.C. to celebrate his foundation of a new colony and had *The Persians* performed in Syracuse. Aeschylus returned to Sicily at the end of his life, by which time the tyrants had been overthrown. He died in Gela in 456 B.C.

The Forms of Tragedy

The masked actors, never more than three, were always men. Early masks were not exaggerated, as are the familiar "comic" and "tragic" masks with up- and down-turned mouths, but were realistic. There were stock character types: the old man, the young girl, the young man, the king, the slave. Masked actors could communicate emotion only through words and gestures, not facial expressions.

Choral song remained an essential element in fifth-century tragedy. The dancers were accompanied by double pipes called *auloi* (a kind of oboe with a hollow vibrating reed). Music was as vital to ancient plays as it is to contemporary cinema but is not represented in surviving texts. Most tragedies have five choral songs called *stasima* (singular, *stasimon*), "songs sung in place," interspersed with portions of dialogue called **episodes,** "side-songs." The action takes place in the dialogue, while choral song offers reflections, not always close, on events in the plot. The presence of a choral song often indicates the passage of time.

The meters of the choral passages are complex, reflecting ancient dance steps, now unknown. They are abstract, impressionistic, and filled with invented words that do not occur elsewhere, impossible without the technology of the Greek alphabet, which made this form of entertainment possible. Modern scholars do not so much read Greek choruses as interpret them (as any comparison of different translations of Aeschylus' *Oresteia* quickly reveals).

The *episodes* of *tragoidia* are in simple meters, starkly different from choral song. The dialogue is often formalized, as when each speaker speaks in turn exactly one line (called *stichomythia,* "speaking line by line"), and reminiscent of ritual, as when two speakers sing a lament or a hymn of victory.

THE CITY DIONYSIA

An archon presided over this major tragic festival. Each year, he chose three tragic and five comic poets and granted each a chorus. The Assembly imposed liturgies on eight rich men, requiring each to pay to train the actors for one of the poets (see Chapter 13, "Democracy and Empire: Athens and Syracuse, 479–431 B.C."). Because of the three-actor rule, each actor performed several parts; Euripides' play *The Suppliants* has twelve speaking parts! If the man paying for the play had political ambitions, he might spend heavily on lavish effects to impress the *dêmos*. Athenian tragedy was intimately involved with democratic politics.

The City Dionysia lasted for five days in late March, at the time of the spring harvest, and was the civic highlight of the year. Two days before the festival, the poets presented a public summary of the plays and introduced the actors. On the day before the festival, the statue of Dionysus was removed from his small shrine near the theater, taken to the countryside, then brought back to the city and set up in the theater to oversee the play. On the first day of the festival was a magnificent procession. Many participants carried large models of erect penises, tributes to Dionysus' life-giving power. At the end of the parade, bulls were killed, the meat eaten, and much wine drunk. Then came choral performances in which men and boys danced while singing. The second day began with another sacrifice, followed by awards to those who had benefited the state. Young men whose fathers died fighting for the *polis* paraded in new armor provided by the state. Then the plays began.

Only one complete group of three tragedies survives, Aeschylus' *Oresteia,* performed in 458 B.C., which tells of Agamemnon's murder by his wife and his son Orestes' revenge and fate. Trilogies by other poets, however, seem to have been related only loosely by theme, if at all. On the fifth day, five comedies were staged. Two days after the festival, the assembly met in the theater to review the conduct of the festival.

As a struggle among poets and their patrons, entertainment at the City Dionysia had a lot in common with athletic contests (see Chapter 8, "Archaic Greece, 700–480 B.C.: Economy, Society, Politics"). In both, contests between the rich entertained the *dêmos;* in both, the winners received symbolic prizes, special wreaths. The real competition was for the honor and glory of serving the *polis,* not for wealth. Ten men drawn by lot from the ten Athenian tribes acted as judges. Their judgments do not always agree with ours: Euripides took first prize only four times in his long career, while Sophocles' *Oedipus the King* (429 B.C.), which many think to be the finest story ever crafted and was for Aristotle the model tragedy, took second prize.

THE THEATER OF DIONYSUS

The earliest tragedies were performed on the south slope of the Acropolis. In the late sixth century, there was no theater, but only an *orchêstra,* a circular "dancing place" outside a small shrine to Dionysus. At the center of the *orchêstra* was a round altar. The audience sat at first on the slopes of the hill, then in permanent stone seats in the *theatron* ("viewing area"), the origin of our word "theater."

A changing hut or *skênê* ("tent"), probably made of wood, was added behind the orchestra. There the actors could change their masks. The *skênê* had a single door through which actors entered and left, and a platform that could be rolled out into the *orchêstra.* This device was probably used for a famous scene in Aeschylus' *Agamemnon* (the first play in the *Oresteia*) in which Clytemnestra murders her husband Agamemnon offstage, inside the *skênê,* then suddenly appears, exulting over his body.

There was probably no stage during the sixth and fifth centuries, but there were special effects. A crane called a *mêchanê* ("device") was attached to the top of the *skênê,* used in Euripides' *Medea* to whisk away the murderess on a chariot "drawn by dragons." Some tragedies ended when the *mêchanê* lowered an actor playing a god down to the earth to resolve a complicated plot. The familiar Latin phrase **deus ex machina,** "god from the machine," comes from this technique and refers to

Figure 15.2 The Theater of Dionysus today, looking southwest. The horseshoe-shaped *orchêstra* is Roman, but the seating is fifth century B.C. The ancient sanctuary to Dionysus lay where the trees are in the picture.

any abrupt ending to a story. In Sophocles' *Philoctetes*, for example, the Greeks must possess Philoctetes' bow in order to take Troy, but he hates them too much to give it up. The hero Heracles, who had once possessed the bow, appears from the *mêchanê* and settles the dispute. At first, there was no scenery of any kind. Aristotle credited Sophocles with inventing painted scenery, presumably wooden panels attached to the front of the *skênê*. But scenery was never important in tragedy.

Surviving ruins of the Theater of Dionysus give us some idea of what it might have looked like in the fifth century, although most of the theater was rebuilt in Roman times. In Figure 15.2, the once round *orchêstra* has taken on a horseshoe shape, according to Roman preference. Ruins of the fourth-century *skênê* are visible in the background.

NARRATIVE STRUCTURE

In Chapter 6, "Homer," we explained that the *Iliad* and *Odyssey* have tripartite plots. They begin with a setup, explaining the situation, leading to the first plot point in which something happens to create conflict. Conflict dominates the middle of the story, until a second plot point opens the final stage, or resolution. We find the same basic structure (or *muthos*, "plot") repeated endlessly in modern novels and films: girl meets boy (beginning), girl loses boy (middle), girl finds boy (end). For all their sophistcation, tragedies worked the same way.

For example, in the setup of Sophocles' *Antigonê* (an-**tig**-o-nē; c. 441 B.C.), King Creon has issued a stern decree: It is a capital crime to bury Polynices (pol-i-**nī**-sēz), who attacked his own city of Thebes with a foreign army and was killed in a duel with his loyal brother Eteocles, who also died. Antigonê buries her brother Polynices anyway. She is caught, arrested, and brought before Creon (the first plot point).

In the middle portion, Sophocles generates conflict at many levels. Antigonê is young; her antagonist Creon is middle-aged. She is female; he is male. He is the king; she is a civilian. He invokes the power of the state; she invokes the power of the family and its obligations. They have one thing in common: Neither will yield. Further conflict appears between son and father when Creon's son Haemon, engaged to Antigonê, pleads for his fiancée. The prophet Tiresias reveals unfavorable omens, but Creon thinks he is taking bribes: thus religion conflicts with the state.

Antigonê is condemned to death and enters a cave where she will die, the second plot point. Conflict can have one of two outcomes. Either a deal is struck between the contenders and the conflict resolved, or one party to the conflict is removed or destroyed. In tragedy we find both outcomes, although the second is more common (hence our word *tragic*). In *Antigonê*, Creon, a late-learner, realizes his error and attempts to forestall the consequences of his actions. Alas, he reaches the cave too late to save Antigonê, who has killed herself; so ends her conflict with Creon. Haemon attempts to kill his own father, then kills himself; so ends the conflict between Creon and Haemon. Creon returns to the palace to discover that his wife has hanged herself, almost an afterthought, as if Sophocles were trying to exaggerate Creon's suffering. Creon is a broken man. The End.

Euripides' *Bacchae* (404 B.C.) provides a more complex example. This time we learn the background to the setup in a prologue, a device invented or elaborated by Euripides, when a god comes on stage to tell us what has happened before the story begins. In this case Dionysus, disguised as a stranger, explains how after a long journey in the East he has returned to his hometown of Thebes to take revenge on his mother's sisters, who slandered his mother by denying that her lover was Zeus. This, then, is a revenge play.

The citizens, including the ancient king Cadmus and the prophet Tiresias (who behave ludicrously in their religious devotion), go into the mountains to revel and adore the power of Dionysus. The stranger (Dionysus in disguise) is arrested and brought before Pentheus, the first plot point: the action turns to the conflict between Pentheus and Dionysus, who face off in a long **agôn**, or "contest," a formal debate common in the middle of Greek tragedies. The *agôn* rhetorically parallels debates in the Assembly and lawcourts, where each side had a chance to speak. They debate in *stichomythia*, "line-by-line talk":

Pentheus: First then tell me who your family is.
Dionysus: I can tell you this easily, without boasting. I suppose you are
             familiar with flowery Tmolus.°
Pentheus: I know of it. It surrounds the city of Sardis.
Dionysus: I am from there, and Lydia is my fatherland.
Pentheus: Why do you bring these rites to Hellas?
Dionysus: Dionysus, the child of Zeus, sent me.

°*Tmolus:* A mountain that rises behind Sardis in Lydia.

Pentheus: Is there a Zeus who breeds new gods there?

Dionysus: No, but the one who married Semelê here.

Pentheus: Did he compel you at night, or in your sight?

Dionysus: Seeing me just as I saw him, he gave me sacred rites.

Pentheus: What appearance do your rites have?

Dionysus: They cannot be told to mortals uninitiated in Bacchic revelry.

Pentheus: And do they have any profit to those who sacrifice?

Dionysus: It is not lawful for you to hear, but they are worth knowing.

Pentheus: You have counterfeited this well, so that I desire to hear.

Dionysus: The rites are hostile to whoever practices impiety.

Pentheus: Are you saying that you saw clearly what the god was like?

Dionysus: He was as he chose; I did not order this.

Pentheus: Again you diverted my question well, speaking mere nonsense.

Dionysus: One will seem to be foolish if he speaks wisely to an ignorant man.

Pentheus: Did you come here first, bringing the god?

Dionysus: All the barbarians celebrate these rites.

Pentheus: Yes, for they are far more foolish than Hellenes.

Dionysus: In this at any rate they are wiser; but their laws are different.

Pentheus: Do you perform the rites by night or by day?

Dionysus: Mostly by night; darkness conveys awe.

Pentheus: This is treacherous towards women, and unsound.

Dionysus: Even during the day someone may devise what is shameful.

Pentheus: You must pay the penalty for your evil contrivances.

Dionysus: And you for your ignorance and impiety toward the god.

Pentheus: How bold the Bacchant° is, and not unpracticed in speaking!

Dionysus: Tell me what I must suffer; what harm will you do to me?

Pentheus: First I will cut off your delicate hair.

Dionysus: My hair is sacred. I am growing it for the god.

Pentheus: Next give me this *thyrsus*° from your hands.

Dionysus: Take it from me yourself. I bear it as the ensign of Dionysus.

Pentheus: We will guard your body within, in prison.

Dionysus: The god himself will release me, whenever I want.

Pentheus: Yes, when you call him, standing among the Bacchae.°

Dionysus: Even now he sees my sufferings from close by.

Pentheus: Where is he? He is not visible to my eyes.

Dionysus: Near me, but you, being impious, do not see him.

Pentheus: (to attendants) Seize him. He insults me and Thebes!

Dionysus: I warn you not to bind me, for I am in my senses and you are not.

Pentheus: And I, more masterful than you, bid them to bind you.

Dionysus: You do not know why you live, or what you are doing, or who you are.

Pentheus: I am Pentheus, son of Echion and Agavê.

Dionysus: You are well-suited to be miserable in your name.°

Euripides, *Bacchae* 460–510 (T. A. Buckley)

°*Bacchant:* A follower of Bacchus (Dionysus).   °*thyrsus:* A phallic staff carried by the followers of Dionysus (see Figure 15.1).   °*Bacchae:* Women followers of Dionysus. °*Pentheus:* A pun in Greek, because the king's name Pentheus sounds like the word *penthos,* "sorrow."

The *agôn* rehearses the play's central conflicts: traditional religion (Pentheus) against religious innovation (Dionysus); cousin against cousin (Pentheus' mother Agavê is the sister of Dionysus' mother Semelê); the ignorant (Pentheus) against the knowing (Dionysus); Greeks (Pentheus) against barbarians (Dionysus); day (Pentheus) against night (Dionysus); state (Pentheus) against religion (Dionysus); masculine (Pentheus) against effeminate (Dionysus); visible (Pentheus) against invisible (Dionysus); the sane/insane (Pentheus) against the insane/sane (Dionysus); the strong/weak (Pentheus) against the weak/strong (Dionysus).

Pentheus imprisons Dionysus, but the god escapes and in a second *agôn* entrances Pentheus, tempting him to spy on the Bacchae abroad in the woodland. The deluded Pentheus agrees (plot point two), which leads to resolution of the plot in Pentheus' dismemberment at the hands of his own mother and aunts.

CHARACTER AND OTHER DIMENSIONS OF TRAGEDY

Tragedies have plots, but also have *characters,* from a Greek word meaning "imprint." We might think of character as the sum of the choices that one makes. Tragedians rarely invented characters from whole cloth, but borrowed them from tradition. Odysseus was the clever man who relied on intelligence, not force; Agamemnon, the braggart who set self-importance above his people's interests; Hector, the family man doomed to a frightful end along with the family he cannot save; and Achilles, the warrior-intellectual who would not compromise ideals for self-interest. Yet within these boundaries the poet was free to invent. For Euripides, as for everyone else, Helen was the lovely seductress, self-pitying but charming, who abandoned husband, family, and reputation from desire for another man. But in his *Trojan Women* (415 B.C.), he makes her refuse to accept responsibility for her choice, blaming Aphrodite (sexual attraction), while in his *Helen,* he says she never went to Troy at all and the whole war was fought over a phantom!

In myths, characters are divine beings, mortals, or even talking animals, but tragic characters are nearly always humans (Aeschylus' Prometheus is an exception). Most are kings and queens; so far as we know, not one of the thousand tragedies performed between about 530 and 400 B.C. focused exclusively on the doings of gods and goddesses. In earlier Near Eastern (nondramatic) literature, by contrast, the principals are usually gods and goddesses (except for the human king Gilgamesh). The tragic characters' high social standing gave their choices gravity and consequence. Hence, Antigonê's choice to bury her brother against King Creon's mandate was a matter of state, not just a family dispute. Pentheus' choice to deny the new god destroyed his dynasty.

Aristotle notes that

> Tragedy is a *mimesis* [representation] of an action that is heroic and complete and of a certain magnitude—by means of language enriched with all kinds of ornament, each used separately in the different parts of the play: It represents men in action and does not use narrative, and through pity and fear it effects *katharsis* [relief] to these and similar emotions. . . .

Necessarily every tragedy has six constituent parts, and on these its quality depends. These are plot, character, diction, thought, spectacle, and song. . . . This list is exhaustive, and practically all the poets employ these elements, for every drama includes alike spectacle and character and plot and diction and song and thought.

The most important of these is the arrangement of the incidents [that is, plot], for tragedy is not a *mimesis* of men but of a piece of action, of life, of happiness and unhappiness, which come under the head of action, and the end aimed at is the *mimesis* not of qualities of character but of some action; and while character makes men what they are, it is their actions and experiences that make them happy or the opposite. . . . The plot [*muthos*] then is the first principle and as it were the soul of tragedy: Character comes second.

Aristotle, Poetics 1449b–1450a (W. H. Fyfe)

Aristotle's concept of **mimesis** ("representation" or "imitation") is the most discussed term in literary criticism. By "*mimesis* of an action that is heroic and complete and of a certain magnitude," Aristotle means that "action" is central to this form of poetry. Other kinds of poetry represent not action, but a point of view or a state of mind. Because of the characters' high status, "what happens" is heroic and has consequences, unlike in some forms of modern literature that focus on people who do not possess power, whose acts lack consequences beyond their personal lives. The *mimesis* is "complete" because the issues raised in the middle portion of the plot, where conflict rages, are resolved in the third portion.

Modern film, to which we have compared tragedy's structure, is a story told in pictures within a dramatic context, with dialogue, but the stories of Greek tragedy, as they have come to us, are told in words. In this respect, tragedy and film are very different. Aristotle distinguishes between the spoken words of the *episodes* within which the action takes place and the choral songs. The story is "acted out," we might say, unlike in epic (which tells the story in the third person) or in film (which tells it in pictures accompanied by dialogue).

When the audience watches the *mimesis* of an action, the members feel pity for what the characters suffer, and they fear that the same fate might befall themselves. Tragedy allowed the audience to feel intense, sometimes disturbing emotions that cannot be experienced in real life without terrible cost. This may be what Aristotle meant by **katharsis,** "relief," a cleansing that audiences feel after experiencing the powerful emotions that a strong drama brings forth. People go to movies to experience tension and release. Dramatic art that does not generate tension is poor dramatic art. Tragedy, therefore, painlessly expands one's experience as a human being. No more effective answer has ever been offered to the censors who, throughout history, have policed entertainment to make it conform to preconceived notions of what is proper.

To Aristotle's penetrating observations, we might add several. Driving the plot is the protagonist's **dramatic need,** something he or she wants. Without dramatic need, there is no action, hence no plot and no drama. Oedipus' dramatic need in *Oedipus the King* is to find the truth about the death of Laius. Antigonê's dramatic need is to bury her brother. Pentheus' dramatic need is to stop the new religion. The tragedians took their technique of story-telling from Homer. Hence, Achilles' dramatic need in the *Iliad* is to avenge an insult; Odysseus' dramatic need is to return home. In the third part of the plot, the resolution, the dramatic need is either met or not, which concludes the action. Oedipus learns who killed Laius; Antigonê buries her brother and pays the price; Pentheus fails to stop the new religion.

TRAGIC PLOTS

It is striking how rarely tragedians drew on the *Iliad* and *Odyssey* for their stories. Instead, they borrowed tales from the more manageable, lost epic poems called the Cyclic Poems, which told the rest of the story of the Trojan War. Tragic plots fall into several types. *Revenge* drives Aeschylus' *Oresteia* (the trilogy consisting of *Agamemnon, Libation Bearers,* and *Eumenides*). Clytemnestra kills her husband Agamemnon because he killed their daughter. Orestes kills his mother Clytemnestra to avenge his father Agamemnon's death. To avenge the matricide, the Furies persecute Orestes. Only enlightened decision by an Athenian lawcourt in the third play can resolve the conflict. In Euripides' *Bacchae,* Dionysus takes revenge on his aunt for slandering his mother. Revenge is a primitive form of justice and appeals to the audience's moral instincts, then as now.

Another recurring plot element is the *foundling.* Oedipus was exposed as an infant, found, raised in a foreign land, then discovered. Foundling stories can reveal the horrors of self-discovery. In Euripides' *Ion,* Ion is exposed as an infant, survives, then as an adult is nearly put to death by his own mother. Another common pattern is the *suppliant* story, where an exile is thrown on the mercy of a foreign potentate, the story of Sophocles' *Oedipus at Colonus.* Oedipus comes as an old man to Theseus of Athens, seeking refuge from his own sons. In Aeschylus' *Danaids,* the fifty daughters of Danaüs, who have murdered their husbands, beg protection from the king of Argos.

Human sacrifice, a form of horror, has high entertainment value and can form an essential plot element. In Euripides' *Iphigenia at Aulis,* Agamemnon prepares to kill his daughter Iphigenia, a fate that she accepts, while in his *Iphigenia among the Taurians,* Iphigenia (saved from sacrifice at Aulis by Artemis) seeks to sacrifice her own brother. Corollary to human sacrifice is the theme of the *bride of death,* where a female virginal victim laments her lot, complaining that death is the only husband she will know. Antigonê makes such a complaint as she enters the cave to die.

Such themes motivate the action that the play represents, as the protagonist works through beginning and middle to the end. Aristotle analyzed the shape this trajectory might take. Tragedy's aristocratic and royal characters rise to high fortune, then in a "turning around," **peripeteia,** accompanied by a "recognition," **anagnorisis,** they come to a "down-turning," **katastrophê** (our "catastrophe"), which reverses fortune. Aristotle speculates on what leads to *katastrophê,* emphasizing **hamartia,** "missing of the mark" or "mistake":

> The structure of the best tragedy should be not simple but complex, and one that represents incidents arousing fear and pity—for that is peculiar to this form of art. It is obvious to begin with that one should not show worthy men passing from good fortune to bad. That does not arouse fear or pity but shocks our feelings. Nor again wicked people passing from bad fortune to good. That is the most untragic of all, having none of the requisite qualities, because it does not satisfy our feelings or arouse pity or fear. . . .

There remains the mean between these. This is the sort of man who is not preeminently virtuous and just, and yet it is through no badness or villainy of his own that he falls into misfortune, but rather through some *hamartia* ["mistake"], he being one of those who are in high station and good fortune, like Oedipus and Thyestes° and the famous men of such families as those. The successful plot must then have a single and not, as some say, a double issue; and the change must be not to good fortune from bad but, on the contrary, from good to bad fortune, and it must not be due to villainy but to some great *hamartia* in such a man as we have described, or of one who is better rather than worse. This can be seen also in actual practice. For at first poets accepted any plots, but today the best tragedies are written about a few families . . . whom it befell to suffer or inflict terrible disasters.

Aristotle, Poetics, 1452b–1453a (W. H. Fyfe)

° *Thyestes:* Brother to Atreus, who fed Thyestes his own children.

Early scholars mistranslated *hamartia* as "flaw," leading to theories of the "tragic flaw." Probably by *hamartia* Aristotle meant misidentification, as when Iphigenia mistook her brother Orestes for a stranger and potential sacrificial victim. Many readers, however, want the word *hamartia* to imply a broader intellectual or moral fault and seek these in tragic characters. In any event, protagonists do not deserve their misfortune, but bring it on themselves through an error of judgment. So Oedipus mistook the man who struck him on the road for a brigand, not realizing it was his own father. His hastiness exaggerated the consequences of this mistake, but he was not morally responsible for the disasters that befell him. Oedipus did not mean to kill his father. Still, had he been less inclined to violence, he might not have done so, and in this sense his *hamartia* has led him to make a wrong decision at a moment of crisis. Agamemnon wreaked violence on Troy, but did not deserve to be murdered by his wife in a bathtub. He made a mistake when he saw her as loving and devoted, when really she was an adulteress with a taste for murder.

The plots in tragedy are a web of family histories. Tragedians showed little interest in great mythic cycles of creation, battles of Titans and Olympians, or the births and loves of gods; the focus was on the passions and horrors of family life. No possibility is omitted: sons kill mothers, wives kill husbands, sons kill fathers, mothers kill children, a father kills his daughter or son or all his children, a daughter kills her father, brothers kill each other, sons kill their stepmothers, mothers expose their infants to die, men and women kill themselves. Sexual trespass is as varied as violence. A son sleeps with his mother, a father rapes his daughter, adultery is rampant, lustful women seduce honorable men (never the reverse), husbands desert their wives and mistresses. Complementing such extreme dishonesty are intense love and devotion between brother and sister, brother and brother, father and son, husband and wife, father and daughter.

CONCLUSION

Two-and-a-half thousand years have passed since Arion or Thespis put on masks and addressed their choruses. Greek tragedy can seem alien and stiff to modern audiences, but those familiar with its conventions can still experience the powerful *katharsis* that Aristotle described. It seems like an unlikely art form for a democratic *polis:* Its characters are royal and aristocratic, and often female, expressing and acting on extreme emotions, and consistently rejecting the cooperative values of the egalitarian city-state. But the tragedians took characters from the heroic age, like Agamemnon and Antigonê, and recreated their lives against the background of contemporary values, which the choruses regularly celebrate. The tragedies asked how great individuals like Odysseus could fit into real, everyday society. Not very well, it turns out.

THE ORIGINS OF COMEDY

We normally think of "comedy" as something that makes us laugh—stand-up comics or TV shows like *Friends*. Literary critics use the word in a more technical sense to mean a genre that may not be funny at all. A comedy is any story that ends happily. In this sense, the *Odyssey* (unlike the *Iliad*) is a comedy, although it is rarely funny. But the Greek word *kômoidia*, "song of the *kômos*," referred to something more specific.

Aristotle's analysis of comedy is lost except for his observations that comedy came "from those leading off phallic songs" (*Poetics* 1449a), just as he claimed that tragedy began "from those leading off the dithyramb." Phallic songs certainly were sung in processions for Dionysus that could also carry large penises, and comic choruses often had large phalluses as part of their costumes. One of the curious features of comedy, the parabasis ("stepping forth"), where the action stops while the chorus sometimes comes forward to insult audience members, may conceivably derive from similar behavior during phallic processions. The evidence for the origins of comedy, however, is even less clear than for tragedy. Scattered accounts suggest that at Athens, Syracuse, and several other cities, performers began turning *kômoi*, a form of drunken revel shown on vases, into true dramas in the late sixth century, but we know none of the details. Western Greeks may have taken the lead. By 500 B.C. or soon after, one Epicharmus was active at Syracuse. His characters were mythical, and he produced burlesques about Odysseus and Heracles, but only fragments survive from his plays. Some ancient scholars thought the small city of Megara was the home of comedy. Still, all surviving examples are Athenian, and we can take Athens as the home of comedy. The first comic victor at the City Dionysia was recorded in 486 B.C., but nothing survives from before 450 B.C. The first complete comedy is the *Acharnians*, produced in 425 B.C., by **Aristophanes** (ar-is-**tof**-a-nēz; c. 460–386 B.C.), one of the funniest men whoever lived. Eleven of Aristophanes' comedies survive complete. We know the names of another thirty-one of Aristophanes' works, but only fragments survive from the dozens of other fifth-century Athenian comics. Scholars call fifth-century Athenian comedy **Old Comedy** to distinguish it from the late-fourth-century plays we discuss in Chapter 21, the New Comedy.[31]

THE PLOTS OF OLD COMEDY

Tragedy drew its plots from heroic myth, and Epicharmus of Syracuse apparently did the same in some of his early comedies, but Aristophanes always produced original (albeit rudimentary) plots, set in the present. Aristophanes usually took an absurd situation in which an ordinary citizen stood in opposition to the mad world around him and, through some crazy scheme, got the better of everyone.

In the *Acharnians* (425 B.C.), a protagonist weary of Athens' war with Sparta makes a private peace treaty. He goes about his business as if there were no war, as for him there is not, declares a free market, and makes a lot of money. In the *Clouds* (423 B.C.), an Athenian impoverished by his son's extravagant ways sends him to Socrates' sophisticated "Thinkshop" to learn debating skills so he can argue his way out of paying the money he owes. In the *Peace* (421 B.C.), the hero flies to heaven on a dung beetle, releasing "peace" from imprisonment in a cave. In the *Birds* (414 B.C.), two disaffected Athenians flee the chaotic city to Cloudcuckooland, the idyllic home of the birds, where they plan a utopian new world. The Olympian gods are brought to their knees when the birds stop the smoke of sacrifice from reaching them. Thus the birds, with their Athenian advisors, become masters of the world. In another harebrained scheme, Athens' women deny sex to their (absent!) husbands and so end the Peloponnesian War, in the *Lysistrata* (411 B.C.). In the *Frogs* (405 B.C.), the god Dionysus, anxious about the decline of tragedy, goes to the underworld to bring back Euripides, who died the year before. After a contest, Dionysus brings back Aeschylus instead, much to Euripides' chagrin.

In all cases, comic plots assume that the world is mad. The protagonist is normally a man (occasionally a woman) of common sense and traditional civic values, but because the world is topsy-turvy, he or she has to do something insane to put it straight. In both the *Lysistrata* (411 B.C.) and the *Assemblywomen* (392 B.C.), women take control of Athens, hysterically funny to Athenian audiences, then institute a sex strike in the first play and introduce communal property (including sexual partners) in the second.

As such stories unfold, the characters and chorus indulge in brutal personal abuse against well-known political figures, no doubt sitting in the audience. In the lost play the *Babylonians* (426 B.C.), Aristophanes attacked the prominent politician **Cleon** (see Chapter 16, "The Peloponnesian War and Its Aftermath, 431–399 B.C.") so brutally that Cleon prosecuted him. Aristophanes' *Knights* of 424 B.C. represents Cleon as a pampered slave who robs and cheats his good-natured but lazy master Dêmos ("the people"). Cleon is worsted by a sausage seller who proves to be even more vulgar—and entertaining to Dêmos—than Cleon himself.

Aristophanes made fun of pretentious Athenians who wanted to be thought special, but also of overzealous democrats. Stupid and clever, rich and poor, young and old, were targets of his wit. His protagonists mean well, but they are full of vanities and foolishness. Aristophanes harks back to an idealized image of Athens in the "good old days" before the Peloponnesian War, lawcourts, the sophists, and other contemporary evils ruined everything.

THE STRUCTURES OF OLD COMEDY

Whereas the structure of tragedy is simple, consisting of alternating spoken portions (*episodes*) and choral song (*stasima*), the structure of Old Comedy is strikingly complex. In tragedy, the chorus rarely interacts with the actors or takes part in the action, but in comedy, the chorus regularly participates in the action. Conversations take place between the actors and the chorus-leader (*chorêgos*). The metrical patterns of the different portions of the play are highly formalized and complex, and of course lost in translation.

The first part of the play is the *prologos* ("speech in front") in which a leading actor warms up the audience and makes clear the general situation. Then comes the *parodos* ("side-road," referring to the entranceways on either side of the *orchêstra*), when the chorus comes in. In tragedy, there were twelve or fifteen members of the chorus, but in comedy, twenty-four. The chorus members introduce themselves by singing a song and by interacting, sometimes violently, with actors already on stage.

Then comes the *agôn*, which like the *agôn* in tragedy is a spirited debate. The victory of the one speaker resolves the conflict raised in the first part of the play and, in a way, the plot of the comedy ends here, in the middle of the play. The protagonist has already satisfied his dramatic need.

Next comes the *parabasis*, sung either by the chorus-leader or the whole chorus. Afterwards, the chorus has little role in the action. In the *parabasis*, the playwright speaks on his own behalf, a kind of sermon on contemporary political or social issues utterly unconnected to the plot, shattering the illusion of dramatic time and setting. You need to know a good deal about contemporary politics and life to understand what Aristophanes is talking about, and for this reason his plays are vital sources for historians. After the *parabasis* comes the sequence of *episodes* that explores the consequences of the protagonist's success, interspersed with choral songs that abuse individual named members of the audience. Here is a typical comic *episode*, the first after the *parabasis* in the *Acharnians*. Having won his point about making a separate peace, the protagonist Dicaeopolis (di-krê-**o**-po-lis, "justice of the city") conducts his free market. A man from Megara, a city near the Isthmus that suffered greatly because of Athenian policy, is so driven to hardship that he attempts to sell his daughters in Dicaeopolis' marketplace, pretending they are pigs. The politically incorrect humor depends on the dual meaning of the Greek word *choiros* (plural *choiroi*), which means either "piglet" or "female genitals," especially the hairless genitals of a young girl:

Dicaeopolis: These stones will mark the boundary of my market. It's open for trade to all the Peloponnesians, to all Megarians and Boeotians too° . . .

Dicaeopolis goes inside and an impoverished Megarian comes up with his two daughters.

Megarian: Hello, Athenian market, dear to Megara. I need you—holy friendship!—like a mommy. You dirty little brats, go get some chow for your poor dad, if you can turn some up. And listen! Give me your undivided bellies: do you want to be sold or starve to death?

Girls: Sold, sold!

Megarian: I'd say the same. But who'd be dumb enough to pay a cent for merchandise like you? So I've cooked up a real Megarian scam:° I'll pass you off as piggies for sale. Put on these piggy-hooves, and look like piggies from a purebred pig. By the God of Traders, if you get home unsold, I'll starve you both to death myself. Now put on these snouts too and climb up into this sack, and do a little grunting and oinking. Make just like piggies at the Mysteries.° I'll yell around for Dicaeopolis. Hey Dicaeopolis, you want to buy some piggies?

°*Boeotians too:* The Athenians had excluded Megarians and Boeotians from their markets as a means of political retaliation.   °*scam:* The Megarians were known for their underhanded ways.   °*Mysteries:* Pigs were sacrificed to Demeter and Persephonê at the mysteries of Eleusis.

Dicaeopolis: What's this? A Megarian?

Megarian: Sure, I've come to trade.

Dicaeopolis: How goes it there?

Megarian: We're always in front of the fire, fasting.°

Dicaeopolis: Feasting, yes that's nice, by god, if there's a live band. . . . Well, what have you got?

Megarian: I got some grade-A piggies.

Dicaeopolis: All right, let's see them.

Megarian: You're gonna like this fine. Go on and feel them. They're nice and soft.

Dicaeopolis: What's this supposed to be?

Megarian: I told you, piggies.

Dicaeopolis: Explain your meaning. Where's this from?

Megarian: From Megara. You say it ain't no piggy?

Dicaeopolis: Doesn't look it.

Megarian: Well I'll be damned. Look, this guy doesn't trust a thing. He says this ain't no piggy. I tell you what. I'll bet you a pound of salt that THIS [points between the girl's legs] is what every Greek calls a piggy.

Dicaeopolis: All right, but it's a human being's.

Megarian: Sure, belongs to me. Whose else you think it is? You wanna hear it squeal?

Dicaeopolis: Why certainly I would.

Megarian: OK now, piggy, make a sound. You won't? You're clamming up, damn you? I swear I'll take you home again!

Girl: Oink oink.

Megarian: That ain't no piggy?

Dicaeopolis: Looks like a piggy now, but when it's grown up it will be a snotch!

Megarian: In five years, I tell you, it'll be just like its momma.

Dicaeopolis: But this one isn't fit for sacrifice.

Megarian: No? How isn't it fit for sacrifice?

Dicaeopolis: It doesn't have a tail.°

Megarian: Too young. But when it fleshes out a bit it'll get the meat that's pink and long and hard. And if you want to rear one, here's another [pointing to the other girl].

Dicaeopolis: Its piggy looks just like the other one's.

Megarian: Why sure, it's got the selfsame mom and dad. And when it fattens up and grows some hair, it'll be a nice piggy to offer up to Aphrodite.

Dicaeopolis: But piggies don't get offered up to Aphrodite.°

Megarian: So piggy's not for Aphrodite? Who else then? And look, the flesh of these piggies is delicious when it's skewered on a spit.

Dicaeopolis: So tell me, can they suck without their mother?

Megarian: Hell yes. They'll suck without their father, too.

°*fasting:* Because they are so poor.   °*tail:* A sacrificial victim could not be deformed, with a pun on "tail" and "penis."   °*Aphrodite:* There were several deities to whom pigs were not sacrificed, including Aphrodite, the goddess of sex and love.

Dicaeopolis: And what do they like to suck on?
Megarian: Anything. Ask 'em yourself.
Dicaeopolis: Here piggy.
Girl: Oink oink!
Dicaeopolis: Would you like to gnaw this hambone?°
Girl: Oink oink.
Dicaeopolis: Then how about a lollipop?°
Girl: Oink oink!
Dicaeopolis: And how about you? Want one?
Other Girl: Oink oink!
Dicaeopolis: They oink so loud when I say lollipops!

Aristophanes, *Acharnians* 729–804 (J. Henderson)

°*hambone:* One of many Greek slang words for penis.   °*lollipop:* In Greek another slang word for penis.

The hilarious scene is typical of Aristophanic *episodes* in its raunchy obscenity, supported by the dramatic pretense of showing how the protagonist has taken advantage of his successful ploy, in this case to create an open market in the midst of war.

CONCLUSION

Drama evolved rapidly, from choral songs in the sixth century B.C. to highly formalized, powerful, and sophisticated performances in the fifth. It was not obvious to Aristotle why this had happened; twenty-three hundred years later, it is more obscure to us. Philosophers tried to make sense of nature and of how debate might generate truth; dramatists explored the same issues by looking at extreme cases, where reason and order broke down. The tragedians presented the spectacle of great individuals trapped in impossible situations; the comedians envisioned the consequences of ludicrous responses to the real world, while addressing contemporary political issues. Drama, like ritual, helped create feelings of solidarity in the community. It was not ritual, but a powerful tool for reflection on the human condition.

KEY TERMS

Aeschylus, 314
tragoidia, 315
Sophocles, 315
Euripides, 315
dithyrambs, 316
Thespis, 317
protagonist, 318
antagonist, 318
Oresteia, 318
City Dionysia, 318
episodes, 319
deus ex machina, 320

agôn, 322
mimesis, 325
katharsis, 325
dramatic need, 325
peripeteia, 326
anagnorisis, 326
katastrophê, 326
hamartia, 326
Aristophanes, 328
Old Comedy, 328
Cleon, 329

FURTHER READING

Tragedy

Csapo, C., and W. J. Slater, *The Context of Ancient Drama* (Ann Arbor, MI, 1995).

Easterling, Pat, *Greek and Roman Actors: Aspects of an Ancient Profession.* (Cambridge, UK, 2002). Superior modern study of many aspects of ancient drama.

Easterling, Pat, ed., *The Cambridge Companion to Greek Tragedy* (Cambridge, UK, 1997). Excellent essays on tragedy as an institution, literary features of the plays, and reception since antiquity.

Else, Gerald F., *The Origin and Early Form of Greek Tragedy* (New York 1972). Presents Thespis as the inventor of Greek tragedy.

Goldhill, Simon, *Reading Greek Tragedy* (Cambridge, UK, 1986). No-nonsense introduction to tragedy, aimed at students more familiar with English literature.

Nietzsche, F. W., *The Birth of Tragedy out of the Spirit of Music*, tr. W. Kaufmann (New York 1968). The German edition of this book, published in 1871, set the stage for the modern appreciation of the role of the irrational in Greek culture.

Pickard-Cambridge, Arthur W., *Dithyramb, Tragedy, and Comedy*, T. B. L. Webster, ed. (2nd ed., Oxford 1962). Thorough treatment of the evidence; indispensable to the study of the subject.

West, M. L., *Ancient Greek Music* (Oxford 1992). The definitive study.

Winkler, John J., and Froma I. Zeitlin, eds., *Nothing to Do with Dionysus? Athenian Drama in Its Social Context* (Princeton 1990). Collection of modern essays addressing the ritual and sociological settings of Athenian drama.

Winnington-Ingram, R. P., *Euripides and Dionysus* (Cambridge, MA, 1948). Contains a detailed examination of Euripides' *Bacchae.*

Comedy

Bowie, A. M., *Aristophanes: Myth, Ritual, and Comedy* (Cambridge, UK, 1993).

Cartledge, P. A., *Aristophanes and His Theatre of the Absurd* (Bristol, UK, 1990).

Dover, K. J., *Aristophanic Comedy* (Berkeley 1972). Pathbreaking analysis of the structures of Old Comedy.

Ehrenberg, V. *The People of Aristophanes* (2nd ed., Oxford 1951). Readable survey looking at Aristophanes' characters as evidence for everyday life in Athens.

Ancient Texts

Aeschylus, *Prometheus Bound and Other Plays* (Harmondsworth, UK, 1961; tr. Philip Vellacott) and *The Oresteia* (New York 1966; tr. Robert Fagles).

Aristophanes, *The Frogs and Other Plays* (New York 1964; tr. David Barrett), *Lysistrata and Other Plays* (New York 1973; tr. Alan Sommerstein), and *The Birds and Other Plays* (New York 1978; tr. David Barrett and Alan Sommerstein).

Euripides, *The Bacchae and Other Plays* (Harmondsworth, UK, 1954; tr. Philip Vellacott) and *Alcestis and Other Plays* (New York 1996; tr. John Davie)

Sophocles, *The Three Theban Plays* (Harmondsworth, UK, 1947; tr. R. Fagles) and *Electra and Other Plays* (Harmondsworth, UK, 1982; tr. E. F. Watling).

CHAPTER 16

THE PELOPONNESIAN WAR AND ITS AFTERMATH, 431–399 B.C.

The Peloponnesian War was an unmitigated disaster, destroying hundreds of thousands of lives and the accumulated wealth of decades. Athens' evolution toward a unified Aegean state collapsed. Persia re-entered the Aegean. Much of Sicily ended up paying tribute to Carthage, while Syracuse chafed under the strongest tyrant Greece ever saw. None of the politicians who led their states to war wanted or expected these outcomes.

Yet Thucydides says that even in 431 B.C., when the war began, the catastrophic nature of the conflict was clear:

> Thucydides the Athenian wrote the history of the war fought between Athens and Sparta, beginning the account at the very outbreak of the war, in the belief that it was going to be a great war, and more worth writing about than any of those that had taken place in the past. My belief was based on the fact that the two sides were at the very height of their power and preparedness, and I saw, too, that the rest of the Greek world was committed to one side or the other; even those who were not immediately engaged were deliberating on the courses that they were to take later. This was the greatest disturbance in the history of the Greeks, affecting also a large part of the non-Greek world, and indeed, I might almost say, the whole of humankind.
>
> Thucydides 1.1 (R. Warner)

Thucydides wrote or revised his account after the war's end in 404 B.C.; perhaps he credited himself with more foresight than he really had. But some Athenians and Spartans opposed the war from the beginning, and debate was fierce. In 431 B.C., Athens dominated the sea; Sparta, the land. The challenge was to convert control of one element into victory on the other. The twenty-seven-year struggle that followed was bewilderingly complicated but consisted of efforts by each side to do just this.

The war had three successive phases. The first (431–421 B.C.) is called the *Archidamian War*, after Archidamos, the Spartan king who invaded Attica each summer. The second phase (421–413 B.C.), known as the *Peace of Nicias*, begins with a treaty negotiated by the Athenian **Nicias** (**nis-ē-as**) and ends with Athens' defeat at Syracuse. The final phase, called the *Ionian War* because most action took place off the Ionian coast, dragged on from 412 to 404 B.C. After Athens' defeat in 404, civil war broke out in Athens, bringing in its train the execution in 399 of Socrates, one of Greece's most original thinkers. Four hundred miles away, in 409 B.C., Carthage invaded an exhausted Sicily, triggering wars that raged throughout the next century.

Nothing was the same after the Peloponnesian War.

THE ARCHIDAMIAN WAR, 431–421 B.C.

Pericles led Athens to war, but to do so he had to persuade the Assembly he could win it. As he saw things, the **Archidamian War** broke out because Sparta saw that left alone, Athens would keep centralizing power until she became irresistibly strong. For Athens, "winning" meant avoiding defeat; stalemate would leave Athens free to resume centralization, and would mean certain ruin for Sparta.

Pericles proposed a simple, two-part plan. First, stay behind the walls, keep the subject cities paying for the fleet, and use the fleet to protect the grain supply. Second, harass the enemy's coasts, seize offshore islands as bases, and keep up the military pressure. The Persian Wars consisted of a few key battles, but this would be a war of attrition. Eventually, Sparta would tire, back off, and Athens could resume her inexorable expansion, Pericles thought.

First Struggles

In summer 431 B.C., as its first act of aggression, the Spartan army invaded Attica, burned and plundered, then halted outside the city's walls. Sparta's strategy was to provoke Athens into a pitched battle. Sparta's superior hoplites would triumph, and Sparta could command the empire's dissolution. But the Athenians stayed behind the city walls and the Long Walls, secure in their access to the sea. The Spartans burned and plundered the countryside, then marched home. They returned in 430, and again in 429, and every year, but (as in the Greek siege of Troy) they could do nothing against the fortifications. So long as the grain ships kept coming from the Black Sea and landed in Piraeus, and the supplies were transported to the city through the Long Walls, Sparta could not defeat Athens (Map 16.1).

In traditional Greek warfare, one hoplite army invaded enemy territory and another marched out to stop it. The Athenians (like Odysseus) suppressed their anger as the Spartans burned crops and farmhouses. The crowding of refugees from the countryside into the space between the Long Walls created highly unsanitary conditions. In the heat of summer in 430 B.C., plague broke out, of which Thucydides gave a precise description. One in four Athenians died. The Athenians turned on Pericles. Morale sank and Athens sued for peace in 430. Receiving no reply, the Assembly dismissed Pericles as general and fined him. Even so, they pursued his strategy, then voted him back into office. But Pericles died of the

Map 16.1 The Archidamian War and the Peace of Nicias. Aegean sites mentioned in this chapter.

plague in 429. Thucydides saw the seed of Athens' defeat in Pericles' unexpected death:

> His successors did the exact opposite [from Pericles' policy], and in other matters which apparently had no connection with the war private ambition and private profit led to policies which were bad both for the Athenians themselves and for their allies. Such policies, when successful, only brought credit and advantage to individuals, and when they failed, the whole war potential of the state was impaired.

This happened because

> Pericles' successors, who were more on a level with each other and each of whom aimed at occupying the first place, adopted methods of demagogy which resulted in their losing control over the actual conduct of affairs. Such a policy, in a great city with an empire to govern, naturally led to a number of mistakes, among which was the Sicilian expedition,[32] though in this case the mistake was not so much an error of judgment with regard to the opposition to be expected as a failure on the part of those who were at home to give proper support to their forces overseas. Because they were so busy with their own personal intrigues for securing the leadership of the people, they allowed this expedition to lose its impetus, and by quarreling among themselves began to bring confusion into the policy of the state. And yet, after losing most of their fleet and all the other forces in Sicily, with revolutions already breaking out in Athens, they none the less held out for eight years against their original enemies, who were now reinforced by the Sicilians, most of whom had revolted, and against Cyrus, son of the king of Persia, who later joined the other side and provided the Peloponnesians with money for their fleet.

And in the end it was only because they had destroyed themselves by their own internal strife that they were forced to surrender.

Thucydides 2.65 (R. Warner)

After Pericles died, his quarreling successors abandoned his limited war aims. Instead of trying to outlast Sparta, they pursued high-risk strategies aiming actually to destroy Sparta and the Peloponnesian League.

The Spartans also explored new strategies. Invading Attica would not win the war, so Sparta looked to her ally Corinth to provide the nucleus of a fleet to defeat Athens at sea. In 429 B.C., the year that Pericles died, the Corinthians engaged the Athenian fleet in the Gulf of Corinth. Fearing the Athenians' skill, the Corinthians formed a circle, rams facing out. The Athenians responded by sailing round and round the circle, occasionally darting in to threaten a ship. One after another, the Corinthian ships backed water to avoid being rammed until they backed into each other, entangling their sterns and losing all order. The Athenians wiped them out.

After this, Sparta avoided naval engagements. When Mytilenê—the main city on the island of Lesbos just off the coast of Asia Minor (opposite ancient Troy), one of Athens' most important allies—revolted in 427 B.C., Sparta offered support but was too afraid of Athens' fleet to deliver any. Pericles' successors became more aggressive, hoping to find allies among the warlike peoples in the western parts of mainland Greece (Acarnania, Aetolia, Ambracia) who could provide enough troops to defeat Sparta in battle. The imaginative Athenian general **Demosthenes**[33] apparently hoped to use these new allies to force Boeotia onto Athens' side, then Corinth, and then defeat Sparta. His plan seemed to be working when in 424 B.C., the Boeotians shattered the new alliance in a pitched battle.

Thwarted in western mainland Greece, the Athenians looked further west, to Sicily (see Map 16.2). As we saw in Chapter 13, "Democracy and Empire: Athens and Syracuse, 479–431 B.C.," Syracuse was reviving as a major power in the 430s, and in 427 a general Sicilian war broke out. The Dorian cities sided with Syracuse (founded by Dorian Corinth) against the Ionian cities. Ionian Leontini north of Syracuse, a victim of Syracusan aggression, appealed to its 433 B.C. treaty with Athens. For the first time, an Aegean power was to intervene in western struggles. By 424 Athens had sixty ships and as many as ten thousand men in Sicily. Alarmed by Athens' imperial intentions, both Ionian and Dorian Sicilians called a secret congress, where, Thucydides says, Hermocrates of Syracuse (about whom we read more later) delivered this warning:

"If we are sensible, we should realize that this conference is not simply concerned with the private interests of each state; we have also to consider whether we can still preserve the existence of Sicily as a whole. It is now, as I see it, being threatened by Athens, and we ought to regard the Athenians as much more forceful arguments for peace than any words that can be spoken by me. They are the greatest power in Greece, and here they are among us with a few ships, watching for us to make mistakes, and, though by nature we must be their enemies, they are, under the cover of a legal alliance, trying to arrange matters to suit themselves. Now if we fight among ourselves and call in the help of the Athenians, who are only too willing to join in whether they are called for or not; if we then proceed to use our own resources in weakening ourselves, thus doing the preliminary work for their future empire, the likely thing to happen is that, when they see us

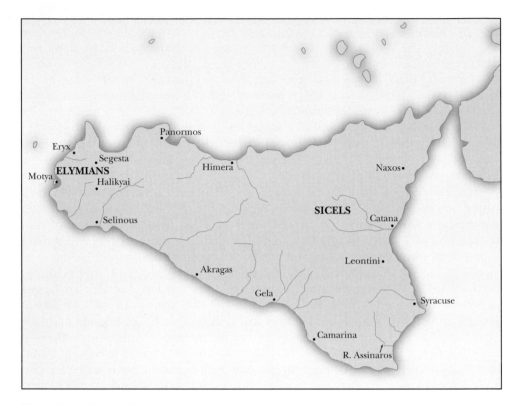

Map 16.2   Sites in Sicily mentioned in this chapter.

exhausted, they will come here one day with larger forces and will attempt to bring all of us under their control."

Thucydides 4.60 (R. Warner)

The Sicilian cities concluded a general peace and sent the Athenians away. When Athens' generals got home, the Assembly prosecuted them for taking bribes: Why else did they fail to conquer Sicily and bring back its hoplites to turn against Sparta? Confident as ever, Athens tried to raise another anti-Syracusan alliance in 422 B.C., but this too failed. Even Athens' vast wealth could not support strategic initiatives on this scale. In 427 B.C., Athens introduced new taxes and in 425 tripled the tribute from the subject cities. Still Athens gained no advantage over Sparta.

Pylos

During a routine mission harassing the coast of the Peloponnesus in 425 B.C., Demosthenes noticed that the northern headland on the bay of **Pylos** (the modern Bay of Navarino), near the famous Bronze Age palace of Homer's Nestor, would make a good base for raiding Sparta and encouraging the helots to revolt. Demosthenes landed a small force and hastily fortified the headland with a wall of driftwood (Map 16.3). When the Spartans heard, they cut short that summer's invasion of

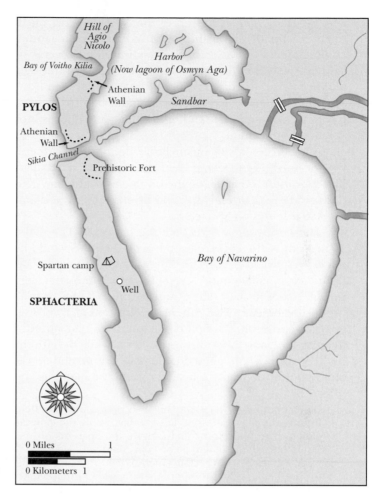

Map 16.3 Map of the Pylos campaign, 425 B.C.

Attica and rushed back to the Peloponnesus. Terrified that the Athenian base would inspire a helot uprising, the Spartans

> made a proclamation that the helots should choose out of their own number those who claimed to have done the best service to Sparta on the battlefield, implying that they would be given their freedom. This was, however, a test conducted in the belief that the ones who showed most spirit and came forward first to claim their freedom would be the ones most likely to turn against Sparta. So about 2000 were selected, who put garlands on their heads and went round the temples under the impression that they were being made free men. Soon afterwards, however, the Spartans did away with them, and no one ever knew exactly how each one of them was killed.
>
> Thucydides 4.80 (R. Warner)

The Spartans sailed their own small fleet into the Bay of Pylos, whose outlet is blocked by the long narrow island of **Sphacteria** except for passageways at either end of the island. They landed 420 hoplites on the island, hoping to barricade the channels at either end so that Athenian ships could not sail into the bay.

The Spartans then sailed up to the Athenian fort on the mainland opposite the northern tip of the island and tried to force a landing. One Spartan ship was commanded by **Brasidas,** who was wounded several times trying to establish a bridgehead. Thucydides noted the peculiarity of this fight: "It was indeed a strange alteration in the ordinary run of things for Athenians to be fighting on land—and Spartan land too—against Spartans attacking from the sea, and for Spartans to be trying to make a naval landing on their own shores, now hostile to them, against Athenian opposition."

After three days of inconclusive fighting, the Athenian fleet, which had sailed farther north after leaving Demosthenes on the headland, returned. The Spartans had forgotten to barricade the entrances to the bay. The Athenian ships sailed in, destroyed the Spartan ships, and by encircling the island with their ships, trapped the 420 hoplites on Sphacteria.

The besiegers had become the besieged. The 420 Spartiates made up about 10 percent of the entire citizen body—their loss would be very grave. Sparta immediately requested a truce. In Athens, **Cleon,** a popular speaker at the height of his influence, persuaded the Assembly to reject the offer, certain that once Athens held the Spartiates hostage, she would get much better terms. Capturing them, however, would not be easy. The Athenians' position at Pylos was almost as difficult as the Spartans' position. Pro-Spartan helots dived beneath the encircling Athenian ships to bring food and water onto Sphacteria, while the Athenian besiegers grew short of both. As the crisis dragged on, the Assembly turned on Cleon, who had opposed the Spartan offer of peace. A heated Assembly debate rapidly spun out of control:

> Cleon pointed at Nicias, the son of Niceratos, who was then general and whom he hated. Putting the blame on him, he said that if only the generals were real men, it would be easy to take out a force and capture the Spartans on the island; certainly he himself would have done so, had he been in command.
>
> At this there was a certain amount of murmuring among the Athenians against Cleon for not being willing to sail now, if the whole thing seemed to him so easy, and Nicias, noticing this and at the same time finding himself attacked by Cleon, told him that, so far as the generals were concerned, he could take out whatever force he liked and see what he could do himself. Cleon's first impression was that this offer was only made as a debating point, and so he was ready enough to accept it; but when he realized that the command was being handed over to him quite genuinely, he began to back out of it, saying that it was Nicias, not he, who was general. He was now in fact thoroughly frightened, because he never imagined that Nicias would have gone so far as to give up his post to him. Nicias, however, repeated his offer and called on the Athenians to bear witness that he was standing down from the command in Pylos.
>
> The Athenians behaved in the way that crowds usually do. The more that Cleon tried to get out of sailing to Pylos, and the more that he tried to take back what he had said, the more they encouraged Nicias to hand over his command and they shouted at Cleon, telling him that he ought to sail. The result was that Cleon, finding that there was no longer any possibility of going back on what he had said, undertook to go on the voyage.
>
> Thucydides 4.38 (R. Warner)

Just before Cleon arrived at Sphacteria, a fire broke out on the island, driving the Spartans to the cliffs on the northern tip. Cut off from water and food, with no prospect of resupply, to Greece's astonishment, the 120 surviving Spartiates surrendered to Cleon. No Spartiate had ever surrendered before.

Brasidas in Thrace

Invasions of Attica were fruitless, and since 429 B.C. Sparta had avoided challenging Athens at sea. By 424, she approached Persia to finance a fleet against Athens, but was rebuffed. In 424, the ingenious Brasidas, who had attacked Demosthenes' fortifications at Pylos, realized that not all Athens' subjects were protected by the sea. Some of the richest lay on the mainland of northern Greece, where Spartan troops could reach them. Dubious of his strategy, fearful of his personality, and depressed by the Pylos incident, the Ephors refused to let Brasidas take any Spartiates north. Undeterred, he set off with just seven hundred helots and a thousand mercenaries. Passing undiscovered through pro-Athenian territories, he suddenly showed up outside Amphipolis, the most important city in the region, and offered generous terms for their surrender.

Athens sent Thucydides (author of the famous history) with ships and men to relieve the city, but hours before he arrived Amphipolis went over to Sparta. Thucydides reports dispassionately that "in this way the city was surrendered, and late on the same day Thucydides with his ships sailed into Eion [a nearby harbor]. As for Amphipolis, Brasidas had just taken it, and was within a night of taking Eion too. If the ships had not arrived so quickly to relieve it, it would have been in his hands by dawn." The Athenian Assembly exiled Thucydides for twenty years. He used this time to write his pathbreaking *History*, one of the great intellectual achievements of the classical cultural revolution.

The fall of Amphipolis shocked the Athenians, who sent Cleon with a large force to regain it. In a great battle outside Amphipolis in 422 B.C., both Cleon and Brasidas were killed. As Aristophanes put it in one of his comedies, "the two pestles that mixed up the war were broken," and the struggle in the north Aegean fizzled out.

Athens and Sparta were exhausted. Despite ten years of bloody sacrifice, neither had a strategy that delivered victory. In 421 B.C. the aristocratic Nicias, the now-dead Cleon's bitter enemy, negotiated a settlement and the return of the 120 Spartiates captured at Pylos. On Pericles' terms, Athens had won: Sparta had failed to break up the empire. Few Greeks seriously thought the struggle was over.

Toward Total War

As Athens and Sparta pursued their ineffective strategies, they grew increasingly desperate and brutal. When Mytilenê revolted against Athens in 427, the Athenians quickly crushed the rebellion, but it terrified them. They could not afford to fight many uprisings like this. The Assembly angrily voted to kill all the men in Mytilenê and sell the women and children into slavery: righteous treatment for foul treachery! They dispatched a squadron to carry out the order.

The next day, stricken with remorse, the Council of 500 called a second meeting. Cleon defended the original decision, but a certain Diodotos, otherwise unknown, spoke vigorously against it. If rebels knew they would die whatever they did, there would be no incentive for them to surrender, and they would fight to the death. Also, with everyone dead, there would be no one to pay taxes.

The Athenians relented, rescinded the order, and sent out a fast ship to overtake the earlier. The second ship reached Mytilenê just as the general was beginning the executions. They would kill only one thousand of the leading citizens, the new decree read, and the others would be spared. Both Cleon and Diodotos argued in terms of expediency—what would help Athens win the war—not in terms of right and wrong. Immediately after describing the cold-blooded debate over Mytilenê, Thucydides turns to Spartan crimes at Plataea, the only city to have helped Athens in the battle of Marathon in 490 B.C. In 427 B.C. Sparta captured Plataea, allied with Athens. The Spartans put the Plataeans on trial, asking each man one question: "What have you done to help the Spartans and their allies in the present war?" Of course they had done nothing. The Spartans executed the 225 captured men and sold the women and children into slavery.

The war's ever-greater brutality inflamed the conflicts within elites and between rich and poor that had divided *poleis* since archaic times. In 427 B.C. a pro-Athenian democratic faction on the island of Corcyra off the northwest coast of Greece defeated its aristocratic rivals in street fighting, then slaughtered everyone they could get their hands on. In one of his most vivid passages, Thucydides describes the breakdown of traditional values in the midst of civil war:

> The Corcyreans continued to massacre those of their own citizens whom they considered to be their enemies. Their victims were accused of conspiring to overthrow the democracy, but in fact men were often killed on grounds of personal hatred or else by their debtors because of the money they owed. There was death in every shape and form. And, as usually happens in such situations, people went to every extreme and beyond it. There were fathers who killed their sons; men were dragged from the temples or butchered on the very altars; some were actually walled up in the temple of Dionysus and died there.
>
> So savage was the progress of this revolution, and it seemed all the more so because it was one of the first that had broken out. Later, of course, practically the whole of the Greek world was convulsed, with rival parties in every state—democratic leaders trying to bring in the Athenians, and oligarchs trying to bring in the Spartans. In peacetime there would have been no excuse and no desire for calling them in, but in time of war, when each party could always count upon an alliance that would do harm to its opponents and at the same time strengthen its own position, it became a natural thing for anyone who wanted a change of government to call in help from outside. In the various cities these revolutions were the cause of many calamities—as happens and always will happen while human nature is what it is, though there may be different degrees of savagery, and, as different circumstances arise, the general rules will admit of some variety. In times of peace and prosperity cities and individuals alike follow higher standards, because they are not forced into a situation where they are forced to do what they do not want to do. But war is a stern teacher; in depriving them of the power of easily satisfying their daily wants, it brings most people's minds down to the level of their actual circumstances.
>
> So revolutions broke out in city after city, and in places where the revolutions occurred late the knowledge of what had happened previously in other places caused still new extravagances of revolutionary zeal, expressed by an elaboration in the methods of seizing power and by unheard-of atrocities in revenge. To fit in with the change of events, words, too, had to change their meanings. What used to be described as a thoughtless act of aggression was now regarded as the courage one would expect to find in a party member; to think of the future and wait was merely another way of saying one was a coward; any idea of moderation was just an attempt to disguise one's unmanly character; ability to understand a question from all sides meant that one was totally unfitted for action. Fanatical enthusiasm was the mark of a real man, and to plot against an enemy behind his back was perfectly legitimate self-defense . . .

Love of power, operating through greed and through personal ambition, was the cause of all these evils. To this must be added the violent fanaticism that came into play once the struggle had broken out. Leaders of parties in the cities had programs that appeared admirable—on one side political equality for the masses, on the other the safe and sound government of the aristocracy—but in professing to serve the public interest they were seeking to win the prizes for themselves. In their struggles for ascendancy nothing was barred; terrible indeed were the actions to which they committed themselves, and in taking revenge they went further still. Here they were deterred neither by the claims of justice nor by the interests of the state. Their one standard was the pleasure of their own faction at that particular moment, and so, either by means of condemning their allies through an illegal vote or by violently usurping power over them, they were always ready to satisfy the hatreds of the hour. Thus neither side had any use for conscientious motives; more interest was shown in those who could produce attractive arguments to justify some disgraceful action. As for the citizens who held moderate views, they were destroyed by both the extremes, either for not taking part in the struggle or in envy at the possibility that they might survive.

As the result of these revolutions, there was a general deterioration of character throughout the Greek world. The simple way of looking at things, which is so much the mark of a noble nature, was regarded as a ridiculous quality and soon ceased to exist. Society had become divided into two ideologically hostile camps.

Thucydides 3.81–83 (R. Warner)

Only victory mattered; massacres, enslavements, and betrayals were simply tools; he who did not use them in pursuit of his own interests was a fool.

THE PEACE OF NICIAS AND THE SICILIAN EXPEDITION, 421–413 B.C.

The **Peace of Nicias** left too many things unsettled. The terms required Sparta to return Amphipolis to Athens, but Amphipolis refused to go, so Athens responded by keeping its fortress at Pylos. The treaty ignored Sparta's allies Corinth, Thebes, and Megara, who refused to sign. War smoldered on in some areas. Spartan allies spoke of breaking from Sparta and even joining Athens.

Within Athens, a young man in his late twenties named **Alcibiades** (al-si-**bī**-a-dēz), an Alcmaeonid, felt personally insulted by the treaty. His family had once represented Spartan interests in Athens, and Alcibiades thought that he, not Nicias, should have negotiated the peace. His family also gave him strong connections with leading men in other cities, and he set about undermining the fragile peace. Alcibiades was one of the extraordinary personalities of this period. Working independently of the Assembly, by 418 B.C. he put together an alliance between Athens, Argos, and other Peloponnesian cities. He achieved by diplomacy what Athens had failed to do in the Archidamian War, assembling such a threatening army that Sparta felt compelled to risk her survival on a hoplite battle, while keeping the risk to Athens at a minimum (only thirteen hundred of the allied troops were Athenian). A great battle at Mantineia in the Peloponnesus showed Sparta's strengths and weaknesses. As at Plataea in 479 B.C., stubborn officers ignored orders they did not like, and when the armies clashed, the Spartan line was already in fragments. As Thucydides explains, "So far as skill in maneuvering goes, the Spartans had had the worst of it in every respect, but certainly they now showed that in courage they had no equals." The Spartans stood their ground and cut down all who came against them. Alcibiades' alliance might have broken the power of Sparta, but by winning the hoplite battle at Mantineia, Sparta restored much of the prestige and influence lost at Pylos.

The Massacre at Melos

In 416 B.C., Athens decided to force the small independent Cydadic island of **Melos** to submit and pay tribute. The Melians had done nothing, but the Athenians worried that the mere existence of an independent island implied Athenian weakness. Athens gave Melos an ultimatum: Join or be destroyed. The Melians replied that they had a defensive alliance with Sparta, who would protect them, and that because they had done no wrong, they would trust in the gods. Thucydides has the Athenian embassy reply with a chilling statement of *Realpolitik*, the way things are in the world of secular power:

> "So far as the favor of the gods is concerned, we think we have as much right to that as you have. Our aims and our action are perfectly consistent with the beliefs men hold about the gods and with the principles that govern their own conduct. Our opinion of the gods and our knowledge of men lead us to conclude that it is a general and necessary law of nature to rule whatever one can. This is not a law that we made ourselves, nor were we the first to act upon it when it was made. We found it already in existence, and we shall leave it to exist forever among those who come after us. We are merely acting in accordance with it, and we know that you or anybody else with the same power as ours would be acting in precisely the same way."

They gave the Melians some good advice:

> "We recommend that you should try to get what it is possible for you to get, taking into consideration what we both really do think; because you know as well as we do that, when these matters are discussed by practical people, the standard of justice depends on the equality of power to compel and that in fact the strong do what they can and the weak do what they must."
>
> Thucydides 5.105, 89 (R. Warner)

The Melians nonetheless rejected Athens' terms. There was a siege, betrayal from within, and a brutal outcome: "The Athenians put to death all the men of military age whom they took, and sold the women and children as slaves. Melos itself they took over for themselves, sending out a colony of 500 men." Sparta did nothing. The Athenians now decided on a new gamble to win the Peloponnesian War.

The Decision to Attack Sicily, 415 B.C.

Despite setbacks in the 420s, Athens had in 418 or 417 B.C. made new alliances with the non-Greek Elymian cities of Segesta and Halikyai in western Sicily (Map 16.2). The powerful Greek city Selinous—allied to Syracuse—constantly tried to expand into Elymian territory, and in 416 the Elymians asked their old ally Carthage for help. The Carthaginians, seeing that intervention would lead to war with Syracuse, refused. Segesta then approached her new ally Athens, saying that if Athens pushed Selinous out of Elymian lands, Segesta would pay all the costs. An Athenian embassy went to Sicily to investigate Segestan resources. Every night, the ambassadors ate off gold and silver plates in a different nobleman's house. The Athenians were impressed, not noticing that there was only one set of plates, passed from house to house. Next, the Segestans showed the Athenians chests of gold and silver in the mountaintop sanctuary of Eryx. Under the top layer of riches there were just rocks, but the Athenians did not look beneath the surface.

The embassy's favorable report set Athens abuzz. The cautious Nicias opposed wild adventures in Sicily, but Alcibiades saw a way to conquer all of Sicily. By 415 B.C., Alcibiades was young, rich, handsome, talented, and impossible to deal with:

> Alcibiades wanted to oppose Nicias, with whom he had never seen eye-to-eye in politics and who had just now made a personal attack on him in a speech. Stronger motives still were his desire to hold the command and his hopes that it would be through him that Sicily and Carthage would be conquered—successes that would at the same time bring him personally both wealth and honor. For he was very much in the public eye, and his enthusiasm for horse-breeding and other extravagances went far beyond what his fortune could supply. This, in fact, later on had much to do with the downfall of the city of Athens. For most people became frightened at a quality in him that was beyond the normal and showed itself both in the lawlessness of his private life and habits and in the spirit in which he acted on all occasions. They thought he was aiming at becoming a tyrant, and so they turned against him. Although in a public capacity his conduct of the war was excellent, his way of life made him objectionable to everyone as a person; thus they entrusted their affairs to other hands, and before long ruined the city.
>
> Thucydides 6.15 (R. Warner)

Nicias and Alcibiades had a furious argument in the Assembly, but Alcibiades convinced Athens to launch her grandest expedition. Thucydides implies that the Athenians, like Xerxes before them, had lost all sense of the limits of their power. With Sparta bloodied but unbowed, Persia waiting in the wings, and Syracuse the third-greatest city in Greece, Alcibiades was talking about conquering all of Sicily, south Italy, and Carthage. But the Athenians "were for the most part uninformed on the size of the island and of the numbers of its inhabitants, both Greek and native, and they did not realize that they were taking on a war of almost the same magnitude as their war against the Peloponnesians."

Nicias tried to dissuade the Assembly by emphasizing what huge forces the expedition would require, only to fuel the Athenians' imperial desires:

> There was a passion for the enterprise that affected everyone alike. The older men thought that they would either conquer the places against which they were sailing or, in any case, with such a large force, could come to no harm; the young had a longing for the sights and experiences of distant places, and were confident that they would return safely; the general masses and the average soldier saw the prospect of getting pay for the time being and of adding to the empire so as to secure permanent paid employment in the future.
>
> Thucydides 6.24 (R. Warner)

The Assembly was uncomfortable with either Nicias or Alcibiades as sole commander, but the pair could not work together. The Assembly therefore appointed *three* commanders: Nicias, Alcibiades, and Lamachus, a grizzled veteran, hoping that each man would compensate for the others' limitations. Instead, they came up with three different plans. Nicias said they should go to Segesta, settle its war with

Selinous, and come home. Alcibiades said they should send heralds to all Sicilian cities except Selinous and Syracuse, raise a general anti-Syracusan league, and conquer the whole island. Lamachus said they should go straight to Syracuse, take it by surprise, and storm it. Eventually, they agreed to Alcibiades' plan.

> This expedition that first set sail was by a long way the most costly and finest-looking force of Greek troops that up to that time had ever come from a single city . . . to the rest of Greece it looked more like a demonstration of the power and greatness of Athens than an expeditionary force setting out against the enemy . . . what made this expedition so famous was not only its astonishing daring and the brilliant show that it made, but also its great preponderance of strength over those against whom it set out, and the fact that this voyage, the longest ever made by an expedition from Athens, was being undertaken with hopes for the future which were, when compared with the present situation, of the most far-reaching kind.
>
> Thucydides 6.31 (R. Warner)

One morning just before the fleet was to sail, the Athenians woke up to a shocking sight. Outside Athenian houses were small statues called **herms,** which turned away evil.[34] A herm (somehow related to the god Hermes) was a block of stone with a face and an erect penis (Figure 16.1). During the night, someone had taken chisels and mutilated the herms. The Athenians feared a plot against the democracy, because the herms symbolized the freedom, manhood, and equality of each Athenian citizen at the head of his houschold. The Assembly rounded up suspects and tortured slaves to gain evidence. They learned nothing about the mutilation, but discovered that a group of young aristocrats had been parodying the rituals of Demeter at Eleusis ("the Eleusinian Mysteries") in drunken parties in their homes. Alcibiades belonged to this group.

Alcibiades' rivals waited until the fleet had sailed, then persuaded the Assembly to recall him to stand trial for his impious behavior. Most of Alcibiades' supporters were with the fleet and would not be able to help him. About to be arrested in southern Italy, Alcibiades jumped ship and fled to Sparta, where he received a warm welcome, with disastrous consequences for all.

The Siege of Syracuse, 415–413 B.C.

Nicias and Lamachus persevered with Alcibiades' strategy. They hoped that the Sicilian cities would join Athens and that Syracuse would give up without a fight. Naxos, an Ionian city in eastern Sicily, welcomed them as saviors, but until some Athenians burst in through a badly closed gate, neighboring Catana refused them entrance, even though it was also Ionian. Segesta paid only half the money promised; in return, Athens did nothing to stop Selinous' war with Segesta. Everyone else turned the Athenians away. Sicilian Greeks feared Syracusan aggression, but they feared the Athenians even more.

Lamachus' strategy was probably right; many Syracusans did not believe the Athenians would attack, and a sudden assault might have broken through the dilapidated walls. Instead, Nicias wasted precious months along the coast unsuccessfully trying to forge alliances. Not until winter did the Athenians assault Syracuse. They landed near the city and won a hoplite battle, but the city's walls were by now too strong to storm.

Figure 16.1 Herm from Athens, circa 520 B.C. This example was a hundred years old at the time of the Sicilian expedition. *National Archeological Museum, Athens/Hellenic Republic Ministry of Culture, Athens, Greece.*

Winter passed. Sparta, on Alcibiades' advice, sent the energetic general **Gylippos** (jī-**lip**-us) to assist the Syracusans. Also on Alcibiades' advice, Sparta fortified the hill of **Decelea** (de-se-lē-a) a dozen miles north of Athens and garrisoned it year round, forcing thousands of Athenian peasants to move permanently inside Athens' walls.

In Sicily, Nicias and Lamachus decided to invest Syracuse with a siege wall while the fleet cut off the city by sea (Map 16.4). Syracuse was as large as Athens, with forty thousand residents, and a tight siege would lead to starvation. The city occupied a small island, Ortygia, bridged to part of the mainland. To the south was the Great Harbor, spacious enough to receive a large fleet. The sea and seawalls surrounded the city, and just before the Athenians arrived, the Syracusans extended the walls on the land side. The walls now ran to the foot of the steep hill north of the city called Epipolai ("land above the city"). Whoever controlled Epipolai would control the city (Figure 16.2). The Athenians built a circle fort at the edge of Epipolai,

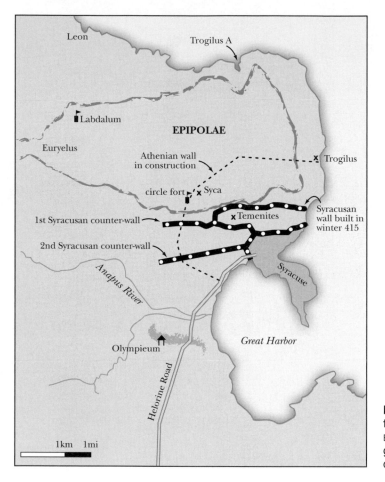

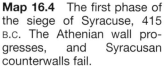

Map 16.4 The first phase of the siege of Syracuse, 415 B.C. The Athenian wall progresses, and Syracusan counterwalls fail.

overlooking the city. They began building walls extending out toward the sea on both sides of the fort, cutting the city off.

The Athenian walls quickly progressed. When the Syracusans tried to build counterwalls cutting across the enemy's construction line at right angles (the standard defensive measure), the Athenians stormed and destroyed them. Lamachus was killed in this fighting, but by now the Athenian siege wall was nearly complete. Syracuse was doomed.

But Nicias was not well; without Lamachus, he allowed progress on the last stretch of the wall across Epipolai to slow to a crawl. When Gylippos, the Spartan commander, approached the city, he learned that the wall was still not complete. Rather than going straight to Syracuse, he sailed to Himera in northwestern Sicily, raised troops, then raced back to Syracuse and attacked from behind, breaking through the unfinished Athenian line and entering the city. The defenders now threw up a new counterwall onto Epipolai, and this time cut the Athenian line, preventing the city's envelopment (Map 16.5). A dozen Corinthian ships evaded the Athenian blockade and sailed into Syracuse's Great Harbor, where on the city side

Figure 16.2 Syracuse as seen from Epipolai. Ortygia, covered by houses, can be seen on the left of the photo; in the center is the Great Harbor.

of the harbor the Syracusans were building new ships to challenge the Athenians at sea. The Athenians had no good beach to bring their own ships ashore, and their waterlogged hulls were decaying.

At the close of summer 414 B.C., Nicias realized the siege was failing. He sent a letter to Athens with an ultimatum: Either send out another force as great as the original, he said, or let him withdraw. Either way, he would resign the command because of ill health. The Assembly voted to send Demosthenes with a new force, but Nicias, they insisted, must remain in command.

Gylippos tightened his grip, capturing Nicias' forts guarding the south end of the Great Harbor. He seized large Athenian stores there. Syracusan ships intercepted and destroyed a convoy bringing timber for the Athenian fleet. Most of the non-Greek peoples of Sicily, who had suffered at the hands of Syracuse and Selinous, now supported Athens, but all the Greek cities on Sicily except Akragas supported Syracuse.

Gylippos no longer aimed just to save Syracuse; he wanted to destroy the whole Athenian force. Gylippos added heavy timbers to the prows of the Syracusan ships. In a decisive battle in the Great Harbor, the heavy Syracusan ships smashed the bows of the Athenian ships, sank many, and forced the Athenian fighters to take refuge within their defenses on land.

At this crucial moment, Demosthenes sailed into the Great Harbor with seventy-three new Athenian ships, five thousand fresh hoplites, and many light infantry. Nicias' men rejoiced as the Syracusans pulled back. Demosthenes soon realized that

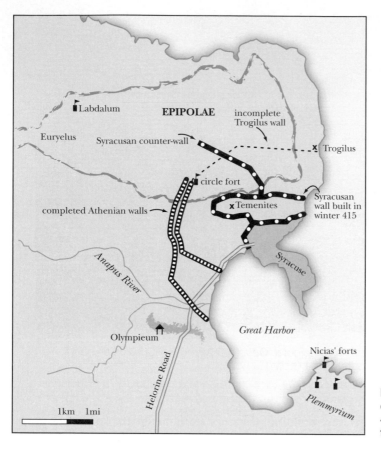

Map 16.5 The second phase of the siege of Syracuse, 414 B.C. The Syracusan counterwall succeeds.

the only chance for victory was to break through the Syracusan counterwall on Epipolai and finish the encirclement. Demosthenes gambled on a night attack. At first, all went well, but the Athenians fell into confusion and were driven off with terrible loss.

It was now impossible for Athens to take Syracuse. They must get away as quickly as possible. But Nicias, who at first deferred to Demosthenes, reasserted his authority. He insisted that traitors were about to betray Syracuse, and in any case he preferred an honorable death in Sicily to execution in Athens on charges of treason.

Vital days slipped away. Sickness spread and morale plummeted. Nicias conceded that Syracuse would not be betrayed to him. He agreed to retreat, but on the evening of August 27, 413 B.C., as the army was packing to pull out, there was an eclipse of the moon, "and Nicias," says Thucydides, "who was rather addicted to divination and such things, said that until they had waited the thrice nine days recommended by the omen-interpreters, he would not even join in any further discussion of how the move should be made."

Twenty-seven days is a long time in war. Gylippos threw a pontoon bridge across the mouth of the Great Harbor, trapping the Athenian ships inside. The

Athenians launched a final, desperate attack on the pontoons, as the two armies watched:

> While the issue of the battle at sea still hung in the balance, great was the stress and great the conflict of soul among the two armies on the shore. . . . For the Athenians everything depended on their navy; their fears for the future were like nothing they had ever experienced . . . as the fight went on and on with no decision reached, their bodies, swaying this way and that, showed the trepidation with which their minds were filled, and wretched indeed was their state, constantly on the verge of safety, constantly on the brink of destruction. So, while the result of the battle was still in doubt, one could hear sounds of all kinds coming at the same time from this one Athenian army—lamentations and cheering, cries of "We are winning" and of "We are losing," and all other great exclamations bound to be made by a great army in its great danger. Much the same were the feelings of the men on board the ships, till finally, after the battle had lasted for a long time, the Syracusans and their allies broke the Athenian resistance, followed them up with great shouting and cheering, and chased them back, clearly and decisively, to the land. And now the whole fleet, apart from the ships that were captured afloat, ran on shore, some going one way, some another, and the men fled from their ships toward the camp. As for the army on land, the period of uncertainty was over, and now one impulse overpowered them all as they cried aloud and groaned in pain for what had happened, some going down to help the ships, while others (and these were the majority) began to think of themselves and how they could get away alive. Indeed, the panic of this moment was something greater than they had ever known.
>
> Thucydides 7.71 (R. Warner)

In panic, some forty thousand survivors in the Athenian force, stationed along the wall on the Epipolai and on the shore of the Great Harbor, abandoned the siege and marched north, hoping to fight their way through to Catana, friendly to Athens (see Map 16.3). The Syracusans guarded the road, and after two days the Athenians turned back, heading southwest for Camarina on the south coast. Everywhere they went, Syracusan cavalry harassed them. Short of food and water under the baking September sun, they struggled as far as the river Assinaros, a swift-flowing river.

> The Athenians hurried on toward the Assinaros, partly because they were under pressure from the attacks made on them from every side by the numbers of cavalry and the masses of other troops, and thought that things would not be so bad if they got to the river; and partly because they were exhausted and were longing for water. Once they reached the river, they rushed down into it, and now all discipline was at an end. Every man wanted to be the first to get across, and, as the enemy persisted in his attacks, the crossing now became a difficult matter. Forced to crowd in close together, they fell on each other and trampled each other underfoot; some were killed immediately by their own spears, others got tangled among themselves and among the baggage and got swept away by the river. Syracusan troops were stationed on the opposite bank, which was a steep one. They hurled down their weapons from above on the Athenians, most of whom, in a disordered mass, were greedily drinking in the deep river-bed. And the Peloponnesians came down and slaughtered them, especially those who were in the river. The water became foul, but nevertheless they went on drinking it, all muddy as it was and red with blood; indeed, most of them were fighting among themselves to have it.
>
> Thucydides 7.84 (R. Warner)

More men died in the retreat than in the whole of the rest of the Sicilian campaign. The Syracusans captured Nicias and Demosthenes and put them to the sword on the spot. They herded the seven thousand or so survivors into deep stone quarries outside Syracuse.

> There were many of them, and they were crowded together in a narrow hole, where, since there was no roof over their heads, they suffered first from the heat of the sun and the stifling closeness of the air; and then in contrast came on the cold autumn nights, and the change in temperature brought disease among them. Lack of space made it necessary for them to do everything in the same spot; and besides, there were the bodies—all heaped together on top of one another—of those who had died from their wounds or from the changes of temperature or from other such causes, so that the smell was unbearable. And at the same time they suffered from hunger and thirst. For eight months the daily allowance for each man was half a pint of water and a pint of grain. In fact they suffered everything that you can imagine might be suffered by men imprisoned in such a place....
>
> This was the greatest Greek action that took place during this war, and, in my opinion, the greatest action that we know of in Greek history—to the victors the most brilliant of successes, to the vanquished the most calamitous of defeats; for they were utterly and entirely defeated; their sufferings were on an enormous scale; their losses were, as they say, total; army, navy, everything was destroyed, and, out of many, only few returned.
>
> So ended the events in Sicily.
>
> Thucydides 7.87 (R. Warner)

SICILY AND THE CARTHAGINIAN WAR, 412–404 B.C.

If the powerful Syracusan fleet that crushed the Athenians in the Great Harbor had attacked Athens in full force in 412 B.C., it might have ended the Peloponnesian War. Hermocrates, the veteran general who dominated the Syracusan democracy since the 420s B.C., was eager to do so. But the city was exhausted. Syracuse's democracy was as divided as Athens', and her leaders squandered success by fighting among themselves. A powerful speaker named Diocles, who distinguished himself during the siege, became the leading man in the Assembly, and in 410 B.C. removed Hermocrates from the generalship. Finally, war threatened from Carthage. As we have seen, the war with Athens began in western Sicily in 416 B.C. when Selinous attacked the Elymian city of Segesta. Segesta had asked Carthage to help, but when Carthage refused, appealed to Athens, who used the request as a pretext for attacking Syracuse. In 410 B.C., Selinous renewed the attack, and this time Carthage agreed to help Segesta.

Carthage had no regular system of military funding as did Athens. She paid for wars by selling treasure and raising loans, then hiring as many mercenaries as possible, for as brief a time as possible. It took a year to prepare a force under these conditions, while recruiters traveled into Spain, Italy, and Libya. In 409, Carthage was ready to attack Selinous. The Greek cities, either complacent or bankrupt after defeating Athens, made no preparations. Carthage's general **Hannibal**[35] shipped perhaps a hundred thousand men and advanced siege machines to Sicily. In just nine days, he smashed through Selinous' defenses. Diodorus of Sicily gives a harrowing description.

> The Selinuntians gathered in the marketplace and all who reached it died fighting there; and the barbarians, scattering through the entire city, plundered everything of value that they found in the houses. They burned some of the inhabitants that they found together with their homes, and without distinction of sex or age they put to the sword those who struggled out into the streets, showing no compassion. They mutilated even the dead according to the practice of their people, some carrying bunches of hands about their bodies and others heads that they had spitted on their javelins and spears....

The savagery of the barbarians spared neither free-born youths nor maidens, but exposed these sad creatures to terrible disasters. As the women reflected on the slavery that would be their lot in Carthage, as they saw themselves and their children in a condition in which they had no legal rights, were subjected to insolent abuse, and forced to obey masters, and as they realized that these masters used an unintelligible speech and had a brutish character, they mourned for their living children as if they were dead.

Diodorus of Sicily 13.57–58 (C. H. Oldfather)

The Syracusans gathered their ships, and Diocles rushed troops to Akragas. But Hannibal was eager to destroy Himera in the north, in vengeance for his grandfather Hamilcar's defeat there seventy-one years before. As he advanced, twenty thousand of the indigenous population joined him. The Sicilian natives had eagerly joined Athens against Syracuse in 415 too, and now Carthage seemed preferable to the Syracusan yoke. Hannibal won a fierce battle outside Himera's walls, and Diocles, worried that Hannibal would make a sudden raid on Syracuse, returned to Syracuse with half the Himerans, all he could get on his ships. Before he could return for the others, Hannibal took the city. He sacrificed three thousand prisoners on the spot where Hamilcar was killed in 480 B.C.

Then Hannibal embarked his army on warships and merchant vessels, and leaving behind sufficient troops for his allies' needs, set sail from Sicily. And when he arrived at Carthage with great plunder, the whole city came out to meet him, paying him homage and honor as one who in a brief time had performed greater deeds than any general before him.

Diodorus of Sicily 13.62 (C. H. Oldfather)

The Carthaginian War might have ended there, leaving Syracuse free to seek revenge against Athens, but in 407 B.C. Hermocrates, who had fled Syracuse in 410, returned. Backed by Persian gold, he hired a thousand mercenaries, assembled refugees from Himera, and tried to force his way back into Syracuse. When he failed, he seized the ruins of Selinous. His ranks swollen by returning Selinuntians, he soon had six thousand warriors. To raise money, he raided the Phoenician cities at Motya on the west coast and Panormos (modern Palermo) on the northwest. He collected the Syracusan corpses that still lay on the battlefield at Himera and brought them back to Syracuse for proper burial, to upstage his rival Diocles. The Syracusans exiled Diocles, as Hermocrates hoped, but refused to recall the dangerous Hermocrates, who launched a coup and was killed.

Hermocrates had caused so much damage to Phoenician settlements that Hannibal decided that only complete victory over Sicily's Greeks could stabilize the situation. With **Himilco**, probably his cousin, he raised another hundred thousand mercenaries, and in 406 attacked Akragas, perhaps the richest of all Greek cities. Akragas had stayed out of the recent wars, and its landowners profited immensely from selling wine and olive oil to Carthage. Diodorus tells us that when one of them won a victory in the Olympic games in 412 B.C.,

he was conducted into the city in a chariot and in the procession there were, not to speak of other things, 300 chariots each drawn by two white horses, all belonging to the citizens of Akragas. Speaking generally, they led from youth onward a manner of life that was luxurious, wearing as they did exceedingly delicate clothing and gold ornaments and, besides, using strigils[36] and oil flasks made of silver and even of gold.

Diodorus of Sicily 13.82 (C. H. Oldfather)

Akragas fell after an eight-month siege. Panic spread through Greek Sicily. Some of the richer Greeks fled to south Italy, while the Syracusans blamed each other for the disasters. Early in 405, a former follower of Hermocrates named **Dionysius** (aged just twenty-five) harnessed popular anger against the generals and persuaded the Assembly to recall its exiles, who were then under obligation to him personally. The democratic Assembly appointed Dionysius as sole general with complete authority and a bodyguard of six hundred (sign of an approaching tyranny).

Himilco now put Gela under siege and defeated Dionysius when he came to its relief. Dionysius told the people of Gela and Camarina that he could not save them; the only option was to fall back on Syracuse. With each Greek city Carthage destroyed, refugees fled to Syracuse, and Syracuse became stronger. If Dionysius could survive the impending Carthaginian attack, he would be sole ruler of the only major Greek city in the west.

For the second time in a decade, Syracuse was besieged, but Himilco found the location as difficult as had Nicias. Plague broke out in camp, and late in 405 or early in 404, he made peace with Syracuse. Greek refugees could return to Selinous, Himera, Akragas, Gela, and Camarina, but they could not have fortifications and had to pay tribute to Carthage. The other Greek cities and the native Sicels were to be autonomous. The Carthaginian War left Dionysius dominant in Syracuse. It also prevented Syracuse from finishing off Athens, giving the Athenians one last chance to win the Peloponnesian War.

THE IONIAN WAR, 412–404 B.C.

The scale of Athens' losses in the Sicilian expedition of 415 to 413 B.C. was gigantic. In 412 B.C., Athens had barely a handful of hoplites, no ships in the docks, no crews to man them, and no money to pay for more. If Sparta could cut off the grain from the Black Sea, Athens would starve. If the grain kept coming, Athens might yet fight Sparta to a standstill (Map 16.6). The strategic crux was the Hellespont straits, linking the Black Sea to the Aegean (Figure 16.3).

Athens' Dark Hour, 412–410 B.C.

The Spartans were burning and plundering Attica year round from the base at Decelea that Alcibiades urged them to set up in 415 B.C. In the chaos, more than twenty thousand Athenian slaves ran away. But Decelea would not decide the war. Far more dangerous was the wave of revolts among Athens' subject cities in 412. The Athenians broke open their "Iron Reserve," a secret hoard of one thousand talents, until now protected by a law condemning to death any man who even proposed spending it. The Athenians managed to assemble enough ships to menace the rebellious subjects. Sparta still had no fleet. When the Syracusans could not offer help, Sparta turned to Persia. For twenty years Persia ignored requests for aid from Athens and Sparta while they bled each other to death, but now King Darius II agreed to help Sparta with gold on one condition—that Sparta surrender Ionia to Persia.

The Spartans agreed. Without losing a single soldier, Persia regained the position it held before 480 B.C.! Then Darius failed at first to deliver the gold he promised, as his two western satraps spent more time feuding with each other than helping Sparta defeat Athens. Alcibiades, still in Sparta, did bring in some Persian

Map 16.6 The Ionian War. Sites mentioned in this chapter.

Figure 16.3 The Dardanelles (the modern strait of Canakkale). The European shore and the narrow entrance to the straits are clearly visible from the Asian shore.

gold, but when Sparta's King Agis discovered that Alcibiades was having an affair with his wife, Alcibiades fled to Persia.

The Spartan-Persian agreement would eventually cut the grain route from the Black Sea to Athens. Aristocratic Athenians said openly that Darius might support Athens if he could deal with an oligarchy rather than a mob. Alcibiades hoped that an oligarchy would recall him to Athens. In 411 a commander in the Athenian fleet named Pisander sailed from Samos, where the fleet was stationed, to Athens to organize an oligarchic coup, and his supporters ran through the streets murdering democratic leaders. In early summer 411, the oligarchic plotters called a meeting of the Assembly *outside* the city walls, knowing that anti-Spartan democrats would be afraid to attend. The rump Assembly voted itself out of existence and authorized a commission of four hundred men to run the city.

The oligarchy of **The Four Hundred** (411 B.C.), as they came to be known, was supposed to draw up a list of five thousand men of property—perhaps twenty percent of the citizen body—who would form the new government of Athens, but they were in no hurry. Instead, they executed their enemies and confiscated their land while simultaneously negotiating with Sparta. The Four Hundred assumed that Sparta would offer favorable peace terms to a friendly Athenian oligarchy. But Sparta now wanted total victory. The Four Hundred negotiated with Persia, but Darius was not interested either. The sailors at Samos rebelled and declared themselves a democratic state in exile. The sailors wanted to return to Athens and restore democracy, but if they did, Sparta, with its small but growing fleet, would cut off the grain supply and win the war. Alcibiades returned from Persia to Samos and persuaded the fleet to stay where it was (and to elect him one of their generals!).

With the trickle of Persian gold that actually reached her, Sparta had now built a second fleet (in addition to a fleet in Ionia), which sailed to Euboea near Athens and raised a revolt. Sparta's Ionian fleet now threatened the Hellespont and the other threatened to blockade the Piraeus. With victory within reach, the Spartans stupidly sailed against neither target. An amazed Thucydides comments that "on this occasion, as on so many others, the Spartans proved to be quite the most remarkably helpful enemies that the Athenians could have had."

While Sparta hesitated, the democrats in Athens quietly overthrew The Four Hundred and officially recalled the resourceful Alcibiades. The Spartan fleet off the coast of Ionia finally moved to block the Hellespont, but the Athenians at Samos defeated them in a savage battle. Shocked, the Spartans consolidated their two fleets into one and abandoned the threat to Piraeus. Against all probability, by autumn of 411 B.C. Athens had regained the initiative.

Athenian Recovery, 410–406 B.C.

At this point, Thucydides' penetrating account of the war breaks off in the middle of a sentence; we will never know why. **Xenophon**, an essayist and friend of Socrates writing around 360 B.C., began his own *Greek History* where Thucydides stops, but does not match his detail or understanding. The war centered on a struggle for the Hellespont. In 410 Sparta sent a new fleet to close it, but after wild adventures (including being captured by the Persian satrap and a dramatic escape from his castle),

Alcibiades led the Athenians in destroying the new Spartan fleet. Sparta's admiral sent a desperate message home: "Ships lost. Mindaros[37] dead. Men starving. Don't know what to do."

Sparta had no strategy except to wait for Persian intervention. A small but effective Syracusan fleet served alongside the Spartans, but the recall of Hermocrates in 410 and the Carthaginian invasion of Sicily in 409 left Sparta to face the Athenians alone. Athens slowly won back her rebellious subjects, and in 407 Alcibiades dared to show his face in Athens, the city that he had betrayed and that had betrayed him. He got a hero's welcome:

> He set sail for home, with the Athenian ships of the line decorated from stem to stern with shields and trophies of war. They towed in their wake the many prizes they had captured, and they carried an even larger number of figureheads taken from the triremes Alcibiades had defeated and sunk. There were no less than 200 of these . . .
>
> When he landed, people scarcely seemed to have eyes for the other generals they met, but they ran and crowded round Alcibiades, crying out and embracing him. As they escorted him on his way, those who could press near crowned him with garlands and the rest gazed at him from a distance, the old men pointing him out to the young. But there were tears mingled with the people's joy as men remembered the misfortunes of the past and compared them to their present happiness, for they reflected that they would never have suffered the Sicilian disaster or any other of their terrible disappointments if only they had left Alcibiades in command of that expedition and kept him at the head of affairs. As it was, he had found Athens all but driven from the seas, while on land she was mistress of little more than the ground the city stood on, with factions raging inside her own walls; and from these forlorn and miserable remnants of her glory he had raised her up again, and not merely restored her dominion over the seas, but made her victorious over her enemies everywhere on land.
>
> Plutarch, *Life of Alcibiades* 32 (I. Scott-Kilvert)

But even then ominous events were unfolding. Darius II of Persia tired of the feuds between his two western satraps and sent his son Cyrus to replace them. Cyrus was not Darius' eldest son, but he wanted to inherit the throne. His arrival in western Asia Minor coincided with the election of **Lysander** (lī-**san**-der) as admiral in Sparta. Charismatic and talented, Lysander forged a friendship with Agesilaos (a-jes-i-**lā**-us), the half-brother of King Agis, and charmed Cyrus. Cyrus wanted Greek soldiers to back him in his coming bid for the kingship in Persia; Lysander wanted Persian money to defeat Athens.

At last with real financial support, Lysander resumed efforts to win over Athens' subject cities. In 406, while Alcibiades was away extorting money to pay his sailors, Lysander scored a minor victory over the Athenian fleet. Alcibiades decided that returning to Athens was too dangerous and fled to a castle he had built near the Hellespont.

Because of Persian gold, Sparta now offered higher pay than Athens, and many sailors deserted. By spring 406, the Athenians had 100 ships, but crews only for 70, while the Spartan fleet had swelled to 140 ships. A Spartan admiral served a non-renewable twelve-month term, but Cyrus refused to deal with Lysander's replacement. The Spartan fleet, nonetheless, swelled to 170 ships and bottled up the Athenians in a harbor on Lesbos, leaving the Hellespont exposed. Desperate, the Athenians melted down their gold statues of the gods to raise cash, and in thirty days built 110 new ships. They offered freedom to any slave who would row (an unprecedented act), and in July 406 B.C. engaged the Spartans at the Arginusae (ar-jin-**oo**-sē) Islands near the Hellespont, between Lesbos and the mainland, the biggest naval battle in Greek history and Athens' greatest naval victory. The Athenians destroyed two thirds of Sparta's fleet and killed the commander.

The Athenians pursued the remnants of the Spartan fleet, but in so doing left over a thousand of their own sailors to drown. A storm arose, and they were unable to recover the bodies of the dead. In Athens, people were overjoyed at the victory but appalled at the treatment of the dead. The Assembly condemned the victorious generals in charge to death, and after an illegal trial, executed six of them (including Pericles' only surviving son). Such was their reward for saving Athens from destruction.

The End, 405–404 B.C.

Sparta despaired of victory and offered peace, but the Athenians rashly refused, assuming that Sparta could not replace such devastating losses. But Sparta restored Lysander, and Cyrus not only came up with money for a new fleet, but put Lysander in charge of Persia's western provinces. With full Persian support, Sparta could now replace any fleet the Athenians could destroy. Without Persian support, a single defeat would be fatal for Athens.

Late in 405, Lysander sailed for the Hellespont, where he captured a good base at the town of Lampsacus on the eastern side of the straits. He waited. To reopen the straits, Athens had to give battle, but the nearest secure harbor with water and food was twelve miles from Lampsacus, too far to be useful, so the Athenians beached their ships at Aegospotami (ē-jus-**pot**-a-mē, "goat river"), directly across the Hellespont from Lampsacus but without food and water (Map 16.7).

By a curious twist, Alcibiades' castle was near Aegospotami. He rode over to the Athenian fleet and warned the generals that they were exposed. They replied, "We are in command now, not you." For four days, the Athenians tried to lure Lysander out to battle. On the fifth day, his patience paid off. Short of food and water, the Athenian sailors scattered in foraging parties. Lysander stormed the Athenian camp, capturing 171 ships on the beach and rounding up 3,000 Athenians as they drifted back with supplies. Sparta's allies insisted on killing them all. Remembering what happened to Athens' victorious generals the year before, all the surviving Athenian generals fled in terror, most to Persia.

Xenophon, who was probably in Athens at the time, says that "as the news of the disaster was told, one man passed it to another, and a sound of wailing arose and extended first from Piraeus, then along the Long Walls until it reached the city. That night no one slept." Lysander clamped the city under a firm siege as disease and starvation set in.

> They had no ships, no allies, and no food; and they did not know what to do. They could see no future for themselves except to suffer what they had made others suffer, people of small states whom they had injured not in retaliation for anything they had done but out of the arrogance of power and for no reason except that they were in the Spartan alliance. They therefore continued to hold out. They gave back their rights to all who had been disenfranchised and, though numbers of people in the city were dying of starvation, there was no talk of peace.
>
> Xenophon, *Hellenica* 2.2.10 (G. Cawkwell)

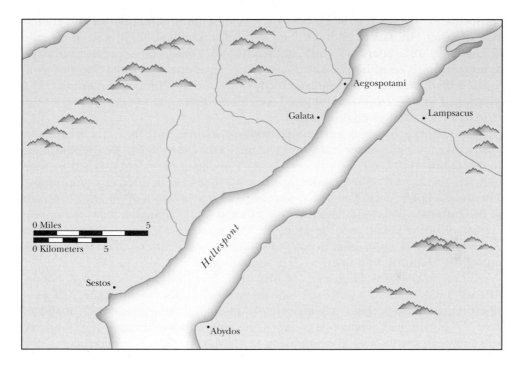

Map 16.7   The Aegospotami campaign.

Then in December 405 B.C., desperate and dying, the Athenians sent one **Theramenes** (ther-**a**-me-nēz) as ambassador to Lysander. Sparta's allies Corinth and Thebes wanted Athens destroyed completely. The men were to be killed and the women and children enslaved. Lysander evidently believed, however, that a weak Athens would be more useful than no Athens at all, to counterbalance Theban and Corinthian ambitions.

The talks dragged on for three months. Theramenes took the best terms he could get to the starving Athenians. They agreed to join the Spartan alliance, destroy the Long Walls and the fortifications of Piraeus, recall the exiled oligarchs, and surrender all but twelve ships.

> After this Lysander sailed into Piraeus, the exiles returned, and the walls were pulled down amid scenes of great enthusiasm and to the music of flute girls. It was thought that this day was the beginning of freedom for Greece.
>
> Xenophon, *Hellenica* 2.2.23 (G. Cawkwell)

AFTERMATH, 404–399 B.C.

The Thirty Tyrants and Athens' Civil War, 404–403 B.C.

As winter approached in 404, the struggle with Sparta had ended. Lysander established a council of thirty oligarchs and ordered them to restore Athens' "ancestral constitution." He wanted the city to survive and be loyal to him personally. He did not care that **The Thirty,** as the Athenians called them, had no interest in the rule of law. They were Sparta's friends, although ready to sate their anger against the democrats in rivers of blood. The Thirty slaughtered their personal enemies, confiscated land, and owed allegiance directly to Lysander. Within a few months, The Thirty had murdered fifteen hundred Athenians (more than one in twenty of the citizens who had survived the war).

The Thirty's behavior generated strong resistance, and they asked Lysander to install a Spartan governor and soldiers for protection. Splits grew within their ranks. **Critias** (**krit-ē-as**), a hardliner, once an associate of Socrates, relied increasingly on force, while Theramenes, at the other extreme, wanted to compromise. Theramenes persuaded The Thirty to make a list of 3000 well-off men (10 percent of the citizens) who would have full rights. Critias then claimed that anyone not on the list could be killed or tortured at will. He prosecuted Theramenes, and when Theramenes gave a powerful speech defending himself, Critias had his name struck off the list, then had him dragged away and poisoned.

By the end of 404, thousands of Athenians had fled the city. Even Thebes—Athens' bitter enemy, who three months earlier wanted to extirpate Athens—offered asylum. In January 403, a group of Athenian democrats set up a small fort near the border with Theban territory. Their numbers swelled to seven hundred, and they seized another hill overlooking the harbor of Piraeus, where many poor, prodemocratic citizens lived. Critias stormed the hill with the few who would actually fight for The Thirty, but was killed. The surviving members of The Thirty asked Lysander to save them from the uprising, but the Spartan kings, worried that Lysander was becoming more powerful than they, instead brokered a treaty with the Athenian rebels, restoring democracy (against every expectation) and removing Lysander's influence. Sparta's internal conflicts had saved Athenian democracy.

The Restored Democracy and the Trial of Socrates, 403–399 B.C.

Since the eve of the Peloponnesian War, Athens had lost a third of her population. Her agriculture and trade were ruined. Those Athenians who survived war, disease, and famine had taken up arms against each other. Even though The Thirty left Athens in 403, many of the Athenians who helped them stayed behind. To avoid revenge killings like those on Corcyra in 427 B.C., the Athenians proclaimed an *amnêsteia,* literally a "not remembering"—the first amnesty in world history. No one except The Thirty themselves and a couple of dozen senior officials could be prosecuted for crimes committed under the oligarchy. Athenians who pursued vengeance had to cloak their intentions.

Socrates was one who fell victim to the raw hatreds in the city. Aged about seventy, he was well known about town. He never wrote anything so we rely on others' impressions. According to his pupil Plato, one of Socrates' friends visited the oracle at Delphi and asked whether anyone was wiser than Socrates. The oracle said no. Socrates was surprised. He did not think the god would lie, yet he felt anything but wise. He began interviewing men reputed to be wise, to find out what the god had meant. But each time,

> I formed the impression that although in many people's opinion, and especially in his own, the man appeared to be wise, in fact he was not. Then when I began to try to show him that he only thought he was wise and was not really so, my efforts were resented both by him and by many of the other people present. However, I reflected as I walked away: "Well, I am certainly wiser than this man. It is only too likely that neither of us has any knowledge to boast of; but he thinks that he knows something that he does not know, whereas I am quite conscious of my ignorance. At any rate it seems to me that I am wiser than he is to this small extent, that I do not think that I know what I do not know."
>
> Plato, *Apology* 21D–E (H. Treddenick)

You do not have to look very hard to see that Socrates' philosophical arguments were also political claims. Democracy assumed that every citizen had political wisdom and that the way to maximize wisdom was for as many citizens as possible to debate questions and participate directly in public affairs. But if no one knows anything, democracy only maximizes ignorance and stupidity, as its enemies have always claimed. Plato explained this in another dialogue, set on the eve of Socrates' execution:

Socrates: But my dear Crito, why should we pay so much attention to what "most people" think? The really reasonable people, who have more claim to be considered, will believe that the facts are exactly as they are.

Crito: You can see for yourself, Socrates, that one has to think of popular opinion as well. Your present position is quite enough to show that the capacity of ordinary people for causing trouble is not confined to petty annoyances,[38] but has hardly any limits if you once get a bad name with them.

Socrates: I only wish that ordinary people *had* an unlimited capacity for doing harm: then they might have an unlimited power for doing good; which would be a splendid thing, if it were so. Actually they have neither. They cannot make a man wise or stupid; they simply act at random.

Plato, *Crito* 43D–E (H. Treddenick)

Back in 423 B.C., Aristophanes made Socrates the main character in his comedy *The Clouds,* representing him as a slippery eccentric sophist who made regular citizens into laughing-stocks and persuaded young men to mock traditional ways. This was funny when the Peloponnesian War was going well. Unfortunately Socrates associated with the wrong people. Alcibiades was prominent in Socrates' circle, and some of The Thirty, including Critias, were admirers or hangers-on: No matter that Socrates (according to Plato) considered oligarchy to be as flawed as democracy or that he defied orders from The Thirty and was condemned to death for it (only the fall of The Thirty saved him). Charges of "corrupting the young" and of "introducing false gods" were now brought against him, the intellectual hero of democracy's arrogant, overeducated enemies.

In Athenian democratic courts of law there were no lawyers or judges. All citizens aged over thirty could serve as jurors. Each day, those who wanted to serve put their names into a lottery. If they were selected, a machine assigned them to a court. Depending on the crimes being tried, juries ranged from 201 to 501 members. The jurors took their seats; the charges were read; the citizen bringing the charges spoke and called witnesses; the defendant spoke and called witnesses; then the citizens voted, guilty or innocent. It was up to the speakers to cite relevant laws, and there was no cross-examination of witnesses. Witnesses testified to the defendant's and accuser's general way of life as well as to what we would consider the facts of the case. Jurors regularly interrupted proceedings with booing, clapping, and abuse. If they found the defendant guilty, some crimes carried fixed penalties. For other crimes, the prosecutor and defendant each proposed a penalty, and the jury voted which to impose. All trials were over in a single day. The law courts were like tragedy in their love of debate and concern with moral issues.

In his dialogue the *Apology*, Plato presents Socrates as giving a sophisticated speech explaining his philosophy and mocking Athens' legal system for relying on superficial forms of knowledge. The vote was close, probably about 265 guilty to 235 not guilty. The prosecutors asked for the death penalty, harsh for these charges but reflecting the high feelings in the city. Socrates, instead of proposing a fine or exile, mockingly proposed that as "punishment" he should receive free dinners for life, like an Olympic athlete, as a reward for his forcing the citizens to think about how to live their lives. The jurors approved the death sentence. A few days later, refusing to escape, Socrates drank a cup of poisonous hemlock—democracy's greatest crime against philosophy.

CONCLUSION

In both the East and the West, the great wars of 480 B.C. had given a few city-states chances to gain greater power than others and to challenge the entire system of autonomous *poleis*. But the resistance to any one city becoming the capital of a larger Greek state remained strong. In the West, Syracuse's power depended on its tyrants' ability to hold the population down, and by the mid-460s that power collapsed. In the East, Athens exploited the other Greeks' fear of Persia to centralize unheard-of resources, develop a sophisticated tax system, and assemble a huge military force. Athens' direct challenge to Sparta in the 450s failed, but the process of centralization continued so that by 431 many Spartans feared that if they did not stop Athens, it would be too late. The next twenty-seven years destabilized the whole Mediterranean, consuming countless lives and vast stores of wealth.

Athens fell, her empire was dissolved, and with it the only opportunity that history offered for one *polis* to become the capital of a larger Greek state. No *polis* ever matched the wealth, power, and organization of Athens before 413 B.C. But Athens' bid for power drove the Greeks to exhaustion. Carthage and Persia nursed their wounds after 479 B.C., then after 410 B.C. reimposed their inexorable wills on the Greek city-states. Seventy years later, Macedon overthrew the Greek city-states of the Aegean, and another seventy years after that, Rome did the same in the West. The fall of Athens was the end of an age.

KEY TERMS

FURTHER READING

Connor, W. Robert, *The New Politicians of Fifth-Century Athens* (Princeton 1971). Excellent account of the evolution of politics in democratic Athens.

———, *Thucydides* (Princeton 1984). Careful reading of this major text, with great sensitivity to nuance.

Finley, Moses, *Ancient Sicily* (New York 1968). Still the only narrative survey of Sicilian history. Tells the main story well.

Green, Peter, *Armada from Athens* (London 1970). Dramatic retelling of the story of the Sicilian Expedition.

Hanson, Victor, *Warfare and Agriculture in Classical Greece* (Pisa 1983; reissued Berkeley 1999). Excellent study showing the limits of the damage Spartan armies could do to the Athenian countryside in the early stages of the war.

Kagan, Donald, *The Peloponnesian War* (New York 2003). The best one-volume survey of the conflict, by the master of military and diplomatic history.

———, *The Archidamian War* (Ithaca, NY, 1974), *The Peace of Nicias and the Sicilian Expedition* (Ithaca, NY, 1981), *The Fall of the Athenian Empire* (Ithaca, NY, 1987). The second, third, and fourth books in a four-volume series, covering the period 431 to 404. A detailed account of the events of the Peloponnesian War.

Lancel, Serge, *Carthage* (Oxford, UK, 1995). A survey of this city's history, including its relations with the Greeks of Sicily.

Lewis, David, John Boardman, John Davies, and Martin Ostwald, eds., *The Cambridge Ancient History*, 2nd ed., vol. 5: *The Fifth Century B.C.* (Cambridge, UK, 1992). Essays by specialists covering 478 through 404 in the Aegean and western Greece.

Munn, Mark, *The School of History* (Berkeley 2000). Good narrative of Athenian politics and intellectual history from 415 through 395.

Wolpert, Andrew, *Remembering Defeat* (Baltimore 2002). Innovative study of how the amnesty of 403 B.C. worked and how Athenian culture recovered from the trauma of civil war.

Ancient Texts

Aristophanes, *The Clouds*. In *Lysistrata and Other Plays* (New York 1973; tr. Alan Sommerstein). Important negative view of Socrates, first performed in 423 B.C.

Diodorus of Sicily, *The History*, books 12 and 13. In *The Library of History* V (Loeb Classical Library; Cambridge, MA, 1946; tr. C. H. Oldfather). Parallel Greek and English texts describing Sicilian history.

Plato, *The Last Days of Socrates* (Harmondsworth, UK, 1954; tr. Hugh Treddenick). Includes the *Apology* and *Crito,* important texts for Socrates' trial and postwar Athenian society.

Plutarch, Lives of Nicias, Alcibiades, and Lysander. In *The Rise and Fall of Athens* (Harmondsworth, UK, 1960; tr. Ian Scott-Kilvert). These biographies contain information on the end of the Peloponnesian War.

Thucydides, *The Peloponnesian War* (Harmondsworth, UK, 1954; tr. Rex Warner). Book 1 describes the years down to 431 B.C.

The Landmark Thucydides (New York 1996; ed. Robert Strassler). Not such a good translation as the Penguin, but the abundant maps and excellent endnotes make it much easier to follow Thucydides' account.

Xenophon, *A History of My Times* (Harmondsworth, UK, 1966; tr. George Cawkwell). Translation of Xenophon's *Hellenica,* the main narrative source for the period 411 to 399 B.C., after Thucydides ends.

Xenophon, *Socrates' Defense.* In *Conversations of Socrates* (New York 1988; tr. Hugh Treddenick and Robin Waterfield). A different version from Plato's of what Socrates said at his trial in 399 B.C.

CHAPTER 17

THE GREEKS BETWEEN PERSIA AND CARTHAGE, 399–360 B.C.

A single story dominated the fifth century B.C.: Athens' and Syracuse's attempts to dominate their neighbors, and the cultural revolutions that their new wealth supported. Their defeats, Sparta's triumph, and the return of Persia and Carthage begin a more complicated period. Once the Athenian empire fell, no one could recreate it. The forty years from 399 through 360 B.C. were filled with bloody, pointless struggles between Sparta (with Persian backing), Thebes, and a revived Athens in the Aegean, and between Syracuse and Carthage in the west. But none could reproduce fifth-century Athens' financial power. To pay for these wars, *poleis* turned more toward their richest citizens. For four centuries, since 800 B.C. power had steadily shifted toward the mass of ordinary male citizens, so that by 400 B.C. democracy was a common form of government. But in the fourth century, as the rich started to shoulder more of the costs of the state's survival, aristocrats gained a new confidence.

A second major change was under way. During the Peloponnesian War, Thessaly, Macedonia, and other large but loosely organized northern and western regions had provided men and materials for Athens and Sparta. In return, they learned the city-states' methods and techniques. In the fourth century B.C., they applied these Greek techniques to their own reserves of manpower and wealth. One northern king was about to turn tables on the *poleis* and bring their political independence to an end.

SPARTA'S EMPIRE, 404–360 B.C.

The Peloponnesian War ended with singing and dancing, as Athens' former subjects celebrated the destruction of her walls as the beginning of liberty. They were to be bitterly disappointed.

Lysander, Agesilaos, and the Return of the Persian Empire, 404–387 B.C.

Athens's power was broken, but Sparta had no intention of setting Greek cities free. As Plutarch explains,

> Lysander suppressed both democratic and other forms of government in the Greek cities of Ionia and left one Spartan administrator in each, and under him ten magistrates chosen from the political associations that he had established everywhere. He followed this procedure just as thoroughly in the cities that had become his allies as in those that had opposed him, and cruising around at his leisure, he established the foundations, in a sense, of a personal supremacy throughout Greece. In appointing these magistrates he was not influenced by considerations of birth or wealth, but simply handed over control of affairs to his own associates and partisans, and gave them absolute power to deal out rewards and punishments. He lent his presence to a number of massacres, and helped drive out his friends' enemies and in this way provided the Greeks with a very unwelcome demonstration of Spartan rule. In fact the comic poet Theopompos chose a particularly inept illustration when he compared the Spartans to barmaids, because they gave the Greeks an appetizing sip of freedom and then mixed vinegar with it. The truth was that the taste was harsh and bitter from the beginning, because Lysander not only refused to allow the people to be masters of their own affairs, but actually delivered the cities into the hands of the most aggressive and fanatical members of the oligarchic faction.
>
> Plutarch, *Life of Lysander* 13 (I. Scott-Kilvert)

By installing oligarchies answering directly to him in Athens' former subject cities, Lysander took control of enormous revenues. He apparently took fifteen hundred talents in cash back to Sparta, kept more than four hundred for himself, and instituted annual tribute of another one thousand talents. No individual Athenian ever controlled such wealth. His power seemed more than human, and some cities set up altars to him as if he were a god—the first time Greeks had so honored a living man. The centuries-old framework of Greek life, which held that all men were roughly equal and none had access to superhuman forces, did not easily accommodate someone as rich and powerful as Lysander. Within a few years, Lysander was campaigning to make Spartan kingship elective, presumably to win it for himself. The kings worried that Lysander was stronger than they and that his followers' brutality would destabilize the new order. Hence the surprising events in Athens in 403 B.C. when the Spartans restored the democracy: As the kings saw it, Lysander was more dangerous than Athenian democracy. Sparta defeated Athens by making a deal with Persia, and in 404 B.C., both Sparta and Persia got what they bargained for. Sparta took Athens' empire while Persia recovered Ionia and secured her northwest frontier. Many Greeks felt that Sparta had sold out Ionia, as in fact she had.

Within weeks of the end of the Peloponnesian War, Darius II died. Egypt rebelled and Darius' younger son (and Lysander's close friend) Cyrus challenged the older son, **Artaxerxes,** for the throne. Cyrus asked for Spartan help. Sparta, welcoming the prospect of a grateful Cyrus on the throne, organized thirteen thousand Greek mercenaries to support him. Cyrus cut through Artaxerxes' defenses. In the final battle, near Babylon, Cyrus' hoplites were victorious, but Cyrus was killed. The only point of the war was to install him on the throne, so his death left ten thousand Greeks marooned in hostile territory a thousand miles from friendly lands. The

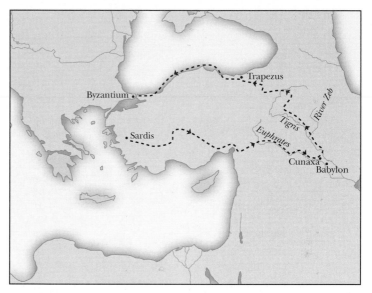

Map 17.1 The March of the Ten Thousand. Cyrus' mercenaries left Sardis in spring 401 B.C. They won a battle at Cunaxa, but Cyrus was killed, and the Greek mercenaries withdrew. The satrap Tissaphernes treacherously captured the Greek commanders at the River Zab, and Xenophon took command of the remaining troops. He led them back to the Black Sea at Trapezus (modern Trebizond), finally returning to Byzantium in early 399 B.C.

Athenian Xenophon (c. 428–357 B.C.), friend of Socrates, was one of the officers. He took command and led the army all the way back to the Black Sea (Map 17.1).

Xenophon wrote a famous (and self-serving) account of their escape, called the *Anabasis,* or "March Up Country." Few Greeks lived more than a day's walk from the sea; now, after walking for months to reach it, fighting all along the way, the battle-hardened Greek veterans rushed into the water of the Black Sea, shouting "*Thalatta! Thalatta!*" ("The sea! The sea!"). Xenophon's triumph came at the same time that the Athenians were putting to death his teacher Socrates. Repelled by this horrible crime, Xenophon enrolled as a mercenary for Sparta, where he lived for the rest of his life, becoming fast friends with its king **Agesilaos.**

The March of the Ten Thousand proved that no Persian army could withstand Greek hoplites in battle. Why, then, should Sparta honor treaties giving Ionia to Persia? Lysander saw no reason, and in 398, after he had maneuvered his lover Agesilaos onto the Spartan throne, freeing Ionia became official Spartan policy.

Setting up Agesilaos as king should have stabilized Lysander's unparalleled power, but he met his match in Agesilaos. The young king ignored his advice, passed him over for commands, and ruined his friends. Agesilaos was determined to break Lysander's power, to save Sparta's traditional institutions. Agesilaos sent Lysander to a minor theater of war, where he died in 395 B.C.

Agesilaos made Ionian freedom his own cause, and in 396 he advanced to Sardis, routing every Persian force and alarming Artaxerxes, who wanted to reconquer rebellious Egypt. Instead of fighting Sparta, Artaxerxes sent agents to Greece with gold. Several Greek cities, disillusioned with Sparta, took Persian money to finance an uprising. The Ephors called Agesilaos back from Asia to fight in Greece, and Artaxerxes achieved his goal without losing a single man.

The Corinthian War (394–387 B.C.), so called because most of the action took place around that city (Map 17.2), pitted Sparta against rebellious Thebes and Corinth (its two closest allies in the Peloponnesian War), a reviving Athens, and

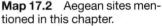

Map 17.2   Aegean sites mentioned in this chapter.

Persia. In a strange reversal, Athens rebuilt the Long Walls, and an Athenian admiral commanding a Persian fleet defeated Sparta's fleet, then ravaged Greece's coasts! The Corinthian War dragged on in a bloody stalemate. Spartan hoplites could win battles, evidently, but only Persian gold could win wars.

The King's Peace, 387–371 B.C.

In 387, Agesilaos conceded this bitter fact and confessed his failure to free the Ionian Greeks (whom Sparta had herself earlier betrayed to Persia). He sought an accommodation. Xenophon records Artaxerxes' terms:

> I, King Artaxerxes, regard the following arrangements as just: 1. The cities in Asia and, among the islands, Clazomenae and Cyprus, should belong to me. 2. The other Greek cities, large and small, should be left to govern themselves, except for Lemnos, Imbros, and Skyros, which should belong to Athens, as in the past. And if either of the two parties° refuses to accept peace on these terms, I, together with those who will accept this peace, will make war on that party both by land and by sea, with ships and with money.
>
> Xenophon, *Hellenica* 5.1.31 (G. Cawkwell)

°*two parties:* That is, Sparta or the alliance against her.

This **King's Peace** (387 B.C.) gave most parties what they wanted. Persia again controlled Ionia and, by banning multicity alliances ("cities . . . left to govern themselves") except Sparta's Peloponnesian League, protected its western borders, allowing Artaxerxes to launch a major (but unsuccessful) invasion of Egypt. Banning alliances also guaranteed Sparta's power within Greece. Athens kept its rebuilt walls and fleet. The Ionians, the losers, were too weak to protest, and no one on the mainland cared enough to restart the war. Thebes, by now Greece's second power, was the other loser. She had controlled the other cities in Boeotia since before 500 B.C., but Thebes' Boeotian League was now dissolved. Thebes would make Sparta regret the insult.

The King's Peace was full of ironies: Sparta had the job of making sure that all cities were free, when it was to free themselves from Spartan tyranny that the Corinthinan War had taken place. In any event, Agesilaos interpreted the treaty as carte blanche to help his friends and hurt his enemies, above all his enemy Thebes. In 382, a Spartan officer named Phoebidas (fē-bi-das) was marching troops past Thebes when a pro-Spartan faction in the city offered him a chance to seize it. Phoebidas did so, in flagrant violation of the King's Peace. Even his colleagues in Sparta were shocked. The Spartans put Phoebidas on trial, but King Agesilaos defended him, saying that he only acted in Sparta's best interests. Phoebidas got off with a fine, which Agesilaos paid; Agesilaos kept the Spartan garrison in Thebes. The pro-Spartan faction in Thebes then executed the leader of the anti-Spartan group for conspiring with Persia—a deeply hypocritical murder, given Sparta's cooperation with Persia under the King's Peace.

In 379 B.C., seven conspirators disguised as *hetairai* stopped by a party that Thebes' pro-Spartan governors were throwing and stabbed them to death. Just twenty-five years before, Thebes had urged Sparta to kill all Athenian citizens at the end of the Peloponnesian War; now Athenian volunteers arrived to expel the Spartan garrison in Thebes. In retribution, a Spartan named Sphodrias (**sfod**-rē-as) decided in 378 to seize Piraeus during the night. But his geography was poor: Dawn found him in a field many miles from Piraeus. The Spartans put the renegade commander on trial, then acquitted him.

So far, the Greeks endured Sparta's arrogance because opposition would (in theory) trigger Persian intervention. Sphodrias' raid was the final straw, and in midsummer 378, the Athenians organized a new naval league. Between sixty and seventy states joined. The Athenians went to great lengths not to upset Persia, specifying that the league was not an alliance, as had been the old league, but an association to help members govern themselves, with the goal of keeping the King's Peace in force for all time. They specified that, unlike in their fifth-century empire, no Athenian could own property in an allied state and that there would be no garrisons or tribute.

Artaxerxes took no action against Athens, no doubt because he was more concerned with reconquering Egypt than with protecting Sparta's position. Even without formal tribute, the new Athenian league financed a fleet that destroyed Sparta's navy in 376 B.C. For nearly thirty years, since 404 B.C., Spartan and Persian fleets had controlled the Aegean, and Athens had had to bow to these powers to preserve its grain supply. Finally, the grain route was secure. Full of confidence, the Athenians decided they did not need Thebes any more. Betraying their recent allies, in 375 B.C. the Athenians helped push through a **Common Peace** that committed all Greeks to the King's Peace, again dissolving Thebes' Boeotian League. Athens stepped aside as Agesilaos plundered Theban territory each summer to force Thebes to recognize the new balance of power.

In 371, Athens called a general congress to reaffirm the Common Peace. Every Greek state signed, but when it came to Thebes' turn, her representative **Epaminondas** (e-pam-i-**non**-das) walked out in protest because Sparta insisted that he could sign only for Thebes, not for the whole of Boeotia. Agesilaos was sick, so his fellow-king **Cleombrotus** led the Spartan army into Boeotia once again to force Thebes back to the negotiating table, and Epaminondas rushed back to Thebes to prepare a defense.

ECONOMY, SOCIETY, AND WAR

The dramatic events of summer 371 B.C. took their significance from long-term social and economic processes. A hundred years earlier, economic changes were making the old style of Greek warfare obsolete. No matter how good Spartan hoplites were, they could not have beaten Persia in 480 to 479 B.C. without the Athenian fleet, which required large amounts of money. Athens could maintain this fleet and build the latest types of fortifications only by creating a state in which many cities paid tribute. Relatively light taxes paid for a powerful fleet and cheap security, which made trade easier, increased overall wealth, and made Piraeus a major market.

In the Peloponnesian War, military spending exploded. Athens tightened its financial organization but constantly needed new income. Generals extorted money from the peoples among whom they campaigned, and there was talk of extracting "loans" from the temple treasuries at Olympia and Delphi. Most cities turned to rich citizens for special contributions, yet archaeology shows that the rich started spending more on expressions of personal status after about 425 B.C. Houses, simple and plain through most of the fifth century, now became elaborate homes with colonnaded courtyards, mosaic floors, and painted walls. Expensive new tombs and a whole array of other elite monuments appeared (Figure 17.1). As the state grew more dependent on the rich to pay for security, the rich asserted greater independence.

Generals experimented feverishly, looking for ways to fight wars more cheaply or, if they had money, to convert it into military victories. Some turned toward inexpensive light infantry (Figure 17.2). The campaigns in mountainous western Greece in the 420s showed that javelin throwers (*peltasts*), archers, and slingers could damage a phalanx on the right terrain. In 390 B.C., Athenian light infantry, working in rough terrain, cut a Spartan regiment to pieces during the Corinthian War. Others tried to exploit the greater prosperity and assertiveness of the rich by recruiting more cavalry.

In the sixth and earlier fifth centuries B.C., few *poleis* could muster more than a few hundred (or just a few dozen) horsemen. By the early fourth century, it was not unusual to put a thousand cavalry in the field. Once cavalry reached such numbers, they could use their speed to outmaneuver and break a phalanx although, having no stirrups, they were always vulnerable to being pushed from the small horses. In another experiment, as early as 424 B.C., Thebes tried massing hoplites on a narrow front twenty-five ranks deep instead of the usual eight, aiming to crash through the opposing ranks before the enemy had time to encircle them. But such tactics were effective only as part of a combined-arms operation using clouds of cavalry and skirmishers to hold back the enemy's wings.

Figure 17.1 Grave stele of Ktesileos and his wife Theano; Athens, circa 400 B.C. The husband stands in a relaxed pose, leaning on a staff before a pediment. His seated wife looks up while languidly holding the edge of her dress. Their names are written below the pediment. Marble, 5 feet high.

Figure 17.2 A Thracian peltast, named after the *peltē,* a light wicker shield often shaped like a half-moon, on a red-figure wine cup, circa 460 B.C. Peltasts wore no armor, but carried several javelins for harassing slow-moving hoplites. Peltasts became important in fourth-century warfare.

All such innovations drove the costs of war higher, but advances in fortification increased expenses even more. Athens had pioneered advanced fortifications with its Long Walls in the 450s B.C., and in the 380s B.C. tried an even more expensive innovation, ringing her whole territory with forts. Greek citizen armies avoided assaulting fortifications because they were unwilling to accept high casualties. In the fourth century, *poleis* responded by hiring mercenaries, who would do things citizens would not, but they raised the cost of war still further. As citizens' military contributions declined, so did their power within their cities relative to the aristocracy, who provided the funds for war.

These economic and social changes shaped the struggles among Sparta, Athens, and Thebes. As the costs of war spiraled upward, no one *polis* could concentrate enough wealth to overwhelm the others without Persian gold. The pointless wars bankrupted everyone and gave further power to the rich. More and more power shifted away from the *poleis* toward the large, loose federations to the north and west. Thessaly, Aetolia, Macedon, and Epirus had been second-rate powers in the fifth century B.C. These *ethnê* (**eth**-nā, meaning "peoples" or "nations"; singular, *ethnos*) had large populations, rich natural resources, and powerful aristocracies, but lacked the organization and civic traditions that would allow them to put hoplites in the field and fleets upon the seas. As the Peloponnesian War expanded, and these societies were drawn into the conflict, a transfer of institutions and techniques began. Through charisma, trickery, and ruthless efficiency, a man named **Jason of Pherae** got control of most of Thessaly in the late 370s. He seemed to come from nowhere, suddenly emerging as a major player:

> So [Jason] returned to Thessaly, a great man indeed. He had been legally appointed Lord of Thessaly; he controlled great forces of mercenaries, both infantry and cavalry, and these forces had been trained to the highest pitch of efficiency. He was greater still in the strength of his alliances, many states being allied with him already and others being anxious to do so too. When one considers that there was no power on earth that could afford to disregard him, one may say that he was the greatest man of his times. . . . the Greeks were really seriously frightened that Jason might seize an absolute and irresponsible power.
>
> Xenophon, *Hellenica* 6.4.28, 33 (G. Cawkwell)

Jason was murdered in 370, and Thessalian power evaporated as his brothers murdered and fought each other. But his rise showed the shape of things to come.

SPARTA'S COLLAPSE, 371 B.C.

Sparta was becoming an anachronism. Lysander wanted to modernize around 400 B.C., but Agesilaos was determined that nothing change. Sparta was obsessed with its past and its traditions. While the population of Greece was growing, the number of Spartiates was falling. A man could be a Spartiate only if he could afford to contribute to his dining group, but Spartan inheritance laws concentrated land in ever fewer hands, meaning that fewer men could afford to be full citizens. There were nine thousand Spartiates in 479 B.C.; by 371 B.C., just fourteen hundred. For all their ferocity, this tiny band could not hold its enemies and allies in line with Persia's support and a widespread belief in Spartan invincibility. Every time Sparta went to war in the fourth century, she risked everything, but the ruling elite refused to broaden the bases for Spartiate citizenship.

Cleombrotus marched against Thebes in 371 B.C. with seven hundred Spartiates and thousands of allies, trusting to his hoplites' morale and skill. In the past, the Thebans hid behind their walls, but that summer Epaminondas gave battle. If he did not, the other Boeotian cities would desert Thebes. The armies met on level ground at a village called **Leuctra.**

Most cities now had strong cavalry, but not Sparta. The expert Theban cavalry drove back the weak Spartan cavalry, whose flight disrupted the Spartan phalanx. Epaminondas had drawn up his hoplites fifty ranks deep as a kind of human battering ram. Their spearhead was the **Sacred Band,** an elite corps reputed to consist of 150 pairs of lovers who would rather die than act shamefully before each other. Like the Spartiates, the Sacred Band were full-time warriors supported at public expense. As always, the Spartans showed astonishing ferocity and bravery, but the Thebans battered them until they fell back to camp leaving behind over four hundred dead Spartiates—more than a quarter of the whole Spartiate population, including Cleombrotus and Sphodrias.

Sparta was broken. Her allies immediately defected to Thebes, and civil war seemed imminent. According to Spartan law, men who retreated in battle forfeited their citizenship and could not marry Spartiate women, but Agesilaos was terrified that if he disenfranchised the three hundred survivors of Leuctra—practically a third of the surviving Spartiates—they would rebel. Rather than change the laws and undermine his own authority, as Plutarch explains it, "he came into the Assembly and announced that the laws must be allowed to sleep on that one day, but that thereafter they must resume their force."

Epaminondas descended on Sparta with forty thousand hoplites, the first time an enemy ever ravaged Spartan territory. Only winter floods swelling the River Eurotas kept Epaminondas from sacking the city. While Agesilaos was fighting internal uprisings that aimed to change the constitution, Epaminondas headed west across the mountains to liberate the helots of Messenia and set up an independent city-state.

When Agesilaos ascended the throne in 398 B.C., Sparta was at the height of her power. She had humbled Athens and threatened the Persian Empire itself. Twenty-seven years later, Sparta had lost everything. Agesilaos used to boast that no Spartan women had ever seen the smoke from enemy campfires. After 371, they knew them too well.

ANARCHY IN THE AEGEAN, 371–360 B.C.

The battle of Leuctra ruined Sparta, but was not enough to make Thebes a major power. Epaminondas had no strategic vision of what to do next. He headed off a Spartan attempt to get Persian aid in 367 B.C., but his anti-Spartan alliance quickly broke up, and petty wars followed everywhere. Thebes fought to keep Thessaly divided after Jason's murder; Athens fought to extend her power over her allies in the Second Athenian League; and Athens and Thebes fought each other. Cities changed sides with bewildering frequency. With no great struggle against Persia or Sparta to galvanize citizens, their participation declined steadily. Bands of marauding mercenaries between jobs soon posed a threat to public safety.

Agesilaos refused to acknowledge the loss of Messenia and remained in a state of war with Thebes. In 362 B.C., it seemed that his chance had come. The city of Mantineia, Epaminondas' major ally in the Peloponnese, broke away from Thebes and asked for Spartan support. Agesilaos, now aged 82, took the small Spartan army to its aid. Epaminondas marched against undefended Sparta while her troops were away. Agesilaos raced back, saving the city only after desperate hand-to-hand fighting in the streets:

> It was Isidas, the son of Phoebidas,° who presented the most striking and astonishing sight, both to the enemy and to his fellow-citizens. He was exceptionally tall and handsome and of an age when the human physique reaches the flower of its beauty, as boyhood merges into manhood. He had just anointed his body with oil and rushed out of his house naked, holding a spear in one hand and a sword in the other, but wearing neither armor nor clothing. Then forcing his way through the midst of the combatants, he threw himself at the ranks of the enemy, striking and laying low all who opposed him. He did not receive a single wound, whether because some god protected him for his valor, or because his height and strength made his enemies believe him to be superhuman. It is said that the Ephors crowned him with a garland for this feat of arms, and then fined him 1,000 drachmas for being so foolhardy as to risk his life by fighting without armor.
>
> Plutarch, *Life of Agesilaos* 35 (I. Scott-Kilvert)

°*Phoebidas:* The same Phoebidas who had captured Thebes in 382 B.C.

No amount of bravery hid the fact that Sparta was now a second-rate power. The main armies clashed at Mantineia a few days later, and the Thebans again broke the Spartan phalanx. As the Spartans turned to run, one of them struck down Epaminondas. Legend had it that with his dying breath he urged Thebes to abandon conquest and make peace. His advice was good. Everyone was exhausted. Thebes could not take Sparta; Sparta could not recover Messenia; and Athens could not recreate its fifth-century empire. Persia might now have intervened decisively in Greek affairs, but was still bogged down fighting to recover Egypt and to suppress revolts among the western satraps. The fall of Sparta had brought on anarchy. Xenophon gave his history of the period 411 to 362 B.C. a telling epitaph:

> The result of the battle [of Mantineia] was just the opposite of what everyone expected it would be. Nearly the whole of Greece had been engaged on one side or the other, and everyone imagined that, if a battle was fought, the winner would become the dominant power and the losers would be their subjects. But the god so ordered things that both parties put up trophies, as for victory, and neither side tried to prevent the other from doing so; both sides gave back the dead under a truce, as though they had won, and both sides received their dead under a truce, as though they had lost. Both sides claimed the victory, but it cannot be said that with regard to the accession of new territory, or cities, or power either side was any better off after the battle than before it. In fact, there was even more uncertainty and confusion in Greece after the battle than there had been previously.
>
> Xenophon, *Hellenica* 7.5.26–27 (G. Cawkwell)

CARTHAGE AND SYRACUSE, 404–360 B.C.

Dionysius I of Syracuse Renews the Struggle against Carthage, 399–393 B.C.

On the face of it, Syracuse was in a much weaker position in 404 B.C. than Sparta (Map 17.3). Carthage had humbled Syracuse, while Sparta had overthrown Athens. But while Sparta faced challenges from Thebes and Athens as well as from Persia, Syracuse had no real Greek rivals. Syracuse had signed a humiliating treaty with

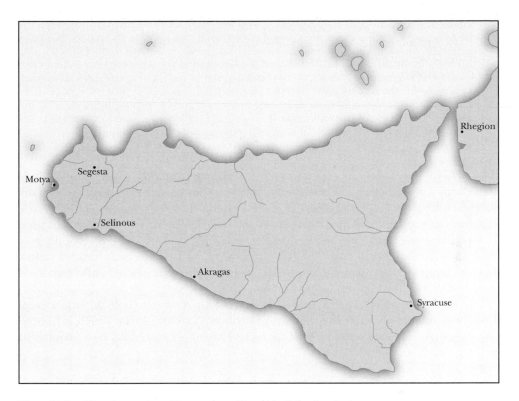

Map 17.3   Sites in western Greece mentioned in this chapter.

Carthage in 405 B.C., but Dionysius had reasons to feel pleased. He had survived; the other Greek cities had been weakened even more than Syracuse; and within Syracuse, he was sole ruler. He set about reviving Syracuse's fortunes.

Dionysius needed to secure Syracuse against external attacks and secure himself against internal threats, such as the cavalry revolt that almost toppled him in 405 B.C. He walled off the old city of Syracuse, the small island of Ortygia separated from the main island by a narrow channel.

There Dionysus could take refuge with his closest supporters and his mercenaries. In the Great Harbor he built dockyards for a new fleet and fortified Epipolai so that Syracuse could not be threatened as easily as in 415 and 405 B.C. He provided pay on a massive scale to the poor and showed his common touch:

> Wishing to complete the building of the walls rapidly, he gathered the peasants from the countryside, from whom he selected some 60,000 capable men and parceled out to them the space to be walled. For each 200 yards he appointed a master-builder and for each 100 feet a mason, and the laborers and common people assigned to the task numbered 200 for each 100 feet. Besides these, other workers, a multitude in number, quarried out the rough stone, and 6,000 yoke of oxen brought it to the appointed place. And the united labor of so many workers struck the watchers with great amazement, since all were eager to complete the task assigned to them. For Dionysius, in order to excite the enthusiasm of the mass, offered valuable gifts to those who finished first, special ones for the master-builders, and still others for the masons and in turn for the common

laborers; and he in person, together with his friends, oversaw the work through all the days required, visiting every section and always lending a hand to the toilers. Speaking generally, he laid aside the dignity of his office and reduced himself to the ranks. Putting his hand to the hardest tasks, he endured the same toil as the other workers, so that great rivalry was engendered and some even added a part of the night to the day's labor, such eagerness for the task had infected the multitude. As a result, against all expectations, the wall was completed in 20 days. It was 4 miles long and of corresponding height, and the added strength of the wall made it impregnable; for there were lofty towers at frequent intervals and it was built of stones 4 feet long and carefully joined.

Diodorus of Sicily 14.18 (C. H. Oldfather)

They did their work so well that parts of the wall stand today.

Dionysius was acting like the tyrants of the sixth century B.C., but in a very different context. Because he controlled the resources of the biggest city in fourth-century Greece, he could hire huge mercenary armies, giving them land confiscated from citizens to create a permanent reserve of exmercenaries to call on in emergencies. He renewed Gelon's and Hiero's policies, attacking Syracuse's smaller neighbors and transporting their citizens to Syracuse. Despite setbacks, Syracuse remained rich and strong, the greatest city on Sicily.

In 399 B.C., while Sparta was secretly backing Cyrus' revolt against Persia, Dionysius openly prepared for war with Carthage. Unlike Sparta, which inherited the Athenian financial system, Syracuse lacked a well-organized tax base. Dionysius resorted to desperate measures to raise large sums in a hurry.

Intending to build a fleet of triremes, Dionysius knew that he would need money for it. He therefore called an assembly and declared that traitors had offered to betray a certain city to him, and he needed money to pay them. The citizens must therefore contribute two staters° each. The money was paid; but after two or three days, Dionysius, pretending that the plot had failed, thanked the citizens and returned to each his contribution. In this way he won the citizens' confidence; so that when he again asked for money, they gave it in the expectation that they would get it back. But this time he kept it for building the fleet.

. . . Again being in need of funds, he asked the citizens to make contributions. When they declared that they lacked money, he brought out the furnishings of his palace and put them up for sale, pretending to be driven to this through lack of funds. At the sale, he made a list of the articles and their purchasers; and when they had all paid up, he just ordered everyone to bring back the articles they had bought.

Pseudo-Aristotle,[39] Economics 2.2.20 (G. C. Armstrong)

°stater: A Persian gold coin worth about twenty drachmas (enough to feed a family of four for three weeks).

Dionysius made extraordinary efforts:

Collecting many skilled workmen, he divided them into groups in accordance with their talents, and put the leading citizens in charge of them, offering great prizes to any citizen who created a supply of arms. He distributed models of each kind of armor among them, because he had gathered mercenaries from many nations; and he was eager to have every one of his soldiers armed with the weapons of his people, seeing that by using such armor his army would cause great alarm, and that in battle all his soldiers would fight best in armor that they were accustomed to. And since the Syracusans enthusiastically supported Dionysius' policy, rivalry rose high to make the arms. Not only was every space—the porches and back rooms of the temples, the gymnasia, and the colonnades in the market square—crowded with workmen, but the making of great quantities of weapons even went on in the most distinguished homes, as well as in public places. . . . With so many arms and ships under construction at one place, the onlooker was filled with utter wonder at the sight. For whenever a man gazed at the eagerness showed in the building of ships, he thought that every Greek in Sicily was engaged in their construction; and when, on the other hand, he visited the places where men were making arms and engines of war, he thought that all available labor was engaged on this alone.

Diodorus of Sicily 14.41 (C. H. Oldfather)

As in his wall-building project, Dionysius ate, slept, and worked with the ordinary people, raising morale. He spent heavily on inventions, including the first effective war catapults, new siege towers, and special ships. He scoured Italy for the best timber and soon had 350 warships, 140,000 shields, helmets, and daggers, and 14,000 breastplates. He offered high rates to attract the best mercenaries, even men from Sparta.

War fever ran high. In the fifth century B.C., Greeks and Phoenicians had coexisted in Sicily, trading and living together, but the bloody struggle of 409 to 405 B.C. changed that. In 398, Syracusans plundered the homes of rich Carthaginians in their city, and Diodorus says that even though the Greeks hated the tyranny of Dionysius, they hated Carthage even more. Hating them for their race, Greeks murdered and tortured Carthaginians wherever they found them.

In 397 B.C., Dionysius invaded Punic[40] western Sicily. He ravaged the country around Segesta, Carthage's strongest native ally, and besieged Motya, a tiny fortified island off the western tip of Sicily. His new catapults and siege towers worked well, and after a long siege, his men stormed the town. The massacre that followed was as horrific as Carthage's destruction of Selinous, Akragas, and other Greek cities a decade before.

Dionysius did not follow up his victory. In 396 B.C., Dionysius' force had dissipated when a vengeful Himilco (the victorious Carthaginian general in the war of 409–405 B.C.) reoccupied western Sicily, then put Syracuse under siege for the third time in twenty years. Dionysius' warmongering was popular a year before, but now that the Carthaginians were camped outside the walls, a popular uprising almost overthrew him. But a plague broke out in the Carthaginian army, which, like the Athenians in 415 to 413 and the earlier Carthaginian force in 405, had pitched camp in an unhealthy swamp.

The plague began with catarrh; then became a swelling in the throat; gradually burning sensations began, pains in the sinews of the back, and a heavy feeling in the limbs; then dysentery took over and pustules spread over the whole body. In most cases this was the course of the disease, but some victims went mad and totally lost their memory. They wandered through the camp, out of their minds, striking anyone they met. In general, as it turned out, even help from doctors was no use because of the severity of the disease and the swiftness of death; for death came on the fifth day or the sixth at the latest, amid such terrible tortures that everyone looked on those who had fallen in the war as blessed.

Diodorus of Sicily 14.41 (C. H. Oldfather)

Dionysius defeated Himilco's disintegrating army and broke up Carthage's fleet. Himilco paid a huge bribe to be allowed to sneak away with the Carthaginian citizens while leaving his mercenaries to die. Back in Carthage, dishonored by defeat, Himilco starved himself to death.

The war dragged on for a few more years until, in 393, the two sides made peace. The King's Peace of 387 B.C. had left Sparta in control of the Aegean, but only as a kind of Persian client. The new Sicilian peace of 393 B.C. acknowledged Carthaginian control of the west, but confirmed Syracuse the undisputed ruler of Greek Sicily.

THE GOLDEN AGE OF SYRACUSE, 393–367 B.C.

Dionysius had not won a resounding victory, but he restored Syracuse's prestige as the only major Greek city in Sicily. He wanted to establish himself as the great man of his age. He contracted polygamous dynastic marriages and brought more western Greeks under his control. In 388 B.C. after a year-long siege, he captured Rhegion on the toe of Italy, Syracuse's rival for a hundred years. Dionysius became protector of most of the Greek cities in southern Italy. Fifty years earlier, there may have been forty thousand people living at Athens; now Syracuse had between fifty thousand and a hundred thousand residents, the largest Greek city in the world.

In 385, emboldened by success, Dionysius intervened in wars between Greek cities far up the Adriatic coast and showed interest in Epirus in northwest mainland Greece. He also supported Sparta in enforcing the King's Peace. As Sparta used fear of Persia to bolster her position in the Aegean, Dionysius used fear of Carthage to keep the Sicilian Greeks in line. Actually fighting Carthage, however, was ruinously expensive. When he miscalculated and had to fight another war between 382 and 374 B.C., Carthage had the better of it.

Like Gelon and Hiero a century earlier, and like the old-fashioned tyrants, Dionysius wanted to impress Aegean Greece with his magnificence. In 388 B.C., he sent his brother with several finely decorated chariot teams to the Olympic games along with professional singers to perform Dionysius' own poetry. Alas, his chariots were not successful, and the Greeks openly mocked the tyrant's verse. Some demanded that he be banned from the Olympics. Undeterred, Dionysius promoted theater and art in Syracuse, bringing Aegean thinkers to his court. Plato visited in 388 or 387. One story (probably invented) says that Plato's philosophizing so irritated Dionysius that he had him thrown in chains and put up for sale in the slave market, where Plato's friends bought his freedom.

Syracuse was big, rich, strong, and cosmopolitan in the 370s B.C. Dionysius won the recognition he craved as a man of letters in 367 when his tragedy, *The Ransoming of Hector*, won first prize in a festival at Athens. Dionysius was so thrilled that, according to one source, he went on a drinking binge that killed him.

ANARCHY IN THE WEST, 367–345 B.C.

Dionysius' rule over Syracuse was personal, and the tyrant-state unraveled after his death. Dionysius I was not the leader of a community of citizens, but a kind of bandit chief using bribes, threats, and trickery to keep the Syracusans under control, and the violence of his mercenaries when those methods failed. His son and successor **Dionysius II** (born around 396 B.C.) shared the first Dionysius' taste for wine and poetry, but lacked his edge, drive, and political skills. He was jealous of one **Dion** (dī-on), Syracuse's main diplomat, tied to the royal family by marriage. Dion, a devoted follower of Plato, was always urging philosophical purity on Dionysius II. Dion talked Dionysius into inviting Plato—now at the height of his fame—back to Syracuse in 367 B.C. Plato apparently hoped to make Dionysius II into the philosopher-king he dreamed of in his celebrated dialogue, *The Republic,* a politically powerful man with philosophical training who would create a perfect society. Dionysius II liked the idea of being an ideal ruler, but liked sex and drinking even more.

Dion and his friends relentlessly pushed Dionysius II to embrace Platonic theory and to renounce tyranny, while Dion's enemies criticized such absurd fantasies. In 366, Dionysius II learned that Dion was talking secretly with Carthaginians. Dion might launch a Carthaginian-backed coup, he feared, but if Dionysius killed Dion, there would surely be other palace intrigues. He could exile Dion, but then he would have a rich and well-connected critic plotting against him. He compromised by sending Dion away while allowing him to keep his property. Dionysius II kept Plato in Syracuse, but Plato kept urging him to surrender his ill-gotten gains and concentrate on virtue. Dionysius finally expelled him from the palace and made him live with the mercenaries. In 360 Plato returned to Athens in disgust, this time for good.

Dionysius II fought another bloody and inconclusive war with Carthage and continued his father's policy of intervening in southern Italy, the Adriatic, and the Aegean, but paying for these wars diminished his power. In 357 B.C., Dion launched the long-awaited coup, leading to a decade of civil war during which Syracuse lost her dominion over the other Greek cities. Carthage's last war against Syracuse ended in 366, after which the Carthaginians (like Persia) found that they could keep the Greeks weak by supporting one faction against another. In city after city, citizens and mercenaries now fought bloody battles for land while bands of exmercenaries wandered the countryside, sacking and pillaging. The population declined as rival warlords devastated the country. Plutarch claims that Sicily's cities were abandoned and that in Syracuse wild animals prowled the marketplace. Around 350, anarchy gripped the west as strongly as it did the Aegean.

CONCLUSION

Greece was passing through tremendous social change, driven in large part by its frenzied wars. States increasingly relied on the rich to finance common security, and a few men of staggering wealth, like Lysander and Jason, challenged entire city-states. Persia and Carthage were the main beneficiaries. Yet despite the backdrop of war, disorder, and fear, most Greeks were better off than before. More of them lived in democracies, and traders filled their markets with exotic goods. Greek explorers visited India and the British Isles, and as we see in Chapter 18, "Greek Culture in the Fourth Century B.C.," artists and thinkers pushed outward the limits of imagination and reason. For all their problems, the Greeks in the mid-fourth century were right to see themselves as the center of civilization.

KEY TERMS

Artaxerxes, 366	*ethnê,* 372
Agesilaos, 367	Jason of Pherae, 372
King's Peace, 368	Leuctra, 373
Common Peace, 369	Sacred Band, 373
Epaminondas, 370	Dionysus II, 378
Cleombrotus, 370	Dion, 379

FURTHER READING

Cahill, Nicholas, *Household and City Organization at Olynthus* (New Haven, CT, 2002). Detailed study of the most fully excavated fourth-century-B.C. Greek city.

Cartledge, Paul, *Agesilaos and the Crisis of Sparta* (Baltimore 1987). Detailed biography of King Agesilaos and sociological analysis of Sparta's decline.

Davies, John K., *Democracy and Classical Greece* (2nd ed., Stanford 1993). Excellent chapters on early-fourth-century Greece.

Lancel, Serge, *Carthage* (Oxford 1995). Survey of Carthaginian history and archaeology.

Lewis, David M., John Boardman, Simon Hornblower, and Martin Ostwald, eds., *The Cambridge Ancient History VI: The Fourth Century B.C.* (2nd ed., Cambridge 1994). Thorough essays reviewing all parts of the Greek world.

Strauss, Barry, *Athens After the Peloponnesian War* (Ithaca, NY, 1986). Excellent study of how the demographic disaster of the Peloponnesian War affected Athenian society.

Ancient Texts

Diodorus of Sicily, *The History,* book 14. In *The Library of History* VI (Loeb Classical Library; Cambridge, MA, 1946; tr. C. H. Oldfather). Parallel Greek and English texts describing Sicilian history.

Plutarch, *Lives* of Agesilaos, Pelopidas, and Dion. In *The Age of Alexander* (Harmondsworth, UK, 1973; tr. Ian Scott-Kilvert). These biographies contain much information on Sparta, Thebes, and Syracuse in the early fourth century B.C.

Xenophon, *A History of My Times* (Harmondsworth, UK, 1966; tr. George Cawkwell). Translation of Xenophon's *Hellenica,* the main narrative source for the years 399 to 362 B.C.

Xenophon, *The Persian Expedition* (Harmondsworth, UK, 1949; tr. Rex Warner). Translation of Xenophon's *Anabasis,* an eye-witness account of the Greek mercenaries' march through the Persian Empire in 399 B.C.

CHAPTER 18

GREEK CULTURE IN THE FOURTH CENTURY B.C.

The social changes that we traced in Chapter 17, "The Greeks between Persia and Carthage, 399–360 B.C." drove momentous cultural changes. We begin with material culture, which became more complex in the fourth century. Most patrons and craftsmen still worked within the classical framework developed in the fifth century, but some experimented boldly. Aristocrats always thought they stood above the masses, and as they accumulated more power—apparently confirming their views—artists and philosophers struggled to make sense of it all.

MATERIAL CULTURE

Sculpture

High Classical sculpture worked magnificently; its canons of proportion, pose, and subject matter seemed almost perfect. Artists who had learned their skills under the old masters could not think of abandoning classicism. But the Peloponnesian War changed art as much as it did everything else. After 404, Athens and Syracuse no longer dominated artistic patronage (Map 18.1). New centers sprang up, providing more room for innovation and diversity and the evolution of the versatile **late classical sculpture.** Some sculptors turned back to what they knew worked. Their statues, echoing early-fifth-century formalism, evoked a more secure age. Figure 18.1 shows Athena. Gone is the clinging drapery of the Peloponnesian War years: the formal folds of her dense, heavy robe and her serious expression look back to the early fifth century, making her seem distant and imposing. But no expert could mistake her for a fifth-century statue: The sculptor tilted her head to the right, adding lightness to the pose.

Map 18.1   Sites mentioned in this chapter.

Figure 18.1   The Piraeus Athena, a bronze statue by an unknown sculptor, cast around 350 B.C. Height 8 feet.

Figure 18.2 Hermes and Dionysus, probably by Praxiteles, circa 340 B.C. Marble. Height 7 ft, 1 in. *Praxiteles (c. 400–300 B.C.E.), "Hermes and Dionysus," c. 350–330 B.C.E. National Archaeological Museum, Olympia, Scala/Art Resource, NY.*

Some patrons wanted statues like this—not copying fifth-century master-pieces, but speaking the same visual language of serenity and reliability. Others wanted the opposite, figures full of energy, verging on the lighthearted, as if cele-brating their escape from the rigid social structures of the fifth century. Fig-ure 18.2, shows the god Hermes with the baby Dionysus. The famous **Praxiteles** (prak-**sit**-e-lēz) probably carved it. Praxiteles did not break with classical forms, but used them to new ends, exaggerating the S-curve pose: Hermes thrusts out his right hip to balance the baby on his left arm. The statue looks unstable, implying movement, and gives a sense that we have caught a moment in a larger story. Praxiteles was famous for giving marble a kind of fluidity, almost a soft focus, as in the smooth junction of Hermes' torso and hips and soft modeling of his jaw. Praxiteles gave his statues long limbs and small heads, making them less realistic but more elegant.

Praxiteles' most famous achievement was to make female nudes acceptable. Since 700 B.C., Greek sculptors had always shown women clothed. Praxiteles' nude Aphrodite of Cnidus, of around 350 B.C., created a sensation. The original is lost, but Roman copies survive (Figure 18.3). The statue stood in a circular open-air shrine in Cnidus in southwestern Asia Minor. It used the soft modeling and S-curves we have already seen, but whereas most statues were made to be seen frontally, Praxiteles carved this one to be seen from every angle. It quickly became the most

Figure 18.3 Roman copy of Praxiteles' Aphrodite of Cnidus. Marble. Height 6 ft, 8 in. The original was carved around 350 B.C. *Aphrodite of Knidos. Roman copy after an original, c. 330* B.C. *by Praxiteles, Marble, H: 6 ft, 8 in. Vatican Museum, Alinari/Art Resource, NY.*

famous statue in Greece. A Roman storyteller described the impact it had on (male) visitors:

When we had enjoyed the plants to the full, we went into the temple [at Cnidus]. The goddess is sited in the middle, a most beautiful work of art in Parian marble,° smiling a little sublimely with her lips parted in a laugh. Her whole beauty is uncovered; she has no clothing cloaking her and is naked except in as far as she nonchalantly conceals her crotch with one hand. The craftsman's art has been so great as to suit the opposite and unyielding nature of the stone to each of the limbs. Charicles,° indeed, shouted out in a mad and deranged way, "Happiest of all gods was Ares who was bound to this goddess,"° and with that he ran up and stretching his neck as far as he could kissed it on its shining lips. But Callicratidas stood silently, his mind numb with amazement.

The temple had doors at both ends too, for those who want to see the goddess in detail from the back, in order that no part of her might not be wondered at. So it is easy for men entering at the other door to examine the beauty from behind. So we decided to see the whole of the goddess and went around to the back of the shrine. Then, when the

°*Parian marble:* Marble from the island of Paros was the most expensive.   °*Charicles:* Charicles, Callicratidas, and "the Athenian" are fictional characters in the story.   °*this goddess:* Homer says that Ares (god of war) had an affair with Aphrodite, but her husband Hephaestus (the lame craftsman-god) trapped him in a net. Charicles says that Aphrodite is so beautiful that being so humiliated was worth it.

door was opened by the keeper of the keys, sudden wonder gripped us at the beauty of the woman entrusted to us. Well, the Athenian, when he had looked on quietly for a while, caught sight of the goddess' private parts, and immediately cried out much more madly than Charicles, "By Heracles! What a fine rhythm to her back! Great flanks! What a handful to embrace! Look at the way the beautifully carved flesh of the buttocks is arched, neither too wanting and drawn in too close to the bones themselves, nor allowed to spread to excessive fat. No one could express the sweetness of the smile of the shape impressed on the hips. How precise the rhythms of thigh and shin extending right to the foot!". . . Charicles was virtually transfixed with amazement, his eyes growing damp. . . .

Pseudo-Lucian,[41] The Lovers 13–14 (K. Kilburn)

Others responded even more passionately. According to one story, a discoloration of the marble on the statue's buttocks marked where one young man gave physical expression to his admiration!

Praxiteles' boldness no doubt shocked conservatives, but was in tune with the times. Within twenty years, female nudes were common, and other sculptors moved even further from frontal views. To patrons and artists living in the rigidly egalitarian societies of the fifth century, it perhaps made sense that there should be just one way to see a statue and that the female form should be hidden. In this brave new, very international world, the same figure might look entirely different, depending on the viewer's perspective. Assumptions that had guided life for four hundred years were dissolving.

Architecture

Architects too were caught between their fifth-century legacy and new demands. Some sculptors made statues more elegant by lengthening their limbs; some architects elongated columns to make taller, lighter, and airier temples. Ornate **Corinthian capitals,** wrapped in leaves and spirals, also lightened the effect (see Figure 9.6). The earliest known Corinthian column is a single example from the Temple to Apollo at Bassai from the mid-fifth century, but by 350 B.C. Corinthian capitals were popular. Compared to the austere Doric and Ionic orders, Corinthian columns look frivolous and fussy, as was much of the art from the fourth century.

Architects experimented with other ways to enhance elegance. A gigantic new temple at Ephesus in Asia Minor sat atop fourteen steps rather than on the two steps of the archaic temple it replaced. Late in the fourth century, architects at Didyma, south of Ephesus, took even more chances: Thirteen steps led up to a forest of columns, leading to an elaborate inner doorway. Then, instead of entering a roofed *cella* as had been normal for four hundred years, the visitor went down steep stairs into an open courtyard with a small *cella* at the end (Figure 18.4). The open-air temple at Didyma cast aside conventional patterns of religious architecture, as did round buildings called *tholoi*[42] (singular, *tholos;* Figure 18.5).

New forms for temples encouraged new uses, and some *tholoi* were used not to honor Olympian gods, but to worship underworld spirits, or even great men. Before the century ended, the kings of Macedonia honored themselves with a giant *tholos* in the sanctuary of Olympia itself.

Experiments with religious architecture and the erosion of earlier boundaries in Greek society between gods and mortals came together in such monuments as the **Mausoleum of Halicarnassus,** counted among the seven wonders of the ancient

Figure 18.4   The inner court of the temple of Apollo at Didyma, begun in 313 B.C. The photo looks over the surprising open inner court toward the steps leading down from the magnificent entrance. The foundations of the *cella* are visible in the foreground.

world. This city—Herodotus' birthplace—was under Persian control from 395 B.C. Around 370, Mausolus was appointed satrap for this part of the empire and made Halicarnassus his capital. Before his death in 353 B.C., Mausolus hired Greek craftsmen to make him the grandest tomb the Aegean had ever seen. It was destroyed long ago, but Roman descriptions and surviving fragments make possible a rough reconstruction (Figure 18.6). The Mausoleum combined a massive base and over-life-sized sculptures with a temple-like second tier, steep roof, and an enormous bronze four-horse chariot at the top. The monument stood 150 feet high, a hint of things to come as non-Greek kings from the edges of the Aegean appropriated the finest classical traditions but turned them to new uses. In the fifth century, great architecture was reserved for gods; no mortal was allowed such monuments. By 350 B.C., if any doubts remained whether great men could challenge the *polis,* the new art styles dispelled them.

For four hundred years, *poleis* poured their greatest energy and wealth into religious architecture. But now Greeks also started spending more on nonreligious civic buildings. The city of **Priene** (prī-ē-nē) on the west coast of Asia Minor, completely rebuilt between 350 and 325 B.C., is a good example. Priene's leaders built a beautiful but small Ionic temple (just 120 by 63 feet) at the top of the site, but spent far more on enormous stoas around the agora, with a council chamber and other public offices along its upper side. A huge theater dominated the town, and an even

Figure 18.5 The marble *tholos* at Delphi, circa 360 B.C.

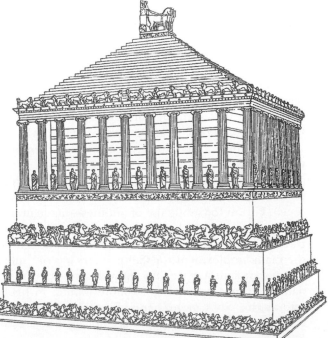

Figure 18.6 Reconstruction of the Mausoleum at Halicarnassus, circa 350–340 B.C. Only the lower walls and pieces of statuary survive. Height 150 feet.

Figure 18.7   Modern model of the city of Priene, circa 325 B.C. The Ionic temple is at the top left. At the center is the agora, with stoas, surrounded by private housing; at the top, the theater; in the foreground, athletic facilities.

larger gymnasium and stadium occupied its lowest area (Figure 18.7). The appearance of Greek cities was changing in the fourth century in line with emerging new social structures.

Painting

We know more about painting in the fourth century than in earlier periods. As before, vase paintings hint at the lost techniques of wall-painters, but after 400 B.C. mosaics of colored pebbles also reproduce the effects of painting, and after 350 B.C. we have actual wall paintings in Macedonian tombs. Dozens of wall paintings from Pompeii and Herculaneum in Italy, preserved when Mount Vesuvius erupted in A.D. 79, also appear to be copies, if sometimes remote, of fourth-century B.C. Greek works.

Two artists who worked at Athens during the Peloponnesian War—Zeuxis (**zūk**-sis), famous for shadowing and delicate gradations of color, and Parrhasius (pa-**rā**-sē-us), known for subtle use of outlines—made important technical advances in the early fourth century; but Athens was now only one of several artistic centers. Artists traveled far and wide, adorning cities from Akragas to Ephesus. In the fifth century, the main employment for wall painters was on public monuments, but during the Peloponnesian War wealthy individuals began hiring these men. Alcibiades scandalized Athens by locking a famous painter in his house until he made it look as fine as the city's monuments. Fourth-century aristocrats marked themselves off from the mass of citizens by building bigger houses and adorning them with mosaic floors, tapestries, and statues. To keep up with fashion, they paid huge sums to hire top artists.

Private money transformed the artists' status. Zeuxis and Parrhasius were famously arrogant. Parrhasius went around in a purple cloak and gold diadem, insulting everyone, while the wealthy Zeuxis claimed that his art was divine and priceless. Such men did not need to beg democratic assemblies for commissions, because they had patrons. Increasingly, painters, sculptors, and architects had more to say to a narrow, highly educated elite who appreciated their work than to fellow citizens.

Red-figure vases give a sense of the new developments, even though the genre declined in the fourth century as the rich shifted to metal plate—even silver and gold—for their dinner parties. Like sculptors, some vase painters clung to fifth-century traditions, while others pursued fluidity and elegance, adding more details, new colors, relief decoration, and gold leaf. To modern tastes, the effect often seems cluttered. Figure 18.8 shows an almost baroque example, made in southern Italy, where the tension between tradition and innovation was so strong that archaeologists divide paintings into two styles, plain and ornate. The ornate style was preferred for large urns to hold the ashes of the dead. On the vase in Figure 18.8, the dead man, standing beside his horse, is shown as part of his own funerary

Figure 18.8 A volute krater (so-called because the handles look like volutes on an Ionic column), circa 310 B.C. This vase, set in its own stand, was used as a funerary urn in a Greek colony in south Italy. Height 48 inches. *Founders Society Purchase, Hill Memorial Fund, William H. Murphy Fund, Dr. and Mrs. Arthur R. Bloom Fund and Antiquaries Fund.*

Figure 18.9 Fragment from a south Italian red-figure krater, circa 350 B.C., with a scene from a tragedy, set in front of a palace. The painter is aware of foreshortening and illustrates sophisticated contemporary stage scenery. Height of fragment 10 in. *Martin von Wagner Museum, University of Wurzburg, Germany.*

monument. Above is a banquet scene. The other side shows a complex assembly of the major deities. The artist tries to give a sense of depth by overlapping the figures. Curling tendrils of filling ornament pack every inch.

Figure 18.9 suggests how fourth-century painters represented depth. It seems to show a scene from a play and reveals how elaborate stage scenery had become. An old man (out of the photo) talks to a young man, while a girl watches through an open door. We look up at the scene, seeing the porch ceiling. A column partly obscures the double doors. The painter used foreshortening, making the girl in the door smaller than the man at the right, but did not use a vanishing point where the lines of the porch converge on some distant spot (the vanishing point in art was not discovered until the Italian Renaissance).

Conclusion

Artists of all kinds simultaneously reflected and reinforced the new social structures emerging in the fourth century. They were caught between the legacy of the fifth century, with its single way of seeing an idealized egalitarian *polis* set apart from the gods, and a new wish to express difference, change, and the power of great men.

PLATO

As in earlier centuries, there were parallels between the creative struggles of visual artists and the achievements of Greek intellectuals. Fourth-century thinkers were also interested in defining a place within the egalitarian *polis* for outstanding individuals, balancing fifth-century traditions with new social forces. But while sculptors, architects, and painters needed rich patrons, philosophers were normally rich men themselves. Thanks largely to **Plato** (c. 427–c. 347 B.C.), Athens' dominance over philosophy grew, rather than declined, in the fourth century.

Plato grew up in a wealthy Athenian family during the Peloponnesian War and, like many men of his background, was drawn to Socrates. After Socrates' shocking execution in 399 B.C., Plato devoted the next fifty years to systematizing and elaborating his master's thought, adding speculations of his own. Because Socrates wrote nothing down, we rarely know whether positions taken in Plato's literary texts belong to Socrates or Plato.

Plato wanted to pursue *aretê* (ar-e-**tā**), "virtue" or "excellence." Within the *polis* he saw two threats. First was democracy, which empowered ignorant people (those who condemned Socrates to death). Second were the sophists' false teachings—that nothing is permanent, values are relative, and knowledge impossible. The structures of contemporary *poleis* encouraged nonsense like the sophists' claims; *poleis* should be placed in the hands of philosophers who understood the Socratic-Platonic way of seeing the world.

Plato's longest works explain how society must change. The ***Republic,*** written probably in the 380s, describes Plato's ideal state; the *Laws,* from around 355 B.C., describes the best that can be accomplished if *poleis* cannot reach that ideal. In either case, a small elite should rule, trained in philosophy, devoting their lives to the citizens' happiness, living without property or families.

Plato justified his arguments by developing the world's first coherent philosophical theory of knowledge. Like Socrates, he asked how we know anything and how we know that we know it. By 360 B.C., aristocrats all over Greece—like Dion, whom we met in Chapter 17—were trying to put his theories into practice; and they remain at the center of philosophical discussion today.

The Theory of the Forms

How can we measure the goodness of a life? It is not enough to say that this or that act is just, or good, or beautiful. To live a good, just, and beautiful life, you must know what goodness, justice, and beauty are, not simply notice alleged examples. Socrates asked, how can we say something is just unless we know what justice is? "Justice," Plato reasoned, is a timeless, eternal thing. The everyday world of the senses is constantly changing, so the ultimate form of justice cannot exist in everyday life. According to Plato's theory of **Forms** (*eidea,* our word "idea"), there cannot be an unchanging world beyond the shifting world we live in. We cannot see the true forms of justice, goodness, and beauty because they exist in another and invisible realm, but they are more real than anything in our experience.

Plato's explanation combined Heraclitus' view that the world is in constant change with Parmenides' notion that reality is unchanging and knowable only through the mind. Objects in the changing everyday world depend on the world of Forms, of which they are dim and inadequate reflections. How can we say that a particular bottle of California chardonnay "is a *good* wine" and that Bob Dylan "is a *good* songwriter," unless both—wine and songwriting—share in an invisible and eternal quality of goodness?

We can grasp the Forms through mathematics. In Greek, *mathêmatika* means "things that are known," that is, through the mind. No one ever saw the square root of two, but it exists and will always exist, independent of the sensual world. Plato argued that the true Forms of goodness, justice, and beauty are equally independent of the world, as invisible as the square root of two.

Plato used stories to explain his sometimes abstract thought. He rejected traditional myths because they lied about reality (saying that the gods were immoral, and other absurdities) and invented his own myths to explain reality. He presents the relationship between the world of the eternal Forms and the everyday changing world in a famous dialogue between Socrates and his friend Glaucon, the **Parable of the Cave**, part of Plato's *Republic*. Socrates speaks first, and Glaucon gives brief replies.

"I want you to picture the enlightenment or ignorance of our human condition somewhat as follows. Imagine an underground chamber, like a cave with an entrance open to the daylight and running a long way underground. In this chamber are men who have been prisoners there since they were children, their legs and necks being so fastened that they can only look straight ahead of them and cannot turn their heads. Behind them and above them a fire is burning, and between the fire and the philosophers runs a road, in front of which a curtain-wall has been built, like the screen at puppet shows between the operators and their audience, above which they show their puppets."

"I see."

"Imagine further that there are men carrying all sorts of gear along behind the wall, including figures of men and animals made of wood and stone and other materials . . . do you think our prisoners could see anything of themselves or their fellows except the shadows thrown by the fire on the wall of the cave opposite them?"

"How could they see anything else if they were prevented from moving their heads all their lives?"

"And would they see anything more of the objects carried along the road?"

"Of course not."

"Then if they were able to talk to each other, would they not assume that the shadows they saw were real things?"

"Inevitably."

"And if the wall of their prison opposite them reflected sound, don't you think that they would suppose, whenever one of the passers-by on the road spoke, that the voice behind them belonged to the shadow passing before them?"

"They would be bound to think so."

"And so they would believe that the shadows of the objects we mentioned were in all respects real."

"Yes, inevitably."

"Then think what would naturally happen to them if they were released from their bonds and cured of their delusions. Suppose one of them were let loose, and suddenly compelled to stand up and turn his head and look and walk toward the fire; all these actions would be painful and he would be too dazzled to see properly the objects of which he used to see the shadows. So if he was told that what he used to see was mere illusion and that he was now nearer reality and seeing more correctly, because he was turned toward objects that were more real, and if on top of that he were compelled to say what each of the passing objects was when it was pointed out to him, don't you think he would be at a loss, and think that what he used to see was more real than the objects now being pointed out to him?"

"Much more real."

"And if he were made to look directly at the light of the fire, it would hurt his eyes and he would turn back and take refuge in the things which he could see, which he would think really far clearer than the things being showed him."

"Yes."

"And if," Socrates went on, "he were forcibly dragged up the steep and rocky ascent and not let go till he had been dragged out into the sunlight, the process would be a painful one, to which he would object, and when he emerged into the light his eyes would be so overwhelmed by the brightness of it that he wouldn't be able to see a single one of the things he was now told were real."

Plato has Socrates imagine the freed prisoner's eyes adjusting to the light until he could see everything and realize that he had mistaken illusions for reality in the realize cave. Socrates continues:

> "When he thought of his first home and what passed for wisdom there, and of his fellow-prisoners, don't you think he would congratulate himself on his good fortune and be sorry for them?"
>
> "Very much so."
>
> "There was probably a certain amount of honor and glory to be won among the prisoners, and prizes for keen-sightedness for anyone who could remember the order of sequence among the passing shadows and so be best able to predict their future appearances. Will our released prisoner hanker after these prizes or envy this power or honor? Won't he be more likely to feel, as Homer says, that he would far rather be 'a serf in the house of some landless man,' or indeed anything else in the world, than live and think as they do?"
>
> "Yes," Glaucon replied, "he would prefer anything to a life like theirs."
>
> "Then what do you think would happen," Socrates asked, "if he went back to sit in his old seat in the cave? Wouldn't his eyes be blinded by the darkness, because he had come in suddenly out of the daylight?"
>
> "Certainly."
>
> "And if he had to discriminate between the shadows, in competition with the other prisoners, while he was still blinded and before his eyes got used to the darkness—a process that might take some time—wouldn't he be likely to make a fool of himself? And they would say that his visit to the upper world had ruined his sight, and that the ascent was not even worth attempting. And if anyone tried to release them and lead them up, they would kill him if they could lay hands on him."
>
> "They certainly would."
>
> "Now, my dear Glaucon," Socrates went on . . . "you won't go far wrong if you connect the ascent into the upper world and the sight of the objects there with the upward progress of the mind into the intelligible realm . . . in my opinion, for what it's worth, the final thing to be perceived in the intelligible realm, and perceived only with difficulty, is the absolute form of Good; once seen, it is inferred to be responsible for everything right and good, producing in the visible realm light and the source of light, and being, in the intelligible realm itself, the controlling source of reality and intelligence. And anyone who is going to act rationally either in public or private must perceive it."
>
> "I agree," Glaucon said, "so far as I am able to understand you."
>
> "Then you will perhaps agree with me that it won't be surprising if those who get so far are unwilling to return to mundane affairs, and if their minds long to remain among higher things. . . . Nor will you think it strange that anyone who descends from contemplation of the divine to the imperfections of human life should blunder and make a fool of himself, if, while still blinded and unaccustomed to the surrounding darkness, he's forcibly put on trial in the lawcourts about the images of justice or their shadows, and made to dispute about the conceptions of justice of men who have never seen absolute justice."
>
> Plato, *Republic* 514e–517e (D. Lee)

Plato's argument struck at the foundations of democracy. A democracy had executed Socrates because it could not understand that he alone saw properly, in the intelligible realm. But Plato was not a simple oligarch: The rich and noble were as deluded as the poor. Only people who had made the painful philosophical ascent to reality understood truth, and they could not explain this to the ignorant masses who had not. The sophists, who claimed to teach wisdom to anyone, were therefore charlatans. Socrates explains to Glaucon that if the Parable of the Cave makes sense, "we must reject the conception of education professed by those [sophists] who say that they can put into the mind knowledge that was not there before—rather as if they could put sight into blind eyes."

Education, the Soul, and the State

Plato based his educational system on his understanding of the soul. The soul is itself a Form, eternal and perfect. When freed from the ever-changing body, the soul directly perceives the world of Forms. Each eternal soul occupies a series of mortal bodies. When the body dies, each soul is judged, then sent for one thousand years to tenfold rewards in heaven or tenfold punishments in the underworld. Then the soul enters a new body, after it drinks from the River of Forgetfulness (*Lêthê*). Philosophy can break through the barrier of forgetfulness so that the soul remembers what it already knew, grasping once more the world of Forms.

Both the *polis* and the soul have three elements, Plato thought, and Justice is their harmonious functioning. The ideal *polis* is like an individual writ large. In a *polis,* the first element is the *rulers,* embodying intelligence and reason. The second is the *warriors,* under the rulers' direction; and the third is the *workers,* in agriculture, commerce, and crafts. In an ideal *polis,* the rulers should live together communally, like the Spartiates (whom Plato admired), own no property, and hence have no interest in profit, which weighs down the soul and disguises its true nature. The justice of the *polis* consists of the three classes accepting their own obligations without coveting or resenting those of another.

Similarly, the individual soul has three parts: reason (like the rulers), desire (like the aggressive soldiers), and will (like the workers, who get things done). Hence we may desire to drink, but reason tells us the water is poisoned. *Will* decides the outcome of the conflict. Many sophists held that the world came from accidental, irrational forces, but the order and harmony of nature convinced Plato that intelligence came first, that very faculty which lives in the human soul and enables the individual to attune its harmonies with those of the greater world.

Plato never presented his philosophy as a system, leading from first principles to necessary conclusions. His task was to lead men toward remembering what their souls already knew. He taught through argument, or dialectic, as Socrates had done. He founded a school called the **Academy** in Athens' suburbs, and wealthy young men flocked there. Philosophy offered students a whole way of life. The process of arguing and reasoning was itself the education they received. Plato presented his theories in simulated written debates between Socrates and other thinkers, often sophists. Most dialogues reach no conclusion about the problems they discuss. Philosophy is a work-in-progress where there are no simple answers, and sometimes no answers at all.

Few fourth-century Greeks liked the authoritarian worlds Plato described in the *Republic* and *Laws,* but the "Socratic method" based on rigorous logic to examine the shortcomings of contemporary thought became the central pillar of rational thought, regardless of cultural context.

ARISTOTLE

The most famous of Plato's students was **Aristotle,** born in 384 B.C. in Stagira, a small town in the north Aegean. His father became court doctor at Pella, the capital of Macedonia, and Aristotle grew up in a royal setting wholly different from the democratic city that shaped Plato's early experience.

Aristotle moved to Athens when just seventeen. He distinguished himself at the Academy, but when Plato died in 347 B.C., the other members chose someone else to fill the master's shoes. Like many fourth-century intellectuals and artists, Aristotle attached himself to a minor king on the fringe of the Persian Empire. He settled near ancient Troy, where he married the king's niece. He did important biological research here, cataloguing over two thousand species of animals and plants. His precise observations would not be equaled until the seventeenth century A.D., and in the 1850s Charles Darwin still found Aristotle one of the most reliable sources of information.

Aristotle seemed destined for a quiet life as a provincial professor until, in 342 B.C., he was summoned back to Macedonia as tutor for the king's fourteen-year-old son Alexander. When Alexander became king in 335 B.C., Aristotle returned to Athens and opened a new school, the **Lyceum** (lī-**sē**-um, named after a nearby shrine of Apollo Lykeios, "Apollo the wolf god").[43] Aristotle did his most important work here between 335 and 323 B.C., the year Alexander the Great died (Figure 18.10).

Figure 18.10 Portrait of Aristotle. Roman copy, circa A.D. 100, of Greek original.

Aristotle's Thought

Unlike his teacher, Aristotle systematized his philosophy. Of over 150 works that he wrote, twenty-five to thirty survive (the authorship of some is disputed); by contrast, all of Plato's writings survive. Aristotle's extant treatises are dry and dense. Several may be lecture notes, not finished compositions. They are comprehensive, analytical, and rigorous, but rarely entertaining. Scholars usually group them into three sets: (i) logic and metaphysics; (ii) nature, life, and mind (including biology, meteorology, physics, and a kind of psychology); and (iii) ethics, politics, and art.

Like Plato, Aristotle argued that true understanding must go beyond sense impressions: There must be first principles that underlie the variety and change in the world. Unlike Plato, Aristotle insisted that the sensual world is nonetheless real, not illusory. To understand anything, he insisted, we must still begin from sensory data. It might seem that experience provides no proper object for knowledge because everything is constantly changing, but by classifying data, organizing them into typologies, we can make sense of life's disorderliness and arrive at laws of nature, general principles that do not change.

Classifying observed data called for more rigorous **rules of logic.** Aristotle began from the principle that contradictory statements cannot be true: *A* cannot be *B* and not-*B* at the same time. People who maintain that contradictory statements *can* in fact be true refute themselves: "Contradictory statements can both be true" means that the contradiction to that very statement is also true, and that contradictory statements *cannot* both be true. Therefore any such statement is "illogical."

In Aristotle's view we do not need invisible Forms existing outside time and space to explain what we see. For example, we can understand "dogs" by examining many of them, discovering what it is that leads us to classify them as dogs, why we think some animals (wolves, dingoes) are like dogs, and why others (spiders, birds) are not; but there is no ideal "dogness" of which all existing dogs are merely pale reflections. Aristotle could not see how Plato's Forms connected to the physical world or explained change in it. The fifth-century atomist philosophers had argued that change was accidental, the result of random motion, but Aristotle also opposed this theory. The true cause or explanation of change, he insisted, lay in its *end*, its purpose (Greek *têlos*), in its **teleology,** "the study of ends."

Aristotle's argument that change was always progress toward some end, and that the end *caused* the change, is called the **theory of potentiality** (Greek *dynamis*, our "dynamic"). An embryo, for example, is not a human but will potentially become one, like its parents. It is the *physis*, "nature," of an embryo to grow into an adult human: As Aristotle wrote, "Natural objects contain with themselves the principles of motion and rest." Humanness is the embryo's end, toward which it grows. That is why its development follows a certain course. The embryo is *potentially* an adult human, even if it died in the womb. Everything has an end, a *têlos*. The *têlos* of humans is to live together in communities; the *têlos* of communities is to maximize happiness; and the *polis* is the type of community that does that most efficiently.

But what causes movement toward the *têlos?* Aristotle abandoned observation and classification and moved toward a purely theoretical account. Nothing can be self-moved, self-caused, because all change is process, a growing toward something that already exists somewhere outside the thing that is changing, its *têlos.* To have a baby girl, you must first have an adult woman. Such must be true of the whole world and its operations. Just as there is an external cause for all change within the world, there must also be an external cause for the world itself, the **Prime Mover,** the ultimate "causeless cause" standing outside the universe, causing everything that happens within it. The Prime Mover is eternal and has always existed. It is the perfection toward which everything strives.

Motion is change from potential to actual, but the Prime Mover is perfect and without potential, containing no motion within itself. Its perfection led Christian thinkers to liken it to God, and the theologian St. Thomas Aquinas (A.D. 1225–1274) used Aristotle's argument as part of his proof of God's existence. But for Aristotle, the Prime Mover had no personality. It was pure mind, life itself, embracing through mind the entire universe for all eternity. The Prime Mover does not know about the things in the world, or even of the world's existence, because the world is characterized by motion and change, whereas the Prime Mover knows no motion or change.

Aristotle organized an account of the universe around the Prime Mover. The earth is at the center, surrounded by invisible spheres made of *aether,* the fifth substance (*quintessence*) after fire, air, water, and earth. The first sphere around the earth belongs to the moon and separates the realms of growth, change, and decay of this world from the celestial realms of eternally perfect, unchanging circular motion. The planets, sun, and moon are lights fixed each in its own sphere, and stars are fixed in the outermost sphere. The spheres rotate, but on different axes in a complex way (explaining the irregular motion of the planets). Beyond the sphere of stars is the Prime Mover, wrapped in eternal self-contemplation, toward which all the things of the world aspire through their *dynamis,* the urge of nature.

Virtually every Greek, Roman, Christian, and Moslem astronomer accepted Aristotle's model until Nicolaus Copernicus (A.D. 1473–1543) argued that the sun is the center of our system, and the physics and observations of Johannes Kepler (A.D. 1571–1630) and Galileo Galilei (A.D. 1564–1642) demonstrated the truth of these claims.

Some of Aristotle's differences from Plato—such as Plato's notion of immortal souls migrating from body to body—seem not to have concerned Aristotle much, but the nature of virtue had to be faced. For Plato, proximity to the Forms explained what was just, good, and beautiful. Because Aristotle denied eternal, external standards, he had to think about right and wrong as purely practical matters. In this context, he made his famous remark that "man is a political animal": Humans are creatures designed to live in the *polis.* Behavior that favored life in the *polis* was "good," whereas behavior that interfered was "bad."

As a rule of thumb, "good" behavior follows the mean between extremes, which constitute "bad" behavior. This **doctrine of the mean** was the key to Aristotle's ethical thought. Courage lies between cowardice and recklessness. Temperance stands between self-indulgence and abstemiousness. Generosity comes between stinginess and extravagance. There is nothing absolutely "good" or "bad" about virtuous behavior, as for Plato, but behaving "down the middle" favors harmony within the *polis.*

> First of all then we have to observe that moral qualities are so constituted as to be destroyed by excess and by deficiency—as we see is the case with bodily strength and health (for one is forced to explain what is invisible by means of visible illustrations).[44] Strength is destroyed both by excessive and by deficient exercises, and similarly health is destroyed both by too much and by too little food and drink, whereas they are produced, increased, and preserved by suitable quantities.
>
> The same therefore is true of temperance, courage, and the other virtues. The man who runs away from everything in fear and never endures anything becomes a coward; the man who fears nothing whatsoever but encounters everything becomes rash. Similarly, he that indulges in every pleasure and refrains from none turns out a profligate, and he that shuns all pleasure, as boorish persons do, becomes what may be called insensible. Thus temperance and courage are destroyed by excess and deficiency and preserved by the observance of the mean.
>
> Aristotle, *Nicomachean Ethics* 2.1 (H. Rackham)

For once agreeing with Plato, Aristotle linked individual virtue—ethics—with its communal pursuit—politics. As he saw it, personal ethics made sense only as part of a *polis:*

> The *polis* is both natural and prior to the individual. For as an individual is not fully self-sufficient after separation, he will stand in the same relationship to the whole as other parts. Whatever is incapable of participating in the association which we call the *polis,* a dumb animal for example, and equally whatever is perfectly self-sufficient and needs nothing from the *polis* (for example, a god), these are not parts of the *polis* at all. Among all men, then, there is a natural impulse toward this partnership. . . . As man is the best of all animals when he has reached his full development, so he is the worst when divorced from law and morals.
>
> "It follows that the *polis* belongs to a class of objects which exist in nature, and that man is by nature a political animal (politikon zôon); it is his nature to live in a *polis.*" The polis was an association formed to pursue the art of living well.
>
> Aristotle, *Politics* 1.2 (T. A. Sinclair)

Aristotle divided the *polis* into component elements: individuals, households, villages, and the *polis* itself. Individuals combine into households, households into villages, and villages into *poleis* because otherwise they are incomplete. Individuals are not autonomous. Male and female, adult and child, and free and slave all need each other and can form appropriate relationships only within larger combinations. All such relationships are natural because the *polis* is humanity's *têlos* and must therefore be natural itself. Children need adults, because otherwise they cannot cope; adults need children, or there will be no more adults. Men and women need each other for reproduction; and the free need slaves because they are a specific and vital form of property:

> The rule of free over slave, male over female, man over boy, are all natural, but they are also different, because, while parts of the soul are present in each case, the distribution is different. Thus the deliberative faculty in the soul is not present at all in a slave; in a female it is inoperative, in a child undeveloped.
>
> Aristotle, *Politics* 1.13 (T. A. Sinclair)

For Aristotle, society was a set of necessary hierarchies making it possible for some members—the male citizens—to pursue the good life. The superiority of men over women, old over young, and free over slave was natural. A state has six needs: food, wealth, arts, defense, religion, and justice. Generating the first three of these requires "slave-like" behavior, so, he reasoned, agricultural laborers, traders, and artisans should be excluded from citizenship. Such men would be citizens in a democracy, of course, but to Aristotle democracy did not reflect nature.

CONCLUSION

The Greek world in the mid-fourth century B.C. was wealthy and complex. It had more people, living at higher standards, than ever before; yet there was a sense of decline. The power and financial efficiency of the Athenian Empire was gone, and mighty Sparta was humbled. After 404 B.C., increasingly expensive and meaningless wars killed thousands and squandered Greece's wealth. In the Aegean, Sparta, Thebes, and Athens strained to dominate, while in Sicily tyrants turned their cities into armed camps. The endless fighting gave more room for Persia and Carthage to assert themselves. Persia funded Sparta and threatened to intervene against anyone who might unite the Aegean; Carthage directly attacked Syracuse and seized western Sicily. To pay for wars on this scale without the benefits of Athenian-style taxation of subject cities, *poleis* surrendered ever more privileges to the rich citizens. By 350 B.C., houses and tombs of the elite were grander than ever. The new aristocrats filled their cities with monuments to their own glory.

Artists struggled to express the specialness of the few without shattering the conventions of sixth- and fifth-century art, which had succeeded so magnificently, while philosophers addressed old puzzles head-on and displaced tragedians and historians as intellectual leaders, generating forms of expression that we still live with today. Fourth-century art, architecture, and painting impressed the Romans more than their fifth-century predecessors had, and Roman copies of fourth-century works inspired the eighteenth-century-A.D. classical revival in western Europe and North America. The questions that Plato and Aristotle asked, the methods they developed, and the answers they offered provide the foundations for modern thought. But, this creative and vibrant world hovered on the brink of disaster. When Plato died in 347 B.C., the system of *poleis* that had flourished since the eighth century B.C. was still recognizable. When Aristotle died a quarter of a century later, that world was gone forever.

KEY TERMS

late classical sculpture, 381
Praxiteles, 383
Corinthian capitals, 385
tholos, 385
Mausoleum of Halicarnassus, 385
Priene, 386
Plato, 391
Republic, 391
Forms, 391

Parable of the Cave, 392
Academy, 394
Aristotle, 395
Lyceum, 395
rules of logic, 396
teleology, 396
theory of potentiality, 396
Prime Mover, 397
doctrine of the mean, 397

FURTHER READING

Plato

Guthrie, W. K. C., *A History of Greek Philosophy*, vol. 4, *Plato: The Man and His Dialogues: Earlier Period* (Cambridge, UK, 1975), and vol. 5, *The Later Plato and the Academy* (1978), have thorough reviews of his work, while vol. 3, *The Fifth-Century Enlightenment* (1969), contains a full account of what is known about Socrates.

Nightingale, Andrea, *Genres in Dialogue* (Cambridge, UK, 1995). Excellent study of Plato in his literary and sociological context, and the emergence of *philosophia* as a distinct way of thinking about Athenian society.

Szlezák, T. A., *Reading Plato*, tr. G. Zanker (New York 1999). Best short book on his thought.

Vlastos, Gregory, *Platonic Studies* (2nd ed., Princeton 1981). Contains several classic papers.

Aristotle

Most scholarship on Aristotle is found in articles in professional journals, but there are several good introductions to Aristotle's thought:

Barnes, Jonathan, *Aristotle* (Oxford 1982). Excellent general survey.

Barnes, Jonathan, Malcolm Schofield, and Richard Sorabji, eds., *Articles on Aristotle* (4 vols., London 1975–79). The proceedings of the triennial *Symposium Aristotelicum;* contains some pathbreaking work.

Lloyd, G. E. R., *Aristotle: The Growth and Structure of His Thought* (Cambridge, UK, 1968). The best short survey.

Jaeger, Werner, *Aristotle: Fundamentals of the History of His Development* (2nd ed., Oxford 1948, reissued 1962; originally published in German, 1923). Advances a theory of the development of Aristotle's thought.

Ancient Texts

Aristotle, *Ethics* (Harmondsworth, UK, 1955; tr. J. A. K. Thomson), *The Politics* (Harmondsworth, UK, 1962; tr. T. A. Sinclair), *Rhetoric* (New York 1984; tr. P. J. Rhodes), *The Athenian Constitution* (New York 1984; tr. P. J. Rhodes), and *De Anima (On the Soul)* (New York 1986; tr. Hugh Lawson-Tancred).

Lucian (Loeb Classical Library; Cambridge, MA, 1982; tr. K. Kilburn).

Plato, *The Symposium* (Harmondsworth, UK, 1951; tr. W. Hamilton), *The Last Days of Socrates* (Harmondsworth, UK, 1954; tr. Hugh Treddenick), *The Republic* (Harmondsworth, UK, 1955; tr. Desmond Lee), *Protagoras and Meno* (Harmondsworth, UK, 1956; tr. W. K. C. Guthrie), *The Laws* (Harmondsworth, UK, 1970; tr. T. J. Saunders), and *Timaeus and Critias* (Harmondsworth, UK, 1971; tr. Desmond Lee).

CHAPTER 19

THE WARRIOR-KINGS OF MACEDON, 359–323 B.C.

By the 350s B.C., *poleis* from Sicily to Ionia were bankrupt and exhausted, and Persia and Carthage were playing the warring Greeks against each other. Jason of Pherae had shown how a strong man might organize one of the larger, looser states around the edges of the Aegean and use its manpower and wealth to overwhelm the *poleis*. **Philip II** of Macedon (Figure 19.1) succeeded where Jason failed. Philip II had prodigious appetites for alcohol, sex, power, and violence. In speeches to the Athenian Assembly in the 340s B.C., his subtlest opponent, **Demosthenes** of Athens,[45] portrayed him as the ultimate lying, murderous tyrant. When Cicero of Rome wanted to abuse his enemy Mark Antony some three hundred years later, he called his attacks *Philippics*, after Demosthenes' masterpieces; when Winston Churchill wanted to awaken Britain to the German threat in the 1930s, he styled himself "Demosthenes" and Hitler "Philip."

He was also brave, intelligent, and determined. He did not shrink from violence, but it was usually his last resort. He broke oaths and tore up treaties, but so did his enemies. He was a realist, ruthlessly pursuing power. He brought unity to Aegean Greece for the first time and set the stage for overthrowing the Persian Empire. Although a Macedonian, and not viewed by the Greeks as a Greek, he spoke Greek and claimed Greek descent. Ironically, his Macedonian son Alexander was to spread Greek culture far beyond the Mediterranean, and we will speak of the Macedonian generals as "Greeks," an appellation they would have gladly approved.

MACEDONIA BEFORE PHILIP II

When Philip came to the throne in 359 B.C., Macedonia was a backwater covering a large area, divided into Upper (western) and Lower (eastern) Macedonia (Map 19.1). Lower Macedonia was a land of plains, watered by wide rivers, with towns and a

Figure 19.1 Ivory head of a middle-aged man, found in Tomb II of the Macedonian Royal Cemetery at Vergina. It dates circa 340–300 B.C. and probably represents Philip II.

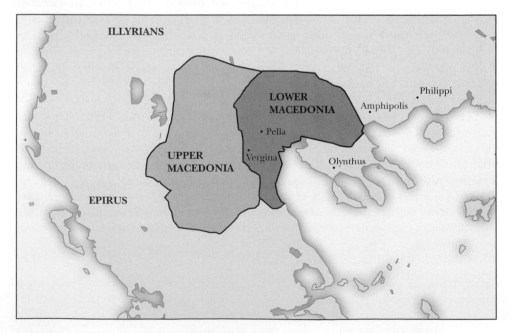

Map 19.1   Sites in northern Greece and Macedonia mentioned in this chapter.

prosperous peasantry. Upper Macedonia, by contrast, was mountainous and wild. Its weather was cooler, and rain fell year round. Culturally, its tribal chiefs looked north and west to mountain peoples as much as to the lowlanders. Macedonia was the Greek cities' bulwark against dangerous movements of peoples in the uplands, but the warlords of Upper Macedonia fought on both sides, resisting mountain raiders or joining them, as the occasion demanded.

Persia overran Macedonia in the 490s, then, after 479, its excellent timber for shipbuilding made it strategically important to Athenians, who dominated Macedonia's weak kings. There was a royal family and an expectation that a king's oldest son would succeed him, but kings hardly differed from their nobles. They dressed, ate, and lived like them, and depended on personal ties and persuasion to mobilize them for war. A new king had to be acclaimed by the army, which the nobles dominated. Unlike the *poleis,* Macedon had little civic solidarity and few farmer hoplites. Most farmers were serfs, better off than Sparta's helots, but the makings of poor infantry. The military striking force was the elite cavalry.

Royal silver mines brought in one talent per day by 500 B.C., giving the king about half the revenue of the fifth-century Athenian empire, not enough to win independence by hiring mercenaries, like Sicilian tyrants. Despite a population of half a million, kings depended on a few hundred noble horsemen, the **King's Companions,** who often preferred fighting each other to following royal orders. Only a king with talent and luck could tame this anarchy. **Alexander I** (498–454 B.C.) was such a man. He became a Persian client-king around 492 and gained some control over his feuding barons. After Persia withdrew in 479, he strengthened the army further and got a better grip on Upper Macedonia. Alexander encouraged the aristocracy to speak Greek and act like Greeks, insisting that the Macedonian royal family originally came from Argos. In a celebrated episode, probably in 476 B.C., he entered the Olympic games, where only Greeks could compete. When (after an argument) the Olympic officials allowed him to race, he claimed this as "proof" that he really was Greek. He tied for first place. But as late as the 420s B.C., Macedonia still struck Thucydides as wild and backward.

Athens wanted to control Macedonian resources. When Athens founded **Amphipolis** in 436 B.C. (the city that Thucydides failed to save from Brasidas in 424), pressure on Macedonia increased. During the Peloponnesian War, Macedonian kings tried to preserve their independence by switching alliances so often that no one knew which side they were on. King Archelaos (413–399) resumed Alexander I's program of Hellenization by building a new Greek-style capital at **Pella** and bringing artists and thinkers there, including Euripides. Archelaos expanded the kingdom, but in the 370s his successor, King Amyntas (392–369 B.C.), fell under the influence of the Thessalian strongman, Jason. Amyntas made concessions to Thebes and Athens, covetous of Macedonia's wealth in timber and metals, and lost much of Upper Macedonia to a hill-people called the Illyrians. Amyntas paid annual tribute to avoid further raids.

Amyntas needed male heirs and took a young wife, Eurydicê. She gave him three sons when he was in his sixties (Philip II was the youngest). Eurydicê began an affair with a noble youth named Ptolemy. She arranged for Ptolemy to marry her daughter Eurynoê (appropriately, "broad-minded") so she could continue sleeping with him without raising suspicion. Emboldened, Eurydicê and Ptolemy now plotted to kill Amyntas, but Eurynoê revealed the plot to her father, who was so shocked he fell down dead! Amyntas' oldest legitimate son, Alexander II, now took the throne in 369 B.C. The army acclaimed him, but Ptolemy prepared a coup. To avoid civil war, uncommitted aristocrats asked Thebes—Greece's greatest power following the battle of Leuctra in 371 B.C.—to arbitrate. The ambassadors favored Alexander over Ptolemy.

Alexander II sent his youngest brother Philip II, aged thirteen, to Thebes as a hostage: If Alexander misbehaved, the Thebans would execute his brother, while if he kept the peace, Philip would form attachments to Thebes. Ptolemy pretended to submit to the Theban arbitration, but as soon as they were gone, he had Alexander murdered at a folk dance. He now married Eurydicê (we hear no more of the unhappy Eurynoê) and announced that he would serve as regent for Alexander II's young brother Perdiccas.

Philip II spent two years in Thebes, living with a top general and moving among the most advanced military thinkers in Greece. His official tutor was a Pythagorean, who advocated vegetarianism, pacifism, and sexual abstinence. Philip was unimpressed. In 367, Thebes sent him back to Macedonia. Now that Philip's brother Alexander was dead, keeping Philip as hostage would hardly restrain the unrelated Ptolemy.

In an unusual display of sentiment, Eurydicê and Ptolemy spared Philip's older brother Perdiccas, but when Perdiccas reached eighteen in 365 B.C. and succeeded to the throne, he did not make the same mistake. He murdered Ptolemy, bringing this extraordinary family saga to an end, and appointed Philip as a provincial governor. In Thebes, Philip had learned the importance of good hoplites, and he now developed an infantry corps for Perdiccas. Copying Theban tactics, Philip trained his men to use spears eighteen feet long and small shields. The long spears held by men in the back ranks protruded ahead of the front ranks, so that the enemy faced a forest of spear points. They fought twenty-four ranks or more deep, against the usual eight or twelve. In 360 B.C., Perdiccas decided to stop paying protection money to Illyria. Relying on his newly trained army, he attacked the Balkan tribesmen in a catastrophic campaign. Perdiccas and four thousand of his men lay dead, leaving Macedonia exposed to the angry Illyrians.

PHILIP'S STRUGGLE FOR SURVIVAL, 359–357 B.C.

Because Perdiccas left no sons, his brother Philip, now twenty-two or twenty-three years old, was the logical heir. The army acclaimed him, but four rivals appeared, and the Illyrians and other neighboring peoples massed to invade. Perdiccas' defeat left Macedonia without an army. Some rivals for the throne were at Pella, whom Philip quickly murdered. Recognizing that the threatening tribes wanted money more than power, he renewed the tribute to Illyria and agreed to a dynastic marriage.

Philip started rebuilding his army. The Thebans probably assumed that Philip, as their former "guest," would favor them. But Philip saw that Athens was stronger in the north than Thebes, and he had something Athens wanted. During Athens' and Thebes' complicated struggle for influence in the north in the 360s, the Macedonians garrisoned Athens' former colony Amphipolis. Three thousand hoplites were sent from Athens to Macedonia to support a rival to Philip's throne in 359 B.C. Athens also negotiated with the powerful northern Greek city of **Olynthus** (see Map 19.1), which offered to help Athens recover Amphipolis. But Philip disposed of the rival claimants to the Macedonian throne, carefully avoiding killing any Athenians. He captured a few, then sent them home, even giving them money for the journey. The Athenians made peace with Philip and asked for Amphipolis back. Philip pulled his garrison out of Amphipolis before signing the treaty, then announced that he did not actually hold Amphipolis, so he could not give it to Athens. Instead, he pledged to help Athens recover the city. But Athens did not get Amphipolis back.

Philip raised a new army of ten thousand infantry and six hundred cavalry. He trained hard, refining Theban tactics. He wanted a strong phalanx that would maneuver to create gaps in enemy lines, which the superior Macedonian cavalry would exploit. Philip tried out his new tactics against the hill-tribes, and for the first time, Macedonian infantry distinguished themselves. Early in 358 B.C., Philip defeated the Illyrians and recovered Upper Macedonia. Just eighteen months after inheriting a kingdom in ruins, Philip's alliance with Athens and victory over Illyria made him secure (for now) from external threats.

Philip had strategic vision. In 359, the real issue was survival, while the Illyrians thought it was money, and the Athenians thought it was Amphipolis. By offering Athens and Illyria what they wanted, he seized what really mattered. He would repeat this maneuver in the years to come.

In 357, Philip seized the metal-rich area of Pangaion in western Thrace, installed up-to-date technology, and was soon extracting a thousand talents a year, as much as the revenue of the Athenian empire at its height. He founded a new city, called Philippi after himself, to protect the mines. In 357, he contracted two new marriages (his third and fourth). So far, his marriages had not given him a viable heir, but his new wife **Olympias** of Epirus would bear a remarkable one.

PHILIP CONSOLIDATES HIS POSITION, 357–352 B.C.

Philip's security depended on his alliance with Athens. If the powerful *polis* of Olynthus attacked him, Athens would intervene to protect her claim on Amphipolis. When Athens set up her Second League in 378 B.C., she promised not to exploit her allies, but constant wars with Sparta and Thebes forced her to break her word. In 357 B.C., three of the most important allies—Rhodes, Cos, and Chios—seceded, initiating the Social War (Map 19.2).[46] Athens could no longer neutralize Olynthus. If Athens' friendship was now useless to him, why not take Amphipolis back? As winter 357 closed in, Philip stormed and captured Amphipolis. Dionysius I of Syracuse had developed new siege engines forty years earlier, which Philip perfected. In the fifth century, by contrast, walled cities were invulnerable unless traitors opened their gates. In the next year, 356 B.C., Olympias delivered a healthy boy, Alexander III; Philip's chariot team won at Olympia; and he defeated Illyria again. The angry Athenians declared war on Philip, but (as he foresaw) were too busy fighting the Social War to act.

Complicated wars still raged between the *poleis*. The heavily politicized **Sacred League,** consisting of various *poleis,* controlled the sanctuary of Apollo at Delphi. In 356 B.C., at Thebes' urging, the League imposed impossibly high fines on leaders of the backwoods territory of **Phocis,** which surrounds Delphi, on trumped-up charges of sacrilege. Thebes hoped to force the anti-Theban leaders in Phocis into exile, thereby increasing the influence of the pro-Theban faction. But Phocis rallied to the men's

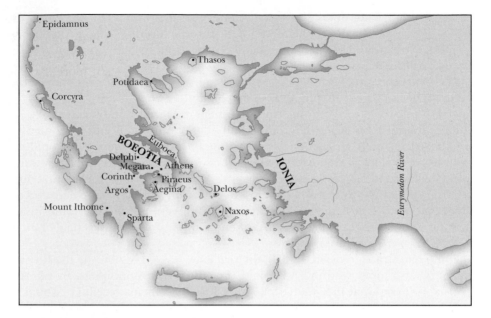

Map 19.2   Aegean sites mentioned in this chapter during Philip's reign, 359–336 B.C.

defense, seized Delphi, took "loans" from its treasures to hire mercenaries, and fought back. Athens and Sparta, looking for ways to damage Thebes, supported Phocis' cause.

In summer 355, Athens conceded defeat in the Social War, and the Second Athenian League dissolved. The Thebans saw that Athens was now too weak to help Phocis, and persuaded the Sacred League to declare war against the Phocians, because they had desecrated Delphi. But with the sanctuary's wealth in their hands, the Phocians offered wages 50 percent above the norm for mercenaries, expanded their army, and drove back the Theban army.

Because complex alliances linked fourth-century *poleis,* various states lined up either behind Thebes or Phocis. Larisa in Thessaly, home to Philip's third wife, was an ally of Thebes and had been fighting the nearby city of Pherae on and off ever since Jason was tyrant fifteen years before. Because Pherae allied with Phocis in the dispute over Delphi, Larisa asked Philip to help them against Pherae. This offered Philip an opportunity. If he defeated Pherae, she would probably ask Phocis for help; and Philip could then pose as the Sacred League's champion, avenging Phocian sacrilege and enhancing his standing among the Greeks.

At first Philip's plan went well, but in spring 353 B.C. the Phocians defeated him, the only serious military defeat Philip ever suffered. Many Greeks thought he was finished. Olynthus broke a recent alliance with him, joining Athens instead. But Philip raised a new army in 352 B.C., captured Pherae, and crushed a Phocian army in Thessaly. Philip drowned three thousand Phocian prisoners on charges of sacrilege and crucified their dead leader's body.

There was nothing to stop Philip marching south through the pass of Thermopylae into central Greece as savior of the Sacred League. He spent the summer annexing Thessaly into the Macedonian state. Athens, Sparta, and their allies fortified Thermopylae, but Philip had other plans.

PHILIP SEEKS A GREEK PEACE, 352–346 B.C.

Philip formulated an ambitious plan to attack Persia. He might have conquered Thebes, Athens, and Sparta, but he admired the vast wealth concentrated in storerooms in the Persian capitals of Persepolis and Susa (see Map 19.3) more. Back in the 390s B.C., the Ten Thousand and Agesilaos of Sparta had showed how hoplites could carve their way through the heart of Persia. By 352 B.C., the western satraps were in revolt and would offer little resistance. Conquering the Greeks was not the best plan, because they would want revenge. Better for them to be allies, identifying their interests with Philip's own. For thirty years, the famous Athenian orator and essayist Isocrates (ī-**sok**-ra-tēz) had argued that Greeks should forget their endless differences and unite behind one city, Athens, against the true foe, Persia. By 352 Athens was no longer a viable leader, but Philip might take that role.

The Sacred War dragged on, splitting Greece into pro-Theban and pro-Athenian camps. Neither Athens nor Thebes could hurt Philip separately, but together they were dangerous. He attempted to win influence in Athens, but the orator Demosthenes violently opposed him. Demosthenes delivered his first *Philippic* in 351, rousing his fellow countrymen to action by claiming that it was their own inaction that had created this monster:

> What could be more startling than a Macedonian fighting a successful war against Athens, and dictating the affairs of Greece? "Philip is dead," comes one report. "No, he is only ill," comes another. What difference does it make? Should anything happen to Philip, Athens, in her present state of mind, will soon create another Philip. This one's rise was due less to his own power than to Athens' inactivity.
>
> Demosthenes, *Philippics* 4.10–11 (A.N.W. Saunders)

Demosthenes thought Athens could be great again if she acted resolutely, but Athens could no longer generate the revenues to compete with states like Macedonia. In 349, Philip moved against Athens' ally Olynthus, perhaps hoping to show that resistance was futile. Demosthenes' rhetoric reached its peak in three speeches called the *Olynthiacs*, claiming that Philip was about to be destroyed by his own evil:

> There is not a state that has tried to make use of him without falling victim to his duplicity. In every case he deceived them, and exploited their folly and ignorance for his own advancement. He has risen on their shoulders, each time they have seen in him a means to their own advantage. He should owe his destruction to the same forces, now that his invariable self-interest has been proved against him. This is the point to which Philip's fortunes have been brought . . . the power which, like his, is rooted in greed and violence will fall in ruin at a word, at the first false step. Never, gentlemen, can lasting power be founded on broken promises and lying words. Such empires stand for one short hour. They may blossom with fair hopes, but time finds them out, and they fade and die. In a house, in a ship, in any structure, it is the foundation that needs most strength. So it is too with the actions of men's lives, which must be founded on truth and justice. And this is not true of the achievements of Macedonia.
>
> Demosthenes, *Olynthiacs* 2.9–10 (A.N.W. Saunders)

Demosthenes urged Athens to find the money somehow, and sail to Olynthus' rescue. Other politicians claimed that although Philip was a tyrant, Athens could work with him. Philip moved his siege engines against the walls of Olynthus. The

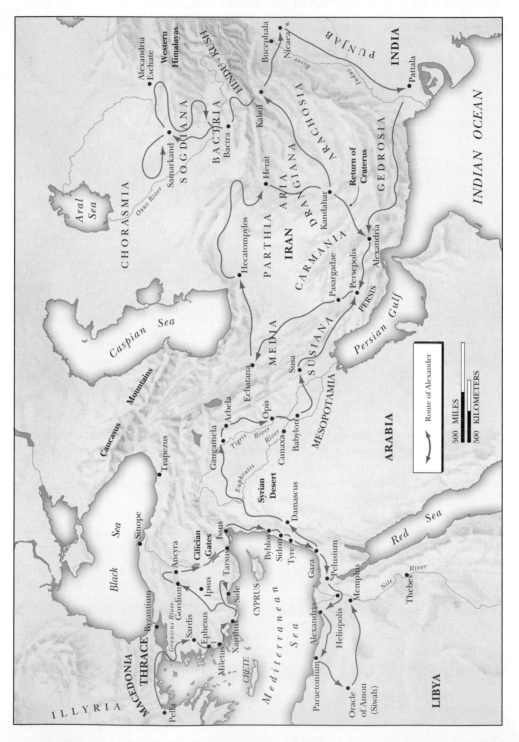

Map 19.3 Alexander's invasion of the Persian Empire.

Athenians voted to send troops to a war closer to home, on Euboea. Philip's supporters betrayed the city from within. He imprisoned the Athenians he found there, sold the Olynthians into slavery, and burned the city to the ground. American archaeologists excavated the ruins in the 1920s and 1930s, and it remains our clearest snapshot of classical Greek urban life (see Figure 2.6).

Philip hoped to negotiate a general peace in Greece, leaving Athens dominant but dependent on his support. The Sacred War against Phocis, still dragging on, made a general peace difficult, because most *poleis* sided either with Thebes or Athens. Demosthenes' attempt to create a broad anti-Macedonian alliance failed because other *poleis* mistrusted Athens. Pro-Macedonians in Athens undermined Demosthenes in 346 B.C. by pushing through their own treaty with Philip. Philip released the Athenian prisoners he took at Olynthus, then persuaded the Sacred League to invite him to finish the war with Phocis. The Phocians had looted ten thousand talents from the sanctuary at Delphi, but in 346 B.C., with the money spent, they collapsed before Philip's attack. Philip hoped to please Thebes (who opposed Phocis) by ending the war, and avoid offending Athens (who supported Phocis) by dissolving Phocis' cities into villages rather than massacring the Phocians. His compromise satisfied no one. The Sacred League invited Philip to preside over the Pythian Games at Delphi, which should have been his crowning moment; but Athens, swayed by Demosthenes' rhetoric, refused to send delegates—a bitter snub from the city of Pericles and Plato.

THE STRUGGLE FOR A GREEK PEACE, 346–338 B.C.

Athens' treaty with Philip divided the city. Anti-Macedonian feelings ran high. In 348 B.C., Aristotle, who had lived in the Macedonian court, felt it wise to leave Athens, and many pro-Macedonian politicians followed his example. Isocrates (now an old man of seventy), who had spent thirty years urging Athens to lead a Greek crusade against Persia, stayed and wrote a new booklet asking Philip to lead the crusade. Philip should build an army from the thousands of landless men and former mercenaries now in Greece, he thought, and after defeating Persia, should settle these mercenaries on Persian lands, ridding Greece of a growing social problem.

Syracuse was in chaos in the 340s B.C., racked by civil wars and declining population. In 345, the people of Syracuse asked for new colonists to be sent from her mother-city, Corinth. The Corinthians responded halfheartedly, sending a disgraced politician named **Timoleon** (tim-ō-lē-on) with just seven hundred mercenaries. Timoleon raised cash in Sicily, and by 338 had deposed all the Greek tyrants and driven Carthage back into western Sicily. In the decisive battle, Timoleon was saved by a thunderstorm that drove hail and sleet into the Carthaginians' faces. Timoleon showed again that for an ambitious man with money to hire mercenaries, anything was possible:

> Timoleon had accomplished what were universally regarded as the greatest and most glorious achievements of any Greek of his time: he was indeed the only man who had actually performed those exploits that the orators of various national assemblies° were

°*Orators of various national assemblies:* For example, Isocrates and Demosthenes.

constantly exhorting their fellow countrymen to attempt. . . . He had shown courage and justice against barbarians and tyrants, and justice and moderation toward the Greeks and his friends; he had set up most of his trophies without causing tears to be shed or mourning to be worn by his fellow-citizens of Syracuse or of Corinth, and in less than eight years he had restored Sicily to its inhabitants, delivered from the strife and disorder that had constantly plagued it in the past.

Plutarch, Life of Timoleon 37 (I. Scott-Kilvert)

Timoleon did what Isocrates preached, leading tens of thousands of Greeks from the Aegean to new land overseas.

Philip must have watched Timoleon's expedition closely as he saw his own chance to act in the east slip away. Philip was making little progress in uniting the Greeks behind him. In city after city, feuds raged between "friends of Philip" and would-be patriots. Meanwhile in Persia, King Artaxerxes III (359–338 B.C.) put down the rebel western satraps and improved the empire's ability to defend itself. Philip, waiting, tightened his control of Upper Macedonia, Thrace, and Thessaly; transplanted populations into new cities; and organized them so he could raise troops more effectively. According to Arrian, a historian writing four hundred years after Philip but using primary sources now lost,[47] Alexander the Great described Philip's achievements in these years as follows:

> "Philip found you a tribe of impoverished vagabonds, most of you dressed in skins, feeding a few sheep on the hills and fighting, feebly enough, to keep them from your neighbors—Thracians and Triballians and Illyrians. He gave you cloaks to wear instead of skins; he brought you down from the hills into the plains; he taught you to fight on equal terms with the enemy on your borders, till you knew that your safety lay not, as once, in your mountain strongholds, but in your own valor. He made you city-dwellers; he brought you law; he civilized you. He rescued you from subjection and slavery, and made you masters of the wild tribes who harried and plundered you; he annexed the greater part of Thrace, and by seizing the best places on the coast opened your country to trade, and enabled you to work your mines without fear of attack."

Arrian, Campaigns of Alexander 7.9 (A. de Selincourt)

Philip's young son Alexander III, aged just fourteen, first tasted battle in these years. Abandoning his strategy of uniting Greece behind a great campaign, Philip moved in 340 B.C. against Byzantium and Perinthus, cities that controlled crossings into the Persian Empire. Byzantium and Perinthus also controlled the grain route from the Black Sea to Athens, so attacking them meant certain war with Athens. Macedonian siegecraft employed mobile towers one hundred feet tall, rapid-fire catapults, and sophisticated tunnels to undermine walls. Philip commented that no one had built a wall so high that gold could not scale it. Neither bombardment nor bribery worked at Byzantium and Perinthus, which had state-of-the-art fortifications and superb natural positions. Athens duly declared war, while Artaxerxes of Persia poured mercenaries and money into the defense of Perinthus and Byzantium.

By autumn 340, Philip knew he could not take Perinthus and Byzantium. Now Athens was the real issue. If he took Perinthus and Byzantium, he would still have to face Athens, but if he defeated Athens, Perinthus and Byzantium would surrender soon enough. He raised the sieges and intercepted a huge grain fleet bound for Athens, causing terrible hardship in the city. In 339 B.C., he persuaded the Sacred

League to declare war on Athens too. Only when he could claim to be acting as the Sacred League's agent, did he attack Athens.

Swinging inland to avoid Thermopylae, he suddenly showed up two days' march from Thebes in spring 338. He demanded that Thebes join the Sacred League and help it punish Athens, but Demosthenes persuaded the Thebans to stand with Athens. In August 338 B.C., he threw his army against well-prepared Athenian-Theban positions at **Chaeronea** (kī-ro-**nē**-a), a village near Thebes. We know little of the battle, except that the eighteen-year-old Alexander charged at the head of the King's Companion cavalry and, smashed the legendary Theban Sacred Band, slaughtered almost to the last man.

In the Athenian line, Demosthenes disgraced himself by throwing down his shield and fleeing. Plutarch says that when he caught his cloak on a thorn bush as he ran, he fell to his knees and begged it to take him alive, before realizing his mistake. A thousand of his countrymen died.

Philip had beaten the finest force the Greeks could assemble. According to one story, he drank himself into a stupor and danced on the piles of Theban dead; another story has him weep on seeing the corpses of the Sacred Band. He sent back the thousand Athenian dead and offered to free the two thousand prisoners he had taken without ransom. Athens still had her fleet and walls and a siege would be difficult and expensive. The Athenians were freeing their slaves to fight, reinforcing their walls, and preparing for a last stand when a messenger announced Philip's terms in the Assembly. The *dêmos* accepted without debate, conferred Athenian citizenship on Philip and Alexander, and put up a statue of Philip in the marketplace.

Thebes, on the other hand, ransomed her prisoners at a high price. Her leaders were banished or executed, a Macedonian puppet government established, and a garrison stationed atop the Acropolis. Athens, Philip reasoned, would now surely secure the Aegean while he marched against Persia, and Thebes was reduced to a second-rank power.

PHILIP'S END, 338–336 B.C.

Philip wanted to be seen as a legitimate leader. He had been careful to act in 338 B.C. as head of the Sacred League, and in 337 he called a conference at Corinth to discuss the future. Only the now-irrelevant Sparta refused to attend. Philip proposed a Common Peace, like that of 371 B.C., with the *poleis* swearing not to act against Macedonia. Macedonian garrisons, later known as "the fetters of Greece," occupied a few strategic spots. He promoted Isocrates' Panhellenism and explained that he merely wanted to avenge Persia's destruction of Greek temples nearly 150 years before. Lured by the promise of plunder, the conference appointed Philip and his heirs as commanders-in-chief.

Artaxerxes had repaired the weaknesses that had made Persia so tempting a target in the early 340s, but just as Philip was cutting down the Thebans and Athenians at Chaeronea, Artaxerxes' grand vizier—a eunuch named Bagoas—murdered him. For two months Persia was in virtual anarchy as Bagoas hunted down and killed claimants to the throne, until only Artaxerxes' youngest son Arses was left. Bagoas restored order by November 338, but left Persia badly weakened.

As Philip foresaw, Byzantium and Perinthos yielded as soon as he defeated Athens, and in spring 336 a vanguard of ten thousand Macedonians crossed into Asia. They met little resistance. The Ionians rose up against Persia. In June 336 Bagoas murdered Arses too and elevated a minor member of the royal family to the throne as **Darius III.** Darius' first act was to force Bagoas to drink the same poison he had administered to others. Persia was in chaos.

Philip sent a man to Delphi to ask the god whether he would conquer Persia. The oracle answered: "The bull is garlanded. All is done. The sacrificer is ready." Philip took "the bull" to be Darius and "the sacrificer" to be himself. Like so many visitors to Delphi, he was mistaken.

To clear up a family dispute, Philip arranged a wedding between his niece and the brother (confusingly, named Alexander) of his fourth wife Olympias. All the dignitaries of Greece came. At the festival's climax, twelve huge statues of the Olympian gods were carried into the arena with a thirteenth statue, at the same scale, of Philip himself. Then came Philip in the flesh, flanked by Alexander his son and Alexander his brother-in-law, all dressed in white. Philip had ordered his bodyguards to stay a few yards back so everyone could get a good view of their entrance. Without warning, one of the bodyguards stepped in front of Philip and drove a short sword into his heart.

Who Killed the King?

The simplest theory to explain Philip's murder is that Pausanias, the assassin, killed Philip for his own reasons. He had once been Philip's lover, but the king abandoned him for a new boyfriend close to Attalus, a powerful nobleman from Lower Macedonia. Pausanias caused a public scene. Philip's embarrassed new lover asked Attalus to punish Pausanias. Attalus invited Pausanias to dinner, got him drunk, then led the rest of the guests in gang-raping him. Attalus then gave Pausanias to his stable boys, who repeated the rape. The much-abused Pausanias appealed to Philip for redress, but the king did not want a feud with Attalus, whose daughter Cleopatra he had just taken as his fifth wife. Pausanias evidently took matters into his own hands. Philip's guards killed Pausanias immediately.

Another explanation places blame on Philip's fourth wife Olympias (Alexander the Great's mother). She suspected that Philip's union with Attalus' daughter Cleopatra was part of a plan to repudiate Alexander and father a new heir. At Philip and Cleopatra's wedding, the proud father Attalus gave a speech praying for a *legitimate* heir for Philip, implying that Alexander was illegitimate. A drunken Alexander threw his wine cup at Attalus, and Attalus threw his back. Philip, drunker than anyone, pulled out his sword and lunged—not at Attalus, who had insulted his son, but at Alexander. When Cleopatra bore Philip a son in summer 336, the danger seemed imminent. Did Olympias (and Alexander) plan Philip's death and persuade the angry Pausanias to do the dirty work?

ALEXANDER THE KING

When news of Philip's death reached Greece, the *poleis* revolted. Athens proclaimed a public holiday. Everyone assumed that pretenders would emerge and civil war drive Macedonia back into obscurity. Like Philip in 359, Alexander faced rivals for the throne, hostile Greeks, and threats from the Balkans. The greatest threats to his power, Attalus and Philip's top general **Parmenio** (par-mēn-ē-ō), were away in Ionia with the advance guard, so Alexander moved quickly. The army in Macedonia proclaimed him king, and he murdered all potential rivals within reach. His mother Olympias killed the two babies that Cleopatra had borne Philip by pressing them face-down into red-hot coals. Cleopatra hanged herself.

The veteran soldiers around the twenty-year-old Alexander advised him that he could not meet all threats at once. He should abandon Greece and defend Macedonia against the Balkans. Alexander feared that Parmenio would claim that in this crisis Macedonia needed experience, not youth, and nominate Alexander's older cousin as king. Alexander had to prove his excellence as a general so he raced south against Greece.

Troops guarded the passes into Thessaly, but Alexander cut steps up the face of towering Mount Ossa and dropped down behind them. Thessaly surrendered, and the Thebans awoke to find Alexander camped outside their walls. They too surrendered. A week earlier, Demosthenes assured Athens that Alexander was "a mere boy"; now Athens capitulated.

Alexander called a meeting of the Greek League at Corinth, which named him general against Persia in his father's place. In six weeks, Alexander had won back Greece without a single casualty. Parmenio recognized Alexander's leadership, but insisted on filling top offices in the army with his own relatives. Alexander agreed—for now.

Early in 335, while the snow lay deep in the mountains, he struck north, pursuing hostile tribes into the interior and across the Danube River. He was gone for months; according to rumor he was dead. Thebes and Athens contacted Persia and revolted once again. Alexander concluded his northern campaign and raced back to Thebes. The first the Thebans knew of it, he was a day's march away. For a few hours, they refused to believe it was him. Then Alexander was upon them, offering generous terms which the Thebans rejected, calling him a tyrant. In a desperate battle, Alexander forced his way into the city and killed six thousand Thebans. He sold another thirty thousand into slavery and burned every house in the city except the home of Pindar, whose poetry he admired. When persuasion fails, turn to terror. Athens surrendered (for the third time since 338). Alexander, the butcher of Thebes, universally hated, no longer feared revolt in his rear. Violence had persuaded the recalcitrant Greeks once and for all.

Alexander's Strategy

The Greek League proclaimed Alexander its avenger, but Alexander wanted to replace Darius and rule the whole Persian Empire. Persians held that the god Ahuramazda chose the Achaemenid family to fight for the light against darkness, saving the world. To rule the empire, Alexander would fulfill the same role. He had to kill or capture Darius, marry a daughter or his widow, and win over the Magi, the powerful priesthood, to achieve this end. The war would be personal, a duel fought through vast armies.

Alexander also had to defeat his own generals, particularly Parmenio, Philip's right-hand man, whose appointees dominated the officer corps. Alexander needed to show that he *personally* made the difference between victory and defeat. He must lead from the front and make brilliant decisions. Throughout his campaigns, Alexander was recklessly courageous. Alexander was more of a man than Darius, and perhaps more than any had ever been.

Alexander also needed money to reward his men. Wages would cost three thousand talents per year (three times the annual income of the fifth-century Athenian empire). Alexander's only inheritance from Philip was a five-hundred-talent debt. He had to borrow from his richest subjects, using royal land as collateral—he mortgaged the kingdom. He paid his debts and set off for Asia with just eighty talents and thirty days' worth of supplies.

Darius' Strategy

Darius could defeat Alexander in battle; he could use money to raise revolts; or he could assassinate Alexander. He had one outstanding general, a Greek mercenary named **Memnon,** who spent 335 B.C. winning back some of the Ionian cities that went over to Parmenio the previous year. But Darius was slow to support the Greek rebellions of 338 through 335, and his fleet was not ready to intercept Alexander's crossing. Most likely, he did not take Macedonia seriously and thought his western satraps would crush Alexander. When Alexander proved him wrong, Darius hesitated, committing neither to Aegean revolts nor to a decisive battle. He seems to have misunderstood the war Alexander brought him.

THE CONQUEST OF PERSIA, 334–330 B.C.

The Opening Moves, 334 B.C.

Alexander claimed that he was avenging the invasion of 480 B.C., and he followed Xerxes' route in reverse. He was the first man ashore in Asia, casting his spear into the beach to claim the land by conquest. He then marched to Troy. Here, he and his lover Hephaistion laid wreaths at what were said to be the tombs of Achilles and Patroclus, then raced naked around them. Alexander dedicated his armor to Athena and took from the temple built on the ancient ruins another suit, guaranteed by the priests to be a relic from the Trojan War itself. Alexander was the new Achilles, and he carried a copy of the *Iliad* everywhere he went.

Desperate for money, Alexander extorted cash from the Ionians, but he needed to fight a battle and capture plunder. Understanding this, Memnon urged the western satraps to avoid battle, retreating ahead of Alexander and devastating the country, but the satraps did not want to tell Darius they had run from Alexander and burned their own territory. They massed their forces near where Alexander crossed, at the **River Granicus** (**gran**-i-kus) (see Map 19.3).

Thousands of Persian cavalry (outnumbering Macedonians three or four to one), stiffened by Greek mercenaries, stood behind the fast-flowing river. The satraps threw back Alexander's efforts to force his way across the river. In a maneuver he would repeat many times, Alexander slipped away by night and crossed the river upstream. Next morning, the armies clashed head-on between the river and the foothills a mile away.

Alexander took a post on the right, wearing the spectacular armor he had taken from Troy so the Persians would see him and send their best cavalry at him. He would be at the heart of the struggle, while Parmenio, on the left, would anchor the Macedonian line. The Persians charged.

> Fortune had brought together in the same place the finest fighters to dispute the victory. Spithrobates, the satrap of Ionia, was a Persian by birth and son-in-law of King Darius. He was a man of high courage, and hurled himself at the Macedonian lines with a large body of cavalry. . . . As the force of this attack seemed dangerous, Alexander turned his horse toward the satrap and rode at him.
>
> To the Persian, it seemed as if this opportunity for a single combat was god-given. He hoped that by his personal gallantry Asia might be relieved of its terrible menace, the famous daring of Alexander arrested with his own hands, and the glory of the Persians saved from disgrace. He threw his javelin first at Alexander with so mighty an impulse and so powerful a cast that he pierced Alexander's shield and drove through the breast-plate. The king shook the weapon off as it dangled by his arm, then applying his spurs to his horse and using the momentum of his charge, he drove his lance squarely into the satrap's chest. At this the adjacent ranks in both armies cried out at the amazing display of manhood. The point, however, snapped off against the breastplate and the broken shaft recoiled. The Persian drew his sword and drove at Alexander; but the king recovered his grip on his lance just in time to stab at the man's face and drive the blow home. The Persian fell, but just at this moment, his brother Rhosaces galloped up and brought his sword down on Alexander's head so hard that it split his helmet and wounded his scalp. As Rhosaces aimed another blow at the same break in the helmet, Cleitus, known as "the Black," dashed up and cut off the Persian's arm.
>
> The Relatives° now pressed in a solid body around the two fallen men. At first they rained their javelins on Alexander, and then closing went all out to kill the king. But exposed as he was to many fierce attacks, he nevertheless was not overcome by the numbers of the enemy. He took two blows on the breastplate, one on the helmet, and three on the shield he had brought from the temple of Athena, but still did not give in, but borne up by his spirit he surmounted every danger. After this several of the other noble Persians fighting against him also fell. . . .
>
> Now that many of their commanders had been killed and all the Persian squadrons were worsted by the Macedonians, those facing Alexander were put to flight first, then the others too. Thus the king by common agreement won the award for bravery and was regarded as the chief author of the victory.
>
> Diodorus of Sicily 17.20–21 (C. B. Welles)

°*Relatives:* An elite core of Persian cavalry.

Alexander's phalanx pushed into a gap in the Persian line which collapsed. Memnon's Greek mercenaries fell back to a low hill. They tried to surrender, but Alexander viewed them as traitors and killed three thousand of them. Memnon escaped.

The Struggle for the Aegean, 334–333 B.C.

Alexander now had money and was loosening Parmenio's grip on the army, but Darius had four hundred ships on the way to Ionia. Alexander's one hundred and sixty ships, with mostly Greek crews of questionable loyalty, could not stop them. Ancient ships had to put into shore every night; if Alexander captured every harbor on the Aegean coast—and then every harbor in the east Mediterranean—the Persian fleet would be useless. Alexander dissolved his own fleet (saving one hundred talents per month) and rushed down the west coast of Asia Minor, storming one harbor town after another, often arriving hours ahead of the Persian fleet. Only at Halicarnassus on the southwest tip of Anatolia, an old city famous as Herodotus' birthplace and for its huge Mausoleum, did Memnon and the Persian fleet arrive first. For weeks, Alexander's siege engines pounded the walls. Memnon's Greek mercenaries resisted, then sailed away. All cities on the Aegean coast were in Alexander's power, if he could only keep them that way.

Memnon pressed Darius to appoint him commander in the west, with money to take the war to Greece. The native Persian generals instead urged staking every-thing on another land battle. While an indecisive Darius massed troops at far-off Susa, Memnon in the west hired new mercenaries. That winter one Ionian city after another went back to Persia. Memnon planned to sail to mainland Greece with three hundred ships. Athens and Sparta were ready to rise against Macedonia.

Should Alexander turn back to defend Greece, or press ahead? From the south-ern coast of Anatolia, he marched his men across high mountains, inland across the Anatolian plain to winter at Gordion, the ancient capital of Phrygia, where supplies were better. The ancient Persian royal road ran through Gordion to Sardis and the Aegean coast two hundred miles away, in case he wished to return there and reclaim the Ionian cities. In the middle of the town was an old ox-cart, said to have been dedicated to Zeus by the great king Midas. Arrian tells the story:

> There was also another traditional belief about the wagon: according to this, the man who undid the knot that fixed its yoke was destined to be the lord of Asia. The cord was made from the bark of the cornel tree, and so cunningly was the knot tied that no one could see where it began or where it ended. For Alexander, then, how to undo it was in-deed a puzzle, but he was nevertheless unwilling to leave it as it was, as his failure might lead to public disturbances. Accounts of what happened differ. Some say that Alexander cut the knot with a stroke of his sword and exclaimed "I have undone it!," but Aristobulus° thinks that he took out the pin—a sort of wooden peg that was driven right through the shaft of the wagon and held the knot together—and thus pulled the yoke away from the shaft. I do not presume to be dogmatic on this subject. In any case, when he and his attendants left the place where the wagon stood, the general feeling was that the oracle about the untying of the knot had been fulfilled. Moreover, that very night there was lightning and thunder—a further sign from heaven; so Alexander, on the strength of all this, offered sacrifice the following day to the gods who had sent the sign from heaven and proclaimed the Loosing of the Knot.
>
> Arrian, *Campaigns of Alexander* 2.3 (A. de Selincourt)

°*Aristobulos:* Aristobulos took part in Alexander's campaign and wrote a history of it after 301 B.C. Only fragments of his book survive.

Alexander gambled that the Aegean would hold. Even if Greece rebelled and invaded Macedonia, it did not matter as long as he took Persia. In spring, Alexander marched southeast across the Anatolian plain and through the towering Taurus Mountains to the broad plain of Cilicia. In mid-July, as Alexander neared Syria, Memnon died of disease. Darius' advisors in Babylon were split, the Persians urging him to abandon the west and his remaining Greek mercenary general insisting they attack Macedonia. The Greek general became so agitated about Persian incompe-tence that Darius flew into a rage and had him executed. Having lost his two best commanders, he blundered again, recalling his mercenaries from the Aegean to join the land army he was assembling, effectively giving up the Aegean.

The Struggle for the East Mediterranean, 333–332 B.C.

Alexander pressed ahead. Darius put a thousand-talent reward on his head. When Alexander dived one day into an icy pool to escape the heat and went into convulsions from shock, no doctor dared treat him, for fear of being accused of treason. Only a Greek friend named Philip came forward.

> [Philip] thought it shameful not to share his friend's danger by exhausting all the resources of his art even at the risk of his own life, so he prepared a medicine and persuaded him to drink it without fear, since he was so eager to regain his strength for the campaign. Meanwhile, Parmenio had sent Alexander a letter from the camp warning him to beware of Philip, since Darius, he said, had promised him large sums of money and even the hand of his daughter if he would kill Alexander. Alexander read the letter and put it under his pillow without showing any of his friends. Then at the appointed hour, when Philip entered the room with the king's Companions carrying the medicine in a cup, Alexander handed him the letter and took the draft from him cheerfully and without the least sign of misgiving. It was an astonishing scene, and one well worthy of the stage—the one man reading the letter and the other drinking the medicine, and then each gazing into the face of the other, although not with the same expression. The king's serene and open smile clearly displayed his friendly feelings toward Philip and his trust in him, while Philip was filled with surprise and alarm at the accusation, at one moment lifting his hands to heaven and protesting his innocence before the gods, and the next falling upon his knees by the bed and imploring Alexander to take courage and follow his advice. At first the drug completely overpowered Alexander and, as it were, drove all his vital forces out of sight; he became speechless, fell into a swoon, and displayed scarcely any sign of sense or life. However Philip quickly restored him to consciousness, and when Alexander had regained his strength he showed himself to the Macedonians, who would not be consoled until they had seen their king.
>
> Plutarch, *Life of Alexander* 19 (I. Scott-Kilvert)

Parmenio advised Alexander to wait for Darius at a place called **Issus,** where he could watch all three passes by which Darius might come through the mountains between Syria and the sea (near the modern border between Turkey and Syria). Alexander was convinced that Darius would come through the southernmost pass. Alexander blocked its entrance, only for Darius to come through a pass further north, cutting Alexander's line of retreat and capturing injured troops whom Alexander had left at Issus. To intimidate the Macedonians, he chopped off their hands and sealed the wounds with boiling tar.

Alexander was trapped between Darius to the north and hostile Phoenician cities to the south. The passes inland were closed. All Darius needed was to hold his position, starve out Alexander, and win the war. Instead, he offered battle, forming up his troops along a two-mile front behind the River Pinarus (Figure 19.2).

Parmenio, on the left, would again anchor the position. The phalanx would advance in the center to pin the Persians down, while Alexander would lead the Companions in a diagonal charge into the heart of the Persian position.

Darius massed his best cavalry on his right. As the Macedonians advanced to within bowshot of the river, he launched them against Parmenio, hoping to break through and roll up Alexander's line. At the same moment, Alexander charged with his Companion Cavalry. The light-armed Persian infantry collapsed, while on the other wing the excellent Persian horsemen drove Parmenio back. In the center, the

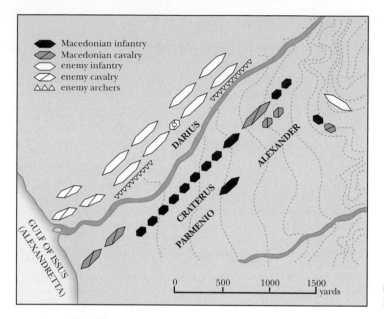

Figure 19.2 The Battle of Issus.

Macedonian phalanx and Darius' Greek mercenaries slaughtered each other in a classic hoplite battle:

> Then the blood really flowed, for the two lines were so closely interlocked that they were striking each other's weapons with their own and driving their blades into their opponents' faces. It was now impossible for the timid or cowardly to remain inactive. Foot against foot, they were virtually engaging in single combat, standing in the same spot until they could make further room for themselves by winning their fight: only by bringing down his opponent could each man advance. But, exhausted as they were, they were continually being met by a fresh adversary, and the wounded could not retire from the battle as on other occasions because the enemy were bearing down on them in front while their own men were pushing them from behind.
>
> Quintus Curtius,[48] *History of Alexander* 3.10 (J. Yardley)

As Alexander's cavalry pressed ahead, a gap opened between them and the Macedonian phalanx. Darius' mercenaries rushed in, taking the Macedonian infantry in their unprotected right flank and killing many. Instead of going to their rescue, however, Alexander swung behind the fight and made straight for Darius (see Figure 19.3).

> Alexander was as much a soldier as a commander, seeking for himself the rich trophy of killing the king. Riding high in his chariot, Darius cut a distinctive figure, at once providing great incentive to his men to protect him, and to his enemies to attack him. [Darius'] brother Oxathres saw Alexander bearing down on Darius and moved the cavalry under his command right in front of the king's chariot. Oxathres far surpassed his comrades in the splendor of his arms and in physical strength, and very few could match his courage and devotion to Darius. In that engagement especially he won distinction by cutting down some Macedonians who were recklessly thrusting ahead and by putting others to flight. But the Macedonians fighting next to Alexander, their resolve strengthened by mutual encouragement, burst with Alexander himself into the line of the Persian cavalry. Then the carnage took on truly cataclysmic proportions. Around Darius' chariot

Figure 19.3 The Alexander Mosaic, about 15 feet long, from a house in Pompeii, destroyed in A.D. 79 by the eruption of Mount Vesuvius. Based on a Hellenistic painting of the Battle of Issus, this mosaic consists entirely of small, cut colored stones. Alexander in his chariot on the left portion of the picture makes straight for Darius right of center, whose eyes seem to meet Alexander's.

lay his most famous generals who had gone down to a glorious death before the eyes of their king, and who now all lay face-down where they had fallen fighting, their wounds on the front of the body. Among them could be recognized Atizyes, Rheomithres, and Sabaces, satrap of Egypt—all generals of mighty armies—and heaped around these was a crowd of lesser-known infantrymen and cavalrymen. The Macedonian dead were not numerous, but they were the bravest of them, and among the wounds received was a sword-thrust to Alexander's right thigh.

By this time Darius' horses had been pierced by lances and were distracted with pain; they had begun to toss the yoke and were on the point of hurling the king from his chariot. Frightened that he might fall into his enemy's hands alive, Darius jumped down and mounted a horse that followed his chariot for this very purpose. He even stooped to throwing off his royal insignia so they could not betray his flight. The rest of his men now scattered in fear. They broke out of the fighting wherever they could find an escape-route, throwing down the weapons that shortly before they had taken up to defend themselves—thus does panic create fear even of things that help.

Quintus Curtius, *History of Alexander* 3.11 (J. Yardley)

By fleeing, Darius lost face. Alexander scooped more than three thousand talents in gold from the Persian camp, bathed in the Great King's jeweled tub, and put on his purple silk robes (even though Darius was very tall, and Alexander rather short). Most important, Alexander captured Darius' mother, wife, and daughters, who for some reason were traveling with the army. Darius could not protect his own women, let alone the Persian Empire. Alexander treated them courteously. When he killed Darius, he could marry his widow and so make a legitimate claim to the throne.

Darius made Alexander an unprecedented offer: In return for his family and peace, he would surrender most of Anatolia. Alexander hid Darius' letter, substituting for it an arrogant note merely offering ransom. The Macedonians were furious, and Alexander wrote back:

> By God's help I am master of your country. . . . Come to me, therefore, as you would come to the lord of the continent of Asia. Should you fear to suffer any indignity at my hands, then send some of your friends and I will give them the proper guarantees. Come then, and ask me for your mother, your wife, and your children, and anything else you please; for you shall have them, and whatever besides you can persuade me to give you.
>
> And in future let any communication you wish to make with me be addressed to the King of all Asia. Do not write to me as an equal. Everything you possess is now mine; so, if you should want anything, let me know in the proper terms, or I shall take steps to deal with you as a criminal. If, on the other hand, you wish to dispute your throne, stand and fight for it and do not run away. Wherever you may hide yourself, be sure I shall seek you out.
>
> Arrian, *Campaigns of Alexander* 2.15 (A. de Selincourt)

Alexander therefore continued securing the Mediterranean coast. The main target was **Tyre,** the great Phoenician city that had founded Carthage four hundred years before. Tyre had the finest harbor in the East Mediterranean. From here, Persian fleets could threaten Alexander's rear. But the city was on an island half a mile off-shore, and Alexander had no ships. The Tyrians mocked his demands for surrender. In February 332, he started building an artificial land bridge two hundred yards wide out to the city. The Macedonians dumped thousands of tons of rock, dirt, and timber into the sea, and the bridge crept out.

The Tyrians tried everything to prevent its completion. They invented special ships that could mount the land bridge and set the Macedonian siege machinery on fire, and wooden towers that tipped burning tar onto the besiegers. Alexander's engineers designed floating battering rams, so the Tyrians dumped debris into the sea to keep them from the walls. The Macedonians then built floating cranes to clear the way. Finally, in July, the mole reached the island. After the most ferocious catapult barrage the world had seen, Alexander's 150-foot-tall siege towers moved against the walls. He led the assault in person, took the city, and sold the thirty thousand survivors into slavery.

Darius had lost the western empire. He had no way to strike at the Aegean, and Alexander's road to Egypt was open. Darius offered Alexander everything west of the Euphrates, legitimate marriage to his eldest daughter, and ten thousand talents.

> Parmenio, according to all reports, declared that if he were Alexander, he would be happy to end the war on such terms and be done with any further adventures. "That," Alexander replied, "is what I would do too, if I were Parmenio; but since I'm Alexander, I'll send Darius a different answer." And send it he did. He had no need, he wrote, of Darius' money, nor was there any call on him to accept part of the continent in place of the whole. All Asia, including its treasure, was already his property, and if he wished to marry Darius' daughter he would do so, whether Darius liked it or not. If, moreover, Darius wanted kindness and consideration at his hands, he must come to ask for it in person. Upon receiving this reply, Darius abandoned all thought of coming to terms and began once more to prepare for war.
>
> Arrian, *Campaigns of Alexander* 2.26 (A. de Selincourt)

Alexander entered Egypt in October 332 B.C. Persia had reconquered the rebellious country only eleven years before, and the Egyptian aristocracy welcomed

Figure 19.4 The Siwa Oasis from the Mountain of the Dead. The salt lake Birket Siwa backed by distinctive high bluffs is visible in the distance.

Alexander as a liberator. They crowned him pharaoh in the ancient city of Memphis. Alexander was proclaimed the son of Ra and incarnation of Horus. By proclaiming Alexander a god, Egyptians handed him a potent propaganda weapon. More ominously, Alexander was starting to believe his own propaganda.

In January 331, Alcxander tested his divine status with a 750-mile round trip to the oracle of Amun far out in the desert at Siwa (Figure 19.4). Greeks identified Amun with Zeus. Alexander claimed on his return that the oracle had confirmed his divinity. He disposed of Egyptian affairs as if the war were won, and marked out a new city called Alexandria to replace Tyre as the East Mediterranean's main harbor, destined to be one of the greatest cities of the ancient world. His governors would rule from here. In April 331, he marched back to Judea, where news arrived that Sparta had revolted. Alexander headed into the heart of the Persian Empire.

The Fall of Darius, 331–330 B.C.

At Babylon, Darius assembled the largest army ever seen in antiquity, perhaps 250,000 strong. Alexander let him pick his spot, the plain of **Gaugamela** (gau-ga-mē-la) near modern Arbela on the upper Tigris. The Persians cleared the plain of rocks and trees so their cavalry and scythe-wheeled chariots could maneuver better. When Alexander arrived, Darius' army outnumbered his own five to one. Darius had as many cavalry as Alexander had cavalry and infantry combined, and thousands of the Persians wore heavy armor. The Persian line was a mile longer than the Macedonian. Whatever Alexander did, he would be outflanked.

Parmenio suggested a night attack, but Alexander scornfully replied, "I will not steal my victory." He needed to defeat Darius in open battle. On the night of September 30, while his army slept, Alexander lay awake. Was there any way to offset the fearful odds? When he finally settled on a plan, Plutarch says,

> Alexander lay down in his tent and is said to have passed the rest of the night in a deeper sleep than usual. At any rate when his officers came to him in the early morning, they were astonished to find him not yet awake, and on their own responsibility gave out orders for the soldiers to take breakfast before anything else was done. Then, as time was pressing, Parmenio entered Alexander's tent, stood by his couch, and called him two or three times by name: when he had roused him, he asked how he could possibly sleep as if he were already victorious, instead of being about to fight the greatest battle of his life. Alexander smiled and said, "Why not? Do you not see that we have already won the battle, now that we are delivered from roving around these endless devastated plains, and chasing this Darius, who will never stand and fight?" And indeed not only beforehand, but at the very height of battle Alexander displayed the supremacy and steadfastness of a man who is confident in the soundness of his judgment.
>
> Plutarch, *Life of Alexander* 31 (I. Scott-Kilvert)

Alexander invented a battle plan that two thousand years later became a favorite of Napoleon's. He angled both flanks backward, making them look even weaker than they were, to entice Darius into attacking them (Figure 19.5). As the Persians

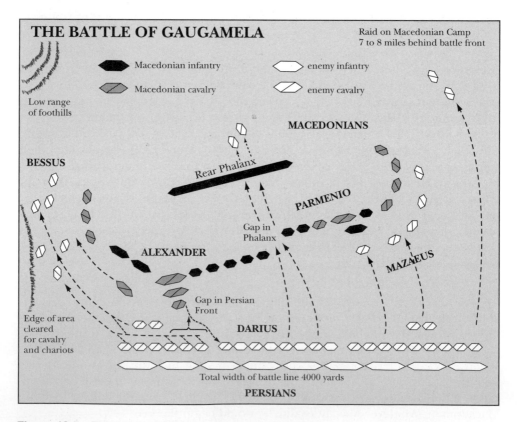

Figure 19.5   The battle of Gaugamela.

found the flanks stronger than they thought, they would (he hoped) commit more men to these fights, thinking they were about to crush the Macedonian wings. At some point, a gap would open in their center. Then Alexander would strike.

The plan depended on perfect judgment and timing. From the moment Darius ordered his right wing forward, Parmenio was under intense pressure and was soon holding off ten times his own numbers. On the other wing, some Persian cavalry broke clear through the Macedonian line and started plundering their camp. Alexander's nerve held, waiting for the moment.

As Darius sent more and more cavalry against Alexander's straining right wing, the ranks in front of the Great King thinned. Forming his men into a wedge, with himself and the Companions at the point, Alexander charged. A quarter of a million men crowded the battlefield, but a few thousand decided the fate of the empire. The Companions hacked through the Persian guard and Darius fled. Alexander wheeled around just in time to save Parmenio's overwhelmed men. The Persians still vastly outnumbered the Macedonians, but with Darius gone and many commanders dead, the battle was lost. Alexander pursued Darius for seventy-five miles to Arbela, where Darius tried to rally resistance. Then he fled east, for the Zagros Mountains.

Darius was supposed to be Ahuramazda's representative, protecting the Truth from the Lie, but he had become a refugee with a few wagonloads of gold and some mercenaries. Babylon surrendered along with Susa, a Persian capital on the plain between the Persian Gulf and the Zagros Mountains. Was the war over? Alexander had avenged the invasion of Greece 150 years earlier and taken massive plunder: At Susa alone he found forty thousand talents in coin! He appointed his friends governors of some of the richest provinces in the world, and the army proclaimed him Lord of Asia.

Yet the Persian elite had not accepted him as Darius' legitimate replacement. To them he was a western barbarian. Alexander found that replacing Darius was more difficult than overthrowing him. He advanced southeast to Persepolis, Persia's most sacred city. There its priests might recognize him. As he approached, he met four thousand Greeks

> whom the Persians had subjected to various kinds of torture. Some had had their feet cut off, some their hands and ears. They had been branded with letters from the Persian script by their captors, who had kept them to amuse themselves over a long period by humiliating them. . . . They looked more like outlandish phantoms than men, with no recognizably human characteristic apart from their voices. Thus they occasioned more tears than they had shed themselves.
>
> Quintus Curtius, *History of Alexander* 5.5 (J. Yardley)

Enraged, Alexander gave the order to loot Persepolis and kill its inhabitants, although the city had surrendered. Then he burned the city, including its magnificent palaces (Figure 19.6). The soldiers might have thought that burning Persepolis meant they could go home. They had marched seven thousand miles and won more plunder than any army in history. But Alexander still had to kill or capture Darius. He set out to march five hundred miles northwest through the rugged Zagros Mountains to Ecbatana ancient capital of the Medes, where Darius was gathering forces.

Before Alexander arrived, Darius fled again. Alexander sent Parmenio to Ecbatana while he pursued Darius with his best troops. Darius hoped to reach the

Figure 19.6 The ruins of the audience hall of Darius and Xerxes in Persepolis, Iran. Built between 518 and 460 B.C.; Alexander destroyed the city in 330 B.C.

rich eastern satrapies of Bactria and Soghdiana (roughly modern Uzbekistan). He had never visited these places before, and their satraps were virtually independent. **Bessus,** Darius' cavalry commander at Gaugamela and one of these eastern satraps, suggested that Darius temporarily hand over command to him so he could win over the other satraps. When Darius refused, Bessus threw him in chains and proclaimed himself king. As Alexander closed in, Darius' little band disintegrated. Bessus ordered Darius murdered, then fled east. Plutarch tells the story:

> The pursuit of Darius turned out to be long and exhausting. Alexander covered more than 400 miles in 11 days, and by this time most of his horsemen were on the verge of col- lapse for lack of water. At this point he met some Macedonians, who were carrying water from a river in skins on the backs of their mules. When they saw Alexander almost fainting with thirst in the midday heat, they quickly filled a helmet and brought it to him. He asked them for whom they were carrying the water. "For our sons," they told him, "but so long as your life is safe, we can have other children, even if we lose these." At this Alexander took the helmet in his hands. But then he looked up and saw the rest of his troops craning their heads and casting longing glances at the water, and he handed it back without drinking a drop. He thanked the men who had brought it, but said to them "If I am the only one to drink, the rest will lose heart." However no sooner had his companions witnessed this act of self-control and magnanimity than they cried out and shouted for him to lead them on boldly. They spurred on their horses and declared that they could not feel tired or thirsty or even like mortal men, so long as they had such a king.
>
> All his horsemen were fired with the same enthusiasm, but only 60 of them, so the story goes, had kept up with Alexander when he burst into the enemy's camp.° They

°*enemy's camp:* Near Hekatompylos ("the Hundred Gates") in northern Iran; see Map 19.3.

rode over great heaps of gold and silver vessels that had been scattered on the ground, passed wagons full of women and children that were moving aimlessly about without their drivers, and at length caught up with the Persian vanguard, imagining that Darius must be among them. At last they found him lying in a wagon, riddled with javelins and at his last gasp. He asked for a drink, and when he had swallowed some cold water that a Macedonian named Polystratus brought him, he said, "This is the final stroke of misfortune, that I should accept a service from you, and not be able to return it. But Alexander will reward you for your kindness, and the gods will repay him for his courtesy toward my mother and my wife and my children. And so through you, I give him my hand." As he said this, he took Polystratus by the hand, and died. When Alexander came up, he showed his grief and distress at the king's death, and unfastening his own cloak, he threw it over the body and covered it. Later, after he had captured Bessus, who had murdered the king, he had him torn limb from limb. He had the tops of two straight trees bent down so that they met, and part of Bessus' body was tied to each. Then when each tree was let go and sprang back to its upright position, the part of the body attached to it was torn off by the recoil. As for Darius' body, he sent it to his mother to be laid out in royal state, and he enrolled his brother Exathres into the number of his Companions.

Plutarch, Life of Alexander 42–43 (I. Scott-Kilvert)

ALEXANDER THE GOD, 330–323 B.C.

By giving Darius a proper funeral and accepting his brother in the Companions, Alexander treated the late king as his predecessor. By punishing Bessus in this very Persian way, he acted as any Achaemenid would toward a regicide. With Darius dead and a story circulating that he had blessed Alexander's succession, Alexander needed only to present himself like a Persian king to win over the empire. Eventually, the Magi and others would follow. But if Alexander acted too much like a Persian, he would offend the Macedonians.

Alexander proceeded cautiously. He started wearing the Persian royal diadem, but not the tiara that went with it; he wore the Persian white robe and sash, but not Asiatic pants; he took over Darius' harem of 365 beautiful women (one for each night of the year), but ostentatiously refused to sleep with them. He used a Macedonian signet ring to seal documents going back to Europe, and a Persian one for imperial affairs.

This strategy did not impress Persians, who expected a king to act like one, or please Macedonians, who despised all orientalism. Alexander decided to change the army from a national force into one loyal to him personally. He disbanded all non-Macedonians, giving each cavalryman one talent as a bonus and each infantryman a thousand drachmas (equivalent to eight and three years' pay, respectively), then offered everyone the chance to re-enlist for a further bonus of three talents! Every soldier was now rich and obligated directly to Alexander for his fortune. The deal cost 12,000 talents, a vast sum by Greek standards, but Alexander had captured about 180,000 talents.

Alexander dealt with his old rival Parmenio, "promoting" him to governor of Ecbatana, removing him from the centers of power. Alexander put Parmenio's arrogant son Philotas under surveillance. When Philotas failed to report rumors of a plot, Alexander arrested him in a midnight raid. The only "proof" of a plot was a letter from Parmenio to Philotas, saying, "First of all take care of yourselves and then of your people—that is how we shall accomplish our purpose." Alexander used the letter to persuade the army to condemn the unpopular man. Under torture, Philotas said Parmenio was behind a conspiracy. Alexander sent assassins through the desert on racing camels to reach Ecbatana before Parmenio heard. They handed Parmenio two letters, one from his son Philotas, the other his own death warrant. Parmenio tore open his son's letter and as he did so the assassins stabbed the great general through the throat. They kept hacking at Parmenio long after he was dead. It was hard for the Macedonians to decide which was worse—that Alexander had murdered his old marshal or that Parmenio might have conspired against his king. As one general put it: "If Parmenio plotted against Alexander, who can be trusted? And if he didn't, what's to be done?"

Alexander pushed deeper into central Asia to crush its unconquered satraps. Early in 329 B.C., he marched through what is now Afghanistan, taking Kandahar and Kabul. No foreign army would repeat this feat until the American invasion of A.D. 2002. When they reached the River Oxus (today on Afghanistan's northern border) in June 329, in one-hundred-degree heat, the troops mutinied and refused to go on. Alexander paid off the oldest veterans and sent them home, then enrolled local troops, who had no qualms about the campaign, and pushed on, leaving behind many of his mercenaries as garrisons in remote new towns (usually called Alexandria).

Alexander grew ever more distant from his Macedonian troops. Tensions erupted in Samarkand (in modern Uzbekistan) in autumn 328 B.C. That day had been a festival of Dionysus, the god of wine.

> It was Alexander's custom to offer sacrifice each year on the sacred day. The story is that on this particular occasion Alexander, for some reason best known to himself, sacrificed not to Dionysus but to Castor and Pollux, the Sacred Twins.° There had been some pretty heavy drinking (another innovation—in drink, too, he now tended toward barbaric excess), and in the course of talk the subject of the Sacred Twins came up, together with the common attribution of their parentage to Zeus instead of Tyndareus. Some of the company—the sort of people whose sycophantic tongues always have been and always will be the bane of kings—declared with gross flattery that, in their opinion, Pollux and Castor were not to be compared with Alexander and his achievements. Others, being thoroughly drunk, extended the invidious comparison to Heracles himself: it was only envy, they maintained, that deprived the living of due honor from their friends.
>
> Now Cleitus° had for some time obviously disapproved of the change in Alexander: he liked neither his move toward the manners of the east, nor the sycophantic expressions of his courtiers. When, therefore, he heard what was said on this occasion (he, too, had been drinking heavily), he angrily intervened. It was intolerable, he declared, to offer such an insult to divine beings, and he would allow no one to pay Alexander a compliment at the expense of the mighty ones of long ago—such a compliment was not for his honor but for his shame. In any case, he continued, they grossly exaggerated the marvelous nature of Alexander's triumphs, none of which were mere personal triumphs of his own. On the contrary, most of them were the work of the Macedonians as a whole.
>
> Alexander was deeply hurt—and I, for my part, feel that Cleitus' words were ill-judged; in view of the fact that most of the party was drunk, he could, in my opinion, have quite well avoided the grossness of joining in the general flattery simply by

°*Sacred Twins:* Brothers of Helen of Troy. Their mother, Leda, produced Castor through a union with her mortal husband Tyndareus, and Pollux from an affair with Zeus. They were honored as heroes.   °*Cleitus:* Cleitus "the Black," who had saved Alexander's life at the battle of the Granicus.

keeping his thoughts to himself. But there was more to come: for others of the company, hoping, in their turn, to curry favor with Alexander, brought up the subject of Philip, and suggested, absurdly enough, that what he had done was, after all, quite ordinary and commonplace. At this Cleitus could control himself no longer. He began to magnify Philip's achievements and belittle Alexander's; his words came pouring out—he was, by now, very drunk indeed—and, among much else, he taunted Alexander with the reminder that he, Cleitus, had saved his life, when they fought the Persian cavalry on the Granicus.

"This is the hand," he cried, holding it out with a flourish, "that saved you, Alexander, on that day."

Alexander could stand no more drunken abuse from his friend. Angrily he leapt from his seat as if to strike him, but the others held him back. Cleitus continued to pour out his insulting remarks, and Alexander called for the guard. No one answered.

"What?" he cried, "have I nothing left of royalty but the name? Am I to be like Darius, dragged in chains by Bessus and his cronies?"

Now nobody could hold him. Springing to his feet, he snatched a spear from one of the attendants and struck Cleitus dead.

Arrian, *Campaigns of Alexander* 4.8–9 (A. de Selincourt)

When the drunken Alexander realized what he had done, he tried to impale himself on the same spear. He fled weeping to his tent, where he refused food and water for three days. Eventually, a Greek soothsayer drew him out by telling Alexander that he stood above normal law and morality: "Do you not know that Zeus has Justice and Law seated by his side to prove that everything that is done by the ruler of the world is lawful and just?" Alexander was starting to believe that he was divine and that he could do anything.

Fighting dragged on for two years against fierce tribesmen in rugged mountain fortresses, but one by one, the chiefs surrendered. In spring 327 B.C., Alexander married Roxane, daughter of one of these chiefs. She was called the second most beautiful woman in Asia, after Darius' widow. Rumor said that Alexander slept with Darius' widow, and that she died giving birth to a stillborn child on the eve of Gaugamela.

Alexander was deliberately merging the Macedonian, Greek, and Persian elites under his own rule. Since Darius' death, he had forced three thousand Macedonians to marry Persians, and he now showed the world that his heir would have central Asian blood. He also enrolled thirty thousand Asian youths in a unit called "the Successors," who were taught Greek and learned Macedonian tactics.

Aggressive egalitarianism marked Macedonian and Greek societies. Persia, by contrast, had an elaborate system for expressing deference. Equals greeted each other with a kiss on the lips, a superior gave a slight subordinate a kiss on the cheek, while a man entering the presence of a greatly superior being threw himself to the ground, with different degrees of groveling, depending on the disparity in ranks. In the Aegean, prostration (in Greek **proskynêsis** [pros-ki-**nē**-sis]) was appropriate only before gods, and then sparingly.

When Alexander admitted Persians to his officer corps, they assumed they should prostrate themselves before him, but the Macedonians thought it unbecoming. Alexander favored *proskynêsis* because the Persians thought it was a Great King's due. If the Macedonians performed it too, Alexander would look more kingly in Persian eyes. But Macedonians thought *proskynêsis* was done only before gods. Callisthenes, Aristotle's nephew and the official campaign historian, openly mocked orders to prostrate himself. After killing Philotas, Parmenio, and Cleitus, adding Callisthenes to the list was easy. According to one source, Alexander had him locked in a cage and dragged behind the army until he died of neglect. Alexander, like his father Zeus, stood above all laws. Many Macedonians thought he had gone insane.

War in India, 327–326 B.C.

A hundred and twenty years earlier, Cyrus had campaigned in what is now Pakistan, and Alexander felt compelled to do the same. The Persians called this area Hindush, and the Greeks called it India; but everyone was vague about what lay there. Greeks said there were tribes with dogs' heads and tails, man-eating monsters, and pygmies with penises as long as their legs (much the kind of things that sixteenth-century Europeans believed about America). Their biggest error was believing that the great river Ocean, thought to flow around the world, lay just past the Indus River. In spring 327, Alexander thought that a month's march would take him to the edge of the world. A year earlier, he told people that he planned to march to Ocean, return to Greece (presumably by sailing on the river Ocean), then begin new campaigns around the Black Sea.

In 327 B.C., the Macedonians struggled across the Khyber Pass in the Hindu Kush Mountains (in modern Afghanistan) and descended into the valley (see Map 19.3). In hard fighting, Alexander was wounded yet again, taking an arrow through the shoulder. He gave further displays of terrible rage: When seven thousand Indian troops surrendered but refused to sign up as mercenaries, he killed them all along with their wives and children. In Indian history books today, the barbarous Alexander is chiefly remembered for this massacre.

In April 326, he entered the kingdom of **Porus**,[49] the strongest king in the region. Porus brought a large army to the River Jhelum, including two hundred elephants (Figure 19.7).

As Alexander headed south to meet Porus, the monsoon broke. The downpour rotted their equipment and flooded every stream. Disease carried off his men. When they reached the Jhelum in June, they found a raging torrent a mile wide with Porus on the other side, blocking the only ford. But Alexander's engineers managed to get half his army across the river by night during a violent thunderstorm.

The battle that followed was one of Alexander's greatest triumphs. After the battle, Alexander saw that his army was falling apart. He had lost some of his best men, and the survivors refused to face elephants again. His beloved horse Bucephalas died, which Alexander had ridden throughout his wars. He named a city after him (still there today; he named another after his dog).

In early July 326, Alexander cajoled his men into advancing again, but they soon realized that the Greek geographers were wrong. They were not coming to the river Ocean at all, but the vast Ganges plain unfolded before them. They reached the River Hyphasis in the Punjab,[50] a tributary of the Indus. Not even Persia's armies had gone further.

Alexander observed that his soldiers were exhausted by their constant campaigns. They had spent almost eight years among toils and dangers, and it was necessary to raise their spirits by an effective appeal if they were to undertake an expedition against the Gandaridae.° There had been many losses among the soldiers, and no

°*Gandaridae:* The inhabitants of the Ganges plain.

Figure 19.7 A worn Macedonian coin from the eastern provinces, bronze, circa 200 B.C., showing Alexander on a horse attacking two men with spears, mounted on an elephant.

relief from fighting was in sight. The hooves of the horses had been worn thin by steady marching. The arms and armor were wearing out, and Greek clothing was quite gone. They had to clothe themselves in foreign materials, recutting the Indians' garments. This was the season also, as luck would have it, of the heaviest rains. These had been going on for seventy days, to the accompaniment of continuous thunder and lightning.

Diodorus of Sicily 17.93 (C. B. Welles)

According to another ancient author, "Alexander's ambition prevailed over reason." He called an assembly, and in driving rain by the mud-filled Hyphasis, gave an impassioned speech about glory and honor, still insisting that they were near the Ocean.

When Alexander ended, there was a long silence. The officers present were not willing to accept what he said, but no one liked to risk an unprepared reply. Several times Alexander invited comment, should any wish to give it and genuinely held different views from those he had expressed; but in spite of his invitation nothing was said, until Coenus,° son of Polemocrates, plucked up his courage to speak.

°*Coenus:* A daring cavalry commander who had distinguished himself at the Jhelum River.

Coenus described the men's exhaustion. He closed:

"Sir, if there is one thing above all others a successful man should know, it is *when to stop.* Surely for a commander like yourself, with an army like ours, there is nothing to fear from any enemy; but luck, remember, is an unpredictable thing, and against what it may bring no man has any defense."

Coenus' words were greeted with applause. Some even wept, which was proof enough of their reluctance to prolong the campaign and of how happy they would be should the order be given to turn back. Alexander resented the freedom with which Coenus had spoken and the poor spirit shown by the other officers, and dismissed the assembly. Next day he summoned the same officers to his presence and angrily declared that although he would put pressure on no Macedonian to accompany him, he himself was going on.

Just as he had done after killing Cleitus, Alexander withdrew to his tent.

For the rest of that day, and for two days following, he refused to allow anyone to see him, even his Companions. His hope was that the various commanders, both of his Macedonians and the allied contingents, might change their minds and become readier to listen to him—for, after all, in a crowd of soldiers such sudden reversals of feeling are common enough. The silence, however, remained absolute and unbroken. The men were angry at Alexander's burst of temper and determined not to let it influence them. But in spite of their obvious hostility, Alexander (according to Ptolemy's° account of the incident) nonetheless offered sacrifice in the hope of favorable omens for the crossing. When, however, the omens proved to be against him, he at last submitted, and, having sent for the most senior officers of the Companions and those who were his closest friends, made a public announcement that, as all circumstances combined to dissuade him from a further advance, he had decided upon withdrawal.

One can imagine the shouts of joy that rose from the throats of that mixed host. Most of them wept. They came to Alexander's tent and called down every blessing for allowing them to prevail—the only defeat he had ever suffered.

Arrian, *The Campaigns of Alexander* 5.27–29 (A. de Selincourt)

°*Ptolemy:* Ptolemy was one of Alexander's generals, who wrote an account of the campaigns. After Alexander's death, this Ptolemy made himself king of Egypt and founded a dynasty.

The Long March Home, 326–324 B.C.

Even now, Alexander would not simply turn around. He built a fleet to sail down the Indus, to return home along what we call the Persian Gulf (see Map 19.3). Just as the fleet was about to sail, thirty thousand infantry and six thousand cavalry arrived as reinforcements, bringing medical supplies and twenty-five thousand new suits of armor. After marching seven thousand miles, they were told to head home again. If the reinforcements hoped for excitement, they were not disappointed. As they sailed down the Indus, they encountered storms, floods, and one hostile tribe after another. The Brahmins stirred up a holy war, calling Alexander a barbaric infidel. Day after day, the Macedonians fought skirmishes and stormed fortresses. The men grew exhausted and finally refused to climb the siege ladders. Only when Alexander himself started up walls did they follow. Morale was near collapse. One day, as they faced yet another castle,

Alexander was already making his move toward the town when a seer began to issue warnings against the siege, which, he said, the king should at least postpone since it was predicted that his life was in danger. Alexander looked at Demophon (that was the seer's name). "If someone interrupted you like this," said the king, "when you were preoccupied with your craft and observing the entrails, I am sure you would consider him an exasperating nuisance." After Demophon replied that this would certainly be the case, Alexander continued: "When I have my mind on weighty matters and not on animal intestines, do you think anything could be more annoying than a superstitious seer?"

Waiting only to give this reply, he ordered the ladders forward and, as the others hesitated, scaled the wall himself. This had a narrow cornice and, on top, in place of the usual crenellated battlements, a continuous parapet blocked passage. Thus the king was hanging, rather than standing, on the parapet, using his shield to parry the missiles falling all round him, for he was the target of projectiles hurled at long range from all the towers about him. His men were unable to reach him because all the projectiles showered from above overpowered them, but finally shame prevailed over their danger, since they could see that by hanging back they were delivering their king to the enemy. Their haste, however, actually retarded their aid: while they all tried to scale the wall before their comrades, they overloaded the ladders, which failed to support them, so that they all fell to the ground and robbed the king of his only hope. Now he stood in total isolation in the face of a huge army.

By now his left arm was tired from swinging his shield round to block enemy missiles. His friends called to him to jump down to them, and were standing ready to catch him.

Alexander jumped, but against all reason, jumped *inside* the city walls, where he took up a position with his back to a giant oak tree, whose branches shielded him from missiles.

Supporting the king in the fight was, first of all, the widespread fame of his name; then there was his desperation, providing a keen incentive to win an honorable death. But the enemy kept pouring onto him and by now he had taken many missiles on his shield, his helmet had been shattered by rocks, and his knees had buckled under the relentless pressure. Accordingly, the Indians standing closest to him rushed at him without due regard or caution. Alexander struck two of them with his sword and they fell dead at his feet.

Then an arrow drove through Alexander's breastbone and lodged next to his heart.

When he received the wound, a thick jet of blood shot out. He dropped his weapons and seemed to be dying. The man who had inflicted the wound therefore ran up to strip the body, all eager and exultant. Alexander felt him put his hands on his body and I suppose the indignity of this final insult brought him round. Summoning back his failing spirit, he brought his sword beneath his enemy and plunged it into his unprotected side.

Three bodies now lay around the king, and the other Indians kept their distance in bewilderment. . . . Finally, after dislodging the defenders in another part of the city, Peucestes appeared, following in the king's steps. When he saw him, Alexander thought Peucestes' arrival meant consolation in death rather than hope of life, and he allowed his exhausted frame to collapse on his shield. Immediately after, Timaeus came up, and shortly after him Leonnatus, and then Aristonos. The Indians, neglecting everything else when they learned the king was within their walls, also converged swiftly on that spot and proceeded to attack Alexander's defenders. Of these, Timaeus went down with many frontal wounds, after a heroic fight. Peucestes, too, had received three javelin wounds, but even so he was using his shield to protect his king, not himself. Leonnatus received a serious neck wound while trying to check a fierce barbarian charge, and fell half-dead at the king's feet. Alexander's last hope lay in Aristonos—but he, too, was seriously wounded and unable to withstand further the violent pressure of the enemy.

Meanwhile a rumor reached the Macedonian main body that the king had fallen. What would have dismayed others stirred them to action. Regardless of risk, they smashed through a gate with pick-axes and, bursting into the city where they had made the breach, they cut down the Indians, more of whom took to flight than dared engage the enemy. Old men, women, children—none was spared. Anyone the Macedonians encountered, they believed responsible for the king's wounds. Mass slaughter of the enemy finally appeased their just rage.

Quintus Curtius, History of Alexander 9.4–5 (J. Yardley)

An emergency operation removed the arrow, but Alexander hemorrhaged. For a week, he seemed likely to die. The Macedonians panicked; "Every difficulty seemed hopelessly insoluble without Alexander to get them through."

> When at last the news came that he was alive, they could hardly believe it, and were unable at first to persuade themselves that he really would recover. Then he wrote them a letter saying that he would soon be visiting them at headquarters, but such was their state of mind that they could not believe it was genuine, and most of them thought it had been forged by his officers and Guards.
>
> Alexander's first thought on learning of this state of affairs was to prevent a breakdown of discipline among the men; so at the first possible moment he had himself carried down to the Hydraotes river . . . when his vessel had nearly reached them, he ordered the awning over the stern to be taken down so that everyone might see him. Even then the troops were incredulous, and supposed that what they saw on board was Alexander's corpse. At last, however, the vessel was brought in to the river-bank. Alexander raised a hand in greeting to the men, and immediately there was a shout of joy, and arms were stretched toward him in welcome or lifted to heaven in thankfulness. So unexpected was the sense of relief that many, in spite of themselves, burst into tears. As he was being moved from the ship, a party of his Guards brought him a stretcher, but he refused it and called for his horse. He mounted, and at the sight of him, once more astride his horse, there was a storm of applause so loud that the river-banks and neighboring glens re-echoed the noise. Near his tent he dismounted, and the men saw him walk. They crowded around him, touching his hands, his knees, his clothes; some, content with a sight of him standing near, turned away with a blessing on their lips. Wreaths were flung upon him and such flowers as were then in bloom.
>
> Arrian, The Campaigns of Alexander 6.12–13 (A. de Selincourt)

Progress down the Indus was marked by even more massacres than their march through Iran. The army was degenerating into a pathological mob. As Arrian said, "The truth is that he was fighting mad." The Indus tribes folded as stories of Alexander's invulnerability spread, and they handed over the Brahmins ("Naked Philosophers," as the Greeks called them) who had led the resistance. Alexander questioned them, asking, "How can a man become a god?" The answer came: "By doing something a man cannot do." He had overthrown Persia, invaded India, and, in July 325, he finally sailed on the Ocean.

Getting home meant crossing the fearsome Gedrosian desert, because only one third of the force could fit on the ships. According to the plan, Alexander would set off walking with most of the men, with camels carrying food. His general Craterus would follow with the ships, bringing more food, when the monsoons stopped. Each night, Alexander would dig wells, and the fleet would use the same wells as they followed. The ships would catch up just before Alexander's food ran out, at the point where mountains blocked the coastal path. The army would then load up with a week's worth of food and swing inland through the worst of the desert (see Map 19.3).

But the monsoon did not drop. The ships set off late and did not appear at the rendezvous. Alexander waited as long as he dared, then headed inland. He sent racing camels ahead ordering the local satraps to meet him with supplies, but none came. Even at night, the temperatures were unbearable, and the only plants were poisonous. Men dropped every moment from heatstroke and dehydration; hundreds died when a flash thunderstorm flooded a dried-up streambed. Hundreds more perished when a sandstorm obliterated all landmarks, leaving them wandering in circles. Of eighty-five thousand who entered the desert,[51] barely twenty-five thousand reached the other side.

More than a year had passed since the mutiny at the River Hyphasis. Few of the veterans who wept with joy when Alexander announced the omens against advance were still alive at the end of 325 B.C., and those who did survive had very different reasons to weep.

THE LAST DAYS, 324–323 B.C.

Alexander's men straggled back into Susa in February 324 B.C. The king needed to organize his conquests and stabilize his authority. While he had spent six years campaigning in the east, his governors had run wild, embezzling huge funds, hiring their own mercenaries, and acting like independent kings. Alexander purged as many as he could, beginning with those who failed to supply him in Gedrosia. He ordered the survivors to dismiss their mercenaries, intending to get control over his subordinates, but filling the countryside with desperadoes. Alexander in summer 324 ordered all Greek exmercenaries to return home and all Greek cities to receive them. However, many mercenaries were Greek outlaws who had been banished and their property divided. All over Greece, hundreds of tribunals had to settle thousands of property, inheritance, and other disputes, which dragged on for a generation.

Back in Babylon, Alexander continued "Persianizing" his army. The Hyphasis mutiny had shown that depending on Macedonian veterans made him vulnerable. He put Iranians into his highest staff and into the Companion cavalry. He assembled the Macedonians at Opis just outside Babylon and announced the senior veterans' demobilization with huge bonuses. Arrian says, "Doubtless he meant to gratify them by what he said," but the veterans took it badly:

> The men already felt that he had come to undervalue their services and thought them quite useless as a fighting force; so, naturally enough, they resented his remarks as merely another instance of the many things that, throughout the campaign, he had done to hurt their feelings, such as his adoption of Persian dress, the issue of Macedonian equipment to the oriental "Successors,"° and the inclusion of foreign troops in units of the Companions. The result was that they did not receive the speech in respectful silence, but, unable to restrain themselves, called for the discharge of every man in the army, adding, in bitter jest, that on his next campaign he could take his father with him—meaning, presumably, the god Ammon.
>
> Alexander was furious. By that time he had grown quicker to take offense, and the oriental subservience to which he had become accustomed had greatly changed his old openhearted manner toward his own countrymen.
>
> °*The Successors:* The thirty thousand Iranians whom Alexander enrolled in 327 B.C. to learn Greek and use Macedonian tactics.

Alexander spoke angrily, telling the troops to leave if they liked; but when they got home and people asked where the king was who gave them such wealth, "tell them, I say, that you deserted him and left him to the mercy of barbarian men, whom you yourselves had conquered. Such news will indeed assure you praise on earth and reward in heaven. Get out of my sight!"

Just as he did after the mutiny at the River Hyphasis, Alexander retired to his tent, refusing food and drink. On the third day, he started putting Persians in charge of the army.

> On the Macedonians the immediate effect of Alexander's speech had been profound. They stood in silence in front of the stage. Nobody made a move to follow the king except his closest attendants and the members of his personal bodyguard; the rest, helpless to speak or act, yet unwilling to go away, remained rooted to the spot. But when they were told about the Persians and Medes—how command was being given to Persian officers, foreign troops drafted into Macedonian units, a Persian Corps of Guards called by a Macedonian name, Persian infantry units given the coveted title of Companions, Persian Silver Shields and Persian mounted Companions being formed, including even a new Royal Squadron—they could contain themselves no longer. Every man of them hurried to the palace; in sign of supplication they flung their arms on the ground before the doors and stood there calling and begging for admission. They offered to give up the ringleaders of the mutiny and those who had led the cry against the king, and swore that they would not stir from the spot day or night unless Alexander took pity on them.
>
> Arrian, *The Campaigns of Alexander* 7.8, 11 (A. de Selincourt)

Alexander made up with his men, but he no longer needed them. He sent eleven thousand Macedonians home, giving one talent to each (enough to buy a farm and some slaves and retire). He drafted more Iranians to replace them and persuaded the departing Greeks and Macedonians to leave behind the Iranian wives he had given to them along with the children they had borne. In twenty years' time, he hoped, the boys would form the nucleus of a new army, loyal solely to their king—himself.

His thoughts turned to further conquest. Early in 324 B.C., he spoke of attacking Italy, Spain, Sicily, and Carthage. He had seven hundred ships built on the Euphrates, to explore India and circumnavigate Africa, and ordered a fleet built on the Caspian Sea, to repeat Darius I's campaign against the Scythians two hundred years earlier. He wanted to conquer Arabia. He had Phoenician ships dismantled and carried overland from the Mediterranean to the Persian Gulf to explore its coasts. In spring 323, he assembled an army at Babylon, determined to occupy the rich kingdoms in the Persian Gulf, who monopolized the spice trade with the Arabian desert.

At the Olympic Festival in 324 B.C., Alexander proclaimed that the Greeks should now worship him as a god. For five hundred years, Greeks had insisted that no man had such privileged links. The Greeks' response was as shocking as Alexander's claim. There were no revolts or violent protests. One Spartan simply said, "Since Alexander desires to be a god, let him be a god." "All right," Demosthenes said, "make him the son of Zeus—and of Poseidon too, if that's what he wants." Alexander likened himself to Heracles, the legendary wandering hero, who (like Alexander) was a son of Zeus, and artists regularly represented him as Heracles (Figure 19.8).

Preparations for the god-king's Arabian campaign were well advanced by May 29, 323 B.C., when, as often, Alexander went to a drinking party. He wanted to

Figure 19.8 Greek coin representing Alexander as Heracles, wearing the skin of the Nemean Lion as a helmet, circa 250 B.C.

go home early, but his cronies talked him into staying and going to another party. There he drank at one go an extra-large cup of unmixed wine. He cried out in pain and was carried home. Next day, he was ill, but eventually got up, bathed, and drank more. After a few days, he discussed the Arabian campaign with his generals, but then his fever returned. He went to bed and on the next day, June 6, gave his general Perdiccas control over administration. Rumors flew that he was dead. His generals had to knock a second door into his room so that the men could file through to see him one last time. Asked to whom he left his empire, Alexander whispered, "To the strongest."

CONCLUSION

Alexander passed through the Near East like a terrible dream. He left a trail of devastation from Thebes to the Indus Valley. Adding up the cities he sacked and casualties in battle, perhaps a million people died in his thirteen years of war. The famines and chaos that followed may bring the total near two million, in a Persian Empire that numbered around twenty-five to thirty-five million before he came— the equivalent invasion of the United States would leave twenty million dead. Alexander came, destroyed, and was gone. Alexander left no heir, just an unborn child in Roxane's belly. The legacy of war would be more war.

Alexander was not only a destroyer. In 340 B.C., the Aegean Sea was the center of the Greek world. By 320 B.C., it was a backwater. What Athens, Thebes, or Sparta did no longer mattered much. The Near East was open to Greek exploration and exploitation. Between 330 and 250 B.C., tens of thousands of Greeks emigrated to make their fortunes in Egypt, Anatolia, and Syria. Standards of living rose, science and learning flourished, and population soared. The Greek-speaking city of Alexandria in Egypt became the cultural center of the Mediterranean and Near East. In most ways, the period 300 to 250 B.C., not the fifth century B.C., was the Greeks' Golden Age. Without Alexander, the shape of Greek history, and of world history, would have been very different.

Alexander seemed to be more than mortal. Five centuries after his death, stories known as the *Alexander Romance* turned him into a superman. The *Romance* was retold in every language of the ancient Mediterranean and Near East and circulated widely in medieval times. Even in early modern times European travelers fully believed the story in the *Alexander Romance,* that in the wilds of central Asia they might yet encounter the unaging Alexander, planning to conquer the world.

KEY TERMS

Philip II, 401
Demosthenes, 401
king's companions, 403
Alexander I, 403
Amphipolis, 403
Pella, 403
Olynthus, 404
Olympias, 405
Sacred League, 405
Phocis, 405
Timoleon, 409

Chaeronea, 411
Darius III, 412
Parmenio, 413
Memnon, 414
River Granicus, 414
Issus, 417
Tyre, 420
Gaugamela, 421
Bessus, 424
proskynêsis, 427
Porus, 428

FURTHER READING

Borza, Eugene, *In the Shadow of Olympus: The Emergence of Macedonia* (Princeton 1990). Archaeological and historical study of Iron Age Macedonia.

Bosworth, Brian, *Conquest and Empire* (Cambridge, UK, 1988). The best scholarly account of Alexander's campaigns.

Ellis, J. R., *Philip II and Macedonian Imperialism* (Princeton 1976). Argues that Philip was always more interested in conquering Persia than in dominating Greece.

Green, Peter, *Alexander of Macedon, 356–323 B.C.* (Berkeley 1973). Probably the best single book on Alexander's career. A gripping read. Highly recommended.

Heckel, Waldemar, and J. C. Yardley, *Alexander the Great* (Oxford 2004). Collection of the key ancient texts about Alexander.

Lewis, D. M., John Boardman, Simon Hornblower, and Martin Ostwald, eds., *The Cambridge Ancient History VI: The Fourth Century B.C.* (2nd ed., 1994), chapters 14–18.

Manfredi, Valerio Massimo, *Alexander: Child of a Dream* (London 2001); *Alexander: The Sands of Ammon* (London 2001). Entertaining novels, telling the story well and sticking close to the facts, though unlikely to win prizes as literature.

Roisman, Joseph, ed., *Brill's Companion to Alexander the Great* (Leiden 2003). Scholarly essays on numerous aspects of Alexander's career.

Wood, Michael, *In the Footsteps of Alexander the Great* (Berkeley 1997). Written to accompany a television series; excellent photos.

Ancient Texts

The Greek Alexander Romance (New York 1991; tr. Richard Stoneman). Translation of fascinating stories about Alexander the Superman.

Greek Political Oratory (Harmondsworth, UK, 1970; tr. A. N. W. Saunders). Speeches by Demosthenes and pamphlets by Isocrates dealing with Athens' reaction to the growth of Philip's power.

Arrian, *The Campaigns of Alexander* (Harmondsworth, UK, 1958; tr. Aubrey de Selincourt). Roman-era history, but drawing on primary sources now lost.

Diodorus of Sicily, *History* books 16 and 17. In *The Library of History* VIII (Cambridge, MA, 1963; tr. C.B. Welles). Parallel Greek and English texts of Diodorus' accounts of Timoleon, Philip, and Alexander.

Plutarch, *Lives* of Demosthenes and Alexander. In *The Age of Alexander* (Harmondsworth, UK, 1973; tr. Ian Scott-Kilvert).

Quintus Curtius Rufus, *The History of Alexander* (New York 1984; tr. John Yardley). Another Roman-era history, also drawing on primary sources now lost.

CHAPTER 20

THE HELLENISTIC CENTURY, 323–220 B.C.

For centuries, the Greeks had lived around the Mediterranean's shores, but now Macedon had cast down the Persian Empire. Tens of thousands of Greeks headed east, forging a new world. Since the nineteenth century, historians have called the period from Alexander's death in 323 B.C. to the suicide of Cleopatra VII, the last major Greek ruler (in 30 B.C.), "Hellenistic." This term has carried a double meaning—first, that Greeks who settled in the Near East brought Greek culture with them, changing native ways; and second, that the new culture was inferior. As classicists saw it, Hellenistic culture lacked the spark of brilliance and vitality that made archaic and classical Greece so special. But the Hellenistic was not an age of decline. During this period, the Greeks dominated a huge empire, invented new cultural forms, made remarkable scientific discoveries, and often lived better than ever before. In most ways, the messy, complicated Hellenistic world feels more familiar to us than the certainties and sharp divisions of classical Greece.

Great regional differences emerged as new centers of Greek wealth sprang up in Egypt, Syria, and Mesopotamia, while the old Greek heartlands in the Aegean and Sicily declined. In the third century B.C., the great powers of classical times—Athens, Sparta, Thebes—were pawns in the games of mighty kings. In many ways, these kings behaved like Near Eastern rulers had since the Bronze Age; instead of the Hellenization of the Persian Empire, we might speak of the orientalization of Greek politics. In other ways, Greek traditions were stronger than ever. Poetry, history writing, philosophy, science, engineering, sculpture, architecture, and painting all flourished, but now in the service of royal courts. In this chapter, we review the political formation of the Hellenistic world. In Chapter 21, "Hellenistic Culture, 323–30 B.C.," we examine its amazing cultural achievements; and in Chapter 22, "The Coming of Rome, 220–30 B.C.," we examine its destruction and absorption by a foreign people.

THE WARS OF THE SUCCESSORS, 323–301 B.C.

Phase I, 323–320 B.C.

Alexander's battle-hardened followers had little time to decide what to do: Never had one man created such an empire so quickly: He died without viable heirs. A new king might take over the empire; a group of kings might divide it among them; or there might be a free-for-all. Alexander's closest male relative was a half-brother born a year before Alexander, the offspring of his father Philip II and a dancing girl. This half-brother, Philip III, was mentally defective. However, Alexander's widow Roxane was pregnant. Later in 323 B.C., she bore a son, known as Alexander IV. It would be years before he could take power. Neither Philip III nor Alexander IV was a plausible successor.

Attempting to avoid civil war or division of the empire, the generals agreed that **Perdiccas,** commander of the Macedonian cavalry, would be "guardian of the kingdom." Shortly before his death, Alexander had sent his general **Craterus** back to Macedonia to depose **Antipater** who was regent there. Thus, Craterus was away from Babylon when arrangements were made, but the other generals, mindful of his power, sent messengers after him. Craterus was appointed guardian for the mentally defective Philip III and the unborn Alexander IV, with orders now to leave Antipater alone.

Perdiccas, Craterus, and Antipater wanted to control the empire as a Gang of Three, but other generals reasoned that the empire could not hold together. Best to grab part of it now. The general **Ptolemy** (**tol**-e-mē) insisted that Alexander wanted *him* to govern Egypt. He raced there and murdered the sitting governor. With the eight thousand talents (fifty-seven pounds of gold!) he found in the treasury, Ptolemy hired mercenaries. In a propaganda coup, he intercepted the procession carrying Alexander's corpse back to Macedonia and brought it to Alexandria, embalmed in honey in a glass-topped coffin. After a traditional pharaoh's funeral, Ptolemy placed Alexander on permanent display.

At the same time, the general **Antigonus,** known as "One-Eyed" from a war injury, took over much of Anatolia, and **Lysimachus** (lī-**sim**-a-kus) took Thrace, roughly modern Bulgaria (Map 20.1). The key players, then, in the first phase of the struggle over Alexander's empire (Table 20.1) were *Ptolemy, Antigonus, Lysimachus,* and the *Gang of Three* (Perdiccas, Craterus, Antipater).

Perdiccas, Craterus, and Antipater were supposed to be preserving the empire, but according to Arrian, "everyone was suspicious of Perdiccas, and he of them." When Perdiccas sent a governor to fight a mercenaries' revolt, the governor was tempted to join it; and when, in September 323, Athens led an uprising against Antipater, who ruled Macedon, it became hard to tell who was on which side. Lysimachus in Thrace and Craterus the regent were conveniently too busy to help Antipater when the Greek rebels besieged him in the Thessalian city of Lamia (hence the revolt is known as the Lamian War). Only after one of Craterus' subordinates defeated the Athenian fleet in spring 322 did Craterus actually support Antipater.

Athens surrendered in August 322. The revolt had been a disaster. Many rich Athenians had preferred peace under Macedon to democratic freedom, and Antipater now executed Athens' democratic politicians. Demosthenes escaped only by committing suicide. Athens had been a democracy since 508 B.C., with only brief

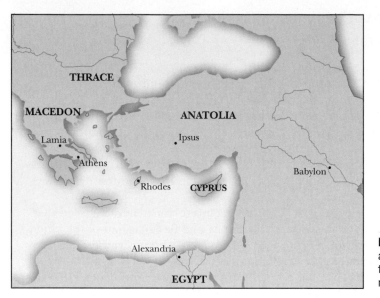

Map 20.1 Main kingdoms and locations from the Wars of the Successors, 320–301 B.C., mentioned in the text.

interruptions in 411 and 404/3, but Antipater now installed a garrison in Piraeus, set up a junta, and deprived twelve thousand out of roughly twenty-one thousand citizens of their votes. Athens remained a center for philosophy and produced some notable artists, but Athenian greatness had come to an end.

The Greeks were not Antipater's only problem. Alexander's mother Olympias wanted her infant grandson Alexander IV, son of Roxane, to be king of Macedon, but Antipater, who hated her, did not. Olympias brokered a marriage between her daughter Cleopatra (Alexander the Great's sister) and Perdiccas, although Perdiccas was already married to Antipater's daughter! The naked ambition of Olympias and Perdiccas alarmed the other generals, but before the generals could act, Perdiccas murdered Craterus in spring 320. Perdiccas overreached by sailing to Egypt and attacking Ptolemy. When two thousand of his men drowned crossing the Nile and crocodiles ate hundreds more, Perdiccas' officers murdered him. They asked Ptolemy to take Perdiccas' place as guardian of the kingdom, but the cunning Ptolemy wanted the empire to dissolve, leaving him in charge of Egypt. He refused the honor.

Phase II, 320–301 B.C.

The surviving generals convened in July 320 B.C., allegedly to decide who would replace Perdiccas in overseeing the empire, but in fact Antigonus (who ruled Anatolia), Antipater (who ruled Macedon), Lysimachus (who ruled Thrace), and particularly Ptolemy (who ruled Egypt) wanted to secure their own positions. They put Antipater in charge of the mentally defective Philip III and the three-year-old Alexander IV. Antipater, Lysimachus, and Ptolemy also wanted to neutralize Antigonus (based in Anatolia), so they put another of Alexander's prominent generals, **Seleucus** (se-lū-kus), in charge of Babylon and the (as yet unclaimed) lands to the east.

In theory, nothing had changed since Alexander died in 323. The empire was united under Alexander IV (or perhaps Philip III) as presumptive king, with a former general, currently Antipater, acting as guardian. In reality, the empire was

Table 20.1   Key players in the Wars of Successors, 323–301 B.C.

Empire-wide Authority

Craterus (died 320 B.C.): guardian for Alexander IV and Philip III
Perdiccas (died 320 B.C.): "guardian of the kingdom"
Alexander IV (323–?310 B.C.): son of Alexander the Great and Roxane
Philip III (c. 357–317 B.C.): son of Philip II; Alexander the Great's half-brother; mentally defective

Local Authority

Macedonia
Antipater (?397–319 B.C.): regent of Macedon, 334–319 B.C.
Olympias (c. 375–316 B.C.): widow of Philip II, mother of Alexander the Great
Cassander (died 297 B.C.): son of Antipater. Rules Macedon from 315 B.C.; proclaims himself king of Macedon c. 305 B.C.
Polyperchon (died c. 300 B.C.): regent of Macedon, 319–315 B.C.

Egypt
Ptolemy I (367/6–282 B.C.): one of Alexander's generals, governor of Egypt 323–305 B.C.; proclaims himself pharaoh in 305 B.C.

Thrace
Lysimachus (c. 355–281 B.C.): Alexander's bodyguard; governor of Thrace and sometimes parts of Anatolia, 323–305; proclaims himself king in 305 B.C.

Western Asia
Antigonus I the One-Eyed (c. 382–301 B.C.): one of Alexander's generals, controls most of Alexander's empire in Asia, 319–301 B.C.; proclaims himself king in 306 B.C.
Demetrius I the Besieger (336–283 B.C.): son of Antigonus I; proclaims himself king in 306 B.C., loses kingdom in 301 B.C., becomes king of Macedon 294–287 B.C., dies in Seleucus' prison
Seleucus I (c. 358–281 B.C.): one of Alexander's generals, satrap of Babylon 321–316 B.C., then again after 312; proclaims himself king c. 305 B.C., takes over most of Antigonus' kingdom after 301 B.C.

breaking apart. Antipater, Lysimachus, Antigonus, and Ptolemy each had his own power base. But Antigonus believed he could reunite the empire by force of arms with himself as king of all.

Antipater, aged nearly eighty, died in 319 B.C. His final disastrous act was to name as his successor a fellow officer, Polyperchon (pol-i-**per**-kon), passing over his own son **Cassander.** The energetic and talented Cassander challenged the succession, and Ptolemy, Antigonus, and Lysimachus supported him. Polyperchon found his own allies, and fighting broke out all over the empire. Antigonus spent three years defeating Polyperchon's allies, scattered from Anatolia to central Asia. He expelled Seleucus from Babylon.

In Macedonia, the slow-witted Philip III had stayed out of politics, but in early 317 his wife Eurydicê announced that Philip III favored Cassander, upsetting not only Polyperchon but Alexander the Great's mother Olympias, who still hoped that her grandson, the five-year-old Alexander IV, would one day rule the whole empire. Olympias formed her own army and invaded Macedon. A female general is highly unusual, but Eurydicê went further than Olympias, putting on armor and leading her own troops into battle—only to be betrayed by them. When she captured Eurydicê, Olympias indulged her cruelty:

> First Olympias placed Eurydicê and her husband Philip [III] under guard and began to maltreat them. In fact she walled them up in a small space and supplied them with what was necessary through a single narrow opening. But after she had unlawfully treated the unfortunate captives in this way for many days, realizing that she was losing favor with the Macedonians because of their pity for the sufferers, she ordered certain Thracians to stab Philip to death. He had been king for six years and four months.[52] But she judged that Eurydicê, who was expressing herself without restraint and declaring that the kingdom belonged to herself rather than to Olympias, was worthy of a greater punishment. She therefore sent to her a sword, a noose, and some hemlock, and ordered her to use whichever of these she pleased as a means of death—neither displaying any respect at all for the dignity of the victim whom she was unlawfully treating, nor moved to pity by the fate that is common to all. Accordingly, when she herself met with a similar reversal, she experienced a death that was worthy of her cruelty. Eurydicê, indeed, in the presence of her attendant, prayed that Olympias might receive similar gifts. She next laid out the body of her husband, cleaning its wounds as well as circumstances permitted, then ended her own life by hanging herself with her girdle, neither weeping for her own fate nor humbled by the weight of her misfortunes.
>
> Diodorus of Sicily 19.11 (R. Geer)

Because of her cruelty Olympias lost support. Cassander invaded Macedonia, promising to pardon Olympias if she surrendered. In spring 315, he stoned her to death.

Polyperchon and his allies had been defeated everywhere except in Greece itself. Here, Cassander and Polyperchon each tried to persuade the *poleis* to support them. In 318, the Athenians overthrew their oligarchy, but in 317 Cassander starved Athens into submission and set up an Aristotelian philosopher named **Demetrius of Phaleron** as dictator. Demetrius revived property requirements for political activity, and for ten years regulated upper-class behavior while dyeing his own hair blond, wearing make-up, and performing prodigious sexual feats with prostitutes of both sexes. Demetrius was evidently no Platonic philosopher-king, but he kept Athens out of wars and repaired the city's shattered finances.

By 314, Polyperchon seemed all but finished. His last significant ally, Seleucus, thrown out of Babylon by Antigonus in 312 B.C., fled to Egypt, where he stirred up trouble by persuading Ptolemy that Antigonus wanted to be sole king of Alexander's empire. Lysimachus and Cassander joined Ptolemy in commanding Antigonus to stop expanding. Antigonus promptly dropped his alliance with Cassander and started helping Polyperchon, still a thorn in Cassander's side. Adopting a policy which Polyperchon began in 318, Antigonus offered in 314 to free the *poleis,* withdrawing Macedonian garrisons and restoring self-rule if they would support him. Ptolemy announced that he also wanted to free the *poleis.* For the next 150 years, "freedom for the Greeks" would be a rallying cry and one more cause of one more ocean of blood.

As the war in Greece wound down, a new front opened in Judea, where Ptolemy defeated Antigonus' son **Demetrius the Besieger** in 312. Exhausted, the major players drew a treaty in 311:

> Cassander, Ptolemy, and Lysimachus made peace with Antigonus and subscribed to a treaty, the terms of which were that Cassander should be general of Europe until Alexander [IV], Roxane's son, should come of age, Lysimachus should be lord of Thrace, and Ptolemy of Egypt and the cities bordering Egypt in Africa and Arabia; Antigonus should be in charge of all Asia and the Greeks should live according to their own laws. But they did not abide by this contract for long, but each one of them put forward plausible excuses for trying to acquire more territory. Cassander saw that Roxane's son Alexander was growing up[53] and that some people were spreading the word in Macedonia that he ought to release the boy from custody and hand his father's kingdom over to him. Afraid for his own safety, Cassander instructed Glaucias, who was in charge of the boy's safety, to assassinate Roxane and the king and conceal their bodies, and not to report the deed to any of the others. Glaucias carried out the orders, and this freed Cassander, Lysimachus, Ptolemy, and even Antigonus from their anticipated fears about the king. For now that there was no one to take over the empire, those who ruled peoples or cities could each entertain hopes of kingship and from now on controlled the territory under their power like kingdoms that had been conquered in war.
>
> Diodorus of Sicily 19.105 (R. Geer)

Thus ended the glorious line of Philip and Alexander the Great, in secret murders and unmarked graves. Cassander had slaughtered a woman and a boy, but no one cared.

The treaty of 311 B.C. meant little. Antigonus apparently decided that the best way to further his plan of uniting the empire was to move into the Aegean, still disputed between Cassander and Polyperchon, and get control of Macedonia. Cassander arranged with Ptolemy for an Egyptian fleet to sail to Athens to deter Antigonus. In 307 B.C., the Athenians saw 250 ships sailing into Piraeus, and, assuming they were Ptolemy's, welcomed them; in fact they belonged to Demetrius the Besieger, Antigonus' son. Demetrius captured the city, and he and Antigonus were poised to take the whole Aegean. The next year, they defeated Ptolemy's fleet near Cyprus.

> After this success the Cypriots for the first time acclaimed Antigonus and Demetrius as kings. Antigonus was immediately crowned, and Demetrius received a diadem from his father with a letter addressing him as king. At the same time when the news reached Ptolemy's followers in Egypt, they also conferred the title of king on him, so as not to appear unduly cast down by their defeat, and this spirit of rivalry proved infectious among the other successors of Alexander. Lysimachus began to wear a diadem, and Seleucus (who had already assumed royal prerogatives when he gave audiences to the barbarians) now adopted the same practices in his interviews with Greeks. Cassander, however, though others addressed him as king, both in letters and in speech continued to sign letters with his own name, as he had always done.
>
> The assumption of these dignities meant something more than the mere addition of a name or change in appearance. It stirred the spirits of these men, raised their ideas to a different plane, and introduced an element of pride and self-importance into their daily lives and their dealings with others, in the same way as tragic actors, when they put on royal robes, alter their gait, their voice, their deportment, and their mode of address. As a result they also became harsher in their administration of justice, and they cast off the various disguises whereby they had previously concealed their power and which had made them treat their subjects more gently and tolerantly. Such was the effect of a single word from a flatterer, which in this way brought about a revolution throughout the world.
>
> Plutarch, *Life of Demetrius* 18 (I. Scott-Kilvert)

Alexander's successors were now independent kings, not loyal servants protecting the empire for Alexander's heir. Could Antigonus reunite the empire by force of arms?

In 305, his son Demetrius besieged the island of **Rhodes** off the southwestern tip of Asia Minor, a major commercial power; no one could dominate the Aegean without it. Demetrius earned his nickname "the Besieger" here, personally designing armored siege-towers a hundred feet tall that rolled forward on wheels sixteen feet across. Each tower held thirty-four hundred men, who could fire in all directions. Plutarch says that "Their sheer size alarmed even his friends, while their beauty delighted even his enemies, and this description is true and not merely elegantly phrased." Demetrius himself wore a suit of iron armor weighing forty pounds. According to Plutarch (in his biography of Demetrius), "to demonstrate the armor's strength and power of resistance, Zoilus, the maker, had a bolt from a catapult shot at one of them from a range of twenty paces. The armor remained unbroken at the point of impact and its surface showed nothing more than a small scratch such as might have been made by an engraver."

But defensive technology had advanced even faster than offensive, and after a brutal year-long struggle, Rhodes' walls still stood. The siege drained both sides, and in 304 Rhodes agreed to be Demetrius' ally. They celebrated their survival by building the Colossus of Rhodes, a 105-foot-tall bronze statue bestriding the entrance to their main harbor, one of the Seven Wonders of the ancient world.

Antigonus and his ferocious son pressed ahead to subdue the Aegean and capture Macedonia. In 302, Antigonus formed a new League of Corinth, explicitly modeled on Philip II's alliance of 338, signaling his intention to unite the Greeks against Cassander in Macedon. Cassander, Lysimachus, and Seleucus banded together to stop Antigonus, and in 301 B.C., the two armies met near the small town of **Ipsus** in central Anatolia. Each side had seventy-five thousand troops, one of the great battles of ancient times. Seleucus also brought four hundred Indian war elephants. Antigonus put his son Demetrius in charge of the cavalry. Demetrius led a great charge and broke through the enemy lines, then pursued too far, leaving Antigonus exposed to the elephants, which trampled Antigonus' guard. The eighty-year-old Antigonus died, almost alone, in a hail of javelins, and with him Alexander's dream of a single empire from the Adriatic to India.

THE HELLENISTIC WORLD AFTER IPSUS

After Ipsus, Ptolemy, Lysimachus, and Seleucus carved up Antigonus' empire "like the carcass of some great slaughtered beast," as Plutarch put it. Although another generation would live and die before the Aegean settled down, the Hellenistic world was taking on its basic configuration (Map 20.2). There were four great kingdoms: Ptolemy ruled in Egypt; Seleucus in Anatolia, Syria, and Mesopotamia; Lysimachus in Thrace and parts of Asia Minor; and Cassander in Macedonia. Demetrius the Besieger had become a king in 306, but Ipsus left him a king without a kingdom. He had vast wealth, with which he hired his own army and fleet, but no territorial base. He lived like a pirate on the high seas. After an orgy of treachery and murder, Cassander's line was extinguished, and Demetrius the Besieger's son finally settled on the Macedonian throne in 276 B.C. In 281 B.C., Seleucus killed Lysimachus in

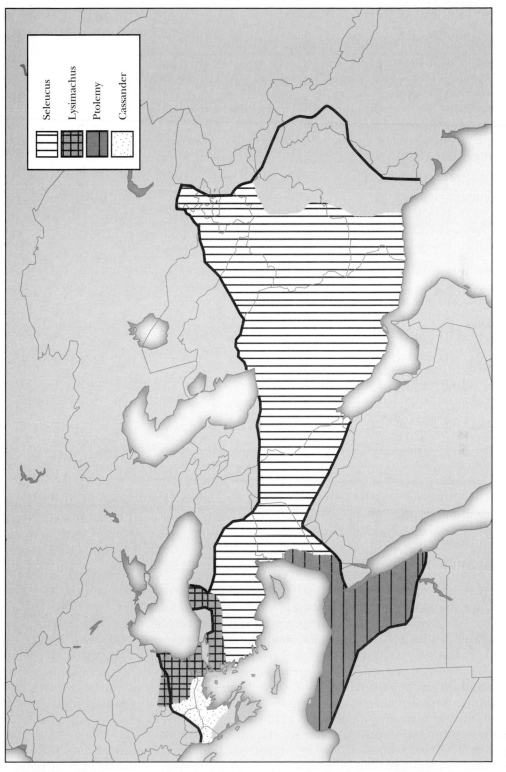

Map 20.2 The Hellenistic world, 300 B.C. Alexander the Great's empire contained everything within the bold lines. A generation later, four of his generals ruled pieces of it: Ptolemy, Seleucus, Lysimachus, and Cassander.

Legend:
- Seleucus
- Lysimachus
- Ptolemy
- Cassander

Table 20.2   Major Hellenistic kings, 306–220 B.C.

Antigonids (ruled western Asia 319–301 B.C.; then ruled Macedonia, 294–287, 276–168 B.C.)
Antigonus I (the One-Eyed), 319–301 (proclaimed king in 306)
Demetrius I (the Besieger), 306–287
Antigonus II, 276–239
Philip V, 221–179

Seleucids (ruled western Asia, 301–63 B.C.)
Seleucus I, 305–281
Antiochus I, 281–261
Antiochus III, 223–187

Ptolemies (ruled Egypt, 323–30 B.C.)
Ptolemy I, 323–283 (proclaimed king in 305)
Ptolemy II, 283–246
Ptolemy IV, 221–204

Thrace
Lysimachus, 323–281 (proclaimed king in 305)

Epirus
Pyrrhus, 306–272

Syracuse
Agathocles, 304–289
Hieron II, 269–215

battle. After his death, the political history of the Hellenistic world was the story of three families—the Ptolemies in Egypt, the Seleucids in Asia, and the Antigonids (Demetrius the Besieger and his descendants) in Macedonia (Table 20.2).

THE SELEUCID EMPIRE

Seleucus ended up with the biggest territory by far, with a population of twenty-five to thirty million and immense geographical variety. In 303 B.C. Seleucus traded territory with Chandragupta, Porus' successor in the Indus Valley, for the elephants who won him the battle of Ipsus, but otherwise he held onto the old Persian Empire (except Egypt).

The Persians had ruled this huge region by interfering as little as possible in its workings. They picked their satraps carefully, then left them to administer their provinces almost as independent kings so long as they paid up on time and provided troops when asked. The result was a patchwork of local institutions, taxes, and customs, governed by separate bureaucracies using different languages. It was a system superbly designed and underpinned by the high religion of Zoroaster, and it functioned for over two hundred years. Alexander replaced the satraps with his own men, as did Antigonus and Seleucus. Seleucus confiscated large estates so the royal family had its own sources of revenue separate from the satraps, and imposed various taxes on the peasants, but otherwise left things alone. Thousands of Greeks and Macedonians migrated to the new territories, where men of talent could get rich. Nineteen out of every twenty administrators mentioned in surviving documents have Greek names, but many of them were members of the old administrative elites, who had learned Greek and took Greek names. The Greek alphabet made possible such shifts in cultural identity, which never went in the other direction. So far as we know no Greek ever learned the native system of writing or the native language (although Cleopatra VII was said to have learned to speak Egyptian).

Hellenization

Hellenization—the adoption of Greek customs in the conquered territories— proceeded partly by Greeks moving to the Near East and partly by local people learning Greek and adopting Greek ways. Under the first two kings, Seleucus I (reigned 305–281 B.C.; see Table 20.2) and **Antiochus I** (an-tī-o-kus; 281–261 B.C.), tens of thousands of young men came east as mercenary soldiers. Many died, or made their fortunes and went home; but most received land and citizenship in a new city in Persia or even farther east. The Seleucids needed such settlements to control the sparsely settled countryside. Gymnasia and agoras were erected in the most unlikely places. A *polis* flourished on what is now the island of Bahrain in the Persian Gulf (Map 20.3),

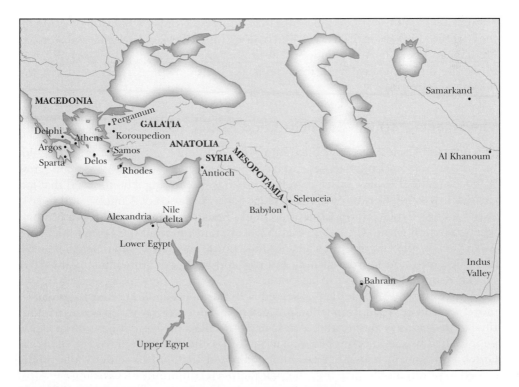

Map 20.3 Third-century-B.C. sites mentioned in this chapter.

and a rich Greek kingdom grew up in Bactria, in modern Afghanistan. One city in modern Uzbekistan not only had the required gymnasium and theater, but also a column base in its agora was inscribed with maxims copied from the sanctuary at Delphi, twenty-five hundred miles to the west! Around 258 B.C., the famous Indian king Asoka, a Buddhist, set up in the Indus River Valley an inscription in Greek and Aramaic, a language and accompanying script widely used for administration in the Seleucid empire, while around 100 B.C. a man with the thoroughly Greek name Heliodorus set up an inscription in Afghanistan to the Hindu god Vishnu.

Seleucus and Antiochus founded much larger cities at the core of the new kingdom. Imitating Alexander, they named the greatest cities after themselves: Seleuceia on the River Tigris near modern Baghdad, and Antioch near the Mediterranean in Syria. These cities swelled to over a hundred thousand, quickly surpassing Athens and Syracuse. From Antioch and Seleuceia on the Tigris, the Seleucids administered rich lands, drawing in money as tax and rent and spending it on palaces, servants, and urban amenities. A dozen other cities with tens of thousands of residents sprang up around them, so that by the late third century B.C., new urban cores had developed in coastal Syria, western Anatolia, and Mesopotamia. Greeks and Macedonians settled predominantly in such cities rather than in the countryside.

Educated Greeks could now travel from Syracuse to Samarkand in central Asia speaking the same language, discussing the same philosophers, looking at similar statues, and drinking the same wine all the way. They could leave Greek lands altogether and still find someone able to discuss Plato in Greek, in India and Carthage. However, if they headed ten miles into the countryside outside Babylon or Antioch, they would find a world barely touched by the Greeks. Assyrian, Babylonian, Median, and Persian rulers came and went, speaking different languages and living in wholly different ways from their subjects. To them, the Greeks were just the newest conquerors.

The Seleucid Zenith: Seleucus I and Antiochus I

The growth of Seleucus' cities filled him with confidence and his coffers with gold. In 301 B.C. overreaching had destroyed Antigonus, lord of the same vast realm; now Seleucus made the same mistake, in the late 280s. Exploiting a family feud that led Lysimachus to murder his own son, Seleucus overran much of Anatolia, and in 281, at the battle of the Field of Crows (in Greek, *Koroupedion,* in western Asia Minor), Seleucus killed Lysimachus, destroyed his army, and reunited the Macedonian and Asian parts of the empire. Just when absolute power seemed within reach, Seleucus' allies betrayed and murdered him. His son and successor Antiochus I (281–261) quickly dropped all claims to Macedonia.

For centuries, Macedonia had served as buffer between Greece and population movements in central Europe. Philip II and his predecessors worried as much about Illyrian invasions as about Athens or Sparta. An unusually large migration of Celtic peoples had begun in central Europe in the fifth century B.C. Some of the Gauls (as Greek and Roman writers called them) searched for land to settle, while others hoped to plunder or to take over the rich southern communities. Crossing the Alps, war parties reached Rome in 390 B.C. and sacked the city—a feat not repeated for another thousand years. Finally driven from Italy, the Gauls rampaged through the Balkans and descended on Macedonia a hundred years after they had burned Rome.

Political divisions in Macedonia undermined resistance to the Gauls, who ravaged Greece in the 270s B.C. and nearly looted Delphi. Others crossed into Anatolia where Antiochus I decisively defeated them in the late 270s, forcing them to settle down (the area was called Galatia after them, as in St. Paul's letter to the Galatians). When he died in 261 B.C., the kingdom of Antiochus was at its zenith, its cities growing, trade booming. Its monarchs were secure.

Crisis and Decline

Economic life increasingly centered on the urban clusters in Syria around Antioch, in the cities along the coast of Asia Minor, and around Seleuceia on the Tigris. After 250 B.C., emigration from the Aegean slowed. With fewer exmercenaries settling in Iran, the isolation of the east increased. Some time around 250, the governors of Bactria started calling themselves kings, ignoring the new king Antiochus II (261–246) in his palace two thousand miles away. A nomadic people named the Parthians had been moving south from central Asia into Iran for some time, and by 230, they controlled large areas.

The loss of eastern revenues made it harder for the Seleucids to support large armies. Other governors asserted themselves. By 240, the ruler of the growing city of **Pergamum** near the Aegean coast was calling himself king, not just defying Seleucus II (246–225), but actually pushing him out of western Anatolia and founding an independent kingdom there.

PTOLEMAIC EGYPT

The country that Ptolemy seized in 323 B.C. was very different from Seleucus' sprawling realm. Ptolemy's Egypt stretched from the flat and marshy Nile Delta for a thousand miles up the river valley, never more than ten to fifteen miles wide, with forbidding deserts on either side (Figure 20.1).

There were always important cultural differences between Upper Egypt ("upper," or south, whence the Nile flows), where indigenous traditions died hard, and Lower Egypt ("lower," or north), the Nile Delta, but the river imposed an enviable unity. The Ptolemies' seven to ten million subjects were squeezed into the most densely populated land on earth, where they could be controlled and taxed.

On his arrival in 323 B.C., Ptolemy I presented himself as a new pharaoh, claiming the ancient prerogatives of Egyptian kingship (though he did not dare use the title "king" among Greeks until 305). Like Seleucus, he kept the old administrative structures largely intact, especially the complex system of taxation of the great temples scattered up and down the Nile. Greek immigrants took many of the top positions and generated royal documents in Greek. Native-born Egyptian scribes, however, continued recording village activities in the Egyptian demotic ("people's") script. The scribes often took Greek names. We know more about local administration in

Figure 20.1 Satellite photo of Egypt. Surrounded by deserts, the Nile makes its valley an oasis of agriculture and abundant life. The valley snakes in a line from modern Lake Nasser behind the Aswan high dam in southern Egypt to the Mediterranean Sea, where it widens into a fertile delta.

Ptolemaic Egypt than in any other ancient country because the dry Egyptian climate has preserved millions of fragments of papyrus (Figure 20.2).

Ptolemy rejected the high stakes of Alexander's whole empire to work on establishing local power. His son **Ptolemy II** (283–246) adopted an old Egyptian tradition and married his sister Arsinoë (ar-**sin**-ō-ē; Figure 20.3), earning the nickname "sister-lover." As in Asia, Greek immigrants came to the cities, above all to Alexandria. According to legend, Alexander personally picked its location in 333 B.C. on a little island at the mouth of the Nile:

> After Alexander had conquered Egypt, he was anxious to found a great and populous Greek city there, to be called after him. He had chosen a certain site on the advice of his architects, and was on the point of measuring and marking it out. Then as he lay asleep he dreamed that a gray-haired man of venerable appearance stood by his side and recited these lines from the *Odyssey:*
>
> > Out of the tossing sea where it breaks on the beaches of Egypt
> > rises an isle from the waters: the name that men give it is Pharos.[54]
>
> Alexander rose the next morning and immediately visited Pharos. . . . When he saw what wonderful natural advantages the place possessed—for it was a strip of land

Figure 20.2 Papyrus business letter in the demotic script, circa 100 B.C. Millions of documents in Egyptian and Greek have been recovered from the sands of Egypt, many of them used to wrap mummified crocodiles.

resembling a broad isthmus, which stretched between the sea and a great lagoon, with a spacious harbor at the end of it—he declared that Homer, besides his other admirable qualities, was also a very far-seeing architect, and he ordered the plan of the city to be designed so that it would conform to this site. There was no chalk to mark the ground-plan, so they took barley, sprinkled it on the dark earth and marked out a semi-circle, which was divided into equal segments by lines radiating from the inner arc to the circumference. . . . While the king was enjoying the symmetry of the design, suddenly huge flocks of birds appeared from the river and the lagoon, descended upon the site, and devoured every grain of the barley. Alexander was greatly disturbed by this omen, but the diviners urged him to take heart and interpreted the occurrence as a sign that the city would not only have abundant resources of its own but would be the nurse of men of innumerable nations, and so he ordered those in charge of the work to proceed.

Plutarch, *Life of Alexander* 26 (I. Scott-Kilvert)

Before Alexander, Egypt had turned inward, but Alexandria provided a gateway to the Mediterranean world comparable to Antioch in Seleucid Syria. Alexandria soon became the greatest city in the ancient world. Before 200 B.C., its population approached half a million. One Greek visitor wrote that

It is inhabited by three classes of people: first, the native Egyptians, a volatile group, hard to control; second, by the mercenaries, a numerous, uncultivated, and overbearing set, it

Figure 20.3 Ptolemy II and Arsinoë. Ptolemy is shown as pharaoh, with the traditional Egyptian double crown and scepter. In his upraised left hand, he holds a symbol of a thunderbolt, like Zeus. Arsinoë also combines Greek and Egyptian conventions. Their names are written above them in hieroglyphs. Painted limestone, circa 250 B.C.

being an ancient practice there to maintain a foreign force which owing to the weakness of the kings had learned to rule rather than obey; and third there are the Alexandrians themselves, a people also not genuinely civilized for the same reasons, but still superior to the mercenaries, for though they are mixed they come from a Greek stock and have not forgotten Greek customs.

Polybius 34.14 (I. Scott-Kilvert)

Greek Alexandrians often looked down on Egyptians. Theocritus, a Sicilian poet who moved to Alexandria in the 270s, described one such character pushing her way through the city, complaining

Gods, what a crowd! How and when are we supposed to get through
this terrible place? Ants, numberless and uncounted!
Many good things, Ptolemy, have been done by you
since your begetter's been with the immortals;°
no criminal now does his mischief, creeping up to someone Egyptian-style,
the sort of games those bundles of deceit used to play before;
they're all just like each other, nasty tricks, all of them cursed.

Theocritus, *Idyll* 15.44–50 (R. Wells)

°*with the immortals:* Since his father Ptolemy I died in 283 B.C.

Alexandria was a place of urban unrest and ethnic tensions. The largest number of Jews outside Judea lived here, and in Alexandria, the Jewish scriptures were

Figure 20.4   The modern lighthouse at Al-Montazah stands on or near the foundations of the great lighthouse of Ptolemy II, one of the Seven Wonders of the ancient world. Portions of its statuary and other fragments were recently found in the harbor. Pharos is no longer an island, but attached to the mainland.

translated out of Hebrew into the Greek version called the *Septuagint,* more widely used than the Hebrew version in the Jewish diaspora and in Judea itself.

Alexandria's vistas were spectacular. Only in the late 1990s did underwater archaeologists discover its ruins submerged by the rising sea. Sailors entering its harbor first saw the famous lighthouse, built of white stone, then behind it tiers of multicolored palaces (Figure 20.4). Pushing through the crowds, they could stroll down Alexandria's boulevards, some one hundred feet wide. Here, all the Old World's goods were for sale—silk from China, spices from Arabia, wines and olive oil from Greece, and the wheat and barley of Egypt. You could listen to philosophers on street corners and visit Ptolemy II's great Museum (Greek *Mouseion,* "home of the Muses"), a combination library, university, and center for artists. The Museum attracted the best intellectuals, including native Egyptians, Jews, and Carthaginians as well as Greeks. The Museum established Greek as the international language of learning, and its librarians set out to obtain a copy of every book ever written in Greek. Virtually all ancient Greek texts that have survived to modern times passed through the library at Alexandria, where they were studied, inventoried, copied, and corrected. All surviving ancient Greek tragedies appear to descend from a complete set compiled in Athens, which Ptolemy II borrowed and did not return. The Museum gave Alexandria a cultural dominance beyond that even of fifth-century Athens, and its influence is still felt today.

The Ptolemies also engaged in massive land-reclamation projects, generating more revenues and providing land where they could settle exmercenaries without dispossessing the natives. The records of one large estate survive from the 250s B.C. The manager experimented with figs, walnuts, peaches, plums, and apricots for sale in Alexandria. His letters reveal a modern enterprise, maximizing profits in competitive markets.

Though the Ptolemies never tried to rebuild Alexander's empire, they intervened overseas to preserve a favorable balance of power. Five "Syrian Wars" against the Seleucids were ruinously expensive, and Ptolemy III had to fight native revolts in Upper Egypt. When Ptolemy IV came to the throne in 221, aged about twenty-three, his kingdom looked strong, but the decline in Greek immigration had ended expansion. Revenues were falling, an inexperienced youth was on the throne, and despite Alexandria's splendor, state power was weakening.

THE ANTIGONIDS: MACEDONIA

For the Seleucids and Ptolemies, the first half of the third century B.C. was a golden age, but not for Macedonia. The people who created Alexander's empire got the least from it. Stability came only in 276 B.C., and even then Macedonia was poorer than her eastern rivals.

Demetrius the Besieger, son of Antigonus the One-Eyed, did not disappear after the battle of Ipsus in 301, but as a pirate king he was always on the move, plundering his enemies. Seleucus, wishing to neutralize Demetrius, married his daughter Stratonicê (even though Seleucus was over sixty and Stratonicê under twenty). When Cassander died in 298 B.C., his family massacred each other, and in the chaos Demetrius the Besieger won back Athens in 297 B.C. In 294, he expelled Cassander's successors from Macedonia, winning himself a proper throne.

Seleucus' son Antiochus, in his early thirties, fell in love with Stratonicê, his stepmother, Demetrius' daughter. When Seleucus found out, he gave his young wife to his son. Now it seemed that a grandson of Demetrius the Besieger, lord of Macedonia, would one day rule the Seleucid Empire. Looking at Demetrius' career, it is easy to see why Hellenistic writers personified **Tychê** (**tī**-kē), "Luck," as a goddess (Figure 20.5).

His victories so alarmed the other kings that in 287 they combined and drove him from Macedonia. Demetrius' despairing wife committed suicide, but he raised a new army and attacked Seleucus. After dramatic adventures, his army disintegrated, and in 285 Demetrius surrendered to Seleucus. After two years of luxurious house arrest, he died of too much drink. In 281 B.C., an estranged son of Ptolemy I murdered Seleucus and seized the Macedonian throne, only to be overwhelmed by the Gauls in 279, whom Demetrius the Besieger's son, Antigonus II (276–239 B.C., grandson of Antigonus I, the One-Eyed) crushed in 276. The Gauls retreated to Anatolia, and Antigonus II took the Macedonian throne. The Antigonids once again controlled Macedonia, but it remained the weakest kingdom. Its most ambitious young men had emigrated to the east. Taxes brought in just one-fifth of Philip II's revenue. In 221, Philip V (221–179 B.C.) took the Macedonian throne. At seventeen, he was even younger than Antiochus III (the Seleucid king, now twenty) and Ptolemy IV (the Egyptian king, twenty-three). These three kings, who would be

Figure 20.5 The goddess Tychê, "luck," here probably representing the city of Antioch on the Syrian coast. Tychê sits atop a male swimmer, probably personifying the Orontes River, which flowed by Antioch. Tychê wears a crown of city walls, because she protects the city, and holds a sheaf of grain, because she brings abundance. Roman copy of a Greek marble statue by Eutychides.

called upon to defend Hellenistic civilization against the Roman storm, were young, inexperienced, and new to the throne.

THE *POLEIS*

When Alexander died in 323 B.C., many Greeks thought the *poleis* would now regain their former and rightful glory. But the *poleis* were too small to compete with the new kingdoms. Since 314 B.C., all Hellenistic kings had preached that the *poleis* should be free, but any king who really allowed Greek freedom would immediately find the *poleis* actively helping his rivals. The real money and power now lay in the great cities of Alexandria and Antioch. Emigration from the Aegean had fueled these cities' growth. When emigration slowed after 250 B.C., it was because population in the Aegean had stagnated and by 150 B.C. was declining. The historian Polybius commented:

> In our times the whole of Greece has suffered a shortage of children and hence a general decrease of the population, and in consequence some cities have become deserted and agricultural production has declined, although neither wars nor epidemics were taking place continuously . . . the cause of this situation was self-evident and the remedy lay within our own power: this evil grew upon us rapidly and overtook us before we were

aware of it, the simple reason being that men had fallen prey to inflated ambitions, love of money, and indolence, with the result that they were unwilling to marry, or if they did marry, to bring up the children that were born to them; or else they would only rear one or two out of a large number,° so as to leave these well off and able in turn to squander their inheritance. For in cases where there are only one or two children and one is killed off by war and the other by sickness, it is obvious that the family home is left unoccupied, and ultimately, just as happens with swarms of bees, little by little whole cities lose their resources and cease to flourish.

Polybius 36.17 (I. Scott-Kilvert)

° . . . *number:* Unwanted children were exposed in the wild to die.

From 800 through 300 B.C., population growth had drawn traders to the Aegean. Now this network was breaking down, and merchants looked to Alexandria and Antioch, not Athens and Corinth. Rhodes, conveniently placed between the Aegean and the east, flourished, and the ancient sacred island of Delos at the center of the Cyclades became an international slave market, capable of processing ten thousand slaves a day. But the old centers shrank and decayed. A third-century B.C. guidebook paints a sad picture of Athens, now reduced to a kind of theme park:

> The city itself is all dry and does not have a good water supply; the streets are narrow and winding, as they were built long ago. Most of the houses are cheaply built, and only a few reach a higher standard; a stranger would find it hard to believe at first sight that this was the famous city of Athens, though he might soon come to believe it. There you will see the most beautiful sights on earth: a large and impressive theater, a magnificent temple of Athena, something out of this world and worth seeing, the so-called Parthenon, which lies above the theater; it makes a great impression on sightseers. There is the Olympieion,° which though only half-completed is impressively designed, though it would have been most magnificent if completed. There are three gymnasia—the Academy, Lyceum, and Cynosarges. They are all planted with trees and laid out with lawns. They have festivals of all sorts, and philosophers from everywhere pull the wool over your eyes and provide recreation. There are many opportunities for leisure and spectacle without interruption. The produce of the land is wonderful and delicious to taste, though in rather short supply. But the presence of foreigners, which they are all accustomed to and which fits in with their inclinations, causes them to forget about their stomachs by diverting their attention to pleasant things. Because of the spectacles and entertainments in the city, the common people feel no hunger, because they are made to forget about food. But for those who have money there is no city comparable in the pleasures it offers.

Heraclides of Crete 1.1–2 (M. M. Austin, no. 83)

° *Olympieion:* A huge temple to Zeus that Pisistratus began around 530 B.C. No one could afford to complete the work until the Roman emperor Hadrian intervened, around A.D. 130. See Figure 22.3 in Chapter 22.

As the *poleis* weakened, pirates swarmed the seas. As trade declined, merchants could not afford to hire protection. The line between piracy and war blurred as *poleis* preyed on each other and Demetrius the Besieger turned pirate king in the 290s.

The cities' impoverishment made them more dependent than ever on the good will of a few rich men. When so much depended on the whims of kings, men who knew them personally mattered more than official embassies, and *poleis* depended on cash infusions from the rich. Historians call these rich benefactors **euergetists** (yū-**erg**-e-tists), "doers of good deeds." Every Hellenistic city has yielded public inscriptions celebrating euergetists' contributions to the community's well-being.

One example from Samos records how the wealthy Boulagoras intervened with Antiochus I, fixed the gymnasium, sent envoys to Ptolemy I, and funded the food supply. Boulagoras doubtlessly acted out of concern for his fellow citizens, but euergetism nevertheless moved political functions from the citizens' collective hands into those of private individuals. With more power, the rich accumulated still more wealth, and the impoverished *poleis* needed them still more.

The new super-rich did not, however, overthrow democracies. Men like Boulagoras accepted that citizens should rule their *poleis* collectively, and more cities called themselves "democracies" in the third century B.C. than ever before. The super-rich could deal directly with kings, and perhaps did not care much what the assembly said. The cities' inability to compete with the Hellenistic kings drove these developments. The advantages of larger political units had been clear since the fifth-century Athenian Empire, and in the fourth century, the Aetolian (ē-tō-lē-an) and Achaean (a-**kē**-an) peoples formed loose federal leagues, the **Aetolian League** and the **Achaean League.** These had assemblies and councils, just like *poleis,* to which *poleis* sent representatives, who elected generals and other officers (Map 20.4).

In the 280s, the Achaeans realized that by acting together their league could stand up to Macedonia. They agreed on common weights, measures, coinage, and laws, and in 245 B.C. elected the daring, young, and rich Aratos (a-**rā**-tus) their general. He set about expelling Macedonian garrisons from Greece. The Aetolians followed suit, even getting control of Delphi. More leagues formed in

Map 20.4 The federal leagues of the third century B.C.

Crete, Ionia, and Thrace as it became clear that to survive in a world of great king-doms, *poleis* must either submit to the Antigonids or Ptolemies, or form competing multicity organizations. Athens and Sparta, perhaps because both had glorious his-tories, resisted absorption into federal leagues. But whereas rich Athenians learned to live with the kings and got the poor to go along with them, Sparta went through a fundamentalist revolt that sought to revive past glories—with disas-trous results.

ATHENS IN DECLINE

During the Wars of the Successors, Athens went through bewildering constitu-tional changes—oligarchy from 322 to 318 B.C., then democracy from 318 to 317, then another oligarchy under Demetrius of Phaleron from 317 to 307. Demetrius the Besieger claimed to reestablish democracy in 307, though in fact he directly controlled politics. A tyrant seized power between 301 and 295, when Demetrius the Besieger returned. Athens was democratic in the 270s B.C., but a narrow clique paid for and directed her festivals and defense, bought grain, and talked Ptolemy II into generous gifts. A secret junta of big property owners dependent on Ptolemy's goodwill in fact ran the city, while a Macedonian garrison held Piraeus.

The cost of dependence on Ptolemy was that he sent Athens, Sparta, and the Achaean League into war against Macedonia in 268. Athens bore the brunt of the fighting and surrendered to Antigonus II in 262 B.C. after a terrible siege. Antigonus expelled Ptolemy's friends and put in a new dictator—by a cruel irony, the grandson and namesake of Demetrius of Phaleron who had ruled the city fifty years before! An assembly met regularly but did little beyond pray for the health of Antigonus and his family.

In 229, a group of euergetists paid off the Macedonian garrison and freed the city. Two wealthy brothers, Eurycleides and Micion, dominated the Assembly for the next thirty years. They understood that Athens was no longer a great power. They avoided depending on any one king and skillfully negotiated a neutral course. They scrapped the fleet and Long Walls to avoid provoking attacks. They recog-nized that Athens could not compete with Macedonia or the Achaean and Aetolian Leagues, and that being attached to any one power would ruin the city. So the Athe-nians, for the first time in their history, retreated into obscurity. Faraway Alexandria easily eclipsed little Athens. By 200 B.C., the city of Pericles was living off its past, a tourist attraction where something once had happened.

SPARTA'S COUNTERREVOLUTION

When the Spartans conquered Messenia in the eighth century B.C., their need to control the helots led them to develop ritualized education, public dining, and the other odd customs we described in Chapter 10, "A Tale of Two Archaic Cities: Sparta and Athens, 700–480 B.C." The loss of Messenia in 371 B.C. removed the ra-tionale for such institutions, but since the Spartans expected to recover Messenia at any moment, they tried to preserve their ancestral ways. They sat out Athens' and Thebes' final stand against Macedon at Chaeronea in 338 B.C., only to launch their own rising in 331, quickly suppressed. Sparta's martial traditions survived, but her young men increasingly fought overseas as mercenaries.

Some Spartans welcomed these changes. A wealthy upper class had emerged since the fifth century B.C., concentrating land in a few hands through strategic marriages and pushing many former citizens out of the Spartiate class. By the third century, these rich families occupied a position rather like the euergetists in other *poleis*. Other Spartans kept asking what had gone wrong. In the 370s, Sparta dominated Greece; now she was a local power. The Spartans did not understand the demographic and economic changes that had undermined their system or the shift of power toward larger political units. As they saw it, the cause of decline was that Sparta had abandoned Lycurgus' noble teachings. They wanted to restore the ancestral constitution, redistribute land to a large Spartiate class, and reinstate ancient simplicity and virtue. Such demands paralleled the wishes of the poor in other *poleis,* but had a unique millenarian quality: If we return to the original covenant that Lycurgus gave us, they fancied, we will rule Greece again.

The tensions between rich Spartans happy with the way things were going and those who sought a Lycurgan renewal broke into the open during the short reign of **Agis III** (ā-jis; 244–241 B.C.):

> Wealth was concentrated in just a few hands, and the city generally was impoverished. In consequence people had no time for any honorable activities: they became subservient, as well as envious and hostile toward those who did own property. Thus there were no more than 700 Spartiates left, of whom perhaps 100 owned land in addition to their lot. Though they lacked rights or resources, the remaining mass of the population continued to squat in the city. They became lazy and unenthusiastic in repelling external attacks, and all the time they kept looking for some opportunity to revolt and change their present condition.
>
> In view of this Agis rightly considered that it would be a splendid achievement to restore a full body of equal citizens, and he began to sound out public opinion. The young men responded quickly, and more eagerly than he had expected: as a group they stripped to show their mettle, as if their clothes represented a way of life which they were all discarding in the cause of liberty. The older men by contrast were more deeply tainted by corruption: most of them, like slaves being returned to a master from whom they had fled, shook with fear at the name of Lycurgus, and criticized Agis for deploring the present condition of the state and for being so eager to restore Sparta's ancient renown.

Agis began his campaign by persuading his mother and her friends to divide their estates among the Spartiates:

> Inspired by the young man's aspirations, the ladies changed their minds and were filled with such great enthusiasm for his noble purpose that together they urged Agis on and told him to proceed faster. At the same time they called in their male friends, asking them to join and to talk to the other women, since they were aware that Spartan men were always subject to their wives and allowed them to interfere in affairs of state more than they themselves did in private ones.
>
> Now at that time most of the wealth at Sparta was in the hands of women, and it was this which made Agis' task troublesome and awkward. For the women opposed him, not only because they would lose the luxury which seemed to them with their lack of taste to be true happiness, but also because they saw that they would be deprived of both the respect and the influence which their wealth afforded them.

Agis thought he was restoring ancestral virtue and bringing Sparta back to Lycurgus' true path. His opponents—including his fellow king Leonidas—saw it differently:

> Leonidas was willing to assist the rich, since he was frightened of the *dêmos* in their enthusiasm for change. He offered no open opposition, but made constant secret efforts to damage the project and wreck it, slandering Agis in discussions he had with the magistrates. According to him, Agis was pledging the property of the rich to the poor as their payment for making him tyrant, and by his land distributions and cancellations of debts was buying plenty of bodyguards for himself, rather than citizens for Sparta.

Agis proposed dividing the land near Sparta into forty-five hundred equal lots, to be distributed among the Spartiates, and the land farther from the city into another fifteen thousand equal lots, to be given to *perioikoi*. When Leonidas persuaded the Elders to block the proposal, Agis overthrew him. The Ephors struck back, saying that debt cancellation and land redistribution were illegal, but Agis announced that the Ephors' opinion mattered only if the two kings disagreed—and because he had deposed Leonidas, that, of course, was not the case. Backed by an armed gang, Agis threw the Ephors out of their official chairs in the agora and replaced them with his own supporters.

> With the king's policy thus going forward without anyone blocking or opposing it, one man, Agesilaos,° now upset and ruined everything. It was that most famous affliction—avarice—which prompted him to wreck a most splendid and most Spartan plan. For although he owned notably fertile and extensive lands, he had also borrowed very heavily. As a result he could not pay off his debts, nor did he want to surrender his land. So he persuaded Agis that it would be too great a revolution of the city if both steps were taken simultaneously, but that if property-owners were first conciliated by remission of debts, then they would cheerfully and peaceably accept the redistribution of land later. . . . So they brought into the agora the debtors' documents, made a single pile of them all, and burned them. Once the flames rose, the wealthy men and creditors were left in deep distress, while by way of mocking them Agesilaos declared that never had he seen a brighter light or a clearer blaze than that.
>
> Then the crowd demanded that the division of land should also be made at once, and the kings gave orders for this to be done. But by constantly alleging pressure of other business and by producing excuses, Agesilaos wasted time until Sparta's allies the Achaeans demanded help, and the expedition fell to Agis.

°*Agesilaos:* Not to be confused with the famous King Agesilaos (400–359 B.C.).

When the poorer Spartans saw the redistribution being postponed so Agis could go on campaign, they felt cheated and Agis' political alliance collapsed.

Agis took refuge in the sanctuary of Athena, but one day when he left the sanctuary to go swimming, his enemies seized him. They strangled him in the state prison; then, hoping to root out fundamentalism, they strangled his mother and grandmother too.

> When the tragedy was made known throughout the city and the three bodies were brought out, the citizens were not sufficiently terrorized to conceal either their grief at these events or their hatred of Leonidas and Amphares:° their opinion was that nothing

°*Amphares:* The man who performed the murders.

more ghastly or more sacrilegious had been perpetrated at Sparta since the Dorians had settled in the Peloponnesus°. . . . Agis was the first reigning king at Sparta to be put to death by Ephors. The course of action he chose to follow was admirable and worthy of Sparta.

Plutarch, Life of Agis 5–21 (excerpts) (I. Scott-Kilvert)

°Peloponnesus: That is, since the beginning of Spartan history.

So ended Agis' bid to revive Lycurgan Sparta. But assassinations could not crush fundamentalism:

Leonidas forcibly removed Agis' wife (who had a newborn infant) from her home and married her to his son Cleomenes: he was not quite of a suitable age to marry, but Leonidas did not want the woman to be given to anyone else. For Agiatis° was heiress to the substantial property of her father Gylippus, as well as being much more beautiful and lovelier than other Greek women, and of equable temperament. The story is that she therefore pleaded hard against being forced, but that once married to Cleomenes, while continuing to detest Leonidas, she did make the man a good, loving wife. For his part, as soon as he married her he fell in love with her, and in a sense sympathized with his wife's devotion to Agis and her remembrance of him. Consequently he often asked about what had happened, and paid careful attention when she explained Agis' purpose and policy.

°Agiatis: Agis' wife.

Cleomenes' (klē-o-me-nēz) tutor was a Stoic philosopher (see Chapter 21) who had written a pamphlet, On the Spartan Constitution. Influenced by him and by Agiatis, Cleomenes decided that Agis' policy was a better response to what had gone wrong in Sparta than his father's support of the status quo. When Cleomenes ascended the throne in 235 B.C., he was determined to act. He decided that victories over the Achaean League, now Sparta's bitter enemy, might give him leverage against the conservative Ephors and win the poor in the Achaean cities over to his side.

Cleomenes defeated the Achaeans in battle in 228, then launched a coup. He assassinated four of the five Ephors and ten of their supporters. Next morning, while the city was reeling from the news, he exiled eighty of the richest men, including many of Agis' enemies. He removed the Ephors' seats from the agora, leaving just one for himself, overthrowing Sparta's ancient traditions in the interests of restoring them. Aided by his wife's and mother's rich female friends, he divided his own family's land and that of the eighty exiles among four thousand new Spartiates and trained them to fight in the Macedonian style, with eighteen-foot spears. He went out of his way to play the part of a traditional Spartan king:

Cleomenes personally set an example to everyone by his own economical, plain lifestyle: it had nothing about it that was vulgar, or superior to ordinary people, so that it served as a public model of restraint—something which gave him a certain advantage in the affairs of Greece. For in their encounters with other kings men were not so much taken aback at all their wealth and extravagance, as disgusted by their arrogance and self-importance, together with the offensive, tactless manner in which they treated those whom they encountered. In contrast those who approached Cleomenes—who really was a king in fact as well as in title—did not see him surrounded by any purple robes or cloaks, or by the paraphernalia of couches and litters; nor did he make the conduct of affairs difficult and slow with a swarm of messengers and doorkeepers, or by means of secretaries. Instead he came out simply dressed to respond to greetings, and talked at leisure in an affable, considerate way to those who made him requests, so that they were entranced and bowled over, and declared that he alone was descended from Heracles.°

°*Heracles:* The Spartans believed that they were all descended from the hero Heracles.

Cleomenes' new army, stiffened with mercenaries, swept through the Peloponnesus. The new Spartiates fought enthusiastically, and the poor in other *poleis* welcomed them. Plutarch says that "The Achaeans were now in turmoil and their cities were on the verge of insurrection. The people in them were hoping for division of land and cancellation of debts." In 226, Cleomenes captured Sparta's ancient enemy Argos. The whole Peloponnesus seemed on the verge of revolution. According to Plutarch,

> there was astonishment at Cleomenes' swiftness and acumen. Those who previously had laughed at his claims to be imitating Solon and Lycurgus with his cancellation of debts and equalization of property were by now totally convinced that he was responsible for the change in the Spartiates' conduct. . . . Just a short time had passed, and they had only just resumed their traditional customs and got back into the way of the famous education, yet already—as if Lycurgus were there in person and conducting their policy— they were offering ample proof of their valor and discipline as they had regained the Peloponnesus and were winning back the leadership of Greece for Sparta.
>
> Plutarch, *Life of Cleomenes* 1–18 (excerpts) (I. Scott-Kilvert)

Aratos, commander of the Achaean League, had won fame in the 240s B.C. for expelling the Macedonians from the Peloponnesus: Now he invited them back. Better to have Macedon dominate the *poleis,* than to let the *kakoi* take over. When Antigonus III's Macedonian troops arrived in 224 B.C., Ptolemy III of Egypt sent money to help Cleomenes. The showdown came in summer 222, at Sellasia (sel-a-**sē**-a), north of Sparta. The Achaean League and the Macedonians slaughtered the Spartans: All but two hundred of Cleomenes' new Spartiates fell. Cleomenes chose not to emulate the valor of Sparta's ancient kings by dying with his men, but fled to Alexandria, hoping that Ptolemy III would help him win back Sparta. But Ptolemy soon died, and his successor, Ptolemy IV, refused help. Furious, Cleomenes tried to topple Ptolemy himself in 219 B.C., but bled to death in chaotic streetfighting. Antigonus, meanwhile, captured Sparta itself. Not even Thebes in 371 had done this. He reversed Cleomenes' innovations and enrolled Sparta in a pro-Macedonian league, then marched home.

Sparta's fundamentalism was out of step with the times. Even if Cleomenes had defeated the Achaean League and redistributed property throughout the Peloponnesus, the great powers waited to intervene. The ancient ideal of the *polis* as a community of roughly equal men had ceased to exist.

THE WESTERN GREEKS: AGATHOCLES OF SYRACUSE (361–289/8 B.C.)

Miles of sea protected western Greece from the Hellenistic kings. The old conflicts dragged on—Carthage against Syracuse; Syracuse against the other Greeks; tyrants against citizens; rich against poor; natives against Carthage, the Greeks, and each other (Map 20.5). A man named **Agathocles** (a-**gath**-ō-klēz), born in 361 in the

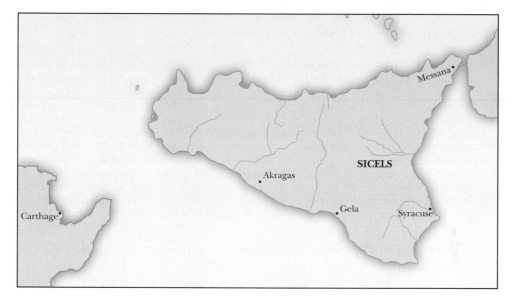

Map 20.5 Sites in the western Mediterranean mentioned in this chapter.

western (Carthaginian) part of the island, was destined to rearrange the balance of power. Moving to Syracuse, he gained influence there by championing the poor and exploiting the fear of Carthage and the Sicels, and by exploiting the hatred of the rich to whip Syracuse's poor into a frenzy. In 316 B.C., they slaughtered four thousand wealthy citizens, while another six thousand fled west to Akragas. The Assembly elected Agathocles commander-in-chief. He canceled debts, redistributed land, and lived in an ostentatiously simple style.

Agathocles' growing power was so alarming that Carthage sent troops to help the exiles. In a great battle in 311 B.C., Carthage shattered Agathocles' army, killing seven thousand men, then put Syracuse under siege. In a bold stroke, Agathocles slipped past the Carthaginian naval blockade with just 13,500 men and made straight for the city of Carthage itself, reasoning that

> if he did this, those in Carthage, who had been living luxuriously in long-continued peace and were therefore without experience in the dangers of battle, would easily be defeated by men who had been trained in the school of danger; that the Libyan° allies of the Carthaginians, who had for a long time resented their taxes, would grasp an opportunity for revolt; most important of all, that by appearing unexpectedly, he would plunder a land which had not been ravaged and which, because of the prosperity of the Carthaginians, abounded in wealth of every kind; and in general, that he would divert the barbarians from his native city and from all Sicily, and transfer the whole war to Libya.
>
> Diodorus of Sicily 20.3.3 (R. Geer)

°*Libyan:* Greeks used "Libyan" to refer to all natives of northwest Africa.

No one had ever attacked Carthage before. When Agathocles wiped out a Carthaginian army, the Carthaginians recalled their best troops from Syracuse and raised the siege by land, though their fleet still blockaded the Great Harbor at Syracuse. The desperate Carthaginians revived horrific religious practices:

> The Carthaginians alleged that Cronus° had turned against them, because in earlier times they used to sacrifice the noblest of their children to this god, but more recently, secretly buying and raising other children, they had sent these to sacrifice instead. But when an investigation was made, it was discovered that some of the sacrifices had been substitutes. When they had given thought to these things and saw the enemy camped before their walls, they were filled with superstitious dread, for they believed that they had neglected the honors of the gods that their fathers had established. In their zeal to make amends for this omission, they chose 200 of the noblest children and sacrificed them publicly; and others who were under suspicion sacrificed themselves voluntarily, to the number of no less than 300. There was a bronze statue of Cronus in the city, extending its hands with the palms up and sloping toward the ground, so that each child that was placed on the arms rolled down and fell into a gaping pit of fire.
>
> Diodorus of Sicily 20.14.4–7 (R. Geer)

°*Cronus:* In Greek myth, Zeus' father. Diodorus equates Cronus with the Phoenician god Baal.

The discovery at Carthage and other Phoenician sites of cemeteries of cremated children, many with inscriptions "offering to Baal," supports such accounts.

Taking Carthage would place Agathocles in the same league as Ptolemy, Antigonus, and Cassander, but back in Sicily Akragas entered the war on Carthage's side and renewed the siege of Syracuse. Late in 307 B.C., Agathocles abandoned the entire army, now suffering in Africa, including his two sons, and sneaked through the blockade with only his close advisors. The forsaken mercenaries murdered Agathocles' sons, then signed up with Carthage.

After many adventures, Agathocles made peace with Carthage and in 304 took the title of king, imitating the Hellenistic monarchs. At least he confirmed that neither Syracuse nor Carthage was strong enough to destroy the other. Agathocles lived another fifteen years. If he could only bring the south Italian Greeks under his dominion, he might finish off Carthage, he thought. He battered many into submission, weakening them for their coming struggle against Rome. Agathocles died in agony in 289 B.C., apparently from cancer of the jaw. Before dying, he abdicated, freeing Syracuse from tyranny and breaking up the kingdom he had created. The west remained a world of *poleis*. Agathocles had more in common with Dionysius I than with Demetrius the Besieger.

PYRRHUS OF EPIRUS

Epirus, in rugged and remote northwest mainland Greece, had been a second-rank power in the fourth century, slower than Macedon to adopt Greek warfare and organization. Olympias, Alexander the Great's mother, came from Epirus. Philip II of Macedonia needed peace with Epirus and went to great lengths to stay friends with her brother, King Alexander of Epirus. In the 280s B.C., their king **Pyrrhus** played a major role. Pyrrhus was a strange and aggressive man. Like Alexander, he loved war for its own sake, sought out enemy commanders for single combat, and made other people's quarrels his own. By 281 B.C., Roman troops were threatening Taras (modern Taranto; Map 20.6), a rich Greek city in southern Italy. The Tarentines asked

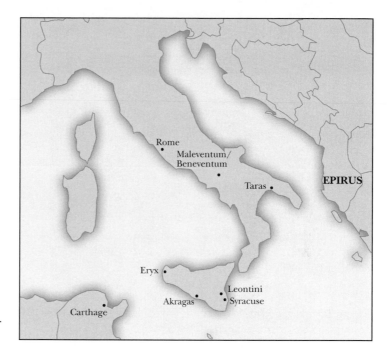

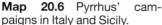

Map 20.6 Pyrrhus' campaigns in Italy and Sicily.

Pyrrhus for help, and Pyrrhus saw a chance to do in the west what Alexander had done in the east.

Despite nearly drowning during the crossing to Italy, Pyrrhus entered Italy in May 280 B.C. The Tarentines struck him as lazy and incompetent, but their enemy the Romans did not. "These may be barbarians," Plutarch has him say to himself, "but there is nothing barbarous about their discipline." He won a difficult battle against them thanks to his twenty elephants, which dismayed the Roman cavalry (Figure 20.6).

The Romans left seven thousand dead on the field to Pyrrhus' four thousand, and many Italian tribes defected to him. Pyrrhus advanced to within forty miles from Rome. He freed his Roman prisoners as an incentive to Rome to strike a treaty. But the stern Roman Senate refused to negotiate and sent back the prisoners, decreeing that any who refused to go would be put to death. Rome then raised a new army.

When the armies clashed again, the battle lasted two days. Pyrrhus' elephants were again decisive. This time, six thousand Romans fell to Pyrrhus' thirty-five hundred dead.

> The story goes that when one of Pyrrhus' friends congratulated him on his victory, he replied, "One more victory like that over the Romans will destroy us completely!" He had lost a great part of the force he had brought with him, with a few exceptions almost all his friends and commanders had been killed, and there were no reinforcements that he could summon from home. At the same time he noticed that his allies were losing their enthusiasm, while the Roman army, by contrast, seemed to be fed, like a spring gushing forth indoors, by a constant stream of recruits, from which they could quickly and easily replace their losses.
>
> Plutarch, *Life of Pyrrhus* 21 (I. Scott-Kilvert)

Figure 20.6 A third-century-B.C. bowl from central Italy showing a war elephant and calf. The design of the tower on the mother elephant's back makes it likely that it represents one of Pyrrhus' elephants.

Hence our expression "pyrrhic victory": Sometimes winning costs so much that you have really lost.

At this crucial moment two messengers reached Pyrrhus. Macedonia was in chaos and he might be able to seize its throne; also, Syracuse, Akragas, and Leontini would submit to him if he led them against Carthage. Torn, he quit Italy for Sicily in 278, defeated the Carthaginians, and stormed the seemingly impregnable fortress of Eryx in the far west. Imitating Alexander, he was the first to scale its walls and jump alone down inside, standing amid a heap of corpses until his horrified troops hacked their way through to him.

In 277, Carthage offered generous terms, but Pyrrhus rejected them. He started conscripting Greeks for a great fleet to invade Africa, but his arrogance so alienated the Greeks that they opened their own negotiations with Carthage to get rid of him. As his position deteriorated, in 276 he suddenly remembered his obligations to Taras. "This gave him a plausible excuse to sail away," Plutarch says, "so that his departure should not appear to be a flight or the result of his having despaired of his prospects on the island. But the truth was that he had failed to master Sicily, which was like a storm-tossed ship, and it was because he was anxious to escape that he threw himself back into Italy."

To escape, Pyrrhus fought tough rearguard actions, at one point accepting single combat with a giant Sicilian despite already being wounded. Pyrrhus split the man's body from skull to groin with one blow. Racing to intercept the Romans, Pyrrhus blundered into defeat at Maleventum (Latin for "Bad Wind") north of Naples. The Romans had learned to send light-armed skirmishers against the elephants, tormenting them with javelins until they panicked and ran back through Pyrrhus' troops, causing chaos. The Romans renamed the local town Beneventum, "Good Wind."

Undismayed, Pyrrhus sailed back to Epirus in 275 and immediately invaded Macedonia, proclaimed himself king, then rushed south to the Peloponnesus. Antigonus immediately recaptured Macedonia. Hacking his way into Argos in 272, Pyrrhus engaged a young man in single combat. The man's mother, hiding on the roof, threw down a roof tile that stunned Pyrrhus. Another Argive ran up and hacked off his head. Plutarch says that

> The general opinion of Pyrrhus was that for warlike experience, daring, and personal valor, he had no equal among the kings of his time; but what he won through his feats of arms he lost by indulging in vain hopes, and through his obsessive desire with what lay beyond his grasp, he constantly failed to secure what lay within it. For this reason Antigonus° compared him to a player of dice, who makes many good throws, but does not understand how to exploit them when they are made.
>
> Plutarch, *Life of Pyrrhus* 26 (I. Scott-Kilvert)

°*Antigonus*: The Macedonian king Antigonus II.

Pyrrhus had attempted to create a new Hellenistic kingdom in the West. Greek fear of Rome and Carthage gave him an entry, but he had to control unruly *poleis* while fighting two great powers. Perhaps he could have saved Taras if he had fought only Rome; or have united Sicily if he had fought only Carthage. When Pyrrhus left Sicily, he sighed, "My friends, what a wrestling ground we are leaving behind for the Romans and Carthaginians."

HELLENISTIC SOCIETY: THE WEAKENING OF THE EGALITARIAN IDEAL

The *polis* was a group of roughly equal men. In the fifth and fourth centuries, it might have been a democracy or an oligarchy, but leaders belonged to a group in which no man was so superior to others that he need not answer to them, and no man so inferior that his voice could be ignored. Wealth, talent, education, or descent should not create barriers within the male community, nor should claims to special intimacy with the gods. Women were a separate race and, regardless of wealth or influence, could never exercise political power. Foreigners and slaves were permanent outsiders; it was almost impossible for either to become citizens.

This ideology suffered during and after the Peloponnesian War, as the cities' incessant demands for money placed ordinary citizens in the debt of the rich. The Macedonian conquests brought previously unimagined wealth and power to the Greek world. By 323 B.C., the old claim that all men were basically equal within their own *poleis* was hard to believe, and *poleis* mattered less within the huge new kingdoms. The Hellenistic world, spread from Sicily to central Asia, was vast and varied. As rigid archaic-classical notions of male citizenship softened, the power of the free poor declined, the rich pulled away from the rest of society, and the super-rich pronounced themselves the equals of gods.

Male and Female

In classical times, Greek women had little social or political power, but in the Hellenistic period, some women, especially queens and the very rich, enjoyed wider horizons. We have seen ferocious warrior-queens like Olympias and Eurydicê, murdering their way to the top and leading armies, and the influence of the royal women around Agis and Cleomenes in Sparta. Arsinoë of Egypt, who married her brother Ptolemy II around 275 B.C., actually ruled jointly with him until her death in 268. She appeared on Egypt's coins and built up Egypt's navy. Her authority was recognized across the Greek world. Royal women's power was greatest when weak men occupied thrones; under strong kings they acted as diplomatic tools, strengthening political alliances through marriage, just as women had throughout the Bronze Age.

Thousands of wealthy but nonroyal women also enjoyed new opportunities. In Sparta, where (unlike in Athens) women could own land, in the 320s women controlled two-fifths of this vital resource; a century later, the proportion was higher. Already in the early fourth century, a Spartan woman's chariot team won a crown at Olympia, and in the third century, rich women all over Greece entered teams. As wealth shifted toward the upper classes, some women accumulated massive resources. Like male euergetists, they paid for public buildings and made loans to their communities, and their cities honored them in return. Women's names were prominent in private loan documents, and in one case a husband had to get his wife's permission before taking a loan. Increased economic power bought political influence and in the third century some women had some voice in making political decisions. In fifth century Athens, no woman had any voice whatsoever.

Human and Divine

In classical times, a vast gulf separated mortals from the gods. If a man did something exceptional, like founding a new city, perhaps after his death—never before—he might be elevated to the status of *hêros*, not so much a god as a glorified ghost. If great leaders like Themistocles or Pericles were more than mortal, what would become of the proposition that all men are equally well qualified for public life? Philip and Alexander posed the first serious threat to conventional distinctions between mortal and the divine. Both claimed descent from gods. When Alexander ordered all Greeks to worship him as a god in 324, most went along out of fear but dropped the cult immediately after his death. When Egyptians crowned Ptolemy I as pharaoh of Egypt, by definition he was the son of the sun-god Ra, although just a general to Greeks. Then in 311, an Ionian Greek city set up a statue of Antigonus I (the One-Eyed) and offered it the same honors as cult images of the gods. Such cults proliferated, of which Plutarch gives an amusing example. In 307, Antigonus' son Demetrius the Besieger sailed into Piraeus and announced he had come to throw out Cassander's puppet ruler, Demetrius of Phaleron.

> When they heard this proclamation, most of the Athenians immediately threw down their shields at their feet and burst into applause. Then with loud cries they called upon Demetrius [the Besieger] to land, acclaiming him as their benefactor and savior. . . .
>
> The gifts Demetrius lavished on the Athenians made his name great and glorious, but the people themselves now began to make it obnoxious by the extravagance of the honors they voted him . . . they were the only people who described Demetrius and Antigonus as savior-gods, and they even abolished the ancient office of *archon*, from whom the year received its name, and elected in his place a priest to officiate at the altar of the savior-gods. They also decreed that the figures of Demetrius and Antigonus should be woven into the sacred robe of Athena, together with those of the other gods. They consecrated the spot where Demetrius had alighted from his chariot and built an altar there, which was known as the altar of the Descending Demetrius. . . .

It was a man named Stratocles who had been the initiator of these extravagant and sophisticated forms of flattery, but the most preposterous of his ideas was the proposal that any envoys sent to Antigonus or Demetrius by public decree or at public expense should be referred to not as ambassadors but as sacred deputies, in the same way as the envoys who conveyed the traditional sacrifices on behalf of the various cities to the great Greek festivals at Olympia and at Delphi. . . .

There was another Athenian whose servility eclipsed even that of Stratocles. This man proposed that whenever Demetrius visited Athens he should be received with the same divine honors as were paid to Demeter and Dionysus, and that whichever citizen surpassed the rest in the magnificence and lavishness of his arrangements for the festival should be granted a sum of money from the public treasury to enable him to dedicate an offering. Finally the Athenians changed the name of the month Mounychion to Demetrion, gave the name of Demetrion to the odd day which falls between the end of the old month and the beginning of the new, and renamed the Dionysiac festival the Demetria.

. . . But the strangest and most exaggerated of all the honors devised for Demetrius was the one proposed by Dromoclides of Sphettos. This man, when the question arose of the consecration of certain shields at Delphi, put down the motion that the people should obtain an oracular response from Demetrius. I reproduce the actual words of the motion, which read as follows:

> May it be propitious. It has been decreed by the people that they shall elect one man from the Athenians, who shall go to the savior-god, and after he has sacrificed and obtained good omens, shall inquire of the savior-god what is the most reverent, decorous, and expeditious manner in which the people may insure the restitution of the intended offerings to their proper places. And whatsoever answer he shall please to give them, the people shall comply with it.

By such absurd flattery, they completely turned Demetrius' head, which even before was not as sound as it should have been.

Plutarch, *Life of Demetrius* 9–13 (excerpts) (I. Scott-Kilvert)

To such depths had sunk the once egalitarian culture of mighty Athens.

When Demetrius fell from power in 287, the Athenians conveniently forgot their adoration, but by now most kings claimed such honors, although some of these ruler cults were mere propaganda, and sometimes Greek collaboration was cynical. In 302, Athens honored three of Demetrius' lieutenants as *heroes,* the old category of semidivinity used only for dead men. By the late third century, hundreds of living men (and some women) were calling themselves *heroes* in inscriptions.

The old gods received few new temples in the third century. Different gods, sometimes new ones, attracted attention. **Asclepius,** the healer-god, was one of the most popular. His devotees claimed miraculous cures and commemorated them with inscriptions:

> Ambrosia from Athens, blind in one eye. She came as a suppliant to the god, and as she walked about the sanctuary she ridiculed some of the cures as being incredible and impossible, that persons who were lame and blind should be restored to health merely by having a dream. But when she went to sleep she saw a vision: she thought the god was standing next to her, saying that he would restore her to health. But she must dedicate in the sanctuary in return a silver pig, as a memorial of her stupidity. Having said this he split open the diseased eye and poured in a medicine. When day came she went away cured.

Syll.[3] 1168, lines 34–41 (M. M. Austin, no. 126)

GIOVE SERAPIDE

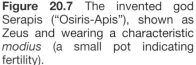

Figure 20.7 The invented god Serapis ("Osiris-Apis"), shown as Zeus and wearing a characteristic *modius* (a small pot indicating fertility).

The Ptolemies even created a new god called **Serapis,** a combination of the ancient Egyptian god of resurrection Osiris and the bull god Apis, but represented like Zeus to appeal both to Greek and Egyptian devotees (Figure 20.7). Cults of certain Egyptian gods, especially Serapis, spread rapidly outside Egypt. Like Asclepius, Serapis came to believers in dreams and provided miraculous cures. Worshipers were initiated into his cult through secret rites that ignored the distinctions of status so important in ordinary life. Serapis can be found in central Asia before 261 B.C.

Great conquerors showed by their deeds that they walked with the gods; even normal aristocrats could describe themselves as semidivine *heroes;* and thousands of men and women initiated into the cult of Serapis believed that they too had privileged access to a supernatural world.

CONCLUSION

The changes in the Greek world between 323 and 220 B.C. were as great as those between 750 and 650 B.C. In the earlier period, the complex of institutions, practices, and ideals that we call the *polis* took shape. In the third century, these institutions crumbled. Traditionalists still resisted god-kings and powerful women, but vast inflows of wealth, a shift in power from poor to rich, and accelerating cultural interactions ruined ancient certainties.

In a way, the third century was the high-water mark of Greek achievement. Alexander had destroyed Greece's ancient enemy Persia. Down to about 250 B.C., emigration from the Aegean drove expansion in the east. There, standards of living were high although they stagnated or declined in the Aegean and the West. The Hellenistic kingdoms were the greatest military powers on earth with nothing to fear except each other. Their royal families lived in astonishing luxury. That would change too.

KEY TERMS

Perdiccas, 439
Craterus, 439
Antipater, 439
Ptolemy, 439
Antigonus, 439
Lysimachus, 439
Seleucus, 440
Cassander, 441
Demetrius of Phaleron, 442
Demetrius the Besieger, 443
Rhodes, 444
Ipsus, 444
Hellenization, 447

Antiochus I, 447
Pergamum, 449
Ptolemy II, 450
Tychê, 454
euergetists, 456
Aetolian League, 457
Achaean League, 457
Agis III, 459
Cleomenes, 461
Agathocles, 462
Pyrrhus, 464
Asclepius, 469
Serapis, 470

FURTHER READING

Cartledge, Paul, and Tony Spawforth, *Hellenistic and Roman Sparta* (London 2001). An authoritative overview by leading scholars on ancient Sparta.

Chamoux, F., *Hellenistic Civilization* (Oxford 2002). Good modern survey.

Green, Peter, *From Alexander to Actium: The Historical Evolution of the Hellenistic Age* (Berkeley 1993). Combines political and military events with cultural and intellectual developments.

Habicht, Christian, *Athens from Alexander to Antony,* tr. D. L. Schneider (Cambridge, MA, 1997). By the leading authority on the history of Athens in the centuries between the fall of the Athenian Empire, in 404 B.C., and the establishment of the Roman Empire.

Hölbl, G., *A History of the Ptolemaic Empire,* tr. T. Saavedra (London 2000). He writes as an authority both on Egyptian religion and archaeology and on the demotic texts, as well as on the Greek sources.

Manning, J. G., *Land and Power in Ptolemaic Egypt: The Structure of Land Tenure* (Cambridge, UK, 2002). Shows how Ptolemaic economic power ultimately shaped Roman Egyptian social and economic institutions.

Momigliano, Arnaldo, *Alien Wisdom: The Limits of Hellenization* (Cambridge, UK, 1975). Entertaining book arguing that in the Hellenistic period the Greeks, Romans, and Jews enjoyed a special relationship that guaranteed their lasting dominance of Western civilization.

Reger, Gary, *Regionalism and Change in the Economy of Independent Delos, 314–167 B.C.* (Berkeley 1994). Applies modern statistical analysis to the detailed inscriptions at the Temple of Apollo on Delos to understand the Hellenistic economy.

Rostovtzeff, Mikhail, *The Social and Economic History of the Hellenistic World* (reprint, Oxford 1993). Classic study by a major scholar.

Sherwin-White, Susan, and Amélie Kuhrt, *From Samarkhand to Sardis: A New Approach to the Seleucid Empire* (London 1993). The first substantial treatment of Seleucid history to appear for fifty years.

Walbank, F. W., *The Hellenistic World* (Boston 1993). Enormously informative, comprehensive, and concise.

Ancient Texts

Austin, M. M., *The Hellenistic World from Alexander to the Roman Conquest* (Cambridge, UK, 1981). Indispensable selection of ancient sources in translation.

Diodorus of Sicily, *History* books 18–20. In *The Library of History* IX (Cambridge, MA, tr. Russel Geer).

Plutarch, *Lives* of Demetrius the Besieger, Pyrrhus, Agis, and Cleomenes. In *The Age of Alexander* (Penguin 1973; tr. Ian Scott-Kilvert) and *Plutarch on Sparta* (Penguin 1986; tr. Richard Talbert).

CHAPTER 21

HELLENISTIC CULTURE, 323–30 B.C.

As large kingdoms, godlike monarchs, and super-rich euergetists characterized the new world of the third century B.C., the *poleis* increasingly became backwaters. Artists and thinkers responded to the new circumstances. The Hellenistic period saw the highest development of Greek mathematics and science, and new forms of philosophy, poetry, and representational art. Greek culture became more complex and in many ways richer than before, reaching from Afghanistan to the Atlantic coast. The legacy of fifth-century classical thought and art remained strong, but creative Greeks pushed their culture in new directions.

It is easy to pinpoint the beginning of Hellenistic culture, because changes were rapid after Alexander's death in 323 B.C., but difficult to define its end. When the Romans gradually took over the East Mediterranean in the last two centuries B.C., they absorbed Hellenistic culture with their conquests. We therefore take the story in this chapter down to 30 B.C., when Rome overthrew the last Hellenistic ruler, Cleopatra VII of Egypt; but on occasion we look further ahead to the second century A.D., when the final fusion of Hellenistic and Roman civilizations took place. We begin with Hellenistic literature, then look at material culture, before turning to philosophy and science, where Hellenistic Greeks made their greatest contributions.

HELLENISTIC HISTORIANS

One Roman scholar commented that the day was not long enough to recite the names of all the historians from this period. These historians wanted to explain why their world had changed so much. They developed new genres of history to understand the times they lived in. Some wrote local histories, rejecting all the attention given to the great kingdoms, but most celebrated the new Hellenistic world, writing for royal courts or the increasingly powerful aristocrats in Rome. Such scholars did not write for popular audiences, as did Herodotus, or for critical, rigorous thinkers, as did Thucydides, but for the leisured rich. Historians developed type scenes, moving descriptions of battles, speeches, plagues, or other moments of emotion, then recycled them regardless of what actually happened. Writers aimed more at moral lessons than at telling the truth about the past. Writers picked great men from the past, selecting (and embellishing) episodes from their lives to provide moral examples to the reader. Plutarch, writing around A.D. 100, whose writings we have quoted repeatedly, explains this tradition well:

> I am writing biography, not history, and the truth is that the most brilliant exploits often tell us nothing of the virtues or vices of the men who performed them, while on the other hand a chance remark or a joke may reveal more of a man's character. . . . When a portrait painter sets out to create a likeness, he relies above all upon the face or the expression of the eyes and pays less attention to the other parts of the body: in the same way it is my task to dwell upon those actions which illuminate the workings of a man's soul. . . . I leave the story of his greatest struggles and achievements to be told by others.
>
> Plutarch, *Life of Alexander* 1 (I. Scott-Kilvert)

The biographers' emphasis on great individuals fitted the Hellenistic world of kings and euergetists, but the rise of universal history was the most important development. Astonished at how Alexander (and later, Rome) drew together previously separate regions through conquest, universal historians sought to understand the entire Mediterranean world. The most important was **Polybius** (c. 200–118 B.C.), who spent many years as a hostage in Rome and wrote a universal history in forty books to explain to Greeks how Rome had come to dominate the world. He based his history on documents, great men's memoirs, and travel, and scorned so-called historians who wrote about places they had never seen. To Polybius, history writing was an analytical craft like medicine, and so different fundamentally from literature:

> The aim of tragedy is by no means the same as that of history, but rather the opposite. The tragic poet seeks to thrill and charm his audience for the moment . . . but the historian's task is to instruct and persuade serious students by means of the truth of the words and actions he presents, and this effect must be permanent, not temporary. Thus in the [tragedian's] case the supreme aim is *probability*, even if what is said is untrue, the purpose being to beguile the spectator, but in the [historian's] it is *truth*, the purpose being to benefit the reader.
>
> Polybius 2.56 (I. Scott-Kilvert)

Few Hellenistic historians reached this level of seriousness. **Diodorus of Sicily,** whom we have also quoted often, was more typical. Writing in the first century B.C. in Egypt, then in Rome, Diodorus also produced a forty-book universal history, but he uncritically copied from earlier writers, often confusing their accounts. He added his own tragic speeches and a strong moralizing tone, praising kings and leaders who seemed to him to act rightly. In their time, Hellenistic historians were hugely influential. By 200 B.C., indigenous historians (writing in Greek) appeared in Persia, Babylon, Judea, Egypt, Carthage, and Rome (Map 21.1). Yet just five books of Polybius and fifteen of Diodorus survive from all this historical writing. Despite the historians' success in their own time, their books were lost as people stopped reading them.

Map 21.1 Sites mentioned in this chapter.

POETRY

The rise of new centers of patronage transformed poetry. Gifted poets flocked to royal libraries and museums, where they earned high pay writing for a small elite of highly educated aficionados. Alexandria was by far the major center. Advised by Demetrius of Phaleron, Ptolemy I endowed a *Mouseion,* or "Temple to the Muses," soon after 300 B.C. He assembled copies of all Greek literature in the world's first great library. He spent lavishly to attract the top men of letters, some of whom produced an official text of Homer. Translated into modern languages, the texts of Homer read in classrooms today go back directly to the Alexandrian edition.

Ptolemy's scholars were sometimes important poets in their own right. **Apollonius of Rhodes,** who directed the Museum (c. 270–245 B.C.), wrote an epic called the *Argonautica* about Jason and the Argonauts' search for the Golden Fleece, the only epic to survive between Homer (eighth century B.C.) and Vergil (first century B.C.). While Homer was an oral poet whose verse was recorded by dictation, Apollonius self-consciously created his poem in writing, borrowing Homer's archaic language but combining it with contemporary, almost avant-garde, literary experiments. He liked to interrupt the action to show off arcane knowledge about rituals or address readers directly about the difficulty of writing an epic. Only the well-educated elite would understand his allusions and subtle wordplays.

Other poets favored brief, intensely crafted works, but wrote for the same well-read urban elite. **Callimachus,** the greatest third-century poet, reputedly engaged in scholarly feuds with Apollonius and famously said, "Big book, big evil" that is, epic was no longer an appropriate vehicle for literary expression. Alexandrian poets invented anagrams to amuse their patrons. For example, the phrase *apo melitas,* "from honey," rearranged the letters of *Ptolemaios,* as Ptolemy's name was spelled in Greek; and *ion Eras,* "Hera's violet," rearranged *Arsinoë,* Ptolemy II's sister-wife. Riddle-poems were popular, in which the riddle's answer was revealed by the poem's shape when the words were written down (poets produced examples shaped like wings, an ax, an altar, and an egg). Sometimes the first letters of the poem's lines were an acrostic that spells out a name.

Such poems appealed to the intellect, but other poets worked to move the heart with short verses in which every word was carefully chosen, as when Callimachus wrote:

> They gave me bitter news to hear and bitter tears to shed.
> I wept, as I remembered, how often you and I
> had tired the sun with talking and sent him down the sky.
> And now that you are lying, my dear old Carian° guest,
> a handful of gray ashes, long, long ago at rest,
> still are your pleasant voices, your nightingales, awake,
> for Death takes all away, but them he cannot take.
>
> Callimachus, *Palatine Anthology* 7.80 9
> (W. Cory, *Ionica,* London 1857, 7)

°*Caria:* A region in southwest Anatolia.

Callimachus was a towering scholar and compiler of information (he wrote a *Catalogue of Persons Conspicuous in Every Branch of Learning and a List of their Compositions* filling 120 scrolls!), but is most famous for his *Hymn to Zeus.* Like Apollonius with his epic, Callimachus revived an archaic poetic form to display learning, pose verbal puzzles, and delight educated readers who could identify his puns and allusions.

Although written in Alexandria, the *Hymn to Zeus* evoked the simpler world of archaic Greece. **Theocritus,** a third-century emigrant from Syracuse, went further still, inventing the bucolic (Greek, "concerning cowherds") poetry filled with nostalgic images of a simple rustic paradise in Sicily and south Italy. He called his poems *Idylls* (Greek, "little pictures"). The poems idealized the countryside for urban elites who had never seen the real thing. The *Idylls* were the product of Ptolemy's Museum; in one of them, Theocritus abruptly abandoned the countryside to write a court poem praising Ptolemy II:

> Uniquely among men of former days
> and men whose warm tracks mark the dusty ways,
> Ptolemy has built shrines with pious care,
> proclaimed his parents gods and set them there,
> chryselephantine° forms, as mankind's friends.
> On their fired altars as each season ends
> he and his consort burn fat oxen's thighs;
> she partners him in filial sacrifice.
>
> Theocritus, *Idyll* 17.121–28 (B. Wells)

°*chryselephantine:* Gold and ivory, used for major religious statues like that of Athena in the Parthenon.

Another new genre was the "novel." Extended prose narrative fiction is not an obvious literary form, especially without the benefit of printing and in a context where all literature was read (or recited) aloud before a small audience. The earliest surviving example is a papyrus fragment of a story about an Assyrian king wooing a fourteen-year-old bride, probably from the first century B.C. Most examples come from Greeks in the Roman Empire, but they are unmistakably Hellenistic in tone. The themes are romantic and lighthearted. A boy and girl fall in love. Before or soon after marriage, fate separates them. The characters endure disasters, incarceration, seduction, rape, torture, and apparent death. In the end they are reunited and they live happily ever after.

Audiences all over the Mediterranean attended tragedies by Aeschylus, Sophocles, and especially Euripides, but these were now "classics," self-consciously performed as great works from the past, rather than a living cultural form. Comedy won a new lease on life, but the New Comedy of late-fourth and third-century-B.C. Athens had more in common with Hellenistic novels than with Aristophanes' Old Comedy. Instead of savage political humor, which had no place in a modern world, they had romantic, lighthearted plots and domestic settings similar to modern television sitcoms. Only a single Athenian New Comedy survives complete, by **Menander** (c. 342–291 B.C.) of Athens, the *Dyskolos* ("Grumpy Old Man").

New Comedy used stock characters (braggart soldiers, greedy pimps, lovestruck young men, lecherous fathers, tricky or faithful slaves) and humorous confusions over identity. A typical plot might involve an aging father and young son competing for the same courtesan, who is owned by a heartless pimp. The courtesan escapes, through her cleverness and the attentions of the father. An object of some kind eventually reveals her to be nobly born and eligible for proper marriage. The play ends with her marrying the young man.

By 200 B.C., drama attracted no leading Greek poets, but it was enthusiastically adopted in other Mediterranean societies. Plautus (c. 254–184 B.C.) and Terence (c. 185–159 B.C.), writing in Latin, brought New Comedy to Roman audiences, and most of our knowledge of the genre comes from their adaptations. A Jewish writer named Ezekiel produced a tragedy about Moses and the Exodus in Euripidean style (probably in the second century B.C.); and in 53 B.C., the king of the central Asian Parthian nomads was watching a performance of Euripides' *Bacchae* when news came to him that his army had defeated the Romans (he used the head of the Roman general as a prop in the last scene!). From Iran to Iberia, anyone with pretensions to culture needed to know Greek and the Greek authors.

Classical tragedy had focused on fate's inevitability, divine vengeance, generational curses, and the paradoxes of humans caught between death and uncertainty. Old Comedy was political satire. But New Comedy and Hellenistic novels used predictable character types to entertain through plots of dizzying complication or melodrama. As the *polis* lost importance, audiences no longer wanted the tensions of citizenship dramatized. The finest poets served royal courts, and educated aristocrats from Sicily to Bactria studied their learned verse, but popular literature—dramas and novels—grew lighter and increasingly divorced from real time and place. Modern readers often criticize Hellenistic histories, New Comedy, and novels for their frivolity and posturing, but non-Greek peoples imitated them more widely than classical literature. They were among the Greeks' most successful exports.

MATERIAL CULTURE

Hellenistic artists perfected techniques that had been developing for half a millennium, and their skills were not equaled until the Italian Renaissance, two thousand years later. The sheer size of the Hellenistic world encouraged regional variations, as royal centers, old *poleis,* and new sanctuaries developed in their own way. Traditionalism, overstatement, playfulness, virtuosity, and sometimes downright bad taste all swirled together, fueled by vast wealth that made anything seem possible. The overall effect was to abandon classical restraint as Greek art served a new world.

Sculpture

As generals transformed themselves into kings, then into gods, they wanted statues to express their new status. Such statues filled royal cities like Alexandria and Antioch, even the *poleis*-comissioned statues of beloved or prominent citizens. Figure 21.1 is a superb statue of the great orator Demosthenes from Athens, commissioned around 280 B.C. when Athenians briefly expelled their Macedonian

Figure 21.1 Portrait statue of Demosthenes. Roman marble copy of a bronze original by Polyeuktos of Athens, circa 280 B.C. Height 6 ft. 7 in.

garrison. Demosthenes is pensive, even gloomy, his brow furrowed, looking puny before the scale of the task facing Athens. His heroism is moral and intellectual, not physical. The statue's base is inscribed

> If your strength had been equal to your will, Demosthenes,
> never would the Greeks have been ruled by a Macedonian Ares.°
>
> Pseudo-Plutarch, Moralia 847A (I. Scott-Kilvert)

°*Ares:* The god of war, referring here to Philip II.

Between 250 and 150 B.C. (sometimes called the High Hellenistic Period), some sculptors sought emotional drama, like the historians and novelists. The finest examples come from Pergamum, a magnificent fortress-city towering a thousand feet above the Ionian coast. Pergamum's King Attalus I (241–197 B.C.) broke away from the Seleucid empire and commissioned a seventy-foot-long group of bronze statues to commemorate his victory over Gallic raiders in 237 B.C., probably showing his cavalry riding them down. The group is lost, but Figure 21.2 shows a marble copy of one statue, known as the Dying Gallic Trumpeter. The fallen warrior, powerfully understated, props himself up on one arm, staring in pain at his broken sword and trumpet as his life ebbs away.

Figure 21.2 The Dying Gallic Trumpeter, a Roman marble copy of one statue from a large group of bronzes set up at Pergamum, circa 220 B.C. On the warrior's right side is a fatal wound, blood gushing forth; his broken sword and trumpet lie by him. Around his neck is a gold torque, a characteristic ornament of the Gauls who invaded Greece from central Europe in the third century B.C.

Figure 21.3   Great Altar at Pergamum. Marble. Begun by King Eumenes II (197–159 B.C.); his successor Attalus II (159–138 B.C.) probably completed it. Once thought to honor Zeus, the monument was probably to Telephus, a local hero. German archaeologists removed the entire altar to Berlin in the nineteenth century.

The original monument must have been astonishing, but King Eumenes II of Pergamum (197–159 B.C.) outdid it with his **Great Altar** of Pergamum (Figure 21.3). Traditional altars were simple structures outside temples, but in this radical combination of architecture and sculpture, the altar replaced the temple. A broad stairway led to an Ionic colonnade, with double doors opening on the actual altar. The friezes on temples were high up, barely visible from the ground, but the innovative architect here put the frieze right before the spectator's eyes.

The frieze narrates the mythical battle of gods and giants. Its unknown designer packed it with detail (archaeologists often call the style "Hellenistic baroque"). Figure 21.4 shows just one panel. On the left, a bearded giant with snakes for legs faces Hecatê, goddess of darkness. The giant hefts a boulder in his right hand while one head of his snake-legs bites her shield. She wields a burning torch like a spear. Hecatê's dog bites one of the giant's legs. A second figure, whose left arm and profile are visible behind Hecatê, imparts a sense of depth. To her right another giant leaves himself uncovered, a target for the goddess Artemis (not shown). The torso and snaky legs of a dying giant are visible beneath the giant's legs. The figures are carved almost in the round, and their muscular bodies even fall out of the frame onto the steps. The composition as a whole and the individual figures within it exude excitement and the drama of cosmic war. The sculptors packed every imaginable device

Figure 21.4 Battle of the gods and giants, from the Great Altar at Pergamum, second century B.C.

into thc frieze, bombarding the viewer's senses with different finishes, draperies, and moods. Originally painted in bright colors (like all statuary), the impression in ancient times would have been very different from that today.

Sculptors everywhere strove for dramatic effects. Figure 21.5 shows the **Nikê** ("victory") **of Samothrace.** Landing from flight, she once stood on a base shaped like a ship's prow, located in a reflecting pool in an open-air sanctuary on the remote northern Aegean island of Samothrace. The statue combines classical features—the drapery recalls the Parthenon frieze—with the new baroque style, in its twisting pose and rich, almost fussy surface detail.

Other sculptors used similar techniques to create very different moods. Figure 21.6 shows a drunken satyr—he has pointy ears, invisible in the picture— caught as he sleeps, perhaps an ornament in an aristocrat's garden. Super-rich Hellenistic aristocrats now decorated their homes with such whimsical statues. In search of novelty, sculptors turned to subjects that would have seemed undignified in classical times: drunks, old people, dwarfs, even hermaphrodites, subject matter that parallels the domestic scenes and melodrama of the New Comedy. Other patrons, by

Figure 21.5 Nikê of Samothrace, circa 190 B.C., marble, height 8 ft.

Figure 21.6 Sleeping satyr, circa 230–200 B.C. Roman marble copy of a Greek original. The statue is known as the Barberini Faun after the family that used to own it. The legs and hanging left arm are restorations.

Figure 21.7 The Venus de Milo, a marble statue of Aphrodite from the island of Melos, carved around 100 B.C. When this statue was displayed in Paris in 1820, it caused a sensation. Height 6 ft., 8 in.

contrast, rejected such whimsy and demanded a return to classical seriousness, as in Figure 21.7, the celebrated **Venus**[55] **de Milo,** an example of Neoclassicism. This Aphrodite strongly evokes Praxiteles' Aphrodite of Cnidus (see Chapter 18, "Greek Culture in the Fourth Century B.C.," Figure 18.7), with a gentle S-curve, and serene, late classical face. The sculptor changed the proportions by moving her waist higher, and whereas Praxiteles' Aphrodite clutches her robe, the Hellenistic sculptor leaves it poised precariously, adding to the figure's eroticism.

Like so much of Hellenistic culture, Hellenistic sculpture profoundly influenced non-Greek peoples, and the Romans above all. Roman copies of Greek originals made possible the rediscovery of Greek art in the eighteenth century.

Architecture

Far more expensive than sculpture, architecture was the medium for display *par excellence* of kings. Alexandria was famous for its palaces, only now emerging from the sea, but it was also famous for its squalid slums. We get the best idea of the splendor of a royal center from Pergamum. Its kings built on a spectacular, virtually impregnable peak. A huge theater dominated the upper city, and spectators at dramas and public meetings could look out over the fertile plans of Ionia (Figure 21.8). Everything about the city was designed for dramatic effect. Terraces

Figure 21.8   The theater at Pergamum and its view across the Ionian plain.

immediately above the theater supported small but cleverly designed temples, the Great Altar of Zeus with its baroque frieze, and the large library, second only to Alexandria's (our word *parchment* is a corruption of the name Pergamum; parchment was invented there as an alternative to papyrus). Royal palaces and barracks for the king's guards occupied the summit. A huge, shady colonnaded porch, or **stoa,** below the theater provided a place to walk among shops, talk, and look out over the plain, and gave architectural unity to the design. Stoas were typical elements of Hellenistic cities.

Old *poleis* like Athens lacked money to compete with the royal centers, but some kings paid for new buildings in Athens to advertise their own wealth and euergetism. Attalus II of Pergamum (159–138 B.C.) built a 126-yard-long, two-storied stoa in Athens (Figure 21.9), containing forty-two shops.

Painting

Just as we know most about New Comedy and sculpture from Roman imitations and adaptations, the best evidence for painting also comes from Italy and again attests to the impact of Greek art across cultural lines. In A.D. 79, Mount Vesuvius erupted, burying the cities of Pompeii and Herculaneum in lava. Since 1738, archaeologists have recovered numerous Roman versions of Hellenistic paintings and mosaics there. Figure 21.10 shows one in a series of Roman wall paintings of Odysseus'

Figure 21.9 Model of the Stoa of Attalus in the Athenian agora, reconstructed by the American School of Classical Studies in Athens (1953–1956). Attalus II of Pergamum (159–138 B.C.) built it around 150 B.C. as a gift thanking Athens for the education he received there. The stoa has a Doric colonnade on the ground floor and an Ionic upper colonnade with a balustrade. Shops ran along the back of the aisle; today it is a museum for finds from the agora.

Figure 21.10 Wall painting from a house in Rome, circa 50 B.C. one of a series of paintings of Odysseus' adventures. This scene shows the giant Laestrygonians hurling rocks at the fleet of Odysseus.

Figure 21.11 Mosaic from Pompeii, signed by Dioscurides of Samos, circa 100 B.C. Dioscurides probably copied the scene from a second-century-B.C. painting. It shows street musicians from an unknown New Comedy. *Museo Archeologico Nazionale, Naples/The Bridgeman Art Library, New York.*

journeys, dating around 50 B.C. The landscape dwarfs the figures. Strong contrasts of light and shade emphasize nature's power over the puny mortals who crawl across earth's surface. The painting probably copied a Greek original of the second century B.C.

Like dramatists and sculptors, painters now enjoyed domestic and even frivolous subjects. Scenes from New Comedy were popular; Figure 21.11, a mosaic found at Pompeii, was signed by its Greek maker, Dioscurides of Samos, around 100 B.C. It too probably copied a second-century-B.C. painting. The mosaicist imitated advanced painting techniques—shading, highlighting, and multiple colors—for a lighthearted scene of masked actors playing street musicians on a narrow stage. He used the new technique of tessellated mosaic, building the scene from precut cubes of stone rather than pebbles.

Mosaics became an important art form in Hellenistic Greece. One craftsman, Sosus of Pergamum, was famous for illusionistic scenes. A famous mosaic showed birds drinking from a basin of water, while another looked like an unswept floor with dinner scraps strewn across it. Sosus' mosaics do not survive, but Figure 21.12, a mosaic from the Roman emperor Hadrian's country estate (A.D. 120), probably imitates his drinking doves.

We rely heavily on vase painting for information about archaic and classical wall painting, but in Hellenistic times, painted pottery all but disappeared. The rich could afford gold and silver plate, which rarely survives because later ages recycled precious metal; poorer people used mold-made black-glazed finewares, which began as imitations of metal vessels. The black-glazed wares are attractive but of course tell us nothing about contemporary painting.

Figure 21.12 Tessellated mosaic from the Roman emperor Hadrian's villa at Tivoli, Italy (circa A.D. 120). It probably copies a famous mosaic by the second-century-B.C. artist Sosus of Pergamum. Length 3 ft, 3 in.

HELLENISTIC PHILOSOPHY

Skepticism and Cynicism

Aristotle had argued that man was a "creature of the *polis*" (*politikon zôon*), but now men lived in a new world of super-rich euergetists and godlike kings. Philosophers wondered how to live a good life in such monarchies. Some sought inner peace by showing how little the chaos of the world mattered; others sought to create alternative, better worlds by rejecting social conventions.

Athens remained a center for literature and sculpture until the 260s B.C., and it likewise dominated early Hellenistic philosophy. The Academy, Plato's philosophical school, gave birth to **Skepticism,** the conviction that nothing can be known about the world for sure. It is nevertheless reasonable to form "plausible impressions" and act as if they are true. In this way the skeptic might function adequately, while remaining tranquil within the chaos around him.

Diogenes (404–323 B.C.) of Sinop, a town on the southern coast of the Black Sea, founded **Cynicism.** Diogenes was called *kynikos* ("doglike") because he ignored social conventions. He owned no clothes, lived in a barrel, urinated where he pleased, and masturbated as the mood took him. He rejected private property and material things. According to a popular story, Alexander the Great went especially to Sinop to offer Diogenes anything he wanted. The philosopher asked Alexander to move because he was blocking the sun.

Diogenes taught that the common lust for wealth, status, and honor was empty. Some Cynics made a living by traveling between *poleis* mocking authority in a kind of oration called a diatribe (the origin of our word).

Epicureanism

Epicurus (341–270 B.C.; Figure 21.13) was born of Athenian parents on Samos. He spent most of his life in Athens, where he studied with Platonists, then in 307 B.C. turned his home into a school known as "the Garden." There his followers—including women and slaves as well as the usual wealthy men—isolated themselves and followed the master's teachings.

We know a good deal about **Epicureanism.** Mount Vesuvius' eruption in A.D. 79 preserved a library of 1,785 papyrus scrolls on Epicurean philosophy in a villa

Figure 21.13 Roman copy of a marble portrait of Epicurus, originally carved around 270 B.C. The sculptor showed him with furrowed brows, expressing the strain of serious thought about the problems of the third century B.C.

that belonged to a relative of Julius Caesar (himself an Epicurean).[56] And the first-century-B.C. Roman named Lucretius wrote a long poem, *On the Nature of Things,* explaining Epicurus' principles. The American Declaration of Independence echoes a principal tenet of Epicurus: "We hold these Truths to be self-evident, that all Men are created equal, that they are endowed, by their CREATOR, with certain unalienable Rights, that among these are Life, Liberty, and the Pursuit of Happiness." Epicurus too insisted that happiness was the goal of life. And what is happiness if not pleasure, but pleasure defined in very specific ways that follow from a larger theory of nature.

Accepting the atomism of Democritus (see Chapter 14, "Art and Thought in the Fifth Century B.C."), Epicurus argued that the universe consists of an infinite number of atoms drifting through space. The atoms have size, shape, and weight, and fall like an endless rain. Left alone, they would never touch, because they fall at the same rate, but (for unclear reasons) they sometimes swerve and strike each other. Because the swerve is unpredictable, Epicurus' universe is not wholly mechanical. His unexplained swerve lies behind what we call "free will," the first attempt to face the problem of free will in a mechanistic universe.

Epicurus' universe is infinite, but comprises an indefinite number of *kosmoi,* "worlds," which come into being through the random collisions of atoms. Each *kosmos* eventually dissolves back into atoms, which continue falling until some swerve and recombine to form a new *kosmos.*

The mind, like everything else, is made of atoms, but finer ones than the body. We perceive objects when a thin film of atoms strikes the sense organs. Our thoughts are material too, made up of these films within our minds. Even the gods are material, but made up, like thought, of very fine atoms. They inhabit the spaces between the stars, but because they live in eternal, undisturbed happiness, they take no interest in our turbulent world and never interfere with its operation. For Epicurus, true happiness meant being undisturbed, like the gods (a state called *ataraxia,* "undisturbedness").

Because we are wholly material, when we die our atoms disperse and we cease to exist. It is therefore foolish to fear death: Because we cease to exist, nothing unpleasant can happen. Epicurus discussed the issue in a letter to a friend:

> The greatest anxiety suffered by the human mind arises from the belief that the heavenly bodies are divine and imperishable, but still are able to desire and act and cause things. Moreover, men cringe in dread as if they were doomed to some unending evil, probably because of the fairy stories they have heard, and await in terror the unfeeling nothingness of death—as if, in truth, that affected us at all! They do not suffer thus because they have thought things out, but through a quite unreasoning panic. Indeed, those who set no limit to their frightened pondering are perturbed as much as or more than men who make only random and careless conjectures on these matters. Real peace of mind means freeing one's self from all these bugbears and constantly remembering the real and supreme truths. . . .
>
> Accustom yourself to the realization that death concerns us not at all. For good and bad exist only by being perceived, and death deprives us of perception. Once we understand this truth, that death does not concern us, even our mortality becomes a source of pleasure: we give up our attempts to add eternity to our span of life here, and can abandon our vain longing for immortality. Life holds no terrors for him who realizes that there are none

in death. This worst of horrors, the fear of death, affects us not at all; for while we are, death is not, and when death is, we are not.

Epicurus, *Letter,* quoted in Diogenes Laertius 10
(H. M. Howe, in MacKendrick/Howe, 1952)

We may wonder that the certainty of dissolution brings comfort, but such was Epicurus' position. He denied religious accounts of the afterlife. Homer's *Odyssey* already related the terrors of the damned—Sisyphus rolling a stone forever up a mountain, Tityus crucified with a vulture devouring his liver, and Tantalus chained in a stream whose cool water he cannot reach. All this was nonsense, Epicurus maintained. The world one sees is all there is, and the pleasure that brings happiness comes from the harmonious flow of the atoms that comprise us.

There are two kinds of pleasure for Epicurus: the positive, such as enjoying food, sex, or music, and the negative, or absence of pain. The second is preferable to the first, because food, sex, and music provide only transitory pleasure, often followed by pain, while avoidance of pain is an appropriate end in itself.

New Comedy and some art turned away from the troubled world into a private sphere, and Skeptics escaped from Hellenistic upheaval by insisting that we can never know what is real. *Ataraxia,* too, was at odds with the ideals of archaic and classical citizenship. Pursuing glory and power only stirs up the atoms and causes pain. Better to seek a quiet, secluded life, in a garden surrounded by flowers.

Stoicism

Zeno (c. 333–262 B.C.),[57] from the Phoenician city of Citium on Cyprus, founded the most influential philosophical school of the Hellenistic Age. He studied with Cynic philosophers, taking several radical ideas from them, then finished his training at the Academy in Athens. Late in the fourth century, he opened his own school in the *stoa poikilê,* "painted stoa," on the edge of Athens' agora.[58] From this meeting place, his philosophy was called **Stoicism.**

Zeno's position was simple: To be happy, we must follow natural law. Those who follow natural law can be happy regardless of circumstance. Stoics ignored pleasure and suffering. Many Roman emperors proclaimed themselves Stoics, and one—Marcus Aurelius (reigned A.D. 161–180)—wrote a major Stoic treatise.

The divine *logos* ("reason, intelligence, God") permeates creation. *Logos* is the same as fate, an intelligent force that determines everything, that causes all things to happen as they do, that gives all things their properties. Stoics therefore reject Epicurus' theory that chance combinations of atoms can explain the world's properties—hardness in a stone, coldness in ice, the smooth pelt of a Great Dane, or human personality. Although the *logos* determines everything, humans remain free and morally responsible. A favorite Stoic image for a human's relationship to moral choice was a dog tied to a moving cart. The dog can choose to run with the cart and do so happily, or he can choose to run the other way, or to the side, or sit down, and be dragged along by the neck. Yet the cart moves on unimpeded. You make your choice and you pay the price. Best to place oneself in harmony with natural law, with the *logos* that pervades and causes the creation. By allowing *logos* to rule your life, you align yourself with the intelligence that rules the universe. That choice, made in agreement with reason, constitutes virtue (*aretê*), the very thing that sophists of the fifth century B.C. claimed they could teach. A virtuous life was a happy one because virtue is its own reward. Those who follow reason are few, of course, the philosophical elite, who form an international community of superior beings, while the suffering masses struggle against reason.

Stoicism justified the educated elites' acceptance of kings in the East and aristocrats in the Roman Empire. One of the most eloquent proponents of Stoicism was **Epictetus,** born into slavery around A.D. 50. After earning his freedom, he taught in Rome. He wrote nothing, but a follower named Flavius Arrian took notes and published them as the *Discourses.* The following selection comments on explicating, by a political example, the Stoic teaching on necessity:

> When the emperor Vespasian° sent word to Priscus Helvidius that he was not to attend a meeting of the Senate, Priscus replied, "You can prevent my being a senator, but as long as I am one I must attend the meetings."
> "Well, then, come but do not speak."
> "If you do not ask for my opinion I shall be silent."
> "But I have to ask for your opinion."
> "And I have to say what seems to me right."
> "If you do I shall have you put to death."
> "Did I ever tell you that I was immortal? You will be doing your part, and I mine. It is yours to kill, mine to die unflinching; yours to banish, mine to depart without grief."
> What good did Priscus do, one man against the emperor? What good does the red border do to the mantle? What else than to be distinguished as color, and provide a beautiful example to the rest?
>
> Epictetus, *Discourses,* 1.2 (W. R. Agard, in MacKendrick/Howe, 1952)

°*Vespasian:* Reigned A.D. 69–79.

Conclusion

Classical philosophers wondered about how we can explain change in the world, and the relationship between substance and form, and how can we know the truth when we have found it. Their speculations often had political repercussions and were tied to the vigorous social life of the *polis.* Hellenistic philosophers asked how one can lead a good life in a world governed by kings who claim to be more than human. Politics, and the *polis* itself, are no longer important subjects for philosophical investigation. The Cynics condemned political endeavor as worthless, while the Skeptics, Epicureans, and Stoics retreated into worlds of private knowledge and virtue. Stoicism nonetheless accommodated public lives lived by powerful men, whose destiny, decreed by fate, was to live in this fashion, and it soon became the most widespread and resilient of the Hellenistic philosophies.

MEDICINE

Medicine and science advanced rapidly after Alexander, supported by the great wealth in royal centers. To understand Hellenistic doctors' achievements, we must look back to Hippocrates of Cos, a fifth-century-B.C. thinker and physician whom we met in Chapter 2, "Country and People."

The School of Hippocrates

Ancient societies had assumed that sickness came from spirit-possession or witch-craft, and that the physician's job was to drive out spirits or to break the sorcerer's spell. Such views remained common in classical Greece (as they are in parts of the world today), but doctors of the Ionian Enlightenment rejected them. Hippocrates (c. 460–c. 370 B.C.) opposed such theories most vigorously. Sixty or seventy texts are attributed to him, most Hellenistic treatises were later given his name. A celebrated essay, *On the Sacred Disease* (probably epilepsy), describes the Hippocratic position on older views. When a person falls down, thrashes about, and afterwards cannot re-member what has happened, most conclude that spirits have possessed the victim, and they therefore call the illness "sacred."

> In my view it is in no way more divine nor more holy than any other disease, but its cause and origin is the same as that of other diseases. From ignorance and wonder men regard its nature and cause as divine, because it is not at all like other diseases. This notion of its divinity is maintained by their inability to comprehend it, and the superficial methods by which it is cured—by such things as purifications and incantations. But if one considers it to be divine because it is wonderful, there are many diseases which are sacred, not just one. As I will show, there are others no less wonderful and marvelous, which nobody imagines to be sacred. . . .
>
> In my own view, they who first called this disease "sacred" were men like the faith-healers, conjurors, and charlatans of our own day who give themselves out as being exces-sively religious and as knowing more than anyone else. Because they had no treatment of the slightest value, they have wrapped themselves in a cloud of superstitious nonsense, rather than admit their inability to effect a cure, saying that the disease is "sacred". . . .
>
> The disease called "sacred" arises from the same causes as other diseases, namely, those things that enter and leave the body, cold weather, the sun, and the changes in climate.
>
> Hippocrates, *On the Sacred Disease* 1.2.21 (J. Chadwick, W. N. Mann)

According to Hippocrates, the physician's main task was to establish a *prognôsis*, a "foretelling" of the disease's course by comparing it with the course of similar sick-nesses. Afterwards, there might be room for theoretical speculation about the causes of disease. We saw in Chapter 2, "Country and People," how Thucydides, who owed much to Hippocrates, applied a physician's eye to the plague that struck Athens in 429 B.C. and to the "disease" of the Peloponnesian War, which afflicted the body politic of Athens. Thucydides' aim of establishing a prognosis of the course of wars paralleled Hippocrates' approach to disease. The following Hippocratic description is typical:

> Apollonius of Abdera.° Although this man had not felt well for a long time, he had not taken to his bed. His abdomen was swollen and for quite a while he had a severe pain in his liver. At this time he became jaundiced and had much gas and his complexion turned pasty. After an injudicious dinner of beef, accompanied by much drinking, he felt hot and uncomfortable and went to bed. He then drank much milk, sheep and goat, both raw and boiled. This was a most unwise thing to do, and much harm resulted from it. His fever grew worse and his bowels passed almost nothing of what he ate; a little thin urine was passed. He could not sleep. Later he developed a severe thirst, and presently fell into a coma. His belly was distended with a painful swelling on the right side just below the ribs. All his extremities felt chilly. He muttered a little, but was out of his mind and could not remember what he said.
>
> °*Abdera:* A city in north Greece.

About the fourteenth day after he took to his bed he had a chill followed by fever and became delirious. He shouted and thrashed about, talking continuously. Then he began to sweat again, and his coma returned. His scanty urine was dark and thin, and his bowels were much disturbed, with bilious, crude, and undigested excreta of various sorts, either dark, thin, and purplish, or greasy, raw, and sharp; sometime it was even of a milky consistency. About the twenty-fourth day he became more comfortable; his symptoms were much the same, but he was partly restored to his senses, although he could not remember anything that had happened since he took to his bed. But soon he went out of his mind again, and his condition deteriorated rapidly. About the thirtieth day he had severe fever with copious thin excrement. He became delirious and lost his voice, and his extremities grew cold. The thirty-fourth day he died. From the time I first saw the patient, his bowels were always disordered, his urine thin and dark. When not in a coma he could not sleep, and was delirious all the time. His extremities were cold, for all this period.

Hippocrates, *Epidemics*, III, series 2, case 13 (J. Chadwick, W. N. Mann)

Apollonius' unwise meal triggered his fatal illness, but the Hippocratic writer did not speculate on the sickness' ultimate cause. Instead of abstract and unprovable theorizing, he accumulated details, which might one day lead to secure knowledge of causes.

Galen

The Hippocratic writings were influential, but learned Hippocratic physicians worked alongside sorcerers, midwives, herb-gatherers, and priests of Asclepius, the god of healing (along with Apollo). There was no such thing as a medical degree or control over medical doctors. The famous Hippocratic oath (see Chapter 2) was merely an effort at self-regulation. Hippocratic writers endorsed traditional practices like dream therapy, when patients slept in sanctuaries of Asclepius to receive the god's healing message.

We know little about Greek medicine in the four centuries between Hippocrates and the time of Christ. The Ptolemies supported human dissections in Alexandria in the third century B.C., allowing one Herophilus to distinguish between the sensory nerves. His technical terms for describing the eye are still used today. He examined internal and sexual organs, distinguished between veins and arteries, and offered a plausible (but inaccurate) explanation of the heart's working. His followers produced increasingly detailed explanations of bodily functions but were handicapped by the limits of the human eye. Without microscopes, they could see that blood flowed in both arteries and veins, but not understand how it got from one to the other.

Over the next three centuries, Herophilus' followers and rivals argued about physiology and to some extent divided into rival medical sects. Our best source of information is the Roman writer **Galen** (A.D. 126–c. 200), who collected all available medical knowledge in an encyclopedia that fills several feet of shelf space in modern libraries. Born in Pergamum, he studied philosophy, mathematics, and medicine. After working in Alexandria and as a doctor for gladiators in his native Asia Minor, he moved to Rome in A.D. 162 and served as personal physician to several emperors.

Deeply influenced by Hippocrates, Plato, Aristotle, Stoicism, and Herophilus, Galen summarized six hundred years of Greco-Roman thinking about health. He was more interested in diseases than patients, and showed his debt to Aristotle by categorizing diseases. He aimed to elicit universals from particulars. He saw the need to build therapy on knowledge gained from dissection and on a theory of how the body worked. In these views, Galen was utterly modern, although many of his assumptions and conclusions were wrong.

Galen depended on Hippocrates in his adoption of the theory of the four humors, or "liquids" (Latin *umor*, liquid), found in some Hippocratic writings. In these theories, health was the result of harmonious interaction between the humors, equated with the four qualities and the four elements of early philosophy: blood (hot, fire), phlegm (cold, earth), yellow bile (wet, water), black bile (dry, air). A predominance of a humor produces the four basic human character types: the *sanguine* ("bloody"), buoyant type; the *phlegmatic*, sluggish type (as when you get a cold and the nose fills with phlegm); the *choleric*, quick-tempered type (*choler*, "yellow bile"); and the *melancholic* ("black bile"), dejected type. Galen thought that disequilibrium among the humors in various organs caused diseases, and he was the first to localize diseases in specific organs.

Galen performed dissections, not of humans, which was no longer allowed, but of animals, then applied his results (sometimes wrongly) to humans. He presented a complex, consistent, philosophically and anatomically sophisticated description of how bodies work, what organs do, and how the heart functions. He was both practical and theoretical, and Galen's anatomy was the best textbook until modern times.

QUANTITATIVE SCIENCE IN THE HELLENISTIC AGE

In ancient Greece, mathematics mostly meant geometry, working with proportions rather than numbers. In early Hellenistic times, **Euclid** (c. 325–250 B.C.) gathered together all that was known about geometry. Some Greek writers said he lived in Alexandria, but we know nothing about his life. Around 300 B.C., he published the *Elements,* the most widely read Greek work in the modern world except for the New Testament. High-school geometry is virtually Euclid's *Elements* with examples and applications.

The *Elements* is a deductive system, arguing from first principles to conclusions. First come *definitions:*

- a point: "that which has no part"
- a line: "length without breadth"

and so forth, applied to unproven statements about planes, right, acute, and obtuse angles, and so forth.

Second come *postulates*—for example,

- that a line can be drawn between any two points
- that a straight line can be extended from either end
- that all right angles are equal

After defining what he means by a geometric element, like a point, Euclid makes various unproven statements about features of these elements. Third come Euclid's *axioms,* or self-evident truths, which may justify statements he has made as postulates. For example, the Euclidean axiom that

two things equal to the same thing are equal to each other

justifies the postulate that all right angles are equal. If they were not, then if *a* equals *b* and *b* equals *c*, *c* would not necessarily equal *a*, which is absurd. Aristotle had shown long before that such contradictions are illogical and hence untrue.

In thirteen books following these preliminaries, Euclid presented his *propositions,* conclusions drawn from his definitions, postulates, and axioms. Propositions, which fell into the categories of plane and solid geometry, themselves generated further propositions, yielding further proofs. Euclid's argumentation remained standard for scientific demonstrations until the end of the seventeenth century.

Numerous exceptional mathematicians followed Euclid, but none more powerful than **Archimedes** of Syracuse (287–212 B.C.). Educated in Alexandria, he spent most of his life at King Hiero II's court in Syracuse. Archimedes used deductions from axioms to make advances in plane and solid geometry, arithmetic, and mechanics. For example, he proved that the volume of a sphere is two-thirds the volume of a cylinder that circumscribes the sphere. He defined the principle of the lever and designed the first compound pulleys and hydraulic screws for raising water. His work on conic sections came close to integral calculus. He is best known for his discoveries in hydrostatics, the study of the equilibrium of liquids at rest and the forces exerted by them. His discovery of what is still called Archimedes' principle is a famous story:

> The discoveries of Archimedes were many and ingenious in widely different fields, but of them all that which I am now going to describe seems to me best to display his unlimited cleverness.
>
> Since the affairs of King Hiero [275–216 B.C.] of Syracuse had prospered and his power had been much increased, he decided to offer a golden crown in a certain temple in thanks to the immortal gods.
>
> He therefore let out a contract to a goldsmith, to whom he paid a fee for making the crown and enough beside for the exact weight of the gold that would be necessary. At the proper time the goldsmith presented a beautifully made crown to the king. Having to judge by the weight of the crown, he used all the gold that had been issued to him. But a little later the king got wind of a story that the goldsmith had abstracted some of the gold and replaced it with an equal weight of silver. Hiero was furious at having been tricked, but he saw no way to prove the theft. He therefore asked Archimedes to think over his problem.
>
> While Archimedes was considering the matter, he went one day to the city baths. There he went into a small pool with an overflow pipe, and while in it he reflected that the submerged part of his body made its own volume of water overflow. Realization of this showed him the principle on which his whole problem hinged, and in his delight he leaped from the pool and ran home without bothering about his clothes, announcing in a loud voice that he had found what he was looking for. As he hurried along he kept shouting in Greek, *"Eureka! Eureka!"*[59] ["I've found it!"].
>
> The story goes on that he took a slab of silver and another of gold, each weighing the same as the crown. He then filled a large pot to the brim with water and dropped in the silver. Water equal in bulk to the silver ran over the edge of the pot. After removing the slab he measured the amount of water it took to refill the pot. Thus he found what weight of silver equaled that of a known bulk of water.

Next he dropped in his slab of gold, removed it, and measured the amount of water need to replace the overflow. It was much less than had been the case with the silver, a difference corresponding to the smaller bulk of the gold, compared with the same weight to silver. Finally he lowered in the crown, and found that more water ran over than had done for the pure gold, although their weights were the same. From the difference in overflows of the crown and the pure gold Archimedes calculated the amount of silver alloyed with the gold in the crown, and thus proved the deceptiveness of the goldsmith.

Vitruvius, *On Architecture* 9.9–12 (H. M. Howe, MacKendrick/Howe, 1952)

Astronomy

Astronomers occupied a middle ground between physicians' meticulous observations and mathematicians' deductions: They observed the positions and movements of stars and planets and reasoned toward theories explaining their observations. In some ways, astronomy was the most successful ancient science when weighed against modern achievements. The Pythagoreans and Aristarchus of Samos (third century B.C.) even calculated that the earth revolved around the sun, although most Greeks resisted this affront to common sense and to Aristotelian cosmology.

The need for reliable calendars drove much early astronomy. Near Eastern observers realized in the third millennium B.C. that the solar year was not an even multiple of cycles of the moon. Around 425 B.C., a Greek named Meton refined a nineteen-year calendar making solar and lunar cycles correspond closely, but not until the Gregorian calendar introduced by Pope Gregory XIII on February 24, 1582 (not accepted in America until 1752), was a calendar devised that corresponds to nature. The Gregorian calendar itself modified the Julian Calendar introduced by Julius Caesar in 46 B.C., which in turn derived from the Egyptian civil calendar of 365 days (but no leap year).

The retrograde movement of planets was a problem for Plato's earth-centered cosmology. It stimulated increasingly complex attempts to reconcile observations with earth-centered models. The Alexandrian **Claudius Ptolemy**[60] (c. 87–150 A.D.) summarized earlier scholarship and added improvements. Ptolemy's book is known as the *Almagest,* a corruption of "the greatest" in Arabic, from the title of an Arabic translation rendered into Latin in the Middle Ages. His model held until A.D. 1543, when Nicolaus Copernicus showed that the sun must be the center of our system, later supported by Johannes Kepler (1571–1630; the first astronomer to understand that some force emanating from the sun holds the planets).

Ptolemy, however, argued that a spherical earth is the center of the universe and does not move. The sun, moon, and planets orbit the earth, not fixed on the surface of an invisible sphere, as Plato and Aristotle thought, but in perfect circles. The planets, while circling the earth, also move in smaller circles, called epicycles, centered on the planet's orbit; the planets' actual courses, therefore, are spirals. That is why planets sometimes appear to go backward, because their epicycle temporarily takes them in the opposite direction from their orbit around Earth (Figure 21.14).

The *Almagest* contains a catalogue of 1,022 stars grouped into forty-eight constellations. Ptolemy believed in astrology, and his authority did much to give it credibility. He also studied the refraction of light. Finally, Ptolemy wrote on geography, producing a map of the world containing Africa, Europe, and Asia (Figure 21.15).

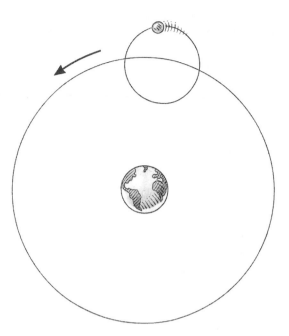

Figure 21.14 Ptolemy's explanation of the retrograde movement of planets: a planet revolves around Earth, simultaneously performing a second orbit.

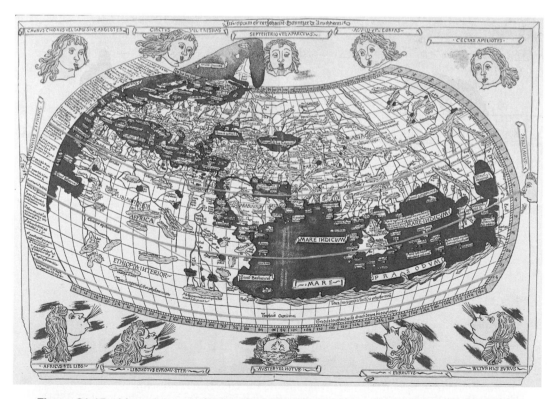

Figure 21.15 Map of the world from the Latin edition of Ptolemy's *Geography,* published at Ulm, Germany, in A.D. 1482. Personifications of the winds surround the globe.

He calculated the size of Ocean, the river that supposedly flowed around the continents (and which Alexander the Great thought he had found in 327 B.C.), but drastically underestimated it—a mistake that had important results when Christopher Columbus set out to sail across the Ocean to India in A.D. 1492.

CONCLUSION

The view of Hellenistic culture as decadent, declining after the Golden Age of Athens, is naïve. In medicine, science, and engineering, Hellenistic thinkers went far beyond those of classical times. In art, literature, and philosophy, they reworked their extraordinary classical heritage within a world utterly changed. Alexander and the Successors took Greek culture to Afghanistan and India, and Greek became a *lingua franca* that served the educated in Carthage and Rome as well as in Athens. Non-Greek peoples adopted and adapted Greek culture enthusiastically, and its impact on the Jews and Romans had profound consequences. There is no way to draw a firm line between Hellenistic culture and what came later; through processes that we discuss in Chapter 22, "The Coming of Rome, 220–30 B.C.," the Roman aristocracy created its own version of Hellenistic culture. They and the Arabs who conquered most of the old Hellenistic world in and after the seventh century A.D. transmitted the Greek heritage to later ages. Hellenistic philosophy, science, and mathematics dominated European thought until the seventeenth century A.D.

KEY TERMS

Polybius, 474

Diodorus of Sicily, 474

Apollonius of Rhodes, 475

Callimachus, 475

Theocritus, 476

Menander, 477

Great Altar, 480

Nikê of Samothrace, 481

Venus de Milo, 483

stoa, 484

Skepticism, 487

Cynicism, 487

Epicurus, 488

Epicureanism, 488

Zeno, 490

Stoicism, 490

logos, 490

Epictetus, 491

Hippocrates, 492

Galen, 493

Euclid, 494

Archimedes, 495

Claudius Ptolemy, 496

Almagest, 496

FURTHER READING

Literature

Feeney, Denis, *The Gods in Epic* (Oxford 1991). Influential study of religion in the Hellenistic and Roman poets.

Gutzwiller, Kathryn, *Theocritus' Pastoral Analogies: The Formation of a Genre* (Madison, WI, 1991). Fine study of Hellenistic epigram and the culture it represents.

Hunter, Richard, *The Argonautica of Apollonius Rhodius: Literary Studies* (Cambridge, UK, 1991). Leads the reader through the most important surviving poem from the Hellenistic period.

Hunter, Richard, *Theocritus and the Archaeology of Greek Poetry* (Cambridge, UK, 1996). Studies the nonbucolic poems and their deep influence on Roman poetry.

MacKendrick, P., and Herbert M. Howe, *Classics in Translation* (vol. 1, Madison, WI, 1952). Invaluable collection of primary sources with introductions and commentary.

Stephens, Susan, *Seeing Double: Intercultural Poetics in Ptolemaic Alexandria* (Berkeley 2003). Innovative analysis of how the Alexandrian poets worked back and forth between Greek and Egyptian cultural traditions.

Art and Architecture

Fowler, B., *The Hellenistic Aesthetic* (Madison, WI, 1990). How the Hellenistic Greeks saw art and what they enjoyed in art.

Pollitt, Jerome, *Art in the Hellenistic Age* (Cambridge, UK, 1986). Fine summary.

Philosophy

Algra, K., J. Barnes, M. Schofield, and J. Mansfeld, eds., *The Cambridge History of Hellenistic Philosophy* (Cambridge, UK, 1999). Essays by various authorities on all the major philosophical schools.

Long, Anthony, and David Sedley, eds., *The Hellenistic Philosophers* (2 vols., Cambridge, UK, 1991). Thorough review clearly presented.

Medicine

Sigerist, H. E., *A History of Medicine* (vol. 2, Oxford 1961). Good discussion of Hippocrates and his influence.

Mathematics and Astronomy

Lewis, Michael, *Millstone and Hammer: The Origins of Water Power* (Hull, UK, 1997). Highlights the application of science to everyday needs in third-century-B.C. Alexandria.

Lindbergh, David, *The Beginnings of Western Science* (Chicago 1992). Exciting, lucid overview, stressing the haphazard, unsystematic progress of scientific discovery.

Lloyd, G. E. R., *Early Greek Science: From Thales to Aristotle* (London 1970), chp. 7. Lloyd traces the Greeks' indebtedness to the Near East.

Netz, Reviel, *The Shaping of Deduction in Greek Mathematics* (Cambridge, UK, 1999). Breakthrough analysis of the formation of Greek mathematical thought.

Neugebauer, Oscar, *The Exact Sciences in Antiquity* (Oxford 1957). Neugebauer was a pioneer in scholarship on ancient science; his books remain invaluable.

CHAPTER 22

THE COMING OF ROME, 220–30 B.C.

We saw in Chapter 19, "The Warrior-Kings of Macedon, 359–323 B.C.," how Macedon, previously despised as a backwater, became a major power in the fourth century B.C. In Italy, Rome likewise grew from a minor city to become the greatest imperial power the world has ever seen. By 280 B.C., Rome so badly frightened the south Italian Greeks that they asked Pyrrhus to cross from Epirus and help them. Fifty years later, Rome had taken over western Greece; fifty years after that, Rome had humbled the Antigonids and Seleucids. The Greeks' story in the second and first centuries B.C. is one of responding to implacable Roman aggression.

Who were the Romans? Why did they expand so relentlessly? And what did this mean for the Greeks? It meant massacres, enslavements, deportations, revolutions, and the collapse of a sophisticated, ancient civilization into anarchic impotence. Millions died and millions more were transported to labor in Italian fields or Spanish mines. Amidst this orgy of violence, Romans absorbed and modified Hellenistic Greek culture, transmitting it to later ages as the basis for modern Western civilization.

THE RISE OF ROME, 753–280 B.C.

Legends said that Rome's story began with the Trojan War; Aeneas, a member of Troy's royal family (and son of Aphrodite) fled west when the city fell, and hundreds of years later, in 753 B.C., his descendants Romulus and Remus founded the city of Rome (Map 22.1).

Archaeology shows that a village was indeed established at Rome in the eighth century B.C. Traditions held that Rome had kings until aristocratic conspirators

Map 22.1 Sites in Italy mentioned in this chapter.

overthrew them in 509 B.C., establishing a **Republic** (Latin *res publica,* "public affair"). Violently opposed to monarchy, a **Senate** ("body of old men") of three hundred aristocrats (serving for life) and a series of **assemblies** made key decisions. Each year, the assemblies elected two Senators as **consuls** ("deliberators"), who oversaw war, finance, and law. Replacing the consuls every year disrupted long-term policy, but the Romans were determined to avoid a return to monarchy. No man must concentrate too much power in his own hands. Roman government in the fifth century B.C. had, therefore, some similarities to Greek systems, notably its hostility to kings. But the rich aristocrats were stronger in Rome than in Greece. They monopolized the Senate and had more votes in the assemblies. The institution of citizenship was correspondingly weak, bringing fewer protections than in Greek cities. The Roman aristocracy's power came largely from its leadership in war. In the fifth century, Rome crushed her central Italian neighbors. Plunder enriched the elite, but instead of ordering defeated enemies to pay tribute, as the Greeks generally did, the Senate had them provide troops for further wars. Rome took land from enemies and colonized it with poor Roman citizens, simultaneously garrisoning defeated states and exporting potential unrest, thus further blurring the boundaries between Romans and non-Romans.

By the time of the Peloponnesian War, Rome was a major Italian power, but 338 B.C.—the year of the battle of Chaeronea—was a turning point. After defeating an Italian uprising, the Senate greatly extended Roman citizenship to the rebels. The Senate was always more pragmatic than the Greek *poleis;* by giving her neighbors a stake in the outcome, Rome made them partners rather than subjects. They henceforth fought for Rome, sharing the spoils of war, while giving Rome inexhaustible manpower. The city of Rome itself grew to a hundred thousand in the fourth century B.C., Europe's greatest metropolis.

Over the next fifty years, Roman armies pushed inexorably into southern Italy. In 282 B.C., the Greeks of Taras asked Pyrrhus of Epirus to help them, as we have seen (Chapter 20, "The Hellenistic Century, 323–220 B.C."). When he arrived in 280 B.C., he was astonished by Roman discipline and ultimately defeated by their resources in manpower. The Greeks did not understand Rome. Even 115 years later, when the Greek historian Polybius came to Rome as a hostage, he was surprised by the Romans' obsession with war. He noticed a sharp contrast between Greek and Roman funerals for the war dead. Greek funerals emphasized the community, treating the war dead as an anonymous crowd, while Roman funerals dwelled on the prowess of individual aristocratic leaders. Polybius concluded that

> the most important consequence of the ceremony is that it inspires young men to endure the extremes of suffering for the common good in the hope of winning the glory that waits upon the brave. And what I have just said is attested by the facts. Many Romans have volunteered to engage in single combat so as to decide a whole battle, and not a few have chosen certain death, some in war to save the lives of their countrymen, others in times of peace to ensure the safety of the Republic. Besides this, there have been instances of men in office who have put their own sons to death, contrary to every law or custom, because they valued the interest of their country more dearly than their natural ties to their own flesh and blood. Many stories of this kind can be told of many men in Roman history.
>
> Polybius 6.54 (I. Scott-Kilvert)

Roman aristocrats prided themselves on puritanical sternness and indifference to luxury. Roman rituals emphasized martial virtues far more than did Greek ceremonies. In the third century B.C., Romans developed their famous game of violence, gladiatorial combat (Figure 22.1), perhaps beginning as a form of human sacrifice at funerals. The religious element had long since disappeared. Members of the audience sat close enough to be splattered with blood and brains as men hacked each other to pieces for their entertainment. For variety, wild animals killed each other, men killed animals, or animals killed men. The only time a hippopotamus was seen in Europe before the eighteenth century was when one was killed in a Roman arena. The demand for wild animals to murder in a public spectacle drove some species in North Africa to near extinction.

In the same years, Romans developed the **triumph,** one of the greatest spectacles in the world. If a victorious general killed more than five thousand in battle, the Senate would vote him a triumphal parade through Rome, displaying his plunder and captives. At first Greeks denied that anything made a man like a god. In the age of Alexander, great conquerors claimed to be gods. Romans made their generals god for a day.

Figure 22.1 Gladiators, from a first-century-A.D. Roman mosaic. In the center, a gladiator named Serpenius spears a lion or leopard. In the upper left, a gladiator lies dead; in the upper right, another fights a wild boar.

ROME, CARTHAGE, AND THE WESTERN GREEKS, 280–200 B.C.

The First Punic[61] War, 264–241 B.C.

In 265 B.C., a civil war in Messana, at the northeast tip of Sicily, widened to draw in Syracuse and Carthage, and the next year one faction asked Rome to help them. For fourteen years, fighting within a shifting and complex system of alliances, Roman and Carthaginian armies devastated Sicily. Many Greek cities were destroyed; Akragas never recovered from a Roman sack in 262 B.C. Only Syracuse flourished, under her cunning tyrant **Hiero II** (reigned 265–216 B.C.), who wisely joined the Romans early on. Carthage and Syracuse had fought each other to a standstill since 409 B.C., but Rome now committed all the wealth and manpower of Italy to the struggle. After twenty-three years of war, Carthage sued for peace, abandoning all claims to Sicily. As Polybius explains,

> the war between the Romans and Carthaginians . . . lasted uninterruptedly for 24 years, and is the longest, the most continuous, and the greatest war of which we have knowledge . . . there were two naval actions in which on the one occasion more than 500 quinqueremes° took part, and on the other nearly 700.° Those who are impressed by the

°*quinqueremes:* Huge warships seemingly with five banks of oars.   °*nearly 700:* The first battle involved some 200,000 men; the second, probably 250,000.

great sea battles of an Antigonus, a Ptolemy, or a Demetrius would doubtless be amazed, if they were to read the account of this war, at the vast scale of the operations it involved. Again, if we consider the size of these quinqueremes compared with that of the triremes with which the Persians fought against the Greeks, and the Athenians and Spartans against each other, we shall find that never before in the history of the world have two such immense forces been ranged against one another at sea. These facts confirm the proposition that I put forward at the beginning of my *History*, that the supremacy of the Romans did not come about, as certain Greek writers have supposed, either by chance or without the victors knowing what they were doing. On the contrary, since the Romans deliberately chose to school themselves in such great enterprises, it is quite natural that they should not only have embarked upon their pursuit of universal domination, but that they should actually have achieved their purpose.

Polybius 1.63 (I. Scott-Kilvert)

Greek Sicily under Roman Rule

The First Punic War finally united Sicily, but under Roman rule, not Syracusan or Carthaginian. The western Greeks' independent history was over: Only Syracuse remained free, as Hiero II's reward for supporting Rome loyally. The Senate had to decide what to do with the Greeks, Carthaginians, and native Sicilians they now ruled. Rather than follow her normal pattern of enrolling the defeated enemies as troops for further wars, Rome made Sicily her first province, a conquered territory governed by the Roman elite. The Senate extended Hiero's system of governance to the whole island. Hiero had copied his system from Ptolemaic Egypt. Unlike most *poleis*, he taxed crops and animals as well as goods coming through his harbors. Two hundred years later, the famous orator Cicero wrote: "The law of Hiero is so carefully framed that neither in the fields, nor on the threshing floors, nor in the barns can the cultivator defraud the collector of one single grain without the severest punishment; nor is it possible for more than the tenth to be extorted from the cultivator against his will."

While Hiero lived, Syracuse enjoyed a Golden Age. The city had shrunk since the fourth century, but still numbered fifty thousand. Hiero built the biggest theater in the world (Figure 22.2), with a beautiful stoa above it and an altar so big that a thousand cattle could be sacrificed on it simultaneously. The poet Theocritus and the great mathematician Archimedes frequented Hiero's court, creating hopes that Syracuse might rival Alexandria as Greece's cultural capital. Excavators have found rich gold and silver ornaments in tombs from these years.

But the war devastated western and southern Sicily. Akragas never recovered, and once-mighty Selinous was abandoned forever after 250 B.C. As Rome grew, it needed food. Italian investors bought up the Sicilian countryside, drove off the peasants, and grew wheat on vast estates called *latifundia* ("broad acres") worked by slaves. Many Greek aristocrats shared in the gains. Luxurious villas, paid for by trade with Rome, sprang up in the second century B.C. The Roman conquest ended the class conflicts that tore Sicilian *poleis* apart in the fifth and fourth centuries B.C. Western Greeks adopted Roman ways, while the Roman elite were imbued by sophisticated Greek culture.

The Second Punic War, 218–201 B.C.

The ever vital Carthage rebounded from the disastrous First Punic War, carving out a new empire in Spain. The famous **Hannibal** (Figure 22.3) had learned from the First

Figure 22.2 The Greek theater at Syracuse, circa 225 B.C. A performance of Aristophanes' *The Clouds* is underway against modern scenery. Beyond lie the modern city and the Great Harbor, where the Athenian fleet was destroyed in 413 B.C.

Figure 22.3 Hannibal, from a Carthaginian coin, circa 215 B.C.

Punic War how manpower and money were decisive. If he cut off hated Rome from her allies, he would starve her of both resources. In 218 B.C., he boldly led an army (including elephants) over the Alps, invading Italy from the north. By 216 B.C., Hannibal had won three shattering victories, and most of Italy and Sicily, including Syracuse, defected to his side. Victory over Rome appeared certain. In 215, Syracuse and Philip V of Macedonia joined him.

The Senate held its nerve. Enough allies remained loyal to continue the war. The Romans adopted a strategy of avoiding battle, wearing Hannibal down with endless marching around Italy while taking the offensive against his allies in Spain and Sicily. In a heroic last stand, Syracuse withstood a three-year siege by the Roman general **Marcellus.** The brilliant Archimedes frustrated Marcellus with fiendishly clever defensive machines:

> Huge beams were run out from the walls so as to project over the Roman ships: some of them were then sunk by great weights dropped from above, while others were seized at the bows by iron claws or beaks like those of cranes, hauled into the air by means of counterweights until they stood upright on their sterns, then allowed to plunge to the bottom, or else they were spun round by means of windlasses situated inside the city and dashed against the steep cliffs and rocks which jutted out under the walls, with great loss of life to the crews. Often there would be seen the terrifying spectacle of a ship being lifted clean out of the water into the air and whirled about as it hung there until every man had been shaken out of the hull and thrown in different directions, after which it would be dashed down empty upon the walls.
>
> Plutarch, *Life of Marcellus* 15 (R. Warner)

Two hundred years earlier, the Syracusans had defeated a terrifying armada from Athens, but this time there was no salvation. Roman determination and manpower slowly prevailed. Syracuse fell in 211 B.C., and with her fell western Greek freedom. Amid the usual horrific scenes of violence, a soldier killed Archimedes—too engrossed in his calculations to notice the soldier's presence in his room, according to legend. Marcellus, a new breed of Roman aristocrat who openly admired Greek culture, wept when he heard that Archimedes was dead. Then he carried Syracuse's greatest artworks off to Rome.

Spain became the major theater of war. A dynamic young Roman named **Scipio** (**sip-ē-ō**, 236–184 B.C.; later nicknamed **Africanus,** "the conqueror of Africa";[62] Figure 22.4) cut a bloody path across Spain. In ferocious battles in Sicily and Spain, the Roman army developed ever-more efficient techniques, placing it ahead of Hellenistic Greek armies in organization and effectiveness. The Romans made an art form of brutality:

> When Scipio judged that a large enough number of troops had entered the town [a Carthaginian base], he let loose the majority of them against the inhabitants, according to the Roman custom; their orders were to exterminate every form of life they encountered, sparing none, but not to start pillaging until the word was given to do so. This practice is adopted to inspire terror, and so when cities are taken by the Romans you may often see not only the corpses of human beings but also dogs cut in half, and the dismembered limbs of other animals. And on this occasion the carnage was especially frightful because of the large size of the population.
>
> Polybius 10.15 (I. Scott-Kilvert)

Figure 22.4 Scipio, marble bust, first century B.C.

By 205 B.C., Scipio had driven Carthage out of Spain. He brought the war to Africa, and in 202 defeated Hannibal—the only loss this great general ever suffered—who had returned from Italy to defend Carthage. Carthage surrendered her fleet and empire. Rome was mistress of the west Mediterranean.

ROME BREAKS THE HELLENISTIC EMPIRES, 200–167 B.C.

Keeping multiple armies in the field year after year was difficult under the old system of annual consulships and under the pressures of war. Marcellus, Scipio, and a few others emerged as "super-generals." They generated wealth and power beyond anything Roman senators had seen before. Conservative Romans worried that they were moving from god-for-a-day generalships toward something like Hellenistic kingship. Radicals wanted to become super-generals themselves by fighting yet more wars. The obvious place to fight new wars was Hellenistic Greece.

As we saw in Chapter 20, young kings had assumed the Hellenistic thrones in the late 220s B.C. (Table 22.1). Instead of preparing to meet Rome, the inexperienced rulers weakened themselves in vicious wars. Antiochus III attacked Egypt, and Ptolemy IV drove him back only by enrolling native Egyptians in his army. The

Table 22.1 Principal Hellenistic rulers

Macedonia
Philip V   221–179
Perseus 179–168

Syria
Antiochus III   223–187

Egypt
Ptolemy IV   221–204
Ptolemy V   204–181
Cleopatra VII   51–30

Egyptians, seeing their own strength, then rebelled, draining Ptolemaic power in a long civil war.

Philip V made an ill-judged alliance with Hannibal in 215. Antiochus III offered Philip support, hoping to drive the Ptolemies out of the Aegean. A terrified Athens, who depended on Egyptian protection, sought Roman assistance against Philip in 200 B.C. Only a few months had passed since the defeat of Carthage, but the Senate voted for war against Philip. In 197 B.C., Rome's general Flamininus shattered the Macedonian phalanx at **Cynoscephalae** (sī-nō-**sef**-a-lē, "dogs' heads") in Thessaly (Map 22.2). Polybius explains how Roman tactics proved superior to the formerly mighty Macedonian army:

> A number of factors make it easy to understand that so long as a [Macedonian] phalanx retains its characteristic form and strength nothing can resist it face-to-face. When a phalanx is closed up for action, each man with his arms occupies a space of three feet square. The spear he carries . . . [is] 21 feet long, and from this we must subtract the space between the bearer's hands and the end part of the spear, which keeps it balanced and couched. This amounts to six feet in all, from which it is clear that the spear will project 15 feet in front of the body of each hoplite when he advances against the enemy gripping it with both hands. This also means that while the spears of the second, third, and fourth ranks naturally extend further than those of the fifth rank, yet even the latter will still project 3 feet in front of the men in the first rank, so long as the phalanx keeps its characteristic order. . . . From these facts we can easily picture the nature and tremendous power of a charge by the whole phalanx, when it advances 16-deep with leveled spears. . . .
>
> With the Romans each soldier in full armor also occupies a space 3 feet wide. However, according to Roman methods of fighting each man makes his movements individually: not only does he defend his body with his own long shield, constantly moving it to meet a threatened blow, but he uses his sword both for cutting and thrusting. Obviously these tactics require a more open order and an interval between men, so in practice each soldier needs to be at least 3 feet from those in the same rank . . . if he is to perform his function efficiently. The result of these dispositions is that each Roman soldier has to face *two* men in the front rank of the phalanx, and so has to encounter and fight against ten spear points. It is impossible for one man to cut through all of these once the battle lines are engaged, nor is it easy to force the points away. . . . It is easy to understand, then,

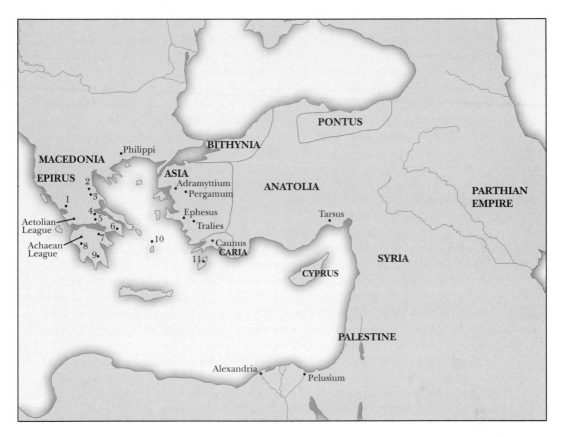

Map 22.2 Sites in the east Mediterranean mentioned in this chapter. Aegean cities: (1) Actium; (2) Cynoscephalae; (3) Pharsalus; (4) Thermopylae; (5) Delphi; (6) Athens; (7) Corinth; (8) Olympia; (9) Sparta; (10) Delos; (11) Rhodes. Kom Ombo lies 350 miles (off the south edge of the map) far up the Nile valley in southern Egypt.

as I said at the beginning, how nothing can withstand the frontal assault of the phalanx so long as it retains its characteristic formation and strength.

What then is the factor that enables the Romans to win the battle and causes those who use the phalanx to fail? The answer is that in war the times and places for action are unlimited, whereas the phalanx requires one time and one type of ground only to produce its peculiar effect. Now if the enemy were compelled to position themselves according to the times and places demanded by the phalanx whenever an important battle was imminent, no doubt those who employ the phalanx would always carry off the victory for the reasons I have given above. But if it is quite possible, even easy, to evade its irresistible charge, how can the phalanx any longer be considered formidable?

Polybius 18.29–31 (I. Scott-Kilvert)

Many Senators had not wanted war with Macedon. They preferred their traditional aristocratic way of life, taking turns to serve as consuls, to becoming a superpower. After Cynoscephalae, their goal was to avoid getting permanently entangled in Greek politics. Flamininus made no attempt to annex Macedonia;

instead, he ordered Philip out of the *poleis,* imposed a fine, and restated the principle of "freedom for the Greeks." But once Rome's armies had entered the quagmire of Greek rivalries, it was not easy to get out. Flamininus brought home fine artworks for his triumph, and some *poleis* set up statues and cults in his honor, as they would to a Greek king. Other Roman generals sought opportunities to gain equal fame.

Antiochus III played into the hands of the Roman war party. He invited Hannibal (who had escaped after the battle with Scipio Africanus) to be his advisor, moved against the Ionian *poleis,* and in 192 B.C. entered mainland Greece to support the Aetolian League in an anti-Roman alliance. Rome responded with overwhelming force, smashing Antiochus' army in the famous pass of Thermopylae in 191, then crossing to Anatolia to destroy another Seleucid army in 189. Hannibal fled, and in 188 Antiochus evacuated Asia Minor, handed over his fleet and elephants, and paid Rome fifteen thousand talents.

Ambitious young senators continued pushing for military commands against Greeks, and Rome's clients in the Aegean simultaneously sought Roman support against rivals. In the late 170s, enemies of Perseus of Macedonia (reigned 179–168 B.C.), Philip V's son, convinced the Senate that he was stockpiling weapons to attack Italy itself. Roman armies again quickly overran Macedonia. There was no vast stockpile of weapons, but the monarchy of Macedon was no more. Still eager to avoid annexations, the Senate split Macedon into four tiny republics in 168 B.C.

In the same year, one of the interminable wars between Egypt and Syria spiraled out of control. The new Seleucid king, Antiochus IV, invaded Egypt and invested Alexandria. The Senate, impatient with Greek kings destabilizing the East, drew up a decree ordering him to desist. They sent the Senator Gaius Popilius with a few officials to deliver the ultimatum.

> When Antiochus had advanced against Ptolemy [V] in order to take control of Pelusium,° he was met by the Roman commander Popilius. The king [Antiochus] greeted him by voice from a distance and offered him his right hand, but Popilius presented to him the tablet he had in his hand containing the senate's decrees, and asked Antiochus to read it first. In my opinion, he did not want to display any mark of friendship before finding out the intentions of the recipient, whether he was a friend or a foe. When the king had read it, he said he wanted to consult with his advisers on these new developments, but Popilius did something in reply which seemed insolent and arrogant to the highest degree. With a vine stick which he had in his hand he drew a circle around Antiochus and told him to give his reply to the message before he stepped out of that circle. The king was astounded at this arrogance. After hesitating for a moment, he said he would do everything the Romans asked from him. Thereupon Popilius and his colleagues shook him by the hand and all welcomed him graciously.
>
> Polybius 29.27 (I. Scott-Kilvert)

°*Pelusium:* In the northeast Nile Delta.

Hence our expression "to draw a line in the sand." A Roman armed only with a stick had humiliated the greatest Hellenistic king. Although Rome had neither annexed nor garrisoned Greek territory, the Senate had in fact incorporated the Greeks into their empire.

CONSEQUENCES OF THE WARS: THE GREEKS

Rome's wars against the Hellenistic kingdoms devastated Greece. More than a million people seem to have been killed or enslaved. In a single raid on Aetolia in central Greece in 187 B.C., Romans carried off golden crowns weighing 112 pounds; 83,000 pounds of silver; 243 pounds of gold; 118,000 Athenian coins; 12,322 coins called Philippics; 785 bronze statues; 230 marble statues; a great amount of armor, weapons, and other enemy spoils, besides catapults and engines of every kind. In 167 B.C. a Roman consul decided to punish Epirus (in northwest mainland Greece):

> Ten leading members of each community [in Epirus] were summoned by the consul, who directed them to have their gold and silver brought out to a public place. The consul then sent cohorts° to all the cities, those bound for the more distant places setting out before those traveling to the nearer, so that they should all reach their destinations on the same day. The tribunes and centurions° had been informed about what was afoot. Early in the morning all the gold and silver was collected; and at the fourth hour the troops were given the signal to plunder the towns. So great was the amount of plunder that each cavalryman received 400 *denarii* in the distribution and each infantryman 200,° while 150,000 human beings were led away into slavery. The walls of the plundered cities—there were about 70 of them—were demolished.
>
> Livy 45.34

°*cohorts:* Military units of about 500 men.   °*tribunes and centurions:* Different ranks of officers.   °*200 denarii:* About twenty months' pay.

In one day, the Romans wiped Epirus, where mighty Pyrrhus once ruled, from the face of the earth.

The Aegean was in any event suffering from depopulation, piracy, and the polarization of wealth (Chapter 20). The Roman wars fed these evils. Indemnities bankrupted cities. Italian moneylenders helped them pay their debts, only to extract still more assets from exorbitant rates of interest. Rome was plundering Greece, turning it into a desert. An angry mob in Corinth almost tore Roman ambassadors limb from limb in 148 B.C. The Senate decided to make an example of Corinth, and for two days in 146 B.C. Roman forces plundered and burned the city, dragging the survivors into slavery. "I was there," Polybius wrote. "I saw paintings trodden underfoot; the soldiers used them for playing dice."

To the Romans the Greeks were unrealistic, constant trouble. When a pretender appeared in Macedonia in 148, claiming to be Perseus' son, Rome lost patience and finally created an Aegean province, with a Roman governor supervising Macedon's affairs. *Poleis* that cooperated, by contrast, did well. Athens had supported Rome since 200 B.C. and was rewarded in 167 with control of the lucrative slave markets on tax-free Delos. After Rome destroyed Corinth, traders relocated to Piraeus, enriching Athens still further. Old political struggles between oligarchs and democrats melted away. The Greek nobles created *latifundia* worked by slaves, built beautiful villas, and commissioned lavish monuments in their own honor. Urban festivals and institutions continued, but citizen assemblies making real decisions were just a memory.

There were more *latifundia* in Sicily than anywhere, and their costs became clear in 134 B.C., when the biggest slave war in history began:

> The Sicilians, having grown very rich and elegant in their manner of living, bought up large numbers of slaves. They brought them in droves from the places where they were reared, and immediately branded them with marks on their bodies. Those that were young they used as shepherds, and the others as need required. . . . Oppressed by the grinding toil and beatings, maltreated for the most part beyond all reason, the slaves could endure it no longer. Therefore, meeting together at suitable opportunities they discussed revolt, until at last they put their plan into effect. . . .
>
> The whole revolt began in the following manner. There was a man in Enna° named Damophilos,° magnanimous in his wealth but arrogant in disposition. This man was exceedingly cruel to his slaves, and his wife Megallis strove to outdo her husband in torture and general inhumanity toward them. As a result, those who were thus cruelly abused were enraged like wild beasts and plotted together to rise in arms and kill their masters. . . .
>
> Thereupon they forthwith collected 400 of their fellow-slaves and, when the opportunity presented itself, they burst fully armed into the city of Enna with Eunus° leading them and performing tricks with flames of fire for them. They stole into the houses and made great slaughter. They spared not even the suckling babes, but tore them from the breast and dashed them upon the ground. It cannot be expressed with what wanton outrage they treated the wives before the very eyes of the husbands. They were joined by a large throng of the slaves in the city, who first visited the extreme penalty upon their masters and then turned to murdering others.
>
> Diodorus of Sicily 34 (C. H. Oldfather)

°*Enna:* A mountain town in the center of Sicily.   °*Damophilos:* Ironically, his name means "friend to the people."   °*Eunus:* An enslaved Syrian priest.

The Romans finally crushed the revolt, crucifying thousands of men, women, and children, their broken bodies hanging on crosses for miles along Sicily's roads.

Rome's armies had as yet scarcely entered Seleucid or Ptolemaic territory, but the Hellenistic political systems were breaking down. The Seleucids lost Anatolia to Rome in 188 B.C. and Judea in 164. By 150, Parthian nomads from central Asia overran so much of Iran that their leaders started calling themselves Persian kings. They captured one Seleucid ruler, and when they killed his successor on the battlefield in 129, the Seleucids gave up all claims to Mesopotamia and Iran. The empire that once stretched from the Aegean to Afghanistan was reduced to parts of northern Syria, often with several men disputing the throne.

Similarly, since 170 B.C., two (sometimes three) Ptolemies claimed the Egyptian throne at the same time. In 131 B.C. Ptolemy VIII (nicknamed "Fatso") and his wife Cleopatra II were fighting for power within Egypt. Cleopatra stirred up riots in Alexandria and persuaded the mob to recognize the twelve-year-old son she and Ptolemy VIII had produced as the true king. She did this because Ptolemy VIII and their son were in Cyprus, leaving her as sole ruler in Egypt. Ptolemy responded by having their son torn into quarters and shipping the parts back to his mother. Soon after, the loving father and mother Ptolemy and Cleopatra were reconciled and ruled jointly for nine years! Despite the anarchy, the Seleucid and Ptolemaic economies still functioned, taxes were gathered, and temples built (Figure 22.5). The Hellenistic kingdoms were tempting targets for Rome's predatory rulers.

Figure 22.5 The great temple in Kom Ombo in southern Egypt, not far from modern Lake Nasser, uniquely dedicated to two gods (Sebek the crocodile god and Horus the hawk god), built during the second and first centuries B.C.

CONSEQUENCES OF THE WARS: THE ROMANS

Wealth poured into the hands of the Roman aristocracy. Rome kept 150,000 men under arms; in any year in the two centuries after 225 B.C., one Italian farmer in eight was serving. Thirteen percent of the adult male citizens were under arms at any moment. The average length of service was seven years, meaning that half of all Roman citizens served in the army at some time. The net effect was a massive migration out of Italy: Down to 146 B.C., roughly a hundred thousand conscripts were killed and twice this number settled overseas. Rich Romans bought up Italian farms weakened by the loss of men, making more *latifundia*. Poor Italians drifted to the city, swelling the urban market for food grown on the slave-run estates. In an irresistible spiral, the rich got richer as the poor lost the little they had.

The richest Romans could now afford to live like Hellenistic kings, although private citizens. When Marcellus captured Syracuse in 211 B.C., he "liberated" many statues and paintings and brought them back to Rome.

> Before this date Rome neither possessed nor was even aware of such elegant and exquisite creations, nor was there any taste for graceful and delicate art of this kind. Instead the city was filled with bloodstained arms and spoils of barbarian tribes, and crowned with the monuments and trophies of victorious campaigns, so that to the unwarlike visitor or to the aesthete she offered almost nothing to gladden or reassure the eye. . . . Marcellus

greatly pleased the common people, because he adorned the capital with works of art which possessed Greek grace, charm, and truth to nature. On the other hand it was Fabius the Delayer° who earned the approval of the older generation, because after he had captured Taras° he neither disturbed nor removed a single monument of this kind. He carried off all the money and valuables which had belonged to the city,° but allowed all the statues to remain in their places.

Plutarch, *Life of Marcellus* 21 (I. Scott-Kilvert)

°*Fabius the Delayer:* A conservative general, called the Delayer because he championed the strategy of avoiding fighting Hannibal, instead wearing him down.   °*Taras:* Fabius recaptured the city from Hannibal in 209.   °. . . *city:* He also sold thirty thousand Tarentines into slavery.

Plutarch says that Marcellus thought "he had taught the ignorant Romans to admire and honor the glories of Greek art," but traditionalists like Fabius thought Marcellus "was teaching them to become lazy and glib connoisseurs of art and artists, so that they idled away the greater part of the day in clever and trivial chatter about aesthetics."

Greek culture became *the* political issue. Some aristocrats admired not only its sophistication, but also that some men were equal to gods—not just for a day, as in a triumph, but permanently. Some generals presented themselves as Hellenistic kings (Figure 22.6).

Education remained essentially Greek, in spite of a small body of Latin texts. Not only was rhetoric quintessentially Greek, but also it had practical consequences for Senate debates, where persuasion was a way to win votes (in addition to bribery and extortion). Plutarch says, "Most of the Romans were well content to see their sons embracing Greek culture and to frequent the society of such estimable men." But conservative Romans thought that the study of rhetoric, "the art of persuasion," would infect them with Greek weakness. Their champion, **Cato** (234–149 B.C.; Figure 22.7),

was afraid that the younger generation might allow their ambitions to be diverted in this direction, and might come to value most highly a reputation that was based upon feats of oratory rather than upon feats of arms. . . . He was opposed on principle to the study of philosophy, and his patriotic fervor made him regard the whole of Greek culture and its methods of education with contempt . . . he pronounced with all the solemnity of a prophet that if ever the Romans became infected with the literature of Greece, they would lose their empire.

Plutarch, *Life of Cato the Elder* 22–23 (I. Scott-Kilvert)

Cato insisted that "Greek literature is worth only a nodding acquaintance, the Greeks are a wicked and most intractable race, their literature will corrupt Rome, their doctors will ruin Rome; in fact the Greeks have taken an oath to kill all barbarians by means of medicine, and include Romans among the barbarians." He was fighting a losing battle. To compete against trained orators in senate debates, Cato needed to speak effectively himself; in fact he had studied Greek literature closely in his youth, memorizing Thucydides and Demosthenes to improve his powers of persuasion.

By the 130s B.C., aristocratic Romans had thoroughly absorbed Hellenistic Greek culture, one of the most important developments in Greek history. Roman tastes in art, literature, and philosophy largely determined what survived from

Figure 22.6 Bronze statue representing a Roman general as a Hellenistic king, circa 150 B.C. The workmanship is Greek, and the pose imitates a famous statue of Alexander the Great, but it seems to portray a Roman—the figure lacks the short cloak normal on Hellenistic royal statues and has a typically Roman stubbly beard and a Roman hairstyle. The heavy musculature follows a style popular at Pergamum. Height 7 ft., 9 in.

ancient Greece. Ambitious Romans quoted Greek poetry (especially Homer), studied and promulgated Stoicism (which appeared to justify traditional values), and switched back and forth between Greek and Latin in everyday conversation. The last words of Julius Caesar, spoken to his friend and assassin **Brutus** were in Greek (*kai su teknon*, "and you, my son?" which Shakespeare translated into the Latin "*et tu Brute?*"). As the Roman poet Horace (65–8 B.C.) put it: "Captive Greece overcame her barbarous captor, and brought civilization to the wild Latins." Ironically, the imperialists who destroyed Hellenistic Greece transmitted her culture to posterity. Yet the Romans were always part of Hellenic culture from the earliest times. The Roman alphabet in which this book is written, is the Italian variety of the Greek alphabet, and Romans knew Greek myths in the sixth century B.C. or earlier. The

Figure 22.7   The Roman statesman Cato in a toga. Life-size, marble, first century B.C.

two-consul system may have been modeled on the dual kingship in Sparta. We rightly speak of Greco–Roman culture. Had Carthage destroyed Hellenistic Greece, it would have been a different story.

NEW ROMAN ARMY

The forms of Roman government, designed to serve a city–state, were strained to the utmost in the 130s B.C. by the need to govern a vast empire. Only a large, standing army could preserve the peace. Traditionally, only farmers served, but as aristocrats bought up Italy's land, the number of farmers declined. Attempts by reformers to redistribute land in the 130s and 120s led to extreme political violence. The pool of recruits steadily shrank, and in 113 B.C., Germanic raiders swept past Rome's small Italian army and plundered northern Italy.

Because rich senators would not redistribute land to increase the number of recruits, an obscure soldier named **Marius** (157–86 B.C.) persuaded the Assembly to abolish property qualifications for military service. His expanded army quickly won its wars and lay the foundations for one hundred years of gory civil war. In the old days, soldiers wanted to finish their service and get back to their farms; their loyalty was to the state. The new soldiers had no farms to retire to; their loyalty was to their commander. He may need to seize land for his troops. For a man prepared to risk everything, anything was possible.

THE AGONY OF THE AEGEAN, 99–70 B.C.

By 100 B.C., Rome was corrupt, violent, and immoral. Rome's Italian allies revolted in 91 B.C., demanding better treatment, and were defeated only after extreme savagery. Resentment burned in the Greek world, and slave wars broke out in Sicily and Athens. The Hellenistic kings were too weak to exploit the chaos, but one **Mithridates** (mith-ri-**dā**-tēz; 121–63 B.C.), a non-Greek ruler of the kingdom of Pontus on the Black Sea coast of Anatolia (see Map 22.2), took up the Greek cause. Mithridates had ruled Pontus quietly for thirty years. Seeing Rome's struggles and the Greeks' anger, he built up a powerful army and in 88 B.C. overran Bithynia, another of Rome's client kingdoms in Anatolia. He defeated two Roman armies, then captured, tortured, and executed a Roman general. He turned the war into an ethnic cleansing, to rid the world of the hated Italian race:

> He wrote secretly to all his satraps and the magistrates of the [Greek] cities [in Asia Minor] that on the thirtieth day they should set upon all Romans and Italians in their towns, and upon their wives and children and their freedmen° of Italian origin. They should kill them, cast their bodies out unburied, and share their goods with King Mithridates. He threatened to punish any who should bury the dead or conceal the living. To slaves who killed or betrayed their masters he offered freedom, to debtors who did the same to their creditors, the remission of half their debt. These secret orders Mithridates sent to all the cities at the same time. When the appointed day came, disasters of the most varied kind occurred throughout Asia,° among which were the following:
>
> The Ephesians tore away the fugitives who had taken refuge in the sanctuary of Artemis, and were clasping the images of the goddess, and slew them. The Pergamenes shot with arrows those who had fled into the sanctuary of Asclepius, without removing them from the statues they were clinging to. The people of Adramyttium° followed into the sea those who sought to escape by swimming, and killed them and drowned their children. The Caunians° . . . pursued the Italians who had taken refuge around the statue of Vesta in their senate house, tore them from the shrine, first killed the children before their mothers' eyes, then killed the mothers themselves and their husbands after them. The citizens of Tralles,° in order to avoid personal responsibility for the crime, hired a savage monster named Theophilos of Paphlagonia to do the work. He conducted the victims to the temple of Concord and there murdered them, chopping off the hands of some who were embracing the sacred images. Such was the awful fate that befell the Romans and Italians in Asia, men, women, and children, their freedmen and slaves, all who were of Italian origin. Thus it was made very plain that it was quite as much hatred of the Romans as fear of Mithridates that impelled the Asiatic Greeks to commit these offenses.
>
> Appian, *The Civil Wars* 12.4.22–23 (J. Carter)

°*freedmen:* Freed slaves who acted as assistants to the Italian financiers.   °*Asia:* That is, western Asia Minor, which had been made a province in 133.   °*Adramyttium:* On the Ionian coast opposite the island of Lesbos.   °*Caunians:* On the southern coast of Asia Minor opposite Rhodes.   °*Tralles:* A wealthy city in Lydia.

Sources say eighty thousand Italians died in one day, a debtors' revolt combined with ethnic hatred. Mithridates even raided the holy island of Delos because there

Figure   22.8 Lucius   Cornelius Sulla, marble, first century B.C.

were many Italians there. He freed thousands of slaves and canceled debts. He took so much plunder that he canceled all taxes on the bankrupt Greeks for five years. The Greeks welcomed Mithridates as a savior. Athens, Sparta, and the Achaean League joined him. In a few months, he had liberated the Greeks and slaughtered the Roman oppressors. A Golden Age was set to begin.

Marius asked the Senate to send him with an army against Mithridates, but the Senate feared his ambitions; whoever led an army of landless men into Greece could use the plunder to make himself the strongest man in Rome. Conservative senators blocked Marius' appointment and chose a younger, apparently more manageable **Sulla** (138–78 B.C.; Figure 22.8). Roman politics was breaking down into gang warfare. Marius' allies threatened to veto Sulla's appointment. Sulla's champions proclaimed a public holiday, so no veto could be issued. Marius' allies declared this illegal, and after their supporters won an armed battle outside the senate house, Marius' allies went ahead with their veto. Marius was officially commander of the army. Sulla raced south to join the fifty thousand troops waiting to sail to Greece. He was an outlaw, taking up arms against the state, and instead of leading the army to Greece, he marched back to Rome. Marius fled. The frightened Senate announced that *Marius* was now the outlaw, and Sulla the legitimate general. Without a trial, they declared Marius a criminal and murdered his supporters in the streets. Sulla sailed for Greece. In January 87, when

Sulla was gone, Marius returned to Rome and forced the Senate to reverse itself. Marius was now consul and *Sulla* was condemned as a criminal. Because no one was paying Sulla's army, he had to extort funds from the Greeks. Landing in Greece in 87 B.C., he hacked his way across the country, invested Athens, and plundered Olympia and Delphi to pay his costs. On March 1, 86 B.C., Athens fell, and Sulla unleashed a frenzy of murder and plunder on Greece's most distinguished city:

> Sulla himself entered the city at midnight, after having thrown down and leveled to the ground the fortifications between the Piraeus Gate and the Sacred Gates. It was a moment made the more terrible by the blowing of trumpets, the blasts of bugles, and the shouting and yelling of his troops who were now let loose by him to pillage and to slaughter, and who poured down the narrow alleys with drawn swords in their hands. There was thus no counting of the slain; to this day their number is estimated simply by the area of ground that was covered with blood. The blood shed in the marketplace alone, without counting the slaughter that took place in the rest of the city, spread all through the Potters' Quarter inside the Dipylon Gate; in fact many people say that it flowed out through the gate and washed right over the suburb outside. And yet, though many indeed perished in this way, equally numerous were those who, out of pity and love for their native city, took their own lives. They thought that their city was doomed to extinction, and this it was that made the best of them give up all hope, and fear the prospect of survival, since they expected from Sulla neither generosity nor ordinary humanity.
>
> Plutarch, *Life of Sulla* 14 (R. Warner)

Sulla carried off everything. Meanwhile, Mithridates needed increasing amounts of money to resist Sulla. He squeezed the eastern Greeks and deported entire cities that would not pay. After two years of rape, murder, burning, and enslavement on both sides, Mithridates and Sulla made a private deal. Mithridates would give Sulla money to pay his soldiers, who would be set free to punish the Greeks who supported Mithridates:

> Sulla distributed his army among all the remaining places and issued a proclamation that the slaves who had been freed by Mithridates should at once return to their masters. As many disobeyed and some of the cities revolted, numerous massacres ensued, of both free men and slaves, on various pretexts. The walls of many towns were demolished. Many others were plundered and their inhabitants sold into slavery. The pro-Pontic faction, both men and cities, was severely punished, and especially the Ephesians, who with servile adulation of Mithridates had treated the Roman offerings in their temples with indignity.

Sulla summoned the leaders of the Greek cities to Ephesus and fined them twenty thousand talents (twice what Carthage had paid in 201 B.C.).

> After he had spoken Sulla apportioned the fine to the cities and sent men to collect the money. The cities, being in financial straits, borrowed it at high rates of interest and mortgaged their theaters, gymnasia, walls, harbors, and every other scrap of public property, being urged on by the soldiers. Thus was the money collected and brought to Sulla, and the province of Asia had her fill of misery.
>
> Appian, *The Civil Wars* 12.9.61, 63 (J. Carter)

Sulla returned to Italy in 83 B.C., leaving the Aegean a wasteland. Cities went bankrupt and could no longer protect themselves. Pirates extorted protection money and enslaved still more. In 69 B.C., pirates attacked the sacred island of Delos and left the ancient shrine in ruins, just twenty years after Mithridates had murdered every Italian there. The once-prosperous market never recovered. The only way for cities to protect themselves was to borrow still more money, often at extortionate rates, and to hire private armies. Adding insult to injury, *poleis* were often compelled to honor Italian moneylenders as euergetists.

By the time Sulla returned to Italy, Marius had died. His cronies were still in Rome, and Sulla technically remained an outlaw. His army, though illegal, was invincible, and rich citizens raised private armies (also illegal) to support him. Sulla took Rome with little fighting. For three years, he ruled as dictator, executing thousands of enemies, taking their land, and settling 120,000 of his veterans on it. He believed these outrages would save Rome. In 79 B.C., he announced that the Republic was restored. He retired and died the next year.

Within months, Sulla's settlement unraveled. The most dynamic new general, Gnaeus Pompeius (known as **Pompey the Great**), was sent as general to Spain in 77 (Figure 22.9). Another Senator, Lucullus, went to Anatolia in 74 to finish the war with Mithridates, and a third, the super-rich Crassus, was given an army in 72 to suppress Spartacus' famous slave revolt. In 71 B.C., Pompey and Crassus won their wars. Rather than repeat Sulla's march on Rome, or fight each other, they forced their own election as consuls for 70, and demanded that the Senate give their veterans land.

Figure 22.9   Pompey the Great, marble, first century B.C.

POMPEY'S GREEK SETTLEMENT, 70–62 B.C.

Sulla left such chaos in the Aegean that the Senate sent commanders there to contain the pirates. When they failed, in 67 the Senate gave Pompey an extraordinary command over the whole Mediterranean Sea and everything up to fifty miles inland. Pompey fell on the pirates with terrifying efficiency, dividing the Mediterranean into thirteen sections and systematically sweeping them from west to east. After just three months he stormed the pirates' lair in southwest Asia Minor and settled the survivors in the cities they had themselves destroyed.

The Senate wanted a Roman new world order. Rome's normal practice was to support local aristocracies, who would govern in Roman interests. But Sulla had crushed the Greek upper classes with debt. Debtors who could not pay—whether individuals or entire cities—fell into the power of their creditors. Many *poleis* were virtual debt-slaves to private Roman financiers (the hated **publicani** of the New Testament). Lucullus, who had been fighting Mithridates in Anatolia since 74 B.C., took aggressive action to ameliorate the terms under which Roman financiers lent money, and within four years most cities were debt free. The influential *publicani* hated him for it. In 66 B.C., the Senate sent Pompey to depose Lucullus and finish Mithridates, who now fled into exile. Dreaming of becoming an eastern Hannibal, Mithridates hoped to cross the Black Sea to the Ukraine, then work his way up the Danube, enrolling central European tribes to murder still more Romans. Roman agents cornered him. Mithridates, now an old man, ordered one of his own soldiers to stab him to death.

The financiers welcomed Pompey in the East, but Pompey realized that Rome must annex what remained of the Seleucid kingdom to end the financial and social chaos. He created four new provinces, restored dozens of cities, and swept away a mosaic of tax exemptions. He kept the Hellenistic distinction between privileged Greeks and native populations, but made everyone pay taxes. He doubled Rome's tax revenue while lowering most Greeks' payments. He marched into Palestine and ended a Jewish civil war.

The Greeks honored Lucullus and Pompey like gods. One *polis* named Pompey "savior and benefactor of the people of all Asia, guardian of land and sea, because of his excellence and goodwill toward them." When he returned to Rome in 62 B.C., the Senate voted Pompey a triumph "over the whole universe" and the unique title "the Great." Pompey had restored order after the disaster of the 80s, saved countless Greek cities from dissolution, and brought peace.

Abuses continued nonetheless. In 56 B.C., Brutus (whom Shakespeare called "the noblest Roman of them all"), who was to assassinate Julius Caesar twelve years later, forced a Greek city in Cyprus to borrow at 48 percent interest, meaning that the size of the debt would double every eighteen months. When the Greeks appealed to Lucullus' law capping interest at 12 percent, Brutus got an exemption from the Senate. When the city elders tried to pay off the loan, the noble Brutus used Roman troops to drive them away. Cicero discusses the situation in a letter in 60 B.C. to his brother, governor of the province of Asia:

> The great obstacle is the money-men: for, if we oppose them, we shall alienate from ourselves and from the Republic a group which has done us most excellent service, and

which has been brought into sympathy with the Republic by our means;° if, on the other hand, we comply with them in every case, we shall allow the complete ruin of those whose interests, to say nothing of their preservation, we are bound to consult.° This is the one difficulty, if we look the thing fairly in the face, in your whole government . . . after hearing the grievances of citizens in Italy [against tax-collectors], I can comprehend what happens to allies in distant lands. To conduct oneself in this manner in such a way as to satisfy the tax-collectors, especially when contracts have been undertaken at a loss, and yet to preserve the allies from ruin, seems to demand a virtue with something divine in it, I mean a virtue like yours.

°*our means:* Cicero had been very active in reconciling the Senate and the publicani.
°*bound to consult:* That is, the Greeks of Asia.

Cicero goes on to justify Roman taxation of the Greeks:

To begin with, that they are subject to tax at all, which is their greatest grievance, ought not to be thought so by the Greeks, because they were so subject by their own laws without the Roman government. Again, they cannot despise the word financier, for they have been unable to pay the assessment according to Sulla's tax without the financier's aid. But that Greek financiers are no more considerate in exacting the payment of taxes than our own may be gathered from the fact that the Caunians, and all the islands assigned to the Rhodians by Sulla, recently appealed to the protection of the Senate, and petitioned to be allowed to pay their tax to us rather than to the Rhodians.° Therefore, people who have always been subject to taxes should not revolt at the name of a tax-collector; nor should those who have been unable to make up the tribute themselves despise it, nor those who have asked for his services refuse them. At the same time let Asia reflect on this, that if she were not under our government, there is no calamity of foreign war or internal strife from which she would be free.

Cicero, *Letters to Quintus* 1.1.11 (E. Shuckburgh)

°*Rhodians:* Sulla had sold to the Greek city of Rhodes the right to collect taxes from neighboring communities. The Rhodians, struggling to pay their own bills to Rome, squeezed these communities hard, making them prefer Roman tax collectors to Greeks.

Romans had killed and enslaved the Greeks, looted their cities, and extorted protection money. Now Cicero expected the Greeks to be grateful. Cicero admired the Greeks, and told his brother, "I shall not be ashamed to go so far . . . as to confess that, whatever I have accomplished, I have accomplished by means of those studies and principles which have been transmitted to us in Greek literature and schools of thought." However, he added,

Among the Greeks themselves you must be on your guard against admitting close intimacies, except in the case of the very few, if such are to be found, who are worthy of ancient Greece. As things now stand, indeed, too many of them are untrustworthy, false, and schooled by long servitude in the arts of extravagant adulation.

Cicero, *Letters to Quintus* 1.1.5 (E. Shuckburgh)

THE END OF HELLENISTIC EGYPT, 61–30 B.C.

The Senate never fully recovered control after Sulla's revolt. When Pompey returned from Greece in 62 B.C., he held a secret meeting with Crassus, the man who had defeated Spartacus' slave army and one of the richest of all Romans, and the young and daring **Julius Caesar**. The three pooled their patronage to subvert the constitution. People called them the *triumviri*, or "Gang of Three." Each gang

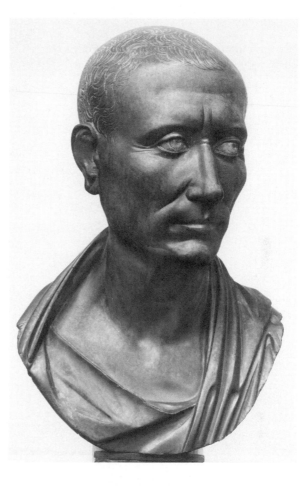

Figure 22.10 Bust of Julius Caesar, circa 47–44 B.C.

member wanted something: Pompey, to settle his veterans and consolidate his position in Rome; Caesar and Crassus, to build their own armies. Caesar wanted a war in Gaul, roughly modern France, while Crassus looked east to the Parthian Empire that had replaced the Seleucids in Iran and Mesopotamia.

Caesar got his command. He borrowed massively to pay his men, and in 58 B.C. left Rome for Gaul one step ahead of his creditors. A brilliant and ruthless soldier (Figure 22.10), he overran Gaul and even raided Britain in 55 and 54 B.C. By the time he was done, a million natives—a third of Gaul's population—were dead or enslaved. Caesar now had a great army, loyal to him alone.

Crassus also got his command, but he blundered into a trap in the Syrian desert in 53 B.C. The Parthians killed him and most of his troops. With Crassus dead and Caesar still in Gaul, Pompey dominated the Senate. He turned on Caesar, challenging the legality of his war in Gaul. Caesar tried to negotiate, but Pompey refused. In 50 B.C., the Senate recalled Caesar. If he returned to Rome without an army, his enemies would kill him; if he refused, he would be an outlaw. Like Sulla before, he marched on Rome. Pompey withdrew to Greece, taking two hundred senators with him. In 48 B.C., Caesar defeated Pompey's army near a village called Pharsalus

Figure 22.11   Portrait of a Hellenistic queen, probably Cleopatra VII. The shape of the nose is reminiscent of the queen's profile on coins. Marble, 30s B.C.

in Thessaly. Surveying the mangled bodies of Rome's aristocracy, Caesar sadly said "*hoc voluerunt*"—"They wanted it this way."

Pompey fled to Alexandria, hoping to fight on from the last Greek kingdom, but he was murdered on the beach as he landed. A few days later, Caesar arrived with four thousand troops. Egypt was in dynastic crisis. Three years earlier, in 51 B.C., the ten-year-old Ptolemy XIII and eighteen-year-old **Cleopatra VII** had become joint rulers, but court factions had shunted Cleopatra aside (Figure 22.11). Caesar only intended to punish Pompey's murderers and collect two thousand talents that Ptolemy owed him, but when Ptolemy was slow to pay, Caesar secretly summoned Cleopatra, thinking he could negotiate with her.

> Taking only one of her friends with her (Apollodorus the Sicilian) Cleopatra embarked in a small boat and landed at the palace when it was already getting dark. Since there seemed to be no other way of getting in unobserved, she stretched herself out at full length inside a carpet, and Apollodorus, after tying up the carpet, carried it indoors to Caesar. This little trick of Cleopatra's, which showed her provocative impudence, is said to have been the first thing about her which captivated Caesar, and, as he grew to know her better, he was overcome by her charm and arranged that she and her brother should be reconciled and should share the throne of Egypt together.
>
> Plutarch, *Life of Caesar* 49 (R. Warner)

The amorous Caesar and the ambitious Cleopatra were lovers during the winter of 48 to 47 B.C., while street battles raged through Alexandria. Ptolemy XIII at first besieged them in the palace. In a ferocious naval battle in the harbor, Caesar's ship was sunk beneath him, and he nearly drowned. Caesar finally outwitted Ptolemy, recovered his money, and left Cleopatra—pregnant with an unborn son—as sole ruler of Egypt. The child would be named Caesarion.

Caesar returned to Rome and attempted to reform the institutions of the state. He instituted the Julian calendar. Twice he publicly rejected kingship. Some senators believed that if they could kill Caesar, they could return happily to the days when the Senate truly ruled. Caesar refused to have bodyguards, and on March 15, 44 B.C.—the Ides of March—Brutus (whom we met extorting money in Cyprus) and **Cassius** led a gang of senators in murdering Caesar as he prepared, ironically, to address the Senate in the Theater of Pompey. Brutus and Cassius expected Rome to rise up, but the conspirators' shouts of freedom echoed down empty streets.

After months of chaos, **Mark Antony** (Caesar's right-hand-man), Lepidus (Caesar's cavalry chief), and **Octavian** (Caesar's nineteen-year-old great-nephew, whom Caesar adopted as a son in his will) formed the Second Gang of Three. The Republic effectively ceased to exist in 43 B.C. The new *triumviri* pursued Brutus and Cassius into northern Greece, just five years after Caesar had pursued Pompey there. In an enormous battle near Philippi in Thrace, they crushed Brutus and Cassius' armies. The young and cunning Octavian soon forced Lepidus into retirement, and he and Mark Antony divided the ancient world between them. Octavian stayed in Rome, controlling the West, while Antony headed east to punish Parthia for destroying Crassus' army a decade before.

Antony needed to pay his men. He ordered the dreaded *publicani* to raise money from the Greeks. Twenty years of slow recovery were washed away in weeks.

> When Antony imposed a second levy on the cities,° Hybreas,° speaking on behalf of the whole province of Asia, summoned up the courage to say this: "If you can take tribute from us twice a year, no doubt you can give us two summers and two harvests." He expressed himself with a certain rhetorical flourish which appealed to Antony's taste, but then he added in blunter language that Asia had already raised 200,000 talents for Antony.° "If you've never received this money," he went on, "you should ask for it from the men who collected it. But if you did receive it and no longer have it, we're ruined." These words made a deep impression on Antony, for he was completely ignorant of much that was done in his name, not merely because he had an easygoing disposition, but because he was simple enough to trust his subordinates.
>
> °*on the cities:* His initial extractions had not raised enough money.   °*Hybreas:* Otherwise unknown.   °*for Antony:* An exaggeration, although huge sums were extracted.

As part of his fundraising campaign in 41 B.C., Antony summoned Cleopatra to meet him. At first, she ostentatiously ignored him, then

> She came sailing up the River Kydnos° in a barge with a poop of gold, its purple sails billowing in the wind, while her rowers caressed the waters with oars of silver which dipped in time to the music of the flute, accompanied by pipes and lutes. Cleopatra herself reclined beneath a canopy of cloth of gold, dressed in the character of Venus,° as we see in her paintings, while on either side to complete the picture stood boys costumed as cupids,° who cooled her with their fans. Instead of a crew the barge was lined with the most
>
> °*River Kydnos:* In southern Asia Minor.   °*Venus:* The Roman goddess of love, equivalent to Greek Aphrodite.   °*cupids:* Venus' boyish companions, who fired arrows of love.

beautiful of her ladies in waiting, attired as Nereids and Graces,° some at the rudders, others at the tackle of the sails, and all the while an indescribably rich perfume, exhaled from innumerable censers, was wafted from the vessel to the river-banks. Great multitudes accompanied this royal progress, some of them following the queen on both sides of the river from its very mouth, while others hurried down from the city of Tarsus to gaze at the sight. Gradually the crowds drifted away from the market-place, where Antony awaited the queen enthroned on his tribunal, until at last he was left sitting quite alone and the word spread on every side that Venus had come to revel with Bacchus° for the happiness of Asia.

°*Graces:* Greek mythical figures.   °*Bacchus:* Dionysus, god of wine and revelry.

She hosted a grand banquet for Antony that evening.

Next day, Antony returned her hospitality with another banquet, but although he hoped to surpass her in splendor and elegance he was hopelessly outdone in both, and was the first to make fun of the crude and meager quality of his entertainment. Cleopatra saw that Antony's humor was crude and gross, belonging to the soldier rather than the courtier, and she quickly adopted the same manner toward him and treated him without the least reserve. Her own beauty, so we are told, was not of that incomparable kind which instantly captivates the beholder. But the charm of her presence was irresistible, and there was an attraction in her person and her talk, together with a peculiar force of character which pervaded her every word and action, and laid all who associated with her under her spell. It was a delight merely to hear the sound of her voice, with which, like an instrument of many strings, she could pass from one language to another.

Instead of attacking Parthia, Antony followed Cleopatra to Alexandria. While his moneymen ran amok in the Greek world, he surrendered to pleasure.

Plato speaks of four kinds of flattery, but Cleopatra knew a thousand. Whether Antony's mood were serious or happy, she could always invent some fresh device to delight or charm him. She engrossed his attention utterly and never released him for an instant by day or night. She played dice with him, drank with him, and hunted with him, and when he exercised with weapons, she watched him. At night, when he liked to wander around the city, stand by the doors or windows of ordinary citizens' houses and make fun of the people inside, she would dress up as a maidservant and play her part in any mad prank that came into Antony's head, for it was his custom to go out disguised as a slave. On these occasions he was always met with torrents of abuse, and was sometimes even beaten up before he returned to the palace, although most people guessed who he was. The fact was that the Alexandrians had a weakness for his buffoonery and enjoyed taking part in these amusements in their elegant and cultivated way. They liked him personally, and used to say that Antony put on his tragic mask for the Romans, but kept the comic one for them.

Plutarch, *Life of Antony* 24–27 (excerpts) (I. Scott-Kilvert)

While Antony played, Octavian plotted. Antony, he said, planned to move the capital from Rome to Alexandria and deliver power to the Greeks. The proud senators would have to prostrate themselves before an alien Macedonian queen.

When Antony finally attacked Parthia, it was a disaster, and the sham triumph he celebrated in Alexandria offended everyone. In 40 B.C., Antony had married Octavian's sister Octavia to strengthen the two men's alliance, but in 37 he bigamously married Cleopatra too (unlike Hellenistic kings, Romans were monogamous). In 32, he divorced Octavia, recognized Caesar's son and his own sons by

Cleopatra as legitimate, and announced that he was dividing the Greek world and Mesopotamia between the boys.

The Senate, under Octavian's control, declared Antony a public enemy. For the third time in seventeen years, a Roman civil war would be decided in Greece. Most former supporters of Caesar backed Antony, but Cleopatra provided troops. Antony dared not take the war to Italy, where Octavian portrayed Cleopatra as an evil woman, but in 31 B.C. he advanced to Actium, a bay behind two promontories on the coast of modern Albania. Octavian crossed to meet him, bottled him up in the harbor, and cut off his supplies. Antony decided to fight his way out by sea, but much of his fleet ignored the order to attack. Panicking, he and Cleopatra fled with forty ships to Egypt, and the rest of Antony's men defected. Octavian sent word that he would give Cleopatra anything she asked if she murdered or banished Antony. She refused. Octavian invaded Egypt. Antony challenged Octavian to single combat, but Octavian replied that Antony had other ways to end his life. As Antony prepared to defend Alexandria, his ships and cavalry deserted.

> Antony retreated to the city, crying out in his rage that Cleopatra had betrayed him to the very men he was fighting for her sake. Then the queen, in terror at his fury and despair, fled to her tomb, pulled up the hanging doors which were strengthened with bars and bolts, and sent messengers to tell Antony that she was dead. Never doubting the message, he said to himself, "Why delay any longer, Antony? Fate has taken away the one excuse which could still make you desire to live." . . .
>
> Now Antony had a faithful servant, whose name was Eros. He had long ago made this man swear to kill him if the need arose, and he now ordered him to carry out his promise. Eros drew his sword and raised it as if he were about to strike his master, but suddenly turned away and killed himself. As he fell at his master's feet, Antony cried out, "That was well done, Eros. You have shown me what I must do." . . . Then he stabbed himself with his own sword through the belly and fell upon the bed. But the wound did not kill him quickly. . . .
>
> When he understood that Cleopatra was still alive, Antony eagerly ordered his slaves to lift him up, and they carried him in their arms to the doors of her tomb. Even then Cleopatra would not allow the doors to be opened, but she showed herself at a window and let down cords and ropes to the ground. The slaves fastened Antony to these and the queen pulled him up with the help of her two ladies in waiting, who were the only companions she had allowed to enter the tomb with her. Those who were present say there was never a more pitiable sight than the spectacle of Antony, covered with blood, struggling in his death agonies and stretching out his hands toward Cleopatra as he swung helplessly in the air. The task was almost beyond a woman's strength, and it was only with great difficulty that Cleopatra, clinging with both hands to the rope and with the muscles of her face distorted by the strain, was able to haul him up. . . . When she had got him up and laid him on a bed, she tore her dress and spread it over him, beat and lacerated her breasts, and smeared her face with the blood from his wounds. She called him her lord and husband and emperor, and almost forgot her own misfortunes in her pity for his. Antony . . . begged her not to grieve over this wretched change in his fortunes, but to count him happy for the glories he had won and to remember that he had attained the greatest fame and power of any man in the world, so that now it was no dishonor to die a Roman, conquered only by a Roman.
>
> Plutarch, *Life of Antony* 76–77 (I. Scott-Kilvert)

This scene moved even the hardened Octavian. He allowed Cleopatra to prepare Antony's body for burial with her own hands. She attempted suicide, then began a complicated negotiation with Octavian, hoping he would let her and

Caesarion rule Egypt as his clients. When it became clear that Octavian would allow no such thing, she again shut herself in the tomb.

> According to one account, an asp° was carried in to her with figs and lay hidden under the leaves in the basket, for Cleopatra had given orders that the snake should settle on her without her being aware of it. But when she picked up some of the figs she caught sight of it, so the story goes, and said, "So here it is," and baring her arm, she held it out to be bitten. Others say that it was carefully shut up in a pitcher and that Cleopatra provoked it by pricking it with a golden spindle until it sprang out and fastened on her arm. But the real truth nobody knows, for there is another story that she carried poison about with her in a hollow comb, which she kept hidden in her hair. Yet no inflammation or any other symptom of poison broke out on her body. Indeed the asp was never discovered inside the tomb, although some marks which might have been its trail are said to have been noticed on the beach on that side where the windows of the tomb looked out toward the sea. . . . Octavian was vexed at Cleopatra's death, and yet he could not but admire the nobility of her spirit, and he gave orders that she should be buried with royal splendor and magnificence, and her body laid beside Antony's.
>
> Plutarch, *Life of Antony* 86 (I. Scott-Kilvert)

°*asp:* Apparently a cobra.

Octavian murdered Cleopatra's sons, annexed Egypt as his private possession, and headed back to Rome. Thus ended the last of the Greek-speaking Macedonian descendants of Alexander.

AFTERMATH

With a flourish, Octavian announced that the Republic was restored. The Senate voted him a new name, **Augustus** ("most revered one"), and proclaimed him *princeps* (**prin**-keps)—not king, but "first citizen." Behind a screen of titles, he ruled the empire for forty-four peaceful, prosperous years. The Greek world slowly recovered. Rome founded new cities and encouraged development. The old Greek independence was gone, but a new, more sedate, and prosperous urban society developed. Its aristocrats built fine theaters, and its famous cities attracted gifts from rich Romans. Athens did well (Figure 22.12). Roman forms of literature and art flourished, sophisticated adaptations of Greek models. Greece's Stoic philosophers and professors of rhetoric earned good salaries in Rome, Gaul, and London, Britain. Emperors sported Greek haircuts and beards and wrote treatises on Stoic philosophy.

The ancient world was ending. Christianity grew from a tiny sect to a major cultural force. As most Jews read the scriptures in the Greek *Septuagint,* so were the founding documents of Christianity written in Greek. In A.D. 312, the emperor Constantine became Christian, and in A.D. 391 Christianity became the empire's official faith. Early Christians claimed that God had revealed to them many of the same ethical precepts that Socrates and Plato reached through reason, but in the fourth century A.D. Christian thinkers argued that revealed wisdom made philosophical learning unnecessary. Christianity was from the beginning a complicated mixture of Greek philosophy, Hebrew traditions, the theology of Paul, and the teachings of Jesus.

Figure 22.12 The temple to Olympian Zeus beneath the Athenian Acropolis, begun in the sixth century B.C. by the tyrant Pisistratus, and finished by the Roman emperor Hadrian (ruled A.D. 117–138).

When the western Roman Empire was breaking up in the third century A.D. under the pressure of population movements from central Asia flooding its frontiers, the urbanized Greek East survived. The western empire broke into Germanic kingdoms in the fifth century A.D., while the Greek-speaking eastern empire went on for another thousand years. Ancient literary genres—history, philosophy, drama—declined after the sixth century A.D., and the Byzantine Empire (as the Greek part of the old Roman Empire is known) in the Balkans was an utterly different world from Pericles' Athens. But while backward western Europe endured its long and depressing Middle Ages, which ignored the achievements of the ancient Greeks, the Greek scholars of Byzantium and the Arabs, who now occupied the formerly Greek cities of western Asia Minor and Egypt, copied out, translated, and passed on the writings of Aristotle and Thucydides.

KEY TERMS

Republic, 501

Senate, 501

assemblies, 501

consuls, 501

triumph, 502

Hiero II, 503

Hannibal, 504

Marcellus, 506

Scipio Africanus, 506

Cynoscephalae, 508

Cato, 514

Brutus, 515

FURTHER READING

Alcock, S., *Graecia Capta* (Cambridge, UK, 1993). Pioneering study using archaeological evidence to understand social change in Hellenistic and Roman Greece.

Astin, A. E., *Cato the Censor* (Oxford 1967). Classic account of Cato's life and struggles against Hellenism.

Badian, E., *Publicans and Sinners* (Ithaca, NY, 1972). Classic study of the *publicani* in the period covered by this chapter.

Badian, E., *Roman Imperialism in the Late Republic* (Ithaca, NY, 1968). An attempt to understand the Romans' perspective on their imperial expansion.

Cornell, T., *The Beginnings of Rome* (London 1994). Detailed review of Roman history and archaeology from the earliest times through 264 B.C.

Gruen, E., *The Hellenistic East and the Coming of Rome* (2 vols., Berkeley, 1984). Detailed analysis of Rome and the Greek world, focusing on Polybius' account.

Harris, W. V., *War and Imperialism in Republican Rome, 327–70 B.C.* (Oxford 1979). Classical analysis, arguing that Rome's expansion was driven by greed.

Hopkins, K., *Conquerors and Slaves* (Cambridge, UK, 1978). Outstanding sociological analysis of the interconnection of war, slavery, economics, and institutions in Rome between the Punic Wars and Augustus.

Lancel, S., *Hannibal* (Oxford 2003). Biography of the Carthaginian general.

Meier, C., *Caesar* (New York 1982). Excellent biography.

Ancient Texts

Appian, *The Civil Wars* (New York 1996; tr. John Carter). A vital but underappreciated source for history of the late Roman Republic.

Austin, Michel, *The Hellenistic World* (Cambridge, UK, 1981). Superb selection of ancient sources.

Livy, *Rome and the Mediterranean* (New York 1976; tr. Henry Bettenson). Books 31–45 of Livy's history of Rome, covering the period 201–167 B.C.

Plutarch, *Lives* of Marius, Sulla, Pompey and Caesar, *The Fall of the Roman Republic* (Harmondsworth, UK, 1958; tr. Rex Warner), and of Fabius, Marcellus, Cato, and Mark Antony in *Makers of Rome* (Harmondsworth, UK, 1965; tr. Ian Scott-Kilvert). Biographies of the major Roman generals involved in the destruction of the Hellenistic world.

Polybius, *The Rise of the Roman Empire* (New York 1979; tr. Ian Scott-Kilvert). The main surviving parts of Polybius' account of Rome and the Greeks.

Suetonius, *Lives* of Julius Caesar and Augustus. In *The Twelve Caesars* (Harmondsworth, UK, 1957; tr. Robert Graves). Highly entertaining biographies.

CHAPTER 23

CONCLUSION

W̲e have crossed a long distance from the end of the last Ice Age to the Roman Empire. In the first millennium B.C. the Greeks created a remarkable culture, became the major power in western Eurasia and in the world, then succumbed to Rome. We are the direct heirs of their achievements, many of which were for all time. We close our explanation by summing up the major phases in the story of ancient Greece.

THE BRONZE AGE (C. 3000–1200 B.C.; Chapter 4)

The Bronze Age provides the prologue. Complex civilizations with large populations, grand monuments, beautiful art, and strong class divisions first developed in the Near East and Egypt. A literate elite with special access to divine power, or gods themselves, oversaw complex divisions of labor and networks of skilled craftsmen and literate officials. The rulers centralized power under palatial control, creating command economies that told people what to produce, then redistributed the produce among groups. Similar systems organized around palaces and temples spread east into Iran and west into the Aegean by 2000 B.C. Minoan and Mycenaean society belonged to the fringes of this Near Eastern world.

THE DARK AGE (C. 1200–700 B.C.; Chapter 5)

Around 1200 B.C., Bronze Age centers burned to the ground all around the east Mediterranean. Populations shrank, and many advanced crafts disappeared. The collapse was most severe in the Aegean. By 1000 B.C., small groups of Greeks huddled around Bronze Age ruins, largely cut off from the outside world. The art of writing was lost, and complex hierarchy collapsed. Greece was separated from the world of Bronze Age palaces, which survived in modified forms in Egypt and the Near East. We know little about the Dark Age, but in some way the Classical Period grew from it.

THE ARCHAIC PERIOD (C. 700~500 B.C.; Chapters 6~10)

All across the Mediterranean, population increased in the eighth century B.C. Trade boomed. Thousands of Greeks emigrated to Sicily, southern Italy, and points further west; thousands more moved to the Black Sea coasts. They tied the Aegean to other regions, and traders exploited the Mediterranean's economic and cultural diversity.

The new colonies and the older communities that dispatched them crystallized as hundreds of small city-states, governed very differently from the communities grouped around the Bronze Age palaces. The principle of equality among male citizens was overriding. The Greek city-states enthusiastically rejected the notion that intimacy with divine power translated into political authority. People believed in gods, built temples, and offered sacrifice, but there was no priestly caste, and there was no scribal class that served the state and served religion.

In some ways, the Greek universe was bleak: Humanity stood alone, without God's guidance. How can we govern society if we are on our own? Assisted by the revolutionary invention of the Greek alphabet, where you can write anything you can say, the Greeks developed increasingly rational forms of inquiry to determine man's place in the cosmos. If there is no source of wisdom outside men's deliberations, then it makes sense to involve as many men in government as possible, not just the elite. The more they moved toward democracy, breaking down barriers within the male community, the more they strengthened the ancient barriers between free citizen men and everyone else: women, foreigners, and slaves, who were imported in increasing numbers.

Through the long centuries between the rise of the Roman Empire and the European Enlightenment, no one much cared about the political, moral, intellectual, and religious problems faced by the archaic Greeks. When in the eighteenth century A.D., west Europeans also began rejecting the claims of divine monarchy and struggled to replace them with reason, citizenship, and equality, historians and politicians were shocked to realize that others had faced similar problems a long time ago.

THE CLASSICAL PERIOD (C. 500~350 B.C.; Chapters 11~18)

As they became economic and military powers, the Greeks drew the attention of the mighty Persian Empire in the east and the rich city of Carthage in the west. Archaic culture had developed in a power vacuum, with few external threats. All that ended in 480 B.C. To resist Persian and Carthaginian attacks, Greeks in the Aegean and Sicily alike formed larger political units. If Greeks had not formed larger units, they would have been forced into such units anyway, as subjects of the all-devouring great empires.

Many Greeks thought that the larger political units after 480 B.C. were temporary, but they were not. Athens and Syracuse created multicity states, which other *poleis* viewed as tyrannical empires. Money flowed into Athens and Syracuse, fueling one of history's greatest cultural explosions. In Athens above all, artists, poets, and intellectuals wondered how a democratic city of equal men could justly rule over others and how great individuals could fit into a society of equals.

The *poleis* became more complex and diverse. The more they expanded their power, the more violent their wars were. The struggle of Athens and Sparta drew in Syracuse, then neighboring peoples in Sicily and Macedonia, and finally Persia and Carthage. The scale of war outstripped the *poleis'* ability to pay, forcing them to turn outward to their mighty imperial foes, and upward, to their own rich citizens. After 404 B.C., when the Athenian empire collapsed, no individual *polis* could compete in the great world. As the rich took more responsibility for security, they chafed at restrictive fifth-century egalitarian ideals.

Classical thought and art captivated Europeans and Americans in the nineteenth and twentieth centuries A.D. The sublime ideals of human potential that its poets, sculptors, and painters expressed struck responsive chords, while Thucydides laid bare the dark recesses of human nature that morally virtuous leaders must master. Politicians, journalists, and artists saw the Greeks through the prism of their own times but also made sense of their own times by studying the Greeks' triumphs and disasters. In some European countries, educators concluded that training in Greek language, history, art, and philosophy was all that young people needed to lead the modern world.

THE MACEDONIAN TAKEOVER (C. 350–323 B.C.; Chapter 19)

The Aegean *poleis,* hungry for manpower and resources, drew northern neighbors into their conflicts. These large, loosely organized societies had previously counted for little in Greek affairs, but in the fourth century they learned to raise taxes, tame their noblemen, and organize armies. In the 370s B.C., Jason of Thessaly almost conquered the Aegean; after 350 B.C., Philip of Macedonia actually did so. Little *poleis* either combined into larger units, like the Aetolian and Achaean Leagues, or ceased to have any importance.

Alexander's rampage through the Near East brought into question a high Greek ideal—that a gulf separates man from god. Alexander supposed that only a god could do what he had done and set out to convince others. His death cut off his extreme vision, but before 300 B.C., even Athens honored some men as gods.

THE HELLENISTIC PERIOD (C. 323–30 B.C.; Chapters 20–22)

Third-century-B.C. artists and thinkers wondered how they could combine Greece's ancient traditions with the realities of great kings ruling famous cities along with millions of non-Greeks. In some ways, the third century was the zenith of Greek cities, which spread all over western Asia, reached record sizes, and decorated themselves as never before. Power shifted steadily toward rich euergetists, and the cities' security depended on kings in Macedonia, Syria, and Egypt.

The old *polis* was gone. Some openly sold citizenship to rich foreigners. The old war between democrats and oligarchs was a thing of the past. Squabbles between little cities like Athens and Sparta had little importance. Stoic philosophers, complex Alexandrian poetry, and the Great Altar at Pergamum belonged to a world utterly changed from the classical.

In the second and first centuries B.C., the sophisticated, wealthy Hellenistic kingdoms were turned upside down by the unstoppable thrust of Roman power. Greeks struggled to understand how this could happen, while their Roman conquerors struggled to make sense of the Greek world they had suddenly mastered. Roman aristocrats absorbed and reformulated Hellenistic culture within their new world order.

Through the nineteenth and twentieth centuries A.D., Hellenistic history was largely neglected. Its kings, empires, fussy buildings, and pedantic professors seemed the antithesis of what made classical Greece important. At the end of the twentieth century, the challenge of globalization and enhanced mobility has made the Hellenistic world look rather familiar. In a world with only one superpower, how should that state use its power for good?

CONCLUSION

We might think of Greek history as the swing of a pendulum. The arc began in the Bronze Age with a society in which status was distributed along a continuum, from exalted king to humble palace servant tied to the land. In the fifth century B.C., the pendulum reached the opposite point of its arc in societies divided sharply between free male citizens and all the others. The free, equal male citizens ruled the *polis,* denying distinctions within their ranks and dominating those who were not male citizens. Around 400 B.C., the pendulum began swinging back to a world of god-kings and complex overlapping hierarchies based on wealth, gender, ethnicity, and religion.

The Greeks lived a remarkable story, an adventure in egalitarianism that has guided intellectuals, artists, and politicians for the last 250 years. The way we now tell the story is quite different from John Keats' idealization of an ancient land that is the source of beauty and truth. The Greeks, like us, were human, finding real solutions for real problems, to the best of their ability. We can judge them if we wish, but better to learn from their mistakes, and their successes. More than two thousand years have passed as we go forward with our own adventure.

CHRONOLOGICAL CHART

10,000 B.C.	**NEOLITHIC PERIOD** ("new stone age") begins in the Near East with the development of agriculture and sedentary communities
4000 B.C.	Sumerian cuneiform writing is developed, c. 3400 Egyptian hieroglyphic writing, Pharaonic civilization emerge, c. 3100
3000 B.C.	**EARLY BRONZE AGE** begins in Greece with introduction of bronze metallurgy, c. 3000–2000 Sumerian cities flourish in Mesopotamia, c. 2800–2340 Minoan civilization flourishes in Crete, c. 2500–1200 Akkadian Empire in Mesopotamia, c. 2334–2220 Sumerian revival, c. 2200–2000
2000 B.C.	**MIDDLE BRONZE AGE** begins with the destruction of communities across the Greek mainland, c. 2000–1600 Old Babylonian Empire in Mesopotamia, c. 1900–1550 **LATE BRONZE AGE** (or **MYCENAEAN AGE**) begins, c. 1600 Hittite Empire rules in Anatolia, c. 1700–1200
1500 B.C.	Phoenician syllabic writing appears, c. 1500 Most likely date for a Trojan War, c. 1250–1200 **DARK** (or **IRON**) **AGE** begins with destruction of Mycenaean cities in Greece, c. 1200–1100
1000 B.C.	Greek colonies are settled in Asia Minor, c. 950–900 Greek colonies in Sicily and southern Italy, c. 800–600 **ARCHAIC PERIOD** begins with invention of Greek alphabet, c. 800 *Iliad* and the *Odyssey*, attributed to Homer, are written down, c. 800–750 Olympic games begin, 776 Rome, allegedly, is founded, 753 Hesiod's *Theogony* is written down, c. 750–700 *Homeric Hymns*, c. 700–500 Cyclic poets, c. 650–500 Age of Tyrants, c. 650–500

Cyrus the Great of Persia, c. 590–530
    Xenophanes, c. 570–460
    Pindar, 518–438
    Simonides, late sixth to early fifth century
Alleged date of the expulsion of the Etruscan dynasty at Rome
    and foundation of the Roman Republic, 510

500 B.C.   Bacchylides, early fifth century
Persians invade Aegean Greece; battle of Marathon, 490
Carthage invades Sicily; Greek victory at Himera, 480
Persians invade Aegean Greece again; destruction of Athens;
Greek victories at Salamis and Plataea, 480–479
CLASSICAL PERIOD begins with end of Persian Wars, 480
    Aeschylus, 525–456
    Sophocles, 496–406
    Herodotus, c. 484–420
    Euripides, 480–406
Roman *Twelve Tables* are committed to writing, 451
    Socrates, 469–399
Peloponnesian War, 431–404
    Thucydides, c. 460–400
Biblical book of *Genesis* reaches present form, c. 400

400 B.C.

    Plato, 427–437
    Hippocrates, c. 400
    Aristotle, 384–322
The Gauls sack the city of Rome, 394 or 390
Philip II of Macedon, Alexander's father, conquers Greece,
    ending local rule, 338–337
Alexander the Great conquers the Persian Empire, 336–323
HELLENISTIC PERIOD begins with death of Alexander, 323

300 B.C.   Callimachus, c. 305–240
    Apollonius of Rhodes, third century

200 B.C.   Three Punic Wars are waged between Rome and Carthage,
    264–241, 218–201, 146
    Plautus, Roman playwright, dies, c. 180
ROMAN PERIOD begins with Roman invasions of Greece,
    200–194, 168, 146
Roman civil wars, Marius-Sulla, Caesar-Pompey,
Augustus-Antony, are waged, 88–31
    Vergil, 70–19
    Livy, 57 B.C.–17 A.D.
Julius Caesar rules as dictator, 46–44
Augustus defeats Antony and Cleopatra at battle of Actium, 31,
    and annexes Egypt, 30
Augustus Caesar reigns, 27 B.C.–14 A.D.

100 A.D.   Plutarch, c. 46–120 A.D.

NOTES

1. In place of the traditional B.C. (before Christ) and A.D. (Latin *anno domins,* in the year of the lord), one sometimes finds B.C.E. (before the common era) and C.E. (common era). Because the systems are conventional (Jesus was probably born in 7 B.C.), we have preferred the traditional usage.
2. A Greek name that was still used until 1919, meaning "the land between the rivers."
3. All Greek states made firm divisions between males and females. When Greeks used expressions like "everyone," "the community," or "the people," they normally meant all freeborn adult males.
4. Better known today by his Roman name Hercules.
5. Until the twentieth century this expression was used for the area we now call the Middle East. We refer to the Near East throughout this book.
6. Cf. p. 17, where Hesiod compares women to drones.
7. We further discuss Greek medicine in Chapter 21, "Hellenistic Culture, 323–30 B.C."
8. No one knows what this last word means. We show such unknown words in italics.
9. *Dactylic* means fingerlike, because the finger has one long joint and two short; *hexameter* means having six divisions.
10. Latin *obligatio,* our "obligation," is from the same root, as are *lig*ament and *lig*ature.

11. Called Arianism, after Arius, a priest of Alexandria (c. A.D. 250–336).
12. *The Origin of Fables,* 1724, published in French by Bernard Fontenelle.
13. As do Latin *anima* and Hebrew *ruach,* which also mean soul.
14. For some reason, water divides the land of the dead from the land of the living, a symbol central to the meaning of the *Odyssey.*
15. The lead tablet is damaged here, and we cannot read this word.
16. The story is told by Philostratus, who lived in the third century A.D.
17. This artist was named nearly one hundred years ago by the great scholar John Beazley, after this pot held in the Berlin Museum.
18. *Esthloi* is another word for *agathoi,* "the good people."
19. From this historical event grew the legend of the ten lost tribes of Israel.
20. When Greeks spoke of Asia, they meant the Near East. The "Indians" whom Darius conquered lived in what is now Pakistan; the "Southern Ocean" is the Indian Ocean.
21. A huge sum of money: at the time, enough to support a family of four for about five years.
22. A phenomenal achievement; the distance is 149 miles. In 1983 a race was held over the same route, and the winner covered it in twenty-two hours.

23. Probably, the Athenians did not know exactly how many Persians they killed. It is rather suspicious that 6,400 = (192/3) × 100; that is, the Greeks believed that for every three of them who fell, a hundred Persians died. This may be roughly accurate, but the round numbers suggest it was a guess.

24. An impossible number—this would be fifteen times the size of the Athenian army at Marathon.

25. Herodotus exaggerates the Persian losses, but they were surely heavy.

26. The first, of course, was in 499 B.C.

27. Two hundred years after Elgin, Greece continued to demand the return of its supreme national treasures, sold by one empire (Turkey) to another (Britain) while the Greeks were powerless.

28. So called after priestesses of Artemis at Karuai, a village near Sparta.

29. Twelve of these begin with the letters A through K and probably represent part of an alphabetically arranged edition of his works.

30. For example, Phrynichus' *Sack of Miletus,* performed in 492.

31. We also hear about "Middle Comedy," but little is known of it.

32. Athens' attack on Syracuse in 415–413, which we discuss later in the chapter.

33. Not the same as the famous orator Demosthenes, whom we meet in Chapter 19, "The Warrior-Kings of Macedon, 359–323 B.C."

34. In theory, there was one outside every house, but archaeologists have found few examples.

35. A distant ancestor of the famous Hannibal who fought Rome between 218 and 201 B.C.

36. Scrapers, usually made of iron or bronze. After exercising, athletes would oil themselves, then scrape the oil, dirt, and sweat off with a strigil.

37. The previous Spartan admiral.

38. They have just condemned Socrates to death.

39. We can tell from the style of this text that it was not written by Aristotle, but the manuscript survived in a group of Aristotle's writings; hence we call the author "pseudo-Aristotle."

40. *Punic* has entered English as a synonym for Carthaginian. It comes from the Latin word *Poenus,* a corruption of the word *Phoenician.*

41. Lucian was a Greek comic writer active under the Roman Empire around A.D. 100–120. *The Lovers* is probably not his work, but the manuscript was preserved with a collection of Lucian's essays, so classicists call the author "Pseudo-Lucian."

42. The term *tholos* is also used to describe the round underground "beehive" tombs of the Bronze Age Greeks.

43. The location of Aristotle's Lyceum was accidentally discovered during preparations for the 2004 Olympic games in Athens.

44. You cannot see virtue, but you can see strength and health.

45. The famous orator should not be confused with the general of the same name who fought in the Peloponnesian War and died at Syracuse in 413.

46. Historians call the conflict that followed (357–355 B.C.) the "Social War" from the Latin word *socius,* meaning "ally," because it was a war between Athens and her allies.

47. His *Campaigns of Alexander* was one of the most popular historical books in the Roman Empire and remains our principal source for information about Alexander's campaigns.

48. A Roman historian of Alexander, writing in the 30s A.D.

49. This is what the Greeks called him; his proper name was probably Parvataku.

50. The modern name is the River Beas.

51. Mostly noncombatants.

52. Diodorus is writing as if Philip had become king when Alexander died in June 323.

53. In 311, when the treaty was signed, Alexander IV was eleven years old.

54. *Odyssey* 4.354–55.

55. The Roman name for Aphrodite.

56. Although carbonized, these scrolls can be read in part and work continues on them today.

57. Not to be confused with Zeno of Elea, who formulated the famous paradoxes in the fifth century B.C. (see Chapter 14).

58. American excavators uncovered its foundations in the 1980s beside the modern train tracks joining Athens with Piraeus.

59. The motto of the state of California, because of the gold rush there in 1849.

60. No connection with the royal Macedonian dynasty of the Ptolemies.

61. Romans called Carthaginians *Poeni,* "Phoenicians," which came into English as Punic. The Roman-Carthaginian conflicts are called the Punic Wars.

62. When Romans said Africa, they meant roughly modern Tunisia.

CREDITS

PRONUNCIATION GUIDE

**ROMAN AND GREEK FORMS OF CLASSICAL NAMES: SPELLING
AND PRONUNCIATION**

The proper names from classical Greece were later transliterated into the Latin
alphabet. In this process a few changes had to be made, and the Latin forms, therefore, are somewhat different from the Greek. Latin is presently broken up into the
Romance languages (Italian, French, Spanish, and Portuguese), each of which has
its own peculiarities of spelling and pronunciation. English is not a Romance language, but its speakers were members of the western Christian Church, which—in
its Roman Catholic branch—used Latin for its liturgy and for almost all of its business down to the mid–twentieth century. In consequence, throughout all western
Europe, Latin was a universal second language for the educated classes for about
fifteen hundred years. For this reason, the most familiar spellings of the proper
names of ancient Greek historical and literary figures are Latinized forms of Greek
names, sometimes further altered in standard English. Because of their familiarity,
these are the forms used (mostly) in this book. About a hundred years ago, however,
some scholars and translators urged a reform of this system and the use of the Greek
forms of classical names rendered in the Roman alphabet, so that one may find tales
about "Klytaimnestra," "Akhilleus," and others. We have occasionally allowed some
of these Greek forms in this book, especially in quoted passages where the names
appear only once or twice. To aid reference, because such Greek forms often appear
in English translations, the following index gives the Greek forms in parentheses
after the Latinized forms.

The principal differences between the Latinized and Greek forms are as follows:

Latin *j* = Greek *i*: *J*ason = *I*ason
Latin *c* = Greek *k*: *C*imon = *K*imon
Latin *ae* or *e* = Greek *ai*: Ga*e*a = Ga*ia*; Clytemn*e*stra = Klyt*ai*mnestra
Latin *e* or *i* = Greek *ei*: Rh*e*a = Rh*ei*a; P*i*sistratus = P*ei*sistratus
Latin *i* = Greek *oi*: Delph*i* = Delph*oi*
Latin *oe* = Greek *oi*: *Oe*dipus = *Oi*dipous
Latin *u* = Greek *ou*: Cre*u*sa = Kre*ou*sa
Latin *y* = Greek *u* (sometimes): Cl*y*temnestra = Kl*u*taimnestra
Latin final *a* = Greek *e*: Athen*a* = Athen*e*
Latin final *um* = Greek *on*: stadi*um* = stadi*on*
Latin final *us* = Greek *os*: Asclepi*us* = Asklepi*os*

Finally, the Greek letter *chi* (χ) is rendered *ch* in Latin but either *ch* or *kh* in the Greek forms.

How ancient Greek names are today pronounced in English is a matter on which people agree to disagree; certainly an ancient Greek would be astonished at the ordinary English pronunciation of his or her name. There is little agreement on how to pronounce the vowels. So one hears the name of the Athenian playwright pronounced as *E*-schylus or *Ē*-schylus or sometimes *Ī*-schylus. Is the famous king of Thebes called *E*-dipus or *Ē*-dipus? With many names, however, there is a conventional pronunciation, which we give in parentheses in the index, as we did in the text. Consonants, which arouse less dispute, tend to follow the following rules in the anglicized forms of words Latinized from the original Greek:

The letters *c* and *g* are "soft" before *e* and *i* sounds (not necessarily letters) and "hard" before *a*, *o*, and *u* sounds in words and names of Greek or Latin origin: for example, *c*enter, *C*aesar, *c*ivic, *c*ycle; *g*entle, Eu*g*ene, a*g*ile, but cate*g*ory, *c*ooperate, *c*uneiform; *g*arrulous, *g*onad, *g*usto. Notice the requirement "in words of Greek or Latin origin": "*g*et" and "*g*ive" are of Germanic origin and do not follow the rule.

The Greek letter *chi* (χ), written *ch*, represented a sound like *k* but pronounced back in the throat; in English it is pronounced like the "hard" *c* in *c*ard," not like the *ch* of "*ch*icken."

Final *e* must be pronounced as a separate syllable: Daph-ñe, Cir-c̄e. To remind the reader of this rule, we place a circumflex over the *e* in such syllables (except for the common Aphrodite): Daphn*ê*, Circ*ê*. Final *es* is also pronounced, as in Achill*ēs*.

Another problem is the accent—where to stress the word. Latin and Greek relies chiefly on pitch and quantity, whereas English depends on stress. Quantity is the length of time it takes to pronounce a syllable; pitch is the register of the voice. Because of the influence of Latin on Western culture, the English accent on proper names follows the rule that governs the pronunciation of Latin: If the next to last syllable is "long," it is accented; if it is not "long," the syllable before it is accented. How does one know whether a syllable is "long" or "short"? If the next-to-last syllable ends with two consonants, or if it contains a diphthong (*-ae-*, *-oe-*, *-au-*, *-ei-*), or if it contains a vowel "long" by nature, it must be accented. Otherwise, the accent goes on the third syllable from the end. But how does one know whether a vowel is long by nature? Unfortunately, only by knowing Latin well can you know whether a vowel is long by nature. A further complication arises from the fact that the combinations of vowels -ae-, -oe-, -au-, and -ei- are not always diphthongs (two vowels pronounced as one) but are sometimes pronounced separately. In these cases we place a dieresis (two superimposed dots) over the second vowel: The mother of Perseus was Danaë, pronounced **dan**-a-ē.

These rules are useful but complex. For many it will be easiest simply to consult the pronunciation given after each name in the text and in the following index, where the syllable to be accented is printed in **bold** characters. Vowels should be pronounced according to this key:

ā = pay
ē = be
ī = wife
ō = no
ū = cute

INDEX

Pontus (Pontos, "sea"), another name for the Black Sea, 26, 120, 198, 202, 280, 517

population, 4–7, 17–19, 24–27, 35, 42–46, 50, 73, 77–82, 194, 196, 203, 204, 209, 221, 251, 272, 274, 279, 280, 283, 285, 306, 353, 360, 362, 372, 373, 379, 403, 409, 436, 446, 448, 451, 455, 456, 459, 506, 523, 529, 532

Poseidon (po-**sī**-don), son of Cronus and Rhea, Greek god of the sea, 52, 68, 111, 112, 114, 130, 132, 136, 145, 146, 253, 305, 317, 434

Priam (**prī**-am. Priamos), king of Troy, 105, 106

Procris (**prok**-ris), daughter of Erechtheus, wife of Cephalus, killed accidentally, 145

Procrustes (pro-**krus**-tēz), enemy of Theseus, 317

Prometheus (prō-**mē**-thūs), a Titan, maker and benefactor of humankind, 32, 129, 217, 267, 324, 333

prophecy, 84, 102, 135, 315

Protagoras (pro-**tag**-o-ras), Greek sophist, fifth century B.C., 217, 220, 293, 312, 400

Protoattic art style, 187, 191

psyche ("breath"), 137, 139

Ptolemy I (**tol**-e-mē, 367–282 B.C.), general of Alexander, first Macedonian king of Egypt, 441, 446, 449, 450; Ptolemy II (reiged 283–246 B.C.), 452–454; later Ptolemies, 457, 458, 462, 468–471, 475, 476, 507

publicani ("tax-gatherers"), 521, 522, 525, 530

Punic (**pū**-nik) Wars, between Carthage and Rome, 504, 506, 530

Pylos (**pī**-los), city in southwest Peloponnesus, where the Athenians captured Spartans in the Peloponnesian War, 62–64, 68–71, 112, 338–343, 363

Pyrrhus (**pir**-us. Pyrrhos), king of Epirus, third century B.C., 446, 464–467, 471, 472, 500, 502

Pythagoras (pith-**ag**-or-as), Greek philosopher, sixth century B.C., 174–176, 191, 290, 291

R

rationality, 7, 438

religion, 10, 52, 74, 86, 91, 117–133, 136, 137, 140–148, 167, 192, 203, 220, 231, 232, 322–326, 399, 460, 471, 498, 532, 534

Remus (**rē**-mus), twin founder of Rome, 500

Renaissance, 77, 390, 478

res publica (rās **pub**-li-ka, "public affair"), oligarchic government at Rome before Augustus, 501

rhapsode ("staff-singer"), 95, 116

Rhea (**rē**-a), a Titan, wife of Cronus, 120, 122, 146

Rhodes (**rōdz**), Aegean island near southwest coast of Asia Minor, 205, 208, 220, 283, 400, 405, 444, 456, 471, 517, 522

Romans, 8, 11, 117, 179, 194, 297, 305, 399, 449, 465–467, 471, 473, 477, 482, 498–517, 521, 522, 526, 528, 530

Romulus (**rom**-u-lus), twin founder of Rome, 500

S

sacrifice, 52, 121, 124–130, 136, 139–146, 163, 245, 253, 254, 266, 320, 323, 326, 329, 331, 341, 416, 426, 430, 464, 476, 532

Salamis (**sal**-a-mis), island near the port of Athens, site of Persian naval defeat in 480 B.C., 206, 210, 258–261, 265–270, 274

Samos (**sā**-mos), island in the east Aegean, 168, 174, 237, 238, 241, 265, 279, 290, 356, 457, 484, 488, 496

Samothrace, island in the north Aegean, 481

Sanskrit, an ancient Indian language, 45

Sappho, Greek poet, sixth century B.C., 29, 30, 41, 155, 226

Sardis, capital of Lydia, 218, 219, 226, 229, 230, 239–241, 244, 248, 253, 322, 323, 367, 416, 472

satrap, Persian governor, 237–239, 273, 357, 386, 415, 419, 441

Scamander River, on the Trojan plain, 100, 105

Schliemann, Heinrich (1822–1890 A.D.), German archaeologist, 60, 99, 100, 116

Scylla (**sil**-la), monster who attacked Odysseus, 110, 114, 115

Scythians, people of the southern Ukrainian steppe north of the Black Sea, 238, 245, 434

secondary products revolution, 46, 90

Selenê (se-**lē**-nē), goddess of the moon, 130, 136

Seleucus I (c. 358–281), one of Alexander's generals; satrap of Babylon 321–316, then again after 312 B.C., 440; Seleucids, 444–449, 454

Semelê (**sem**-e-lē), daughter of Cadmus and Harmonia, beloved by Zeus, mother to Dionysus, destroyed by lightning, 144, 323, 324

Semites, 88

Senate, in ancient Rome, 501, 510, 514, 517–523, 525, 527, 529

Sesklo, Neolithic site in Greece, 47

One Classic Text Deserves Another

For more than 50 years, Penguin has been the leading publisher of classics in the English-speaking world. We are pleased to provide adopters of *The Greeks: History, Culture, and Society* with the opportunity to package this text with Penguin Classics titles, such as the ones below, at a significant discount. Contact your local Prentice Hall representative for details at *www.prenhall.com*. For a complete listing of Penguin Classics go to *www.penguinputnam.com*.

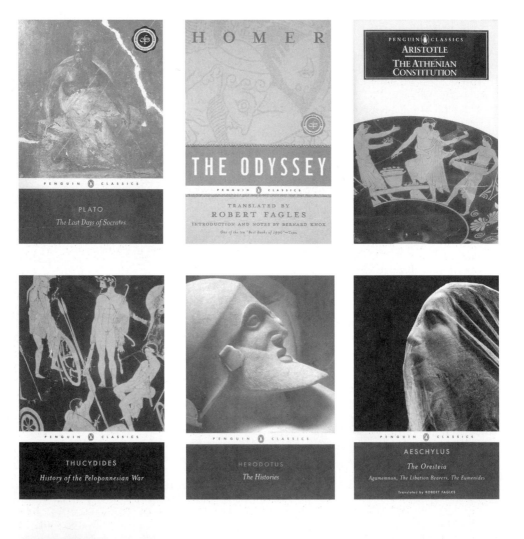